DATE DUE

DEC. 01.1998			
GAYLORD			PRINTED IN U.S.A.

ECONOMICS

Institutions and Analysis

Second Edition

Gerson Antell

When ordering this book, please specify:
either R 297 H
or Economics: Institutions and Analysis, Hardbound Edition

Dedicated to serving

our nation's youth

AMSCO SCHOOL PUBLICATIONS, INC.

315 Hudson Street   New York, N.Y. 10013

About the author

Gerson Antell was assistant principal for social studies at Hillcrest
High School and chairperson of the department of social studies at
Seward Park High School, both in New York City; a member of the
board of directors of the New York City Council on Economic
Education; and director of the New York City Developmental
Economic Education Project (DEEP). At present he is coordinator
of programs in economics for Junior Achievement, Inc.

Gerson Antell is coauthor of *Current Issues in American
Democracy*, *Economics for Everybody*, and *Western Civilization*.

Acknowledgments

We gratefully acknowledge the following sources of photographs:

facing page 1: Craig Aurness/Woodfin Camp; 3: Burk Uzzle/Woodfin Camp; 5: AP/Wide
World; 8: Bill Owens/Archive Pictures; 22: Rick Smolann/Stock, Boston; 24: Fredrik D.
Bodin/Stock, Boston; 31: Jerry Berndt/Stock, Boston; 35: Leif Skoogfors/Woodfin Camp;
44: Ginger Chih/Peter Arnold; 46: J. R. Holland/Stock, Boston; 60: Sybil Shelton/Peter
Arnold; 74t: Tyrone J. Hall/Stock, Boston; 74b: David Aronson/Stock, Boston;
76: The Bettmann Archive; 82: Culver Pictures; 92t: H. Morgan/Stock, Boston;
92b: Randy Matusow; 108: New York Stock Exchange Archives; 112: Edward C. Topple/
New York Stock Exchange; 128t: Christopher S. Johnson/Stock, Boston; 128b: Jean C.
Pigozzi/Archive Pictures; 132: Culver Pictures; 148: Georg Gerster/Photo Researchers;
155: Lionel Delevingne/Stock, Boston; 164: Joe Munroe/Photo Researchers; 168: Earl
Dotter/Archive Pictures; 169: AP/Wide World; 171l: Christopher Morrow/Stock, Boston;
171r: Cary Wolinsky/Stock, Boston; 183: Hazel Hankin/Stock, Boston; 197: UAW Solidar-
ity; 200: Jason Laure/Woodfin Camp; 212: Charles Gupton/Stock, Boston; 215 AP/Wide
World; 254: Peter Menzel/Stock, Boston; 258t, b: Bureau of Engraving and Printing; 272:
Barbara Alper/Stock, Boston; 278: Library of Congress/Photo Researchers; 292: Historical
Pictures Service, Chicago; 304: Mike Mazzaschi/Stock, Boston; 314: Charles Cocaine/
Photo Researchers; 316: George Bellerose/Stock, Boston; 339: Christopher Brown/Stock,
Boston; 355: Randy Matusow; 359: AP/Wide World; 368: Ray Ellis/Photo Researchers;
380: Syd Greenberg/Photo Researchers; 386: Steve Potter/Stock, Boston; 394: Arthur
Glauberman/Photo Researchers; 402: U.S. Army; 408t: William Carter/Photo Researchers; 408b: Patricia Hollander Gross/Stock, Boston; 416: James H. Karales/Peter Arnold;
419: Frank Siteman/Stock, Boston; 421: Buckminster Fuller Institute; 431: Dean Abram-
son/Stock, Boston; 436: Joe Munroe/Photo Researchers; 445: Tom McHugh/Photo Researchers; 462: Nicholas Sapieha/Stock, Boston; 467: Elizabeth Hamlin/Stock, Boston;
473: Michael Hayman/Stock, Boston; 487: Peter Menzel/Stock, Boston; 506: Kenneth
Murray/Photo Researchers; 518: Denny Lorentzen/Swedish Information Service; 528:
Bernard Pierre Wolff/Photo Researchers; 531: AP/Wide World.

Preface

ECONOMICS: INSTITUTIONS AND ANALYSIS, Second Edition, is a thoroughgoing revision of a well-proven basic economics text for high school students. We carefully scrutinized all aspects of the first edition—text, illustrations, and exercises—to determine whether they were still appropriate for students of economics today. As a result of this review, we dropped some topics, either lengthened or shortened many others, and added a great many new topics. Throughout this new edition, we have tried to personalize the material with references to everyday experience, but not at the expense of correctness and precision.

While every effort has been made to bring the text into line with the latest economic thinking, we have retained the basic approach to the development and presentation of subject matter that made the first edition both accessible and teachable. The first two units deal with economics: the fundamental questions all economic systems must answer, the American free enterprise system, the laws of supply and demand and market price, and the production process. Succeeding units deal with the roles of business, labor, and government in the American economic system; money and banking; the business cycle, gross national product, and fiscal and monetary policies. Taking a more personal approach, we next examine the problems that young consumers will face in the American economy. We discuss personal budgeting, savings and investing, insurance, advertising, and government protection for the consumer. In the final two units, we study national economic issues and the global economy.

Among the important additions to this second edition are:

- Seventy-five photographs and cartoons especially selected to sharpen students' economic understanding.
- Ninety new graphs and charts.
- Greatly expanded tabular material.
- An expanded exercise section following each chapter, which includes content and interpretation questions about special readings and illustrations.
- A completely new text feature-reading program.

The text feature-readings include historical-biographical sketches of the makers of economic thought from Adam Smith to recent Nobel

Prize winners; personal-economics readings about checking accounts, income taxes, and consumer complaints; short mini-readings (one page or less), for comprehension of a subsidiary topic or a current economic problem; and long feature-readings (from two to four pages) that develop further understanding of the text. Each long reading is accompanied by exercise questions. Teachers may use these readings as they see fit, and assign them on the basis of students' interests and abilities.

For many students, a course in economics has all the appearance of a journey into the unknown. Unlike mathematics, English, and history—subjects taken many times before—economics is new to young people. Yet, as they start to read and learn, students will begin to see that economics is familiar: it is the study of how people and societies use their limited resources to satisfy their unlimited wants. In this second edition, as in the first, we have made every effort to explain the special language of economics in terms that students will quickly comprehend.

If providing basic literacy in economics is the first goal of this book, a second, equally important goal of economics education must be training for citizenship. Economic topics and issues are discussed again and again on television and radio, and in books, magazines, and newspapers. The positions taken on these economic issues by candidates for public office have a direct bearing on the success or failure of the candidates at the polls. How the electorate perceives economic problems and the proper solutions to them inevitably affects the kind of leadership it chooses.

Thus, economic understanding is critical to the success of democracy, since that knowledge, or lack of it, will be reflected in the quality of those who are chosen to govern. This conclusion, stated some years ago by a task force of leading economics educators, is still valid today:

> In the final analysis, the effectiveness of government depends on the capacity and understanding of the people. For it is the people who, through their votes and other influences, determine within broad limits the scope and nature of government policies. If they are to exercise their great political power responsibly and effectively, more of our people must know more about our economy and must learn to think about economic issues objectively and rationally.[1]

The author would like to express his gratitude to the many teachers and students whose comments and suggestions are reflected in this new edition, and to his wife, Diane, whose understanding and support contributed to the happy completion of this work.

---

[1] *Economic Education in the Schools: A Report of the National Task Force on Economic Education* (New York: Committee for Economic Development), p. 7.

Contents

UNIT I   Economic Reasoning

Chapter 1   *Economics: The Basic Questions*   1

The Factors of Production   2
The Three Fundamental Questions of
    Economics   5
Economic Systems: Society's Answer to What, How,
    and Who   8
Economic Goals of Our Society   12

Chapter 2   *Demand, Supply, and Market Price*   20

Demand   20
Supply   29
How Prices Are Determined   34

UNIT II   The Free Enterprise Economy
of the United States

Chapter 3   *The United States Economic System*   45

The United States Economic System Rests Upon
    Certain Institutions   46
The Role of Government   49
The Interdependence of Economic Society   51
Specialization and the Economy   52
The Circular Flow of Economic Activity   52
Adding Government to Our Model   54
The United States Economy Is a Market
    System   57
How the Price-Directed Market System Works   59
Evaluation of the Market System   63

Chapter 4   *Production and Productivity*   71

What Ingredients Determine the Output of
    Goods and Services?   72
How Productivity Is Increased   75

Combining the Factors of Production:
   What Are the Proper Proportions?   76
The Economies and Diseconomies of Scale   81

UNIT III   The Role of Business

Chapter 5   *How Business Firms Are Organized*   93

The Single Proprietorship   93
The Partnership   94
The Corporation   96

Chapter 6   *How Corporations Obtain Funds*   106

Earnings   106
Loans   106
The Stock Market: Equity Financing   107
Corporate Securities: Stocks and Bonds   108
How Stocks and Bonds Are Sold to the Public   110
Buying and Selling Stocks and Bonds   113
Specialized Markets   116
Securities and Exchange Commission   117
Financial Statements: Balance Sheet and
   Income Statement   117

Chapter 7   *Monopoly and Imperfect Competition*   122

Monopoly   123
Imperfect Competition   129

Chapter 8   *Big Business and Government Control*   142

Business Combinations: Past and Present   143
Government Regulation of Business: The Antitrust
   Laws   149
Antitrust Today: Too Little or Too Much?   152
Public Utilities: Natural Monopolies Requiring
   Government Regulation   154
What the Regulatory Agencies Do   156
Public Enterprise: Government Ownership   157
Countervailing Power   158

UNIT IV   The Role of Labor

Chapter 9   *The Labor Force in Our Economy*   165

Overview of the Labor Force   165
Work and Income   168
Factors Affecting the Demand for Labor   170

Factors Affecting the Supply of Labor   171
Nonmarket Forces and the Determination
    of Wages   172
The Distribution of Income   175
Poverty in America   176
Programs to Fight Poverty   180

Chapter 10   *Labor Unions in Our Economy*   190

Highlights From the History of Labor Unions   190
Basic Aims of Unions   193
The Collective Bargaining Process   195
When Collective Bargaining Fails   198
Current Problems of Labor Unions   202

UNIT V   The Role of Government

Chapter 11   *The Growing Importance of Government*   213

Reasons for the Growth of Government   213
Federal Budget   217
A Look at Expenses in the Federal Budget   218
State and Local Finances   224
Impact of Government Spending Upon the
    Economy   226

Chapter 12   *Taxation*   230

Why Are Taxes Necessary? The Functions of
    Taxation   230
What Are the Ingredients of a Good Tax
    System?   231
Who Should Pay Taxes?   232
Federal Taxes: The Individual Income Tax   234
Other Federal Taxes   242
State and Local Taxes   247
Incidence of Taxes: Who Really Pays the Tax?   249
Grant-in-Aid Programs   250
Is the Nation's Tax System Working Well?   251

UNIT VI   Money, Credit, and Banking

Chapter 13   *Money in Economic Society*   255

Money: Historical Background   255
Functions of Money   256
Characteristics of Money   257
What Kinds of Money Do Americans Use?   257

Near Moneys   261
How Currency Is Produced and Distributed   263
Monetary Standards in United States History   264

Chapter 14   *Banks and Banking*   267

The Origins of Banking   267
The Business of Banking   268
Commercial Banks   269
Thrift Institutions   269
Commercial Banks and the Creation of Money   270
Keeping Our Banks Safe   277
The Role of the Federal Reserve System   279

Chapter 15   *The Fluctuating Value of Money*   289

How the Value of Money Is Measured   289
How Inflation Affects the Economy and
    People's Lives   291
What Are the Causes of Inflation?   296
How the Government Fights Inflation   298

UNIT VII   Promoting Economic Stability

Chapter 16   *Measuring the Nation's Economic
    Performance*   305

The GNP: Total Output of Goods and
    Services   305
The Gross National Product as Total
    Expenditures   306
The Gross National Product as Total Income   309
Limitations of the GNP   316

Chapter 17   *The Level of Economic Activity*   321

The Business Cycle: The Ups and Downs of
    the American Economy   321
The Great Depression   323
Theories on the Causes of Business Cycles   326
Aggregate Demand, Full Employment, and
    the Price Level   330
Analyzing the Gross National Product   332
Economic Fluctuations May Be Cumulative   335

Chapter 18   *Managing the Nation's Economy*   343

What Are the Goals of Economic Policy?   343
Fiscal Policy   344

Fiscal Policy and the National Debt   347
The Controversy Over Deficit Financing   349
Monetary Policy   350
The Federal Reserve Regulates the Money
    Supply   351
Monetary and Fiscal Policy Summarized   358
Limitations of Fiscal Policy   358
Limitations of Monetary Policy   360

UNIT VIII   Personal Economics

Chapter 19   *Personal Savings and Consumer Credit*   369

Personal Savings   369
Where Do Consumers Keep Their Savings?   371
Providing for Financial Risk Through
    Insurance   380
The Economic Implications of Savings   382
Consumer Credit   383
What Kinds of Credit Are Available to
    Consumers?   385
Shopping for Credit   387
Getting and Keeping a Good Credit Rating   388

Chapter 20   *How Can Consumers Get More for
    Their Money?*   392

Income Management for Consumers:
    The Personal Budget   392
Shopping Guidelines for Consumers   394
Information for Consumers   396
Protection for Consumers   397
Consumerism—The Consumer-Action
    Movement   400
Advertising and the Consumer   401

UNIT IX   Living Issues in the United States Economy

Chapter 21   *The Economics of Cities*   409

Our Growing Urban Population   409
Current Problems of the Metropolitan
    Areas   412
Meeting the Cities' Problems   420

Chapter 22   *The Economics of Farming*   427

The Miracle of United States Farm
    Production   427
Supply, Demand, and Resource Use of
    Agriculture   430
Government and the Farmer   433

Chapter 23   *Economic Growth and the Quality of Life*   442

What Is Economic Growth?   442
What Is the Importance of Economic Growth?   443
What Are the Ingredients of Economic
    Growth?   444
Government and Economic Growth   450
The Controversy Over Economic Growth   452

UNIT X   The Global Economy

Chapter 24   *International Trade*   463

International Trade and Economic
    Specialization   464
Barriers to World Trade   470
Why Do Nations Restrict International Trade?   471
Evolution of American Trade Policy   475
World Trade Since 1945   476
Multinational Corporations and the
    "Globalization" of Businesses   478

Chapter 25   *Financing International Trade*   486

Exchange Rates   486
How Are Exchange Rates Determined?   488
The Balance of Payments   491

Chapter 26   *Other Economic Systems*   502

Iow We Compare Economic Systems   503
Coordinating Economic Activity:
    The Market vs. the Plan   504
What Tools Are Available to Economic Planners?
   507
Karl Marx's Economic Thought   510
Communism in Practice: The Soviet Union   514

Sweden: The Middle Way   517
Hungary: Market Communism at Work   520
Comparing Economic Systems   520

Chapter 27   *The Less Developed World*   525

Why Are Many Countries "Less Developed"?   525
Why Are the Less Developed Countries
      Poor?   527
A Program for the Less Developed Countries   530
How Less Developed Countries Pay the
      Costs of Development   532

Illustrations and Tables   536

Glossary   539

Index   548

Features

Makers of Economic Thought

Adam Smith   10
David Ricardo   78
Joan Robinson   130
Thomas Robert Malthus   178
Alfred Marshall   294
John Maynard Keynes   328
The First Nobel Prize in Economics Is Awarded   456
Karl Marx   512

Personal Economics

Filing an Income Tax Return   240
Your Checking Account   376
How to Write a Letter of Complaint   398

Developing Economic Understanding

The Production Possibilities Curve   14
Costs, Revenues, and Profits in the Process of Production:
    A Hypothetical Case Study   84
The Micrin Mouthwash Story: A Study in Product
    Differentiation   136
The Role of Consumers in Utility Regulation   154
The Social Security System   222
The Underground Economy: A Drain on Us All   243
The Business Cycle and Economic Indicators: How Do We
    Know Where We Are?   324
The Multiplier, the Accelerator, and the Paradox of Thrift 337
The Quantity Equation of Exchange   352
Supply-Side Economics   362
Automation: Promises and Problems   445
The Economics of Pollution   454
The Money Without a Country: Eurodollars, Petrodollars,
    and Other Eurocurrencies   496
Input-Output Analysis   508

Mini-Readings

Have Unions Been Responsible for Higher Wages?   206
The Flat Tax: A Proposal to Simplify the Income Tax   239
What Is Money? Ask M1, M2, M3, or L   262
Aggregate Demand and Full Employment   331
Does Federal Borrowing "Crowd Out" Business?   356
The Laffer Curve: How to Cut Taxes and Increase
    Government Revenue   361
The Power of Compound Interest   375
Government Regulatory Agencies: When Does Regulation
    Become "Too Much Regulation"?   405
To Grow Or Not to Grow   458
How Important Is Foreign Trade?   469
The Debt Crisis of the Less Developed Countries   533

Exercise Readings

The Concentration Ratio: A Measure of Competition   140
Antitrust Today: What Constitutes "Restraint of Trade"?   161
Payments-in-Kind: A New Approach to an Old Problem   440
Love Canal: A Landmark in the History of Environmental
    Pollution   461

Scarcity of natural resources forces all societies to make economic choices.

UNIT I

Economic Reasoning

CHAPTER 1
Economics: The Basic Questions

Have you ever gone shopping for clothes with $75 in your wallet, only to find that the things you wanted to buy added up to something around $150? Did you go home empty-handed? Perhaps not, for like many people in that situation you might have tried to squeeze the greatest satisfaction out of your $75 by buying only those items that you needed most.

Economists refer to the things people want as either *goods* or *services*. *Goods* are *tangible* things (you can see them and touch them). *Services* are the *intangible* things that have value. Haircuts, medical care, and education are examples of services. As goods and services are used to satisfy our wants, they are *consumed*. For that reason those who buy goods and services are called *consumers*, and the act of consuming is called *consumption*.

The ingredients that go into the production of goods and services are *productive resources*, or the *factors of production*. Whereas human wants are virtually unlimited, the productive resources needed to satisfy those wants are relatively scarce. Thus, *scarcity* is a fact of life, one which every individual and institution must deal with by choosing among resources.

Economics is the study of how people and societies use their limited resources to satisfy their unlimited wants. Or, to put it another way, economics is the study of how people make a living.

This chapter opens our study of economics. First we shall look at the factors of production and the questions that must be answered before these factors can begin to create goods and services. Economic systems represent the answers to those questions and are our next topic. Finally, we shall discuss our nation's economic goals.

THE FACTORS OF PRODUCTION

All human wants cannot be satisfied at the same time. People's wants are unlimited, but the factors of production are limited. This section discusses the four factors of production—human resources, natural resources, capital, and management—and shows how they are related to human wants and needs.

1. Human Resources. When economists talk about human resources, labor, or the work force, they are describing the people whose efforts and skills go into the production of goods and services. Without human resources goods and services could not be produced.

People affect the production of goods and services in two ways. First, the size of the work force affects the amount of goods and services produced. If a country has too few workers, it will be unable to make full use of its other resources. It may then encourage its citizens to have larger families or it may promote immigration.

Numbers of workers alone, however, do not determine how much a society can produce. Even more important is productivity, which is the amount each worker produces in a specified time. Productivity is determined largely by the availability of machinery, equipment, and *skilled* workers. India's population is nearly three times as large as that of the United States, yet India produces barely one-twentieth the amount of goods and services that the United States does. United States productivity is so much higher than India's because the United States has more and better machinery and skilled workers than India.

2. Natural Resources. Natural resources are materials obtained from the land, sea, and air, and include soil, minerals, fish, wildlife, water, and timber. (Economists sometimes use the word "land" to mean natural resources of all kinds.)

In order to benefit from their natural resources, a people must have a use for them and the means of obtaining them. For centuries the Native American western Shoshones dwelling near present-day Salt Lake City eked out a meager existence from the land. They ate seeds, roots, and an occasional rabbit or grasshopper, and had only the simplest shelter and clothing. Today, the same land produces not only abundant vegetables, beef, and dairy products, but also valuable minerals such as gold, copper, and lead. The reason for this difference in the use of natural resources lies in our present advanced technology, which has conquered this once barren land with irrigation, drought-resistant crops, and modern machinery and know-how.

Some regions of the world have a low *standard of living* because they have few natural resources. In economic terms, standard of living refers to the quantity and quality of goods and services that are

Factors of Production. In this photo of a construction site, three of the four factors of production are visible. Can you identify them?

consumed by an individual or a society. The only way to improve the economies of these lands is to strengthen their other productive factors—labor, capital, and management. Switzerland, Denmark, and Japan have limited natural resources but still have a high standard of living because their other resources are highly developed.

Although all natural resources are limited, some can be replaced or *renewed* while others cannot. Forests can be replanted. Streams and woodlands can be restocked. But mineral ores and fuels cannot be replaced. They are *nonrenewable* resources. In recent years shortages of some resources and the disappearance of others have led many governments to pass laws conserving their natural resources and to seek international cooperation to protect world supplies.

3. Capital. The machines, tools, and buildings that are used to produce goods and services are called *capital,* or *capital goods.* A shirt factory is a form of capital because it produces shirts. A commercial airplane is another type of capital because it provides transportation services. Schools, too, are a type of capital because they help provide a service: education. The term "capital" as it is used here should not be confused with money, which in other contexts is also called "capital." Money does not produce goods; machines, tools, and buildings do.

Economics: The Basic Questions **3**

Capital is eventually used up or worn out, a process called *depreciation.* If new capital is not produced to replace capital that has depreciated, fewer goods can be produced. In order to increase production, a nation must produce more or better capital goods than are needed merely to make up for depreciation. If a country has $100 billion in capital goods that will last twenty years, at the end of one year one-twentieth of the capital goods, or $5 billion, will have been used up. This $5 billion will have to be replaced just to have as much capital at the end of the year as there was at the beginning. Thus in order to *increase* its capital, the nation will have to spend more than $5 billion. The production of capital goods is called *capital formation.* Because capital goods are so vital to the production of goods and services, capital formation is an essential economic process in all societies.

How Capital Formation Takes Place. Unlike consumer goods (such as food, clothing, and shelter), capital goods do not satisfy human wants immediately. Instead, they are used in the production of other goods—either consumer goods or other capital goods. Capital produced in the present satisfies human wants at a future time. Since there is a limit to the amount a nation can produce at any one time, capital formation requires a decision to do without some consumer goods now in order to have more later.

In the United States, capital formation takes place when companies use part of their profits to expand their operations or when individuals and businesses or other private institutions put their savings into banks, government bonds, insurance, or the stock market. The financial institutions receiving these savings will seek to lend them out. The effect is to provide a reservoir of surplus funds that can be used for the purchase of capital goods. Thus, a business in need of a new machine can call upon a local bank for a loan to finance the purchase.

4. Management. For a business to function, some person or group has to bring together the three factors of production that we discussed above: natural resources, labor, and capital. This function is called *management.* It is performed by persons known as *entrepreneurs* (enterprisers) who invest their money in a business to make a profit. Entrepreneurs are the owners of a business. They see that the business operates efficiently and may hire managers to handle the day-to-day affairs of the business. Although we are used to identifying the management of a business with its owners, in economic terms managers are themselves a special form of labor.

THE THREE FUNDAMENTAL QUESTIONS OF ECONOMICS

Since all the factors of production are limited, individuals, businesses, and governments must make economic choices by answering three fundamental questions:

What goods and services should be produced?

How should they be produced?

Who should receive the goods and services that are produced?

1. What Goods and Services Should Be Produced? Even if everyone able and willing to work had a job and every factory, mine, and shop were working full time, we still could not produce enough to satisfy the nation's wants. With our resources fully employed, production in one area could be increased only by decreasing production in another area. If a shopping center is built on what was once farmland, that land can no longer be used to grow food. Labor that is working on the construction of a sports arena cannot be employed at the same time to build a hospital.

Economists refer to this trade-off of one activity for another as the *opportunity cost* of the choice. If you choose to play basketball on a summer afternoon instead of going swimming, an economist would say that the opportunity cost of your basketball game was the

Opportunity Cost. In 1980, the baseball superstar David Winfield (left) signed a contract to play for the New York Yankees for a record-setting $1.5 million a year for ten years. Express this cost to Yankee owner George Steinbrenner (right) as an opportunity cost.

"This one could be converted into 104 schoolhouses. How many would yours make?"
Langley in *The Christian Science Monitor* © 1969 TCSPS

afternoon's swim. Similarly, the opportunity cost of the shopping center was that many acres of farmland.

The characters in the political cartoon above are discussing opportunity costs. Can you identify those costs? What nations do the two characters represent?

2. How Should Goods and Services Be Produced? There is more than one way to make an automobile, build a school, or explore for minerals. The method of production depends on how the factors of production are combined. In producing automobiles, management must decide to what extent the introduction of labor-saving machinery will cut costs and improve output. In building a new school, city planners must determine whether they want a sprawling one-story school, which will require much land, or a multistoried building, which will increase construction costs. In exploring for minerals, mining companies must decide which technique of extraction will yield the least waste as compared to the total output and cost of operation.

6   *Economic Reasoning*

How goods are produced often affects the entire society. In parts of our country the destruction of forests, the overgrazing of grasslands, and the misuse of croplands have resulted in soil erosion and floods. Our production methods have led to the pollution of lakes, streams, and air. The increasing use of machines and the advent of automation have changed the entire character of our labor force and have made it harder for the unskilled to find jobs.

Some person or group must decide what combination of resources is to be applied to the production of goods and services. The answers will vary from nation to nation because of differences in resources, technological know-how, and culture. In some nations the lack of certain resources accounts for the heavy use of hand labor instead of machinery. Cultural values can influence the use of human resources, as in countries where it is considered wrong for women to work.

Another factor that affects how goods and services are produced is the efficiency of a nation's industries. In the 1970s our nation's steel companies chose not to adopt the most modern methods of production that had been developed in Japan. As a result, the Japanese steelmakers were able to undersell American steel in world markets. Meanwhile the United States Congress enacted laws requiring American manufacturers to buy steel from American firms. Consequently, American consumers had to pay more for the automobiles, refrigerators, and other goods that were made with the costlier American steel. The effect of these higher prices was to restrict purchases of new steel products and thus reduce the standard of living.

3. Who Shall Receive the Goods and Services Produced? Since it is not possible to produce enough of everything to satisfy everyone, we must ask, "Who shall receive the goods and services produced?"

Should everyone have an equal share? Or should some people be allowed to have more than others? Should goods and services be awarded according to people's contributions to society? Or should goods and services be divided according to need? If people are to be paid in accordance with their contributions or needs, how are these to be measured? Who will do the measuring?

In the United States, a neurosurgeon's income may be twenty times that of a schoolteacher. In Great Britain a neurosurgeon may earn only four times as much as a schoolteacher, and in China the difference may be less than two times.

Among the wealthiest men and women in America are successful professional athletes. In many other countries, however, professional athletes could hardly earn a living. America answers the question "Who shall receive the goods and services produced by the economy?" in one way, Britain answers it in another, and China in still another.

What, How, and Who. How has this ice cream shop answered the basic economic questions, what, how, and who?

ECONOMIC SYSTEMS: SOCIETY'S ANSWER TO WHAT, HOW, AND WHO

All societies, past and present, have had to seek answers to the fundamental economic questions of *what, how,* and *who.* Each society adopts an economic system to deal with these questions. Most economic systems can be classified as traditional, command, or market economies or as a combination of these.

1. Traditional Economy. The feudal society of the Middle Ages in Europe was a traditional economic system. The questions *what, how,* and *who* were decided by the church, by guilds, and by custom. Under this essentially agricultural system, the basic economic unit was the feudal manor, which was owned and ruled by a landlord who was usually a member of the nobility or clergy. The landlords decided *what* goods would be produced. Their decisions were influenced by the simple needs of their peasants, by the more elaborate demands of their own families and any other high-born people on their estates, and by the customs of the day.

Custom also influenced *how* goods were produced. Profession was usually determined by birth: A man worked at the job of his father. Women tended the home and cared for children. Peasants worked their lands in accordance with time-honored tradition, and invention and innovation were discouraged. In the villages, the guilds closely

8   *Economic Reasoning*

regulated the production of goods. They not only set standards of quality but also determined quantity and price.

Who would receive the goods depended upon their station in life. The peasant was given just enough to keep body and soul together, while the nobility enjoyed the few comforts and luxuries of the age. In accordance with custom, people were expected not to attempt to improve their status, for this was settled once and for all at birth.

Tradition did not account for all the economic life of feudal society. There were also traveling merchants whose activities more closely resembled the market economy described below. Local rulers sometimes made economic decisions for the areas they controlled, thus creating an economic system resembling a command economy. Few economic systems exist in pure form. Elements of traditional, command, and market economies are found to some degree in all societies.

2. Command Economy. In a command economy, the fundamental questions of *what, how,* and *who* are decided by a central authority, usually the government. The degree of power exercised by the government varies from one country to another. In some countries the government holds absolute control over the political and economic life of its citizens. In the Soviet Union, China, and Cuba, for example, the government is in the hands of political dictatorships, and the will of the people is subordinate to the will of the rulers. In other countries, such as Sweden, India, and Israel, the government makes many economic decisions, but the leadership must regularly seek reelection and therefore remains responsible to the people.

All countries have some element of centralized planning. In the United States, the federal government continuously influences the economy through its powers to tax and to spend money, and government on various levels exerts control over such services as education, transportation, mail, medical care, and defense.

3. Market Economy. Quite the opposite of the centrally directed command economy is the decentralized market economy. Here the major decisions as to *what, how,* and *who* are made by individuals and businesses and, to a lesser extent, the government. Buyers and sellers make their wishes known in a *marketplace,* which is any place where goods are bought and sold. The marketplace is something like a polling booth: buyers are in effect "voting" for the goods they purchase. The sellers, in order to make the largest possible profit, try to satisfy the wants of as many buyers as they can.

Although no country has a pure market economy, the United States economy is primarily a market economy. The following chapters focus on the operation of the market system.

ADAM SMITH
The Wealth of Nations (1776)

The year 1776 was a landmark in the history of the West for at least two reasons. First, a new vision of political freedom was proclaimed in the American Declaration of Independence. Second, a new vision of economic freedom was heralded. In 1776 a Scottish author, Adam Smith, published *An Inquiry Into the Nature and Causes of the Wealth of Nations*. So great was Smith's impact upon Western thinking that he came to be known as the "father of modern economics."

Born in Scotland in 1723 and educated at Oxford University in England, Smith returned to his native land to teach for a time at the University of Glasgow. In 1763 he began a three-year tour of Europe, during which he met with a number of prominent thinkers. Returning to London in 1766 Smith spent the next ten years writing *The Wealth of Nations*. In 1778 Smith was placed in charge of the customs house in Glasgow, and he held that post until his death in 1790.

In Adam Smith's time, most European nations followed the doctrine of *mercantilism*. The mercantilists believed that money—that is, gold and silver—was the source of wealth. Governments, therefore, ought to do everything they could to build up their nations' supply of the precious metals. Since most governments followed the mercantilists' doctrine, they enacted laws whose purpose was to enlarge their nations' supplies of silver and gold. These laws limited the economic activities of their colonies and prohibited, or sharply restricted, the export of precious metals.

Smith strongly disagreed with the mercantilists. Wealth, he said, sprang from the production of goods and services, not from the accumulation of gold and silver. People cannot eat precious metals, nor can they be sheltered by them in storms, or warmed by them in winter. Those who would measure the true wealth of a nation, Smith said, should look to the amount of goods and services available for each of its citizens, not the size of its treasury.

How then can a government encourage the production of the greatest quantity of goods and services? Here is where Smith's break with mercantilism is most clearly seen. Government, he wrote, could serve

the economy best by *keeping its hands off business*. To the French who had first proposed such a policy the idea was described as *laissez-faire* (literally, "let them do"). François Quesnay, a French economist, had advocated *laissez-faire* in connection with the French government's farm policies. Smith expanded Quesnay's concept to apply to a nation's entire economy. *Laissez-faire* achieved enormous popularity in England as a result of *The Wealth of Nations,* and the term is still in use today.

Why should government allow businesses to conduct their affairs without interference? Left to their own devices, Smith said, business people would seek to make the greatest profits by turning out the greatest quantity of goods and services at the lowest possible prices. These low-cost goods and services would have to benefit society as a whole. Smith put it this way: "The businessman intends only his own gain; however, he is in this . . . led by an invisible hand to promote an end which was no part of his intention. . . . By pursuing his own interest, he frequently promotes that of society more effectually than when he really intends to promote it."

The "invisible hand" which Smith saw guiding business along a path of public good was, in reality, the pursuit of profits. The "chase" took place in a *market* subject to the laws of *supply* and *demand,* which we shall discuss in Chapter 2. To allow these laws of the marketplace to function, Smith espoused the philosophy of *laissez-faire.* But Smith was also a realist. He recognized that government would have to intervene in the economy to preserve competition and to protect the general welfare.

The Wealth of Nations deals with many other subjects besides *laissez-faire,* among them labor, production, income distribution, rent, and taxation. Later economists would look to Smith's ideas as the springboard for the development of their own theories in each of these fields.

Smith's influence was dramatized in 1983 when the Nobel Prize in Economics was awarded to Gerard Debreu of the University of California at Berkeley. (See page 456 for a discussion of the Nobel Prizes in Economics.) Debreu's prize was awarded in recognition of his work on one of economics' fundamental questions: How do prices operate to balance what producers offer for sale with what buyers want? Debreu developed a mathematical foundation that could be used to demonstrate the laws of supply and demand in action in a modern economy. In this way, the invisible hand of the eighteenth century has become a mathematical reality in the twentieth century.

ECONOMIC GOALS OF OUR SOCIETY

The economic system a society adopts depends largely on its economic goals. Most Americans want a system to provide the following:

1. Economic Freedom. Americans have guarded their traditional economic freedoms as carefully as their political freedoms. Workers in the United States take for granted their right to accept or reject a job. In some nations, workers do not have this right. American workers can form labor unions that are free to strive for better working conditions—another economic freedom not enjoyed in all nations.

Economic freedom includes the right to spend or save money as one wishes and to own the goods one has purchased. It also includes the right of business people to own property and make a profit. Of course, our economic freedoms, like our political freedoms, are limited by rules of law. The right of business people to run their own firms does not permit them to produce or sell merchandise that would endanger the health or safety of others.

2. Economic Justice. Most Americans agree that all persons should have equal economic opportunity regardless of nationality, age, sex, race, or income level. There is far less agreement, however, on how to make this goal a reality. Not everyone agrees on what constitutes equal economic opportunity or on what steps should be taken to insure it.

For example, the average income of nonwhites and females in this country is far below that of white males. In an effort to raise the income of those groups, the federal government and some state governments have required that companies under government contract give preference in hiring to minorities and women. Critics label such programs "reverse discrimination" since the programs deny jobs solely on the basis of sex and race.

Most Americans also agree that everyone should have a fair share of the nation's goods and services—that is, there should be a fair distribution of income. But what constitutes a fair share is a matter of divided opinion. The government seeks a fairer distribution of income by taxing wealthier individuals and groups at a higher rate and distributing some of that wealth to the needy.

3. Economic Efficiency. A nation must make the best use of its resources to provide the greatest quantity of the goods and services that its citizens want. How well it achieves that goal is a measure of the nation's economic efficiency.

4. Economic Stability. A period of economic stability is one in which changes in the level of prices, employment, and business activity are modest. In stable times, prices of most goods and services remain at levels that people can afford, and jobs are plentiful. An important economic goal, therefore, is to maintain stable prices and employment.

Unfortunately, there have been times when the United States has experienced periods of economic decline and periods of inflation. During an economic decline, business activity falls off, workers lose their jobs, and many resources lie idle. When the decline is severe, as it was during the 1930s, it is called a depression. A milder decline is known as a recession.

Inflation is a general rise in prices. During inflation, people find that unless their incomes are increasing as fast as prices, they cannot buy as much as before. Inflation is particularly cruel for people with fixed incomes such as pensions.

The hardships resulting from depression and inflation led Congress to take action to maintain national economic stability. The Employment Act of 1946 declared that it is the responsibility of the federal government "to promote maximum employment, production, and purchasing power." Later chapters in this book discuss how our government tries to maintain the nation's economic stability.

5. *Economic Security.* People like to know that in times of illness or unemployment and in old age, they and their families will be provided for. They may set aside a portion of their earnings in the form of savings, insurance, and other investments for that purpose. Many business firms and labor unions provide their employees and members with insurance and retirement plans.

Because economic security is so important and many people could not otherwise obtain it, all levels of government have established programs to offset the risks resulting from loss of income. Examples of such programs are social security, unemployment insurance, welfare, and savings deposit insurance.

Nations also seek to provide economic security for their citizens through international agreements. For example, when in 1979 the United States was faced with a serious shortage of oil because of the difficulties it was having with Iran, the Carter administration negotiated an agreement with Saudi Arabia to supply the difference.

6. *Economic Growth.* Most people want more of the goods and services that make for a rising standard of living. But the society as a whole can obtain more only if it is producing more. An increasing output of goods and services is called economic growth.

Some people question whether unlimited economic growth is desirable. Along with the benefits of unlimited production of goods and services, there are also serious dangers. For example, as production increases, pollution and the loss of natural resources also increase.

DEVELOPING ECONOMIC UNDERSTANDING

The Production Possibilities Curve

The production possibilities curve illustrates in graphic form the economic concepts of scarcity and opportunity cost. Scarcity may be the most significant word in economics. Scarcity compels individuals and societies to choose from among the things they want. If they choose one combination of goods and services, they must give up another. Let us illustrate the problem of scarcity by considering an imaginary country we will call Ravinia. A tiny nation, Ravinia produces two categories of goods: necessities and luxuries.* In a recent survey Ravinian economists determined the following:

1. With the labor force fully employed and producing nothing but necessities (food, clothing, and shelter), 600 million tons could be turned out in one year.

2. With the labor force fully employed and producing nothing but luxuries (jewelry, yachts, and candy), 110 million tons could be created in one year.

3. If Ravinia chose to turn out both luxuries and necessities, various combinations of each could be produced.

Table 1.1 shows that if Ravinia chose to produce 300 million tons of

* Necessities are those goods and services needed to sustain daily life. Luxuries are items that add comfort and pleasure to life but can be done without.

TABLE 1.1   Production Possibilities in Ravinia

If necessities produced are	the maximum production of luxuries could be
600 million tons	0
550 ″ ″	40 million tons
500 ″ ″	55 ″ ″
400 ″ ″	80 ″ ″
300 ″ ″	90 ″ ″
150 ″ ″	100 ″ ″
0	110 ″ ″

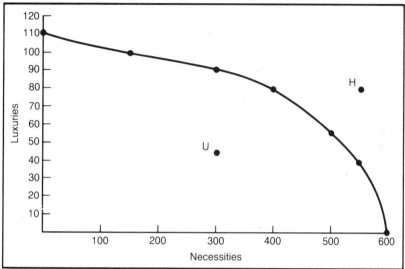

FIGURE 1.1   Production Possibilities in Ravinia

necessities in a given year, it could also generate up to 90 million tons of luxuries. Suppose, however, that the Ravinians wanted more than 90 million tons of luxuries—say, 100 million tons. Would they be able to produce the additional 10 million tons of luxuries? Yes, but in so doing they would have to take some of the resources that had been engaged in the production of necessities and shift them to luxury production. The table tells us that producing 10 million more tons of luxuries would result in a 50 percent reduction in the production of necessities. In economic terms, the opportunity cost of producing an additional 10 million tons of luxuries would be 150 million tons of necessities.

By transferring the information in the table to a graph and connecting the plotted points, we can create a production possibilities curve, as shown in Figure 1.1. A production possibilities curve depicts the possibilities for production when all resources are fully and effectively employed. In actuality, a nation is likely to produce less than it is capable of producing.

Suppose, for example, that Ravinia's present production is at point U. At U the nation is producing 300 million tons of necessities and 45 million tons of luxuries. These amounts are well below Ravinia's capacity, and the Ravinians have fewer goods and services available to them than the economy is capable of producing.

Suppose, however, that the Ravinians wanted to produce 550 tons of

necessities and 80 million tons of luxuries, as depicted by point H. Would that be possible?

Figure 1.1 shows that it would not be possible under present conditions to expand production to point H. The production possibilities curve indicates a limit beyond which production cannot expand using current resources. Expanding the economy beyond the production possibilities curve would require additional resources. Increasing the size of the labor force or acquiring more and better tools and equipment could lead to increased production. So too could improved management techniques or better government. For the nation's economic planners, the production possibilities curve represents a limit they must constantly strive to exceed.

1. Explain the statement that "*scarcity* may be the single most significant word in the field of economics."
2. Define a production possibilities curve.
3. According to the table, how many tons of luxuries could the Ravinians have produced in a year that they turned out 400 tons of necessities?
4. What are *opportunity costs*?
5. What would be the opportunity cost to Ravinia if it chose to increase its production of necessities from 500 to 550 tons at a time when its resources were fully employed?
6. You have been asked by the Ravinian government for your opinion as to the state of its economy. Current production levels stand at 200 tons of necessities and 80 tons of luxuries a year. What would you tell the Ravinians? Explain your answer.
7. Ravinia is now producing 500 tons of necessities and 50 tons of luxuries. It would like to hold its production of necessities at current levels and increase production of luxuries to 80 tons. What are Ravinia's chances of success? Explain your answer.

EXERCISES

Multiple Choice

Select the answer that correctly completes the question.

1. When a nation's resources are fully employed with maximum efficiency, additional machinery (a) cannot be produced under any circumstances (b) can be produced, but only under government supervision (c) can be produced, but only if the production of something else is reduced (d) can be produced, but only by privately owned industries.

2. All of the following are factors of production *except* (a) land (b) money (c) labor (d) capital.

3. Because wants are unlimited but resources are limited, society must *economize*. This means that society must (a) use its resources in such a way as to get the most out of them (b) save as much money as possible (c) keep its budgets balanced (d) limit the use of its resources.

4. All economic systems *must* provide answers to three of the following questions. Which question is not *necessarily* a concern of every economic system? (a) What goods and services should be produced? (b) Who will receive the goods and services that are produced? (c) How can goods and services be fairly distributed among all the people? (d) How shall the factors of production be combined to produce goods and services?

5. The *opportunity cost* of an increase in the local police force is (a) the cost of the additional police salaries and benefits (b) the cost of training new recruits (c) the amount by which taxes will be increased to pay for the additional police (d) the goods or services that will be given up in order to hire the additional police.

6. *Productivity* is a measure of (a) output per worker (b) the amount of resources available (c) the level of inflation (d) the value of goods and services.

7. The process whereby capital goods are produced is called (a) custom (b) consumption (c) centralized planning (d) capital formation.

8. A firm sets aside funds for *depreciation* to (a) prepare for a decline in business (b) provide for the replacement of worn-out capital

(*c*) cover increasing labor costs (*d*) insure against falling prices of its goods.

9. Even though a nation possesses few natural resources, it may nevertheless have a high standard of living because (*a*) needed natural resources may be purchased cheaply (*b*) many goods and services can be produced without natural resources (*c*) the nation's other resources are highly developed (*d*) the people live very simply.

10. "In country X, a person's future is determined at birth. People do the same jobs that their parents and grandparents did. Goods are produced according to time-honored methods and distributed to people according to their rank or social position." What kind of economy is being described in this quotation? (*a*) market economy (*b*) traditional economy (*c*) command economy (*d*) underdeveloped economy.

11. Skyscrapers are found in large cities but not in small towns. Economists would explain this in terms of (*a*) differences in architectural taste between city and country (*b*) the relatively low construction cost of tall buildings as compared to those of one or two stories (*c*) the lower cost of labor in cities (*d*) the scarcity and high costs of land in cities.

12. Economists differentiate between *goods* and *services*. Which of the following represents payment for a *service*? (*a*) 95 cents for a hamburger (*b*) $10 for a haircut (*c*) $8.95 for a textbook (*d*) $9,000 for a new automobile.

Essay Questions

1. Some people claim that a command economy is more efficient than the United States market economy. In support of this position, they remind us that in time of war the United States government has found it necessary to assume wide economic powers. These powers included controlling prices, wages, and hours of work, along with rationing certain goods that were in short supply. (*a*) Identify and explain two reasons why you agree or disagree that a command economy is more efficient than our market economy. (*b*) Give two reasons why you think the United States abandoned central planning after World War II.

2. Economic decisions are likely to be influenced by the *opportunity costs* that they incur. For each of the following questions, answer yes or no and explain your answer in terms of opportunity costs. (*a*) Should the United States undertake a program to land astronauts on Mars? (*b*) Should your community build a new hospital? (*c*) Should your family buy a new automobile (in addition to any it may already own)? (*d*) Should the federal government give financial support to the United States Olympics team?

3. "People cannot eat machinery or factory buildings. That is why poor countries should concentrate on agriculture and leave manufacturing to the industrialized nations." Explain why you agree or disagree with this statement.
4. "If there were no sanitation workers to remove and dispose of our garbage, the incidence of disease and death would increase. By contrast, if professional sports were abolished, there would be no effect upon public health or longevity. How then can you explain why professional athletes earn so much more than sanitation workers?" How would you respond to this statement?
5. Why is economics sometimes called the "science of choice"?

CHAPTER 2
Demand, Supply, and Market Price

"You mean you bought another watch?"

"I know, I already own two watches, but at the price I simply couldn't pass this one up."

"I just took a job at VendorsMart."

"VendorsMart? That's a department store. I thought you were working for Gold Star Clothing."

"I was until VendorsMart offered me twice as much as I was making at Gold Star."

"I'm looking for a new ten-speed bike."

"I thought you already owned one."

"I did. But Gloria offered me so much money for it that I had to sell it to her."

There are many reasons why people decide to make a purchase, take a job, or sell something. Whatever the reasons, one element that is always present is *price*. If the price is too low, sellers will not sell. If the price is too high, buyers will not buy. Prices play a crucial role in our economic system. To understand how a nation's economy functions, it is necessary to have some understanding of the nation's price system.

This chapter describes the forces that determine the price of a good or service. Economists call these forces *supply* and *demand*. Our discussion will consider demand and supply and will then examine how they interact to establish *market price*.

DEMAND

Many people would like to own a new sports car, wear designer clothes, or take a trip to China. To the economist these desires are merely wishes that have no economic significance. But if a person steps forward with the necessary money and says, " I will pay $30,000 for a sports car now," our economist would identify this as *demand*. Demand is the desire to purchase a particular item at a specified price and time, *accompanied by the ability and willingness to pay.*

Demand Schedule. The quantity demanded varies with the price of an item. Suppose, for example, that on October 3 you were to survey a class of 30 students to find out how many would like to purchase chocolate ice cream cones that would be delivered immediately at a price of $1.25 each. Two hands might go up. But if the price you quoted was 80 cents, 23 hands might be raised. Up to a certain point, the lower the price went, the more students would be willing to buy. In tabular form, the demand might look like Table 2.1. This table, showing the varying demand for a particular item at different prices, is called a *demand schedule.*

TABLE 2.1   Demand for Chocolate Ice Cream Cones
Monday, October 3

Price	Number of Cones Students Will Buy
$1.40	1
1.25	2
1.10	6
.95	12
.80	23
.65	45

Demand Curve. The demand schedule shown above can be illustrated with a demand curve. A demand curve is a line graph that shows the amount of a product that will be purchased at each price. *On all of the following graphs, the vertical axis measures price per unit (P), and the horizontal axis measures number of units, or quantity (Q).* In Figure 2.1 on page 22, the demand curve D slopes downward and to the right. The points on the curve correspond to the demand schedule for chocolate ice cream cones. A demand curve thus shows how much of a commodity will be sold at any given price. ·

The Law of Demand. The Law of Demand says that as the price of an item decreases, the quantity demanded will increase. Conversely, as the price increases, the quantity demanded will decrease. As the price of a product goes down, (*a*) more people can afford to buy the product, (*b*) people tend to buy larger quantities of the product, and (*c*) people tend to substitute the product for similar products that are either more expensive or less desirable. Similarly, as the price of a

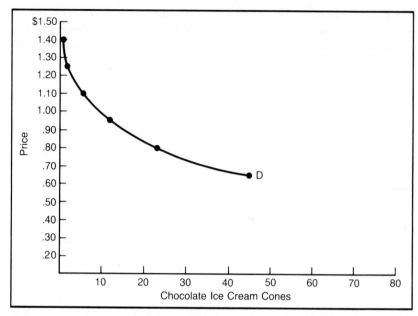

FIGURE 2.1   Demand Curve for Chocolate Ice Cream Cones on October 3

product goes up, (*a*) fewer people can afford to buy the product, (*b*) people tend to buy smaller quantities of the product, and (*c*) people tend to substitute cheaper products. The Law of Demand can be generalized as follows: *The quantity demanded varies inversely with changes in price.*

Law of Demand. What factors will affect the demand for hot dogs and ice cream?

In our example, the Law of Demand determined how many chocolate ice cream cones would be sold at each price. As the price of the cones was reduced, more students were interested in buying them. The lower price attracted some students who had not been planning to spend any money. Others who would have purchased one cone at a higher price bought two or more at a lower price. And still others who had been planning to buy a candy bar or a piece of cake after class decided to eat ice cream instead.

Storekeepers are well aware of the Law of Demand. That is why they lower prices when they want to clear out merchandise. Butchers know, for example, that some consumers who would not buy steak at $4.50 a pound will buy it for $3 a pound. They also know that some consumers who are willing to pay $4.50 a pound will buy more at $3 because at the lower price they will substitute steak for other foods such as chicken and fish.

Principle of Marginal Utility. When we conducted our ice cream cone study, we in effect made each member of the class ask the question, "Do I want to give up some of my purchasing power in order to have an ice cream cone?" Anyone about to make a purchase must ask a similar question. Once you have spent a sum of money on one purchase, that sum is no longer available to you for any other purchase.

Why does a buyer choose one product instead of another? Assume, for example, that you have 40 cents with which you plan to buy either chewing gum or candy. After a few moments' consideration in front of the candy counter, you decide to buy the gum. Why gum and not candy? The economist would explain this choice in terms of *utility*. Utility is the measure of satisfaction one gets from the use of a good or service. When you chose the chewing gum, you decided that it would better satisfy your wants than a candy bar. In economic terms, the utility of chewing gum was greater than the utility of a candy bar.

Economists have devised the concept of *marginal utility* to help explain the spending patterns of consumers. Marginal utility is the degree of satisfaction a consumer gets from each *additional* purchase of a product or service. (The word "marginal" has several meanings in economics. In this case it means "additional.")

People will buy something if they expect the purchase to yield them more satisfaction (utility) than something else. In the example of the chocolate ice cream cones, many students were willing to buy a second, a third, or even a fourth cone if the price was low enough. But as the ice cream was consumed, it became less satisfying. By the time the second or third cone was downed, the thought of still another

Marginal Utility. Suppose that this is the second hamburger that the consumer has purchased within the last hour. What would be the marginal utility to her of a third hamburger?

cone was less appealing. In economic terms, each additional cone had less utility than the preceding one. This phenomenon is summarized in the Principle of Diminishing Marginal Utility, which states that each additional purchase of a product or service by a given consumer will be less satisfying than the previous purchase.

The Principle of Diminishing Marginal Utility applies to almost any product. One overcoat may be a necessity, two or three desirable; but what would induce you to buy four or five? Each new purchase will be less satisfying than the one before. It will have less utility. You will be less willing to give up something else to buy an additional overcoat. You may still be induced to buy another coat, but only at a lower price.

Elasticity of Demand. The Law of Demand is clear: Fewer items will be bought at a higher price than at a lower price. But the Law of Demand does not tell *by how much* the quantity demanded will increase or decrease at different prices. If the price of milk doubles, less milk will be sold. Similarly, if the price of steak doubles, consumers will buy less steak. But will the sales of milk and steak fall by the same percentage? For example, if milk sales drop 20 percent when the price doubles, will steak sales also drop 20 percent when the price of steak doubles? Certainly not. The population as a whole can do without steak far more easily than it can do without milk. Even at the higher price, the demand for milk will be greater than the demand for steak, and the decline in steak sales will be far greater than the decline in milk sales.

If the prices of milk and steak *drop* by 50 percent, more of both products will be sold, in accordance with the Law of Demand. But the percentage increase in steak sales will probably be far greater than that of milk sales. The reason is that after consumers purchase what they consider a sufficient amount of milk, they will still be willing to buy more steak.

One way to measure the degree of demand is through the concept of *elasticity*. Elasticity of demand describes the percentage change in demand that follows a price change. The more demand expands or contracts after a price change, the greater the elasticity of the demand. The demand for most goods and services may be described as either relatively elastic or relatively inelastic. When a drop in the price of an item causes an even greater percentage increase in demand, we say that the demand for that item is relatively elastic (the demand has "stretched" a great deal). When a drop in price results in a decrease or only a small increase in demand, we say that the demand is relatively inelastic. The same holds true for increases in price. Demand is considered elastic if a rise in price results in a large drop in demand, and inelastic if a rise in price results in a relatively small drop in demand.

Elasticity of demand can also be measured by the amount that price changes affect total *revenue* (dollar sales). If a decrease in price results in an increase in revenue, the demand for the item is said to be elastic. If, however, a decrease in price results in a decrease in revenue, the item is said to be inelastic. Similarly, if an increase in price results in a decrease in total revenue, the demand is elastic; and if an increase in price results in an increase in revenue, the demand is inelastic.

Suppose that your local supermarket reduced the price of both milk and steak by 50 percent. Before the sale, milk was selling for 80 cents a quart and steak at $4 a pound. At those prices the store sold 200 quarts of milk and 60 pounds of steak each day. At the sale prices, customers bought 350 quarts of milk and 175 pounds of steak per day. This information is summarized in Table 2.2.

TABLE 2.2   Demand for Milk and Steak

	Price (P)	×	Units Sold (Q)	=	Total Revenue (TR)
Milk	$0.80		200		$160.00
	.40		350		140.00
Steak	$4.00		60		$240.00
	2.00		175		350.00

Table 2.2 shows that total revenue from the sale of milk fell from $160 to $140 when the price of milk was reduced. This indicates that the demand for milk is inelastic. Total revenue from the sale of steak, however, increased from $240 to $350. This shows that the demand for steak is elastic.

What Makes Demand Elastic or Inelastic? When we ask why some items are subject to elastic demand and others are not, we are really asking why price changes affect the purchase of some things more than of others. Usually, if one of the following conditions is present, the demand for a good or service will be elastic (sensitive to price changes):

1. The item is considered a luxury. If consumers regard an item as something they can live without, they are less likely to buy it if the price is high. But because most consumers want luxuries, they will consider buying them if the price drops enough. An item considered a luxury need not be costly in dollars; for example, a person with a modest income might consider fresh flowers, a bottle of cologne, or a taxi ride as luxuries. Also, what is considered a luxury by one person may be a normal or even a necessary expense for someone else—for example, plane tickets, meals in restaurants, or expensive clothes. If a product or service is considered a luxury by a large number of consumers, it will be subject to elastic demand.

2. The price represents a large portion of the family income. An automobile, a house, and a personal computer represent a significant portion of most family incomes. Therefore a rise in the price of such items will discourage many consumers from buying them. But because of the greater utility of many costly items, a decrease in their price will cause a significant increase in sales.

3. Other products can easily be substituted for it. Because chicken or some other meat may be substituted for steak, many people will shift to it if the price of steak goes up. Similarly, if the price of steel rises, manufacturers and builders will substitute other materials such as aluminum or concrete. But there are no good substitutes for gasoline, and therefore the demand for it is likely to be inelastic.

4. The items are durable. Furniture, appliances, and automobiles are relatively long-lasting. Since they are often major household items, many consumers will purchase them if the price is low enough. But because they are durable, people will tend to "make do" with them rather than replace them if the price is high.

What Is the Significance of Demand Elasticity? The elasticity of demand for a good or service is an important factor in many business and government decisions. Suppose, for example, that a local bus

TABLE 2.3   Demand for Bus Service

	If the fare is	and the number of passengers is	total revenue will be
Present	$1.00	10,000	$10,000
Elastic demand	1.20	7,500	9,000
Inelastic demand	1.20	8,500	10,200

company whose fares are regulated by the government finds itself in need of additional funds. Should the company apply for a fare increase? The answer would depend upon the elasticity or inelasticity of demand for the bus service.

Table 2.3 shows that if the demand for the bus service was elastic, a 20 percent fare increase might lead to a 25 percent reduction in riders and a decrease in earnings. But if demand for the bus service was inelastic, a 20 percent fare increase might lead to only a 15 percent loss in riders and an increase in earnings. In order to decide whether or not to apply for the fare increase, the bus company must know the degree of elasticity of demand for its service. The same is true for any firm or government.

When the cost of one fare was $1, the A&B Bus Company carried a total of 10,000 riders daily, for a net income of $10,000. A 20 percent fare increase would raise the cost of a ride to $1.20. If the ridership fell by 25 percent, the company would carry 7,500 passengers daily and would net $9,000. If the ridership fell by only 15 percent, the company would carry 8,500 passengers daily and would net $10,200.

What Economists Mean by an "Increase" or a "Decrease" in Demand. Certain events can make people more willing or less willing to pay a price than they once were. When this happens, the demand for goods or services at *all* prices is affected. If buyers are willing to take more items at each price, we say that there has been an increase in demand. When buyers are willing to buy less than they once did, we say there has been a decrease in demand.

To illustrate increased demand, let us return to our classroom sales of chocolate ice cream cones. Table 2.1 on page 21 describes the demand for ice cream cones on October 3. But it is now June 11, and

Demand, Supply, and Market Price   **27**

TABLE 2.4 Demand Schedule for
Chocolate Ice Cream Cones
Monday, June 11

Price	Number of Cones Students Will Buy
$1.40	6
1.25	9
1.10	18
.95	30
.80	45
.65	66

the community has been suffering through a week-long heat wave. The temperature has been above 90 degrees for most of the day, and there is still an hour to go before final dismissal. In October, cones that sold for $1.40 each found only one buyer. Today, six students would pay $1.40. At 95 cents as many as 30 cones would be bought, and at 65 cents sales would jump to 66 cones, since many of the pupils would consume two or three cones. The demand schedule for June 11 is shown in Table 2.4.

This demand schedule can be plotted as a demand curve. (See Figure 2.2.) D represents the demand in October, while D_1 represents the demand in June. We can see that when demand changes, the entire schedule shifts. Because the change in this case was an increase in demand, the curve shifted to the right. Had there been a decrease in demand, the curve would have shifted to the left.

In the previous example, a rise in temperature caused an increase in the demand for chocolate ice cream cones. There are many other things that can cause a change in demand. What effect do you think each of the following situations would have on the demand for a given product?

1. An increase in the price of substitute products.
2. An increase in most people's income.
3. A change in the taste of buyers.
4. The expectation that the price of the product will fall soon.
5. The appearance of a new substitute product.
6. The fear that the nation will soon suffer a depression, in which many businesses will collapse and many persons will be unemployed.

SUPPLY

Neil Simi, the economics teacher at North High, opened the day's lesson with an experiment.

"Class, how many of you are wearing wristwatches?" Twenty-eight hands went up.

"You may have noticed this paper bag sitting on my desk," Mr. Simi continued. "This bag contains one hundred dollars in one-dollar bills. I will give this bag of money to any one of you in exchange for your wristwatch. Will you please raise your hand if you would be willing to sell me your watch for a hundred dollars." The teacher counted the raised hands and wrote the number 27 on the chalkboard.

"Brenda," Mr. Simi said, "I noticed that you did not raise your hand. Don't you want to sell me your watch?"

"No, because it cost much more than a hundred dollars only a few months ago."

"I see," the teacher replied as he peered into the bag.

"Class," he went on, "I seem to have made a terrible mistake. I thought I had one hundred dollars in this bag. Actually, it looks more like fifty. Let us start over again. Who would sell me his or her watch for fifty dollars?" Once again Mr. Simi counted the raised hands, wrote the total, 15, on the board, and looked into the bag. With feigned surprise, he took a smaller bag out of the paper bag.

FIGURE 2.2   Demand Curve for Chocolate Ice Cream Cones on June 11

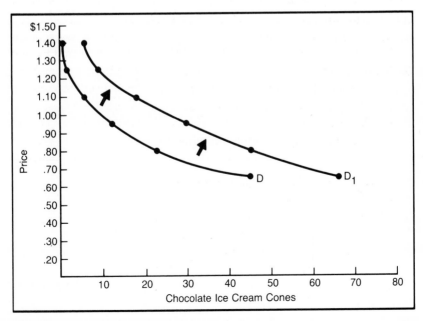

"Oh, this is embarrassing," he said. "I thought I had just money in this bag, but I see I packed my lunch in it too. I don't believe there's more than twenty dollars here. Will anyone sell me a watch for twenty dollars?"

Five hands went up, and the number was duly noted.

Mr. Simi reached into the bag and started counting off bills. ". . . seven, eight, nine, ten! Well, it seems I have only *ten* dollars here. Does anyone want to sell his or her watch for ten dollars?"

Only one hand was raised this time. The teacher placed the number 1 on the board.

"Bill," Mr. Simi said to the remaining seller, "it looks as if you have the only watch I will be buying today. Here is your ten dollars."

"On second thought, Mr. Simi," said Bill, "I think I will hold on to my watch. You can keep the ten dollars."

Why did Bill suddenly refuse? Perhaps the name *Monopoly* printed on the money Mr. Simi offered him changed Bill's mind.

Mr. Simi's experiment demonstrated the economic concept of supply. Economists use the term *supply* to describe the amount of goods or services offered for sale at a particular price. As the price that Mr. Simi offered for a wristwatch went down, fewer watches were offered for sale. Just the opposite would have happened if Mr. Simi had offered $10 to start and had increased the price: More watches would have been offered for sale.

The dress shirts worn by members of the United States Army are produced by several different manufacturers in accordance with specifications prepared by the military. Let us assume that a survey was taken among the manufacturers to see how many shirts each could provide at various prices. The supply schedule returned by one of the manufacturers is shown in Table 2.5.

TABLE 2.5 Supply Schedule for Army Shirts

At a price of	seller will offer
$ 6	8,000
8	8,600
10	9,600
12	11,200
14	14,000

Law of Supply. An auctioneer asks for bids on this antique bicycle. Why will an old, obsolete bicycle from the 1890s command a higher price than most new, ten-speed bicycles of the 1980s?

The Law of Supply. Both the wristwatches and the army shirts illustrate the Law of Supply: *The quantity of a commodity supplied varies directly with its price.* The number of units offered for sale increases as the price increases. There are two reasons for this. First, the higher price enables producers to increase their output even though it may cost them more to produce each item. And second, less efficient producers will be lured into the market to produce the commodity because at the higher prices even they will be able to earn a profit.

The supply schedule in Table 2.6 lists the number of skateboards that manufacturers are willing to sell at the prices indicated. The schedule shows that at a price of $15 each, only 8,000 skateboards

TABLE 2.6   Supply Schedule for Skateboards
March 1

At a price of (per board)	sellers will offer (thousands)
$15	8
25	22
35	30
45	36
55	38
65	39
75	40

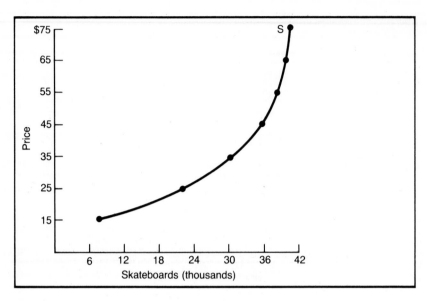

FIGURE 2.3 Supply Schedule for Skateboards on March 1

will be offered for sale. At $75 each, however, 40,000 skateboards will be offered. Why are sellers willing to offer so many more skateboards at the higher price? One reason is that at a price of $75, manufacturers can afford to take on the extra help and pay for the overtime necessary to increase output to 40,000 skateboards. Another reason is that manufacturers of related products such as hockey sticks and roller skates will find it worth their while to cease making those goods and start making skateboards instead.

A supply schedule, like a demand schedule, can be plotted on a graph. In Figure 2.3, the supply curve S, which slopes upward to

TABLE 2.7 Supply Schedule for Skateboards
October 1

At a price of (per board)	sellers will offer (thousands)
$15	10
25	30
35	40
45	50
55	55
65	56
75	60

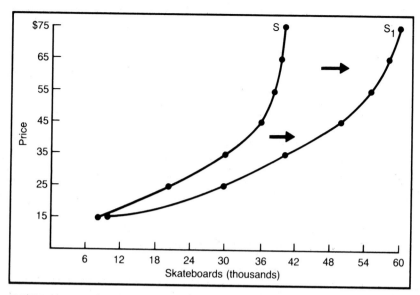

FIGURE 2.4 **Supply Schedule for Skateboards on October 1**

the right, summarizes the information contained in our skateboard supply schedule.

Changes in Supply. Suppose that skateboard manufacturers discovered that they could turn out fiberglass boards that were better than wooden boards and less expensive to manufacture. This would enable producers, large and small, to increase their production so that more boards would be available for sale at each price. The supply of skateboards would increase. Table 2.7 summarizes such a possibility.

If we plot this increase in supply in Figure 2.4, the curve (S_1) will shift to the right.

Suppose that instead of a decrease in costs, the industry experienced an increase resulting from an increase in wages. What would happen to the supply schedule and the supply curve?

Elasticity of Supply. Like demand, supply is subject to elasticity. The supply of some commodities is more sensitive to price changes than the supply of others. If a change in price brings about a larger change in supply, the supply is said to be elastic. If a change in price produces a smaller change in supply, the supply is said to be inelastic.

Manufactured goods generally are subject to greater supply elasticity than goods provided by nature. Skateboard manufacturers might be able to increase their output of boards by asking their employees to work overtime. Dairy farmers, however, could not expect such cooperation from their herds. Therefore, an increase in milk production would take longer than an increase in skateboard production.

Demand, Supply, and Market Price

The amount of natural resources available is usually limited. While some resources such as trees and wildlife can eventually be replaced through reforestation and conservation, others have absolute limits. For example, some additional land can be created by draining swamps or damming rivers, but for the most part we have to make do with the land we have. Minerals such as petroleum, iron, and copper also are subject to relatively inelastic supply. The output of minerals is limited by the expense of the equipment need to extract them, the size of the known deposits, and the uncertainty of discovering new sources.

HOW PRICES ARE DETERMINED

Our discussion of demand and supply has thus far concentrated on the number of items buyers and sellers are willing to consider at different prices. We have seen that the amount of goods and services that buyers and sellers are willing to exchange fluctuates with changes in price. What people are willing to do, however, is not always what they are able to do. You may be willing to buy an imported ten-speed bicycle for $5, but since no one is likely to sell you one at that price, you will probably not be able to buy one.

The price at which goods and services may actually be bought or sold is called the *market price*, or *equilibrium price*. The following discussion describes how market price is determined.

Supply, Demand, and Market Price: Bringing It All Together. In describing how the forces of supply, demand, and price come together, we shall be dealing with a model of *pure competition*. A *model* is a theoretical system that is used to study actual events. Under pure competition, the following conditions exist:

1. There are many buyers and sellers acting independently, and no single buyer or seller is big enough to influence the market price.

2. Competing products are practically identical, so that buyers and sellers of a given product are not affected by variations in quality or design.

3. All buyers and sellers have full knowledge of prices being quoted all over the market.

4. Buyers and sellers can enter and leave the market at will. That is, buyers are free to buy or not to buy; sellers are free to sell or not to sell.

In the following discussion we shall assume these conditions in order to show how prices of goods and services are set in the United States market system.

Equilibrium Price. How do the sellers and buyers of skateboards finally arrive at a stable, mutually acceptable price?

How Supply and Demand Determine Price. As the price increases, the number of items offered for sale (the supply) increases, but the quantity that buyers are willing to buy (the demand) decreases. There is only one price at which demand and supply are equal. On a graph, this price is shown by the point where the demand and supply curves intersect. Because it is the price at which supply and demand are equal, the price at which goods are sold is sometimes called the *equilibrium price.* Because it is established in the market, it is also called the *market price.*

To summarize: *The price at which sales take place is the price at which the amount demanded is equal to the quantity supplied.*

Table 2.8 shows the demand for skateboards on March 1. If we add the supply schedule for this day, we will have Table 2.9. The

TABLE 2.8   Demand Schedule for Skateboards
March 1

At a price of (per board)	buyers will take (thousands)
$15	48
25	36
35	30
45	24
55	20
65	14
75	6

Demand, Supply, and Market Price

TABLE 2.9   Demand and Supply Schedule for Skateboards March 1

At a price of (per board)	buyers will take (thousands)	sellers will offer (thousands)
$15	48	8
25	36	22
35	30	30
45	24	36
55	20	38
65	14	39
75	6	40

demand and supply schedule in Table 2.9 shows that at a price of $35, the number of skateboards offered by manufacturers is equal to the number that buyers are willing to take. This information is illustrated graphically in Figure 2.5. Point M, which lies at the intersection of D and S, identifies the market or equilibrium price. The figure shows that this price is $35 and that 30,000 boards can be sold. As long as demand and supply do not change, this is the *only*

FIGURE 2.5   Demand and Supply Schedule for Skateboards on March 1

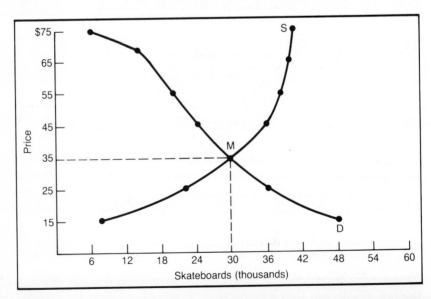

Economic Reasoning

price at which all the boards produced can be sold. At any higher price, there will be sellers with leftover skateboards that they can sell only by lowering the price. At a price lower than the market price, buyers unable to find any boards but willing to pay more will bid the price up until they too are satisfied. All sellers willing to sell at the market price *or less* will be satisfied, and so will all buyers willing to pay that price *or more*.

What about those buyers who will not (or cannot) pay more than $25 per board, and those sellers who will not sell for less than $45? They will neither buy nor sell because the market price is too high for the buyers and too low for the sellers. At the equilibrium or market price, the "market is cleared"—that is, all possible sales are made. For any new price to be established, there will have to be a shift in supply, demand, or both.

Effect of a Change in Demand Upon Market Price. Suppose that a panel of distinguished doctors announced that skateboarding was the key to good health and long life. Suppose also that this report received nationwide publicity and that prominent people in all walks of life were soon observed skateboarding to and from work and social activities. Many thousands of people might now be willing to pay more than in the past to take up the hobby. The demand for skateboards would increase dramatically. The new demand schedule is illustrated by line D_1 in Figure 2.6. The new demand curve intersects our supply curve S at a higher point, M_1, and the new market price is $45.

FIGURE 2.6   Increased Demand for Skateboards

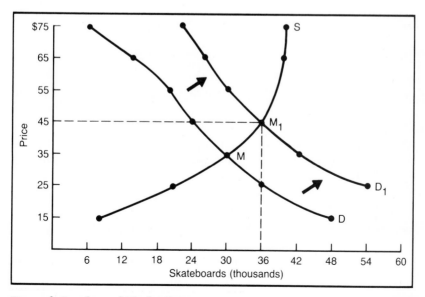

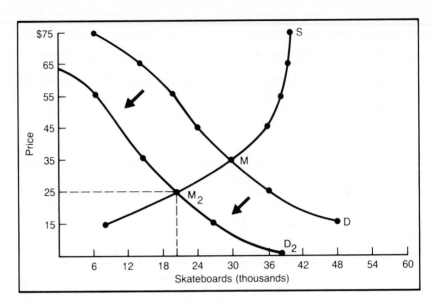

FIGURE 2.7 Decreased Demand for Skateboards

Suppose, however, that our panel of doctors announced that skateboarding was harmful to health. Very likely the demand for skateboards would fall off, and the demand curve would shift to the left. In Figure 2.7, curve D_2, which intersects S at M_2, represents the new, lessened demand for skateboards. The curve shows that as demand decreases, market price also decreases. Common sense tells us that this will be so. Manufacturers must sell what they have produced. If fewer people want a product while its supply remains constant, suppliers must lower the price to attract buyers. We can express this principle in general terms: *Price varies directly with changes in demand.*

Effect of a Change in Supply Upon Market Price. How is market price affected if supply increases or decreases while demand remains constant? Earlier in the chapter, we described how an improved way of making skateboards might result in an increase in supply. The effect of such an increase was to make more boards available for sale at every price and to shift the supply curve to the right. In Figure 2.8, S_1 represents an increase in supply. The new market price, M_1, is lower than the old price, M.

Suppose that the price of ball bearings rose sharply and there was a decrease in the supply of skateboards. In Figure 2.9, S_2 represents the new supply schedule. The curve has moved to the left, and M_2, the new market price, is higher than M. Again common sense tells us that if fewer items are available for sale, the price per item will increase.

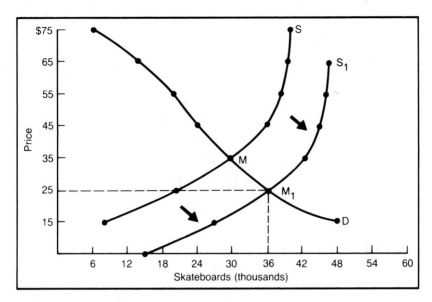

FIGURE 2.8 Increased Supply With Market Price M₁

The same principle applies to any product or service. If large quantities of diamonds were suddenly discovered and made available for sale, the price of diamonds would fall. When certain fruits and vegetables are in short supply, their prices rise. Thus, price increases when supply decreases, and price decreases when supply increases. In general terms: *Price varies indirectly with changes in supply.*

FIGURE 2.9 Decreased Supply With Market Price M₂

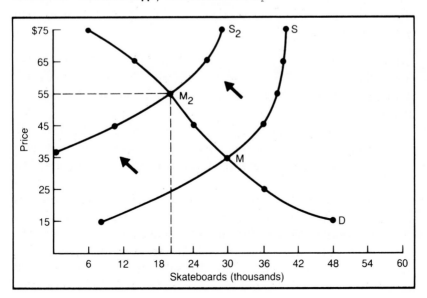

To What Extent Do Supply and Demand Affect Price? So far our discussion of market price has been based on a model of pure competition in which price is determined entirely by supply and demand. Our model has the following characteristics: (1) there are many buyers and sellers, (2) similar products are assumed to be identical, (3) all buyers and sellers have full knowledge of market conditions, and (4) buyers and sellers can enter and leave the market at will.

In the actual economy, however, these conditions are met very seldom. The supply of an item may be controlled by only one company or by a handful of firms. Similar products are often not identical, and even when they are virtually identical, advertising and other factors influence consumers to prefer one product over another. Buyers may not know that they can get the same item for less under a different brand name or at the store next door. For these and many other reasons, the laws of supply and demand do not operate in real life the way they do in the model.

If pure competition is a laboratory concept that rarely exists in real life, why do we discuss it? The reason is that in spite of its limitations, competition does give us an insight into some of the forces that control prices. Although in the actual economy we may never see all four conditions of pure competition, we may see one or two, and in those instances supply and demand will affect prices. Prices are important because they keep the market functioning, and the market system is at the heart of our economy. The United States economic system is discussed in detail in Chapter 3.

EXERCISES

Multiple Choice

1. When the supply of a commodity increases while the demand remains the same, the market price will (*a*) rise (*b*) fall (*c*) stay the same (*d*) vary directly with the change in supply.
2. Which of the following would probably lead to an increase in the demand for bricks? (*a*) an increase in the price of lumber, which could be used as a substitute for bricks (*b*) a decrease in the income of potential home builders (*c*) an increase in the wages of bricklayers (*d*) an increase in the price of bricks.
3. Which of the following would *not* have the same effect as the other three on the amount of beef consumed? (*a*) a rise in the price of lamb (*b*) a fall in the price of beef (*c*) an effective

advertising campaign on the part of pork producers (*d*) an effective advertising campaign on the part of beef producers.

4. Which of the following is subject to the greatest elasticity of demand? (*a*) postage stamps (*b*) bread (*c*) personal computers (*d*) chewing gum.

5. When described in connection with supply and demand schedules, an increase in demand means that (*a*) the price will fall (*b*) buyers will take a larger quantity at all prices than before (*c*) the demand for the product has become more elastic (*d*) the demand curve slopes downward.

6. Where there are many competing firms, an increase in demand may be expected to result in (*a*) a decrease in production (*b*) no change in production (*c*) an increase in production (*d*) the elimination of inefficient firms.

7. The supply of which of the following commodities is most elastic? (*a*) eggs (*b*) plastic toys (*c*) gold (*d*) corn.

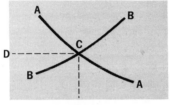

FIGURE 2.10

(Base your answers to questions 8–10 on Figure 2.10.)

8. In the graph, A represents (*a*) the supply curve (*b*) the demand curve (*c*) equilibrium (*d*) the market price.

9. In the graph, D represents (*a*) the supply curve (*b*) the demand curve (*c*) the demand schedule (*d*) the market price.

10. In the graph, B represents (*a*) the supply curve (*b*) the demand curve (*c*) equilibrium (*d*) the market price.

11. Suppose the law required that all the wheat grown in the United States had to be sold for $3 per bushel. Which of the following illustrations would portray this situation?

(a) (b) (c) (d)

12. The price of product X increased at the same time that the quantity of the product sold decreased. Which of the following could have accounted for the price increase? (*a*) an increase in supply (*b*) an increase in demand (*c*) a decrease in supply (*d*) a decrease in demand.

13. Both the price and the quantity sold of product Y fell during the past year. Which of the following could have accounted for this decline? (a) an increase in supply (b) an increase in demand (c) a decrease in supply (d) a decrease in demand.

14. Which of the following events is most likely to result in a decrease in the demand for product Z? (a) a decrease in consumer income (b) news that product Z is often used by the President of the United States (c) an increase in the price of product W, which is often used as a substitute for product Z (d) a public announcement that the price of product Z will double sometime next year.

Graphing Supply and Demand

Price	$16	14	12	10	8	6	4	2
Quantity	6	10	16	24	30	40	50	80

1. Construct a curve based on the data in the above chart. You may use graph paper for more precise plotting of points.
2. Is this a demand or a supply curve?
3. Why does the curve slope downward?
4. On the same graph, construct another curve using the following data.

Price	$16	14	12	10	8	6	4	2
Quantity	48	44	40	36	30	20	0	0

5. Does this curve represent supply or demand?
6. Why does this curve slope upward?
7. What is the equilibrium or market price?
8. Why can the market price not be $40?

Matching Questions

Match each item in Column A with the item it defines in Column B.

Column A

1. This increases as a good or service becomes more desirable.
2. When we have this, a small price change will lead to a big change in the amount that people will buy.
3. According to this, you could sell bathing suits in the winter by lowering the price.
4. You will find this at the point at which supply and demand are equal.
5. Economists use this to describe an additional item of a good or service.
6. When plotted on a graph, its curve slopes upward (from left to right).

Column B

a. supply
b. utility
c. elastic demand
d. law of demand
e. marginal unit
f. equilibrium

Essay Questions

1. For each of the five possible events described below, tell (1) how the event would affect either the supply of or the demand for the italicized product and (2) how the event would affect the price of the product. (a) Yields decline as *corn* crop is hit by mysterious blight. (b) The wearing of *hats* is again becoming fashionable among American men. (c) Only two days are left to buy a *turkey* for Thanksgiving, and food markets have many unsold turkeys. (d) *American automobile* manufacturers show great interest in the rise in European wages. (e) Midwestern drought forces ranchers to rush their *cattle* to market.

2. In terms of the laws of supply and demand, explain each of the following: (a) the difference in price between diamonds and rhinestones (rhinestones are glass copies of diamonds) (b) the difference in price between a loaf of bread baked today and one baked yesterday, and (c) the difference in price between roses in January and roses in June.

3. When a clothing store has had a fire, the store will usually reduce the price of smoke-damaged merchandise. Explain why consumers will buy this clothing even though it smells of smoke.

4. In a certain town, there were, until last year, five bakeries and five florists. Since then, however, one firm bought out all the bakeries, and another firm bought out the florists. Both companies have now decided to increase their prices. Which will be able to introduce the greater price increases, the bakery or the florist? Why?

Consumer choices in the marketplace determine the kinds and quantity of goods that businesses produce.

UNIT II

The Free Enterprise Economy of the United States

CHAPTER 3

The United States Economic System

As you walk down the aisles of your local supermarket, do you ever wonder how all the packaged foods, household products, and fresh produce got there? Many of the items traveled hundreds, even thousands, of miles and underwent a number of processing changes before arriving on the shelves. Yet in most cases there is a constant supply of those foods and other goods that you normally purchase. As soon as one lot of goods is sold, a fresh supply appears as if by magic. If you choose to hold off on a purchase today, there is a good chance that the product you want, or a similar product, will still be available next week or a month from now. The nearest department store, too, always seems to have a wide and fairly predictable variety of items for sale.

The nation's supermarkets and department stores bring us such a steady stream of goods and services that we have come to take all these products for granted. Large and varied as they are, however, the stocks of these stores represent only the tiniest fraction of the $3 trillion worth of goods and services that are produced annually by the United States economic system. Incredibly, too, this enormous outpouring functions without having been designed or operated by any single individual or agency. Somehow, the 115 million people involved in running the economy are able to do so without central direction. And although our economy is not perfect, it succeeds in meeting the economic needs and many of the wants of most of our citizens, and serves the needs of many other countries as well.

How does our economic system function with no centralized management? How do the people of the United States answer the fundamental economic questions facing all societies: *What* goods and services should be produced? *How* should they be produced? *Who* should receive the goods and services produced?

THE UNITED STATES ECONOMIC SYSTEM RESTS UPON CERTAIN INSTITUTIONS

The economic system of the United States is known as *capitalism,* or the free enterprise system. Capitalism is an economic system under which the means of production are privately owned, and the fundamental questions of *what, how,* and *who* are answered by the market, rather than an economic plan. Capitalism is founded on certain principles, or institutions, the most important being private property, freedom of enterprise, freedom of contract, the profit motive, competition, and consumer sovereignty. Let us examine each institution as it exists in our economic system.

1. Private Property. All persons in the United States have the right to own not only personal property (movable possessions) but also land, factories, farms, and businesses. Within certain limits set by law, property owners may use their property as they wish, and they may dispose of their property by either selling it or giving it away.

Free Enterprise. Explain how this shoe-car and shop window illustrate four characteristics of a free market: (1) private property, (2) profit motive, (3) competition, and (4) consumer sovereignty.

Property rights are subject to certain limitations. The government may tax the owners and inheritors of property. Under *eminent domain*, the government has the right to force people to sell their private property so that it may be used for a public purpose. The Fifth Amendment to the Constitution provides that such property shall not be taken "without just compensation." Limitations on the use of private property are imposed to protect the rights of others. Individuals have the right to own television sets and watch the programs of their choice, but they do not have the right to turn the sets up to full volume at three o'clock in the morning. Similarly, the right to own an automobile does not include the right to drive it recklessly or without a valid license.

2. Freedom of Enterprise. The principle of free enterprise allows individuals to enter any legal business and conduct it as they see fit. However, this right is not unlimited. Certain businesses are exclusive monopolies awarded by the government to specific companies. For example, public utilities such as gas and electric companies cannot be organized without explicit government approval. Furthermore, people may not enter certain professions without meeting required qualifications, and most business owners must obtain licenses from the government and must pay fees. Business people are also limited by laws that safeguard consumers and ensure fair competition.

Despite such limitations, the individual has considerable freedom to select, organize, and operate a business. In many other parts of the world, this right does not exist, and only the government or certain select individuals may own or operate business enterprises.

3. Freedom of Contract. An important institution in the United States economy is the right of individuals to make business agreements. These agreements, or *contracts,* are considered so important that they can be enforced by the courts. If people did not have to live up to their business agreements, it would be difficult for the economy to function. Workers might find that they were paid less than they were promised, and firms might refuse to fill orders unless they were paid in advance.

Here, too, freedom is limited. Contracts dealing with an illegal act such as gambling are not enforceable in the courts. Also, many contracts cannot be enforced against minors and the insane.

4. The Profit Motive. Profits are what remain after the costs of doing business are deducted from the income derived from the sale of goods and services. The desire to maximize profits (achieve the greatest possible return) is the principal motivating force behind business activity in the United States.

A business is established only if an enterprising person or a group believes it will be profitable. Once a business is under way, the search for profits determines how it is run. A business can continue to operate only as long as it continues to make a profit.

In addition to producing an income for its owners, the profits of a business are its single most important source of capital. Capital funds pay for the modernization and expansion of an enterprise and in that way keep it competitive and growing. In the long run, then, profits can benefit the whole society by making possible the production of increasing amounts of goods and services at lower costs.

5. *Competition.* In an economic sense, competition refers to the rivalry among buyers and sellers for goods and services. Like profits, competition helps to drive the wheels of capitalism.

Competition encourages producers to keep their prices low. The ice cream maker who has to charge $4 a pint in order to make a profit will not stay in business long when other brands of comparable quality are being sold for less than half that amount. Also, if businesses are to maintain competitive prices, they must keep their costs low. Hence, competition encourages producers to be efficient.

Competition may occasionally lead to abuses. It may, for example, result in wasteful duplication, as when a new business enters a field already overcrowded with sellers. There have been times, too, when competition has led firms to engage in ruthless and unfair practices to secure an advantage over their rivals.

Despite its hazards, however, competition is an important institution of the United States economy. In competing with one another, sellers put forth their best efforts. And buyers, knowing that many firms are competing for their dollars, help keep standards high by seeking out the best prices and the finest quality.

6. *Consumer Sovereignty.* In a competitive economy there is *consumer sovereignty.* This means that consumers determine what will or will not be produced. For example, if consumers are unwilling to purchase purple ball point pens, manufacturers will stop producing them. If consumers want yellow ball point pens, manufacturers will quickly produce yellow pens.

Consumers' likes and dislikes are expressed in a kind of election that is held in the marketplace. Consumers "vote" for a product by buying it, and they vote against other products by not buying them.

The most successful businesses are those that can "anticipate the market" by correctly predicting what consumers will buy. Therefore, businesses frequently use advertising to shape consumer demand.

Two decades ago, few parents would have thought of buying disposable paper diapers for their infants. In those days diapers were made of cloth. The development of the disposable diaper was, however, followed by huge advertising campaigns that created a demand for the product. Now people buy more disposable diapers than cloth ones.

Consumer sovereignty can be limited by government policy. If the government requires titanium—a scarce metal—for its own purposes, titanium will probably not be available for consumer products. Consumer sovereignty is also limited when there are only two or three producers of a product. Most light bulbs, for example, are manufactured by three producers who can pretty much determine the size, shape, wattage, and price of their products.

THE ROLE OF GOVERNMENT

According to classical economic theory, government should play only a small role in a capitalist economy. Adam Smith, the eighteenth-century economist, believed that government had four primary responsibilities:

1. To provide for the national defense.
2. To protect its citizens and provide for a system of justice.
3. To provide for public works and institutions that could not be operated profitably by private enterprise.
4. To collect taxes so as to pay for the cost of government.

In reality, government plays a far larger role in capitalist economies than Adam Smith envisioned. Twenty percent of our nation's output of goods and services is created by government—federal, state, and local. In creating this wealth, government employs 20 percent of the nation's work force and accounts for 25 percent of the personal income earned by our citizens. Because of government's substantial involvement in the economy, economists often describe our capitalist system as a *mixed economy*. This means that the economy is a mix of both private enterprise and government enterprise.

There are several reasons why government's involvement in the economy goes far beyond that conceived by Adam Smith:

1. Economic problems such as inflation and unemployment affect the entire nation. Most people agree that such problems are very much government's business and that government has a general responsibility to help keep the economy running.

2. Government participation is needed to prevent wasteful economic competition among public utilities. Since it would be econom-

ically unsound for several local telephone, gas, or electric companies to compete for identical markets, the government licenses, or *franchises,* only one company to do business. Government agencies closely regulate public utilities to ensure that they provide satisfactory service at fair prices.

3. Developments in transportation, communication, science, and health, all undreamed of in Adam Smith's day, have created problems that only government seems able to solve. The Federal Trade Commission and dozens of other specialized government agencies are directly involved in the nation's economic life.

4. With the vast changes that science and technology have brought about in the environment have also come problems that could not have been foreseen in the eighteenth century. Chemical wastes from modern factories create problems for the public which no single business can solve. Citizens have looked to government to protect them from the dangerous effects of pollution and to preserve dwindling resources.

5. The fortunes—and misfortunes—of billion-dollar industries that employ thousands of workers can directly affect large segments of the American economy. Towns, cities, and entire regions have suffered when major industries have cut back production or shut down. Such economic disasters have led to greater government involvement in the economy. In 1979, it appeared that the Chrysler Corporation, one of the nation's three largest automobile manufacturers, might fail. Congress voted to save the company from bankruptcy with a $1.5 billion guaranteed loan. The jobs of 137,000 Chrysler employees were saved, as were those of thousands of other workers whose companies supplied Chrysler's manufacturing plants and sold and serviced its automobiles.

6. One of the basic assumptions of the capitalist system is that the public will benefit from healthy competition among firms. When competition becomes unfair, however, weaker firms and the public may suffer. Government has assumed the responsibility of seeing that business "plays by the rules" in its competitive activities.

7. Still another reason for the growing participation of government in the economy has been the shift in attitude of Americans from one of "rugged individualism" to one of "entitlement." Until the 1930s it was generally believed that individuals and families should solve their own problems. Individuals who were unable to meet their own needs would be referred to private charities. Since the Great Depression of the 1930s, however, attitudes have changed. Today, most people believe that any needy person is entitled to receive some government

aid. Government-sponsored entitlement programs such as social security, unemployment benefits, and Medicare help to relieve people of the financial burdens associated with old age, unemployment, and illness.

Operating within the framework of its unique system of private enterprise with government participation, the United States economy has reached levels of output never before attained by any society. Some people might argue that this achievement should be credited solely to private enterprise or to the government. But others believe that it is the blending of the two that has accounted for our nation's prosperity. The following pages tell more about the interplay of private enterprise and government activity in the United States economic system.

THE INTERDEPENDENCE OF ECONOMIC SOCIETY

Jack and Mildred Green live in an apartment in a large city with their two children, Teddy and Laura, ages fifteen and thirteen. Jack works as a mechanic for a bus company, and Mildred is a manager in a law firm. Teddy and Laura go to school. On a typical day, the Greens consume many of the same goods and services as other families in their income bracket. They spend money for food, clothing, utilities (such as telephone, gas, and electricity), recreation, a car, a television set, and all the many other items that go along with modern living. They also use such government-provided facilities as schools and highways.

It is likely that the Greens produce practically none of the goods and services they consume. They live in a society where work is so specialized that few people are able to provide for more than a tiny fraction of their own needs. Mr. Green repairs buses, while Mrs. Green helps run a law office. In addition, both parents work at raising their children and caring for their home. How are the Greens able to obtain the hundreds of goods and services that they need and want in order to live comfortably?

The Greens, like 235 million other Americans, must count on the efforts of many other people to provide them with most of their needs. This dependence on the labor of others was not always the rule in society. In prehistoric times, people relied upon their own efforts and nature's abundance to provide what they needed. Frontier families in this country had to grow their own food, build their own homes, and make their own clothing. Even today, in certain agricultural societies, each family provides most of the goods and services it consumes.

SPECIALIZATION AND THE ECONOMY

The economic independence seen in primitive agricultural societies is not possible in the United States today. In modern civilization, jobs are highly specialized. Workers perform one specialized task and depend on other workers to provide them with the things that they need.

There are many advantages to specialization. By concentrating on one activity, workers produce more because they become highly skillful at what they do. In addition, specialization encourages the efficient use of capital. If a business needs a delivery truck only twice a week, it would be wasteful for the business to purchase and maintain its own truck. The business can use its capital more efficiently by hiring the services of a company that specializes in making deliveries. Specialization also promotes *innovation* (new ways of doing things). Just as individual workers become more efficient at their specialized tasks, so companies that produce only a few products are able to develop machines, factories, and production techniques that will increase production, improve quality, and lower costs.

Specialization is possible only where markets are large enough to support them. In New York City, there are dozens of shops which sell only handbags and others that sell only the finest grand pianos. But driving through many small towns in Vermont, you won't find a single shop selling pianos of any kind. The market (number of potential customers) is too small in a Vermont town to support highly specialized shops. On the other hand, in a huge city like New York or Chicago, there are thousands of potential buyers for pianos. Such a market can support dozens of piano shops. Stated as an economic principle: *The degree of specialization is limited by the extent of the market.*

How is it that 115 million people working at thousands of different tasks are able to produce the hundreds of thousands of different goods and services that people want? And how are these goods and services distributed to where they are needed? We shall try to answer these questions in the following pages.

THE CIRCULAR FLOW OF ECONOMIC ACTIVITY

People receive income from a number of sources and spend it in a variety of ways. Workers receive wages and buy consumer goods. Business owners receive profits and pay their employees and suppliers. Landlords receive rent and purchase maintenance services and fuel for their buildings. Lenders earn interest and spend part of it on new loans or other investments. No matter how money is earned, it returns to the economy when buyers purchase the things they need or want.

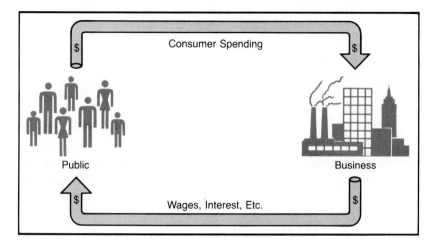

FIGURE 3.1 Circular Flow of Money Between the Public and Business

This stream of funds, which is constantly passing back and forth between the public and the businesses of the country, is pictured by economists as a circular flow. Figure 3.1 represents the circular flow of funds between the public and business. Businesses send out funds to the public in the form of wages to employees, rent to landlords, and other payments. The public, as consumers and investors, sends the money back to the business community.

There is not only a circular flow of funds between business and the public; there is also a circular flow of goods and services. The goods and services produced by business are purchased by the Greens and other consumers. Consumers in turn sell their productive services to business—in the Greens' case, to a bus company and a law firm. The flow of goods and services is shown in Figure 3.2. Business

FIGURE 3.2 Circular Flow of Goods and Services

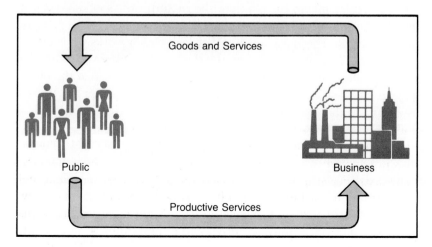

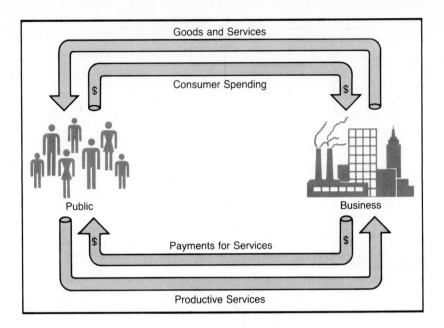

FIGURE 3.3 Circular Flow of Money, Goods, and Services

provides goods and services to the public, and the public provides productive services (land, labor, capital, and management) to business.

Now we have two circular streams moving in opposite directions. One carries money from the public to business and back again; the other carries goods and services between the same parties. These two flows are combined in Figure 3.3.

ADDING GOVERNMENT TO OUR MODEL

Until now we have limited our discussion of economic activity to the public and business. To complete the picture, we must add government. The public's relations with government are similar to its relations with business. The bus company that Jack Green works for is owned by the city. The city uses his productive services to provide a service to the public—in this case, transportation. The money that the public pays to the bus company in the form of fares is used by the city for wages and other payments to the public. Other city income such as tolls and sales taxes returns to the public in a similar way.

In Figure 3.4, the inner loop represents the money flow between the public and government. The upper portion of the inner loop represents the taxes that the public pays to provide government with the major part of its income. The lower portion of the inner loop indicates the payments that government makes to the public in the form of wages, rent, interest, and so on.

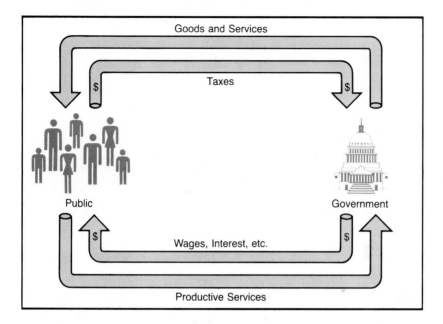

FIGURE 3.4 Circular Flow of Money, Goods, and Services Between the Government and the Public

The outer loop of Figure 3.4 shows (top) the flow of government goods and services to the public, and (bottom) the flow of productive services of individuals who provide labor or other services to the government.

A similar flowchart would represent the economic exchange between business and government. Productive services flow from business to government—as, for example, if Mrs. Green's law firm were to do some legal work for a government agency. Businesses also provide government with goods, such as office furniture, paper, and helicopters. Productive services flow from government to business, as when businesses use the Postal Service to send and receive mail. Money flows from government to business in the form of fees (such as those charged by Mrs. Green's law firm), wages, and other payments. Money flows from business to government as taxes, tolls, postage, and so on.

Using the preceding information, we can construct a chart showing the circular flow of goods and services, and of money, between business and government. If we combine the relationships described in Figures 3.1–4, we get a picture of the general flow of economic activity among the three major sectors of our economy: government, business, and consumers (the public). This economic activity is shown in Figure 3.5 on page 56.

These circular flowcharts give us a bird's-eye view of the economy and help us to see how changes in one part of the economy may affect

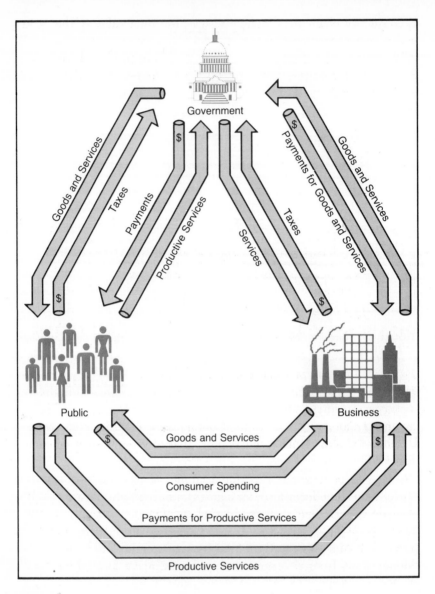

Labels in figure: Government, Goods and Services, Taxes, Payments, Productive Services, Services, Taxes, Payments for Goods and Services, Goods and Services, $, Public, Business, Goods and Services, Consumer Spending, Payments for Productive Services, Productive Services

FIGURE 3.5 Circular Flow of Economic Activity Among the Public, Business, and the Government

the other parts. For example, when we read in the newspaper that the government plans to increase spending, we will understand that this could lead to an increase in the size of the total economic flow. Similarly, a reduction in the amount of goods and services purchased by the public will reduce the amount of income received by business and will thus reduce the size of the total flow of spending.

Gross National Product. The size of the streams of money, goods, and services that flow between consumers, business, and the public is constantly changing. Economists call the total value of the goods and services produced in a single year the *gross national product* (GNP). Since the goods and services that were produced were paid for by either consumers, business, or government, the GNP can be expressed mathematically as follows:

$$C + I + G = GNP$$

where: C = consumer spending
     I = business spending (investment)
     G = government spending

Economists describe the study of these flows and the factors affecting them as *macroeconomics*. By contrast, *microeconomics* is the branch of economics that focuses on the economic behavior of individual units in the economy such as a single household, firm, or industry. In other words, macroeconomics deals with the economy as a whole, while microeconomics studies its parts.

THE UNITED STATES ECONOMY IS A MARKET SYSTEM

How do the suppliers in an economy know what goods and services to produce and in what quantities to produce them? In traditional economies of the past, production was determined by custom and by various authorities such as the church, the nobility, and guilds. In command economies such as the Communist economies of the Soviet Union and Cuba, a small group of political leaders makes the economic decisions.

But the United States economy is a *market system* or, to be more precise, a *price-directed market system*. No church or guild decides whether a steel manufacturer should build a new refinery or shut down one of its plants. No dictator tells American manufacturers how many blue, brown, and red sweaters to produce. Although the United States economic system has elements of both traditional and command economies, most economic decisions are made in the marketplace. Now let us see how the market system fits into the picture.

Markets Defined. Chapter 2 explained that market price, or equilibrium price, is the price at which demand equals supply—that is, buyers are willing and able to buy, and sellers are willing and able to sell. A *market* is any place or situation in which goods are bought and sold. Buyers and sellers need not meet face to face in the market. Purchases and sales may be made over the telephone, by mail, or through brokers or agents. In the stock market, millions of shares of stock are bought and sold daily in behalf of buyers and sellers who will probably never meet.

Some markets are international—that is, they consist of buyers and sellers from many parts of the world. In recent years, the international petroleum market has received much attention. Americans discovered that the prices charged by oil producers in the Middle East directly

FIGURE 3.6   Role of Markets in Our Economy

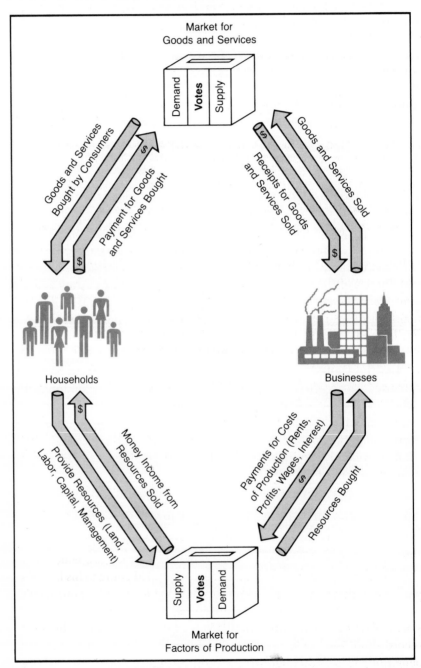

affected their own standard of living. Less dramatic but as important are the international markets for such commodities as rubber, gold, wheat, and cotton.

Other markets cover a smaller territory. Goods such as food and clothing that are produced and consumed in the United States are said to have a national market. Services such as haircuts and auto repairs are part of a local market.

Dollars as Votes in a Market Economy. Circular flowcharts can illustrate the role of markets in the economy. Figure 3.6 shows the flow of goods and services between businesses and the public (households). In addition, the figure shows the markets that are involved in the money transactions.

Figure 3.6 likens markets to an election. In the upper half of the flowchart, households "vote" for the things they want by casting their "ballots" (money) for goods and services at a certain price. Businesses put up their "candidates for office" (the goods and services they produce) so as to attract the greatest number of "votes" (dollars). The votes represent demand and the candidates represent supply. As sales are made, businesses receive the "votes" of the electorate (consumers' dollars), and their "candidates" (their goods and services) are either elected (purchased) or defeated (not purchased).

In the lower half of the flowchart, the roles are reversed: Households are the sellers and businesses the buyers. Here the "candidates" running for election are the factors of production supplied by households: labor, buildings, and machinery. The "votes" are the dollars paid by businesses for the factors of production. Money flows from firms as part of their cost of doing business, and households receive payments in the form of wages, rent, interest, and profits.

What does the circular flowchart tell us about markets? Markets provide the "polling place" for buyers and sellers. Out of the never-ending round of elections, the prices at which goods and services will be sold are determined.

HOW THE PRICE-DIRECTED MARKET SYSTEM WORKS

Like many other teenagers, Teddy and Laura Green are concerned with keeping up with their friends. Teddy stopped going to his father's barber and now uses a stylist who cuts hair in the latest fashion. Laura recently talked her parents into buying her a stereo so that she could start collecting her own records. When Mrs. Green visited the local record shop, she was amazed to see how many albums catered to her daughter's taste. Although Mrs. Green recognized only a few of the

Market System. What motivates competing record companies to supply the record albums that these buyers want?

names on the albums, the proprietor told her that all of the albums were selling well—in fact, business had never been better.

How is it that Teddy Green was able to find a hair stylist who offered the latest look, and Laura Green had no difficulty locating the records she wanted? Was it because some government official had directed that barbers be assigned to certain neighborhoods where stylish haircuts were in demand? Did a board of supply prepare a list of recordings that were to be stocked by the nation's record shops? Not at all. The decisions to supply the goods and services that consumers like Teddy and Laura were most willing to pay for were made by thousands of individuals and business firms acting in their own behalf. Taken together, the economic decisions made by the nation's business enterprises and those who buy from them have come to be known as the market system.

Prices. Teddy Green's hair stylist, who has become very popular, recently raised his price to $18 per haircut. To Teddy, who had been paying less than $5 at the barbershop his father uses, this price is too high. Teddy therefore decides to give up style in favor of thrift. He would rather use the money he saves to buy some new clothes. Laura meanwhile is excited because the record store just announced a half-price sale. She can hardly wait to go and stock up. In both cases, the decision to buy or not to buy depended upon price. So important is price in the United States economy that economists often describe it as a price-directed market system.

Almost every decision in our economy is influenced in some way by price. Consumers compare the prices of goods they want to buy.

Workers try to get the highest price, or wage, for their labor. Producers consider the prices, or cost, of the items that go into production and the prices they will charge for the goods and services they produce.

Our economy relies on the price system to answer the fundamental questions of *what* goods and services will be produced, *how* they will be produced, and *who* will receive them.

The Market System Determines What Goods and Services Will Be Produced. How does it happen that there is such an ample supply of Laura Green's favorite albums at the record store? The answer is that storekeepers stock records that they believe will sell. If customers want records that are not in stock, proprietors will quickly order those records from their suppliers.

What is true for this local record shop is also true for many other consumer businesses. Business people try to give their customers the goods and services their customers are most willing to pay for. But it is not only the consumers' willingness to buy, but also the price they are willing to pay, that determines whether or not producers will find it profitable to sell an item. Hence the fundamental economic question of *what* goods and services will be produced is ultimately decided by the prices that consumers are willing to pay for the products they buy.

The decision as to what capital goods should be produced is reached in much the same way. As explained in Chapter 1, capital goods are used in the production of other goods. Capital goods include machines, tools, and factories. If producers believe that sales of a particular product will increase, they will try to get new and better facilities for producing it. Thus, if Laura Green and other teenagers convince record producers through their buying habits that sales will continue to soar, these manufacturers will build new factories and place orders for new machinery for the production of recordings.

Most businesses make some attempt to influence consumer demand through advertising. In some cases, advertising expenses account for a large portion of the cost of a product. Futhermore, advertising alone has been proved to be profitable, regardless of the merits of the product. From the standpoint of *what* goods and services are produced, however, it does not matter whether consumer demand is the result of clever advertising or rational judgment. One way or the other, it is the consumer who decides *what* will be produced.

The Market System Decides How Goods and Services Will Be Produced. Businesses seek to make the greatest possible profits from their operations. Since profits represent the difference between the selling price and total costs, a sure way to increase profits is to reduce costs. It is the never-ending search for lower costs that has led business firms to seek the most efficient method of operation. Specifically, entrepreneurs try to find the most efficient combination of the four factors of production: natural resources, labor, capital, and management. In the recording industry, for example, manufacturers may have to decide whether to replace some workers with automatic packaging machinery. The final determination as to how to combine labor and capital will be influenced by each producer's estimate as to which combination will result in the greatest profits. These and lesser decisions are made every day by all of our nation's entrepreneurs. It is they who determine *how* goods and services will be produced.

The Market System Decides Who Will Receive the Goods and Services Produced. In order to purchase goods and services, people must be able to pay the price. Normally, people acquire their income by selling goods and services. For example, Mr. Green gets paid for his services in repairing and maintaining buses, and Mrs. Green receives wages for her work in the law firm. Other forms of income are interest from loans, profits from a business, and rent.

In most cases, the size of a person's income determines the amount of goods and services the person can receive. Income level generally depends upon two factors: the demand for the good or service the person is selling and the number of people offering the same good or service. Certain city real estate is in great demand, and because of its scarcity there are generally few landowners offering comparable property. Therefore, such real estate can command high rents. By contrast, there is small demand for certain property in rural areas, and many landowners are seeking to rent such property; rents are therefore low. Similarly, skilled workers receive higher wages than unskilled ones because they are in demand and because they have fewer competitors.

Thus, the market system, by determining the level of individual income, establishes *who* can receive the goods and services the economy has produced.

But as we saw in Chapter 2, demand depends not only on ability to pay, but also on willingness to pay. Teddy Green, his sister Laura, and their parents all have the ability to purchase a wide variety of goods and services. But although he had the money, Teddy decided he could not afford $18 haircuts. Laura could have spent her money on clothes, but she chose instead to stock up on her favorite records at a half-price sale. She wanted her parents to buy her a video cassette recorder, but they did not want to spend the money for it. In short, goods and services produced by our economy are distributed to those people who are able *and willing* to pay for them.

The Market System Is Not the Only Determinant of What, How, and Who. Earlier in this chapter we described the United States as a "mixed economy" because economic decisions are made as a result of government participation as well as market forces. We listed several ways in which the government affects the economy, including the production of 20 percent of the nation's goods and services.

Custom and personal taste are other examples of nonmarket forces that influence our economy. If income were the only consideration, workers would always move to those areas that pay the highest wage for their specialty. In fact, however, most people prefer to remain in the region where they have been living and working, even though they might earn more elsewhere. Likewise, entrepreneurs who have been doing business "their way" for years may not want to change their methods, even though change might result in higher profits.

The market economy that we have described assumes that many firms are competing against one another. In real life, however, there is often only one producer or a handful of producers of a particular good or service in the market. In the absence of competition, sellers are not as hard pressed to sell their goods at the lowest possible prices. The seller of hot dogs at the ballpark can charge a few cents more for frankfurters because there is no one else inside the stadium to charge less.

Labor unions are among the nonmarket forces that make our system a mixed economy. Through collective bargaining, unions may influence who will be hired and help set wages, hours, and benefits. In these circumstances, wages will not be determined solely by the competition of employers for workers and of workers for jobs. In some cases, unions may exercise a virtual monopoly over the industries or firms that employ their members.

EVALUATION OF THE MARKET SYSTEM

Advantages. Those who favor the market system, or free enterprise, make the following claims to support it:

1. The market system is the most efficient economic system yet devised. In their quest for profits, all producers of goods and services, be they wholesalers or retailers, must compete with one another for the consumer's dollar. In these efforts, they (the producers) must always be able to offer goods and services of comparable quality at the lowest possible prices. As a result of this competition, producers

must constantly strive to improve their products and their production methods. Those who succeed are rewarded with profits; those who fail are forced out of business. Meanwhile, society benefits from the efficient use of its scarce resources, and the economy gets the goods and services it wants.

Households, too, in selling the factors of production (labor, buildings, and machinery) to businesses, will seek to offer excellence in order to command a good price, and will economize in order to make the best use of their own funds. As consumers, households are free to select from among competing products; hence, they will encourage producers to offer the best products at the lowest prices.

2. The market system is more sensitive to consumer demand than other economic systems. Because businesses are out to make profits, they seek to provide the public with what it wants. Through the price system, consumers "vote" their demand for specific goods and services by purchasing the products they want that are offered at prices they are willing to pay. At the same time, consumers pass by products that they either do not want at all or find too expensive or of inferior quality. Because businesses are free to adjust their marketing and manufacturing policies as they see fit, they are able to respond quickly to changes in consumer demand. The firms that are best able to meet consumer demand will be the most successful.

3. The market system provides the most individual freedom and the least direction and control by government. Not only are businesses free to respond to consumer demand; they are also free to shape consumer demand through advertising. Also, in purchasing the factors of production, businesses are free to seek the best quality at the lowest prices.

As consumers, individuals are free to purchase the goods and services they want. No law says that only certain people may own automobiles or that consumers in a given area may purchase goods only from certain stores. As workers, individuals are free to do any type of work for which they are qualified or to start businesses of their own.

To a certain extent, the freedom of the market system serves to correct abuses. For example, if a business tries to overcharge consumers or sell inferior merchandise, consumers will simply shift their business to its competitors.

4. The market system gives the best rewards to those who contribute the most to it. Under a price system, those who make the most money are able to get the most goods and services. Businesses offer the highest pay to those managers, salespeople, and other workers who contribute most toward increasing company profits.

Hence workers seek to develop those skills and talents that will make them most valuable to their employers.

Disadvantages. The market system is not without its faults. Some of the more serious criticisms of the market system are discussed below.

1. The market system does not provide many of the goods and services needed by society. No individual or group would be willing or able to pay for the construction of public roads, schools, and hospitals. Nothing in the price system insures that natural resources will be preserved or life and property protected. Yet such public facilities and services are as necessary as food, clothing, and all the other products that are supplied through the market system.

Why does the market system fail to provide essential public goods and services? The reason is that people are willing to buy products if they acquire the right to *exclusive* use of those products, but they are not willing to pay for goods and services whose use by the public cannot be prevented or excluded. Food, clothing, games, and entertainment are private goods and services; they can be enjoyed only by those who pay for them. Streets, police protection, public health services, and the like are *public goods and services;* they benefit us all whether we pay for them or not. But since those who use public goods and services cannot be made to pay for the cost of providing them, private sellers will not produce them.

Therefore, where public rather than private goods and services are concerned, society must find some way other than the interaction of the laws of supply and demand to determine *what* things to produce, *how* to produce them, and *who* will receive them.

2. The market system does not adequately provide for the needs of all the people. Critics often point to the large number of people living in poverty in the United States—in a recent year, an estimated 32 million persons. While the market economy probably does a good job in rewarding the most efficient and productive citizens, it does not provide equally for many less able groups such as children, the aged, and those whose lifelong experience of poverty has left them powerless to provide adequately for themselves and their families. Critics maintain that all people are entitled to a decent standard of living, regardless of the size or importance of their contribution to the economy.

3. The market system is likely to experience periods of expansion and contraction of business activity. Widespread unemployment and personal hardship often accompany the contraction of business. Unlike other economic systems, in which workers are guaranteed jobs

regardless of business conditions, the United States market economy has witnessed numerous periods of high unemployment. In recent years, the federal and state governments have taken an active role in economic affairs to lessen the impact of those periods. As a result there has been no repetition of the American experience of the 1930s when, in the words of President Franklin Roosevelt, "one-third of a nation" was "ill-housed, ill-clad, ill-nourished." Although government action has helped to compensate for swings in the business cycle, critics maintain that the need for such government intervention reveals a weakness in the market system.

4. The market system cannot account for the cost of many harmful *externalities,* or side effects of doing business. Certain resources, such as air, water, and soil, are often available without cost to the producers of goods and services. Producers who use free resources often do so without regard to efficiency or the effect on the rest of society.

Consider, for example, the coal-powered manufacturing facility that spews harmful pollutants into the atmosphere. To the economist, both the coal that powered the machinery and the air currents that carried off the smoke are resources. But they are significantly different kinds of resources. On the one hand, coal, which is privately owned, must be paid for by those who use it. Coal, therefore, is one of the costs of doing business. Air, on the other hand, belongs to all of us. The cost of cleaning it up does not have to be paid by those who pollute it.

To an economist, coal represents an internal cost that is part of the expense of doing business. By contrast, air is an externality, or *external cost.* Externalities are paid for by society as a whole. Since the market system does not impose a penalty for polluting the air, the coal-powered manufacturing facility has no economic reason for changing its policies and would only reduce its profits if it invested in antipollution devices. Thus, the argument that competition and the market system promote efficiency is true only if there are no externalities in the production process.

5. The laws of supply and demand ignore the importance of one's contribution to society. In allocating income to society's members, the impersonal market-price mechanisms do not consider the true or lasting value of one's contribution to society. On any number of occasions one may read that a popular entertainer or an outstanding athlete earned more in a year than a distinguished scientist, artist, or national leader. Why do you think this is so?

While most economists would agree that some balance ought to be established in our economic system between government intervention and free enterprise control, there is wide disagreement as to just what that balance should be. You will read in later chapters about government laws and other nonmarket forces that set limits on many of the activities of buyers and sellers. As students of economics and as citizens in a free society, you will have many opportunities to think about this question and to express your opinion on it.

EXERCISES

Matching Questions

Column A	Column B

Column A

1. consumer sovereignty
2. profits
3. freedom of contract
4. competition
5. mixed economy
6. external cost
7. entitlement

Column B

a. our nation's blend of private enterprise and government participation
b. the right to own income-producing property
c. a government program to help certain needy groups
d. principle that the customer determines the nature of the market
e. income remaining after expenses have been paid
f. paid by society as a whole rather than a single producer
g. the right to make legally binding agreements
h. rivalry stimulated by the quest for profits

Multiple Choice

1. Where is the greatest degree of economic specialization likely to be found? (*a*) in a small agricultural country (*b*) in a large agricultural country (*c*) in a large metropolitan area of the United States (*d*) in a poor rural area of the United States.
2. "The degree of specialization is limited by the extent of the market." This means that (*a*) the larger the market is, the less specialization there will be (*b*) economies can produce only as many goods as they can sell (*c*) a compact economy is more efficient than one spread over a large geographic area (*d*) specialization limits the size of the demand.
3. In a market economy, which of the following forces will be most influential in determining the number of pairs of brown as compared to black shoes a manufacturer will produce? (*a*) gov-

ernment directives (b) decisions by production supervisors (c) consumer demand (d) labor union policy.

4. In which type of economic system are consumers most likely to determine what goods will be produced? (a) market economy (b) traditional economy (c) command economy (d) wartime economy.

5. How goods are produced in a market economy is determined chiefly by (a) individual business people (b) the government (c) monopolies (d) labor unions.

6. Which of the following best explains why skilled workers are paid more than unskilled ones? (a) There are more skilled workers than unskilled. (b) There are more jobs for skilled workers than for unskilled. (c) The demand as compared to the available supply is greater for skilled than for unskilled workers. (d) Skilled workers work harder than the unskilled.

7. Which of the following statements is most valid? (a) If the price consumers are willing to pay for an item declines, more of that item will be produced. (b) If consumers are willing to pay more for an item, less will be produced. (c) If consumers are willing to pay more for an item, more will be produced. (d) Producers will try to turn out goods at the fastest rate possible regardless of cost.

8. The circular flow of spending will be affected by (a) an increase in business spending (b) a decrease in government spending (c) an increase in consumer spending (d) all of the above.

9. In the circular flow of economic activity, we see that business (a) receives no money from the government (b) receives goods and services from the public (c) sells more goods to the government than to the public (d) receives money from both the public and the government.

10. The role of the government and tradition in the American economy indicates that (a) we have a command economy (b) we have a traditional economy (c) the market system is not the only determinant of economic decisions in the United States (d) our economy is inefficient.

11. America's best tennis players will earn far more as professional athletes than its best handball players because (a) tennis is a more strenuous game than handball (b) people are willing to pay more to see professional tennis than professional handball (c) tennis is more of an American game than handball (d) tennis costs more to play than handball.

12. Eminent domain is the right of government to (a) take private property (b) levy taxes (c) print money (d) build roads.

13. Which of the following statements is a major criticism of the market system? (a) It rewards inefficiency and waste. (b) It is insensitive to changes in consumer tastes and wants. (c) It fails to deal with certain harmful side effects of production. (d) It encourages the overproduction of goods and services that no one really wants.

Essay Questions

1. Base your answers to the following questions on the cartoon (Figure 3.7). (*a*) Explain the meaning of the cartoon. In your explanation, make reference to the two buildings. (*b*) Each of the "pillars" in the cartoon has certain limitations. For example, private property rights are limited by eminent domain. (1) Explain how eminent domain limits one's right to own property. (2) Identify and explain three other limitations on the "pillars" of the United States economy.

2. Assume that three members of the nation's leading rock group were recently seen at a popular disco wearing buttoned shoes. Consequently, many fashion-conscious young men and women have sought to do the same. (*a*) How would the public inform shoe manufacturers that it wanted shoes with buttons? (*b*) What economic factors would shoe manufacturers consider before deciding to produce the buttoned models? (*c*) What economic groups other than shoe manufacturers are likely to be affected by the public's decision to wear buttoned shoes? Explain your answer.

3. *How* goods and services are produced is very much influenced by the expectation of profit. (*a*) Under what circumstances might theater owners substitute counters and sales clerks for soda, popcorn, and candy-vending machines? (*b*) What factors might an insurance company consider before it replaced five clerical workers with one computer system? (*c*) What factors would a dress manufacturer take into consideration in deciding where to locate a new factory?

FIGURE 3.7

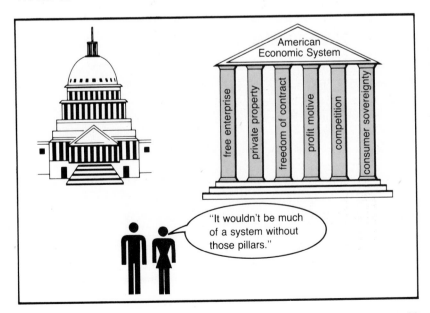

4. "The degree of specialization is limited by the extent of the market." (*a*) Explain the meaning of this statement. (*b*) How would this statement be illustrated by the fact that the United States can support a major commercial aircraft-manufacturing industry whereas Switzerland has none? (*c*) In view of this statement, how is it possible for Japan, which prohibits the use of citizens band (CB) radios by its own citizens, to be the world's largest manufacturer of CB radios?
5. The American marketplace has often been compared to a giant voting booth in which consumers cast their ballots for the goods and services of their choice. Explain this concept.
6. Critics have charged that the market economy (1) fails to provide goods and services that are needed yet are unprofitable and (2) imposes certain harmful effects, or "externalities," upon the public at no expense to those who caused them. (*a*) Explain these arguments. (*b*) Tell whether you agree or disagree with them.

CHAPTER 4

Production and Productivity

"Oh, I remember when I was your age—those were the good old days."

How often have you heard your parents or other adults speak lovingly of times gone by—the good old days—when, to hear them tell it, life was simpler and more pleasant? Perhaps things were better for some of us at an earlier time. But on the whole, Americans are living much better than their grandparents did. A few figures will illustrate our claim.

In 1914, when the average factory workweek in the United States was 55 hours, workers were earning less than $16 per week. (Because of price changes due to inflation, this sum would be equivalent to around $80 today.) Factory workers in the 1980s work fewer than 40 hours while earning an average of more than $300 a week. Today's workers earn more because businesses produce more than they did in the early 1900s. Hence, Americans in the 1980s have more goods and services than their parents and grandparents had.

In 1927, for example, it took the average worker 275 working hours to earn enough to buy a washing machine. Today 65 hours of work will pay for that appliance. Similarly, it took some 413 hours to earn enough to purchase a refrigerator in 1927, whereas today's worker can earn enough to buy one in 93 hours. In the 1920s a worker had to save about 11 months' salary to buy a car. A factory worker today can buy an automobile with four months' wages.

One hundred years ago half the population of the United States lived on farms. It took that many people to feed and clothe the nation because farms were smaller then, and farming methods were far less advanced. Today, fewer than 5 percent of us are farmers, yet our farms are able to feed and clothe us better than ever before, and much of the rest of the world as well.

The increased output of goods and services can be illustrated by referring to the gross national product, which we discussed in Chapter 3. United States production—the total output of goods and services—which passed $3 trillion in 1982, is the greatest the world has ever

"I suppose it's not *that* much if you see it in the context of a three-trillion-dollar economy."
Drawing by Dana Fradon; © 1982 *The New Yorker Magazine, Inc.*

seen. Our production is nearly twice that of our closest competitor, the Soviet Union, and five times that of the world's most populous nation, China.

WHAT INGREDIENTS DETERMINE THE OUTPUT OF GOODS AND SERVICES?

What enables the United States to produce more goods and services than any other nation? In general, the amount that a nation can produce depends upon two factors: (1) the amount and quality of available resources, and (2) the ability to use those resources. Let us examine these factors more closely.

1. The Amount and Quality of Available Resources. We described in Chapter 1 the productive resources that go into the making of goods and services. These resources are *land*, or natural resources such as soil, water, and minerals; *labor,* or "human resources"; and *capital*—the factories, machines, and equipment that are used in producing goods and services. An incredibly wealthy nation, the United States is blessed with a plentiful supply of all three types of resources. We have an abundance of fertile land, minerals, water, and other natural resources. We have a sizable and skilled labor force. And we have more machines and factories than any other nation.

Like every other modern nation, however, the United States cannot supply itself with everything it needs. Indeed, about 10 percent of the goods and services we consume each year are imported from abroad. Of this amount, a little more than half goes into the production of manufactured goods. The importance of our foreign trade was highlighted in the 1970s when America's supplies of petroleum and other energy resources began to dwindle. Since then, the nation has had to import substantial amounts of crude oil each year to supply its energy needs. The efforts have been successful enough so far to allow the United States to consume over 25 percent of the world's annual output of energy resources.

But even with increasing imports, the United States is limited in its supply of goods and services. As other nations increase their production, and world supplies of raw materials become scarcer, we may have to learn to make do with fewer goods and services. This brings us to the second factor in production: *productivity*.

2. The Ability to Use Resources. Productivity measures how well we use our resources to produce goods and services. Not only has our economy been producing *more* every year than the year before, but, because of our improving technology, it has also accomplished this with less human effort for each item produced. For that reason, American workers have been able to work fewer hours, take longer vacations, *and* receive higher pay than ever before. Economists explain this phenomenon as a result of the nation's rising productivity. Like a batting average, which measures a ballplayer's hitting ability, productivity measures the nation's ability to produce goods and services.

Output. One way to express productivity is in terms of the number of units an employee can produce in an hour, or *output per employee-hour*. Suppose, for example, that a chair factory employing five workers produces 160 chairs in an eight-hour day. Output per employee-hour in this case would be four: 160 chairs divided by eight hours equals 20 chairs per hour, and 20 chairs divided by five workers equals four chairs per worker-hour. Suppose, however, that either by rearranging the manufacturing process or by using new machines and techniques, the factory increased its output to 30 chairs per hour with the same number of workers. In that case we would say that output per employee-hour, or *productivity*, had risen by 50 percent.

The benefits of increased productivity may be shared in several ways. If the benefits are used to increase production (the total output of goods and services), living standards will rise. If they are used to

Output per Hour. These two cash registers illustrate changed technologies in the distribution and sale of groceries. How does the computerized machine increase a clerk's output per hour?

shorten the workday, workers will benefit. At an optimum level, increased productivity can lead to both shorter working hours and a higher standard of living.

United States productivity has been growing since the 1930s. From the 1950s through the 1960s, productivity gains averaged around 4 percent a year. (This figure is larger than it seems at first because gains in productivity are like compound interest. A 4 percent growth rate will double the nation's gross national product in less than twenty years.)

In the 1970s, however, the United States' growth rate began to slip. By 1973 the rate was less than 2 percent a year, and by 1980 it had fallen below one percent per year. As a result, our standard of living, which until 1972 was the world's highest, also began to slip, so that the nation now ranks about fifth.

HOW PRODUCTIVITY IS INCREASED

In Unit VII we shall explore the reasons why United States productivity declined in the 1970s and early 1980s, and we shall discuss ways to reverse the trend. But first let us explain what it takes to increase productivity. In the process we shall be talking about workers' skills, management's skills, capital investment, and technology.

1. Workers' Skills. Since productivity measures the efficiency of the labor force, workers are the key to increases in productivity. Increasing productivity must rely upon a labor force capable of applying new techniques and operating new machinery. The computers and other high-technology machines associated with modern society can be effectively employed only if the nation's labor force is available to operate and service them. Thus private industry spends huge sums to train its employees in the use of new equipment, for without trained people, new technology would be useless.

2. Management's Skills. Management, sometimes described as the "power behind the desk," is another essential ingredient in any effort to increase productivity. There are many different ways in which equipment may be used, some more efficient than others. The vital decisions in this area have to be made by the managers, and their ability therefore has a direct relationship to the overall efficiency of the economy. A successful manager will find the right answers to such questions as: What equipment should we use? What production methods should we use? How can we time our production so as to meet the needs of our market? Which plant layout will enable our workers to achieve the greatest output?

3. Capital Investment. Capital, you remember, refers to the machines, tools, and buildings that are needed to create goods and services. How much workers can produce will be limited by the type, amount, and quality of machines and tools available to them. Until a decade or so ago, the productivity of clerical employees in business depended largely upon their skills in the use of mechanical adding machines and typewriters. In the business world today, office skills have been increased many times by such new machines as electronic typewriters and calculators and high-speed copiers. Even though this equipment is often costly, the additional expense is quickly offset by the increased output of each worker.

4. Technology. The type and quality of capital goods is so important in increasing productivity that we treat it as a separate factor. *Technology* refers to the use of tools, materials, machines, and power

Productivity. In the 1890s, this Nebraska farm family could harvest far more wheat than a Pennsylvania farm family of the 1790s. What developments contributed to the increase in farm productivity?

sources to enable workers to perform tasks more easily and productively. There are about 40 percent fewer coal miners today than there were in the 1950s. Despite this decline in numbers of workers, coal production in the early 1980s was about one-third greater than it was thirty years ago. How was it possible for fewer miners to dig more coal? The answer is technology. Technology involves using something other than the human body (that is, tools or machines) to accomplish a task. When people long ago discovered how to move a boulder with a pole pivoting on a rock rather than simply trying to push the boulder with brute force, they were applying technology to solve a problem. Just as the pole enabled primitive humans to move a boulder more easily, so new tools and machinery enable today's miners to outproduce their counterparts of just thirty years ago.

To increase productivity, industry is constantly adding to its stock of new equipment. In addition, many firms spend large sums on research and development of new processes and products. By the 1980s, spending on new plant and equipment amounted to $200 billion a year, and another $43 billion was invested in research and development.

COMBINING THE FACTORS OF PRODUCTION: WHAT ARE THE PROPER PROPORTIONS?

Suppose we have a specific amount of money with which we are going to set up a shoe factory. What do we need? You will probably think

The Free Enterprise Economy of the United States

of a building and machinery, workers and a management staff, and raw materials such as leather, thread, canvas, and nails. Working within our budget, we must decide how many and what kind of machines to buy and how many workers to hire. We could buy or rent the most modern automatic equipment and hire a few highly skilled workers to operate it, or we could buy or rent less expensive machinery and hire more workers. We could hire skilled leathercrafts workers, or we could try to get along with less-skilled machine operators. The kind of management we want to set up is also open to many questions, as is the type of raw material we want to use. We can choose to make our shoes from anything from a plastic leather substitute to the rarest animal skins. An almost infinite number of combinations of capital, labor, management, and raw materials is possible, and each leads to different results. We will, of course, try to make the largest possible profit, and we are seeking the combination that will yield this result.

Law of Diminishing Returns. Let us assume that we have hired one worker for our factory, who is able to turn out 50 pairs of shoes a day. We then decide to hire a second worker and discover that, as a result of this addition to the work force, production is increased to 110 units. This leads us to hire a third worker, with the result that 180 pairs of shoes are turned out. So far, as we have added workers, not only has total production increased, but so has productivity (output per worker). Table 4.1 summarizes these results. If we assume that our workers are about equal in skills and ability, the increased productivity must be due to more efficient use of the machinery resulting from the addition of workers. But let us see what happens as we continue to add workers.

TABLE 4.1   Output With One to Three Workers

Number of Workers	Output per Day	Net Increase From Each Additional Worker	Output per Worker
1	50	50	50
2	110	60	55
3	180	70	60

DAVID RICARDO
The Principles of Political Economy and Taxation (1817)

The economic order first described by Adam Smith was studied and enlarged upon by those to whom we now refer as economists of the classical school. Second only to Smith in importance among the classical economists was David Ricardo (1772–1823). The son of an affluent London stockbroker who disowned him when he married outside his religion, young Ricardo opened his own brokerage firm and was so successful in this endeavor that by the time he was thirty-five he was able to retire a rich man. In later years, Ricardo went on to become a large landholder and member of Parliament. His most important work, *The Principles of Political Economy and Taxation*, is generally regarded as the best theoretical statement of classical economics.

Two topics that received special attention in the *Principles* were income distribution and economic growth. Income, Ricardo said, was distributed to landlords, workers, and entrepreneurs (business persons) in the form of rents, wages, and profits, respectively. Left to their own devices, entrepreneurs would expand their operations to the fullest in order to earn the greatest profits. This investment (business spending) would create jobs for workers, whose wages would be pushed up to whatever level was required to attract the needed supply into the labor market. With their wages rising, workers could afford to marry and have families. In that way, they would create their own competition by adding more people to the labor force. The addition of these new workers would push down wages to that point where workers would earn just enough to survive.

Meanwhile, the population growth would have induced farmers to open their less productive land to cultivation. This would increase food prices and, of necessity, wages, since workers had to be paid enough to subsist. Unfortunately for the entrepreneurs, wage increases would have to come out of their profits. For their part, entrepreneurs could be expected to expand their operations as best they could through their investment in additional capital. This would lead them to employ additional workers at still higher wages, and the cycle would be repeated.

What a dismal picture Ricardo painted! Here were workers, bound to a life of bare subsistence by what came to be called the "iron law of wages," doomed because of their propensity to have children. Here, too, were entrepreneurs standing by helplessly as rising food prices pushed up the wages they had to pay at the expense of their hard-earned profits. Only the landlords seemed to benefit, for as the population grew so too did the prices they could charge for their crops and the rents they earned on their lands.

One way out of the dilemma for the entrepreneurs (there was no way out for the workers, in Ricardo's view) was to bring down food prices by importing less expensive grain from other European countries. Unfortunately, this remedy could not be applied because England's Parliament, the lawmaking body, was controlled by the land-owning nobility, whose primary source of income was from agriculture. In the early nineteenth century, by way of protecting themselves from foreign competition, they sponsored a series of laws (the so-called Corn Laws) that levied high taxes on grain entering England. The effect of these taxes was to make the price of imported grain higher than the price of English grain.

In the midst of this dilemma, Ricardo's work provided the theoretical ammunition needed by the middle class, which wanted these laws repealed. What Ricardo did was to introduce the Law of Comparative Advantage. This law, which is often cited by economists in defense of free trade, states that under certain circumstances two nations can benefit from trade even if one of them produces everything at lower costs than the other. (See Chapter 24.) In a well-known example, Ricardo demonstrated that it was to the mutual advantage of England and Portugal for England to export wool to Portugal and to import Portuguese wine in return, even though Portugal could produce both wool and wine at a lower cost. Over the years, the strength of the English middle class grew so that by 1846 it was able to bring about the repeal of the hated Corn Laws.

The passage of time has made obsolete much of what Ricardo had to say about the economy. Nevertheless, many of his theories and methods were employed by later economists as the starting point for the development of their own ideas, and his place in history is assured.

TABLE 4.2 Output With Four to Seven Workers

Number of Workers	Output per Day	Net Increase From Each Additional Worker	Output per Worker
4	240	60	60
5	280	40	56
6	300	20	50
7	280	− 20	40

Table 4.2 shows that at a certain point the net increase in production for an additional worker begins to decline. This point is called the *point of diminishing returns*. We reached the point of diminishing returns when we hired our fourth worker. Although our total output of shoes increased from 180 pairs to 240, the additional worker added fewer pairs (60) than the last previous additional worker (who had added 70). The reason that this happened was that there were not enough machines for the additional workers. They could relieve the operators occasionally or do chores for them. But, because they could not spend full time at the machines, their output could not be as great as that of the first workers hired. The economist would say that the average amount of the fixed resource (the capital, or machinery) available to each unit of labor (each worker) declines as more labor is added. (Here labor is called a variable resource.)

Furthermore, as we continue the experiment, we reach a *point of negative returns*, where the workers start to get in each other's way and total output falls off. In the example above, we would have reached the point of negative returns when we hired our seventh worker.

The phenomenon we have described is known as the *Law of Diminishing Returns*. It states: "As additional units of a resource are applied to fixed resources, output may at first increase, but a point will be reached beyond which the extra output resulting from the same addition will become less and less." In our illustration the fixed resources were land and capital, and we added additional units of labor.

We could have shown the Law of Diminishing Returns for capital by assuming a factory in which all shoes were made by hand and observing the effect as machinery in increasing quantities was added.

At first, productivity would increase as workers took advantage of the new machines. But if we continued to add machinery while keeping the same number of workers, productivity would begin falling off as we reached the point of diminishing returns. Why? Simply because there would be more machines than the workers could operate. Note that in this case we would be measuring productivity in terms of output per machine instead of output per worker.

In putting together the factors of production, managers have to consider diminishing returns because there may come a point at which it becomes uneconomical to expand output. In the case of our shoe factory, for example, we saw that if management were to continue to try increasing the output of shoes simply by hiring more workers, the factory would eventually lose money. To increase our output of shoes without raising the cost per pair, we must increase several or all of the factors of production. Under certain circumstances, we can even decrease the cost per pair as we increase production.

THE ECONOMIES AND DISECONOMIES OF SCALE

In the case of the shoe factory, production reached a maximum of 300 pairs a day. But production could be increased beyond this point by adding new or more efficient plant and equipment. Before a firm decides to expand its capacity, it has to consider both the advantages and the disadvantages of growing larger. Economists call these pluses and minuses the *economies and diseconomies of scale.*

Advantages of Growing Larger—The Economies of Scale. In large-scale production as well as in small business, a firm must constantly concern itself with increasing its productivity and reducing its costs. That is, the firm must be prepared to review its methods of doing business so as to get the greatest output from its available resources. One way to increase productivity and lower the cost per unit is to grow larger and thereby enjoy the benefits of the economies of scale. There are several reasons why these economies take place.

Division of Labor, or Specialization. It is a rare factory worker who has a hand in the manufacture of a product from beginning to end. Were you to visit any plant today, you would more than likely see workers involved solely in one or two stages of the total production process. For example, if the factory you visited was one that manufactured gasoline-powered lawn mowers, one group of workers might be seen preparing the motor for installation. A second group might be doing the electrical wiring, while a third might oversee the

Division of Labor. Henry Ford pioneered in the timesaving process of making automobiles on an assembly line. How does this 1930 picture of a Ford assembly line illustrate the principle of division of labor?

stamping and painting operations. Final assembly and packaging might be the responsibility of two other groups.

This breaking down of the total production process into a series of simpler tasks is known as the *division of labor,* or *specialization.* Among the many advantages of specialization are the following: (*a*) The worker need be trained to perform only one operation or process. Therefore, with little training, a worker can become highly skilled at one job. (*b*) Because the task has been subdivided, it is easier to perform. In a television factory, only a highly trained worker would be able to assemble an entire set. By dividing the tasks, however, the firm is able to hire less-skilled workers at a lower wage. (c) Supervisory and management responsibilities may also be subdivided. Like other workers, supervisors and managers will be able to attain a higher level of expertise in a few specialized tasks than they would if they were responsible for production from beginning to end.

Quantity Discounts. The large firm can frequently obtain its raw materials at lower cost than the small one. Suppliers are eager to keep their biggest customers and may offer discounts for quantity purchases.

Availability of Specialized Machinery. Large-scale production and the division of labor permit the use of specialized machinery. Large firms can afford to purchase such machinery, and division of labor makes the employment of specialized equipment practicable. For example, when certain workers are used to make only crankshafts for automobiles, it becomes economically attractive to buy a machine to assist in this one operation. If the same workers also had to work on the engine block, the crankshaft machine would stand idle part of the time and thereby represent a waste of capital.

Easier Access to Credit. Big businesses find it easier to borrow than small ones. One reason is that the large, successful firms are better known, and consequently lending institutions and the public are more willing to lend them money. Also, their size makes them appear to be less of a risk. This easy access to capital funds makes it easier for large firms to expand their operations.

Research, Development, and By-products. As businesses grow, they can afford to hire the best brains available to conduct elaborate research programs. Research has led to the development of many new products and methods of production. In addition, profits have been increased through the discovery and development of by-products. These are goods produced along with the major items of production from materials that once may have been considered waste. Orange peel, for example, used to be discarded by juice processors. When industrial research discovered that orange peel could be made into fertilizer or feed, the juice industry acquired a profitable by-product. Furthermore, big business is able to invest in the equipment needed to produce by-products. For example, large meat-packing companies have been able to produce glue, fertilizers, and soap—by-products that smaller meat-packing firms could not afford to produce.

Costs, Revenues, and Profits in the Process of Production: A Hypothetical Case Study

The management of the Miracle Lantern Company, whose advertising slogan "If it works, it's a Miracle" is known by millions, has been unhappy with company earnings in recent months. In an effort to increase profits, Miracle has engaged a firm of economic consultants. As a first step the consultants prepared an analysis of the company's operations and its methods of production.

The process of production at Miracle is fairly simple. Lantern cases are stamped out by a specially designed machine at one end of an assembly line. From there the products are moved along by a conveyor belt. On either side of the belt, two workers assemble the parts of the lanterns. At the end of the assembly line, a third worker packs the finished products for storage or shipment. Meanwhile, the office staff attends to other functions of the business such as advertising, sales, payroll, and administration. Production has been running at 900 lanterns a week.

The consultants found that the plant had a peak capacity of 1,500 units a week and that peak capacity would be attained with a total of nine workers. *Capacity* refers to the maximum number of units that can be produced with present machinery and production methods or, as economists say, "in the short run." Why didn't Miracle simply hire six more workers and thus reach peak capacity? Because hiring new workers would also increase costs. Peak capacity does not necessarily mean the greatest profits.

Miracle would be able to increase production beyond its present capacity "in the long run" by acquiring additional plant, equipment, or both. But such an action would be a major decision entailing large risks. In hiring consultants, the firm wanted to explore first the possibilities for short-run improvement.

The consultants next examined Miracle's costs of production. They looked first at the *fixed costs*, also known as "overhead"—those costs that remain unchanged regardless of the number of units produced. Fixed costs include such expenses as rent, real estate taxes, and interest on loans. Miracle's fixed costs totaled $2,000 a week and had to be met whether the firm produced one lantern or a thousand.

The other category of costs of production are *variable costs*—those that increase or decrease with the number of inputs. Variable costs include such expenses as wages (workers can be laid off when business

TABLE 4.3 Cost Analysis of Miracle Lantern Company

1	2	3	4	5	6	7	8
			TOTAL COSTS			AVERAGE COSTS PER UNIT	
Inputs	Output	Fixed	Variable	Total	Fixed	Variable	Total
0	0	$2,000	$ 0	$2,000			
1	200	2,000	500	2,500	$10.00	$2.50	$12.50
2	500	2,000	1,000	3,000	4.00	2.00	6.00
3	900	2,000	1,500	3,500	2.22	1.67	3.89
4	1100	2,000	2,000	4,000	1.82	1.82	3.64
5	1275	2,000	2,500	4,500	1.57	1.96	3.53
6	1350	2,000	3,000	5,000	1.48	2.22	3.70
7	1425	2,000	3,500	5,500	1.40	2.45	3.85
8	1475	2,000	4,000	6,000	1.35	2.70	4.05
9	1500	2,000	4,500	6,500	1.33	3.00	4.33

is slow and rehired when orders increase), power, raw materials, and income taxes. The consultants found that Miracle's variable costs were currently $1,500 per week.

Table 4.3 summarizes the consultants' findings. Column 1 shows the number of inputs, which in this case are workers on the production line, to be applied to the production of lanterns. The numbers end at nine because with nine workers the plant can produce and package its full capacity of 1,500 lanterns per week. Hiring more than nine workers would not result in any additional output because the machine simply cannot produce more than 1,500 lanterns a week.

Column 2 tells us the number of lanterns that will be produced weekly at each level of input. Note that output follows the *Law of Diminishing Returns* (see page 80). As workers are added, productivity, or output per worker, will at first increase and then, after reaching the point of diminishing returns, decrease. Can you tell at what point Miracle Lantern reached diminishing returns?

Column 3 lists the fixed costs of the operation. Variable costs (Column 4) increase, as you can see, with the number of units produced. Total

costs (Column 5) represent the sum of Columns 3 and 4, fixed and variable costs.

Columns 6, 7, and 8 show the average fixed, variable, and total costs per unit as inputs are increased from one to nine. Average costs are found by dividing total costs by the number of lanterns produced. As output increases, average fixed costs will decrease because the total cost will be spread over more and more units. Miracle's average fixed costs (Column 6) will drop from $10 to $1.33 per unit as the work force increases from one to nine. Average variable costs (Column 7), on the other hand, are subject to diminishing returns. Although costs will decrease at first, they will increase once the point of diminishing returns has been reached. Total average costs (Column 8) are the sum of average fixed and variable costs (Column 6 plus Column 7).

Thus far we have discussed only the costs of running the company. Before the management of Miracle Lantern can make any intelligent decisions, it must know the effect of these costs on profits. As we know, profits are what remains after the costs of doing business have been subtracted from the income, or *revenue*. To assist management in its analysis, the consulting firm gathered the information in Table 4.4, which was added to the original presentation.

At the beginning of this case study, we said that Miracle was producing 900 lanterns a week. If the company can sell whatever quantity it chooses to produce (up to its capacity), what level of production would you expect management to decide upon?

If you said 1,275 units, you would be correct, because at that level the firm would make the greatest profit. Table 4.4 shows that in order to achieve an output of 1,275 units per week Miracle Lantern will have to hire two more workers, for a total of five.

1. Define each of the following: (a) capacity (b) fixed costs (c) variable costs (d) revenue.
2. The reading lists rent, real estate taxes, and interest as examples of overhead expenses. Identify one other kind of fixed cost that Miracle Lantern might have to meet in addition to these three.
3. The reading classifies income taxes as a *variable expense* while real

TABLE 4.4 Revenue Possibilities of Miracle Lantern Company at a Variety of Input Levels

With this number of inputs (workers)	output per week (number of lanterns) will be	sold at a price of (each)	revenue will be	minus total costs of	equals net profit of
0	0				
1	200	$5	$1,000	$2,500	− $1,500 (loss)
2	500	5	2,500	3,000	− 500 (loss)
3	900	5	4,500	3,500	1,000
4	1,100	5	5,500	4,000	1,500
5	1,275	5	6,375	4,500	1,875
6	1,350	5	6,750	5,000	1,750
7	1,425	5	7,125	5,500	1,625
8	1,475	5	7,375	6,000	1,375
9	1,500	5	7,500	6,500	1,000

estate taxes are classified as a *fixed expense*. How do you account for this difference?

4. According to the data contained in Table 4.3, (a) when did Miracle reach the point of *diminishing returns*? (b) What happened to average fixed costs per unit as output increased from 900 to 1,425 lanterns?

5. According to the data contained in Table 4.4, (a) how many workers would be needed to give Miracle the greatest profit? (b) What would happen to profits if output were increased from 900 to 1,500 lanterns per week?

6. What would Miracle Lantern have to do if it wanted to increase output beyond its present capacity of 1,500 lanterns per week?

Disadvantages of Large Size—The Diseconomies of Scale. As a firm grows, it may pass the point where the economies of scale are effective and reach a point of diminishing returns. That is, the increase in income resulting from the firm's expansion will be less than its cost of operation. There are two reasons for the diseconomies of scale.

Decline in Management's Effectiveness. As plants grow larger, more managers must be hired to administer and supervise the operation. If the cost of an additional manager is no longer justified by a resulting increase in net profit, the company has reached the point of diminishing returns in mangement effectiveness.

Increased Cost of Resources. As firms grow larger, so too does their need for the factors of production. The demand for more labor, more raw materials, and more electricity will, in time, push up the costs of these resources. In this way some of the savings coming from size will be lost.

EXERCISES

Multiple Choice

1. When productivity is rising, (*a*) foreign competition increases (*b*) prices must also rise (*c*) business profits fall (*d*) there is an opportunity to improve the standard of living.
2. Before modernizing, the Chelsea Video Games Company employed twenty workers and produced 200 games a day. After modernizing, the company laid off five workers and is now producing 300 games a day. As a result of modernization, productivity (*a*) was doubled (*b*) increased by 50 percent (*c*) remained the same (*d*) declined.
3. All of the following will increase productivity *except* (*a*) efficient use of natural resources (*b*) working overtime (*c*) employee training programs (*d*) improved machinery.
4. When, as workers are added to a production line, the point of diminishing returns is reached, (*a*) total output will decline (*b*) output per employee will decline (*c*) total profits will decline (*d*) the factory should hire more workers.
5. The best way to increase productivity is to (*a*) hire more workers and increase hours (*b*) obtain more capital and better management (*c*) raise prices (*d*) employ all the factors of production more efficiently.
6. As a result of our nation's increasing productivity, (*a*) most goods

are cheaper today than they were years ago (b) more goods are available per person than years ago (c) goods are made better by machine than they were by hand (d) output per employee-hour has decreased.

7. Which of the following is an example of a fixed cost? (a) rent (b) electricity to power machinery (c) commissions on sales (d) raw materials.

8. In industries with high overhead costs, increasing production tends to lower (a) the return on investment (b) total variable costs (c) overhead costs per unit (d) total operating costs.

9. The Kilroy Bicycle Company has fixed annual costs of $100,000 and variable costs of $10 per bicycle. If output is increased from 5,000 to 10,000 bicycles per year, the total cost of producing each bicycle will be reduced from (a) $30 to $25 (b) $30 to $20 (c) $20 to $10 (d) $20 to $15.

10. The division of labor provides all of the following advantages *except* that (a) the training of workers is simplified (b) work tasks are easier to perform (c) workers tend to develop greater pride in their work (d) supervisory and managerial responsibilities may be subdivided.

11. The Clamalot Seafood Company was considering the purchase of an additional automatic packaging machine for its frozen fried clams. Studies revealed that the new machine would increase output but would also increase the cost per package. The company would most likely (a) purchase the machine because it would require fewer workers (b) purchase the machine because it would result in increased output (c) not purchase the machine, because it would result in increased cost per package (d) not purchase the machine, because it would not really be needed.

12. Which of the following situations is an example of a diseconomy of scale? (a) A company goes out of business because of a decreased demand for its product. (b) A company becomes so large that it has to expand into new quarters. (c) A company finds that it is spending more on new managers than it is earning in additional profits. (d) A company is receiving more orders than it can fill.

Essay Questions

1. "If productivity advances had stopped in 1945, American workers today would have to put in a sixteen-hour day to pay for the goods and services that they can buy with eight hours of work." Explain this statement. Give *three* reasons for the advances in productivity since 1945.

TABLE 4.5 Automobile Battery Production

Number of Workers	Output per Day	Output per Worker	Net Increase From Each Worker
1	50	50	50
2	120	60	70
3	210		
4	260		
5	300		
6	330		
7	350		
8	360		
9	351		

2. After acquiring the equipment for the production of automobile batteries, a manufacturer hired one worker to operate it. This resulted in a day's production of 50 batteries. The next day the manufacturer hired a second worker, and total output rose to 120 batteries. Continuing the procedure, the manufacturer found that three workers could produce 210 units. Eventually, the manufacturer hired a total of nine workers. Table 4.5 gives partial data on the company's productivity. (a) Complete the table. (b) At what number of workers did the operation reach the point of diminishing returns? (c) At what number of workers did the manufacturer reach negative returns? (d) What additional information would be necessary in order to determine how many workers the manufacturer should employ?

3. A manufacturer of motorcycle batteries has a plant capacity of 100,000 batteries per year. Overhead costs are $500,000 per year, in addition to which there are variable costs of $10 for each unit produced. Sales have been running at 50,000 units per year at a wholesale selling price of $25. Recently, a large mail-order department store offered to purchase an additional 50,000 batteries a year, which it would market under its own name. The store offered to pay the manufacturer $20 per battery. (a) Should the manufacturer accept the offer? Explain. (Assume that 50,000 units continue to be sold to the other customers at $25 each.) (b) Suppose that the department store offered to buy the entire output of 100,000 batteries at $15 per battery. Should the manufacturer accept the offer? Explain.

4. Explain why firms with high overhead costs frequently spend large sums for (*a*) research and development and (*b*) advertising.
5. Read the selection and answer the questions that follow.

Robots: The Way to Productivity Gains in the Japanese Auto Industry

Two of the nastiest jobs in an automobile factory are body welding and spray painting. Welding sets off volleys of sparks and clouds of acrid smoke that assault the senses, while painting fills the air with hazardous paint particles and solvent fumes. In Japan, automobile workers need never face these unpleasant and dangerous tasks, however, because they are now performed entirely by robots.

The willingness of the Japanese to apply the latest technology, including the use of robots, to the manufacture of automobiles has resulted in dramatic productivity increases. According to a recent United States Department of Transportation study, the Japanese were producing cars at a cost of $1,000 to $1,500 less per car than American manufacturers. It remains to be seen whether the American auto industry will be able to catch up with Japanese technology.

(*a*) What does the use of robots for welding and painting have to do with productivity? (*b*) Why should Japanese productivity interest American automobile manufacturers? Explain your answer. (*c*) The welding robots used by the Japanese automakers cost approximately $40,000 each and were good for about three years before they wore out and had to be replaced. Each robot could weld about 1½ times as many cars in a day as a person. Under what circumstances would it pay for an American factory to replace its workers with robots?

Even the smallest businesses may incorporate to reduce the risk of unlimited liability.

UNIT III

The Role of Business

CHAPTER 5

How Business Firms Are Organized

Perhaps the most distinctive feature of the American free enterprise system is the extent to which it is privately owned. Unlike Socialist and Communist economies, in which the government owns most of the means of production, nearly 90 percent of the goods and services produced in the United States comes from private sources. In 1982, for example, when domestic production of goods and services amounted to $3,012 billion, $2,689 billion was produced by privately owned business firms.

The organization of business firms may take one of three forms: the *single proprietorship*, the *partnership*, or the *corporation*. The single proprietorship is a business owned by one person, while a partnership is a business association of two or more owners. Single proprietorships and partnerships are sometimes referred to as *unincorporated businesses*. A corporation is a business made up of a number of owners (stockholders), which is authorized by law to act as a single person. In the pages that follow, we will be taking a look at the advantages and disadvantages of each of these three forms of business organization.

THE SINGLE PROPRIETORSHIP

When Richie Jones got out of the Army, he decided to use his savings to go into business for himself. He leased a store in his old neighborhood and set up a small grocery. He worked long hours, opening and closing the shop himself, and he had to do all the ordering of goods and waiting on customers. But the business was Richie Jones' own, so anything he earned from it belonged to him. And he was responsible only to himself.

The kind of business that Richie had set up was a *single propri-etorship*, or an individually owned business. The single proprietorship is the most common form of business in the United States. Indeed, almost 80 percent of our nation's enterprises have adopted this form. The most common single proprietorships are the small businesses in a community: the small housewares and electronics shop, the shoe repair store, the hair stylist, the fast-food stand.

Advantages of the Single Properietorship. One virtue of the single proprietorship is its simplicity. No legal forms or agreements are needed to start the business, and the owner can close down the business at will. The other forms of business organization usually require the services of lawyers both to start up and shut down.

Another benefit of the single proprietorship is the appeal of working for oneself. Richie Jones could probably have found a job working in a grocery store, but he would not have been his own boss. As sole proprietor, Richie can run the business the way he wants.

A major attraction of the single proprietorship is the opportunity to make a *profit*. If Richie Jones worked for someone else, he would receive wages that were more or less fixed. As the owner of his own business, however, he has a chance to increase his income by increasing his profits. There is no limit to the amount of profits that a successful business can earn.

Disadvantages of the Single Proprietorship. The single proprietor has the advantage of making all the decisions but also assumes all the responsibility. Richie may hire assistants, but he alone is responsible for everything that happens in his store. Furthermore, although as proprietor Richie hopes to make a profit, he may instead incur a loss. The 8,000 businesses that have failed annually in recent years testify to the risk involved in all private business.

The size of a single proprietorship is limited by the amount of money the proprietor has and is able to borrow.

Single proprietorships are subject to limited life, which means that the business terminates when the owner dies. They are also subject to *unlimited liability*, meaning that there is no limit to the amount of money that the proprietor can lose. Thus, if a business is unable to pay its debts, personal funds and other assets of the proprietor can be seized for payment.

THE PARTNERSHIP

Let us return to Richie Jones and his grocery store. Richie was growing tired of the long hours and responsibilities of his business. He had hired two clerks to wait on customers during the busy time of the day, but he still had to work a full week himself, and he was still solely responsible for the business. Besides, his employees did not have the same interest in the business as he had.

One day, Bill Brown, one of Richie's oldest and closest friends, dropped by to say hello. For several years, Bill had spent his summers working as a cook at a resort hotel. In the course of the conversation Bill told Richie that he had saved up some money with which he was hoping to open a luncheonette or a small restaurant.

"Hey, that gives me an idea," Richie exclaimed. "Why don't you come into business with me? The store next door is vacant, and we could expand in there and add a take-out food section."

"You might have something, Richie," Bill replied. "I was nervous about going into business on my own. This way we'd be able to help each other out."

After some further talks in which the details were worked out, Richie and Bill drew up an agreement and formed a partnership to replace Richie's single proprietorship. A *partnership* is a business organization that is owned by two or more persons, each of whom is known as a partner. The partners may divide their responsibilities and share the business profits in any way they see fit. Under the terms of their agreement, Bill Brown put up some cash, and the two men agreed to divide the profits equally. Soon thereafter work began on the store expansion, and a new sign appeared in the window announcing the creation of the "B&J Food Emporium."

Advantages of the Partnership. When he went into business with Jones, Brown brought with him a number of valuable assets. One asset was the additional money that enabled the store to expand. A principal advantage of the partnership over the single proprietorship is that the available capital is increased by whatever amount the additional partners bring in.

Additional partners may also bring special skills into a business. In this instance, Brown's experience as a cook will help him create and manage the take-out food department. Furthermore, the partners will be able to share the problems that are certain to come up and perhaps deal with them more effectively together than either could alone.

Still another advantage of the partnership is that it provides for coverage when one of the owners is ill or on vacation. Finally, partnerships, like single proprietorships, may be easily organized and are not subject to special federal taxation.

Disadvantages of the Partnership. The principal disadvantage of the partnership as a business organization can be summed up in two words: *unlimited liability.* In the event that the business fails to pay for itself, any partner or group of partners can be held personally responsible for the payment of all its debts.

Suppose, for example, that a few years after they formed their partnership, Jones and Brown approached their former classmate and mutual friend Jenny Green to ask her for money to modernize their store. Jenny agreed to invest $10,000 in exchange for a 10 percent share in the partnership. Because she was fully occupied with her own responsibilities, Jenny made it clear that she wanted to remain a "silent partner." Although entitled to 10 percent of the profits, she would leave the management of the firm to Jones and Brown.

A year later, Jones and Brown found that they were losing so much money that they could no longer pay their debts and had to close down the business. The firm owed its suppliers $20,000, and neither Jones nor Brown had any way of paying even part of this debt. Green, however, had about $25,000 in a savings account. The creditors found out about this account and sued Green for the full amount of the firm's debt. Even though she was only a 10 percent partner and had had little or no say in the management of the business, her status as a partner made her fully liable for the firm's debts, as Jones and Brown were. Merely because she happened to be the only one of the three who had any funds, she had to use those funds for payment of the firm's debts. The court required her to pay off the entire $20,000 debt.

A second disadvantage of the partnership is that its life is limited. When a partner dies or resigns, a whole new partnership must be formed.

Another drawback to the partnership is that the amount of capital it can raise is limited to the wealth of the individual partners, the earnings of the business, and loans. While the addition of new partners is a possible source of new capital, many people are reluctant to enter into a partnership because they would be liable for the debts of the business.

Finally, a partnership is risky because there is always a chance that the business will be hurt by a conflict between partners. Disagreement among partners is a frequent cause of business failure. Even when disagreements between partners do not actually threaten the existence of the business, they can hamper its progress. For example, finding new partners can be difficult, since they must be approved by all the others.

THE CORPORATION

As we have seen, the advantages of unincorporated businesses such as the single proprietorship and the partnership are matched by certain disadvantanges—notably unlimited liability, limited life, and restrictions on size due to the difficulty of raising new capital. To avoid these disadvantages, businesses may turn to another type of business organization: the corporation.

What Is a Corporation? A *corporation* is a business firm that is created by authority of a state or federal *charter*. The charter gives the firm the right to do business and issue shares of stock representing ownership of the business. Anyone owning one or more shares is a part owner of the corporation. If, for example, a corporation issues 1,000 shares of stock, then a person owning 100 shares owns 10 percent of the business.

A unique feature of the corporation is that it is legally separate and distinct from the people who own it. In a legal sense, the corporation itself functions in many ways like a person. It can, for example, enter into contracts. Thus a performer signing a contract with a motion picture corporation is making an agreement with the corporation rather than with a particular person. A corporation can also sue or be sued and must pay taxes. Because of these attributes, the corporation has sometimes been described as an artificial person.

Advantages of the Corporation. Let us return to the time when the B&J Food Emporium was seeking to raise money from Jenny Green. Suppose that instead of going into business as a partner, Green had asked that Jones and Brown establish their business as a corporation. Under the terms of Green's proposal, Jones and Brown would each hold 45 percent of the stock while Green would receive 10 percent of the shares in exchange for her $10,000 investment.

The two partners liked Green's proposal and asked their lawyer to apply for a charter from their state. Soon they received permission to incorporate and had a new sign placed over the front of the store: "B&J Food Emporium, *Inc.*"

Why had Green insisted that B&J incorporate before she agreed to invest in the business? The answer is that incorporation provides certain advantages that are lacking in other forms of business enterprise.

Limited Liability. Because the corporation is legally separated from those who own it, the stockholders cannot be held liable for its debts. If the business should fail, the most that the stockholders could lose would be whatever they had paid for their stock—that is, their investment. Thus, if B&J as a corporation were to fail with $20,000 of unpaid debts, Jenny Green would lose her initial $10,000 investment, but the creditors could not take her savings, as they could under the partnership.

The British place such importance on the concept of limited liability that they identify corporations with the *Ltd.* (Limited) designation rather than our familiar *Inc.* (Incorporated). Because the possibility of personal loss is limited, it is far easier to induce people to invest in corporations than in partnerships. This feature is particularly important to corporations that are seeking to expand, for it makes the sale of their stock a practical way to obtain additional funds.

Transferability of Shares. When the members of partnerships want to sell their holdings, not only must they find people who are willing to buy their portions of the business, but the buyers must also be acceptable to the other partners. Futhermore, once these conditions have been met, new partnership agreements have to be drawn up. This process can be difficult, costly, and time-consuming. In a corporation, however, stockholders cannot usually veto the sale of stock to anyone. All that stockholders have to do to sell their shares is to sign over their stocks to buyers. Moreover, in the case of the large, publicly held corporations, shares may be sold almost instantaneously through the organized stock exchanges (see Chapter 6). This transferability of stock shares, which facilitates the finding of buyers, is another reason why it is easy for corporations to raise capital.

Unlimited Life. Shares of stock in a corporation—in other words, ownership of the corporation—may be easily transferred from one person to another. Such transfers occur daily in the nation's stock exchanges. The easy transferability of stock gives a corporation *unlimited life*—that is, the life of the corporation is not limited to its ownership by any particular person or persons. Even after the death of one or more of its stockholders, the corporation continues to function. Unlimited life makes the corporate form attractive to investors because it reduces the chances of business failure and because it enables them to leave their shares of the business to their heirs. Unlimited life also allows corporations to borrow funds for long periods of time.

Ease of Obtaining Capital. The ability to obtain funds from sources other than earnings is a significant advantage of the corporation over the single proprietorship and the partnership. Because of its limited liability and unlimited life, and the ease with which stock shares can be bought and sold, a corporation usually has little difficulty attracting new capital through stock sales. Corporations are also usually considered a good risk for loans by banks and other large lending institutions. In addition, many corporations are able to borrow funds from the public through the sale of bonds. A *bond* is a kind of long-term IOU on which the corporation promises to repay a sum of money in a year or more, in addition to interest. Those who own bonds are *creditors* of the corporation, whereas those who own stock are *part owners.*

Tax Advantages. Corporations must pay taxes on their income, but at a lower rate than individuals. Therefore self-employed persons and businesses with substantial earnings frequently incorporate themselves to avoid the high personal income taxes they would have to pay as individuals or unincorporated businesses. Such tax savings apply only to undistributed profits of the corporation—those not paid out in dividends. Income from dividends is subject to personal income taxes like any other personal income.

Disadvantages of the Corporation. Despite the advantages of incorporation, most business firms are not incorporated. As you can see from Figure 5.1 on page 100, unincorporated businesses outnumber incorporated ones by nearly five to one. Some of the factors that discourage business owners from incorporating are:

Subject to Double Taxation. Unlike the earnings of unincorporated businesses, which are not taxed, corporate profits are taxed by the federal government and also by some states. In addition, if corporate earnings are distributed to stockholders in the form of dividends, these earnings are taxed a second time by the personal income tax. In small corporations, in which most of the stock is held by the few people who are actually running the business, double taxation can significantly reduce the attractiveness of the corporate form.

Difficult to Organize and Maintain. Although the actual costs of incorporating are not great, they can seem unnecessary when added to the already large expenses involved in setting up a new business. Similarly, many entrepreneurs prefer to avoid the paperwork required in organizing and maintaining a corporation. They may not want to bother hiring an attorney or issuing stock. Finally, some small-business people may simply not understand the corporate form and may fear some loss of control in the need for a state charter and regular accountability.

The S Corporation and Small Businesses. In an effort to aid certain small businesses, Congress added Subchapter S to the Internal Revenue Code. Subchapter S allows the owners of small corporations (those with twenty-five or fewer stockholders) to use the corporate organizational form but to be taxed as though the firm were a single proprietorship or a partnership. The owners of an S corporation, as it is called, enjoy the limited liability of the corporation without incurring its tax disadvantages. They declare any corporate profits as personal income and pay taxes on that amount, but they avoid the additional tax on corporate profits that regular corporations incur.

Because it is a corporation, however, the S corporation is liable to the other disadvantages of corporations discussed above. It is therefore likely that unincorporated firms will continue to outnumber incorporated firms.

How Large Corporations Are Organized. Corporations generate the major share of business activity in this country. (See Figure 5.1.) They account for 88 percent of the receipts and 77 percent of the profits earned by American industry. Almost all of the nation's mining and manufacturing is conducted by corporations, and corporations employ over 60 percent of the labor force—some 67 million people in 1982.

Although corporations vary in size from the small, family-operated business, in which there may be only one or two stockholders, to huge enterprises employing tens, even hundreds, of thousands of workers and owned by similar numbers of stockholders, it is the largest firms that play the most important role in our economy. In 1981 the 500 largest industrial corporations accounted for $1.8 trillion in sales—about 62 percent of the gross national product for that year.

FIGURE 5.1   Business Organizations and Receipts, 1980

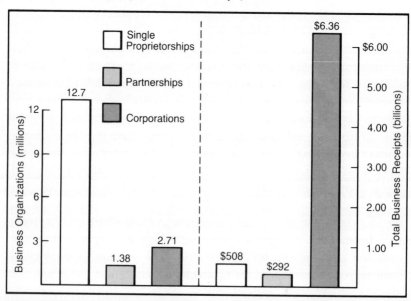

The Role of Business

The largest of these giant corporations was Exxon, with $103 billion in sales. Exxon was owned by 686,000 stockholders and had 177,000 employees.

Giant corporations like Exxon have organizational and operational problems quite different from those faced by small, closely held corporations. Although each of Exxon's 686,000 stockholders is a part owner of the corporation, it would hardly make sense for all the stockholders to try to run the day-to-day affairs of the business. The average person is not likely to have much knowledge of the petroleum industry or the techniques of managing a big business. It would be difficult enough just getting 686,000 stockholders to agree to anything. Over the years, large corporations have developed an operating framework that has allowed them to deal effectively with both day-to-day and long-range problems while, at the same time, looking after the interests of their stockholders. The key elements in this framework are the *board of directors* and the *officers*.

Board of Directors. The board of directors is the direct representative of the stockholders. In electing the board, stockholders are usually entitled to one vote for each share of common stock they hold. In this way, voting power is assigned in accordance with the size of one's holdings. Thus, in a corporation with 100,000 shares of stock outstanding, a person with 25,000 shares of stock will be entitled to cast 25,000 votes (one-fourth of the total).

Typically, the board's primary concern is with the overall well-being of the corporation. The board does not generally get involved with the day-to-day business of the firm. Managing the company is left to the officers, who are selected by the board.

One major responsibility of the directors is the financing of the corporation. They decide, for example, what portion of the profits will be distributed to the shareholders as dividends and how much will be reinvested in the business. They also decide whether or not the firm is to seek additional funds from outside sources, and if so, what means should be used.

The board is also expected to prepare reports for the shareholders summarizing the company's activities.

The Officers. It is the officers, selected by the board, who actually run the corporation. They usually include the president, the various vice presidents in charge of major aspects of the business, a secretary, and a treasurer. The officers hire the personnel and conduct whatever operations are necessary to the functioning of the organization. Figure 5.2 on page 102 summarizes the relationship between the stockholders, directors, officers, and personnel of the firm.

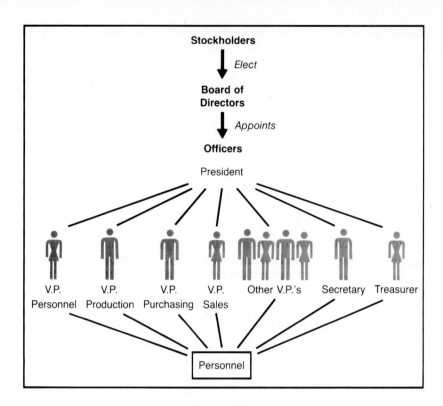

FIGURE 5.2 Organization of a Typical Corporation

Separate Ownership and Control. Stockholders own part of the corporation whose stock they hold. In a large corporation, however, the stockholders have little or no control over the affairs of the company because no single shareholder owns enough shares to influence company policy. Thus, the holder of 100 shares of Exxon is merely one of the company's 686,000 stockholders. One stockholder controls only a tiny fraction of all the outstanding shares, and that person's views concerning company policy will probably be of little consequence to the elected management. For this reason, a stockholder who does not like the way the company is run will most likely sell the stock rather than fight management.

Actual control of the corporation lies in the hands of the few large stockholders who control the election of the board of directors. Obviously, any person owning more than 50 percent of all the stock would have absolute control because that person could name the entire board. Usually, however, a controlling share is achieved with far less than half the stock. Indeed, ownership of 10 to 15 percent of the total stock is usually enough to control a large corporation.

How is it possible for an individual holding only a fraction of the total shares of stock to control a company? This is accomplished through the use of proxies. A *proxy* is a written authorization giving another person the right to vote one's share of stock at a stockholders' meeting. Most stockholders are willing to let the business continue in its present course because they are not interested in its day-to-day operations, do not understand how the business functions, or feel that their opinions would not significantly influence the management of the company. For this reason they will usually give their proxies to the present management. In this way, the management remains in power indefinitely, because it can control more than 50 percent of the firm's voting strength by combining its own shares with those of its proxies.

Some economists have been critical of the fact that ownership and control in the large corporation are so far apart. They argue that it is not right that stockholders are almost powerless to change the course set by management. Others, while conceding that stockholders have little if any control over their company, argue that this is as it should be. Modern-day business is so complex that only experts can make intelligent decisions pertaining to it. Thus people investing in a large corporation willingly turn over control of their investment to the management team in exchange for the opportunity to share in the profits and growth of the company. Besides, these economists point out, it is possible for groups of stockholders to get together in an attempt to oust the management. While this is usually a very difficult undertaking, such actions by stockholders have been successful from time to time.

Although stockholders in large corporations have had little or no control over the day-to-day affairs of their companies, most large corporations in the United States have prospered. It would appear, therefore, that the separation of ownership from control has not presented a serious handicap to their operation or growth.

EXERCISES

Multiple Choice

1. Who owns a corporation? (*a*) stockholders and bondholders (*b*) stockholders only (*c*) bondholders only (*d*) the board of directors.
2. Which form of business organization is most common in the United States? (*a*) single proprietorship (*b*) partnership (*c*) corporation (*d*) government monopoly.
3. A partner may be forced to pay the debts of the partnership out of his or her own funds. This illustrates which disadvantage of

the partnership? (a) limited life (b) limited capital (c) unlimited liability (d) double taxation.

4. In a large corporation the common stockholders generally do all of the following *except* (a) receive a share of the profits (b) manage the everyday affairs of the business (c) elect the board of directors (d) own the business.

5. Limited liability, unlimited life, and a charter are characteristic of (a) single proprietorships (b) partnerships (c) most small firms (d) corporations.

6. The phrase "separation of ownership and control" is used to describe the situation in corporations in which (a) the stock dividend rate is fixed (b) bondholders can outvote stockholders (c) no voting stock is issued (d) ownership of common stock is widely distributed.

7. "Double taxation" refers to the fact that (a) corporations have to pay both federal and state taxes (b) corporations pay income taxes, and the earnings that they pay out in dividends are subject to personal income taxes (c) that part of a corporation's earnings that is not distributed as dividends is subject to an excess profits tax (d) corporations pay income taxes and sales taxes.

8. Which statement is correct? (a) Corporations generate the major share of the nation's business activity. (b) Most businesses are corporations. (c) Corporations are always owned and operated by the same people. (d) Most corporations are public utilities.

9. The board of directors is elected (a) by the stockholders on a basis of "one person, one vote" (b) by the stockholders according to the number of shares of voting stock they hold (c) by the combined vote of bondholders and stockholders (d) by the incumbent board of directors.

10. In a corporation, a proxy (a) is the head of the corporation (b) transfers a stockholder's voting rights to someone else (c) gives a stockholder the right to vote in the election for the board of directors (d) is the stockholders' share of the corporation's profits.

11. Which type of business organization would be appropriate for a firm owned by three persons who want both limited liability *and* exemption from corporate income taxes? (a) a single proprietorship (b) a partnership (c) an S corporation (d) none of the above.

12. Which of the following is the most attractive feature of the single proprietorship? (a) the ease with which ownership can be transferred (b) its ability to expand across state boundaries (c) the ease with which it can be organized (d) its access to stock market money.

Essay Questions

1. Answer the following questions for (a) the single proprietorship, (b) the partnership, and (c) the corporation. (1) How is the business formed? (2) How long can the business last? (3) Who is

responsible for the everyday affairs of the business? (4) What are two disadvantages of this form of business? (5) How does the business obtain capital?

2. In a recent election for the board of directors of a large corporation, the efforts of a new group that had been formed to unseat the existing board failed, and the incumbents were reelected. The victors argued that this was evidence of "corporate democracy." The losers argued that it demonstrated how difficult it is to defeat the "insiders." Explain both points of view, supporting each with *two* arguments.

3. Upon graduation from television repair school, Harry Zoltan opened a small shop as a single proprietor. A few years later he was approached by an old friend, Bill Paseo, who offered to put $5,000 into the business in exchange for a 50 percent interest. Harry agreed, and the partnership of Zoltan and Paseo was opened. (*a*) Explain *three* factors that might have led Zoltan to start his business as a single proprietorship. (*b*) Explain *three* reasons why Zoltan was willing to take Paseo in as a partner. (*c*) Suppose Zoltan and Paseo decided to incorporate their business. What *three* advantages would this offer to the partners?

4. Barbara Harrison and Frances McCreedy were partners in Computer Cosmos, a retail store selling personal and small business computers and software. Under the terms of their partnership agreement, both women invested an identical amount of money and were to share equally in the profits.

   Unfortunately, the business failed to show a profit. Indeed, by the end of the second year it was so heavily in debt that the partners decided to call it quits. After selling their furniture, fixtures, and inventory—the proceeds of which were used to pay a portion of their debts—$9,000 in debt still remained.

   "I hate to tell you this, Barbara," Frances said, "but I invested every cent I had in the store. I don't have a penny to my name."

   "All I have," said Barbara, thinking out loud, "is the $10,000 I've been saving to buy a new car."

   (*a*) How much, and from whom, will Computer Cosmos' *creditors* (the people to whom the $9,000 is owed) receive? (*b*) Suppose that instead of organizing as a partnership, Harrison and McCreedy had formed a corporation; how would you then answer question (*a*)? (*c*) If the women had decided to incorporate, they most likely would have formed an S corporation. Explain why.

CHAPTER 6
How Corporations Obtain Funds

Money has been called the fuel that drives the machinery of industry. Money pays for the day-to-day expenses of doing business and enables a firm to grow. As long as an adequate supply of money is available, a company is likely to remain healthy. Should the supply of money be reduced or shut off, however, the firm will wither and eventually fail.

As you might expect, funds for the day-to-day operations of most businesses come from their earnings. But where do the larger firms get the money they need to replace worn-out or obsolete buildings and equipment (capital) or to expand the scope of their operations? There are three sources of such funds: earnings, loans, and the sale of shares of stock, or equity financing. (See Figure 6.1.)

EARNINGS

Earnings, or *profits,* are what is left after the expenses of doing business are deducted from the receipts (money taken in). One of these expenses, *depreciation,* represents the money that is set aside to replace worn-out or obsolete plant and equipment. After taxes have been paid, the remaining earnings are available for distribution to the stockholders and for use by the corporation. In recent years, corporations have looked to their *retained earnings,* or *undistributed profits* (the earnings that were not paid to the stockholders as dividends), to provide some 60 percent of their new funds.

LOANS

Businesses have three ways of borrowing money. They may receive credit from the firms with which they trade; they may borrow from institutions that make corporate loans, such as banks or finance companies; or they may sell corporate bonds. Bonds are long-term certificates of indebtedness (see the discussion of corporate securities below). Borrowing is the second largest source of corporate funds.

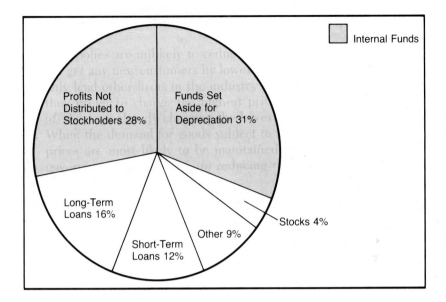

FIGURE 6.1   Sources of Corporate Funds, 1980

THE STOCK MARKET: EQUITY FINANCING

You have probably heard of the stock market, where shares of stock in the nation's major corporations are bought and sold. Daily newspapers carry news about the stock market and listings of stock prices from the two major stock exchanges on Wall Street in New York City. Radio and television also report on the stock market.

In amounts of money involved, the sale of stock—also called *equity financing*—is the least important source of new capital for business. In recent years, stock sales have accounted for just a few cents out of every dollar invested by industry in new capital. But to those corporations that rely on the sale of stock to finance their business activity, equity financing is extremely important. It is also important to the millions of Americans who own or are thinking of buying shares of stock and to corporations that plan to raise capital by equity financing in the future.

In a more general way, the fortunes of the stock market mirror how the people of the United States view their economy. Indeed, economic analysts look to trends in the stock market to assess the national mood. If the American public is feeling optimistic, it is likely to increase its investments in the stocks and bonds of American businesses. These increased investments result in a general upward trend in prices in the securities markets. If there is a general spirit of gloom, market prices are likely to drop as the public sells off its stocks and bonds.

In view of the tremendous interest that trading in corporate securities seems to stimulate, we shall take a closer look at the process.

CORPORATE SECURITIES: STOCKS AND BONDS

One of the factors that sets the corporation apart from the single proprietorship and the partnership is the corporation's legal right to sell securities in the form of stocks and bonds. As we have seen, stocks represent ownership in a corporation. Bonds, however, are issued in exchange for loans. Thus the stockholder is a part owner of a firm, while the bondholder is a creditor.

1. Stocks. Most corporate stocks are *common stocks.* They entitle their owners to a voice in the selection of the board of directors. Holders of common stock may also share in the profits of the company. Suppose, for example, that the directors of a corporation set aside $3 million of the corporation's profits for distribution to its stockholders. If there are one million shares of common stock outstanding, the stockholders will receive $3 in *dividends* for each share of stock they hold. If the business should fail or for any other reason be dissolved, the holders of common stock would receive their share of whatever was left after all the debts of the business were paid. If nothing was left at that point, the stockholders would, of course, receive nothing.

Some corporations issue *preferred stock* in addition to common stock. Holders of preferred stock are entitled to a fixed dividend

Common Stock Certificate. Why would anyone want to own one of these certificates?

whenever the board of directors decides to pay it. Holders of common stock do not receive dividends until the holders of preferred stock are paid. If the preferred stock is *cumulative preferred* and the corporation fails to pay any dividends for a year, it must pay double dividends to the preferred stockholders before any dividends are paid to the common stockholders. Consider the following example:

The Miracle Flashlight Company issued 100,000 shares of cumulative preferred stock paying annual dividends of $1 per share. There were also one million shares of common stock outstanding. In 1983 no dividends were paid. In 1984 the board of directors set aside $700,000 from profits for payment to stockholders. The money was distributed as follows: Holders of preferred stock received $2 per share: $1 for 1984 plus $1 for 1983, when no dividends were paid. This payment left $500,000 for distribution to the holders of common stock, or 50 cents for every share of stock they owned.

If a corporation is *liquidated* (dissolved and all the assets sold for cash), the creditors will be paid first. The holders of preferred and common stock, in that order, will receive their share of whatever is left. Usually, holders of preferred stock do not have the right to vote in the election of the board of directors.

2. Bonds. Corporate bonds represent a debt of a corporation, and the holder of a bond is a creditor. A bond is thus a kind of IOU. It is a promise by the corporation to repay a specified sum (usually $1,000) at the end of a specified number of years. During this time, the corporation is required by law to pay interest to the bondholders.

An important difference between interest and dividends is that corporations are legally obliged to pay interest on their bonds but are not legally obliged to pay dividends on their stocks. Interest is therefore treated like any other cost of doing business. Corporations may fail to pay dividends without serious consequences, but failure to meet interest payments could force a company into bankruptcy.

If the company fails, bondholders will be paid off before any of the stockholders. Sometimes specific property such as a factory or land is pledged as security for the bonds, in which case they are called *mortgage* bonds. *Debenture* bonds rely on the general credit of the corporation.

A common assumption made by investors is that all bonds are safer than stocks or that all mortgage bonds are safer than all debentures. This is a mistake, however, because the safety of any corporate security depends upon the company that issues it. Thus the common stock of a well-established, profitable corporation is likely to be safer than the mortgage bond of a newly formed gold-mining company that has not been able to find any gold.

3. Government Bonds. You may be familiar with the Series EE savings bonds issued by the United States government. The most popular of these bonds sells for $25 and pays $50 when held for a specified period of time. Like corporate bonds, government bonds are evidences of debt. When you purchase a savings bond, you are lending money to the United States government. In exchange for the loan, the government promises to return your principal plus interest on a specified date.

All levels of government—federal, state, and local—sell bonds from time to time. While methods of payment, interest rates, and denominations differ depending on the type of bond, all bonds are issued in exchange for a loan and represent a promise to repay the loan with interest.

HOW STOCKS AND BONDS ARE SOLD TO THE PUBLIC

Initial Sale to Underwriters. When a corporation decides to sell its stocks or bonds to the public, it usually goes to an *investment bank,* which underwrites the issue. Underwriting means that the bank, which specializes in this kind of activity, buys the entire issue of stocks or bonds. The corporation can then use the funds without any further concern over the sale of the securities. The bank, in turn, sells the securities to the public at a price that will yield it a profit. Sometimes an issue is so large that a group of investment bankers will form a *syndicate* for the purpose of underwriting the issue.

State and local governments also use investment banks to market their bonds. The federal government sells its securities through the Federal Reserve System.

Those who buy stocks and bonds from underwriters are free to sell them any time they choose. But neither the issuing corporation nor the initial underwriter is likely to buy them back; hence there is a need for organized markets in which securities may be sold. *Stock exchanges* and the *over-the-counter market* fill that need. They provide a mechanism by which stocks and bonds can be traded at a moment's notice.

Securities Markets. The stocks and bonds of the nation's largest corporations are generally traded in securities markets known as *stock exchanges.* The largest of these markets is the New York Stock Exchange, and the second largest is the American Stock Exchange, both located in New York City. There are other exchanges in major cities around the country, but the New York Stock Exchange is by

52-Week High	Low	Stock	Div	Yld %	PE Ratio	Sales 100s	High	Low	Last	Chg.
26	18½	ClvClf	1.00	5.1	...	155	20¼	19⅝	19⅝	- ⅛
23	13¾	ClevEl	2.40	15.0	4	5254	16⅛	15⅞	16	......
61½	46½	ClvEl pf	7.40	14.4	...	z2780	51¼	50½	51¼	+ ¼
19⅝	10¾	Clevpk	.60	3.9	15	62	15¼	14⅛	15¼	+ 1⅛
17¼	14¾	Clvpk pf	2.23	13.1	...	153	17	17	17	......
22⅜	14¾	Clvpk pf	1.84	10.4	...	38	17¾	17¼	17¾	+ ¼
31	22½	Clorox	1.20	4.7	8	1636	26	25⅜	25½	- ⅜
30⅞	22½	CluettP	1.00	3.9	8	23	25⅞	25⅝	25⅝	- ¼
35⅞	12¼	Coach s	.40	2.5	5	566	16⅝	16¼	16¼	- ⅛
39¼	23½	Coastal	.40a	1.3	6	754	30⅜	29¾	30¼	+ ¾
64⅜	47⅜	CocaCl	2.76	4.6	14	3649	61⅜	60¼	60⅜	- ⅛
38⅝	26⅛	ColeNt	.52	1.3	16	325	38⅝	38⅝	38⅝	.....
40	9⅝	Coleco		...	...	1456	15⅛	14⅝	14¾	+ ⅛

FIGURE 6.2 How to Read Stock Market Tables Columns 1 and 2 list the highest and lowest prices at which the stock traded during the past 52 weeks. Prices are quoted in dollars and fractions of dollars per share (note that ⅛ equals 12½ cents). During the year, Clorox ranged in price from $22.50 to $31 per share. The name of the company issuing the stock (Column 3) is followed by the annual dividend (Column 4), here $1.20 per share. (Listings are of common stock unless the letters *pf*—meaning preferred—follow the stock's name.) Yield (Column 5) is the percentage return in the form of dividends due to an investor who purchased the stock at the day's closing price. Thus $1.20 (the annual per share dividend) is 4.7 percent of $22.50 (the closing price of one share of stock). Column 6, Price-Earnings ratio, is the number of times by which the company's latest 12-month earnings per share must be multiplied to obtain the stock's current selling price. (The PE ratio is 8.) In Column 7, the number of shares sold during the reported trading day is listed in hundreds (in this case, 1636 equals 163,600 shares). Columns 8–10 (High, Low, and Last) refer to the trading price range during the day. In this case, the high was $26 per share, the low was $25.37½, and the closing price was $25.50. Change (Column 11) is the difference between this day's closing price and the previous day's closing price (here the price was ⅜, or 37½ cents, lower).

far the most important. Indeed, the total value of its sales is greater than the combined total of the stock sales in all the other markets. Figure 6.2 explains how stock market transactions are reported in a daily newspaper.

In the nation's stock exchanges, securities are bought and sold through an auction system. Brokers representing the buyers and sellers offer their wares to the highest bidder and call out their own bids in an attempt to acquire stocks for their clients at a favorable price.

In order to qualify to have their stocks "listed" (traded) on the national exchanges, firms must meet certain standards regarding size and financial security. Not all firms seeking to sell their stocks to the public meet these standards. Accordingly, many corporations sell their stocks either in the regional exchanges or *"over the counter."* The over-the-counter market consists of the many brokerage firms

New York Stock Exchange. Why do stock prices go up and down?

throughout the nation that buy "unlisted" stocks from special dealers and sell them to investors. (The role of brokers in securities sales is explained further on page 113.)

Over-the-Counter Market.   The over-the-counter market handles the stocks of relatively small firms and of most banks, insurance companies, and mutual funds. It also handles the sale of all securities being offered to the public for the first time. The securities of more than 40,000 firms may be bought and sold over the counter. The stocks of fewer than 3,000 firms are traded on the floors of the New York and American stock exchanges.

As with the stock exchanges, over-the-counter transactions are publicly reported the instant they take place. This reporting is made possible by the National Association of Securities Dealers Automated Quotations, or NASDAQ system. NASDAQ is a computer system that enables firms trading in the over-the-counter market to keep informed of the availability and selling price of securities.

Why are securities markets needed? One reason is that investors would be unwilling to buy stocks or bonds if there were no easy way to sell them later. Corporations would then find it excessively costly to sell their securities.

Another reason securities markets are needed is that they enable us to know the value of individual stocks and bonds. This knowledge is indispensable to investors who own or are thinking of buying securities. It is also important to the economy as a whole because it serves to withdraw money from areas where it is no longer needed and transfer it to areas where it is needed. For example, if the outlook for new-car sales is poor at a time when there is an increasing demand for personal computers, the value of automobile-industry securities will probably decrease, while the value of computer-industry securities will increase. Firms in the computer industry will then have an easier time raising new money through the sale of securities than firms in the auto industry.

BUYING AND SELLING STOCKS AND BONDS

People who wish to buy or sell stocks or bonds must use the services of a *brokerage firm*—a company of securities-sales specialists known as brokers. Brokers buy and sell securities in behalf of their clients and receive a commission, or fee, for their work. When a customer places an order for a stock listed on an exchange, the broker relays it to the brokerage firm's representative on the floor of the exchange. There the broker's representative meets with others who are trading the same security and either buys or sells according to the customer's instructions.

The price at which a security is sold depends upon the supply of and the demand for that security. If the security is in great demand, its price will be pushed up. If the demand for the security falls, so too will its price. Similarly, if few want to sell a security, the short supply will push prices up; if many want to sell, the oversupply will push prices down. Whatever the price, none of the money that changes hands after the first sale goes to the corporation that issued the security.

Why People Buy Stocks. Stock ownership in the United States is not confined to the wealthy. In 1980, for example, some 30 million Americans, representing one out of every five adults, owned shares of common stock. Why have so many people invested in the stock market? Most people who buy stocks do so for one or more of the following reasons:

Dividends. The profits earned by a corporation may be distributed to its shareholders in the form of dividends. Many individuals and institutions that invest in common stocks do so in order to share in these dividends.

Capital Growth. The value of a stock is not fixed but fluctuates with changes in supply and demand. Many people invest in common stocks because they expect that in time the stocks will be worth more than they paid for them. Such an increase in value is called *capital growth.*

Stocks increase in value for a number of reasons. One reason is business performance. If a corporation's sales and profits increase, its value and the value of its stock will rise. The value of a stock also increases because of public expectations. If investors expect a corporation to do well, the demand for its shares will increase and so will the value of those shares. Still another reason why individual stocks increase in value has to do with the value of stocks in general at a given time. When most investors are feeling optimistic, the prices of securities tend to rise.

Speculation. Because the price of stocks fluctuates from day to day, it is possible to profit from these movements *if one can correctly predict them.* Although the difference between an investor seeking capital growth and a speculator may not be too clear, the general distinction is that the speculator usually seeks to profit in the short run at some risk, while the investor is looking for long-term growth with little risk. Also, investors generally profit only from an upward trend in the price of their stocks, while speculators can profit from either an upward or a downward movement in stock values if the movement can be correctly predicted.

Speculators generally use two tactics: buying long and selling short.

Buying Long: The "Bulls." Speculators who believe that the value of a particular stock will rise are called "bulls." They hope to profit from this rise by *buying long*—that is, by buying the stock immediately and selling later at a profit. Let us assume that the price of XYZ common is now 24½. (Stock prices are quoted in dollars and fractions of dollars. Thus 24½ = $24.50 per share. Had the price been 24⅜, it would have been equal to $24.375 per share.) A bull purchases 200 shares at 24½. If the price then goes up to 30¼ and our speculator sells, there will be a gross profit of $5.75 per share, or $1,150.00. Brokerage fees and certain taxes have to be deducted from this profit. Of course, if the price of the stock falls to below 24½, our speculator will lose money.

Selling Short: The "Bears." "Bears" are speculators who expect the price of a particular stock to decline and who hope to profit by *selling short*. This step is accomplished by selling borrowed stock and buying it back later for return to the lender. If the stock goes down, the bear will profit. We may illustrate this process as follows:

Frank Jones feels that the stock of Maypak Corporation is overvalued and that its price will fall soon. Jones does not happen to own any Maypak stock, and since he expects its price to fall it would not be profitable for him to purchase the stock. But if he *borrows* the stock, he can sell it at its present price, then buy it back later at a lower price (if the price of the stock does indeed fall) and thus make a profit. Jones therefore orders his broker to sell 100 shares of Maypak short at the current market price of 50¼. What actually happens is that the broker lends the stock to Jones, sells it for him, and credits Jones's account for $5,025. A week or so later Jones proves correct in his prediction, and the price of Maypak falls to 43. He orders his broker to close out the transaction. The broker buys back the borrowed stock at the new, lower price of $4,300, withdrawing that amount from Jones's account. This leaves Jones with a profit of $725, from which must be deducted brokerage fees, taxes, and a rental fee for the borrowed stock, which he returns to the broker.

Of course, it is also possible to lose money in this kind of transaction. Indeed, in a short sale there is no limit to the amounts speculators can lose if they are wrong, because there is no limit to the prices to which their stocks could climb. For example, if the price of Maypak stock in the above example climbed to 80, Jones would have to pay $8,000 for shares for which he received only $5,025—a loss of $2,975.

Margin. Stocks may be purchased partly on credit, called *buying on margin*. The margin, or percentage that a buyer has to put up in cash, is established by the Federal Reserve Board and since 1934 has fluctuated between 40 and 100 percent.

Buying and Selling Bonds. Like stocks, bonds may be sold in organized exchanges or over the counter. And as with stocks, the price is determined by how much buyers are willing to pay and how little sellers are willing to accept. Figure 6.3 on page 116 explains how bond market transactions are reported in a daily newspaper.

The price of a bond is influenced chiefly by two factors: its safety and its rate of interest. If the public has any doubts about the ability of the borrower (the issuer of the bond) to pay either the principal or the interest, the bond's price will tend to fall. The price will also tend to fall if the rate of interest of the bond is less than the rate of interest prevailing in the economy. For example, in order to sell a $1,000

Bonds	Current Yield	Sales in $1,000	High	Low	Last	Net Chge
Fuqua 7s88	7.9	13	89	89	89	+ ½
Fuqua 9½s98	13.8	6	69	69	69	+ 1
Fuqua 9⅞97	13.3	12	74⅜	74⅜	74⅜	+ ¾
GTE 10½07	cv	31	104½	103½	104½	......
Gelco 14⅝99	15.4	13	95¼	95¼	95¼	− ⅜
Gelco 14s01	cv	15	96	96	96	......
GnATr 5¾99	cv	73	62½	62	62½	+ ½
GCinem 10s08	8.8	11	115	114	114	− 1½
GnEl 7½96	10.6	15	70½	70½	70½	......
GnEl 8½04	12.1	11	71	70⅜	70⅜	− ⅝
GEICr 8.6s85	8.8	25	98¼	98¼	98¼	− 7-32
GEICr 8¼86	8.7	110	95⅛	94¾	94¾	......
GEICr 8¼97	11.3	12	73	71¾	73	+ 3¾

FIGURE 6.3   How to Read Bond Market Quotations In Columns 1 and 2, the name of the firm issuing the bonds (General Electric) is listed in abbreviated form, followed by the bonds' rate of interest and the year in which they mature. These GE bonds pay 8½ percent of their $1,000 face value, or $85, in interest yearly. When they mature (come due) in the year 2004, the bonds will be worth $1,000 each to their holders. Column 3 lists the Current Yield, the rate of return on investment based on the purchase price. Newspaper quotations use the closing (or last) price in calculating the current yield. Since the closing price was $703.75 (from Column 7, explained below) and the bonds paid $85 in interest, the yield was 12.1 percent (because 85/703.75 = 12.1). Column 4, Sales in $1,000 units, tells us the number of units worth $1,000 in face value that changed hands. In this instance, GE bonds worth $11,000 in face value were sold. Columns 5–8 show the trading price range during one day. Bond prices are found by multiplying the published figures in the tables by $10. Thus the high price was $710, and the low and final prices were $703.75. Net Change is the difference between the previous day's closing price and the closing price on the day reported. Here the closing price of 70⅜ (or $703.75) was ⅝ of $10, or $6.25, less than the closing price on the previous day.

bond that paid 8 percent interest at a time when the prevailing rate on other bonds was 12 percent, one would find that the price would have to be lowered to considerably less than $1,000.

SPECIALIZED MARKETS

Although we have discussed only securities exchanges, similar markets exist for commodities such as wheat, barley, rye, coffee, tin, and silver. If you examine the financial pages of your local newspaper, you will see many other markets listed. Because trading in these markets requires far more specialized knowledge than trading in the securities of large corporations, the specialized markets are not as popular with the public.

SECURITIES AND EXCHANGE COMMISSION

The Securities and Exchange Commission was created by an act of Congress in 1934. The purpose of the commission is to protect the public against deception or fraud in the selling of securities.

Caveat Emptor. The SEC does not say what it thinks of a particular investment. Rather, it subscribes to the principle of *caveat emptor*— "let the buyer beware." It would be inappropriate for a federal agency to seem to be either endorsing or condemning any particular corporation. But just as important, trading in securities is subject to so many variables of interpretation and chance that no single body could safely set itself up as an authoritative source of advice for investors.

The SEC requires that most companies wishing to sell their securities to the public file certain pertinent financial information. Failure to do so, or the publication of false or misleading information by a corporation, is punishable by fine, imprisonment, or both. It is up to investors to examine the financial reports of companies they wish to invest in. If they then make foolish decisions, they probably deserve their fate. For example, if a worthless mining company informs the public of the true facts in financial statements, then people who lose their money by investing in the company have no one to blame but themselves. The SEC has also established certain procedures designed to prevent any person or group from manipulating stock prices. Unfortunately, these safeguards have not always proved effective.

FINANCIAL STATEMENTS: BALANCE SHEET AND INCOME STATEMENT

Two of the most important sources of financial information about a firm are the *balance sheet* and the *income statement* (or *profit and loss statement*).

Balance Sheet. The balance sheet summarizes the financial condition of a firm. It deals with three areas of information: assets, liabilities, and net worth.

Assets represent anything of value that is owned by a business, including cash on hand or in the bank, plant and equipment, merchandise, and furniture and fixtures.

Liabilities represent the obligations, or debts, of a company. These include unpaid bills and salaries, borrowed money, and mortgages on the building or equipment.

TABLE 6.1 Sunshine Launderette Balance Sheet December 31, 19___

Assets		Liabilities and Net Worth	
Cash	$ 7,000.00	Accounts payable	$ 1,480.00
Machinery	12,200.00	Unpaid taxes	1,000.00
Supplies	350.00	Total liabilities	2,480.00
Truck	2,400.00	Owner's equity	19,470.00
Total	21,950.00	Total	21,950.00

The difference between what a firm owns and what it owes is its *net worth*, or *owner's equity*. This may be stated as:

Assets − Liabilities = Net Worth

For convenience, accountants transpose liabilities when drawing up the balance sheet, in the following manner:

Assets = Liabilities + Net Worth

Table 6.1 is an illustration of a typical balance sheet.

Income Statement. An *income statement* (Table 6.2) summarizes the activities of a business over a period of time (usually a quarter or a year). As you can see from Table 6.2, the income statement sets out the total income and its source. It then shows the expenses that were

TABLE 6.2 Precise Stationery Company Income Statement For the Year Ended December 31, 19___

Sales		$141,000.00
Cost of goods sold		84,500.00
Gross profit on sales		56,500.00
Operating expenses		35,930.00
Net income from operations		20,570.00
Other income	$750.00	
Other expenses	240.00	
Net other income		510.00
Net income		21,080.00

incurred by the firm. Total expenses are subtracted from total income to determine the company's profit (or loss). Income statements may also show how the profits were divided among taxes, dividends, and retained earnings.

Limitations of Financial Statements. Financial statements are useful, but they have limitations. Some of the more important limitations are:

1. They are a record of past events, not a forecast of the future. Past success does not guarantee future success.

2. They may not reflect the changing value of money resulting from inflation or deflation.

3. Some of the values may be based not on fact, but opinion. For example, some companies may assign a value to their name because experience has shown that their reputation attracts customers. This will show up as "goodwill" in the asset section of the balance sheet. Similarly, the values assigned to such items as "depreciation" and "inventory" may not be accurate in terms of present-day market conditions. "Total assets" are supposed to give some idea of what the firm would be worth if it were forced to liquidate. If the inventory (the goods waiting to be sold) were valued at a higher price than they could actually be sold for, the figure would make the firm appear to be worth more than it is.

As stated at the beginning of this chapter, borrowing is a major source of corporate funds; and the sale of stocks, though it represents only a small percentage of corporate funding, has a great impact on investors and the economy in general. Corporations are required by law to make certain financial information available to potential lenders or investors. This information is presented in the corporation's income statement and balance sheet. The wise lender or investor will obtain and carefully study these statements before risking money in a loan or an investment.

EXERCISES

Multiple Choice

1. Corporations obtain most of the funds that they need for expansion from (a) the sale of stocks (b) the sale of bonds (c) short-term borrowing (d) their undistributed profits.
2. The holder of one share of stock in a corporation is (a) a creditor (b) a debtor (c) an owner (d) an officer of the corporation.

3. The holder of a corporate bond is (*a*) a creditor (*b*) a debtor (*c*) an owner (*d*) an officer of the corporation.
4. Preferred stock is like (*a*) a bond in that the dividends must be paid regularly (*b*) a bond in that the holder of the stock is a creditor of the corporation (*c*) common stock in that dividends will increase as profits increase (*d*) common stock in that there may be times when the board of directors decides to pay no dividends.
5. When a corporate security is registered with the Securities and Exchange Commission, this means that (*a*) the SEC has approved the security as a safe investment (*b*) certain financial information has been filed with the SEC (*c*) the SEC may act as a broker for the corporation (*d*) the public may inquire of the SEC as to its opinion of the advisability of purchasing the security.
6. All of the following information is contained in a balance sheet *except* (*a*) assets (*b*) liabilities (*c*) net worth (*d*) total sales.
7. In economics, the term "depreciation" is most frequently associated with (*a*) a firm's buildings and equipment (*b*) a decline in production (*c*) declining sales in time of inflation (*d*) a decline in the market value of a stock.
8. Which information is contained in a corporation's income statement? (*a*) net income (*b*) accounts payable (*c*) value of the firm's factory (*d*) total liabilities.
9. To "sell short" means (*a*) to sell fewer stocks than one owns (*b*) to sell stock that one owns because one expects the price to fall (*c*) to sell stocks one does not own (*d*) to sell stock for less than its market value.
10. To "buy on margin" means (*a*) to buy long (*b*) to buy over the counter (*c*) to buy stocks in the hope of selling at a profit in the near future (*d*) to buy stocks with borrowed funds.
11. A corporation pays a dividend on its common stock (*a*) every year (*b*) when the interest becomes due (*c*) whenever its board of directors votes to do so (*d*) whenever it earns a profit.

Essay Questions

1. On January 12, the following transactions took place:
   Robert Allison, convinced that Dr. Pepper stock was undervalued, instructed his broker to buy 200 shares.
   Margo Bromley, believing that General Electric stock was undervalued, purchased 100 shares of GE stock.
   Patrick Chin thought that General Motors was in for a bad year and ordered his broker to sell 100 shares of GM common short.
   These transactions took place at the closing price for January 12:

Dr. Pepper	12¾
General Electric	97½
General Motors	35

Three months later Allison, Bromley, and Chin closed out their stock transactions at these prices:

Dr. Pepper	18½
General Electric	90¼
General Motors	70

(a) Identify the bulls and the bears in these transactions. (b) How much money did each of the three speculators earn or lose? (Ignore commissions and taxes in calculating your answers.)

2. The Boswash Computer Company, Inc., has the following securities outstanding:

$1 million in 10 percent mortgage bonds, due 2001

2 million shares common stock

Last year the company's profits totaled $1.75 million after all interest payments were made, including debt on the bonds. The board of directors voted to distribute $1 million to the common stockholders as dividends. (a) How much was paid in interest to the bondholders? (b) How much did a holder of 100 shares of common stock receive in dividends? (c) In connection with the bonds issued by the corporation, explain the meaning of "due 2001." (d) Suppose that next year Boswash Computer fails and the company is liquidated. After all the corporation's debts are paid, $1.2 million remains. How will this sum be divided?

CHAPTER 7

Monopoly and Imperfect Competition

"Oh, no!"

"What's the matter?"

"The car won't start."

"No wonder. Look at the gas gauge. It says 'E'—the tank's empty."

As every driver knows, an automobile cannot run without gasoline. Just as gasoline provides the energy to drive a car's engine, so prices produce the energy that makes our economy run. Prices and the price system determine *what* goods and services will be produced, *how* they will be produced, and *who* will receive them.

Because prices are so important, economists try to learn as much as they can about them. Prices are affected by many factors. Stock prices may fluctuate daily, as you learned in Chapter 6, but the price of a telephone call or a bus ride is likely to remain unchanged for years. Unbranded aspirin costs less than the one with the well-known name, while the candy bars at the checkout counter all seem to sell for the same price. In recent years, the high price of borrowing money has pushed interest rates so high that business firms are threatened with extinction. And yet, at the other extreme, low prices for farm goods in the recent past have brought many farmers close to bankruptcy.

In some nations of the world, nearly all prices are set by the central government. In the United States, the government sets the price of a few goods and services, but most prices are established in the marketplace by the competition among buyers and sellers.

In Chapter 2 we described the largely theoretical situation of *pure competition* in which market price is determined exclusively by the forces of supply and demand. We said that such a state of pure competition would have to be based on the following set of four assumptions:

1. There are many buyers and sellers acting independently, and no one alone is big enough to influence the market price.

2. All products competing with one another are practically identical so that it does not matter which item the buyer takes or the seller offers.

3. All buyers and sellers have full knowledge of prices being quoted all over the market.

4. Buyers and sellers can enter and leave the market at will.

While the concept of pure competition provides us with a useful framework for the discussion of economic problems, it is of limited value in describing real situations. In reality, the conditions required for pure competition hardly ever occur. The prices we pay for food, clothing, entertainment, and everything else that goes into daily living were not determined in a market like the New York Stock Exchange. But they were subject to some kind of competition. This competition normally lies somewhere between pure competition, with its many buyers and sellers and free flow of information, and *monopoly*, in which one seller controls the entire output of a good or service. Between these extremes falls a wide range of market conditions, which economists have called *imperfect competition*. Most economic activity today would be described as imperfect competition.

To get some idea of the different levels of imperfect competition that characterize most of our economy, it will help us to understand the two extremes of competition: pure competition and monopoly. We examined pure competition in Chapter 2; in this chapter we shall consider monopoly. Later, we will discuss the two major forms of imperfect competition: monopolistic competition and oligopoly.

MONOPOLY

Strictly speaking, a monopoly exists when there is only one seller of a particular good or service and when there is no substitute for that good or service.

Even in a pure monopoly, the laws of supply and demand continue to function. That is, the point at which the supply and demand curves intersect still determines the market price and the amount of goods that will be purchased. Monopolists can set market prices because they have control over the entire supply. (Monopolists do not control demand, however.) In setting prices, monopolists know that the amount they can sell will be determined not by them but by the demand curve representing the buyers' wishes.

The curve in Figure 7.1 on page 124 represents the buyers' demand. The monopolist can select any price along that curve, and buyers will have to pay that price if they want the product. The quantity sold will be determined by the price.

As a practical matter, a monopoly can exist even if there is more than one supplier of a commodity. A monopoly will occur if one supplier controls a large enough share of the total output to be able

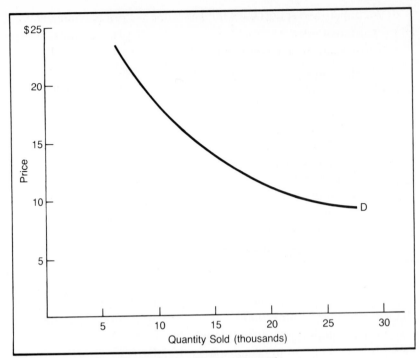

FIGURE 7.1 Market Price Under Conditions of Monopoly

to determine the market price. An example was the American Sugar Refining Company, which in the 1890s controlled all but one of the sugar-refining plants in this country and 90 percent of the nation's sugar output. The company's power was so great that sugar prices stood at whatever level it selected.

Legal Monopolies. Although most monopolies are illegal in the United States, certain specific types are permitted.

Patents and Copyrights. In a recent court decision, a federal jury ordered Sears, Roebuck & Company, one of the nation's largest retail chains, to pay $5 million to the inventor of a quick-release socket wrench. The court held that Sears had marketed the hand tool without properly compensating its inventor, who held a *patent* on it. A patent is a legal monopoly granted to an inventor by the federal government. Most patents remain in effect for four to seventeen years.

A *copyright* is an exclusive right that protects such people as authors, composers, publishers, and artists from having their works reproduced, displayed, or performed without their permission. The United States Copyright Office in Washington, D.C., registers all claims to copyrights.

Patents and copyrights are granted in order to stimulate innovation, cultural achievement, and scientific progress. By placing limits on the number of years that patents and copyrights are in effect, the law prevents the establishment of permanent monopolies on inventions and creative works. Works that are no longer protected by copyright are said to be in the *public domain.*

Public Utilities: Natural Monopolies. Certain industries that are vital to the public health and welfare do not lend themselves to competition. For example, if there were four or five competing telephone companies in one city, individuals and businesses would have to keep four or five telephones in their homes and offices or else be unable to call persons and organizations that subscribed to different services. And imagine the confusion as competing firms tore up streets in order to maintain their equipment.

Other industries in which competition would not be in the public interest include such services as gas, electricity, water, and public transportation. Because a community is best served if there is only one firm in each such field, the state or city permits one company to have a monopoly by granting it a *franchise*, or exclusive license to do business. Such *natural monopolies*, which may be publicly or privately owned, are subject to extensive governmental regulation.

Government Monopolies. Americans have traditionally distrusted private monopolies. They have, however, been more willing to accept monopolies owned and operated by their governments. The United States Postal Service, state turnpikes, and municipal transportation facilities are all examples of government-owned monopolies. The reasons why some industries tend to be owned by government are varied. Custom and tradition have played a part. As a general rule, however, government has stepped in where private industry has been unable or unwilling to function because the anticipated profits did not justify the risk.

Market Price Under Conditions of Monopoly. A firm that holds a monopoly may choose any point along the demand curve for its product's market price. Naturally, the higher the market price selected, the fewer will be the number of items sold. Which price will the monopolist select? The highest possible price? The lowest? Neither. Monopolists will try to select the price that yields the most profit.

Let us suppose that ABC Pharmaceuticals, Inc., holds the patent, and therefore the monopoly, on the manufacture of the nation's most effective treatment for athlete's foot. The product is called Spray

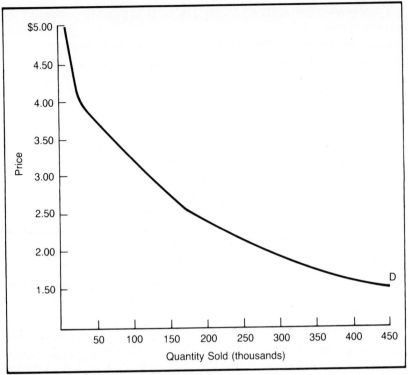

FIGURE 7.2 Market Demand for Spray Away

Away and is sold in nonaerosol cans. Upon conducting an extensive survey, ABC's economists have developed a graph (Figure 7.2) depicting the demand for the product.

The market survey enabled ABC's accountants to prepare an analysis of the effect of price on the firm's profits, which is shown in Table 7.1. After studying the results of the market survey and the price analysis, ABC's management decided to charge $3 a can, because at that figure it would earn the biggest profit.

What Is Wrong With Monopolies? With the exception of the legal monopolies described above (such as public utilities, patents, and copyrights), monopolies are generally outlawed in this country. There are several reasons why monopolies are forbidden.

1. The market price under conditions of monopoly is almost always higher than it would be in a competitive market. Under a monopoly, the price of an item is limited only by the degree of elasticity of demand for the item.

In Chapter 2 we explained that necessities are subject to *relatively inelastic demand.* In a monopoly, the seller has far greater freedom

TABLE 7.1 ABC Pharmaceuticals, Price-Sales Analysis

At a price per can of	we could sell this number of cans (thousands):	gross income of	minus costs of	would leave us with a profit of:
$5.00	5	$ 25,000	$ 60,000	− $ 35,000 (loss)
4.50	20	90,000	85,000	5,000
4.00	25	100,000	88,000	12,000
3.50	75	262,500	163,000	99,500
3.00	125	375,000	206,000	169,000
2.50	175	432,500	300,000	132,500
2.00	275	550,000	500,000	50,000
1.50	450	675,000	837,000	− 162,000 (loss)

to raise prices of necessities than of goods that are subject to more elastic demand. If the public can easily do without the product, demand will quickly fall off as prices are raised. But if the item is a necessity for which there is no adequate substitute, buyers will be under greater pressure to pay the price asked. Thus the owner of the only oasis in a desert could command a very high price for a glass of water.

Let us return to the pharmaceutical company, which has just decided to charge $3 a can for its foot spray. Were the item not a monopoly, the market price would have been something less than $3—say, $2.50. At that price consumers would have bought an additional 50,000 cans. If the price had been $2, consumers would have bought an additional 150,000 cans. In either case consumers would have had the use of more cans of the foot spray than they have when the product is sold as a monopoly. Thus, by making goods and services more expensive than they would otherwise be, *monopolies reduce the standard of living.*

2. Monopolies are more likely to waste resources than competitive firms. Since monopolies do not have to worry about competition, there is less pressure on them to find more efficient methods of production.

3. Monopolies are less sensitive to consumer demand than their competitive counterparts. We noted in Chapter 3 that consumer sovereignty is one of the principal features of the American free enterprise system. In their quest for profits, firms seek to outrace

Elastic and Inelastic Demand. Which of these products, bread or luxury cars, is subject to greater elasticity of demand?

their competitors by better providing for consumer wants. This is less true in the centrally planned Communist countries, such as the Soviet Union, where state-owned firms can provide consumers with goods and services on a take-it-or-leave-it basis. In much the same way, because they are the only suppliers, monopolists are under less pressure to cater to consumer tastes.

4. Monopolies may be in a position to force workers to acccept lower wages than they might receive in a competitive market. Where there are several competing firms, workers will refuse to work for

those firms whose wages are below normal. This choice may not be possible in a monopoly.

5. Monopolies may increase the likelihood of economic recession or depression. Monopolies tend toward *price rigidity*—the maintenance of prices at a certain level even when demand is falling. The only way to maintain prices in the face of falling demand is to reduce production. Then workers are laid off, people have less money to spend, and there is a general decrease in demand for goods and services. When this occurs throughout the nation, we have the beginnings of a business slump. (Business cycles are discussed in Chapter 17.)

6. Monopolies are often accused of unfair competition. Because of their desire to maintain and extend their control over the market, monopolists have at times taken unethical steps to eliminate competition. Sometimes monopolists have sold their goods at a loss so as to force their competitors into bankruptcy. Once the competitors were eliminated, the monopolists charged whatever price they wished. At other times, monopolists have used their huge buying power to make suppliers dependent on the monopolists' business. Then the monopolists could force their suppliers to sell to them for less than they charged the monopolists' competitors. Some monopolists have even been able to cut off their competitors' supply of raw materials or credit by buying up all that was available.

7. Monopolists may use their economic power to achieve political power. They do this by using their great wealth to support legislators and legislation favorable to their interests. Through such influence, monopolies can easily outweigh the efforts of the unorganized public and thus push through legislation that may not be in the public interest.

IMPERFECT COMPETITION

Thus far we have described the two extremes of a market economy: (1) pure competition, in which there are many buyers and sellers and no one firm is big enough to influence prices, and (2) monopoly, in which competition is absent and one seller has absolute control over the market price. Our economy provides only a few examples of pure competition (such as the stock market and commodity exchanges) or of pure monopoly (your local electric company comes close to our definition). But we have many examples of *imperfect competition;* in fact, almost all businesses fall into this category. Economists recognize two major forms of imperfect competition: *monopolistic competition* and *oligopoly.*

MAKERS OF ECONOMIC THOUGHT

JOAN ROBINSON
The Economics of Imperfect Competition (1933)

When the English economist Joan Robinson (1903–1983), began her studies of the market system, it was generally believed that sooner or later all trade would take place under conditions of "perfect competition." According to the theory of "perfect competition," no individual buyer or seller could become big enough to determine prices. The lure of profits, it was assumed, would always attract competition, and for that reason monopoly would not survive for any length of time.

Although the theory worked on paper, perfect competition simply did not exist in real life. Much of the world's trade was being carried on by giant monopolies and oligopolies whose conduct did not match that of the "perfect competition" model. Joan Robinson demonstrated this disparity between theory and reality in *The Economics of Imperfect Competition* (1933).

The book was written shortly after Joan Robinson joined the faculty of Cambridge University, where she had been a student. In outlining her theory of *imperfect competition,* Robinson demonstrated how product differentiation and consumer preferences gave certain companies the ability to manipulate prices despite the presence of competing firms. In other words, under imperfect competition, giant firms gained monopoly-like, or as Robinson put it, "monopolistic," powers.

In Robinson's view, monopolistic competition posed a threat to society as a whole. By restricting production in order to maintain unnecessarily high prices, monopolists deprived the public of the goods and services it might otherwise have enjoyed. Worse still, she went on, fewer goods and services resulted in fewer jobs, declining income, and less consumption. In other words, the end result would be economic recession. Robinson called for vigorous regulation of the economy by the national government as a way of preventing what she viewed as abuses of the market system.

Although many economists disagreed with her conclusions, Joan Robinson continued to be occupied by the central economic questions of the day until her death. Robinson helped elucidate John Maynard Keynes' economic theory (see Chapter 17) in her *Introduction to the Theory of Employment* (1937), discussed overall economic growth in *The Accumulation of Capital* (1956), and was the author of *Economic Philosophy* (1962) and *Introduction to Modern Economics* (1973).

Monopolistic Competition. How many gas stations are there in your neighborhood—one? five? twenty? Whatever the number, if your family members are like most people, they will prefer to buy their gas from one or two stations in particular. The quality of service, the brand of gasoline, and convenient location attract patronage. For one or more of these reasons, your family may even be willing to pay a cent or two more for their gas.

Gasoline, haircuts, toothpaste, furniture, and shoes are but a few of the goods and services sold under conditions of *monopolistic competition.* This term describes a market in which many firms in an industry sell a similar product. Under monopolistic competition, although sellers are influenced by the law of supply and demand, they have some say in determining the price at which their goods or services will be sold. The major factor that gives sellers some control in setting prices is *product differentiation.* Product differentiation is a *perceived* difference in quality between products that are essentially alike. Advertising, product design, and packaging can all make one product more attractive to buyers than another, virtually identical, product. Or consumers may prefer one product over a similar competing product because of individual taste or because "our family has always used Brand X."

As an example, let us consider aspirin. Because all aspirins are made according to the same formula, one brand is about the same as another. Yet not only do a half dozen or so brands appear on the shelves of drugstores and supermarkets, but the best-selling brand is also the most expensive. Apparently, more people feel that their aches and pains will be relieved by Brand X than by any other aspirin, even though the others are essentially the same. Why are people willing to pay more for one brand of aspirin than for another? The secret ingredient is advertising. Because Brand X has been made to appear unique in the minds of consumers, it has achieved a kind of minor monopoly and can therefore sell for more than competing brands.

Thus, if consumers think that one brand is better than another (whether it is or not), the sellers of that item will be able to charge more than their competitors because they have, in effect, a monopoly on their own product. Some buyers will actually choose the more expensive brand *because* it is more expensive. They will assume that if the product costs more, it must be of better quality. There is, of course, a limit to the amount that sellers can charge. If a seller raises its price too high, the consumer may decide to forgo that brand and take "second best."

Product Differentiation. How did the Campbell's Soup Company create demand for its new product in this 1920s advertisement?

Market Price Under Monopolistic Competition. Under monopolistic competition, many firms in an industry compete with one another. The cosmetics, soap, cereal, and soft drink industries are common examples. The typical firm in these industries concentrates not upon underselling its competitors, but rather upon convincing the public that there is something special about its product. Success is measured by the extent to which the public insists on the company's brand. The stronger the insistence, the greater is the company's ability to raise prices. Convincing the public through advertising is expensive, however, and must inevitably affect the cost of the product. In one year, one well-known cosmetics company had advertising costs amounting to 40 percent of its sales. Such costs are reflected in higher prices, which the public may not be willing to accept. Therefore, in setting their price under monopolistic competition, company managers have to consider the following:

Product Differentiation. How can the company convince the public that its product differs from similar competing items?

Selling Costs. How much should be spent on advertising to achieve product differentiation and convince the public that this product is superior to all the others? Companies can predict with some accuracy that the more they spend to promote their product, the more it will sell. But they must also be aware that the additional costs of advertising will eventually exceed the additional profits they will earn as a result of the advertising.

Price. With one eye on the demand schedule and the other on costs, the seller will attempt to select the price that will yield the greatest profit.

Does Monopolistic Competition Benefit the Economy as a Whole? Critics of monopolistically competitive markets have argued against the large expenditures for advertising that this kind of competition requires. They claim that such costs lower living standards by compelling consumers to pay more for goods and services than would otherwise be necessary. They argue that if competing companies did no advertising, their products could be sold at a lower price.

Supporters of monopolistic competition point with pride to the well-stocked shelves of America's supermarkets. They argue that the wide choice offered to consumers raises people's standard of living instead of lowering it. People have different tastes, and in a free society they should be able to choose from among similar products to suit their tastes. Production might be more efficient if there were only one brand of soap, one brand of cereal, and one brand of shampoo. But if everyone looked alike, ate alike, and smelled alike, life would be a lot duller.

Supporters of the system also contend that as a result of the extensive advertising and promotional campaigns sponsored by industry, the public is kept informed about the goods on the market. Moreover, the heavy investment in advertising has made the communications media that the advertisers support (such as television, magazines, and newspapers) less expensive to the general public.

Oligopoly. *Oligopoly* is the domination of the market by a few large firms. Cigarettes, electrical appliances, chewing gum, steel, cement, aluminum, and containers are all examples of industries in which a few producers supply almost the entire market. Some of these industries sell differentiated products, while others sell products that are identical in every respect. For example, producers of chewing gum, cigarettes, or electrical appliances will attempt to convince customers that their particular brand or model is different from, and better than, all the others. United States Steel, however, makes no claims that its steel is better than that of Bethlehem Steel. In the steel industry, as in the cement and aluminum industries, there are few competitors because of the huge amount of capital needed to set up such businesses.

Market Price Under Oligopoly. How are the prices of steel, cigarettes, or any other oligopolistic product determined? Because a small number of large producers dominates each field, each company knows that if it cuts its prices, the other firms will do likewise. If, for example, the Brand A Cigarette Corporation reduced its prices by 10 percent, Corporations B, C, and D would probably follow suit. Since the number of cigarettes consumers smoke does not seem to depend upon price, it is likely that the major effect of the price cut on all four companies would be to reduce their profits. Therefore, oligopolies generally avoid price competition in favor of product differentiation, price leadership, or even collusion.

Product Differentiation. We have already noted that certain kinds of oligopolistic industries lend themselves to product differentiation. Sony goes to considerable expense to convince the public that its television sets are better than and different from those of Zenith or Panasonic. Maytag does the same in promoting its clothes washers. But in either industry one firm seldom claims that its product is priced below that of its competitors.

Price Leadership. It is usually illegal for companies to get together to establish prices. However, there is no law to prevent one company from announcing a price change and all other companies in the industry from "following the leader" with the identical change. When this is a generally accepted practice, it is described as "price leadership."

Collusion. Because there are few competitors in an oligopolistic market and because price competition is expensive and pointless in the eyes of the oligopolist, there has always been a strong temptation for competing companies to get together and set prices. Most such activities are illegal under the antitrust laws, but there have been cases where "pools" and "cartels" were created for this purpose.

Administered Prices. From what we have said about imperfect competition, we can see that most prices are set not by independent market forces but rather by business firms themselves. Such prices that are set by the seller are known as *administered prices.*

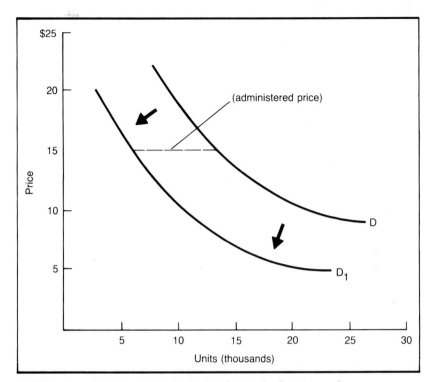

FIGURE 7.3 Administered Price Under Conditions of Falling Demand

It is characteristic of administered prices, such as those of the cigarette industry, that they are maintained at one level for a fairly long time. This price maintenance is made possible by the control the seller has over supply. During times of falling demand, the seller need only cut back on production to maintain prices at existing levels. (See Figure 7.3.)

Government, too, may administer prices. The prices of phone calls from your home and from pay telephones are approved by a government agency. Bus fares, electricity rates, and other public utility charges are also set by government action. "Fair trade laws" permit manufacturers to set minimum prices below which their goods may not be sold.

Critics of administered prices argue that such artificially high prices force consumers to pay more for their purchases and tend to keep inefficient producers in business. Supporters of administered prices point out that if large companies were forced to lower prices every time demand slipped, many of these firms would be forced into bankruptcy. Many workers would lose their jobs, and the economy as a whole would suffer. Administered prices therefore lend stability to the economy.

Monopoly and Imperfect Competition   **135**

The Micrin Mouthwash Story: A Study in Product Differentiation

The mouthwash industry is big business, with sales running into the hundreds of millions of dollars annually. Several years ago Johnson and Johnson introduced a new mouthwash, Micrin Blue, which quickly captured about 15 percent of the market and soon threatened to outsell the industry leader, Listerine. But fifteen years after its entry into the field, Micrin's sales had fallen to less than one percent of the industry's totals, and Johnson and Johnson took it off the market.

The rise and fall of Micrin Blue serves as an interesting case study of product differentiation in action.

Micrin's initial success was no mere stroke of good luck. Johnson and Johnson had spent $15 million in advertising and market research to launch the project. The firm chose a blue color to distinguish the product from the amber, red, and green of its three leading competitors, and packaged the product in a distinctively shaped apothecary bottle.

The secret of Johnson and Johnson's success, however, became the source of its undoing. The ingredients of mouthwash are not costly; all it takes is a solution of water, alcohol, and glycerine to which coloring and flavoring are added. But the most important ingredient in the manufacture and sale of mouthwash, and also the most expensive, is advertising.

Warner-Lambert, manufacturer of Listerine, decided to spend twice the amount on advertising that Johnson and Johnson spent advertising Micrin. Listerine turned an apparent liability into an asset. While other mouthwash manufacturers stressed the personal attractiveness their products would impart and referred disparagingly to the mouthwash that tasted like "medicine," Warner-Lambert capitalized on Listerine's "medicinal" taste by claiming health-giving properties for the product.

Monopsony and Oligopsony. Most restrictions on pure competition come from sellers who are able to impose some limitations on the market. These restrictions range, as we have seen, from monopolistic competition to monopoly. But suppose that we had a situation in which there were only one employer of navigational-instrument technicians in an entire region, or only one refinery to which sugarcane

At about the same time, Procter and Gamble introduced a new green-colored product called Scope, which was marketed as "the good-tasting alternative." Scope also appealed to both the "medicinal" and "sex-appeal" markets, and so rose quickly to second place after Listerine in the marketing race. Meanwhile, other manufacturers brought out new products or new campaigns that were targeted at the "good-taste" and "sweet-breath" markets. Thus Lavoris stressed its "pucker power," and Colgate 100 became "the mouthwash for lovers."

Experts are still debating why Micrin failed. Perhaps its color was against it. As one advertising executive said, "There never has been a successful *blue* mouthwash." The reason may have been Johnson and Johnson's reluctance to spend enough on advertising to maintain the product's number-two position in the field. The failure to establish Micrin as either a medicinal or a sexy mouthwash may have contributed to the product's failure.

Whatever the reason for Micrin's demise, no one suggested that its effectiveness as a mouthwash could have had anything to do with it. Product differentiation may actually have worked against Micrin's chances for success.

1. What is meant by *product differentiation?*
2. Why was Micrin colored blue?
3. What is the most expensive ingredient in the manufacture and sale of the best-selling mouthwashes?
4. (a) Identify and explain three reasons why Micrin lost its number-two position in mouthwash sales. (b) Which of the three reasons listed above would you say was the most important? Why?
5. "Product differentiation enables a manufacturer to carve a monopoly out of a segment of a market." With reference to the market for mouthwash, discuss this statement.

growers could sell their crops. In such a situation, in which there is only one *buyer* in the market, we have what economists call *monopsony.* Like monopolists, monopsonists can exercise great influence over the market price, in this instance because they control demand. By reducing their demand for an item, monopsonists can force suppliers to lower their prices. The quantity and price that monopsonists are willing to accept depend upon the supply curve in much the same way that the amount and price that monopolists are willing to offer depend upon the demand.

Oligopsony is a market in which there are few buyers. A classic example is the cigarette industry, in which a handful of companies buy the major share of the tobacco that is grown in this country.

EXERCISES

Multiple Choice

1. Prices are usually lowest for a product when (*a*) only one company produces it (*b*) many competing companies produce it (*c*) labor unions are strong where it is produced (*d*) it is produced under monopoly conditions.
2. If two giant corporations are manufacturing the same product and selling it for the same price, which condition is most likely to exist? (*a*) One of the companies has a monopoly on the product. (*b*) The products are about equal in quality. (*c*) The companies are competing in terms of quality of product rather than price. (*d*) The companies are owned by the same stockholders.
3. Which series is arranged in order from the most competitive situation to the least competitive situation? (*a*) perfect competition, monopoly, monopolistic competition, oligopoly (*b*) monopolistic competition, oligopoly, perfect competition, monopoly (*c*) monopoly, perfect competition, monopolistic competition, oligopoly (*d*) perfect competition, monopolistic competition, oligopoly, monopoly.
4. In selecting their selling price, monopolists pick (*a*) the highest price at which they can sell their merchandise (*b*) the price that is determined by consumer demand (*c*) the price that will give them the largest profit (*d*) the price at which they would sell the most merchandise.
5. All other things being equal, monopolists will have the greatest freedom to set prices if (*a*) the demand for their product is elastic (*b*) many substitutes are available for the product (*c*) the demand for the product is inelastic (*d*) the firm is a public utility.
6. Monopolistic competition takes place when (*a*) consumers come to regard two nearly identical products as being quite different (*b*) monopolies compete with each other (*c*) many firms sell a similar product (*d*) only two or three firms manufacture a product.
7. Product differentiation enables businesses to (*a*) charge more than they would under perfect competition (*b*) have as much freedom to set prices as under conditions of monopoly (*c*) spend more on

advertising than their competitors (d) improve the quality of their products.

8. Oligopolies are unlikely to reduce prices because (a) they would not get any new customers by lowering their prices (b) this would only lead other firms in the industry to lower their prices too (c) they prefer to charge the highest price they can get away with (d) they are already charging the lowest possible price.

9. When the demand for goods subject to administered prices falls, prices are most likely to be maintained at existing levels by (a) government intervention (b) reducing the supply (c) advertising (d) collusion.

10. Monopsony exists where (a) there are relatively few sellers (b) there is only one seller (c) the sellers set the market price (d) there is only one buyer.

11. Which one of the following arguments has been advanced as a reason why monopolies are harmful to the public? (a) Monopolies reduce the standard of living by keeping prices artificially high. (b) There is less pressure on monopolies to conserve resources. (c) Monopolies may use political power in ways that are not in the public interest. (d) All of the above.

12. What do a *patent* and a *copyright* have in common? (a) Both grant the holder a legal monopoly. (b) Both provide government with an important source of revenue. (c) Both are issued by state governments. (d) Both protect the rights of authors and composers.

13. Which is the principal reason why a new company does not compete with the electric company in your community? (a) the cost of starting up a competing electric utility (b) the government franchise protecting the existing utility (c) the patents and copy-rights held by the present company (d) the shortage of workers.

14. Last night the network news reported that one of the nation's largest manufacturers will increase its prices next week. The other manufacturing firms in the industry are soon expected to follow suit. Even without knowing what the product is, what would you assume to be true about the industry? (a) It produces consumer goods. (b) It produces producer goods. (c) It has many manufac-turing firms. (d) It has very few firms.

Essay Questions

1. In a certain city, all of the record shops charge the same prices for their records. Competition, however, is quite brisk, and the stores frequently advertise on the radio. (a) Since all the stores are charging the same prices for their merchandise, what tech-niques might each one adopt to differentiate its products and service from the others? (b) What kind of competition does this illustrate? (c) Advocates of other economic systems have argued that it is wasteful for firms to compete in the sale of identical products. Give *two* arguments to counter this point of view.

2. Under conditions of oligopoly, there tends to be an absence of price competition. As a result, when one of the giant firms raises its prices, other companies follow suit. Give *two* reasons why smaller firms do not keep their prices at the lower level and thereby capture a larger share of the market.

3. Since a handful of firms produce nearly all of the nation's supply of light bulbs, the home-lighting industry is often cited as an example of an oligopoly. Stock markets, by contrast, serve as models of perfect competition. Westinghouse is a producer of light bulbs, and its stock is sold on the New York Stock Exchange. Which would you say is more likely to *fluctuate* (move up and down), the price of Westinghouse light bulbs or the price of its common stock? Why?

4. List the names of the sponsors of three commercial television programs you watched recently. What kind of competition is practiced by the industries of each of the sponsors?

5. Recently a well-known record and tape distributing company was fined $10,000 and an official of the company was sentenced to serve a year in jail. The company was convicted of selling "pirated" records and tapes. The pirated recordings had been made illegally at various live musical performances and sold to the public without the knowledge or consent of the performers, their agents, or the recording companies that had them under contract.

   (*a*) What federal law had the distributor broken? (*b*) Who was harmed by the sale of the records and tapes? in what way? (*c*) Dorothy Darvas had what she thought was a terrific idea. She planned to use her new video cassette recorder to record movies from her television set and sell the copies to her friends. When Dorothy mentioned her plan to her Aunt Frieda, who is a lawyer, her aunt said, "You had better forget the idea, Dorothy. What you plan to do is against the law." What did Aunt Frieda mean? (*d*) Why does the law grant inventors, artists, and writers monopoly powers over their works?

6. Read the selection and answer the questions that follow.

The Concentration Ratio: A Measure of Competition

To what extent is the United States economy dominated by large firms? One yardstick that can be used to answer this question is the *concentration ratio*. The concentration ratio is the percentage of an industry's output produced by its four largest firms. (See Table 7.2.) Many economists define an *oligopoly* as an industry having a concentration ratio of 50 percent or more (meaning that 50 percent or more of the industry's output is in the hands of four firms). For example, while there are 62 manufacturers of flat glass, the industry has a concentration ratio of 90 percent. That is, the four largest producers manufacture 90 percent of the industry's output, while the remaining 10 percent is divided among the other 58 manufacturers. The flat-glass industry thus falls under our definition of an oligopoly.

TABLE 7.2   Competition in Selected Industries, 1981

Industry	Number of Producers (establishments)	Concentration Ratio (percentage of output produced by four largest firms)
Aerospace	1,280	61
Book publishing	1,744	18
Bread and cake	3,062	33
Concrete (ready-mixed)	5,433	5
Dairy products	3,731	27
Farm machinery and equipment	264	89
Motor vehicles	322	93
Sawmills and planing mills	7,544	17
Soft drinks	2,192	75
Sporting and athletic goods	1,878	21
Telephone and telegraph	264	89
Women's and misses' dresses	6,953	8
Zinc	6	80

Source: *1982 U.S. Industrial Outlook,* **Department of Commerce**

The concentration ratio by itself can be a misleading measure of monopoly power. One would think, for example, that the photographic industry, with a concentration ratio of 75 percent, was dominated by an oligopoly. Such domination does not exist, however, because foreign sales, particularly by Japanese firms (which are not included in the concentration ratio) make the photographic industry highly competitive. At the other end of the scale is the concrete block and brick industry, with a concentration ratio of only 4 percent. Although no concrete block or brick firm dominates the national market, in many cases the local producer has considerable control over prices. Why? Because most buyers are unwilling to bear the cost of having heavy concrete blocks shipped more than a short distance.

(*a*) (1) Identify the three industries with the *greatest* amount of competition among those listed. (2) Identify the three industries with the *least* amount of competition among those listed. (*b*) With reference to one of the industries you identified in answer to question *a* (1), why do you suppose this industry is so much more competitive than the others? (*c*) With reference to one of the industries you identified in answer to question *a* (2), what would account for the lack of competition in this industry? (*d*) "Concentration ratios can be a misleading measure of competition or the lack of competition." Explain this statement.

CHAPTER 8

Big Business and Government Control

One reason why Adam Smith is called the "father of modern economics" (see page 10) is that so much of what he wrote in the 1770s about economics is still valid today. Consider, for example, the following statement, adapted from his famous work, *The Wealth of Nations:*

> People in the same business seldom meet without having the conversation ending in a conspiracy against the public, or in a scheme to raise prices.

Smith went on to suggest that it would be government's responsibility to see that business "played by the rules" if the laws of supply and demand in a free enterprise system were to operate properly. Would he still hold that view if he were alive today? Before answering, consider the following events:

1961. Twenty-nine of the nation's largest electrical manufacturing firms (including Westinghouse and General Electric) were convicted of conspiring to fix the prices of electrical equipment. One result of these schemes was an increase in the cost of almost every power-generating station built in the United States during the period of the conspiracy. The companies paid $2 million in fines, and seven executives served brief jail sentences.

1976. Forty-seven executives from twenty-seven companies pleaded "no contest" to the charge of fixing the prices of cardboard boxes. The president of the giant Container Corporation of America was fined $35,000 and spent fifteen days in jail.

1979. Brink's, Inc. and Wells Fargo Armored Service pleaded "no contest" to the charge of allocating customers and rigging bids in the armored-car protection business. The firms were fined $625,000 and $375,000, respectively.

1981. After the federal government accused the Sunkist Company of monopolizing the citrus fruit industry, rigging prices, and preventing others from entering the field, Sunkist Growers signed a settlement agreement. Under the terms of the agreement, Sunkist agreed to sell off one of its major processing plants. It also promised to provide the new owners with the produce they would need to be truly competitive.

In each of the above cases a large corporation used its economic power to reduce competition and raise prices. These activities prompted many Americans to heed the 200-year-old warnings first raised by Adam Smith and to call for increased government regulation of big business.

The defenders of big business claim that the *economies of scale* resulting from mass production serve to raise the American standard of living. Too much government interference, they say, could increase the cost of doing business, make goods and services more expensive, and reduce the standard of living.

How can abuses by big business be controlled while the economic freedom needed for efficient large-scale production is preserved?

BUSINESS COMBINATIONS: PAST AND PRESENT

American business boomed in the years following the Civil War. New methods of production and the development of a fine transportation system made it profitable for industry to grow in size and expand its markets. As the scale of production grew, so too did the cost of doing business. In many industries, firms that could no longer afford to expand lost their ability to compete and were forced into bankruptcy. Those firms that remained in business sought to increase their sales in order to meet overhead costs and make larger profits. Sometimes, the severe competition led to *price wars*, in which firms took turns cutting prices in order to undersell their competitors.

Consumers loved price wars, but businesses were hurt by them. Seeking a better way to reduce or eliminate competition, some business owners (or "captains of industry," as they were romantically called in the 1800s) thought it better to cooperate with one another than to compete. Over the years they developed strategies by which they manipulated prices so as to increase profits. The most notable of these strategies, known as *business combinations*, are described below.

1. Pools. An early form of business combination was the *pool*. This was an agreement between two or more firms to share the market for their products and to fix prices. A number of industries established pools in the 1870s and 1880s, but the railroads made the greatest use of them.

Pools lost their popularity in the 1890s. Since they were informal (and usually secret) agreements, they could not be enforced. When one or more of the member firms broke the rules by underselling the pool or invading the territory of the other members, the pool ceased to exist. In addition, the Interstate Commerce Commission Act of

1887 specifically outlawed railroad pools. In their place a new device was developed whose name would become synonymous with monopoly: the trust.

2. Trusts. In 1882 John D. Rockefeller's Standard Oil Company developed a new kind of business organization known as the *trust.* Holders of controlling shares in forty competing oil firms representing 90 percent of the oil industry turned their shares over to a group of trustees in exchange for trust certificates. The trustees coordinated the activities of the forty firms so as to eliminate the remaining competition and fix prices. The former stockholders received their share of the profits in the form of dividends on the trust certificates they held.

Trusts soon developed in other industries, including cottonseed oil, linseed oil, whiskey, sugar, lead, and cordage. The trusts all had the same goal: to increase profits by reducing competition.

Unlike pools, trusts were not organized in secret. Public opposition to trusts soon resulted in action by Congress and the courts. The Sherman Antitrust Act of 1890 and the Clayton Act of 1914 outlawed trusts that were "in restraint of trade." Several courts around the country made trusts illegal in their states.

3. Holding Companies. After trusts were outlawed, *holding companies* became the most important means by which companies combined to reduce competition. A holding company is a corporation organized for the purpose of owning or "holding" a controlling interest in other corporations. As mentioned earlier, controlling interest is ownership of or control over more than 50 percent of the voting stock of a corporation.

In Figure 8.1, Companies A, B, and C are controlled by Holding Company X. If each company is worth $100,000 as represented by 100,000 shares of stock at $1 per share, an investment of $50,001 (which we shall call $50,000) will give the purchaser control of the

FIGURE 8.1   Holding Company X

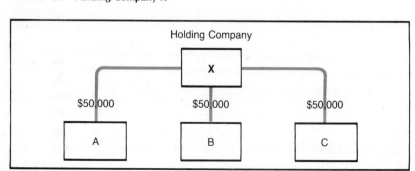

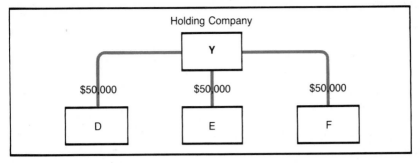

FIGURE 8.2 Holding Company Y

firm. With $150,000, therefore, Holding Company X will have acquired control of A, B, and C.

Assume identical conditions for Holding Company Y and Companies D, E, and F, as shown in Figure 8.2. We now have two holding companies, each with stock worth $150,000 that controls corporations whose value totals $300,000. Suppose now that another holding company is created and that it acquires 51 percent of Holding Company X for $75,000 and 51 percent of Holding Company Y for $75,000. Figure 8.3 shows that this new holding company, which we shall call Z, has acquired control of corporations whose total value is $600,000.

We can see that control of Holding Company Z could be obtained with an investment of $75,000 and that this would mean control of $600,000 worth of corporations. The technique of building up control of corporations through the use of holding companies on several levels is called *pyramiding*. Companies X and Y, which control operating firms, are called *first-level* holding companies. Company Z is a *second-level* holding company because it holds control of first-level holding

FIGURE 8.3 Holding Company Z

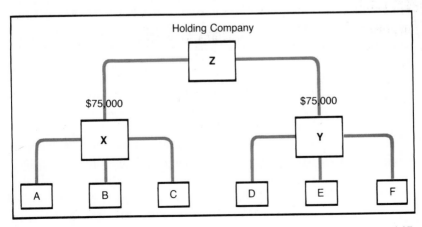

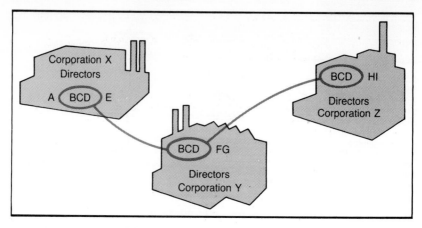

FIGURE 8.4 Interlocking Directorate

companies. In the case of public utilities, holding companies beyond the second level are illegal.

4. Interlocking Directorates. When the same people sit on the boards of directors of several firms, these firms are said to have *interlocking directorates.* In Figure 8.4, directors B, C, and D sit on the boards of Corporations X, Y, and Z.

While many kinds of interlocking directorates have been declared illegal, others are legal and are used at times to coordinate the operations of two or more companies.

5. Cartels. When independent firms formally agree to stop competing and work together to establish a monopoly, they have created a *cartel.* The two essential ingredients in a cartel are production and price. By limiting production to an agreed level, the cartel seeks to gain the same kind of control over prices as a monopoly. This kind of collusion is generally illegal in the United States, but it is legal in most other countries. The world's best-known cartel is the Organization of Petroleum Exporting Countries (OPEC). In just a dozen years, beginning in 1970, OPEC was able to raise the price of crude oil from $1.40 to $34 a barrel.

6. Mergers. In recent years the most common form of business combination has been the *merger.* A merger occurs when one corporation is absorbed by another. The absorbed company may remain intact as a division of the parent firm or it may lose its identity completely. Sometimes, an entirely new company is formed from a merger of two or more firms. Such was the case when the Nash and Studebaker automobile companies merged to become American Mo-

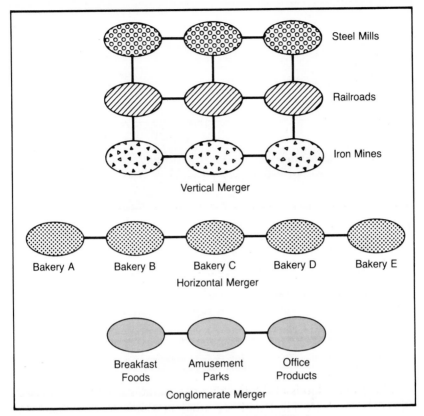

FIGURE 8.5 Vertical, Horizontal, and Conglomerate Combinations

tors. Mergers are generally classified as *horizontal, vertical,* or *conglomerate.* (See Figure 8.5.)

The Horizontal Merger. In a horizontal merger, two or more companies engaged in the same line of business are brought under one management. Such a combination is designed primarily to reduce competition and lower certain kinds of overhead. Competition is reduced because the firms that are combined were formerly contending with each other for business. Overhead can be reduced because functions that were duplicated can now be combined—for example, while formerly each company may have had a bookkeeper and secretary, now one administration office can be established for all. Furthermore, the great buying power of the new firm may reduce the cost of the merchandise that it purchases.

The Vertical Merger. In a vertical merger, two or more firms that are engaged in various stages of marketing or manufacturing the same

Mergers. The San Francisco headquarters of Transamerica Corporation. Transamerica operates a car rental service, sells insurance, and manufactures electronic instruments. What type of business combination does Transamerica represent?

item are brought together under a single ownership. United States Steel, for example, owns its own iron mines, shipping companies, and steel mills. This process of bringing together different stages of production under one management is also called *integration*.

The Conglomerate Merger. A conglomerate merger combines companies producing unrelated products. Thus, the Continental Can Company, which now calls itself Continental Group, acquired firms in the insurance, forestry, and gas industries. Companies become conglomerates for various reasons. Some business people see conglomerate mergers as a way of spreading or cushioning the impact of hard times. When business is bad for one industry in a conglomerate, it may be better for another industry in the same conglomerate.

Other reasons for conglomerate mergers include the following: (1) to gain entry into a line of business at lower cost than if the acquiring company had to start fresh; (2) to buy a company, undervalued by the stock market, at a bargain price; (3) to take advantage of loopholes in the tax laws; (4) to invest surplus funds; and (5) to benefit from the economies of size while staying within the law. Recent court decisions indicate that the government is more likely to approve conglomerate mergers than horizontal or vertical mergers because conglomerate mergers are less likely to reduce competition.

"Merger mania" has been an important factor in American business in recent years. More than 20,000 manufacturing and mining firms were acquired by mergers during the 1960s and 1970s. While most of these companies were small by American standards, nearly 400 of them had assets in excess of $10 million. The large number of mergers has raised questions about what government policy toward business combinations is and ought to be. Before we discuss policy questions, however, we shall briefly review the history of America's attitude toward business combinations and monopoly.

GOVERNMENT REGULATION OF BUSINESS: THE ANTITRUST LAWS

We have already mentioned that the growth of business after the Civil War led many industries to form pools, trusts, and holding companies in an attempt to control the market for their products. The Standard Oil Company, for example, gained control of 90 percent of the nation's oil industry. This control was achieved by a number of questionable strategies. For example, after obtaining control of a large number of refineries, the company was able to force railroads to grant lower rates to it than to its competitors. In this way, Standard Oil was able to sell its oil at lower prices. With the power to undersell the competition, Standard Oil was able to demand that independent firms merge with it or face a price war that they could not win.

Oil is not the only industry dominated by a single company in the late nineteenth century. By 1904 one giant firm in each of eighty of the nation's industries controlled 50 percent or more of the production of those industries. Public opposition to the increasing power of the monopolies led to demands for government regulation of business. At first, only state governments responded, but it soon became apparent that regulation could not be successful unless the federal government was also involved. In the Wabash Case (1886), the Supreme Court held that only the federal government could regulate industries engaged in interstate commerce. As a result of this decision, Congress in 1887 passed the Interstate Commerce Act to regulate railroads.

Since the late nineteenth century, government regulation of monopolies has taken three forms:

1. The government permits monopolies in which normal business competition would not be in the public interest. Public utilities, transportation industries, and others are permitted to function as

monopolies. Recognizing that the legal power of a monopoly can be abused, however, the government has established close *regulation* of these industries through agencies such as the Interstate Commerce Commission.

2. In a few instances, *public ownership* has been instituted in which the government owns and operates a business enterprise.

3. Where the goal has been to promote competition, laws have been passed to ban monopolies and monopolistic practices. Because the first targets of the laws against monopolies were the trusts, these laws are still known as *antitrust* laws.

Sherman Antitrust Act (1890). The first law to regulate the activities of monopolies was the Sherman Antitrust Act. It declared that "every contract, combination . . . or conspiracy, in restraint of trade . . . is illegal." In addition, the act contained penalties for those who violated the law. Its purposes were to hinder the growth of large business combinations that would be able to exercise monopoly powers, and to prevent agreements between two or more companies for the same purpose.

The law was upheld in the Addyston Pipe Case of 1899, in which the federal government relied upon the conspiracy clause of the Sherman Act to prevent an association of pipe manufacturers from secretly fixing prices. Using powers granted by the Sherman Act, the government broke up a number of other companies, including the Standard Oil Company.

Despite these achievements, however, several glaring weaknesses in the Sherman Act made the passage of further legislation necessary. For one thing, while the law prohibited the restraint of trade, it did not spell out what constituted "restraint." This was brought home in 1911, when the Supreme Court announced the *"rule of reason,"* in which it proclaimed that only "unreasonable" restraint was illegal. The effect of this was to make enforcement of the law even more difficult. Not only did the government have to prove that a combination was in "restraint of trade," but it also had to prove that this restraint was "unreasonable." Another major weakness of the Sherman Act was its failure to provide for any agency to enforce it. Furthermore, labor leaders argued that the law was being used to destroy unions because the courts held some union activities to be in unreasonable restraint of trade. To correct these shortcomings, Congress passed in 1914 the Clayton Antitrust Act and the Federal Trade Commission Act. Two later acts dealt with discounting and mergers.

Clayton Antitrust Act (1914). The Clayton Act strengthened the Sherman Act by describing certain illegal monopolistic practices:

Price Discrimination. The law declared it illegal for a supplier to charge one customer more than another for the same quantity and quality of goods or services.

Tying Contracts. The Clayton Act outlawed the "tying clause," a device which required a buyer to agree not to deal with competing firms. The "tying contract" had been used by manufacturers with monopolies in one product to compel their customers to buy all their products. For example, a company with a monopoly on the manufacture of a particular kind of duplicating machine had required that distributors of its machine carry only its brand of ink and paper. The Clayton Act forbade this means of extending a monopoly.

Intercorporate Stockholding and Interlocking Directorates. Companies could not hold stock in competing firms if the effect would be to lessen competition or create a monopoly. Similarly, the law outlawed interlocking directorates where they served to lessen competition.

In addition, the Clayton Act exempted most activities of labor unions from the provisions of the antitrust laws.

Federal Trade Commission Act (1914). This act established the Federal Trade Commission (FTC) to carry out the provisions of the antitrust laws. The commission is empowered to investigate practices it believes to be illegal and to issue "cease and desist" orders. Offending firms must either comply with the orders or appeal to the courts to have them set aside. Since the law was first enacted, the duties of the FTC have been expanded to include the supervision of advertising practices.

Robinson-Patman Act (1936). The purpose of this law was to protect small firms, particularly retailers, from larger competitors and chain stores. The law prohibited sellers from giving bigger discounts to their large customers than their smaller ones unless it could be shown that the discounts were justified by actual cost economies.

Critics argued that the effect of the Robinson-Patman Act was almost the reverse of the Sherman and Clayton acts because it served to protect sellers at the expense of consumers. The critics claimed that although the Robinson-Patman Act protected small firms by reducing the monopoly power of larger ones, it reduced competition and increased the prices paid by consumers.

Celler-Kefauver Antimerger Act (1950). This act was designed to plug a loophole in the Clayton Act that permitted virtually any kind of merger to take place. Celler-Kefauver declares mergers illegal if they "substantially lessen competition or tend to create a monopoly."

ANTITRUST TODAY: TOO LITTLE OR TOO MUCH?

Antitrust legislation and enforcement have been the subject of debate ever since the passage of the Sherman Act in 1890. Some have said that government has done too little to curb the power of big business, others that government has done too much. The following are arguments of those who believe that government has not done enough to curb the power of big business.

1. There have been approximately 7,000 mergers in the past decade. This figure alone is evidence of the failure of government to curb the growth of big business.

2. Government efforts to regulate big business and enforce the antitrust laws are poorly organized and underfinanced. Responsibility for the enforcement of the antitrust laws is shared by the Federal Trade Commission and the antitrust division of the Department of Justice. This has led to some confusion, for the two agencies often do not coordinate their efforts. Government efforts are also hampered, the critics say, because federal agencies must rely upon limited budgets and less experienced staff members than those available to the giant industries. In a recent case brought against an oil company, for example, the government was represented by five lawyers while the oil company was defended by 103 lawyers. And, in an action brought against the American Telephone and Telegraph Company, the government spent $15 million while AT&T spent $360 million in its defense.

3. The growth of the largest corporations through conglomerate mergers threatens the American political system. Recently, changes were made in the tax laws to enable oil companies to retain a larger percentage of their profits. The reason for the changes was to provide the oil companies with funds they would need to explore for new sources of oil. But, critics claim, the additional funds were used instead to acquire companies operating in fields unrelated to the oil industry. Meanwhile, as their assets have grown, big oil companies, along with other industrial giants, have been spending more and more money on public relations campaigns and political activities. In this way the oil companies seem to be seeking public and government support for legislation favorable to their special interests.

Those who claim that the government has done too much to curb the power of big business and that "big is not necessarily bad" argue as follows:

1. In the name of promoting competition, the antitrust laws have

152

prevented companies from making horizontal mergers that could have reduced costs, increased productivity, and benefited consumers. In 1966 the Supreme Court ruled that a merger between Von's, a Los Angeles supermarket chain, and one of its competitors was a violation of the Clayton Act (*U.S. v. Von's Grocery Co.*). Critics of the Court's decision argued that the merger would have allowed Von's to reduce its costs and pass the savings along to the public and that the proposed merger was hardly a monopoly situation, since there were at that time nearly 4,000 single-store operators in the retail food business in Los Angeles. The merger would have given Von's 7.4 percent of total grocery sales in Los Angeles but would still have made the chain only the *second* largest in town (Safeway was larger).

2. The antitrust laws have curtailed the ability of American firms to compete successfully in international markets. In some cases, the courts have held American firms guilty of violating United States laws for their activities abroad. United States companies therefore have a tendency to "play it safe" abroad by doing business as if they were at home. This caution puts them at a disadvantage in competing with foreign firms that do not have to worry about United States antitrust laws.

3. The antitrust laws have also curtailed the ability of United States firms to compete with foreign companies here at home. Although the courts penalize United States companies for growing too big, in many cases the foreign competition is even bigger. General Motors, for example, accounts for 64 percent of total United States automobile production, but it makes up less than 45 percent of all United States auto sales. Some of the balance of the sales comes from other American manufacturers, but a large portion comes from Japanese and European imports. Some economists argue that United States companies should be as free to compete with foreign oligopolies as the foreign companies are free to compete with us.

4. Many of the cases prosecuted by the government cost too much, take too long, and should not have been started in the first place. In 1982, for example, the Justice Department asked the courts to dismiss a thirteen-year-old case it had been prosecuting against International Business Machines (IBM) because, the department said, the case was "without merit." The case had cost the government over $13 million, and although IBM did not disclose how much it had spent in its defense, the amount was probably far greater. Also in 1982, the Federal Trade Commission dropped a ten-year-old case it had been pursuing against the nation's three largest producers of cereals, again because the case was "without merit." The case had cost the FTC some $6 million to prosecute.

5. Even when the government achieves its purposes, it is not

"The courts have ruled, sir, that we must divest ourselves of the Watson Company and Copper Fittings, Inc., sell off thirty percent of our mining interests, and get you a smaller desk."
Drawing by Dana Fradon; © 1982 *The New Yorker Magazine, Inc.*

always clear whether the public benefits. In what may have been the largest antitrust suit in history, American Telephone and Telegraph Company, the nation's largest corporation, agreed in 1982 to *divest* itself of (sell off) its local telephone companies. These twenty-two companies were worth $80 billion and represented two-thirds of AT&T's total assets. As a result of that government "victory," consumers may have to pay more for their local telephone service. And it now appears that AT&T will be in a position to earn more than ever before because local telephone service was the least profitable aspect of its business.

Despite the criticisms leveled against them, however, the antitrust laws have remained relatively unchanged over the years. And the laws are still enforced. For example, in a 1982 decision, the Supreme Court refused to permit a takeover of Marathon Oil's marketing and refining facilities by the Hess Oil Company.

PUBLIC UTILITIES: NATURAL MONOPOLIES REQUIRING GOVERNMENT REGULATION

Certain industries are considered *natural monopolies* because competition in them would be especially wasteful. We have already described the confusion that would result if there were more than one phone company in the same area. Telephone companies are not the only natural monopolies. Electricity, gas, water, communications, and transportation also fall into this category.

Companies in the above industries are usually called *public utilities*. These are privately owned businesses that are directly involved with the public interest. For example, a privately owned bus company, operating on a prescribed route with a *franchise* (license) to be the only carrier on that route, would be classified as a public utility. Clearly, competition between several bus companies racing each other to the corner to pick up passengers would not be in the public interest. For similar reasons, airlines and trains may be classified as public utilities. Television and radio stations are given monopolies over specific wavelengths for broadcasting because they, too, are involved with the public interest, and competition could tie up limited transmission space.

Because they hold monopolies over vital public services, public utilities would be in a position to exploit the public were they not subject to regulation. Therefore, local governments have established agencies to supervise transportation services such as buses, subways, and taxicabs. State agencies supervise the telephone, power, water, and gas companies to whom they have issued franchises. The federal government regulates interstate power projects, airlines, railroads, radio, television, and other forms of communication and transportation. All the regulatory agencies, be they local, state, or federal, have similar aims. These aims are summarized in the following discussion.

Regulation of Public Utilities. Why is the business of generating and selling electricity considered a public utility?

WHAT THE REGULATORY AGENCIES DO

1. Establish Minimum Levels of Service. If you do not like the service you have been receiving from your electric, gas, or water company, you can complain about it, but you cannot take your business elsewhere. In the absence of competition, regulatory agencies supervise the activities of public utilities. Of major concern to these agencies are the quantity and quality of the services provided by the companies they regulate.

In exchange for their franchise, public utilities must agree to serve an entire area. If a particular service provided by a utility is no longer profitable, the company must first obtain permission from the regulatory agency before it may discontinue the service. For that reason families living in remote areas will receive electric and telephone service even though the utilities providing the services may be losing money on those installations. Of course, the utilities' losses will be made up by profits earned from services to nearby customers.

Regulatory agencies also establish guidelines about the *quality* of service. Among the areas of regulation are minimum standards of pressure and purity for drinking water, air conditioning and heating requirements for passenger trains, safety equipment requirements for home installations of utility services, and the like.

2. Set Industry Rates. The most important function of the regulatory agencies is to establish rates (prices) for the industry. Rate-setting is also the agencies' most difficult function. What, for example, is a fair price for a phone call? What fares should bus or taxicab companies be allowed? What are reasonable gas or electric rates? These are the kinds of questions that must be answered by the commissions that regulate the utilities.

Ideally, public utility rates should permit a company to provide the public with the kind of service it wants and still make a profit. Therefore, rates are generally calculated so as to give the company a "fair return" on its capital. Just as you might expect to receive 6 to 7 percent interest on your savings account, so too will a business seek to make a certain percentage of profit on the money it has invested. Regulatory agencies are thus faced with two fundamental questions: What constitutes a "fair" return? What is the real value of the investment?

Fair Return. Because a fraction of a percent rise or fall in the rate of return could mean a difference of several million dollars of profit each year, setting fair rates can be a difficult task. Regulatory commissions have found no simple way to establish a fair rate of return.

Value of the Investment. Let us assume that a fair return has been determined to be 13 percent of the total investment. The question will now arise as to the real value of the utility's investment. The cost of replacing equipment today may well be much higher than the original price of the equipment. The utility will argue that the rate of return should be based on the replacement value of the plant and equipment rather than on the original cost. Consider the case of a utility company that spent $100 million for equipment twenty-five years ago but would have to spend $500 million to replace it today. At a 13 percent rate of return, the company would make a profit of either $13 million on its original investment or $65 million at replacement cost.

Although commissions and courts have agreed that public utilities are entitled to a "fair return on a fair value" of their property, they have never set down hard-and-fast principles for determining either. Instead, each case is decided on its own merits.

PUBLIC ENTERPRISE: GOVERNMENT OWNERSHIP

Although public utilities are normally privately owned companies that are regulated by agencies of the government, in some instances it has been found necessary for the government to own and operate an enterprise. Cities own and operate transportation systems, hospitals, and docks. Some states operate light and power companies. On the federal level, the Tennessee Valley Authority (a coordinated regional power complex) and the Postal Service are notable examples of publicly owned businesses. While it is argued that government is not likely to take advantage of the public by engaging in unfair practices, Americans have traditionally been reluctant to expand government ownership for the following reasons:

1. Economic power may lead to excessive political power.
2. Because there is no profit motive, government enterprise tends to be inefficient and lacking in initiative.

The proponents of government enterprise have answered with the following arguments:

1. Because it has no profit motive, a government-owned business is less likely to take advantage of the public by engaging in unfair business practices.
2. The alternative to government enterprise is often a private monopoly, which is harder to control than a publicly owned business. Furthermore, a private monopoly can also be inefficient because of the absence of competition.

The Role of Consumers in Utility Regulation

As you have read, the power to regulate utilities is delegated by government to various public service commissions. In recent years, however, consumer groups have assumed an increasingly important role in making utilities more responsive to the needs of the general public. In the 1970s, Ralph Nader, one of the nation's leading consumer advocates, urged the formation of Residential Utilities Community Action Groups for two purposes:

1. To lobby for reasonable utility rates and
2. To oversee the activities of the regulatory agencies so that they represent the interests of consumers as well as those of the local utility.

As consumer activism increased in the 1960s and 1970s, its effect was felt by utilities around the country. In North Carolina, for example, consumers' demands resulted in the passage of laws lengthening the waiting period before certain kinds of rate increases could be put into effect. State constitutional amendments were proposed in Arkansas, Colorado, and Ohio to require that members of public service commissions be elected rather than appointed. Consumer groups in Michigan struggled to overturn Public Service Commission rulings that permit automatic rate increases.

Between 1975 and 1982, consumer opposition to the use of nuclear energy for generating electricity resulted in the cancellation of plans to construct some sixty-nine nuclear plants around the country. In addition,

COUNTERVAILING POWER

We have described how government has used its lawmaking power to limit the power of large corporations. Economist John Kenneth Galbraith has identified another force through which government and other large power blocs in the society limit the power of big business. He has called this force "countervailing power."

For example, when large producers of automobile tires seek to sell their products to large buyers such as Sears, Roebuck or Montgomery Ward, they do not enjoy the same degree of price-setting power as

many nuclear power plants that were nearing completion were prevented from "going on line" (beginning operations). By the mid-1980s, for example, it appeared that the $4 billion nuclear energy plant at Shoreham, New York might never be permitted to open. Similar opposition also prevented the opening of nuclear plants at Marble Hill, Indiana; Moscow, Ohio; Rockford, Illinois; and Seabrook, New Hampshire.

While consumer groups have not achieved everything that they set out to accomplish in the field of public utility regulation, they are more active than ever before and are having an impact on the industry. Largely because of their efforts, it now appears that public service commissions may have to allow consumers an increasing role in the regulation of utilities.

1. Who is Ralph Nader?
2. What have been the goals of consumer groups with respect to their local public utilities?
3. Let us suppose that your state legislature is considering a bill that would grant automatic rate increases to your local electric utility company. These rate increases would enable the utility to keep up with rising costs caused by inflation. Write a letter to your representative in the legislature expressing your reasons why you are in favor of or opposed to such a bill.
4. Why have consumer groups in many communities opposed the construction of plants that use nuclear energy to generate electricity?
5. Why is the privately owned public utilities industry subject to more government regulation than virtually any other industry?

they would if they were selling to smaller buyers. Big buyers offset the monopolistic power of big producers, in effect requiring them to offer their wares at reasonable prices.

Big labor unions are also among the forces that limit the power of big business to set wage rates, even where there are only a few employers of certain kinds of labor. Thus the giant automobile, steel, and rubber industries must all bargain with some of the nation's most powerful labor unions.

Countervailing power therefore describes the development of large power blocs of suppliers, customers, labor, and government that have tended to offset the monopolistic powers of big business. Though economists are not agreed as to how effective countervailing power has been, it must be considered one of the forces restricting monopoly power in the United States.

EXERCISES

Multiple Choice

1. A major flaw of the Sherman Antitrust Act was that it (a) was ineffective against labor unions (b) could not be used to break up a monopoly (c) gave too much power to a government agency (d) failed to give a clear definition of "restraint of trade."
2. The Clayton Act strengthened the federal government's power to regulate monopolies by (a) giving it authority to regulate advertising (b) identifying certain specific acts by business as being illegal (c) permitting sellers to set minimum, or "fair trade," prices for their merchandise (d) outlawing conglomerate mergers.
3. In its effort to expand, the Sweet Tooth Candy Store, Inc., acquired the stores of six of its competitors in various parts of town. In this way, Sweet Tooth was building a (a) horizontal (b) vertical (c) conglomerate (d) circular combination.
4. Business was so brisk for the Sweet Tooth Candy Stores that the management bought a nearby factory, thereby enabling the firm to make its own candy. This was a (a) horizontal (b) vertical (c) conglomerate (d) circular combination.
5. A few months ago, the Sweet Tooth Candy Company, Inc., was acquired by one of the nation's largest producers of wire and sheet metal. This was a (a) horizontal (b) vertical (c) conglomerate (d) circular combination.
6. Pools and cartels (a) are formed when two or more firms sell their stocks to another firm (b) are a form of merger (c) eliminate competition between member firms by dividing the market (d) hold controlling shares of stock in competing firms.
7. Holding companies (a) are formed when one company is absorbed by another (b) hold controlling shares of stock of other companies (c) are companies that have representatives on the boards of directors of competing firms (d) supervise public utility companies in behalf of local governments.
8. Which of the following is a cartel? (a) OPEC (b) the Japanese automobile industry (c) American Telephone and Telegraph, Inc. (d) the Dallas Cowboys football team.
9. The federal government has attempted to eliminate monopolies chiefly in order to (a) keep the private sector of the economy

from getting too big (b) decrease the size of public utilities (c) ensure competition (d) increase the number of small businesses.

10. Which has been an important business trend in the United States in recent years? (a) the decline of railroad pools (b) the rise of cartels (c) a reduction in the concentration of power of large corporations (d) the diversification of interests and holdings by large corporations.

11. Which of the following laws first declared any "contract, combination . . . or conspiracy in restraint of trade" to be illegal? (a) Interstate Commerce Act (b) Sherman Antitrust Act (c) Clayton Antitrust Act (d) Federal Trade Commission Act.

12. Government agencies regulate each of the following aspects of an electric utility's business *except* (a) the selection of its personnel (b) the rates it charges its customers (c) the territory served by the utility (d) the quality of the utility's service.

13. Telephone rates are established (a) solely by the officers of the telephone company (b) solely by the stockholders of the telephone company (c) in accordance with guidelines established by governmental agencies (d) by the laws of supply and demand.

14. In establishing the rates that public utilities may charge, government agencies will permit them to charge (a) whatever will give the utilities the largest profit (b) enough to permit the utilities to pay 10 percent dividends to their stockholders (c) enough to earn a fair return (d) just enough to break even.

Essay Questions

1. Read the selection and answer the questions that follow.

Antitrust Today: What Constitutes "Restraint of Trade"?

Any "combination or conspiracy in restraint of trade," in the words of the Sherman Antitrust Act, is against the law. But what constitutes a combination, a conspiracy, or restraint of trade? For years the government and the courts have wrestled with this question, and their answers have varied with the times. Present-day policy is illustrated in two recently settled cases. In the first case the Justice Department decided that the actions of the accused were not a violation of the law and dropped the case. In the second case, the government prosecuted to the full extent of the law.

In the first case, the government decided in 1982 to drop its thirteen-year-old suit against the International Business Machines Corporation. In 1969 the Justice Department had charged IBM with monopolizing the computer industry. The suit asked the courts to break up IBM into smaller companies so as to separate its manufacturing, sales, and software operations from the control of a central authority. Over the years, however, important developments in the computer industry changed the government's attitude toward IBM.

IBM no longer dominated the computer industry, as it once had. Between 1969 and 1982, new generations of minicomputers and personal or microcomputers were developed by new companies. Although IBM was a major competitor, the competition was fierce. It was anybody's guess which company would win the sales race. In addition, foreign competition, particularly from Japan, was expected to further erode IBM's position in the computer industry. These changes in the market prompted the Justice Department to drop its case, even though IBM continued to be the largest firm in the industry.

In the 1970s, the Justice Department undertook a major crackdown on electrical contractors in the construction industry. When contracts are awarded on government and public utility projects, sealed bids are normally solicited, and the firm presenting the lowest offer is hired for the job. Justice Department investigators discovered that unscrupulous electrical contractors had secretly arranged to divide up the work among themselves. Designated "losers" deliberately submitted higher bids than those picked in advance to be winners.

By 1982 the prosecution had led to the imposition of some $37 million in fines against the contracting firms and prison terms for more than a hundred of their executives.

In comparing the case involving the electrical contractors with the IBM case, we see that the principal concern of the government was the freedom of the marketplace. The scheme by the contractors to eliminate real bidding served to create a monopoly. In the IBM case, however, competition in the computer industry was not threatened, and so the case was dropped.

(a) What changes in the marketplace caused the government to drop its antitrust suit against IBM? (b) Do you think the electrical contractors deserved the punishment that they received? Explain your answer. (c) Critics have charged that antitrust laws often place American firms at a competitive disadvantage with foreign companies. How might this argument have been applied if the government had not dropped its suit against IBM?

2. Over the years a number of strategies were developed by big business to combine and coordinate the activities of what had formerly been independent firms. These activities included forming *pools, trusts, holding companies,* and *mergers.* Critics of these efforts say that their true purpose was to reduce competition so as to enable powerful firms to control prices and increase profits. Defenders, however, argue that business combinations enable firms to increase their *economies of scale,* which are likely to be passed along to consumers in the form of lower prices. (a) Explain how pools, trusts, holding companies, and mergers promote business combinations. (b) How might it be argued that business combinations reduce production costs and thus raise the standard of living? In your answer, refer to the *economies of scale.* (c) How might it be argued that business combinations are created for the purpose of reducing competition and increasing profits?

3. Although the United States has traditionally been committed to the principle of free enterprise and the market system, it has adopted a different philosophy in the case of the public utilities.

TABLE 8.1   Principal United States Antitrust Laws

Name of Law	Date Enacted	Basic Provisions
Sherman Antitrust Act		
Clayton Antitrust Act		
Federal Trade Commission Act		
Celler-Kefauver Antimerger Act		

These firms are told what they may charge their customers, where they may operate, and the kind of service they must maintain. (*a*) Why are public utilities subject to special regulations? (*b*) Why may regulatory agencies not be willing to grant rate increases requested by public utilities? (*c*) Under what circumstances would you say that the power company serving your community would be entitled to a 10 percent increase in its electricity rates?

4. Congress has enacted a number of laws to limit the growth of monopoly power and outlaw certain undesirable business practices. On a separate sheet of paper, complete Table 8.1 of antitrust laws.

5. A government official recently described the Robinson-Patman Act as "a dreadful piece of legislation, very anticompetitive in its effects." (*a*) What reason did the speaker have for describing Robinson-Patman as "anticompetitive"? (*b*) Would you agree or disagree that Robinson-Patman is "a dreadful piece of legislation"? Explain your answer.

6. Since certain giant firms can set the price structure for entire industries, some critics have called for government regulation of prices in those industries. Would you favor such regulation? Defend your answer.

In the morning rush hour, more American workers commute to office and service jobs than to manufacturing jobs.

UNIT IV

The Role of Labor

CHAPTER 9

The Labor Force in Our Economy

Most of us will spend a part of our lives in the labor force. The United States government defines the labor force as all the people sixteen years of age and older who are working for money or looking for paid work.

Since 1950, significant changes have taken place in the labor force. These changes are summarized in Figures 9.1 to 9.3 on pages 166 and 167. Take a few moments to look them over before you read on.

OVERVIEW OF THE LABOR FORCE

Size of the Labor Force. Figure 9.1 shows that the labor force has been growing since 1950. One reason for this growth is that the nation's population increased from 152 million in 1950 to 232 million in 1982, so there were simply more people looking for jobs. But another reason for the growth of the labor force is that the United States economy itself grew, and as a result more jobs were created. Finally—and this was unique in the history of American labor—the number of women in the labor force increased by more than 50 percent, as Figure 9.2 shows.

Occupations in the Labor Force. As the labor force has grown, the kinds of jobs that people perform have changed, as Figure 9.3 shows. For purposes of comparison our data are grouped under the headings *white collar, blue collar, service,* and *farm* occupations. White-collar occupations are those in the professional, technical, clerical, sales, and managerial categories. Blue-collar work, by government definition, includes craft, operative, and labor jobs. Service occupations

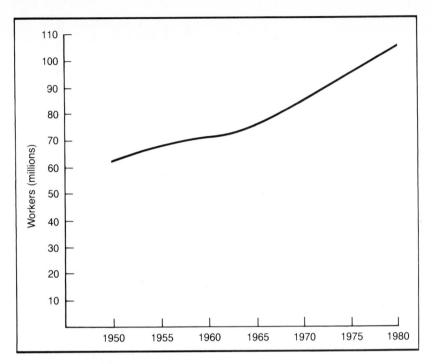

FIGURE 9.1 Growth of the Labor Force, 1950–1980

include such categories as firefighters, building service workers, cosmetologists, and restaurant workers. Finally, farmers, farm operators, and farm laborers are all included under the umbrella of farm occupations.

FIGURE 9.2 Women in the Labor Force, 1900–1980

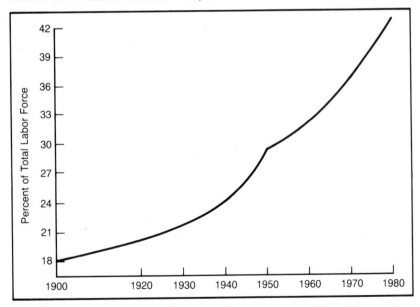

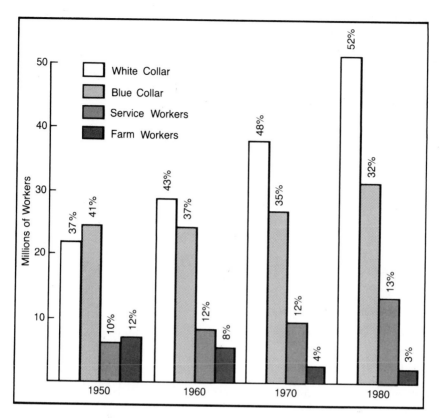

FIGURE 9.3 Occupations of Employed Workers, 1950–1980

Labor Force Trends. Growth rates have differed considerably among the occupational groups in the labor force. White-collar workers, once only a small proportion of the total labor force, today represent about half the total of all workers. The number of service workers has also risen rapidly. The blue-collar work force has grown, but slowly, and the number of farm workers has actually declined.

The reasons for these changes in the labor force are to be found in the *technological revolution*—a term used to describe the rapid changes in the ways of producing goods and services. The technological revolution has replaced many workers with machines, but it has also created many new jobs operating and servicing the machines. White-collar jobs have become more important and blue-collar jobs relatively less important. The increasing demand for protective services and cleaning and maintenance services, and the more frequent use of restaurants, beauty salons, and leisure services, have made the service workers category the fastest growing section of the labor force. Because of the spectacular growth of farm productivity, fewer farmers are able to feed more people than ever before; hence, fewer and fewer farm workers have been needed over the years.

WORK AND INCOME

How Are Wages Determined? Wages vary widely from one occupation to another. These variations are illustrated in Table 9.1, which lists the median weekly earnings of workers in the principal job categories in 1981. (A median figure indicates that half the workers in each category earn the amount shown or more, and half earn the amount shown or less.) By doing some simple arithmetic, you can see that nonfarm laborers earned an average of $12,376 that year ($238 × 52 = $12,376), while managers and administrators earned over $21,000.

TABLE 9.1 Median Weekly Earnings of Full-Time Workers, 1981

Professional and technical workers	$377
Managers and administrators, except farm	407
Sales workers	306
Clerical workers	233
Craft and kindred workers	352
Operatives, except transport	242
Transport equipment operatives	303
Nonfarm laborers	238
Service workers	192
Farm workers	179

Distribution of Income. Why does a star performer like Diana Ross receive more income for one hour of work than a skilled machinist earns in six months?

Why do some jobs pay more than others? An economist would answer this question by discussing first the "market forces" of supply and demand and then certain "nonmarket forces."

The Laws of Supply and Demand Affect Wages. The nation's best football and basketball players earn a handsome living. But this is not the case with its outstanding water polo and volleyball stars, who would have a difficult time earning a living at their sports. Why is it that top athletes in some sports can command enormous salaries, while others, equally talented, cannot? The reasons lie in the very limited number of truly outstanding athletes *and* the willingness of the public to pay to see them perform. In other words: The supply of and the demand for athletes as workers create a market situation that pays high wages.

What is true for athletes applies to other jobs and professions as well. We have noted that managers and administrators earned more than laborers. We can use our knowledge of supply and demand (as described in Chapter 2) to explain this difference in wages. The supply of laborers as compared to the demand for them is far greater than the supply of and demand for managers, administrators, and professional and technical workers. It also follows that if millions of Americans clamored to see professional water polo at its best, salaries in that sport would rise to the point where talented athletes would seek to make their living at it.

But supply and demand as applied to people rather than goods and services are subject to certain factors that require further explanation.

The Labor Force in Our Economy   **169**

FACTORS AFFECTING THE DEMAND FOR LABOR

Demand, you will recall, refers to the number of units that buyers will take at a particular price. When we apply the concept to labor, we are speaking of the number of workers that firms will hire at a particular wage.

The number of workers an employer is willing to hire at a particular wage depends on (1) the demand for the employer's merchandise or service, and (2) the productivity of each additional worker.

1. Demand for Goods and Services. If consumers stop buying a particular item, the demand for workers to produce that item will probably decline. For example, if you are a saddle-maker, the chances are that far fewer jobs are available to you than would have been a century ago. Because the demand for the goods and services being produced influences the number of workers employed, the demand for labor is called a *derived demand.*

2. Productivity. The second factor affecting the demand for labor is its productivity. Employers can afford to pay a worker no more than the worker adds to the firm's income. For example, if the addition of one worker will add $60 in income per day, the employer can afford to pay the worker any wage up to $60 daily. A wage above that figure will result in a loss to the firm.

If, because of improved technology, the worker in the example above were able to produce $100 worth of additional income daily, the firm could afford to pay a wage up to $100 per day.

Productivity sets only the upper limits to the amount of wages that workers are likely to earn. If in one week a company with ten workers produces goods worth $4,000 more than the cost of raw materials, rent, and capital, the employer will not be able to pay these ten employees more than an average of $400 each. The employer would certainly be willing to pay them less than $400 because this would add to profits.

Economists sometimes use the term *marginal productivity* in describing the value of the worker's output. In this case they are referring to the *marginal,* or last, worker hired. In theory, workers will be added until the point is reached where the extra income added by the last worker hired is equal to the worker's wage. Economists express this by saying that workers will be hired until *marginal revenue is equal to marginal costs*—that is, until the value of the additional production is equal to the cost of the last worker hired. For this reason, the demand for labor varies inversely with wages. In other words, if wages were reduced while everything else remained the same, employers could afford to hire more workers.

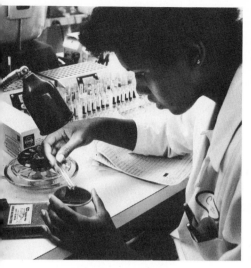

Supply of Labor. What factors affect the supply of workers in the occupations shown here?

FACTORS AFFECTING THE SUPPLY OF LABOR

By the supply of labor we mean the number of workers available to perform a particular job at a specified wage. As is the case with goods, the supply curve for labor slopes upward; that is, the number of workers will increase as wages rise and decrease as wages fall. This is logical because as wages in one field increase, workers in other fields will be attracted to it. If, for example, nurses in private hospitals were paid more than those in public hospitals, nurses would leave public service for the higher paying private jobs. Similarly, if wages in an industry fall, workers will move to higher paying jobs in other industries.

Wages alone cannot determine the total supply of labor in a particular field. Supply is subject to a number of other factors, including the following:

1. Attractiveness of the Job. Some jobs carry more prestige or are more appealing than other jobs paying similar salaries. Many persons prefer office work to more strenuous jobs though office work may pay no more, or even less. Also, writers and artists tend to feel so strongly about their work that they often stay in their field even though they might earn more money elsewhere.

2. Skill Required. Only a limited number of people have the skill or talent required for certain jobs. No matter how well the job pays, not everyone can become a singing star or professional ballplayer.

The Labor Force in Our Economy   **171**

3. *Required Training.* Some occupations have much longer training periods than others. Young people who want to be physicians may have to spend an additional eight to ten years in school after they graduate from high school. Other professions and technical fields also require extensive training beyond high school. Because many people cannot afford the time or money necessary, the greater the amount of training required for a particular job, the smaller the supply of workers available.

4. *Mobility.* Employers in certain parts of the country may find it difficult to hire enough workers. Merely raising wages slightly may not help attract workers to the region because workers usually like to stay where they are. In the early 1980s, for example, there were shortages of workers in certain computer-related jobs on the West Coast. During the same period, however, some workers in the midwestern and northeastern United States who possessed the needed skills were reported as unemployed. People are naturally reluctant to leave their friends and families or move their children from one school to another. The willingness of workers to move "to where the jobs are" is described as their *mobility.* The lack of mobility accounts in part for the pockets of poverty in some regions.

NONMARKET FORCES AND THE DETERMINATION OF WAGES

While supply and demand, the so-called market forces, are major factors in determining wage levels, they are not the only ones. In some instances other factors, or nonmarket forces, also have an impact. These include the following:

1. *Labor Unions.* When labor union negotiators and company management sit down to negotiate wages, the laws of supply and demand often fade into the background. Instead of supply and demand, the relative strengths of labor and management are likely to dominate the proceedings. If, for example, union members are in a position to weather a long strike, they may be able to extract a substantial wage increase from the employer. If, however, the workers cannot afford the loss of income that a work stoppage would impose, or if the employers are well organized throughout the industry, the unions will be under pressure to keep their salary demands down.

Although labor-management negotiations are largely guided by nonmarket forces, both labor and management are still subject to the laws of supply and demand. Business must show a profit in order to survive. This places a limit on the amount that can be paid out in wages. Similarly, there is a bottom-line salary below which qualified workers will simply quit or refuse to apply for jobs. The role of labor unions is discussed at length in Chapter 10.

2. Government Legislation. Government laws can affect wage levels. Regardless of the conditions of supply and demand, employers must pay the minimum wage of $3.35 an hour established by federal law. Similarly, many workers must be paid higher rates for overtime whenever they work more than the maximum number of hours per week established by the law. Other laws limit the supply of labor by banning the employment of children in many industries and requiring that children attend school until they reach a certain age.

Civil rights laws and other government legislation require that workers receive equal pay for equal work. The purpose of these laws is to prevent discrimination on the basis of race, religion, nationality, or sex. The extent to which such laws are enforced will, therefore, affect the job market and wages.

3. Discrimination. Certain groups in this country earn more than others. We can show, for example, that blacks and Hispanics earn less than whites, and that women earn less than men (see Figure

FIGURE 9.4 Median Weekly Earnings of Full-Time Workers, 1982

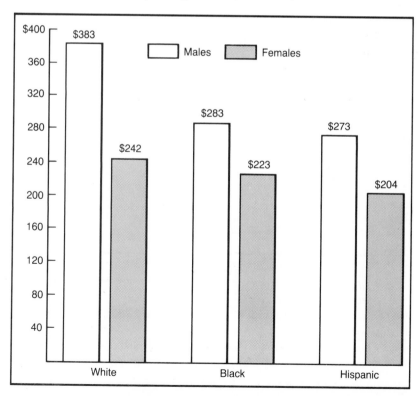

TABLE 9.2 Median Income of Families, by Selected States, 1979

Rank	State	Median Income
1	Alaska	$31,037
2	Nevada	25,457
3	Colorado	25,228
. . .	. . .	. . .
21	Iowa	22,567
22	Ohio	22,528
23	New Hampshire	22,335
. . .	. . .	. . .
48	Arkansas	18,493
49	Maine	18,074
50	Mississippi	17,672

9.4). Although there are a number of reasons for these differences, *discrimination* is a major cause of wage differences. Discrimination in employment—the favoring of one group over another in hiring, salary, or promotion, for reasons that have nothing to do with ability to learn and perform job skills—is a violation of both federal and state laws.

4. *Geography.* Where people live and work affects their earnings because wages differ from one part of the nation to another. This is illustrated in Table 9.2, which ranks the top, middle, and bottom three states according to median family income.

TABLE 9.3 Median Personal Income, by Sex and Educational Attainment, 1970–1980

Highest Level of Education Completed	Males			Females		
	1970	1975	1980	1970	1975	1980
Elementary school	$ 5,400	$ 6,500	$ 8,900	$ 1,800	$ 2,600	$ 4,200
High school	8,800	10,200	14,600	3,400	4,200	6,100
4 yrs. college	12,100	14,400	22,200	5,400	7,000	11,700
5 + yrs. college	13,400	17,500	26,900	7,900	10,100	15,100

TABLE 9.4 Percent of Income Received by Each Fifth and the Top 5 Percent of Families, 1950–1981

Income Rank	1950	1960	1970	1981
Lowest fifth	4.5	4.9	5.5	5.0
Second fifth	12.0	12.0	12.0	11.3
Middle fifth	17.4	17.6	17.4	17.4
Fourth fifth	23.5	23.5	23.5	24.4
Highest fifth	42.6	42.0	41.6	41.9
Top 5 percent	17.0	16.8	14.4	15.4

5. *Education.* People who have completed many years of school earn more, on the average, than those who have completed fewer years. How much more the better educated earn is illustrated in Table 9.3. These income figures are in keeping with the Law of Supply, since those with the most schooling are fewest in number.

THE DISTRIBUTION OF INCOME

The distribution of income in the United States—and in every other country, for that matter—is unequal. There are always some people who will earn more than others. This inequality is illustrated in the discussion that follows.

A commonly used measure of income distribution ranks household earnings from the lowest to the highest incomes. The total number of families is divided into equal fifths, and the total income earned by each group is tallied. Statisticians then calculate what *percentage* of the total income of all five groups is represented by each group total. These percentages and the percentage of total income received by the top 5 percent of households are illustrated in Table 9.4.

The Lorenz Curve. Economists and statisticians often illustrate the distribution of income with the *Lorenz curve* (Figure 9.5 on page 176). This curve shows how much of total earned income goes to each portion of the nation's population. In Figure 9.5, the vertical and horizontal dimensions are scaled in units of 20 percent up to a total of 100 percent. The horizontal axis represents individuals or families in a given year, while the vertical axis represents the share of total income that the individuals or families received.

In Figure 9.5, a diagonal line at a 45° angle to the horizontal axis represents perfectly equal income distribution. At any point along

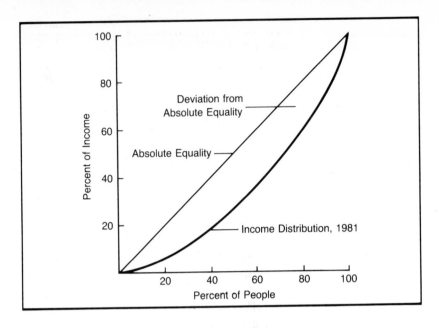

FIGURE 9.5   Lorenz Curve

this 45° line, the percent of the population is exactly equal to the percent of the total income earned. Thus 10 percent of the population is shown as earning 10 percent of the income, 30 percent of the population as earning 30 percent of the income, and so on. Plotted against this theoretical line is the Lorenz curve showing the *actual* distribution of income. The distance between the theoretical and actual illustrates the deviation from absolute equality, or the degree of inequality, in income distribution that year. Figure 9.5 portrays the theoretical and actual income data in a Lorenz curve.

POVERTY IN AMERICA

For one group of people, the question of income distribution is not simply an academic one. These are America's poor, who are represented at the bottom end of the Lorenz curve described above. In 1981 there were, according to the United States Bureau of the Census, some 32 million poor people living in this country. That amounted to some 11 percent of the nation's families.

The poor, according to government definition, are people whose cash incomes fall below certain set minimums. This minimum income, or poverty level, is adjusted from year to year to account for changes in prices. (See Figure 9.6.) In 1981 the poverty level ranged from $4,620 per year for a person living alone, to $9,287 for a family of four, to $18,572 for a family of nine or more persons.

The Role of Labor

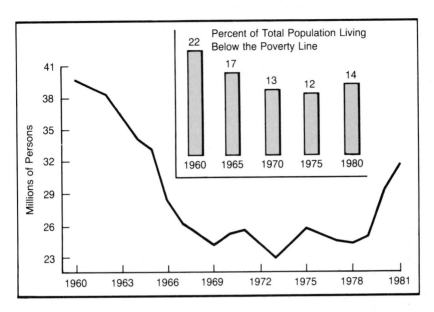

FIGURE 9.6 People Living Below the Poverty Line, 1960–1981

Who Are the Poor? As indicated by Table 9.5, certain groups suffer a much higher *incidence* (rate of occurrence) of poverty than the national average. These groups are:

Members of Minority Groups. In a year when 11 percent of the nation's families were classified as poor, the poverty rates for blacks and Hispanics were 31 percent and 24 percent, respectively.

TABLE 9.5 Poverty Status, by Households, 1981

	Number of Households Below Poverty Level	Poverty Rate (Percent of Group Shown)
All households	6,851,000	11.2
White	4,670,000	8.8
Black	1,972,000	30.8
Hispanic	792,000	24.0
Head of household:		
15 to 24 years old (black, Hispanic)	419,000	55.3
65 years and older (black, Hispanic)	291,000	24.2
Female, no husband present	3,300,000	34.6

THOMAS ROBERT MALTHUS
An Essay on the Principle of Population (1798)

Adam Smith and other writers of the eighteenth century saw a world in which natural forces were working everywhere to benefit humanity. Indeed, the underlying justification for *laissez-faire* (the policy in which government kept its hands off business activities) was that it would allow people to do, in Smith's words, "that . . . which is advantageous to the society." In 1798, however, a work titled *An Essay on the Principle of Population* was published. Written by Thomas Robert Malthus, an English minister, its views served to mark economics as the "dismal science."

Malthus' central thesis was that the population always increases more rapidly than the food supply. With not enough food to go around, large sections of the population are doomed to go hungry or starve. The reason for this dilemma, Malthus explained, is that the population increases in a *geometric progression*. For example, a married couple (two people) have two children and increase to four people; four would increase to eight; and eight to 16, and so on in geometric progression. The food supply, on the other hand, is limited by the amount of available land and the quantity of seed, fertilizer, and labor applied to it. Although the total food supply could be increased in time, it would do so in an *arithmetic progression,* as for example: two, four, six, eight, ten. Figure 9.7 illustrates the *Malthusian Theory.*

With population increasing at a faster rate than the food supply, there comes a point when the number of people is greater than the amount of food available to feed them. What happens once the population outstrips the food supply? Malthus foresaw a "season of distress" when the shortage of food will push prices to such a high level that many people go hungry or starve. In the wake of the famine, disease, and war that would surely follow, Malthus predicted that fewer people would marry, and as a consequence, the birthrate would decline. Meanwhile, the abundant supply of cheap labor combined with high food prices would encourage farmers to increase their output. In time, therefore, the supply of food would be equal to the needs of the population, and marriages and births would return to normal. And then what? Population growth would once again surpass the food supply, and the dreary cycle would be repeated.

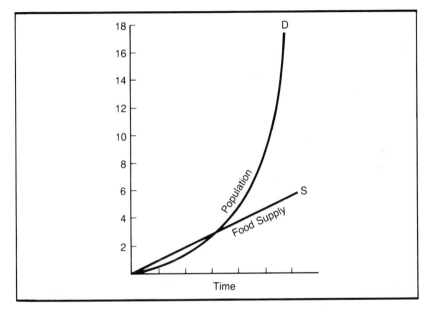

FIGURE 9.7 Food Supply and Population Growth According to Malthus

Was Malthus correct? Is Planet Earth doomed to a perpetual state of overpopulation? Are famine, disease, and death the unavoidable consequences of the difference between the world's limited resources and humanity's unlimited capacity to reproduce?

History at first seemed to refute Malthus' predictions. Using the biological and technological advances of the Industrial Revolution, farmers in the United States and Europe were able to provide more than enough food for the people of the Western world. Meanwhile, changing social attitudes among the industrialized nations slowed population growth. These two developments, which Malthus did not foresee, enabled European and North American nations to escape his predictions.

But the less developed countries (LDCs) have not been so fortunate. A recent study predicted that the world's population will jump by 55 percent to 6.35 billion people by the end of this century, *and* 90 percent of that growth will take place in the poorest nations. On an even gloomier note, the study predicted that the number of malnourished people in the LDCs could reach 1.3 *billion* in the year 2000.

Over 185 years ago, Malthus wrote: "The power of population is infinitely greater than the power in the earth to produce subsistence for man." Thirty years ago most economists thought Malthus was wrong. Today they are not so sure. What is your opinion?

Family Households Headed by Women in Which There Is No Husband Present. Families in which the head of the household is a woman and there is no husband present show a significantly higher incidence of poverty. Some 35 percent of the families in those circumstances were poor.

Households Headed by the Young or the Elderly. One in every two black and Hispanic households headed by persons 15 to 24 years old was poor. Households headed by persons 65 years of age or older were somewhat better off. However, the poverty rate of the elderly— 24 percent—was still twice the national average.

PROGRAMS TO FIGHT POVERTY

Government programs to fight poverty fall into one of two categories. The first category, the income maintenance group, seeks to transfer enough income to the poor to raise them above the poverty line. The second category, sometimes described as labor-market strategies, fights poverty by reducing its causes.

The Income Maintenance Approach. Some income programs provide money, while others offer income *in kind* (in the form of goods and services). Income maintenance may be in the form of *social insurance* or *public assistance*.

Social Insurance. Social security and unemployment compensation are the principal social insurance programs. Like private insurance plans, these programs provide money benefits paid out of premiums. Social security premiums are shared by both the employer and the employee. Premiums for unemployment insurance are paid by the employer alone. See Chapter 12 for a full discussion of the social security program.

Public Assistance: The Welfare Programs. Social insurance programs protect those who have contributed to them or who have earned coverage during their working years. But what about the millions of needy people who for one reason or another are not covered by social insurance? Help for most of these people is available in the form of public assistance or, as it is more commonly known, welfare. The most important welfare programs are Supplemental Security Income, Aid to Families With Dependent Children, Food Stamps, and Medicaid.

Supplemental Security Income (SSI). SSI assures a minimum monthly income to needy people who are 65 or older, blind, or

"Every time I think we've climbed above the poverty line, they raise it."
Marvin Kuhn in *The East Hampton Star*

disabled and who are not covered by the social security program. Eligibility for SSI is based on one's income and assets.

Aid to Families With Dependent Children (AFDC). AFDC is the largest and costliest of the welfare programs whose benefits are paid in cash. The federal government sets the general standards of eligibility for AFDC and contributes more than half of the program's funds. The administration of the program itself, however, is in the hands of the states. Their contributions, like their benefits, vary from state to state. In 1979 AFDC payments for a family of four ranged from $1,440 per year in Mississippi to $6,552 in Hawaii.

Food Stamps Program. Food stamp coupons are issued to needy persons who can exchange them for food at any market. Over 20 million Americans, at least half of them under eighteen years old, received food stamps in 1982. The total cost of the food stamps program that year was $11 billion.

Medicaid. All persons in the SSI and AFDC programs, as well as certain other needy persons, are eligible for health care under the Medicaid program. Since each state designs its own program, the requirements for coverage and the benefits vary. In general, Medicaid pays for both medical and hospital care as well as for a variety of health-related services. Some states also provide dental care, eyeglasses, and physical rehabilitation for Medicaid recipients. Medicaid costs are shared by the federal government, the states, and localities.

Labor-Market Strategies. The programs described above attack the symptoms of poverty by transferring additional income to the poor. Most of the money spent by government to fight poverty has gone into these transfer programs. Other strategies have sought to reduce the causes of poverty. These strategies are described below.

Government Investment in Human Capital. "Human capital" is the economists' term to describe the physical and mental skills of the labor force. One of the chief problems faced by the poor is that they frequently have fewer marketable skills and less education than the rest of the population. For this reason federal, state, and local governments have sponsored programs to improve the job skills and education of the labor force.

One such program is the *Job Corps.* The Job Corps functions out of residential training centers. There, some of the most educationally and economically disadvantaged youth are given an opportunity to complete their education and learn a trade. The Work Incentive program (WIN) has provided persons receiving AFDC assistance with training, job counseling, and day-care services for their children.

A number of government-sponsored programs have joined with private enterprise in providing training and on-the-job experience for disadvantaged workers. A proposal before Congress in the early 1980s called for a program to create urban "enterprise zones." By reducing taxes and eliminating certain government regulations on business activities, this program would attract private enterprise into low-income areas and thus create jobs for the areas' residents.

Still another ingredient in human capital is the physical health of the labor force. Since disability and illness reduce an individual's ability to earn a living, the government's efforts to improve the nation's health and safety also help to reduce poverty and unemployment. Medicare, Medicaid, and the public health services represent the government's commitment to these goals. And while permanent disabilities cannot be undone, many can be prevented. Congress created the Occupational Safety and Health Administration (OSHA) in an effort to prevent job-related injuries and illnesses.

Efforts to Reduce Discrimination. We have mentioned that poverty is greatest among certain minority groups and women. Discrimination is a major cause of this poverty.

Affirmative Action. In the past, what has prevented women from being hired as construction workers? How do women benefit from affirmative action?

Discrimination against minorities and women has been declared against the law. Title VII of the Civil Rights Act of 1964 prohibits discrimination for reasons of race, color, religion, national origin, or sex where the effect of such discrimination is to affect access to jobs. The same act created the Equal Employment Opportunity Commission to enforce its provisions.

Another approach that has been used to reduce discrimination is known as *affirmative action.* The affirmative action plan sets a quota, or minimum number, of women and minority persons who must be hired as jobs are filled. The federal government has required some of its contractors to maintain affirmative action programs. The effect of affirmative action is to allow some minority members and women to obtain jobs that would otherwise have been given to white males. Critics of affirmative action have termed it "reverse discrimination" on the grounds that solely because of their race or sex, less qualified persons may displace more qualified ones. Those favoring affirmative action say that it serves to correct centuries-old racist and sexist practices.

Efforts to Promote Economic Stability. Poverty is an even more serious problem during periods of national economic troubles than it is when business is expanding and jobs are plentiful. From 1978 to 1982 economic growth in the United States nearly stopped. Record numbers of business firms closed down, and unemployment reached the highest levels since the Great Depression of the 1930s. This period of economic difficulty also resulted in a 7 million increase in the number of people living in poverty.

The Employment Act of 1946 committed the federal government to an active role in promoting economic stability, growth, and *full employment.* Once a year the Council of Economic Advisers sends to the President a report giving detailed recommendations on how best to achieve the act's goals. Generally, these recommendations involve government spending and taxation policies, which are discussed in Chapter 18.

Criticisms of Present Welfare Programs. About eight cents out of every dollar spent by government goes for welfare benefits. Critics of the welfare system claim that this amount is too high. Money is wasted on programs whose services overlap, and too many people who are not truly needy are receiving government funds.

Many observers are concerned about the different ways in which welfare is distributed to people with similar needs. These differences were highlighted in a recent study by the President's Council of Economic Advisers. The study revealed that a single-parent family of four with no earnings could obtain benefits in New York City that were more than twice as large as the benefits available to the same family in Mississippi. Certain families and individuals received fewer benefits than others. So, for example, childless couples and single people who were not aged or disabled were ineligible for any benefits other than food stamps, regardless of how little they earned.

The current welfare system, it is claimed, discourages people from finding jobs. Welfare does not provide the poor with the training they need to qualify for good jobs. In some states a week's work at the minimum wage amounts to less than welfare benefits, with the result that people working at the minimum can "get a raise" by going on welfare. Moreover, earnings serve to reduce the amount of welfare benefits received *and* are subject to social security and withholding taxes.

Critics charge that the welfare system is inefficient, complex, and expensive to run. The result is, according to the Council of Economic Advisers, that the needy poor "become frustrated, and their rates of [labor force] participation decline."

Can the Problem of Poverty Be Solved? In 1964 President Lyndon Johnson told the nation that it was the "policy of the United States to eliminate the paradox of poverty in the midst of plenty." It would now appear that that policy was a failure. Despite the expenditure of hundreds of billions of dollars over the past two decades to rid the nation of poverty, more than 32 million Americans are poor.

Some have argued that the very nature of democratic government works against the poor. Normally, in a democracy those with similar interests and needs come together to bring their problems to the attention of government. Concerning poverty, however, those with most to gain—the poor—are least able to organize politically.

We may be certain that efforts will continue to be made to help the poor. Whatever these efforts are they will cause controversy, and the elimination of poverty will for the foreseeable future remain a dream unfulfilled.

EXERCISES

Multiple Choice

1. Which of the following best summarizes the changes that have been taking place in the labor force? (*a*) The proportion of blue-collar workers has been increasing while that of white-collar and female workers has been decreasing. (*b*) The proportion of blue-collar and white-collar workers has been increasing while that of female workers has been shrinking. (*c*) The proportion of blue-collar, white-collar, and female workers has declined in recent years. (*d*) The proportion of white-collar and female workers has been increasing while that of blue-collar workers has decreased.
2. The demand for workers in an industry tends to rise as (*a*) the supply increases (*b*) the supply decreases (*c*) the demand for the goods produced increases (*d*) productivity falls.
3. According to economic theory, it will pay employers to hire additional workers (*a*) until the point of diminishing returns is reached (*b*) until the value of the additional production is equal to the cost of hiring the last worker (*c*) so long as marginal costs are greater than marginal revenues (*d*) until production exceeds demand.
4. Workers who have more education than others generally earn more money chiefly because (*a*) educated workers are more likely to belong to unions (*b*) the supply of educated people is limited

(c) people with more education have a higher standard of living (d) they deserve higher wages.

5. Which of the following is likely to affect the level of one's earnings? (a) one's education (b) one's sex (c) one's residence (d) all of the above.

6. The Lorenz curve is used to demonstrate (a) the tradeoff between unemployment and the inflation rate (b) the relation between education and income (c) the inequality in income distribution (d) the number of households living below the poverty level.

7. According to the government's definition of poverty, Family A was classified as poor while Family B was not. But families A and B had identical earned income last year. Which of the following might explain this discrepancy? (a) Family A spent its money unwisely. (b) The cost of living affected Family A more than it did Family B. (c) Family A had less education than Family B. (d) Family A had more members than Family B.

8. Which of the following household groups is *least likely* to be poor? (a) households headed by females in which there is no husband present (b) households headed by white males (c) black and Hispanic households (d) households headed by a person with less than a high school education.

9. Which program provides income *in kind* rather than in actual money income? (a) Aid to Families With Dependent Children (AFDC) (b) Supplemental Security Income (SSI) (c) Food Stamps (d) Unemployment Insurance.

10. Which of the following people is classified as a white-collar worker? (a) a machinist in a factory (b) a teller in a bank (c) a farmer in Iowa (d) a bus driver.

11. Which of the following people is classified as a blue-collar worker? (a) a machinist in a factory (b) a teller in a bank (c) a farmer in Iowa (d) a waitress in a restaurant.

12. Which job category has lost the largest percentage of workers over the past thirty years? (a) blue collar (b) white collar (c) service (d) farm.

13. According to the Lorenz curve (Figure 9.8) (a) income is more equally distributed in Country A than in Country B (b) Country A is wealthier than Country B (c) income is more equally distributed in Country B than in Country A (d) Country B is wealthier than Country A.

Essay Questions

1. Table 9.6 summarizes some of the principal changes that have taken place in the composition of the labor force since 1950. (a) What changes have taken place in the total number of persons employed in the United States? How would you account for these changes? (b) Among the major categories (white-collar, blue-

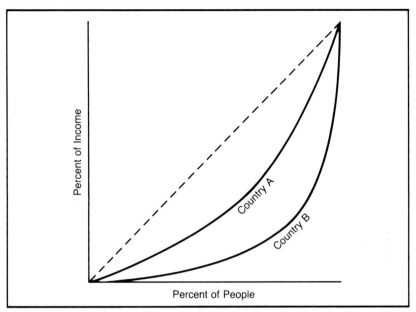

FIGURE 9.8 Lorenz Curve

collar, service, and farm workers), which group showed the greatest percentage increase? How would you account for this increase? (c) Which major category showed the greatest percentage decrease? How would you account for this decrease?

TABLE 9.6 Employed Persons by Major Occupation Group, 1950–1980 (in percentages)

	1950	1960	1970	1980
White-collar workers	37.5	43.4	48.3	52.2
Professional and technical workers	7.5	11.4	14.2	16.1
Managers, officials, and proprietors	10.7	10.7	10.5	11.2
Clerical workers	12.8	14.8	17.4	18.6
Sales workers	6.5	6.4	6.2	6.3
Blue-collar workers	38.8	36.6	35.3	31.7
Craftsmen and foremen	12.8	13.0	12.9	12.9
Operatives	20.2	18.2	17.7	14.0
Nonfarm laborers	5.8	5.4	4.7	4.6
Service workers	10.8	12.2	12.4	13.3
Farm workers	12.9	7.9	4.0	2.8
Total (in thousands)	**59,648**	**65,778**	**78,678**	**99,303**

2. Study Figure 9.9 below and answer these questions. (*a*) (1) Which job categories have the *highest* proportions of women? (2) Which job categories have the *lowest* proportions of women? (*b*) To what extent would you agree or disagree with the statement, "The information contained in this illustration is evidence of *sexism* (prejudice against women) in the labor market"? Explain your answer.

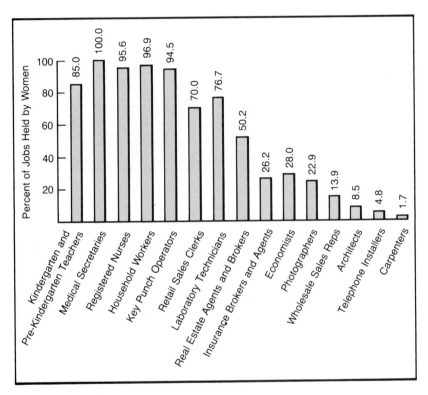

FIGURE 9.9   Women in Selected Occupations, 1982

3. Proposals or programs designed to help the poor generally fall into one of three categories: programs that seek economic growth, programs that seek a redistribution of income, and programs that seek to remove the causes of poverty. (*a*) Explain how *each* of the three approaches tries to reduce poverty. (*b*) Cite an example of a specific program that would fall into *each* of these three categories.

4. Agree or disagree with *each* of the following statements and present *two* arguments to support your position in each case. (*a*) Private enterprise can do more than the federal government to end poverty. (*b*) If federal spending for defense is reduced, most of the available funds should be used to aid the poor. (*c*) The

The Role of Labor

problem of poverty cannot be solved. (*d*) The United States should inaugurate a system of children's allowances for poor families. (*e*) The problem of poverty should be dealt with on a local rather than on a national level. (*f*) It is unfair to ask working people to pay taxes to support those living on welfare.

CHAPTER 10

Labor Unions in Our Economy

Today about 22 million Americans, approximately one worker in five, belong to labor unions. Large and powerful unions are now as much a part of American economic life as large and powerful corporations.

It was not always this way. Historically, unions have had a long struggle gaining strength and recognition. In the past, they were viewed by most business managers as a threat. After all, a major goal of unions was to put pressure on employers to raise wages and improve working conditions. Such demands, if granted, would add to an employer's costs. But from a worker's point of view, wages were often unreasonably low, and joining a union seemed the only practical way of getting an employer to deal fairly with employees.

To understand the role of labor unions today, we need to know something of their history from colonial times to the present.

HIGHLIGHTS FROM THE HISTORY OF LABOR UNIONS

Labor unions existed even in colonial times. These early unions consisted of only a few members who worked in the same trade and lived in the same community. For example, workers in the print shops of Philadelphia joined together in 1786 to force employers to raise wages. But they were not joined in their strike either by workers in other trades (barrelmakers, weavers) or by workers in the print shops of New York and Boston.

Before the Civil War, unions were small, local, and poorly organized. They had great trouble persuading employers to bargain with union representatives instead of bargaining directly with each individual employee. The union way of negotiating an employment contract is known as *collective bargaining*.

Rise and Fall of the Knights of Labor. Unions increased in size as a direct response to the increased size of business corporations. After the Civil War, railroad companies spanned whole regions of the country and wielded enormous power. How could workers hope to bargain for better employment contracts from these corporate giants?

190

One answer was to organize unions on a national scale, instead of on the small, local scale of an earlier time.

The first national union to achieve any real success was the Knights of Labor. Founded in 1869, the Knights conducted several strikes against railroad companies, which ended in wage increases for union members. Total membership in this national union grew to an impressive 700,000 by 1886. This achievement was followed, however, by a period of equally spectacular decline, and the Knights of Labor soon passed out of existence.

Rise of the American Federation of Labor. One national union that endured into our own time was founded in 1881 by a cigarmaker named Samuel Gompers. This was the American Federation of Labor or AFL. Gompers learned from the mistakes of earlier union leaders. He organized the AFL as an association of smaller, already existing craft unions. These unions (cigarmakers' unions, carpenters' unions, wheelwrights' unions, and so on) maintained their separate identities within the larger organization. Only skilled workers within a trade were eligible for union membership.

Gompers insisted that the AFL concentrate on bread-and-butter issues such as higher wages, shorter hours, and better working conditions. When political candidates of either major party offered to support these goals, they received the AFL's endorsement. Because of these tactics, the AFL was the most successful labor organization of its time. Its membership grew steadily to a peak of almost 4 million immediately following World War I.

The Opposition of Business and Government. Despite the growth of the AFL, unions were still at a serious disadvantage in their dealings with powerful corporations. Before the presidency of Franklin Roosevelt in the 1930s, government laws tended to hurt unions and help business.

The courts, for example, severely limited union activity by means of *injunctions.* An injunction is a court order that directs a person or group to stop committing certain acts. In the 1890s, state and federal courts regularly issued injunctions to stop unions from carrying out strikes.

United States Presidents and state governors also tended to give more help to employers than to union organizers. Striking workers often clashed with nonunion "strikebreakers," and battles sometimes raged outside factory gates. Government authorities frequently sent troops and militia to stop the violence by arresting union leaders. The presence of troops made it easier for business managers to crush a strike. In 1892, for example, unionized steelworkers called a strike against the Carnegie steel mills at Homestead, Pennsylvania. The governor responded to the violence at Homestead by sending state militia to break the strike.

A New Deal for Labor. Government's negative attitude toward unions changed slowly in the early decades of the twentieth century. President Theodore Roosevelt urged business leaders to treat labor more fairly. Most important, under President Woodrow Wilson, Congress passed the Clayton Act in 1914. This act specifically exempted labor unions from being broken up by federal antitrust suits. Before the Clayton Act, unions had been sued under the Sherman Antitrust Act of 1890 as "conspiracies in restraint of trade."

But the laws which most dramatically improved the status of unions were enacted during the Great Depression in the 1930s. To help Americans cope with the depression, President Franklin Roosevelt thought that unions should be protected and encouraged by laws of the federal government. As part of his New Deal program, he signed into law two acts of Congress which enabled unions to grow into extremely large and powerful organizations. One law was the Wagner Act of 1935 (also called the National Labor Relations Act). The other was the Fair Labor Standards Act of 1938.

In effect, the Wagner Act changed the balance of power between labor and management. It guaranteed all workers the right to organize and join unions and the right to bargain collectively. Unfair labor practices by management were defined, and a National Labor Relations Board (NLRB) was created to enforce the provisions of the law. The NLRB could conduct elections in a factory to determine whether workers wanted to be represented by a union.

The Fair Labor Standards Act was the second of Roosevelt's major labor laws. The act established a national minimum wage of 25 cents per hour and a maximum workweek of 44 hours, which in a few years rose to 40 cents and fell to 40 hours, respectively. Workers who put in more than the maximum workweek were to be paid overtime at a rate one and a half times their normal wages.

Rise of the CIO. Until the 1930s, unskilled and semiskilled workers in steel mills and other mass-production industries had been generally left out of the union movement. They could not join the AFL because they did not belong to any skilled trade group. But the passage of the Wagner Act in 1935 made it possible to organize all wage earners in an entire industry.

This was the goal of labor leader John L. Lewis who, in 1935, helped to form the Committee for Industrial Organization. At first

Lewis's group was only a committee within the AFL. It set out to found "vertical" unions in major mass-production industries. Such unions were to include all the workers within an industry regardless of the job they performed. The older, "horizontal" unions had grouped workers of similar skills. Quarrels between Lewis and leaders of the AFL caused Lewis to break away and create, in 1938, a new federation of industrial unions. This was the Congress of Industrial Organizations, or CIO.

The two organizations competed with each other for members, and so became increasingly alike. The AFL brought in many unskilled members, while the CIO recruited some highly skilled workers. Much energy was wasted in settling disputes between the rival unions. Factory workers often quarreled among themselves about whether to be organized by the AFL or by the CIO. To avoid these troubles, the great rivals decided in 1955 to merge into one organization—the AFL-CIO.

By this time, unions had gained tremendously in membership and power. There were 17 million union members in 1955 compared to just 3 million members in 1930. Fully one-third of all nonagricultural workers in the United States then belonged to a union. This was the high-water mark of union growth. In recent years, as we shall see, the percentage of union workers in the labor force has declined significantly.

BASIC AIMS OF UNIONS

1. Higher Wages. Of primary concern to all unions are the so-called bread-and-butter issues of wages and hours. In presenting their demands for higher wages, unions usually rely on one or more of the following arguments:

Profits and Ability to Pay. Unions believe that the workers are entitled to share in the company's prosperity and thus frequently claim that large profits justify wage increases.

Equal Pay for Equal Work. If workers performing identical or similar jobs in other companies or industries are earning higher rates of pay, unions will argue that their members should be brought up to that level. This is fair, they claim, because, if the job is worth so much to one company, it should be worth that much to another.

Productivity. If the productivity of workers is increasing for technological or other reasons, unions argue that the workers should share in these gains.

Rising Cost of Living. Because the general level of prices has been rising for over four decades and will probably continue to rise, workers' current wages will probably not be able to buy as much in the future as they can today. Economists take this into account when they speak of *real* wages as compared to *money* wages. Money wages are the earnings that workers receive in dollars and cents. Real wages take into account the goods and services that the money wages can buy. They are calculated by comparing wages to a base year. Suppose, for example, that workers earned $300 per week during the base year and the cost of living has increased since then by 50 percent. They would now have to earn $450 per week in money wages to realize $300 in real wages.

In order to protect their members against increases in living costs, unions frequently base their wage demands on changes in the price level. They may also ask for an *escalator clause* in their contract. Escalator clauses tie money wages to the cost of living in order to keep real wages constant. Thus, if the cost of living should rise by 10 percent in the course of the year, wages would automatically be raised by 10 percent or some fraction.

2. Shorter Hours. Just as unions have striven to increase their members' wages, so, too, have they sought to reduce the number of hours worked. This effort has been directed toward the reduction of both the number of hours worked each day and the number of days worked each year. Whereas in the early New England textile mills the average workweek ran to 72 hours, the present-day nonfarm workweek averages about 35 hours. Unions claim much of the credit for this reduction in working hours.

3. Union Shop. During collective bargaining, a union attempts to gain more than improved wages and hours. Among its primary goals will be the establishment of a union shop. For its part, management would prefer an *open shop*, in which workers are free not to join the union.

A compromise between the union shop and the open shop is the *agency shop.* Under this arrangement, nonunion workers are required to pay dues to the union as long as they work in the shop, but they do not have to join the union. The agency shop eliminates the "free rider," the worker who does not pay dues.

4. Checkoff. Another contract provision commonly sought by unions is the checkoff. It provides that dues will be deducted automatically from the workers' pay and sent on to the union.

5. Union Label. Attached to goods produced by union labor is a label. Unions try to induce the public to look for this label before making purchases.

6. Job Security. One of the main objectives that workers expect unions to achieve is job security. Union contracts usually provide that workers may not be dismissed without good reason. In case of layoffs, most contracts provide that workers with the most *seniority*, or years of service, will be the last to leave. Recently, unions have also tried to achieve a form of *guaranteed annual wage*. In some contracts, this has taken the form of *supplementary unemployment benefits*, which are payments by the employer to laid-off workers.

7. Fringe Benefits. The benefits not directly connected with wages or the job are called fringe benefits. They include items pertaining to health, welfare, vacations, and retirement. In recent years fringe benefits have made up an increasing percentage of the total labor costs of employers. Many shops, for example, pay the full cost of health insurance programs for their employees. Although the cost of this insurance does not appear in workers' pay envelopes, it nonetheless represents added income.

8. Grievance Machinery. Once a labor contract is drawn up and in force, disagreements may arise between the employer and the employees over many kinds of questions. A worker may feel that a supervisor has been unfair, or management may claim that the union has not been living up to its responsibilities. Whatever the dispute, most labor contracts provide for *grievance machinery*, which outlines the methods by which disputes can be resolved. This machinery usually involves hearings with the right of appeal to a higher level. The final appeal under many union contracts is to an *impartial arbitrator*. Under the procedure of arbitration, an impartial third party, the arbitrator, hears both sides of the argument and renders a decision that is binding on both parties.

THE COLLECTIVE BARGAINING PROCESS

1. Achieving Recognition. Before a shop is organized, there are usually some workers who would like to be represented by a union and others who are either uncertain or would prefer to remain independent. The situation may be further complicated if two or more unions are seeking to organize the same workers. Under the terms of the National Labor Relations Act, a union can ask the NLRB to "certify" it as the official bargaining agent for a particular shop. If there is any apparent objection, the NLRB is authorized to conduct an election to determine who, if anyone, should represent the employees. Having won a majority of the votes in such an election, a union is certified by the NLRB as the sole bargaining representative for its members, and the employer is legally bound to bargain in good faith with that union.

2. Union Contract: Collective Bargaining. Once it has been designated as the exclusive bargaining agent, the union will seek to negotiate a labor contract. This contract is a written agreement between the employer and the union representing employees, which sets the conditions of employment (compensation, hours, and working conditions) and the procedure to be used in settling disputes.

Representatives of the union and of management sit down to hammer out an agreement through collective bargaining. This process is the backbone of labor-management relations. More than 90 percent of union contracts are drawn up entirely as a result of these kinds of discussions. There are times, however, when collective bargaining breaks down, and disagreements between employer and employee become difficult to resolve. Labor relations then become the focus of television newscasts and newspaper headlines. This is understandable because strikes are more exciting than agreements. But peacefully

"Now, I'm a reasonable fellow, but it seems to me that in case after case and time after time in these labor disputes the fairer, more enlightened position has always been held by management."
Drawing by Stan Hunt; © 1982 *The New Yorker Magazine, Inc.*

Aims of Unions. Union negotiators prepare to present their case to management for an improved employment contract. What issues are they most likely to discuss?

negotiated agreements in the United States average about 300 a day, while there are fewer than 3,000 strikes a year.

Usually, collective bargaining takes place between the officials of a single company and the union. Sometimes, however, unions bargain with more than one company at a time. Collective bargaining normally will follow one of these patterns:

Local Bargaining. Where companies in a particular industry do not normally compete outside their own community, collective bargaining usually takes place on a community basis. Retail food stores in Peoria, Illinois, do not compete with those in Columbia, South Carolina. Therefore, food merchants in those towns may negotiate separately with the local unions.

Pattern Bargaining. In certain industries a few very influential companies control major portions of the market. Consequently, whatever they do will probably be followed by the other firms. United States Steel, General Electric, and General Motors are typical of the companies with which unions negotiate in the expectation that the agreements reached will "set the pattern" for other companies in the industry.

Industrywide Bargaining. If one trucking company could sign a union contract in which its drivers were paid less than those working for other firms, this company would be in a position to undersell its competitors. This would not take place under *industrywide* bargaining, in which representatives of all firms negotiate one union contract for the entire industry. This kind of negotiation benefits both management and labor. Management is protected against unfair competition from companies having lower labor costs. By preserving competition, unions help keep competing firms in business, thus protecting the jobs of their members.

WHEN COLLECTIVE BARGAINING FAILS

Although the overwhelming number of union contracts are worked out through collective bargaining, there are times when collective bargaining fails to bring about an agreement between management and the union. When face-to-face bargaining breaks down, the choices that remain usually involve either intervention by a third party or the application of some form of "arm-twisting."

Federal Laws That Regulate Unions. Following World War II, several important laws designed to regulate unions were enacted.

Labor-Management Relations Act (Taft-Hartley Act, 1947). The Taft-Hartley Act limited the activities of labor unions in a number of ways. (1) The act defined certain labor practices as "unfair." (2) The act outlawed the *closed shop* but did permit the *union shop*. In both instances all workers in a plant must belong to the union that is recognized as their bargaining agent. In a closed shop, which was legal under the Wagner Act, workers had to be union members before they were hired. But in a union shop, nonunion workers are permitted to join the union after they have been hired. (3) The act required that a union give the company sixty days' notice before going on strike. Moreover, in an industry that affects the national welfare, the President of the United States can request a court injunction delaying the strike an additional eighty days. (4) Union leaders were required to submit reports of union finances.

Labor-Management Reporting and Disclosure Act (Landrum-Griffin Act, 1959). This law sought to reduce corruption in labor-management relations and improve democratic procedures in unions. It guaranteed the workers' right to participate in the union's affairs and to elect their officers. The embezzlement of union funds was made a federal offense.

Right-to-Work Laws. "Right to work" means that workers may hold jobs without being required to join unions. Some nineteen states, located mostly in the South and Midwest, have enacted these laws.

How Unions Put Pressure on Management. In seeking to achieve their goals, labor unions may use a variety of tactics.

Strike. A strike is a work stoppage for the purpose of gaining concessions from management. It is labor's most powerful weapon because of the financial penalties it imposes upon the employer. Of course, a strike also costs the workers a loss in income. For this reason, they will have to feel that the potential gain from a successful

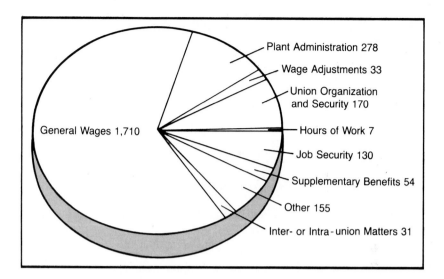

FIGURE 10.1 Major Issues in Strikes, 1981

strike will outweigh the expense of lost wages. Major issues in strikes in a recent year are shown in Figure 10.1. Ways of settling strikes are described on page 202.

Picketing. Picketing takes place when workers march in front of a business with signs, usually to proclaim the existence of a strike. The objectives of picketing are to: (1) discourage workers from entering, and (2) arouse public sympathy and urge the public not to patronize the struck business.

Boycott. A boycott is a refusal to buy goods from a company whose workers are on strike. Unions ask their members and their families to "spread the word" to boycott the struck company's goods. They may also call upon the general public to cooperate in the action. The objective is to add to the financial pressure on the employer by reducing the company's sales. Because the pressure is being applied to the company being struck, this tactic is called a *primary boycott.* When the same pressure is put on a company whose workers are not on strike but which is doing business with the struck company, we have a *secondary boycott.* If, for example, the workers of the Rifle Towel Company were on strike and they and others refused to buy Rifle towels, we would have a *primary boycott.* However, should the union order its members not to have any dealings with stores selling Rifle towels, this would be a *secondary boycott.* Certain types of secondary boycotts have been made illegal by the Taft-Hartley and Landrum-Griffin acts.

Labor Unions in Our Economy   **199**

Union Tactics. Cesar Chavez, organizer of the United Farm Workers Union, addressing a group of unionized hotel workers in New York City. What was he asking them to do?

Slowdown. When workers deliberately reduce their output in order to force concessions from their employer, this is called a slowdown. However, since the workers are not on strike, they can continue to draw their wages.

Political Action. Although labor has not organized its own political party, unions do try to induce their members to support political candidates whose views the unions consider as favorable. As long as unions can continue to achieve most of their aims through collective bargaining and through their present political activities, labor will probably not attempt to field a third party. Like management, however, unions lobby for the passage of legislation that will strengthen their position.

Illegal Methods. Unions have resorted to tactics that either were never legal or have since been declared illegal. Among the most common of these were the following:

Secondary Boycott. This tactic is described above.

Strong-Arm Methods. Unions have been guilty of hiring thugs to coerce management into accepting their demands. The extent and nature of these illegal activities were revealed in the investigations conducted in the 1950s by the McClellan Committee of the United

States Senate. The findings of this committee ultimately led to the passage of the Landrum-Griffin Act.

Jurisdictional Strike. A jurisdictional dispute occurs between two unions over the question of which one has authority over a particular job. For example, should the worker who removes a part of a costume from the stage during a play be a member of the Costumers' Union or the Stagehands' Union? While at one time such a dispute might have led to a strike, such a strike is now outlawed as an unfair labor practice by the Taft-Hartley Act.

How Management Puts Pressure on Unions. In the past, employers relied upon a number of techniques to maintain as much control as possible over the operations of their businesses. These efforts were usually directed toward weakening the power of unions and getting the government to pass laws that would help accomplish this. Many of the tactics once used by management have been declared illegal and are, therefore, no longer practiced. Furthermore, most employers have accepted the idea of working with unions and have done their best to maintain cordial relations with them. Nevertheless, the occasional breakdowns in labor-management negotiations have led management to take certain steps against unions. The following are some of the more important tactics of management:

Lockout. A lockout is the shutting down of a plant by management in the hope of bringing the workers to its terms. Although the effect is the same as a strike in that work has been suspended, management hopes to be in a better position than labor to afford the temporary financial loss. In recent years, the lockout has sometimes been followed by a permanent shutdown of operations and a move to a region of the country where unions are weaker. The possibility of such a move puts pressure on the union to come to terms.

Injunction. An injunction is a court order prohibiting a certain action. In a labor dispute, it can sometimes be used to halt a strike. The use of the injunction in labor disputes was sharply limited by the Norris-La Guardia Act.

Strikebreakers. One way for an employer to break a strike is to hire workers to replace the striking union members. It is legal to hire strikebreakers, or "scabs" as the unions call them. However, some states require that strikebreakers be informed that they are being used to replace workers on strike.

Political Activity. By persuading government to pass laws that limit the power of unions, industry has tried to maintain a strong bargaining position. Unions point to the right-to-work laws as examples of legislation favoring management.

Public Relations. Industries have founded or supported organizations such as the National Association of Manufacturers and the Chamber of Commerce of the United States. These groups have sought to present management's point of view to the public and have lobbied for legislation favorable to management. In addition, companies buy newspaper advertisements and time on radio and television to present their side of a labor dispute.

How Strikes May Be Settled by Third Parties. There are three major methods of settling disputes between labor and management with the aid of outside parties.

Fact-Finding. A fact-finding board is usually appointed by the government. It investigates the issues, makes a report, and, in many cases, suggests solutions. Its recommendations are not necessarily binding.

Mediation. In mediation, the third party brings together the two parties in the dispute, listens to their arguments, and perhaps offers a solution. The compromise proposals suggested by the mediator, however, are not binding on either party. (This procedure is also called "conciliation.")

Arbitration. In the arbitration method of settling labor disputes, a third party gives a decision that is binding on both sides. Arbitration is rarely used to negotiate labor contracts. More frequently, it is used as the final step in the handling of a grievance arising out of the interpretation of an existing contract.

When, as sometimes happens, both bargaining and third-party intervention fail, we may expect to see union and management applying whatever forms of pressure they have available to force the other side to accept their demands. It is during these periods that the public most frequently reads or hears about labor-management relations.

CURRENT PROBLEMS OF LABOR UNIONS

1. Decline in Labor Union Membership. Although the number of workers belonging to unions has increased over the years, membership as a percentage of the total labor force has declined. This trend is summarized in Figure 10.2. The reasons most frequently cited for the decline in union membership are as follows:

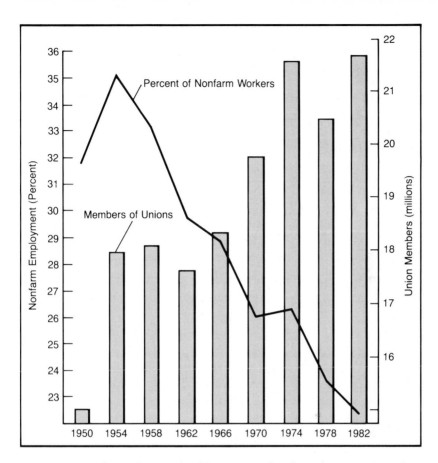

FIGURE 10.2 Labor Union Membership, as a Total and as a Percent of Nonfarm Employment, 1950–1981

Growing Number and Importance of White-Collar Workers. White-collar workers, who usually work in offices or behind counters, include professional, managerial, clerical, and sales workers. Unlike the blue-collar workers who provided the bulk of union membership in the past, white-collar workers have traditionally been reluctant to join unions.

In recent years, the number of white-collar workers has been increasing rapidly. In 1956 they outnumbered blue-collar workers for the first time. By the early 1980s the white-collar labor force was four times larger than the blue-collar labor force.

Corruption and Crime in Unions. Another reason for the decline in union membership is the publicity surrounding recent and past instances of corruption and crime within labor's ranks. Because of the widespread interest in these investigations, which ultimately led to passage of the Landrum-Griffin Act, many workers became fearful of joining unions. (See further discussion on page 208.)

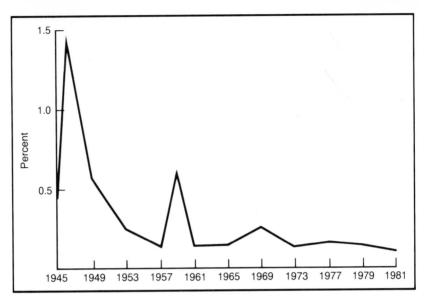

FIGURE 10.3   Work Time Lost Because of Strikes, 1945–1981

Economic Recession and Layoffs. The sharp decline in business activity in the late 1970s and early 1980s cost many union workers their jobs and discouraged others from joining labor unions.

2. Strikes. The amount of time lost because of work stoppages is far less than the public seems to believe. In 1980, for example, the time lost because of strikes was 0.14 percent of the total time worked. Indeed, as indicated by Figure 10.3, in only one year since 1945 has the working time lost because of strikes gone above one percent of the total time worked. In this regard union leaders remind us that the time lost because of strikes is tiny as compared to the number of workdays lost through unemployment. (See Figure 10.4.)

Despite the relatively light cost of strikes, certain industries are so closely related to the public interest that even the briefest stoppage can become intolerable. If, for example, a strike should shut off public transportation, or garbage removal, or milk delivery, the public welfare is directly involved. Also, the American economy is so

FIGURE 10.4   Work Time Lost Because of Strikes and Unemployment, 1981

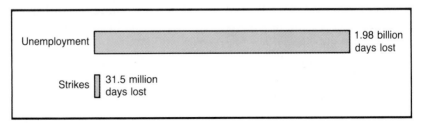

specialized that, if one segment of it fails to function, many others will feel the pinch. A strike in the steel industry will eventually be felt by all industries that use steel. Similarly, a tire strike will affect automobile production, and a stoppage by dockworkers that shuts down the waterfront will inevitably leave its mark on many other industries and their workers. Thus, despite the relatively small number of strikes in the United States, their impact is widely felt. Furthermore, because the public is often affected by strikes, it frequently adopts a hostile attitude toward the strikers.

As we have seen, the Taft-Hartley Act permits the federal government to obtain an injunction that can delay a strike for eighty days if the national welfare is involved. Of course, at the end of the eighty-day period, the workers can go on strike. When the law was passed, however, it was hoped that during the "cooling-off" period the negotiating process would continue and a strike be avoided. These negotiations could involve fact-finding, mediation, or arbitration. In extreme cases of national emergency, as during wartime, the government has seized and operated plants that were on strike. This is a last-resort measure that most lawyers feel is unconstitutional during peacetime.

3. *Public Employees and the Right to Strike.* "There is no right to strike against the public safety by anybody, anywhere, any time." So declared Calvin Coolidge, then governor of Massachusetts, to Samuel Gompers some sixty-five years ago. The issue that Coolidge raised is still being debated. Do public employees—people working for a branch of government—have the right to strike?

Most states have declared strikes by their public employees illegal, and laws threaten strike leaders with fines and imprisonment. Similarly, the federal government has prohibited strikes by its employees. Despite these prohibitions, however, there were over 1,500 strikes by state and local employees between 1977 and 1979.

Strikes by public employees have been outlawed for several reasons. First, such strikes threaten the public safety or public order. If police officers or fire fighters were to walk off their jobs, there would be a clear threat to the safety of lives and property. Second, the smooth operation of society depends upon the continuing operation of its government. When public transportation stops running, or garbage rots in the streets, or taxes remain uncollected, then society as a whole is disrupted.

Third, public-sector workers (those who work for government) have an unfair advantage as compared to workers in the private sector (in business, farming, and industry) because public employers do not have to earn a profit in order to stay in business. In other words, private-sector strikers are limited in the size of a pay raise that they can expect to win by the ability of the firm to earn enough to offset wage costs. If, because of a wage increase, a firm had to raise prices to the point where it lost money, it could be forced out of business. Thus the firm's need to cover its wage costs is the ultimate check on union power.

This need for profitability does not exist in the case of government employees. Even if a government pays its workers twice what they deserve, business will go on as usual, and only the taxpayers will suffer. It therefore follows that in the absence of the ultimate check provided by the marketplace, government employees ought not to be allowed to back up their wage demands with a strike, or the threat of a strike.

Public-employee unions received a major setback in 1981 when

Have Unions Been Responsible for Higher Wages?

One question that economists have been debating has been whether or not unions have raised the general level of wages. We can see from Table 10.1 that wages have been rising dramatically.

TABLE 10.1   Average Weekly Earnings of Nonagricultural Workers

1937	$ 21.83
1951	57.86
1961	82.60
1971	126.54
1981	255.20

Would these increases have taken place if there had been no unions pushing for them? We can summarize these opposing points of view as follows:

UNIONS HAVE NOT AFFECTED WAGES.   In arguing that unions have not affected wages, economists refer to statistics showing that the share of the nation's income going to labor has changed little in the past fifty years. In fact, the portion of the total national income paid out in wages went up only 4 percent between 1929 and 1981.

the Professional Air Traffic Controllers Organization (Patco), representing the traffic controllers at the nation's major airports, threatened an illegal strike unless its demands were met. The government refused and the union struck. Some 12,000 Patco members were fired and the union was fined. It remains to be seen whether Patco's experience will have a carry-over effect on the actions of other public-employee unions.

4. Economic Recession and "Givebacks." The economic recession (a period of business decline) of the late 1970s and early 1980s was particularly hard on industries such as automobiles, rubber, steel, and trucking, which had the greatest concentration of union members. The United Automobile Workers (UAW) alone lost over 300,000 members between 1979 and 1982 because of layoffs in the auto plants.

While admitting that unions can force *money wages* up, these economists insist that, unless productivity also increases, there can be no general increase in *real wages*. When a union forces management to grant a substantial wage increase, management will have to raise prices, reduce costs, or both. When prices are increased throughout the economy, the inflationary situation may wipe out all wage gains. If, on the other hand, businesses are unable to increase prices, they may choose to reduce their costs by laying off workers. Still another alternative that some businesses have chosen in the face of large wage increases was to shut down the plant. Only if a general wage increase is accompanied by a rise in productivity will workers throughout the nation be better off than before. The rise in productivity will permit management to pay higher wages without raising prices and without laying off workers.

UNIONS HAVE AFFECTED WAGES.   Turning to the other side of the argument, we find economists who contend that, if there had been no unions to force increases, labor's share of the nation's income would have been smaller than it is. As proof, they cite statistics showing that wage rates have gone up substantially in recently organized industries. The fact that some employers increase wages in order to avoid unionization further demonstrates the ability of unions to raise wages. It is also argued that, if there were no unions, workers would have no assurance that they would share in productivity gains. In other words, if a corporation increased the productivity of its plant by 10 percent, it would not have to share its increased profits with its workers unless a union compelled it to do so. Furthermore, unions have argued that by insisting on higher wages, they encourage management to become more efficient and to increase productivity.

Adding to unions' woes were the difficulties experienced in organizing efforts. In shop elections held by the National Labor Relations Board to decide whether a union would represent the workers, unions won about 45 percent of the elections in the 1980s as compared to 60 percent in the 1960s.

The pressure for "givebacks" in many of the contracts negotiated during the recession years was another problem for union leadership. Givebacks are concessions of wages and benefits previously won by unions. Sometimes, givebacks were demanded and granted in an effort to keep troubled companies from going bankrupt. In one notable instance, workers at the Chrysler Corporation granted $622 million worth of concessions to help keep the automaker in business. In 1981–1982 employees in the rubber, trucking, meat-packing, and airlines industries, in efforts to save their jobs, accepted substantial cuts in salaries.

While a period of recession, in which some workers are laid off and others are forced to give back hard-won gains, serves to discourage many workers from joining unions, it may also strengthen the resolve of other workers to stick with their unions. Said one union member, "Just think what might happen to us if there were no union in times like these."

5. Crime and Corruption in Labor Unions. We have already noted that the nationwide attention given to crime and corruption in the labor movement may have been a factor in declining union membership. Justice Department data show that from 1973 to 1980 some 450 union officers and employees were convicted of serious crimes involving their labor activities. Other investigations have linked four major unions with organized crime and led to charges of corruption against 300 union locals.

In fairness, however, it should be pointed out that nearly all of the nation's elected labor leaders and 75,000 union locals have neither been charged with crimes nor linked with corruption. Some union leaders claim that news stories focusing on the criminal activities of a small minority within labor's ranks are evidence of the news media's hostility.

Dishonest union officials "caught in the act" are far more likely to receive attention in the nation's press than business executives who do something equally dishonest.

EXERCISES

Matching Questions

1. The National Labor Relations Board (NLRB) holds elections to determine if this is to take place.
2. Issued by a court of law ordering persons to stop certain acts.
3. Third-party decisions are binding when this is applied.
4. Provides for union dues to be withheld from members' pay.
5. Labor would like shippers to look for this identification.
6. Union tactic that reduces output without a walkout.
7. Prohibits union shops.
8. Establishes working conditions for many firms at one and the same time.
9. Third-party decisions are *not* binding when this is applied.
10. The method by which most labor contracts are negotiated.

a. union recognition
b. industrywide bargaining
c. checkoff
d. union label
e. collective bargaining
f. injunction
g. right-to-work law
h. yellow-dog contract
i. arbitration
j. slowdown
k. mediation
l. grievance machinery

Multiple Choice

1. About what proportion of the labor force belongs to unions? (*a*) about 80 percent (*b*) less than 75 percent but more than 50 percent (*c*) less than 50 percent but more than 25 percent (*d*) about 20 percent.
2. In the labor disputes of the late nineteenth century, the cause of labor in the United States was frequently hampered by (*a*) government activities that favored management (*b*) Communist infiltration of labor unions (*c*) resentment against sit-down strikes (*d*) the violent tactics pursued by the leaders of the Knights of Labor.
3. When a strike threatens the national health and safety, the President of the United States may (*a*) forbid the strike (*b*) request an injunction to halt the strike temporarily (*c*) impose a settlement (*d*) provide for government operation of plants threatened by the strike.
4. Which practice of labor is now often forbidden? (*a*) injunction (*b*) secondary boycott (*c*) strike (*d*) political activity.
5. In recent years, unions have been affected by (*a*) an increase in

job opportunities for unskilled labor (*b*) the growing importance of blue-collar jobs as compared to the rest of the labor market (*c*) the decline in the importance of white-collar work (*d*) the increasing number of white-collar workers.

6. "Real wages" are (*a*) hourly wages remaining after taxes have been deducted (*b*) the quantity of goods and services that can be purchased with one's money wages (*c*) a worker's total income from all sources (*d*) what remains out of wages after a sum has been set aside for savings.

7. In a union contract with an escalator clause, a rise or fall in wages is dependent upon a rise or fall in (*a*) output (*b*) productivity (*c*) living costs (*d*) the unemployment rate.

8. In which type of shop do nonunion workers join the union after being hired? (*a*) union shop (*b*) open shop (*c*) closed shop (*d*) agency shop.

9. Which of the following is a weapon of management? (*a*) lockout (*b*) picketing (*c*) strike (*d*) boycott.

10. In an agency shop, workers (*a*) must belong to the union before they can be hired (*b*) must join the union after they have been hired (*c*) do not have to join the union and need not make any contribution to it (*d*) need not join the union but must pay it a periodic fee.

11. Most labor contracts are arrived at as a result of (*a*) a strike (*b*) picketing (*c*) collective bargaining (*d*) arbitration.

12. In a jurisdictional strike, the striking union tries to (*a*) compel management to increase wages (*b*) compel management to recognize it rather than another union (*c*) improve working conditions (*d*) reduce the hours of work.

13. The first law to guarantee the right of collective bargaining was the (*a*) Clayton Act (*b*) National Labor Relations Act (Wagner Act) (*c*) Taft-Hartley Act (*d*) Landrum-Griffin Act.

14. The law that set minimum hours and wages was the (*a*) Fair Labor Standards Act (*b*) Wagner Act (*c*) Taft-Hartley Act (*d*) Landrum-Griffin Act.

15. According to Figure 10.3, on page 204, working time lost because of strikes between 1961 and 1981 amounted to (*a*) 20 percent of the time worked (*b*) 10 percent of the time worked (*c*) between 5 and 10 percent of the time worked (*d*) less than one-half of one percent of the time worked.

16. Strikes by government employees are (*a*) just as legal as those by any other workers (*b*) usually illegal (*c*) rare in this country (*d*) more likely to occur than strikes by private workers.

Essay Questions

1. In recent years there have been increasing numbers of strikes by public employees such as teachers, sanitation workers, and air traffic controllers. In most instances, these strikes were in violation

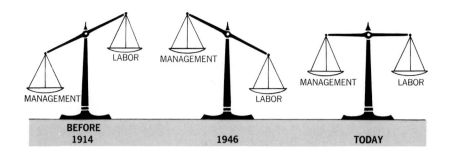

FIGURE 10.5 Balance Between Labor and Management in 1914, 1946, and 1984

of antistrike laws. (a) Identify and explain two reasons why many states and the federal government have outlawed strikes by their employees. (b) Do you believe that public employees ought to have the right to strike? If your answer is "yes," explain why. If your answer is "no," explain some procedures you might suggest for settling disputes between government and its employees.

2. Assume that the union representing the workers in a large bakery has just signed a contract with management. Summarize under the following headings some of the provisions that the agreement is likely to include: (a) union recognition (b) conditions of work (c) grievance procedures (d) wages (e) job security (f) fringe benefits (g) other provisions.

3. Some people have suggested that labor disputes could be settled through the introduction of compulsory arbitration. (a) Explain the meaning of the proposal. (b) Give *two* reasons why you either agree or disagree with the suggestion.

4. (a) Assume that you are on your union's negotiating team and have been asked to prepare arguments supporting your wage demands. Explain *three* arguments that you would use. (b) Since you will have to anticipate management's reaction to your presentation, explain the arguments that management is likely to raise in rejecting your demands.

5. There are those who claim that the balance of power between labor and management has followed the pattern summarized in Figure 10.5, above. (a) Give *three* arguments to show that labor was at a disadvantage in the years before 1914. (b) Give *two* arguments to show that in 1946 labor had the upper hand in its relations with management. (c) What events have taken place in the years since 1946 to "restore the balance of power" between labor and management?

6. (a) With reference to the period either from 1900 to 1920 *or* 1935 to 1957, account for the growth that took place in the labor union movement at that time. (b) With reference to the period either from 1920 to 1933 *or* 1970 to the present, summarize the factors that account for the decline in the labor movement in those years.

Education is the most expensive function of state government—and probably the most important.

UNIT V

The Role of Government

CHAPTER 11

The Growing Importance of Government

In the United States, government exists on three levels at the same time: the federal or national government, the governments of the fifty states, and thousands of local governments. Although their scope and power differ enormously, each level, through its powers to tax and to spend, affects the entire economy. Over the past half-century, government participation in the economy has grown dramatically. This growth is illustrated in Figure 11.1 on page 214, which shows the following:

1. Total spending by all levels of government increased from $12 billion in 1932 to more than $1 trillion in 1982.

2. Total government purchases of goods and services increased from 14 percent of the gross national product in 1932 to 21 percent by 1982.

3. The number of persons on government payrolls increased from 3 million in 1932 to 16 million in 1982.

The more important reasons for the spectacular increase in government spending are discussed in this chapter.

REASONS FOR THE GROWTH OF GOVERNMENT

1. National Defense. The United States assumed an immense financial burden in this century by fighting two world wars and limited wars in Korea and Vietnam, and by undertaking the leadership of the free world after 1945. These costs are reflected in the nation's outlays (expenditures) for national defense as well as many other activities designed to limit the spread of power by the Soviet Union and its allies.

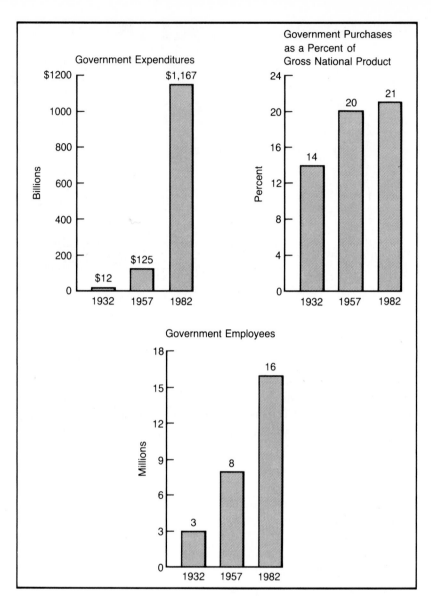

FIGURE 11.1   Growing Importance of Government: 1932, 1957, 1982

If, in addition to military programs, interest on the national debt is included, the total accounts for 37 cents out of every dollar spent by the federal government in 1982, or over $270 billion. The national debt is the amount of money the federal government has borrowed over the years. Payments for interest on the national debt have been included in the category of national security since this debt exists primarily because of the wars the United States has fought and the nation's international and defense programs.

Impact of Government on Workers. Can you identify four ways that the economic welfare of these Pittsburgh steelworkers is influenced by policies of the federal government?

2. Population Growth. The United States has a much larger population now than at the turn of the century. The population has grown from 76 million in 1900 to 123 million in 1930 and 228 million in 1980 (the date of the last census). In 1984, the United States population was over 235 million. Thus numbers alone account for part of increased government expenditures. More people require more services, such as schools, police and fire protection, roads, sewers, water lines, and power services—in short, more of everything that government provides.

Not only has the population been growing, but the proportion of the elderly has also been increasing. In 1930, for example, about 5 percent of the total population was over 65 years of age. By 1980 the elderly constituted over 11 percent of the total. The reasons for this increase may be found in advances in science and medicine. Life expectancy has been extended from an average of 59.7 years for a person born in 1930 to 73.8 years for a person born in 1979. Longer lifespans for the population have added to the cost of government, which now pays retirement benefits for longer periods of time and cares for more elderly persons.

3. Changing Attitudes Toward the Role of Government. Before the Great Depression of the 1930s, most Americans would have accepted the saying that "that government is best which governs least." Generally, the government was expected to provide little more than physical protection and the operation of certain activities that were not profitable for private enterprise, such as schools, post offices, and highways. Since the 1930s, however, the various levels of government have assumed a substantial interest in the economic and social well-being of their citizens. Governments now finance extensive and costly programs of assistance in the areas of unemployment, old age, health and welfare, housing, and social problems.

Government programs that provide financial assistance do so through what are known as *transfer payments.* These payments are government expenditures that do not involve the purchase of goods and services. Instead, they move or "transfer" funds from one section of the economy to another. Social security, unemployment compensation, welfare payments, and veterans' benefits are examples of government transfer payments.

Government has also been called upon to assume some of the economic risks that in other times were taken by private individuals and corporations. Now, for example, when you make a deposit in a savings bank, you will see a sign proclaiming that your money will be protected by the Federal Deposit Insurance Corporation, a government agency. Similarly, the government will guarantee mortgage payments to banks and other lending agencies, and wages to many persons out of work. Some of these programs are self-supporting. Nevertheless, in operating these programs, the government does incur expenses that inevitably add to its total expenditures.

4. Rising Living Standards. Thanks to the nation's enormous capacity to produce goods and services, people in the United States are living better today than ever before. As a consequence, governmental expenditures for services have also had to improve. Two-lane roads have been replaced by six-lane highways. Schools require more costly equipment and larger staffs than in the past. In these and in many other areas, citizens have come to expect more from their government.

5. Advances in Science and Technology. The federal government supports a variety of scientific and technological projects. These include basic research in science as well as such aerospace achievements as the space shuttle and communications satellites. Costs have been averaging about $7 billion annually.

6. Inflation. Since 1940 prices in general have increased nearly seven times. Thus the government has had to pay higher costs for all the services it provides. For this reason, a substantial amount of the greater expenditures of government does not result from expanded services but rather from increasing costs.

7. Shift From a Rural to an Urban Society. In recent years there has been a rapid growth in the size of cities and suburbs. You have heard about bad housing, high crime rates, and inadequate transportation in the cities. These and other urban problems have added enormous financial burdens to all levels of government. (See Chapter 21 for a detailed look at the economics of cities.)

8. Economic Growth. The American economy of the 1980s is much larger than it has ever been. From a low of $56 billion in 1933, the gross national product climbed to over $3 trillion in 1982. While this growth has made it possible for government to spend more, it has also been accompanied by the need for more government regulation and the demand for more government services.

FEDERAL BUDGET

Many individuals and families find that they are able to get more for their money if they plan their spending in advance by drawing up a *budget*. A budget is a financial plan summarizing anticipated income and expenses. In drawing up its budget, a family may find that its expenditures will be less than its total income. In this case, the amount left over, or *surplus*, could be put into some form of savings. If, however, the anticipated expenses are greater than the family's income, the family might have to cut out or reduce certain expenditures. If expenses then equal income, the budget is said to be *balanced*. On the other hand, if the family feels that it has to spend more during the period than it expects to earn, it would have to make up the difference, or *deficit*, either by borrowing the money or by using savings. (We shall discuss personal budgeting further in Chapter 20.)

Governments, too, prepare budgets. The federal budget is prepared by the Office of Management and Budget, an executive agency. This agency goes to work fifteen months or so before the budget is to go into effect, so as to enable the President to present the budget to Congress by January of each year. Federal budgets run from October 1 to September 30 of the following year. This twelve-month period is known as a *fiscal year*. January 1 to December 31 is called a "calendar year."

In preparing the budget, the Budget Office gathers all the information it can find on anticipated expenses and income. As one would expect, thousands of items are listed in the budget, which usually runs to many hundreds of pages.

The budget that the President presents to Congress is merely a

TABLE 11.1 Receipts and Outlays of the Federal Government (billions of dollars)

Year	Receipts	Outlays
1955	$ 65.5	$ 68.5
1960	95.5	92.2
1965	116.8	118.4
1970	192.8	195.7
1975	279.1	324.2
1985 (est.)	750.9	932.1

recommendation. Congress may revise either expenses or revenue upward or downward. For example, Congress may refuse to allocate funds for a program recommended by the President, or, less often, it may vote more funds for a program than the President has asked. Congress may also raise or lower taxes beyond what the President has recommended. After Congress has made all its changes, it passes the budget in the form of appropriations and revenue laws.

Because a budget is drawn up in advance of the fiscal year, it is merely a forecast of what is expected to happen, not a summary of what actually does happen. There are two main reasons for this discrepancy:

1. The unexpected may happen. Sometimes a crisis at home or abroad will cause an unanticipated increase in expenses. In the 1960s the Vietnam War proved to be far more costly than the Budget Office or Congress had expected. Similarly, the recession and high unemployment of the late 1970s and early 1980s required emergency appropriations to help millions of unemployed workers and their families.

2. Income depends upon business conditions. Unlike the income of a family living on a fixed salary, government income fluctuates. This happens because tax revenues depend upon the incomes of individuals and businesses. If times are bad, incomes will fall off and so will the taxes that government collects.

According to Table 11.1, in what year was the federal budget most nearly in balance? In what years was there a surplus? a deficit?

A LOOK AT EXPENSES IN THE FEDERAL BUDGET

Table 11.2 summarizes the principal items of income and expense in the federal budget for 1982. Almost all of the income earned by the

TABLE 11.2 Federal Budget, 1982
(billions of dollars)

RECEIPTS

	Amount	Percent of Total
Individual income taxes	$297.7	47.2
Social insurance taxes and contributions	201.5	31.9
Corporation income taxes	49.2	7.8
Excise taxes	36.3	5.8
Earnings of Federal Reserve System	15.2	2.4
Customs duties	8.9	1.4
Other	22.3	3.5
Total Receipts	$631.1	

OUTLAYS

	Amount	Percent of Total
Income security	$248.3	33.5
National defense	187.4	25.3
Interest on the national debt	84.7	11.4
Health	74.0	10.0
Education, training, employment, and social services	26.3	3.6
Veterans' benefits and services	23.9	3.2
Transportation	20.6	2.8
Agriculture	14.9	2.0
Natural resources and environment	12.9	1.7
International affairs	10.0	1.3
Community and regional development	7.2	1.0
General science, space, and technology	7.1	1.0
General-purpose fiscal assistance	6.4	.9
General government	4.7	.6
Administration of justice	4.7	.6
Energy	4.7	.6
Commerce and housing credit	3.9	.5
Total Outlays	$741.7	

Budget Deficit: **$110.6 billion**

government came from taxes, which will be described in Chapter 12. In this discussion we shall focus on items of expense, or "outlays."

Budgets tell us something about what a government regards as important and unimportant. Governments, like private citizens, have limited resources and must therefore pick and choose from among many needs and wants. By comparing the budget of one year with that of another year, and by examining the items within a particular budget, we are able to see a government's priorities.

Following are explanations of the principal categories of expenditures in a typical federal budget.

Income Security. The largest item in the federal budget is income security. In 1982 over 33 percent of total budget outlays were for income security, while in 1956 outlays were but 14 percent of the total. In the past 25 years federal social insurance protection has been extended to virtually all Americans who are aged, poor, disabled, or unemployed.

National Defense. Funds for national defense support the activities of the armed forces. These moneys pay the salaries of more than 2 million men and women in uniform and buy the weapons and equipment needed to fulfill their mission. From 1941, the year that the United States entered World War II, until 1973, national defense was the largest single item of expense in the budget. Since that time defense has ranked second, after income security.

Interest. Interest is the cost of borrowing money. In recent years, the money needed to pay the interest on the public (national) debt has reached astounding proportions. Whereas in 1900 the public debt stood at $1.3 billion, or $16.60 for every man, woman, and child in the nation, by 1982 the total had passed the $1 trillion mark, or $4,300 per person. Nearly all the $82.5 billion set aside for interest payments in 1981 was a result of this huge debt. How the government borrows money is discussed in Chapter 18.

Health. Federal involvement in the nation's health began with the creation of the Public Health Service in 1798. Federal support for health services grew rapidly in the mid-1960s when the Medicare and Medicaid programs were established. The $66 billion spent on health services by the federal government in 1981 represented well over one-quarter of the nation's total health expenditures.

Education, Training, Employment, and Social Services. The major objective of the programs in this category is to help individuals who require assistance in obtaining education, job skills, job information, and supportive services such as counseling and child care.

Veterans' Benefits and Services. Among the costs of past wars are the benefits now provided to the veterans of those wars and their families. Benefits pay for education, pensions, and health services.

Transportation. Funding for these programs is used to support ground, water, and air transportation facilities.

Agriculture. The major part of the moneys allocated to agriculture is used to support farm prices. (Price-support programs for farm products are described in detail in Chapter 22.) A second goal of the government's agricultural programs is to improve the production and marketing of farm products.

Natural Resources and Environment. Various federal programs attempt to curb pollution of the land, air, and water; conserve and develop minerals, timber, and other natural resources; and preserve natural areas, historic sites, and fish and wildlife.

International Affairs. The United States plays an active leadership role in international affairs because national well-being depends, in part, upon events beyond our borders. Funding for these activities falls into four categories: (1) foreign economic and financial assistance; (2) military assistance to allies and other friendly nations; (3) administration and conduct of foreign affairs; and (4) foreign information and exchange activities.

Community and Regional Development. The federal government sponsors a number of programs that attempt to revitalize the nation's housing. (Most of the money for this purpose is channeled through state and local governments.) Other programs provide disaster relief and insurance and assist in the development of business opportunities in economically depressed or declining communities.

General Science, Space, and Technology. The goals of the government's science, space, and technology programs are to: (1) expand scientific knowledge through support of basic research in all fields of science; (2) promote technological innovation in industry; (3) develop a greater understanding of the solar system and the physical universe through space exploration; (4) develop and demonstrate practical, economic, and productive applications of space technology.

General-Purpose Fiscal Assistance. This aid is given to state and local governments without restrictions on how the money is to be used. Cities and states use this money to increase public services, reduce debts, or lower taxes.

The Social Security System

Every month the federal government mails more than 35 million green checks to beneficiaries of the social security system. Social security is the nation's basic method of providing a continuing income when family earnings are reduced or stop because of retirement, disability, or death. About nine out of every ten persons working today are covered or in the process of being covered by social security. Coverage comes in the form of *Old Age, Survivors, Disability, and Health Insurance (OASDHI)*. OASDHI benefits include the following:

RETIREMENT PAYMENTS. Workers may start receiving retirement checks as early as age 62.

DISABILITY PAYMENTS. These payments are sent to workers who become severely disabled before age 65.

SURVIVORS BENEFITS. If a worker dies, payments go to certain members of his or her family.

HEALTH INSURANCE. *Medicare,* as health insurance is commonly called, is a two-part program that provides hospital and medical insurance to people 65 years of age and older, and the same services to the severely disabled at any age. The hospital insurance part of Medicare helps pay the cost of inpatient care and certain kinds of follow-up hospital care. The medical insurance part of Medicare helps pay the cost of physicians' services and certain other medical expenses not covered by the hospital insurance.

UNEMPLOYMENT INSURANCE. Most workers who have lost their jobs are entitled to receive *unemployment compensation.* These benefits, which vary from state to state, are paid out of a fund created by a payroll tax on employers and by contributions from the federal government. Benefits averaging about $100 a week run for a limited time only. At the present, the limit generally ranges from twenty weeks to a year.

FINANCING SOCIAL SECURITY

Workers, their employers, and self-employed people pay social security taxes. This money pays for the administrative expenses and the current benefits of the program. In turn, when people who are presently working and paying taxes are eligible for benefits, they will receive them from taxes paid by working people at that time.

Hospital insurance is also financed out of social security taxes. Medical insurance, however, is paid for in part by additional premiums collected from the people who have elected to enroll in the program, and partly by the federal government.

SOCIAL SECURITY FACES A CRISIS

Social security is, as we have noted, a pay-as-you-go system. That is, the benefits paid this year will come from the proceeds of this year's payroll taxes. As long as the economy and the labor force were expanding, as they were until the 1970s, the system worked. Congress even saw fit to increase benefit payments so that they would keep up with cost-of-living increases. These payments were to be financed out of increases in the social security tax rate. But the economy began to slow down just about the same time. Unemployment increased, and with fewer workers employed, taxes had to be raised still further to keep up with the benefit payments. In addition, the number of workers eligible for benefits was also growing. While in 1960 only 9 percent of the population was 65 years or older, in 1981 the proportion had reached 11 percent, and by the year 2000 it is expected to grow to 12 percent.

By 1983 it was clear that, in order to save the social security system, Congress would have to enact important changes in the law. Congress chose both to increase taxes and reduce benefits. Under the terms of the new legislation, the tax paid by employers and employees was scheduled to increase nearly 2 percent, to 15.3 percent, by 1990. In addition, retired people in the middle-income and upper-income brackets will have to pay income taxes on a portion of their pensions. Other changes reduced cost-of-living increases and raised the age at which young workers today will be eligible to receive full retirement benefits. Between the years 2003 and 2027, the retirement age will gradually rise from the present 65 years to 67 years.

1. About what percentage of the labor force is covered by social security?
2. What is OASDHI?
3. Summarize the benefits provided under Medicare.
4. Briefly summarize: (a) Since 1960, what has happened to the nation's birthrate and life expectancy? (b) How have these changes affected population distribution by age? (c) What problems have these trends created for the social security program?
5. What steps did Congress take in 1983 to save the social security system?

General Government. The funds in this category are used to carry out the everyday business of government as it is conducted by the White House and Congress.

Administration of Justice. This category provides the funding needed to finance the activities of the federal law enforcement agencies (such as the FBI), the courts system, and the *correctional* (prison and probation) facilities.

Energy. In the years following the end of World War II, America's economic growth was fueled by inexpensive, readily available crude oil. The pattern of continuous growth changed markedly after 1971 when domestic oil production reached its peak. Since that time the nation has had to rely more and more on expensive imported petroleum to meet its needs.

Funding for energy supports the programs designed to (1) protect the security and independence of the nation's energy supply; (2) promote energy production and conservation; (3) develop renewable sources of energy; and (4) increase the safety of nuclear power and the long-term disposal of nuclear wastes. (For a further discussion of pollution and economic growth, see Chapter 23.)

Commerce and Housing Credit. This category includes federal programs designed to assist small businesses and to provide credit for people wishing to purchase their own homes.

STATE AND LOCAL FINANCES

Ever since the end of World War II in 1945, government participation in the economy has increased dramatically. Spending by the federal government rose from $36 billion in 1946 to $657 billion in 1981, or multiplied 19 times over. As great as this increase in federal spending was, however, it was exceeded by state and local spending, which increased 35 times over, from $11 billion to $380 billion, during the same period. (See Table 11.3.)

TABLE 11.3   Government Spending in Selected Postwar Years (billions of dollars)

Year	State and Local	Federal
1946	$ 11	$ 36
1964	69	118
1981	380	657

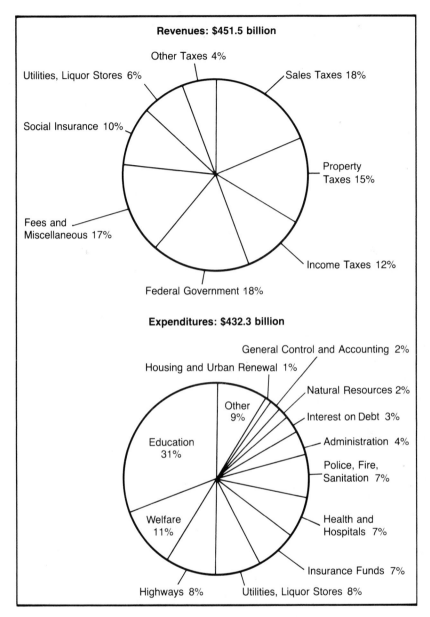

Revenues: $451.5 billion

Other Taxes 4%
Utilities, Liquor Stores 6%
Sales Taxes 18%
Social Insurance 10%
Property Taxes 15%
Fees and Miscellaneous 17%
Income Taxes 12%
Federal Government 18%

Expenditures: $432.3 billion

General Control and Accounting 2%
Housing and Urban Renewal 1%
Other 9%
Natural Resources 2%
Interest on Debt 3%
Education 31%
Administration 4%
Police, Fire, Sanitation 7%
Welfare 11%
Health and Hospitals 7%
Insurance Funds 7%
Highways 8%
Utilities, Liquor Stores 8%

FIGURE 11.2   Combined State and Local Government Budgets, 1980

Bear in mind that in describing "state and local governments" we are talking about more than 91,000 individual units. In addition to the 50 states, there are 3,000 counties, 18,000 municipalities, 35,000 townships and special districts, and 35,000 school districts. For this reason any description of their finances is, at best, a generalization.

With this in mind, we can draw certain conclusions about how the states and localities earn and spend their money. Table 11.4, by comparing data for 1946 and 1980, shows the enormous increases in state and local revenues and expenses. Figure 11.2 on page 225 shows the percentages of income received from various sources and how states and localities allocated their expenditures.

Sources of Revenues. In recent years, sales and property taxes, which are described further in Chapter 12, have been the principal source of tax revenues for states and localities. These governments in addition receive a sizable amount of money from the federal government, as you can see in Figure 11.2 and Table 11.4.

Expenditures: Education and Welfare. The largest single item of state and local expenses is for education, which accounts for 31 cents out of every dollar spent. State and local governments have expanded their welfare programs to aid the needy, the unemployed, the aged, and the physically handicapped. As a result welfare programs are now the second largest category of expense.

IMPACT OF GOVERNMENT SPENDING UPON THE ECONOMY

Resources employed for one purpose cannot be used for another. For example, if the nation's factories and workers are concentrating on producing military goods, production of civilian goods is sharply limited.

When our best scientists are using their energies for the exploration of space, they are not available to study other problems. In other words, when government decides to spend its money in one way, the resources it consumes are no longer available to produce other goods and services. In this way government directly affects how many of the nation's resources will be allocated (used).

The other sectors of the economy also affect resources—whatever they consume is no longer available. The difference, however, is that in the case of government spending the decision to spend or not to spend is more likely to take into consideration its effect upon the public.

TABLE 11.4 State and Local Government Finances, 1946 and 1980 (billions of dollars)

REVENUES

	1946	1980
Taxes:		
Property	$ 5.0	$ 68.5
Sales and gross receipts	3.0	79.9
Individual income	.4	42.1
Corporation income	.5	13.3
Other	1.3	19.6
Utilities and liquor stores	2.0	25.6
Retirement and unemployment insurance funds	1.5	43.7
Federal government grants-in-aid	.9	83.0
Fees for services	1.4	75.8
Total Revenues	$16.0	$451.5

EXPENDITURES

	1946	1980
Education	$ 3.4	$132.2
Highways	1.7	33.3
Public welfare	1.4	45.6
Health and hospitals	.9	32.2
Police, fire, and sanitation	1.1	32.4
Natural resources, parks, and recreation	.5	12.0
Housing and urban renewal	.1	6.1
Interest on debt	.4	14.7
Administration	.7	15.4
Utilities and liquor stores	1.7	36.2
Insurance funds (retirement and unemployment)	1.3	28.8
General control and accounting	—	8.7
Other	.9	33.7
Total Expenditures	$14.1	$432.3

EXERCISES

Multiple Choice

1. The principal reason for the growth of the federal debt in the years since 1900 has been (a) depressions (b) wars (c) the decline of tax receipts (d) reckless spending by the federal government.
2. Approximately how large is the federal debt *per capita?* (a) $1,000 (b) $2,000 (c) $3,000 (d) over $4,000.
3. The largest item of federal expenditures in recent years has been for (a) income security (b) space exploration (c) national defense (d) education.
4. The largest item of state and local expenditures in recent years has been for (a) income security (b) crime prevention (c) highway construction and maintenance (d) education.
5. A government's *budget* is a (a) summary of the money that was spent in previous years (b) statement of expenditures and income that took place during the preceding year (c) plan of income and expenses for the year to come (d) law to prevent the government from spending more than it earns.
6. When the government expects that its income will be more than its expenditures, (a) the budget will be described as "balanced" (b) there is a "deficit" in the budget (c) there is a "surplus" in the budget (d) the budget is said to be "allocated."
7. In recent years, expenditures by state and local governments (a) have been growing at a faster rate than federal expenditures (b) have remained about the same (c) have been growing, but at a slower rate than federal expenditures (d) have been declining.
8. Scientists who take part in the space shuttle program are not available to work on problems at home. This illustrates (a) the superiority of government-sponsored programs (b) the laws of supply and demand (c) the effect of government spending upon the allocation of resources (d) the law of diminishing returns.
9. Which of the following terms describes most of the yearly federal budgets illustrated in Table 11.1, on page 218? (a) balanced (b) deficit (c) surplus (d) allocated.
10. According to Table 11.2, on page 219, which taxes are the principal source of revenue for the federal government? (a) individual income taxes (b) corporation income taxes (c) social insurance taxes (d) excise taxes.
11. According to Table 11.4, on page 227, which item is the principal source of revenue for state and local governments? (a) individual income taxes (b) property, sales, and gross receipts taxes (c) federal grants (d) fees for services.
12. Approximately what percentage of the gross national product is

accounted for by government spending? (*a*) 5 percent (*b*) 10 percent (*c*) 20 percent (*d*) 40 percent.

13. Which of the following is an example of a *transfer* payment? (*a*) the army's purchase of 100 new tanks (*b*) a salary increase for postal workers (*c*) an allocation of funds to pay for a new high school (*d*) a social security payment to a retired person.

Essay Questions

1. Two speakers are discussing government spending and the American economy.

   SPEAKER A: "America has to decide what it wants to do first: land an astronaut on Mars, eliminate poverty at home, or stop the spread of communism."

   SPEAKER B: "With a three-trillion-dollar GNP, America can do anything it wants, provided it stops wasting its resources."

   (*a*) Explain the point of view held by each speaker.

   (*b*) With which speaker would you agree? Why?

2. "That government which governs best, governs least," summarizes the attitude probably held by most people during most of the nineteenth century. Since that time, however, the federal government has played an ever-expanding role in the nation's economy. (*a*) With reference to *three* events or developments that took place since 1900, show why the role of the government in the economic life of the nation was expanded. (*b*) In your view, was this expansion of governmental activities necessary? Explain your answer by referring to the events or developments described in (*a*).

3. Spending by state and local governments increased by over 35 times between 1946 and 1980. Identify and explain three reasons why the cost of government increased so dramatically.

4. Study a copy of the budget of your state or community for a recent year. With reference to its contents, answer the following questions: (*a*) What is the principal source of income for the state or community? (*b*) What is the principal item of expense? (*c*) Which expenditures do you think ought to be increased? Why? (*d*) How would you propose to pay for these additional items of expense? Which community groups do you suppose would object to your proposals?

CHAPTER 12

Taxation

Federal, state, and local governments combined raise some $750 billion in taxes each year, or about $3,000 for every man, woman, and child in the nation. This is a large bite out of personal income, and for that reason we must ask several questions. Why are taxes necessary? Who should pay them? What kinds of taxes do Americans pay? Is our tax system fair?

WHY ARE TAXES NECESSARY? THE FUNCTIONS OF TAXATION

1. Paying for the Cost of Government. As we saw in Chapter 11, the costs of government have been rising at a rapid rate as the responsibilities of government have increased. Costs will probably continue to mount as modern living becomes increasingly complex. Of course, some of the costs may be met out of charges levied for government services. Whenever you pay a toll to ride on a bridge or through a tunnel, you are paying a fee to some government for the transportation service it is providing. Similarly, those persons who live in the region serviced by the Tennessee Valley Authority, and who receive electricity from the government-owned utility, pay a fee for this service. Government may also pay some of its expenses by borrowing. Nevertheless, by far the most important source of income to all levels of government is taxes. Currently, taxes account for about 95 percent of federal and 60 percent of state and local income.

2. Redistribution of Income. When governments levy taxes, they are in effect taking income away from those who pay them. If some of these funds are then transferred to others, there is, in effect, a redistribution of wealth from those paying taxes to those receiving aid. Certain taxes, most notably the federal income tax, are designed with this principle in mind. For this reason, persons with higher incomes pay a larger percentage in taxes than those earning less money. Indeed, it has been estimated that one-fifth of all American families pay no income tax at all because their income falls below the

230

taxable minimum. Also, taxes are placed on "luxuries" on the theory that the poor will not have to pay them. The proceeds from either income taxes or "luxury" taxes can be used to pay for programs which help people with inadequate incomes.

3. Promoting Certain Industries. You will recall from your study of American history that protective tariffs—taxes on goods entering the country—were used to keep out foreign goods in order to stimulate the development of the nation's infant industries. The government still uses the tariff to protect certain of the nation's industries from foreign competition.

4. Influencing Consumer and Business Spending. Taxes may be used to make it either easier or more difficult for people to spend money. As we shall see in Chapter 17, the level of economic activity can be influenced by the amount of purchasing power in the hands of business and consumers. By either raising or lowering taxes, government can influence this purchasing power. For this reason, the federal government looks to taxation as one of the tools that it can use in its efforts to stabilize the economy.

Since taxes may discourage spending, governments have attempted to limit the consumption of certain goods by placing relatively high taxes on them. The taxes on tobacco and liquor are quite high partly for this reason. That is, many legislators have felt that people should be discouraged from drinking or smoking. Most authorities would probably agree that the attempt to restrict the consumption of these two items through the use of taxation has been a failure. Nevertheless, the taxes remain in force because they do provide all levels of government with a substantial source of income.

WHAT ARE THE INGREDIENTS OF A GOOD TAX SYSTEM?

In his *Wealth of Nations* (1776), Adam Smith set forth certain *criteria*, or standards, for judging a nation's tax system. To this day, economists refer to these standards in their evaluation of taxes.

1. Fairness. The first standard Smith set forth was that taxes should be fair, and taxpayers should believe that they are fair. For this reason, Smith called for the payment of taxes in proportion to income.

2. Clarity and Certainty. Everyone should be able to understand what the rate of the tax is and how it is to be paid. Smith felt that people would be more willing to pay their taxes if they knew what was expected of them. If, on the other hand, the tax was whatever the collector felt like charging, as was frequently the case in eighteenth-century Europe, people would be tempted to avoid it.

3. *Simplicity and Efficiency.* If the cost of collecting a tax was more than its yield, there would not be much point to levying the tax. Taxes should be easy to collect, difficult to evade, and inexpensive to administer.

To this list of Smith's standards, modern economists have added the following, which they consider an essential ingredient of any tax system:

4. *Flexibility.* Taxes should adjust to economic conditions. In times of general prosperity, people can afford to pay taxes that at other times might be a hardship. Business taxes that at one time are reasonable might at another time be oppressive.

Ideally, taxes should adjust themselves automatically to the state of the economy. In reality, however, few taxes are able to do this, but we can cite the income tax as a step in the right direction. When business booms and people's earnings increase, the income taxes they pay increase automatically. Similarly, during periods of recession and business decline, the tax bite is automatically reduced because people are earning less.

WHO SHOULD PAY TAXES?

In his first principle of taxation, Adam Smith raised what was, and still is, a most difficult question: "What makes a tax fair?" Or, to put it in another context: "Who should pay taxes, and in what amount?" Two approaches to this problem have emerged over the years: the *benefits-received principle* and the *ability-to-pay principle.*

1. *Benefits Received.* According to the *benefits-received* theory, taxes should be paid by those persons who benefit from the way in which the money will be spent. Thus a gasoline tax, the proceeds of which are used to pay for the building and maintenance of highways, is eminently fair, for the purchaser of gasoline obviously makes use of highways. In similar fashion, a bridge toll is fair if it is used to pay for the bridge's construction and maintenance. However, this theory has severe limitations. A tax to benefit the poor could not be paid by the poor. People with children in school could not very well be the only ones expected to pay for public schools. Public hospitals would be nonexistent, since patients who can afford hospital care usually go to private hospitals, and patients who use public hospitals could not support them.

2. Ability to Pay. If all taxes were based on the benefits-received theory, services would be denied to the people most in need. It is widely agreed, therefore, that taxes should be levied in accordance with a person's *ability to pay* them. This means that the people who are best able to afford to pay taxes should pay more than others. The "graduated" income tax is the classic application of the ability-to-pay principle because the percentage paid increases with a person's income.

Although most people would agree that the fairest method of taxation is one that is based on the ability-to-pay principle, exactly what constitutes "ability to pay" is not easily determined and has led to widespread controversy. This leads to the question of what kind of rates are most equitable: *progressive, proportional,* or *regressive.*

Progressive Taxes. The rate (percentage) of a progressive tax increases as the taxpayer's income increases. The federal income tax is an example of such a tax. Thus in 1982 a person with a taxable income of $6,500 paid $608 in taxes, which represented a rate of 9 percent. A person with a taxable income of $100,000 paid $41,318 in taxes, or 41 percent.

Proportional Taxes. The proportional tax would apply the same rate to all persons regardless of income. Suppose the rate were 30 percent. Then the person with a $15,000 income would pay a tax of $4,500, and the person with $150,000 would pay $45,000. This may seem fair on the surface, because the taxpayer earning $150,000 is paying ten times the tax of the taxpayer earning $15,000. However, if we apply *Engel's Law,* we find that a proportional tax is more of a burden to the poor than to the rich. (Ernst Engel was a nineteenth-century German statistician who pioneered studies of consumer behavior.)

According to Engel, the lower a family's income, the greater the percentage the family has to spend on the necessities of life. For example, a family of four earning $15,000 might have to put 70 percent of its income into food, clothing, and shelter, whereas a family of four earning $150,000 might be spending only 30 percent of its income for these necessities. The poor family has only $4,500 (30 percent of $15,000) available for luxuries, and the $4,500 tax payment takes it all. The wealthy family, on the other hand, has $105,000 (70 percent of $150,000) to spend on luxuries. The tax payment of $45,000 would take less than half of this total. In other words, the proportional tax took all the money available for luxuries from the poor family and less than one-half that amount from the rich. The unfairness of a proportional tax can be dramatized even further if we assume that the family earning $15,000 has to spend 90 percent of its income for necessities. In this case, taxes would actually take away some necessities from the low-income family.

The nearest thing to a proportional tax in this country is the social security tax, in which all wage earners pay the same percentage of their income. It is not a true proportional tax, however, since it is applied only up to a limited amount of income.

Regressive Taxes. A tax that takes a larger fraction from a low-income family than from a high-income family is called a regressive tax. Although the United States has no tax that specifically sets out to tax persons with low incomes at a higher rate than those with high incomes, some of our taxes are regressive in their effect.

The most common regressive taxes are sales and excise taxes. For example, the sales tax on a new automobile and the excise tax on gasoline are the same for all buyers, no matter what the buyers' personal incomes. But the *amount* of the tax represents a higher *percentage* of a poor family's total income. By applying Engel's Law to these situations, we see that regressive taxes are even more damaging to lower income families and individuals than are proportional taxes.

What Kinds of Taxes Do We Pay? We saw in Chapter 11 (Tables 11.2 and 11.4) the principal taxes collected by each of the three levels of government. The individual income tax is the principal source of revenue for the federal government. Sales and gross receipts taxes rank first with the states, and property taxes are by far the most important source of income to the localities.

FEDERAL TAXES: THE INDIVIDUAL INCOME TAX

The individual income tax, as the principal source of revenue for the federal government, is the tax with which most Americans are familiar. The income tax is a *progressive tax*—the percentage levied increases as one's income increases. In a recent year, for example, a married person paid 11 percent in taxes on income in excess of $3,400 but not more than $5,500. The tax rate increased until it reached a maximum of 50 percent on income over $162,400. (See Tax Rate Schedule, Table 12.1.)

As you can see from the tax schedule, each successive rate applies only to the income earned in excess of the preceding tax bracket. If, for example, a family's income increased from $18,000 to $24,000, the family would be moved into a higher tax bracket. In this case the

TABLE 12.1 Tax Rate Schedule Y, Married Taxpayers and Qualifying Widows and Widowers

IF LINE 5 IS:		THE TAX IS:	
Over	but not over		of the amount over
$ 0	$ 3,400	0	
3,400	5,500	— 11%	$ 3,400
5,500	7,600	$231 + 12%	5,500
7,600	11,900	483 + 14%	7,600
11,900	16,000	1,085 + 16%	11,900
16,000	20,200	1,741 + 18%	16,000
20,200	24,600	2,497 + 22%	20,200
24,600	29,900	3,465 + 25%	24,600
29,900	35,200	4,790 + 28%	29,900
35,200	45,800	6,274 + 33%	35,200
45,800	60,000	9,772 + 38%	45,800
60,000	85,600	15,168 + 42%	60,000
85,600	109,400	25,920 + 45%	85,600
109,400	162,400	36,630 + 49%	109,400
162,400	—	62,600 + 50%	162,400

family would find itself in the 22 percent bracket, whereas it was formerly in the 18 percent category. But the higher rate would apply only to that income it earned above the $20,200 level. For that reason taxpayers in a higher bracket are always left with more money after taxes than those in a lower bracket.

In calculating how much they must pay in income taxes, most families refer to the *tax tables* printed in the government's tax instruction booklet. In consulting the tax table from a recent year on page 236, we see the progressive feature of the income tax in action. A family with taxable income of $28,000 earned four times as much as one with an income of $7,000, but the former had to pay over 10 times as much in income taxes ($429 vs. $4,547). Meanwhile, a family with taxable income of $49,000 had to pay $11,624 in taxes. This amounted to over 27 times the amount paid by the family with $7,000 in taxable income.

Although the highest tax rates fall upon the rich, most of the tax revenue provided by the individual income tax comes from *middle-income* people. The latter, whose incomes in 1980 ranged from

TABLE 12.2 Tax Table for Persons With Taxable Incomes of Less Than $50,000

IF 1040A, LINE 19, OR 1040EZ, LINE 7 IS—		AND YOU ARE			
At least	but less than	Single	Married filing jointly	Married filing separately	Head of a household
		YOUR TAX IS			
7,000					
7,000	7,050	645	429	757	583
7,050	7,100	652	436	766	590
7,100	7,150	660	442	774	598
7,150	7,200	667	449	783	605
7,200	7,250	675	455	791	613
. . .					
28,000					
28,000	28,050	5,797	4,547	7,217	5,309
28,050	28,100	5,813	4,560	7,237	5,324
28,100	28,150	5,829	4,573	7,257	5,338
28,150	28,200	5,845	4,586	7,277	5,353
28,200	28,250	5,861	4,599	7,297	5,367
. . .					
49,000					
49,000	49,050	14,299	11,624	16,627	13,161
49,050	49,100	14,322	11,644	16,651	13,183
49,100	49,150	14,344	11,664	16,675	13,205
49,150	49,200	14,367	11,684	16,699	13,227
49,200	49,250	14,389	11,704	16,723	13,249

$20,000 to $50,000, paid almost half of the $213 billion collected that year. (See Table 12.3.)

The Income Tax in Everyday Life. The concept of an income tax seems simple enough. The government takes a certain percentage of each person's earnings in taxes. (See Figure 12.1 on page 238.) The amount paid varies directly with income. Much of the responsibility

TABLE 12.3 Federal Personal Income Taxes Collected, by Income Range, 1980 (billions of dollars)

Adjusted Gross Income		Taxes Collected (billions)		Percent of All Income Tax Collections	
Under $5,000		$ .5		.2	
$5,000 to $10,000		8.3		3.9	
$10,000 to $15,000		16.9		8.0	
$15,000 to $20,000		22.6		10.6	
$20,000 to $25,000	middle-	25.7		12.1	
$25,000 to $30,000	income	24.4	$103.9	11.5	48.9%
$30,000 to $50,000	families	53.8		25.3	
$50,000 to $100,000		29.5		13.8	
$100,000 to $500,000		24.2		11.4	
$500,000 to $1,000,000		3.0		1.4	
$1,000,000 and over		3.9		1.8	
Total Collected		$212.8			

for maintaining the tax system is left to individual taxpayers, who are expected to keep records, report income, calculate their taxes, and make payments. Employers routinely withhold income taxes from their employees' wages. Therefore, even the manner of payment has been made fairly painless.

The income tax system is really quite simple. Or is it?

In reality, there are often substantial differences between gross income and the income that is subject to taxation. These differences exist for three reasons. (1) Not everything that one receives as income is subject to taxation. (2) People may reduce their taxable incomes by applying certain exemptions and deductions. (3) Some taxpayers can reduce their liability still further by applying credits against their tax bill.

Income Not Subject to Taxation. Welfare benefits, inheritances, and most social security payments are examples of the kinds of income that need not be reported to the Internal Revenue Service (IRS). (The IRS is the federal government agency that collects taxes and enforces the tax laws.) Also tax-exempt are the interest payments on certain state and municipal bonds and most of the profits known as *long-term capital gains*. The latter are the moneys earned from the sale of property held for more than a year.

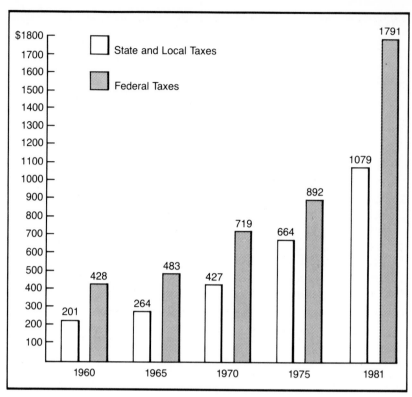

FIGURE 12.1   Tax Revenues per Capita, 1960–1981

Exemptions and Deductions. All taxpayers are entitled to exemptions of $1,000 each for their living expenses and those of each of their dependents. Thus a couple with three children may take $5,000 in exemptions against taxable income. The effect of these exemptions is to relieve millions of low-income persons from income tax liability. Exemptions also reduce the administrative burden of collecting many small sums.

Other exemptions are also known as deductions and may be taken to reduce the amount of income subject to taxation. Regardless of the size or nature of their earnings, all taxpayers are entitled to a standard deduction. This deduction ranges from $1,700 if the taxpayers are married and filing separately from their spouses, to $2,300 if they are single, and $3,400 if they are married and filing jointly with their spouses. The deduction is known as the "zero-bracket amount," because it has the effect of leaving many people in a "zero" tax bracket—of owing no taxes. Deductions may also be taken for state and local income and sales taxes, property taxes, interest on debt, charitable contributions, and medical expenses. Other deductions are allowed for certain business and professional expenses.

Income Tax Credits. After adjusting their incomes to eliminate those items not subject to tax, and reducing that amount by the deductions and exemptions to which they are entitled, taxpayers then calculate their taxes on the remaining balance. This amount too may be reduced by taxpayers who are entitled to certain credits. Tax credits have two purposes. One purpose is to encourage certain activities, such as the modernization of home heating systems to save energy, contributions to political campaigns, and participation in job programs. In each instance part of the taxpayers' expenses may be applied against taxes owed. The second purpose of tax credits is to aid directly such special groups as the elderly with limited incomes and working families with dependent children.

Opinions Differ on the Income Tax. People who favor the personal income tax stress its progressive character and the effect this has on

The Flat Tax: A Proposal to Simplify the Income Tax

Much of the controversy surrounding the individual income tax results from the complex loopholes, deductions, credits, and incentives that have crept into the system over the years. Most of these methods to reduce taxes would be eliminated by the *flat tax*, a proposal that has attracted considerable attention. Simply stated, a flat tax applies a single rate to all income above a certain level. Virtually no deductions or exemptions are permitted. Since people would be taxed on the full amount of their earnings, tax rates could be significantly lower than they are now. A flat-rate system, its supporters claim, would discourage many of the schemes (some legal, some not) to avoid paying taxes.

Opposition to the flat-tax proposal comes from people or groups who benefit directly from the deductions and loopholes in the present laws. Charitable organizations fear losing income if contributions are no longer tax-deductible. State and local governments worry about what will happen to their borrowing ability if the interest on their bonds is no longer exempt from taxation. The real estate industry foresees a decline in home sales and building if mortgage interest payments cannot be deducted from taxes.

Similarly, people who represent the interests of the poor and the needy are wary of the flat tax. They fear that the elimination of those features of the tax law favoring the less fortunate (like the $1,000 exemption for each dependent, and the tax credits for the elderly) would cause many hardships.

PERSONAL ECONOMICS

Filing an Income Tax Return

If you held a job last year and earned more than $3,300, you are required by law to file an income tax return. If you earned less than $3,300, but *income taxes were withheld from your wages,* you are entitled to a refund of that money. In order to obtain it, you must file a tax return.

Employers must by law withhold a portion of their employees' wages in each pay period and send these moneys to the government. When individuals file their returns, they calculate how much they owed in taxes on the previous year's income. The difference between the amount withheld and the amount owed is either returned to the taxpayer (if there was an overpayment) or paid to the government (if the amount withheld was not sufficient to cover the total amount of taxes owed).

Although preparing an income tax return can sometimes be quite complicated, it is a simple matter for most single people with part-time jobs. If you fall into this category (and either earned over $3,300 or had income taxes withheld last year), you will want to file a Form 1040EZ Income Tax Return. Figure 12.2 shows just how simple the 1040EZ is to prepare.

In 1984 Jean LaRue had a job after school and during the summer at the local supermarket. In the course of the year, Jean earned $4,940 at the supermarket and paid $401 in withholding taxes. Jean also has a savings account that paid $184 in interest last year. Over the year Jean gave money to several charities and was able to deduct $5 for these contributions.

Jean completed the 1040EZ as is shown in Figure 12.2. As line 2 indicates, interest earned on savings accounts and other sources is subject to taxation. But a portion of one's donations to charity may be deducted from taxable income (line 4).

The federal government allows each taxpayer a $1,000 exemption for living expenses. That amount appears on line 6.

The total earnings subject to income taxes are entered on line 7 of the return ($4,119). The amount of tax that Jean owes on total earnings is found in the tax table accompanying the 1040EZ instruction booklet. In this case, Jean owes $208.

As we know, $401 was withheld for taxes by Jean's employer (line 8). The difference between what Jean owes and what was withheld is $193, which Jean will receive by refund check from the federal government.

Department of the Treasury · Internal Revenue Service

Form 1040EZ Income Tax Return for
1984 **Single filers with no dependents** (0)

OMB No. 1545-0675

Name & address

If you don't have a label, please print:

Please write your numbers like this.

1234567890

JEAN LA RUE
Write your name above (first, initial, last)

1563 MAIN STREET, N.W.
Present home address (number and street)

OGDEN, UT 84403
City, town, or post office, state, and ZIP code

Social security number

462 05 1397

Presidential Election Campaign Fund
Check box if you want $1 of your tax to go to this fund. ▶

☑

Figure your tax

1 Wages, salaries, and tips. Attach your W-2 form(s). | 1 | 4 940 00

2 Interest income of $400 or less. If more than $400, you cannot use Form 1040EZ. | 2 | 184 00

Attach Copy B of Form(s) W-2 here

3 Add line 1 and line 2. This is your **adjusted gross income**. | 3 | 5 124 00

4 Allowable part of your charitable contributions. Complete the worksheet on page 19. Do not write more than $25. | 4 | 5 00

5 Subtract line 4 from line 3. | 5 | 5 119 00

6 Amount of your personal exemption. | 6 | 1 000 00

7 Subtract line 6 from line 5. This is your **taxable income**. | 7 | 4 119 00

8 Enter your Federal income tax withheld. This should be shown in Box 9 of your W-2 form(s). | 8 | 401 00

9 Use the tax table on pages 29-34 to find the **tax** on your taxable income on line 7. Write the amount of tax. | 9 | 208 00

Refund or amount you owe

10 If line 8 is larger than line 9, subtract line 9 from line 8. Enter the **amount of your refund.** | 10 | 193 00

Attach tax payment here

11 If line 9 is larger than line 8, subtract line 8 from line 9. Enter the **amount you owe.** Attach check or money order for the full amount, payable to "Internal Revenue Service." | 11 |

Sign your return

I have read this return. Under penalties of perjury, I declare that to the best of my knowledge and belief, the return is true, correct, and complete.

Your signature | Date

X Jean LaRue | 4/1/85

For Privacy Act and Paperwork Reduction Act Notice, see page 38.

FIGURE 12.2   Tax Return 1040EZ for 1984

income distribution. By taking more from the wealthy and less from the poor, the income tax helps to break down income differences. The tax also helps the economy, because more people are left with the purchasing power they need to buy the goods and services produced by the nation's industries.

Critics of the income tax seem to fall into two categories. The first group maintains that the income tax discriminates in favor of well-to-do people. Numerous deductions and credits reduce the amount of individual income that is subject to taxation. These *tax loopholes*, as they are called, enable many people to avoid paying taxes that they could—and sometimes should—pay. So, for example, wealthy individuals in the 50 percent tax bracket can convert much of their income to long-term capital gains, which are subject to a maximum tax of only 20 percent. Similarly, a person with $1 million to invest could buy municipal bonds. These bonds would give the investor a return of $100,000 or more each year in tax-free interest (with, of course, a promise to return the $1 million when the bonds mature).

Other critics of the income tax argue that it discriminates against the rich and thereby discourages incentive and investment. Suppose, for example, that our wealthy person had been considering the investment of $1 million in a new factory. Our investor learned that a 25 percent return on investments was reasonable. This would amount to $250,000 a year.

"Sounds great," you say. "After all, $250,000 is a lot of money."

But wait—our investor is in the 50 percent tax bracket. That would leave only $125,000 after taxes. Compare this to an investment in tax-free bonds, which might return $100,000 or more each year at *substantially less risk*.

After comparing the alternatives, the investor chose to skip the factory and put the money into bonds. Incentive and private investment were discouraged.

In reply to these arguments, supporters of the income tax say that many of the so-called tax loopholes (capital gains provisions and deductions for charitable contributions) stimulate investment and promote the general welfare.

OTHER FEDERAL TAXES

1. The Corporate Income Tax. About 10 cents of every dollar raised by the federal government comes from the income tax on corporations. Like the individual income tax, the corporate income tax is based on a simple principle: The taxes on net profits increase proportionately with the size of the profit. Defining what constitutes net profit can

The Underground Economy: A Drain on Us All

"I can paint your apartment next week. But you should know that I work only *for cash*."

"Why?"

"I do not want to report it on my income tax."

"But that is illegal."

"Yes. But if you do not tell, no one will find out."

There is a sector of the United States economy whose activities are not included in government statistics on the gross national product, the consumer price index, the economic indicators—or anything else, for that matter. This sector is known as the "underground economy." Its participants conceal the income from their activities because they are attempting to evade paying taxes on this income, the activities themselves are illegal, or both.

Who are these income producers in the "underground economy"? Some are criminals whose unlawful activities will land them in jail once they are caught. Far more of them, however, are people from many walks of life who have found ways to conceal from the government the financial details of their otherwise legal activities. Shopkeepers and professionals who fail to ring up cash sales or report cash payments fall into this category. So, too, do those who fail to report their tips or who trade one thing of value for another.

How large is the underground economy? Any estimate as to the size of unreported and illegal transactions must remain just that, an estimate. Government economists, however, have arrived at some figures that are astounding. Starting with the assumption that all underground activity relies upon the use of cash, they have compared the amount of currency required to conduct the reported volume of business with the amount actually in circulation. The excess of cash provided the basis for the estimates of the size of the underground economy and amounted to between 10 and 15 percent of the reported gross national product, or *$350 to $500 billion a year.* (This amount is more than the combined GNPs of Finland, Greece, Iceland, New Zealand, Norway, Portugal, and Turkey.)

"What," you ask, "has all this got to do with me? Why should I care if some people are getting away with not paying their taxes?"

Unfortunately, the underground economy hurts us all. For one thing, it means that fewer of us must share the cost of government. Thus the

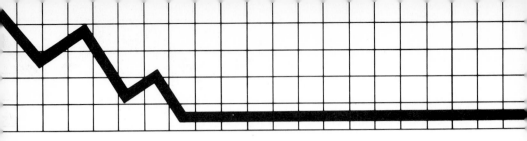

taxes we pay are higher than they would be if all taxpayers paid their fair share.

The underground economy also gives government planners and others a distorted picture of the economy as it actually exists. This distortion, too, places us all in jeopardy. For example, the federal government relies upon certain data when deciding whether to increase or decrease the nation's money supply. If, because of the $400 billion in the underground economy, the government errs in its planning, an inflation that might otherwise have been brought under control will continue.

Finally, a large sector of the labor force may be more interested in money earned in the underground economy than in money earned in the legitimate economy. The money that is escaping taxation may be valued more highly by its producers than taxable income. If this is true, productivity may be adversely affected. If, for example, the refrigerator assembly line worker pays less attention to a daytime job than to an after-hours, cash-only appliance-repair business, the worker's daytime efficiency may be affected.

Most Americans still report their earnings and pay their taxes in full when they are due. But it appears that the burden of paying for those who are not meeting their obligations is becoming heavier.

1. What is meant by the "underground economy"?
2. According to the pie chart (Figure 12.3), what were the sources of income in the underground economy?
3. Why is the underground economy described as a "drain on us all"?
4. "Any estimate of the amount of money circulating in the underground economy will always be more a guess than a *fact*." Explain this statement.
5. How does the underground economy complicate the government's job of monitoring our nation's economy?

become quite complicated, however, and frequently requires the services of accountants and lawyers.

The corporate income tax has also received the following criticisms:

1. The corporate tax subjects the owners of corporations (the stockholders) to double taxation because corporations are taxed on their profits, and the stockholders are taxed on the dividends they receive from those profits.

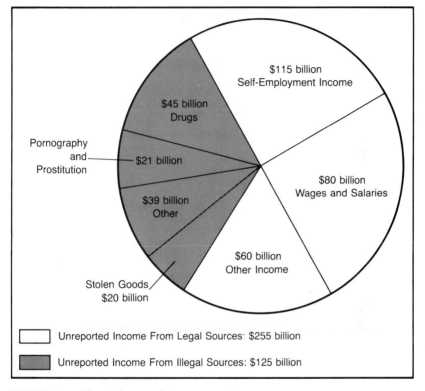

FIGURE 12.3   The Underground Economy, 1981

6. In what way does the underground economy pose a threat to American *productivity?*

7. What do you think should be done about the underground economy? Explain your answer.

2. The corporate tax discourages economic growth because the money taken by government might have been used by corporations to expand their production.

3. Unlike the individual income tax, which cannot be shifted, the incidence of the corporate tax is uncertain. Some or all of the corporate income tax may be passed on to consumers in the form of higher prices, thereby increasing the cost of living.

Taxation

Those favoring the corporate tax argue that the government is able to tap a source of revenue that might otherwise avoid taxation. Since corporations do not have to distribute all their profits, were it not for the income tax, money that the corporations retained would not be taxed. Stockholders could then use the capital gains provisions of the individual income tax law to cash in on those savings some time in the future.

2. Excise Taxes. Excise taxes are levied on the manufacture or sale of particular goods or services. These taxes account for 6 cents out of every dollar collected by the government. Those who pay an excise tax usually pass its cost along to the final consumer. If competition is strong or the product is subject to relatively elastic demand, however, producers are likely to absorb some or all of the excise tax themselves.

Politicians are frequently attracted to excise taxes because people are often unaware that they are paying them. Excise taxes thus are likely to be regressive. While many items are subject to an excise tax, nearly three-fifths of the government's receipts come from taxes on alcoholic beverages, gasoline, and tobacco. These are mass-consumption goods, on which poor families spend a larger percentage of their incomes than wealthy ones. However, when taxes are levied on luxuries such as yachts and furs, they are neither as regressive nor as lucrative.

3. Estate and Gift Taxes. The estate tax is levied on a person's property at the time of death. The purpose of the tax, in addition to raising revenue, is to prevent the creation of a class of idle rich people who acquire wealth and property through inheritance rather than their own efforts. Most people are not affected by estate taxes because the law allows a sizable exemption. Meanwhile, the truly wealthy can use a variety of legal accounting devices to reduce the impact of the estate tax.

The gift tax was created to prevent wealthy persons from giving their property away so that their heirs would escape paying estate taxes. Thus, gifts in excess of specified limits are subject to federal taxation.

4. Social Security Tax. The social security tax (known as FICA, for the Federal Insurance Contributions Act) is a payroll tax designed to pay the costs of the old age, survivors, and unemployment insurance features of the social security program. About 30 cents out of every dollar received by the federal government comes from the social security tax. Wage earners and their employers pay the same percentage of the workers' salaries into the social security system. The social security tax is sometimes described as an income tax in reverse because it taxes income only *under* a certain limit ($57,000 in 1990).

STATE AND LOCAL TAXES

1. Sales and Gross Receipts Taxes. "Let's see now. These items you've bought add up to $15.65. The tax on that amount is $1.25. So the total bill is $16.90, please." Everyone who lives in a state or community that has a sales tax will recognize this dialog. *Sales taxes* are levied on the value of certain retail sales of goods and services. These taxes are usually added as a percent of the sales price. Sales taxes are collected and forwarded to the government by the seller, and they are paid by consumers who are informed at the time of sale that the tax is being added to their bill.

Gross receipts taxes are business taxes levied by certain states and communities. These taxes are calculated as a percentage (usually a fraction of one percent) of a firm's receipts from wholesale as well as retail activities. Gross receipts taxes may or may not be shifted. When these taxes are shifted, the buyers are likely to be unaware that they paid them.

Sales and gross receipts taxes are the principal sources of income to the states. Sales taxes are popular among the states because they are easy to collect and administer, and because they yield much money. As we have previously noted, sales taxes are often regressive in that they constitute a heavier burden for the poor than the rich. In order to make the sales tax less regressive, many states and localities exempt certain necessities such as food, medicine, and rent.

Sales taxes are not as responsive to economic growth or contraction as the income tax. As a consequence, the states and localities using this tax have found that their revenues have not risen with prosperity. This is true because, as income increases, people tend to spend more of their income for services and to put a larger percentage of it into savings.

A major criticism of gross receipts taxes is that they favor firms doing business outside the state. Receipts from out-of-state sales may not be taxed by a state because of a provision of the federal Constitution.

2. Property Taxes. As we saw in Table 11.4, property taxes are a major source of income to state and local governments. These taxes fall into two categories: *real property taxes,* which are levied upon homes and land; and *personal property taxes,* which are levied on such items as jewelry, furniture, securities, clothing, and automobiles. Of the two, the tax on real property is by far the more important.

In administering this tax, the locality *assesses*, or evaluates, each taxpayer's holdings. This total *assessment* serves as the basis for the establishment of the tax rate. Thus, if the community needs $1 million in revenue for the coming year and the total assessed valuation of all the taxpayers' holdings is $100 million, the tax rate for that year will be one percent.

The property tax rate is applied uniformly throughout a community regardless of the taxpayer's ability to pay. It is therefore often particularly regressive. For example, if two families live in identically assessed homes, they will both pay the same tax. However, it is quite possible for one family to be wealthier than another. The tax can cause special hardships for a family with many children that needs a large home but is not particularly rich, or for an elderly couple with a limited income.

Property taxes have also been criticized for lacking a uniform method of assessment. As a result, some property may be overvalued and some undervalued. In general, studies have shown that smaller properties are more likely to be overvalued than larger properties. This again tends to make the tax regressive. In addition, personal property is easy to hide and therefore may go unassessed and untaxed.

It has also been pointed out that it is difficult to adjust the property tax to the times. Thus people have lost their property for failure to pay taxes because the tax was not adjusted to reflect periods of depression or decreasing values resulting from declining neighborhoods.

Some critics also complain that the property tax discourages home improvement because this increases the value of property and, therefore, the homeowner's taxes.

Opposition to the property tax came to a head in 1978 in California when Proposition 13 was passed overwhelmingly in a statewide referendum (vote). Proposition 13 required that property taxes be rolled back to the level of former years and limited the amount by which these taxes could be increased.

Ever since, the success—or lack of it—of Proposition 13 has been the subject of debate both in and out of California. On the one hand, its advocates say that the tax reductions have attracted so many new businesses and jobs to the state that tax revenues have actually risen and government services have been maintained or even increased over earlier years.

On the other hand, critics argue that Proposition 13 has been a disaster. They claim that important government services have been reduced or curtailed in many communities. And California itself, which had an income surplus before 1979, has run a deficit every year since then. This deficit is a direct result, critics claim, of

"Hutchins, what on earth gave you the notion that we want the rich to get poorer and the poor to get richer?"
Drawing by Handelsman; © 1984 *The New Yorker Magazine, Inc.*

California's reduced ability to collect taxes and the need to help the many communities hurt by Proposition 13.

3. Highway Taxes. These taxes are classified under the benefits-received theory and are levied in the form of gasoline taxes, license fees for motor vehicles, and tolls. Highway taxes often raise more than the cost of highway maintenance and construction, whereupon the surplus is put into the general fund of the state or locality.

4. Income Taxes. These taxes are in use in most states and in a few localities. Income taxes currently account for about one-quarter of the tax dollars raised by the states and 6 percent of the funds raised by localities.

5. Inheritance Taxes. These taxes are similar to the estate taxes levied by the federal government.

6. Payroll and Business Taxes. Collected in a variety of forms by the state and local governments, payroll and other business taxes are often used to finance unemployment insurance programs, as well as health, disability, and retirement programs.

INCIDENCE OF TAXES: WHO REALLY PAYS THE TAX?

In many cases, the person who turns tax money over to the government is not the person who really paid it. This occurs when the person paying the tax is able to *shift* the burden to someone else. If you look at the sign on the gasoline pump at a gas station, you will see that the price quoted includes a certain amount of money that will be turned over to the government. In this case, the person who actually pays the tax is you, the consumer of the gasoline.

The *incidence* of taxation refers to who really pays the tax. *Shifting* describes the process of passing the tax on to someone else. Taxes that can be shifted to other persons are *indirect taxes.* Taxes that cannot be shifted are *direct taxes.*

Indirect Taxes. These taxes are usually levied on goods and services rather than on people, and for this reason they are easier to shift. Excise taxes, sales taxes, and tariffs are examples of indirect taxes because the person who pays the tax to the government is usually able to shift the burden to someone else.

Although sales taxes are usually added to the posted price, excise taxes and tariffs are not. Instead, the latter are included in the posted price, and for that reason buyers are frequently unaware that they are paying the taxes. This explains why excise taxes and tariffs are frequently referred to as "hidden taxes."

Direct Taxes. The personal income tax, the property tax on a private home, and the inheritance tax are all examples of direct taxes that are levied on persons and cannot be shifted.

Effects of Tax Incidence. The question of tax *incidence* is important because it affects the economy as a whole. Suppose, for example, that a tax is levied on wheat. Will the cost of the tax be passed on to the consumer in the form of higher bread prices? Will the cost be absorbed by the farmers in lower profits? Or will the cost be taken up by the millers and bakers or by their employees (in the form of lower wages)? Any of these alternatives, or a combination of them, is possible. We might also wonder about the impact of a wheat tax on competing products such as rye and oats.

Before enacting a new tax law, governments generally try to determine what the incidence of the levy will be. Unfortunately, no one has yet devised a foolproof method of predicting how a tax will be shifted, and for that reason it is not possible to predict with 100 percent accuracy the economic effects of new tax legislation.

GRANT-IN-AID PROGRAMS

Grants-in-aid are sums given for a specific purpose by the federal government to states and localities, or by states to localities. Though not a tax, a grant is a very important source of income. In 1981 federal grants-in-aid totaled $85 billion, or a little more than 20 percent of the total receipts of the states and localities.

The use of grants-in-aid is another example of how the power to tax can be used to redistribute income, for the grants usually go to areas that are in need. For example, federal grants-in-aid have been given to states to help them set up child care centers, provide unemployment insurance, and aid the handicapped. Grant-in-aid programs are also valuable in that they can stimulate the states into taking action in fields that they had neglected in the past. This is accomplished by including "matching" provisions according to which federal aid is given only if the states also make an appropriation. The Interstate Highway Act set up a program of this kind by granting nine dollars of federal funds for every dollar of state funds appropriated for the construction of highways.

In similar fashion, states give financial aid to their cities, counties, townships, and special districts. In recent years, most of this assistance has been for education.

IS THE NATION'S TAX SYSTEM WORKING WELL?

People frequently complain about the taxes they pay. Taxes are hardly a new problem. Even the Bible discusses them. Despite their antiquity, however, taxes are of as real concern to present-day Americans as they were to the ancients. Government spending has reached record high levels, and the end of this growth does not seem to be in sight. Since taxes represent the share of the total cost of government that all citizens must bear, it is only natural that they should want to feel that their shares are fairly apportioned. Indeed, history has shown that taxpayers may be expected to react quite vigorously if they feel that they are being discriminated against while other groups are favored. Both the American and French revolutions illustrate the often devastating consequences of economic inequity.

Equity, or fairness, is not the only concern of taxpayers. They know that tax programs may also be used either to stimulate or to slow down the economy. Because there are times when one or the other action is called for, they want to feel that those responsible for making the decisions are doing so with wisdom.

While many economists would agree that our tax system has performed its role adequately, virtually all of them would like to see improvements in it. Governments on all levels appear to share this view, for the existing tax structures are a subject of persistent study and discussion.

EXERCISES

Multiple Choice

1. Last year A earned $5,000, B earned $50,000, and C earned $500,000. Under the terms of a special tax passed that year, A paid $50, B $500, and C $5,000. What kind of tax did they pay? (*a*) regressive (*b*) progressive (*c*) proportional (*d*) none of these.

2. Suppose that instead of paying the taxes described in Question 1, A paid 10 percent of income, B 25 percent, and C 50 percent. The tax would now be described as (*a*) regressive (*b*) progressive (*c*) proportional (*d*) none of these.

3. Suppose that instead of the taxes described in 1 and 2 above, it was announced that in the interest of fairness, all families would pay the same tax, $100, regardless of income. Such a tax would be (*a*) regressive (*b*) progressive (*c*) proportional (*d*) none of these.

4. Which type of tax falls most heavily on families with low incomes? (*a*) personal income tax (*b*) inheritance tax (*c*) sales tax (*d*) bridge and highway tolls.

5. Which of the following types of revenue is based upon the benefits-received principle? (*a*) income tax (*b*) sales tax (*c*) property tax (*d*) highway tolls.

6. Base your answer to this question on the information contained in Table 12.3, on page 237. Suppose the government increased everyone's income taxes by 10 percent. Which of the following income categories would give the government the greatest amount of revenue? (*a*) $15,000 –$20,000 (*b*) $500,000 to $1 million (*c*) $1 million and over (*d*) under $5,000.

7. In the United States, taxation may be used to accomplish all of the following *except* (*a*) redistribute income (*b*) reduce purchasing power (*c*) discourage the consumption of specific goods (*d*) promote the purchase of particular brands of merchandise.

8. Which of the following is the best example of an ability-to-pay tax? (*a*) income tax (*b*) sales tax (*c*) property tax (*d*) bridge and highway toll.

9. The incidence of taxation refers to (*a*) the size of a tax (*b*) the importance of a tax (*c*) the group responsible for collecting a particular tax (*d*) the group that actually pays a tax.

10. The process of passing taxes on to others is called (*a*) incidence (*b*) shifting (*c*) buck-passing (*d*) a nuisance tax.

11. A tax that cannot be passed along to someone else is called (*a*) an indirect tax (*b*) a direct tax (*c*) an excise tax (*d*) a tariff.

12. The tax yielding the most revenue to cities, towns, and villages is (*a*) the income tax (*b*) the sales tax (*c*) the property tax (*d*) an excise tax.

13. A commonly heard criticism of high progressive income tax rates is that (a) they fall more heavily on the poor than the rich (b) they tend to stifle incentive at the upper levels (c) they are regressive at the upper levels (d) they are too difficult to collect.

14. States that rely most heavily on sales and excise taxes for their income have had difficulty in paying for the cost of government in recent years because (a) these taxes are difficult to collect (b) these taxes are indirect (c) taxpayers are able to avoid payment by shopping out of state (d) tax receipts do not automatically expand with the growth of the economy.

15. The property tax is regressive because (a) it is terribly old-fashioned (b) it is based upon assessed valuation, not income (c) the rich pay heavier taxes on their homes than the poor (d) property assessors do not allow for changes in the cost of living.

Essay Questions

1. Although it is commonly thought that the most important job of the federal income tax is to pay for the cost of government, of equally great significance for the economy as a whole are some of its other functions. Among these we would include the following: (a) The income tax places resources in public, rather than in private, hands. (b) The income tax influences the pattern of income distribution. (c) The income tax affects the level of total private spending in the economy. Show how the federal income tax seeks to achieve *two* of these functions.

2. According to Adam Smith and others, a good tax should have the following features: (1) fairness (2) clarity and certainty (3) convenience of payment (4) ease of administration (5) flexibility. With reference to *three* of these criteria, evaluate the (a) personal income tax (b) sales tax (c) real estate tax.

3. In recent years, states and localities have had increasing difficulty in meeting the rising cost of government. (a) By comparing their sources of income with those of the federal government, discuss the reasons why they are having these financial difficulties. (b) What proposal would you suggest that would help states and localities obtain adequate revenues?

4. In 1980 United States citizens with incomes of $1 million or more were able to reduce the amount of their income subject to taxation by applying deductions that averaged $505,000 per return. Explain the meaning of the statement.

5. There are those who argue that the income tax works a particular hardship on the wealthy and for that reason is harmful to the nation. Others claim that the income tax favors the wealthy over other income classes. Explain each of these points of view.

Money should be durable, portable, divisible, uniform, easily recognizable, and relatively scarce.

UNIT VI

Money, Credit, and Banking

CHAPTER 13

Money in Economic Society

Suppose that a modern-day Robinson Crusoe were to find himself on a desert island, completely out of touch with civilization. Suppose that, in his search for food and water, he were to come upon a chest containing a million dollars in United States currency. Would his situation be improved? Hardly. What could he buy on an uninhabited island? Our Robinson Crusoe would have learned a fundamental lesson in economics: Money has value only when it can be exchanged for goods and services. With no one from whom to buy (and with nothing to buy), a million dollars would be worthless.

If money did not exist, the only way that a person could acquire things would be to exchange something of value for the desired items. Such an exchange is called *barter*.

The barter system works well on a simple level when, for example, someone with a hunger for fish and a rabbit to swap can find a person with a fish and a yearning for rabbit stew. But barter has serious shortcomings. Consider, for example, the case of the farmer with a cow to swap. If the farmer wants a dozen eggs, how will the egg seller make change? What will the farmer do if the egg seller does not want a cow?

MONEY: HISTORICAL BACKGROUND

The invention of money eliminated the problems of the barter economy. *Money is anything that is generally accepted in payment for goods and services.*

Many things have served as money in the past. The ancient Romans used salt. The Aztec in Mexico used cacao beans. Fishhooks, arrowheads, and shells were money to some Native Americans, as were furs and tobacco to the European explorers and colonists in the New World. During World War II, American prisoners of war developed a mini-economy based on the use of cigarettes as a kind of money.

Because money was generally more acceptable if it was durable and easy to carry, metallic money became popular early in the history of civilization. Around the year 2500 BC, the Egyptians produced one of the earliest kinds of metallic money in the form of rings. About 400 years later, the Chinese began using gold cubes as money. The first metal coins were struck in the eighth century BC by the Lydians, a people who lived in Asia Minor.

The first people to develop paper money were the Chinese; Marco Polo reported on its use in the late 1200s. During the late Middle Ages, merchants and other travelers sought to protect themselves from highway robbers by exchanging their gold coins (which the robbers wanted) for goldsmiths' receipts (which were useless to the robbers). The receipts could be exchanged back to coins by designated goldsmiths in other cities. In time, the receipts became so popular that people used them to pay debts without bothering to exchange them for coins.

FUNCTIONS OF MONEY

If money is doing its job, it will perform the following functions:

1. Medium of Exchange. With money, a woodcutter who wants shoes does not have to find a shoemaker who wants wood. Or, to use a more modern example, a welder who wants shoes does not have to find a shoestore owner who needs some welding. The welder can sell his services to anyone because the money that he receives in payment will also be accepted by the owner of the shoestore, who can then exchange it for the things she wants. In this way, money serves as a medium of exchange.

2. Standard of Value. Money provides a convenient standard with which we can express the value of different items. Thus a paperback book selling for $5 is equal in value to ten candy bars selling for 50 cents a piece. All goods and services can be measured by the yardstick of their monetary value.

3. Store of Value. Because money can be saved for future use, it provides a store of value. Thus our egg merchant can save the money earned from the sale of eggs and use the savings at a later date to buy an expensive item.

CHARACTERISTICS OF MONEY

We have already indicated that anything can be called money if it is generally accepted by society. Experience has shown, however, that good money will possess the following characteristics:

1. Durability. Money should have the ability to stand up under use.
2. Portability. Money should be light enough to be carried.
3. Divisibility. Unlike an egg, money should be capable of being divided into change.
4. Uniformity. Every unit of money should be similar to every other unit of that denomination.
5. Ease of Recognition. Money should be identifiable as such by everyone who sees it.
6. Relative Scarcity. In order to be usable, money should be scarce. If it is too easily obtainable, people will be able to pay whatever price is asked, and prices will continue to rise until money becomes worthless.

Gresham's Law. In the sixteenth century, the English financier Sir Thomas Gresham observed that when two or more kinds of money having the same nominal value circulate, the one considered more valuable is hoarded and disappears from circulation. Since that time the principle that "cheap money drives out dear (expensive) money" has been known as *Gresham's Law*.

During and immediately following the Revolutionary War, the American colonists saw Gresham's Law in action, as metallic money all but disappeared from circulation. What had happened was that people spent the distrusted paper dollars issued by the Continental Congress and hoarded silver and gold coins, which they felt had more certain value.

WHAT KINDS OF MONEY DO AMERICANS USE?

1. Currency. Currency is money issued by the federal government. Anyone else or any other group or organization attempting to produce money is guilty of *counterfeiting*, which is a serious offense. All United States currencies are *legal tender*. This means that they must be accepted in payment for debts. Thus, if you owe a store $1,000, it does not have to accept your jewelry or even your check in payment, but it must accept your currency.

Currency-Making. This government printing press can manufacture sheets of currency at the rate of 7,000 an hour. How does the government protect itself against counterfeiters?

All United States currencies are known as *fiat* money. This money has value because the government says it does, not because of its intrinsic (natural) value. Thus a dime consists of copper and nickel, which would be worth far less than ten cents if the dime were melted down for its metallic content. Similarly, the paper upon which a $5 bill is printed is hardly worth anything at all. While there once was a time when the "melt value" of coins was close to their face value, and a certain quantity of precious metal (gold and silver) "backed" paper currency, this is no longer the case (see page 264 for a further discussion).

$10,000 in Fiat Money. The government no longer prints currency in denominations larger than $100. It is legal, however, to spend any $10,000 bills you may happen to have in your possession.

There are, then, two kinds of currency presently in use in the United States: *coins* and *paper currency.*

Coins, or "Fractional Currency." Pennies, nickels, dimes, quarters, and half-dollars, our *fractional currency,* are produced primarily for the convenience of making change. In addition, a small number of coins worth $1 are also produced. Coins are *token* money, so called because their metallic value is far less than their face value. In all, coins make up about 3 percent of the nation's money supply.

Paper Currency. Virtually all the paper currency in circulation today is in the form of *Federal Reserve notes.* These notes are issued by the twelve banks of the Federal Reserve System (the Federal Reserve is discussed in Chapter 14). Figure 13.1 is a drawing of a typical $10 bill. We can identify it as a Federal Reserve note by the name that appears on the top line, in the black seal, and the green serial numbers. On rare occasions you may come across a bill with red serial numbers, a red seal, and the name "United States note" printed at the top. This bill is issued by the Treasury Department. United States notes had their origins as the "greenbacks" that were issued during the Civil War. The government still prints and circulates a small quantity of notes.

Returning to our illustration, we note the words identifying the currency as legal tender immediately below and to the left of our country's name. The bill was printed by the Bureau of Printing and Engraving (whose name you will not find) of the Department of the Treasury (whose seal is to the right of the portrait of Alexander

FIGURE 13.1 $10 Bill

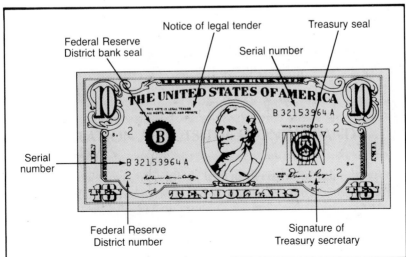

Hamilton). The round seal that appears to the left of the Hamilton portrait designates the issuing Reserve bank by name and by an alphabet letter. The district's number is located about an inch from each corner.

Paper currency makes up about 25 percent of the money supply.

"Twenty-five percent? Wait a minute! Didn't you say that coins make up less than three percent of the money supply? That accounts for only about a quarter. Where do the other three-quarters come from?"

The answer, very simply, is "checks." Most transactions are paid for by checkbook money.

2. Checkbook Money. Although we tend to think of paper currency and coins as money, they represent but a fraction of the total money in circulation. Indeed, if the nation's total currency supply were equally divided, it would come to only $600 for every person in the country. Most transactions are paid for by *check*. Technically, checks are orders written by individuals or firms directing banks to pay specified sums to their legal holders. People who have money on deposit in accounts that offer check-writing privileges have the right to order banks to make payments. These accounts are sometimes described as "checkable" ones.

Most checkable accounts (over 75 percent of the total) are held in *demand deposits* in the nation's commercial banks. Other accounts with check-writing privileges are available from thrift institutions (mutual savings, savings and loans, and credit unions) as well as from the commercial banks. Unlike demand deposits, which pay no interest, these checkable accounts offer interest on part or all of the balance in the account. The best-known interest-bearing checking account is the negotiable order of withdrawal (NOW). (See Chapters 14 and 19 for fuller discussions of banking services and savings plans.)

The total value of all the checks that could be written at any point in time is equal to the value of the deposits in checkable accounts. This information is contained in data relating to the money supply published by the federal government.

3. Traveler's Checks. Travelers do not like to carry large sums of money with them, yet they can expect to have difficulty in cashing personal checks. For that reason many people purchase *traveler's checks*, which are widely accepted both at home and abroad. Traveler's checks are issued by a few large banks and certain specialized firms such as American Express and Thomas Cook and can be purchased at most banks. Since traveler's checks are as usable as checkable

**TABLE 13.1 Money Supply, 1982
(billions of dollars)**

Currency		
Coin	$ 16.2	
Paper currency	116.6	
Total currency		$132.8
Checkbook money		
Demand deposits	$239.8	
Other checkable deposits	101.3	
Total deposits		341.1
Traveler's checks		4.2
Total money supply		$478.1

Source: *Federal Reserve Bulletin*

accounts, they are included in government data as a component of the money supply.

The money supply of the United States in 1982 is summarized in Table 13.1.

NEAR MONEYS

Money has been called the "lifeblood" of the economy because, like its human equivalent, the proper circulation of a healthy product is vital to the economy's survival. Just as physicians follow changes in their patients' blood pressure, so do economists look to the ups and downs of the money supply for telltale signs of trouble in the nation's economic health. In at least one respect, physicians have an easier time of it because blood is clearly defined and easily identified. Such is not the case with money.

There is no question that paper currency and checkable accounts are "generally acceptable in payment for goods and services" and so fall within our definition of money. Problems arise, however, over the status of other assets that are easily converted into cash. For example, a shopper cannot walk into a store, plunk a bankbook down on the counter, and ask the clerk to wrap up an article worth $100. The shopper could, however, *withdraw* $100 from a bank account

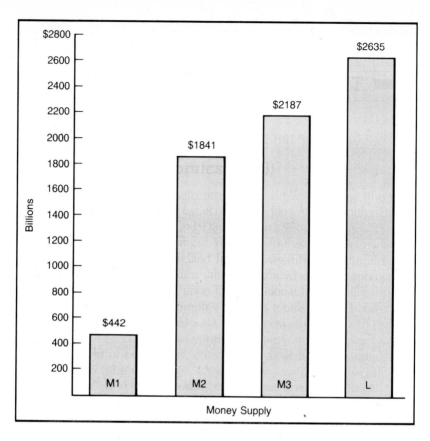

FIGURE 13.2 Measures of the Money Supply, 1981

and pay for the item a short time later. Similarly, a person with an account in a money market fund could easily withdraw $100 to finance a purchase. Some economists argue that assets like savings accounts, government bonds, and money market funds are so easily converted

What Is Money? Ask M1, M2, M3, or L

Although it may sound like a visitor from outer space, M1 is the name given by the Federal Reserve System, the nation's central bank, to its most frequently used definition of money. M1 is the total of all the currency, checkbook money, and traveler's checks in circulation on any given day. M2 adds individual savings accounts and money market funds, as well as certain foreign assets, to the M1 total. M3 is equal to M2 plus business and other large savings accounts, and L adds savings bonds as well as certain private and government securities to the M3 total.

to cash that they can be regarded as currency or any other form of money. Others look upon these assets as "near moneys" because they are not as *liquid* (easily converted to cash) as currency and checkable accounts.

The federal government has worked out a compromise by compiling four sets of measures of the money supply: M1, M2, M3, and L. (See Figure 13.2.) Near moneys are not included in M1, the most frequently consulted statistic on the money supply. They are, however, included in the broader definitions provided by M2, M3, and L.

HOW CURRENCY IS PRODUCED AND DISTRIBUTED

One of the more fascinating visits that you can make in Washington, DC is to the Bureau of Printing and Engraving. There you will see the elaborate process by which our paper money is printed. Although the Bureau of the Mint also has its offices in Washington, you will not be able to see any coins being produced there because coins are manufactured ("minted") at plants in Philadelphia, Denver, and San Francisco. The question that might well come to mind at this point is, "How do these coins and this paper money get into the hands of the public?" This is accomplished by the nation's banks, which act as intermediaries between the government and the public in the distribution of the currency. Individuals obtain currency from their banks either by cashing checks or making withdrawals from their accounts. "Well," you ask, "how do banks get the currency?"

Just as individuals maintain bank accounts upon which they can draw when they are in need of funds, so, too, do many commercial banks. For their part, however, commercial banks keep their savings, or "reserves," in the Federal Reserve bank in their district. Whenever a private commercial bank runs short of currency, it can draw upon its account with the Federal Reserve and replenish its stock. The Federal Reserve banks get their supply of paper money and coin from the Treasury Department's Bureau of the Mint and Bureau of Printing and Engraving.

The unique thing about this system is that the amount of currency in circulation at any one time is determined by the needs of business and the public. When, for example, people demand a great deal of cash, as they do during the Christmas season, they will go to their banks and make withdrawals. When the currency supplies of the banks run low, the banks may then draw additional stocks of Federal Reserve notes and coins from their accounts in the Federal Reserve banks. With the end of the buying rush, merchants and other persons with excess cash deposit it in their local banks, and these, in turn, return it to their accounts in the district banks.

MONETARY STANDARDS IN UNITED STATES HISTORY

As we have seen, any number of things can be used for money. Societies have used grains, shells, glass, stones, arrowheads, and furs for this purpose. The particular material that is used for this purpose is called the *monetary standard*.

From its earliest days until 1900, the United States was on a *bimetallic monetary standard*. This means that two metals—gold and silver—served as the basis for our money. Each dollar, the basic unit of our currency, was said to be worth a certain quantity of gold or of silver. It could be exchanged for either of these metals.*

From 1900 until 1933, the United States was on the *gold standard*. This meant that the dollar was defined in terms of gold (25.8 grains, 9/10 fine, or about $21 for one ounce of gold), and that the government stood ready to buy or sell gold at this price. During the Great Depression, most of the world, including the United States, went on a *modified gold standard*. The federal government forbade private ownership of gold and ordered everyone holding gold to exchange it for paper money. The government then raised the official price at which it would buy gold from $21 to $35 an ounce. Foreign governments could either buy or sell dollars at this price, and the Federal Reserve System was required to hold some gold as a reserve or "backing" for the dollars it circulated.

This modified gold standard came to an end in August 1971 when the United States announced that it would no longer sell its gold for dollars even to foreign governments. Gold is now being treated like any other commodity (such as wheat, rubber, or tin) in the United States. Both private individuals and the federal government may buy or sell it at will at a price determined in the marketplace. As for American currency, it has value because the government *says* it has value—that is, by *fiat;* and because people are willing to accept it. Economists call this a *paper money* or *fiat currency* standard.

In the absence of precious metals on which to base its value, the dollar is now measured by its purchasing power—that is, what it can buy. Purchasing power, however, is subject to change, and so we look to our government to direct the efforts to stabilize the dollar. The fluctuations in the purchasing power of the dollar and the federal government's efforts to stabilize the dollar are the subjects of Chapters 15, 17, and 18. Before we deal with these subjects, however, we shall discuss the role of banks in our economy.

---

* The term "dollar," derived from the German "taler," was adopted because our hostility to everything English following the Revolution prevented us from adopting the British unit of currency, the *pound*.

EXERCISES

Multiple Choice

1. Which of the following supervises the printing of paper money and the minting of coin? (*a*) the Federal Reserve System (*b*) Fort Knox (*c*) the United States Treasury (*d*) commercial banks.

2. During the Revolutionary War, the colonists spent their paper money, which had been issued by the Continental Congress, and hoarded their metallic currency. This activity was an illustration of (*a*) barter (*b*) legal tender (*c*) counterfeiting (*d*) Gresham's Law.

3. Under what circumstances might peacock feathers be called "money"? (*a*) if they were very rare (*b*) if they were all identical in size and shape (*c*) if everyone accepted them in payment for goods and services (*d*) if they could be easily divided into equal parts so as to "make change."

4. Money provides a "store of value" because it (*a*) can be used to buy valuable goods in stores (*b*) is easily carried (*c*) may be saved for future use (*d*) packs a great deal of value into a small volume.

5. Savings accounts and government bonds are described as "near money" because they (*a*) are closely connected with banks (*b*) can easily be converted into cash (*c*) can be used as legal tender (*d*) can be used as security for loans.

6. Most of the currency in circulation is issued by the (*a*) Federal Reserve System (*b*) United States Treasury (*c*) commercial banks (*d*) Bureau of the Mint.

7. Each of the following is an example of currency *except* (*a*) a dime (*b*) a $1 bill (*c*) a check for $5 (*d*) a penny.

8. In totaling the value of the nation's money supply, which of the following items would *not* be included? (*a*) paper currency (*b*) demand deposits (*c*) traveler's checks (*d*) corporate stocks and bonds.

9. M1, M2, and M3 are (*a*) measures of the money supply (*b*) agencies of the Treasury Department (*c*) the British Secret Service (*d*) Federal Reserve bank branches.

10. The agency directly responsible for the production of coins in the United States is the (*a*) Federal Reserve System (*b*) Bureau of the Mint (*c*) Bureau of Printing and Engraving (*d*) Congress.

11. Which of the following is primarily responsible for the amount of currency in circulation at a particular time? (*a*) the Treasury Department (*b*) public demand (*c*) the nation's supply of gold and silver (*d*) the Federal Reserve System.

12. Which of the following best describes America's monetary system at the present time? (*a*) paper money standard (*b*) silver standard (*c*) gold standard (*d*) bimetallic standard.

Essay Questions

1. During the Roman Era, the merchants of Rome frequently traveled into the provinces to trade with the barbarian tribes. Summarize the trading difficulties that probably arose in this barter economy.

2. During World War II, American prisoners of war used cigarettes as a form of money. Cigarettes could be used to purchase anything that was for sale in the prison camps. Practically, however, money should possess the qualities of durability, portability, divisibility, uniformity, easy of recognition, and scarcity. In terms of these six criteria, discuss the advantages and disadvantages of cigarette money in this prison economy.

3. Throughout history, the most popular form of money has been gold. (*a*) Give *three* reasons why gold has been such a popular form of money. (*b*) What would happen to the value of gold if it were discovered that it could easily be made at home on the kitchen stove? Explain your answer. (*c*) Suppose that a nation has issued gold coins and that for some reason the value of gold is now rising. What will the holders of the gold coins most likely do with them? Explain your answer.

4. Exactly what constitutes the nation's money supply has been a matter of disagreement among economists and government officials. (*a*) What is money? Define. (*b*) Why do economists and others have difficulty in measuring the nation's money supply? (*c*) What difference does it make how much money is in circulation at any particular time? (*d*) Explain the differences between M1, M2, and M3.

CHAPTER 14
Banks and Banking

As money replaced the barter system in civilized societies, the development of banking inevitably followed. History's earliest written records inform us that the temples of ancient Babylonia were used to protect the savings of private citizens. In later years private individuals and families held funds for safekeeping, made loans, and exchanged one kind of foreign coin for another for the peoples of the ancient world. With the expansion of trade during the late Middle Ages, several large banking houses were established in Italy, Germany, and the Netherlands.

THE ORIGINS OF BANKING

An important form of banking had its origins in the 1600s in England. A number of London goldsmiths undertook to store gold and other valuables for merchants. In exchange for these deposits, the goldsmiths issued receipts that entitled the holders to the return of their property on demand. At first the merchants expected to receive in return the exact bag of gold that they had left on deposit. In time, however, they came to accept the idea that it really did not matter which gold they received as long as it was equal in amount. When this happened, the merchants' gold receipts could be accepted by others in payment for goods and services. In that way these receipts became a kind of paper currency. In time, too, the goldsmiths discovered that they were never confronted by all their customers asking for their money at one and the same time. What usually happened, the goldsmiths noted, was that on any given day the amount of gold withdrawn was more or less equal to the amount brought in for deposit. It therefore followed that they could safely lend out a portion of their deposits and in that way add to their profits (by charging interest on the loan). Naturally, the more they lent the greater would be their profits, and so, many goldsmiths began to offer interest to their depositors as a way of attracting additional funds. Of course, in order to earn a profit, the interest paid for deposits was less than that charged on loans. Modern banking still follows many of the principles that were developed by the goldsmiths.

Banking, as developed by the goldsmiths, was a primitive institution that served only the rich people in the community. Today's banks, by comparison, employ some of the most sophisticated electronic equipment to serve the financial needs of the entire community.

THE BUSINESS OF BANKING

On a typical banking day, the people transacting business at a bank are there for various reasons. Some people are making deposits to or withdrawing money from their savings or checking accounts. Others are applying for loans, purchasing government bonds, or paying utility bills. There are those who have come to the bank to buy traveler's checks, visit their safe deposit boxes, or buy foreign currency. Modern banks offer so many services that some people call them "financial supermarkets."

Banks that directly serve the public are usually classified as either commercial banks or thrift institutions. Thrift institutions (or "thrifts," as they are more commonly known) include savings and loan associ-

FIGURE 14.1 Number and Assets of Banking Institutions, 1980

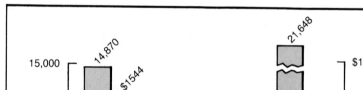

ations, mutual savings banks, and credit unions. The relative importance of each is illustrated in Figure 14.1.

COMMERCIAL BANKS

With over $1.5 *trillion* in assets, commercial banks are the nation's most important financial institutions. One reason for their dominance is that they are the only banks that can provide business firms with checking accounts. (Although the thrifts also offer checking accounts, these accounts are available only to individuals and nonprofit organizations.) Consequently, there is hardly a firm that does not have an account with a commercial bank.

The accounts upon which checks are drawn are payable on demand, and for that reason are known as *demand deposits*. This distinguishes them from savings accounts, which are known as *time deposits* (because banks can, but rarely do, ask for notice of a depositor's intention to withdraw funds). Because checks written against demand deposits are immediately acceptable, they are considered a form of money (see Chapter 13). This brings us to the second reason for the preeminence of commercial banks: *They have the ability to create money.*

When commercial banks grant *short-term* loans (those that mature in less than a year), the amount is usually added to the borrowers' checking accounts. But checking accounts, or demand deposits, are as we have noted a form of money. Thus the commercial banks have created money when they grant loans.

Commercial banks, in common with the thrifts, offer many other services to their customers. While the extent of these services varies, "full-service banks" are likely to offer the greatest variety. Among these services are saving accounts (time deposits), safe deposit boxes, and Christmas Clubs. They also sell a variety of credit instruments such as traveler's checks, money orders, and bank drafts. Some banks maintain trust departments for those who want their wealth managed for the benefit of others. So, for example, in drafting a will, a person might name a commercial bank as trustee of an estate. Upon the person's death the bank will invest or distribute the money and property in accordance with the will.

THRIFT INSTITUTIONS

1. Savings and Loan Associations. The largest of the thrifts in assets are the savings and loan associations (S&Ls). A savings and loan association is interested primarily in home financing. Therefore, virtually all its loans are in the form of long-term *mortgages*. A mortgage in this instance is a loan that is secured by that property which was purchased with the borrowed money. Dividends or interest are paid to depositors out of the earnings generated by the association's loans and other activities.

While the services offered by savings and loan associations are not as extensive as those offered by commercial banks, they go well beyond simple savings and home loan activities. As part of their array of financial services, many of the S&Ls now offer interest-bearing checking accounts, credit cards, and retirement plans as well as traveler's checks, government bonds, and consumer loans.

2. Mutual Savings Banks. Depositors in a mutual savings bank are part owners of the bank. Theoretically, this gives them a voice in the management of the bank and a claim against its assets in the event of *liquidation* (that is, when it is sold off after going out of business). In practice, mutual savings banks are operated by professional managers with very little direction from their depositors.

The principal function of mutual savings banks is to accept deposits and use those funds to make loans. Depositors entrust their savings to the banks for safekeeping and for income, which is paid in dividends and interest.

In recent years the mutual savings banks have entered into competition with the commercial banks by offering many of the services that were once the commercial banks' alone. For example, the mutual savings banks now offer both regular and interest-bearing checking accounts to individuals and nonprofit organizations. Although the bulk of their lending is still in the form of long-term real estate mortgages, they also offer short-term consumer credit, financial services like investment and retirement accounts, credit card services, and safe deposit boxes.

3. Credit Unions. Some 45 million Americans are members of the nation's 22,000 credit unions. Credit unions are established by groups such as business organizations, labor unions, universities, fraternal orders, and neighborhood associations. They accept savings deposits from members who thereby become entitled to borrow when the need arises and, in some cases, open checking accounts. Because their operating costs are usually lower than those of banks and S&Ls, credit unions are able to pay slightly higher rates of interest to their depositors and to charge less interest for their loans.

COMMERCIAL BANKS AND THE CREATION OF MONEY

We have already noted that commercial banks hold a special position in the economy because of their unique ability to create money. They do so by making certain types of loans which are added to their *demand deposits.* Like other businesses, banks must earn profits in order to survive. Since the principal activity of banking is the granting of credit, the interest earned on their loans is the banks' primary source of income. Banks get most of the money that they lend from their depositors. Were all their depositors to appear at one and the same time to withdraw their money, there simply would not be enough on hand to go around. Experience has shown, however, that such demand withdrawals never happen. While on any given day some people will want to withdraw money, others will make deposits. For that reason, banks have to keep only a fraction of their total deposits on hand to meet their customers' needs. The remainder can be safely lent to qualified borrowers. The portion of its deposits that the bank keeps on hand is known as its *reserves,* and the process is known as *fractional reserve banking.*

Loans and Discounts. The bulk of the loans granted by commercial banks are short-term ones granted to business firms. Business loans are generally made for the purpose of earning income for the borrowers. Businesses then use part of this income to pay back their loans.

As a general practice, banks *discount* commercial loans. Discounting means that the banks deduct the interest in advance. The balance is then added to the customers' checking accounts.

Suppose, for example, that John Spratt, who owns a toy store in the neighborhood, finds himself short of cash at just the time when he should be building up *inventory* (stock of merchandise) for the Christmas season. He estimates that if he could borrow about $15,000 sometime in June it would enable him to place his order in time to receive delivery well before the holidays.

Spratt discussed his problem with Ms. Hubbard, the lending officer at New City National, his local bank. Ms. Hubbard and other bank officers had known Spratt for many years and were confident that he would be able to sell his merchandise and repay his loan. Thus they approved his request promptly. For his part, Spratt was happy to learn that he would now have the capital he needed to build up his inventory. The bank was also pleased because it stood to earn interest on the loan.

On June 15 John Spratt signed a *promissory note* (a legal IOU) at New City National Bank in the amount of $15,000 payable in eight months at a 16 percent interest rate. The bank *discounted* the note by deducting the interest and crediting the balance to Spratt's company's checking account. At 16 percent, the interest on a $15,000

Deposits and Balance Sheets. This customer of a Boston bank is making a computerized deposit. How will this deposit affect the bank's balance sheet?

loan for eight months (two-thirds of a year) is $1,600.* Thus, Spratt received $13,400 which was credited to his account. Eight months later, on February 15, Spratt was expected to repay the $15,000 in its entirety.

Let us pause for a moment to explore the effect of this transaction. When New City National granted John Spratt his loan, it increased the amount of its demand deposits by $13,400. No one arrived at the bank to deposit that sum—it was created by the bank. But demand deposits, you will recall, are a form of money. Thus, it can be said that the loan increased the nation's money supply by that amount. The source of the increase was the bank's decision to give Spratt a loan.

The Commercial Bank's Balance Sheet. One way to summarize the principal activities of commercial banks is to examine a typical balance sheet (Table 14.1). Although this statement is very much simplified,

---

* The equation for the calculating of interest is

$$I = P \times R \times T$$

where:

P = principal, or the amount of the loan
R = rate (of interest on the loan)
T = time (in years or fractions of a year).

Thus, in the example above:

$$\$15,000 \times 16/100 \times 8/12 = \$1,600$$

$\quad\quad\;\;$ P $\quad\quad\quad$ R $\quad\quad\;\;$ T $\;$ = Interest charged on the loan

TABLE 14.1 Balance Sheet, New City National Bank
June, 19___

Assets		Liabilities and Net Worth	
Cash in vault	$ 200,000	Deposits	$6,400,000
Reserve account		Capital stock	1,600,000
with Federal Reserve	2,600,000	Surplus and un-	
Loans	3,200,000	distributed profits	1,200,000
Securities	2,800,000		$9,200,000
Building and			
fixtures	400,000		
	$9,200,000		

we have included the most significant items that typically appear. The balance sheet, you recall, is usually laid out so that Assets = Liabilities + Net Worth. Assets represent what is "owned" by the firm; liabilities represent what is "owed"; net worth represents the difference between the two and belongs to the owners.

Assets. The assets of the New City National Bank total $9.2 million. These are made up of the following items:

Cash in Vault. Though most of a member bank's reserves are kept on deposit in a Federal Reserve bank, some coin and currency must be kept on hand to meet the demands of depositors wishing to make withdrawals. The amount of cash that a bank has to keep on hand fluctuates according to weekly or seasonal demand.

Reserve Account With Federal Reserve. Since the New City National Bank is a member of the Federal Reserve System, the bulk of the bank's reserves is kept in the nearest Reserve bank as required by law. (The Federal Reserve System is explained below, pages 279–285.) As we can see from the balance sheet, the bank has some $2.6 million in its reserve account. Together with the $200,000 in the vault, this accounts for a total of $2.8 million in reserves.

Loans. Loans represent money owed to the bank. They are assets because, even though the bank does not have possession of the funds, it nonetheless has a claim on them. Because most of the profits earned by banks come from their loans, banks are understandably interested in building up this aspect of their business. In addition to self-liquidating business loans, banks lend money to consumers to help finance the purchase of such items as automobiles and major appliances. Other important customers for bank loans are people who want to buy homes or who want to improve their property.

Securities. After satisfying reserve requirements and lending out money, a bank may still have some funds left. Most banks try to place these funds in some form of investment that will earn interest but that may easily be converted to cash. Ideally suited to this purpose are the short-term bonds of the federal government. These are called "short-term" because they usually mature in less than a year. Because they may be bought or sold at almost a moment's notice, short-term bonds are sometimes referred to as the *secondary reserves* of the bank. In addition to these securities, banks may "balance their portfolios" by purchasing longer-term government bonds—federal as well as state and local. These bonds mature in from five to twenty years and pay a higher rate of interest than short-term bonds. Finally, banks may invest in the bonds of certain very secure corporations.

We can therefore see that banks are largely engaged in financing business activities (through loans to business), real estate purchases (through mortgage loans), consumption (through loans to consumers), and government spending (through the purchase of government bonds).

Building and Fixtures. Like all other banks, New City National has had to make an investment in its premises. This investment, as you can see, was estimated to be worth $400,000.

Liabilities and Net Worth. Turning to our statement of liabilities and net worth, we observe the following:

Deposits. The deposits are the principal obligation of a bank. They represent money that belongs to depositors, and for this reason they are considered liabilities. In recent years, deposits in commercial banks have been about equally divided between time and demand deposits.

In our simplified statement, the remaining items make up the net worth of the bank.

Capital Stock. The capital stock is equal to the par value of the shares of stock held by the bank's stockholders. *Par value* was the value assigned to the stock at the time the bank was organized.

Surplus and Undistributed Profits. The *surplus* represents the amount paid in by the shareholders in excess of the par value when the stock was first issued. *Undistributed profits* are, as the name suggests, those profits that have not been paid to the shareholders.

How a Commercial Bank Expands Deposits. Commercial banks create money, you recall, by granting loans that wind up as demand deposits and are circulated in the form of checks. As these funds are spent, they have an impact on the total economy that goes well beyond the size of the initial loan. We can demonstrate this impact by tracing a single transaction as it passes through a local commercial bank and the national banking system. Let us assume that, at the very moment that a new bank opened its doors for business, a customer walked in to deposit $10,000. This deposit will appear on the bank's balance sheet as follows:

ASSETS		LIABILITIES	
Reserves	$10,000	Deposits	$10,000

Eager to start earning profits, the bank will want to lend as much of its reserves as possible. How much it can legally lend will depend upon the amount that the Federal Reserve System requires be held on reserve. Assuming that the Federal Reserve has established a *reserve ratio* of 20 percent, the bank will have to set aside at least $2,000 (20 percent of $10,000). The remaining $8,000 is available for loans.

Sure enough, the very next customer—the head of a small corporation—applies for and is granted an $8,000 business loan, which is credited to the corporation's checking account. This transaction is reflected in the bank's balance sheet, as follows:

ASSETS		LIABILITIES	
Loans	$ 8,000	Deposits	$18,000
Reserves	10,000		

Let us pause to observe what has happened.

Acting on a fundamental assumption of banking—that all depositors will not ask for their money at one and the same time—the bank lent the bulk of its first customer's deposit. Reserves are still $10,000 because no withdrawals have been made. The corporation has a credit of $8,000 in its checking account, which it will soon spend. Deposits, which stood at $10,000 before the loan, are now $18,000, *even though no one brought in an additional $8,000.* Where then did the additional $8,000 come from? It came from the bank itself: it manufactured a deposit by granting a loan. Since the $8,000 is in the form of checkbook money, the nation's money supply has been increased by that amount.

How the Banking System Expands Deposits. The corporation that borrowed the $8,000 did so for a specific purpose. In this case we will assume that the $8,000 all went to one supplier, the Hickory

Dock Company. Hickory deposited the check in its bank, which, for the purpose of convenience, we will call the second bank. The second bank's balance sheet will reflect the $8,000 deposit as follows:

ASSETS		LIABILITIES	
Reserves	$8,000	Deposits	$8,000

The first bank's balance sheet will now look like this:

ASSETS		LIABILITIES	
Loans	$8,000	Deposits	$10,000
Reserves	2,000		

The second bank will now be able to lend out an additional $6,400 (80 percent of $8,000). When added to the borrower's checking account, the loan will be reflected with the following additions to the bank's balance sheet:

ASSETS		LIABILITIES	
Loans	$6,400	Deposits	$14,400
Reserves	8,000		

Just as the original loan moved on to a second bank, this second loan could be deposited in a third bank, which could then lend up to $5,120 of the $6,400 deposited (80 percent of $6,400 = $5,120). Theoretically, this loan could move through the banking system until the last cent was set aside in reserve. At this point, we would observe that a total of $40,000 had been lent as a result of the initial $10,000

TABLE 14.2 Progress of $10,000 Through the Banking System

Bank	Deposits	Required Reserve	Loans
First	$10,000.00	$ 2,000.00	$ 8,000.00
Second	8,000.00	1,600.00	6,400.00
Third	6,400.00	1,280.00	5,120.00
Fourth	5,120.00	1,024.00	4,096.00
Fifth	4,096.00	819.20	3,276.80
Sum of remaining banks	16,384.00	3,276.80	13,107.20
Total	$50,000.00	$10,000.00	$40,000.00

Money, Credit, and Banking

deposit, and that total deposits had expanded to $50,000. We should also note that, although no one bank lent out more than its excess reserves, the banking system as a whole expanded deposits by five times the original deposit. Table 14.2 summarizes the progress of the $10,000 deposit as it moved through the banking system.

We should note that the reserve ratio is quite significant in determining the amount of money in circulation. If, for example, the ratio were 25 percent, then an initial deposit of $10,000 would permit total deposits to be expanded to only $40,000. On the other hand, a 10 percent reserve ratio would permit expansion of deposits up to $100,000. The Federal Reserve's Board of Governors can therefore use its control of the reserve ratio to influence the amount of money in circulation.

Contraction of Deposits. Just as a deposit of cash leads to a great expansion of deposits throughout the banking system, so the withdrawal of funds would have the opposite effect. If a bank has no excess reserves and some money is withdrawn, it has to take steps to replace the reserves by either calling in loans or selling securities. If the funds that were withdrawn from one bank are placed in another bank, then the banking system as a whole would not lose. However, if the money is not deposited in another bank, then the total of all deposits in the economy would be reduced. If the reserve ratio is 20 percent, then total deposits would be reduced by $5 for every dollar withdrawn.

KEEPING OUR BANKS SAFE

In the early 1930s, during the Great Depression, bank failures were unfortunately a fairly common occurrence. Over 1,300 banks closed their doors in 1930, 2,300 in 1931, and in 1933 the number passed 4,000. In those days a bank failure was something to be feared by all depositors, for it could mean the loss of their lifetime's savings.

The picture has changed dramatically since those times. While bank failures are still with us (there were 83 during the ten-year period from 1971 to 1980), people with savings in those banks were almost completely unaffected. Two of the most important reasons for this dramatic turnaround are the introduction of deposit insurance and the closer regulation of banking practices.

Deposit Insurance. Virtually all accounts in both commercial and savings banks are now insured up to $100,000. Because of the alarming number of bank failures during the 1929–1933 period, it was felt that some action would have to be taken to protect investors and restore

Bank Panics. In 1884 New York's Wall Street was the scene of panic when banks could not meet their obligations to depositors. What government institutions have been created since then to prevent financial panics?

the public's faith in banks. Accordingly, in 1933 Congress established the Federal Deposit Insurance Corporation (FDIC). Its function is to pay back depositors of a bank that is unable to continue in business. All member banks of the Federal Reserve System must join the FDIC. In addition, nonmember banks may also join provided that they live up the FDIC's standards of sound banking practices.

Premiums to support the FDIC's insurance fund come from the participating banks and are based upon the size of their deposits. The major importance of this agency lies in its psychological effect upon depositors. They no longer feel compelled to stage a "run on the bank" at the first rumor of a failure.

Much of the same kind of security is available to depositors in savings and loan associations by another governmental agency, the Federal Savings and Loan Insurance Corporation. Insurance for savings in most credit unions is provided by the National Credit Union Administration. Both the FSLIC and the NCUA insure accounts up to $100,000.

Regulating the Banks. The Federal Reserve System has broad powers to supervise its member banks and to lend them money in times of difficulty. State-chartered banks are subject to regulation by state banking authorities. Bank examiners scrutinize the books and opera-

Money, Credit, and Banking

tions of the institutions in their state periodically with a view toward preventing difficulties before they occur.

Banks and the Economy. Most people think of banks when they want to set aside savings, borrow money, or open a checking account. However, because of their ability to expand or contract the money supply, banks are also very much involved with the total economy. This involvement accounts for the federal government's special concern with the nation's banks. One of the more important results of this concern has been the creation of the Federal Reserve System, which is described below.

THE ROLE OF THE FEDERAL RESERVE SYSTEM

The principal business of banks, we have learned, is to lend to qualified borrowers the funds that are brought to them for safekeeping by depositors. On most banking days, requests for withdrawals can be handled out of the day's deposits. Every now and then, when withdrawals are greater than their deposits, banks will simply use the reserves that they keep on hand for that purpose to satisfy their customers' demands. Of course, banks maintain but a fraction of their total deposits as reserves. It is therefore theoretically possible for so many withdrawals to be made at one and the same time that a bank may not be able to meet its obligations. When an unusually large number of depositors descend upon a bank to withdraw their money, there is said to be a "run on the bank." When heavy withdrawals occur in many banks nationally, the phenomenon is described as a "panic."

Historical Background of the System. Runs and panics were recurring problems in the years before the creation of the Federal Reserve System in 1913. It was the custom in those days for smaller banks around the country to deposit their reserves in major money center banks for safekeeping and to earn interest. For their part, the money center banks used the deposits for loans to business.

Problems developed at certain times when many smaller banks sought to withdraw their reserve funds at the same time. This created a kind of run on the money center banks, which had to call in their loans to satisfy their small-bank depositors. Unfortunately, the delay frequently forced several smaller banks that had run out of cash to close their doors. As word of the bank closings spread, depositors elsewhere demanded their savings, creating another round of requests for their reserves by the smaller banks, followed by more delays and bank closings, and a national panic.

The worst of the bank panics occurred in 1907. Money all but disappeared from circulation during the height of the crisis, and many Americans were forced to barter for the things they needed. In the aftermath of the disaster, a Congressional committee was formed to investigate the causes of bank panics and to propose remedies. After years of study and debate, Congress recommended that the nation adopt some form of *central banking.*

A central bank is created by the government for the purpose of servicing and coordinating commercial banks and of regulating the supply of the nation's money and credit. Although the major nations of the world had long recognized its advantages, our country was without a central bank from the expiration of the Second Bank of the United States in 1836 until passage of the Federal Reserve Act in 1913 created the Federal Reserve System.

Structure of the Federal Reserve System. The Federal Reserve Act created a central banking system consisting of twelve Federal Reserve banks rather than just one bank. This was done for two reasons. First, Congress feared the consequences of placing too much financial power in the hands of one bank. Second, Congress felt that the particular needs and interests of various regions of the nation could best be served by a decentralized banking system.

Another feature of our banking system is that each Reserve bank is owned by the member banks in its district, all of which are required to purchase its stock. Control of the system, however, is in the hands of the government, whose primary objective is to serve the needs of the economy. Despite this the Reserve banks will earn a profit every year because of the large quantities of income-producing government securities they acquire in the course of their operations.

FIGURE 14.2   Structure of the Federal Reserve System

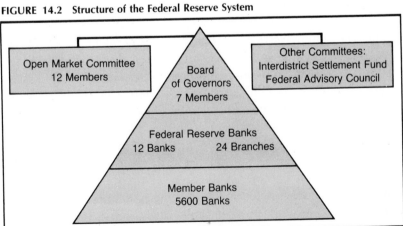

The organization of the Federal Reserve System, or the Fed, as it is more commonly known, can be compared to a pyramid. (See Figure 14.2.) At the apex (highest point) is the seven-member Board of Governors. Below the board are the twelve Federal Reserve banks and their twenty-four branches, while at the base stand the approximately 5,600 commercial banks that are "members" of the system.

The Board of Governors. The seven members of the Board of Governors are appointed by the President of the United States with the advice and consent of the Senate. The term of their appointment is fourteen years. The chairperson of the board is appointed from among the members by the President for a four-year term.

The Board of Governors supervises the many activities of the Federal Reserve System. In addition, the board establishes and oversees the nation's *monetary policies*—that is, its programs to regulate the supply of money and credit.

The Federal Reserve Banks. The twelve Federal Reserve banks are "bankers' banks" in that they are primarily concerned with servicing the member banks within their districts. All but two of the Reserve banks maintain branches that cover particular parts of their districts. (See Figure 14.3 on page 282.)

Member Banks. By law, all national banks (those holding charters from the federal government) must be members of the Federal Reserve System. Many of the larger state banks as well as some of the smaller ones have also joined, so that now about 40 percent of the nation's 14,000 commercial banks are members. These banks hold approximately 80 percent of the banking system's demand deposits.

The Federal Open Market Committee. The Open Market Committee is the most important policy-making group of the Federal Reserve. The committee directs the purchase and sale of government securities as a means of regulating the nation's supply of money and credit. Members of the Open Market Committee include the seven members of the Board of Governors and five of the Reserve bank presidents.

Other Committees. With so many complex responsibilities, the Federal Reserve looks at a number of other committees to undertake major tasks. Among these, for example, is the Federal Advisory Council, a twelve-member committee of bankers that meets several times a year to advise the Board of Governors on matters of current interest.

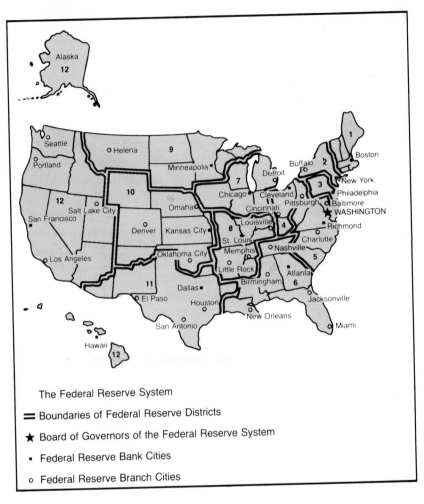

The Federal Reserve System

= Boundaries of Federal Reserve Districts

★ Board of Governors of the Federal Reserve System

▪ Federal Reserve Bank Cities

○ Federal Reserve Branch Cities

FIGURE 14.3 Districts of the Federal Reserve System

Operation of the Federal Reserve System. The Federal Reserve System has two functions. The first function is to provide the federal government and the American public with a number of basic banking services. The second function is to regulate the flow of money and credit so as to contribute to economic growth and stability. Of the two, the second function, which involves the Federal Reserve's control over monetary policy, is the more important and will be treated in full in Chapter 18. The Federal Reserve's banking services are discussed below.

District Banks Hold the Nation's Banking Reserves. We have said that all banks (including both members and nonmembers of the Federal Reserve System) must keep a portion of their deposits on hand to satisfy the withdrawal demands of their customers. Banks keep a small portion of their reserves as currency and coin to meet the day-to-day needs of their customers. The rest of the banks' reserves must be kept on deposit in the Federal Reserve district banks. Since 1980 the Federal Reserve has paid interest on these accounts. Banks may draw on their district bank reserve accounts whenever they exceed reserve requirements. Funds on deposit also provide a pool from which loans are made to local and other district banks.

District Banks Act as Fiscal Agents for the Federal Government. The Federal Reserve banks act as bankers for the federal government. Just as an individual uses a commercial bank for deposits and withdrawals, so the government employs the Federal Reserve banks for the deposit of its receipts and the payment of its obligations. If you or someone in your family receives a check from the federal government, take a look at it to see on which district bank the check is drawn.

District Banks Provide Currency for Circulation. As we have already observed, almost all the currency in circulation is in the form of Federal Reserve notes. One of the principal advantages of this form of money is that it is *elastic*—its supply will automatically expand or contract as necessary. When people need cash, they can withdraw it in the form of Federal Reserve notes from their accounts. When the member banks run short of cash, they can replenish their supply merely by drawing additional currency from their accounts at the district bank. During periods of contraction, the opposite takes place, and money is returned to the district banks and removed from circulation.

In order to grow, the nation's economy requires an ever-increasing supply of currency. This need is satisfied in the same way as the seasonal demand for currency. That is, as the public requires more cash, it will turn to its local banks, which, in turn, will call upon the Federal Reserve System to provide the currency needed for everyday business.

District Banks Are Clearinghouses for the Collection of Checks. We have already noted that the largest portion of money in circulation at any time is *checkbook money*, or *demand deposits*. One of the reasons why this form of money has become so popular is that business people know they will be able to deposit a check in a bank and have the amount credited to them in only a few days—even if the check has been drawn on the bank located at the other end of the country. This has been made possible by the Federal Reserve System, whose nationwide facilities are used for the clearance and collection of checks.

Let us suppose that Brown gives Jones a check for $100 drawn upon the First National Bank of Middletown, New York, in which Brown has an account. Jones deposits the check in the People's National Bank of Newburgh, New York, which is located in the same Federal Reserve district as Middletown. Jones's account is credited with $100. At this point we see that the People's National Bank of Newburgh has given Jones $100 in exchange for a check. It now wants to get its money back by presenting the check to the First National Bank of Middletown for payment. This could be accomplished by mailing the check to Middletown. However, this would hardly be a practical procedure since the First National Bank probably received hundreds of checks from dozens of banks on this day. The paperwork involved in settling with each bank individually would be staggering. What the bank does instead is to send the check to the clearinghouse at the Federal Reserve bank in its district. Here the account of the People's National Bank of Newburgh is credited with $100, and the amount is deducted from the account of the Middletown bank. The check is then forwarded to Middletown, where the bank deducts the sum from Brown's account and sends Brown the canceled check.

When a check is drawn on a bank located in a different district from the bank in which it is deposited, the local Federal Reserve bank will collect from the first bank's Federal Reserve bank. This is done through the Interdistrict Settlement Fund, located in Washington, DC, which acts as a clearinghouse for the Federal Reserve banks.

Clearing checks is an enormous, steadily growing task. According to recent estimates, the Federal Reserve processes over 30 billion checks a year. The job has been made possible largely by the development of computers and electronic data processing equipment.

District Banks Transfer Funds From One Part of the Country to Another. The Federal Reserve System maintains a communication center in Culpeper, Virginia, whose function is to transfer funds by wire from one part of the country to another. This center, which contains several computers that are designed to transmit messages in rapid fashion over special telephone lines, makes it possible to move large sums of money almost instantaneously. So, for example, a national firm with headquarters in San Francisco, California, can transfer funds to its branch office in Raleigh, North Carolina, in a matter of hours. The firm does this by requesting its San Francisco bank to wire the funds to its Raleigh bank. The San Francisco Reserve bank deducts the amount from the balance of the firm's commercial bank. The Richmond Reserve bank (in whose district Raleigh lies) adds those funds to the reserve balance of the firm's bank in North Carolina, which then credits the firm's account. The Reserve banks will then settle by means of an entry on the books of the Interdistrict Settlement Fund.

The Fed Influences Economy Activity. The second major function of the Federal Reserve System is to help the nation achieve its major economic goals of full employment, price stability, and economic growth. The Federal Reserve does this by regulating the supply of money and credit. Toward that end, the Fed has a number of monetary tools that it can use at its discretion. These tools will be described in Chapter 18.

EXERCISES

Multiple Choice

1. "Fractional reserve banking" describes the system in which banks (*a*) keep a portion of their deposits on reserve (*b*) keep all their deposits on reserve (*c*) may lend out sums equal to their deposits (*d*) may lend sums equal to their total deposits plus a fraction beyond this amount.
2. A basic assumption on which banks operate is that (*a*) not everyone is entitled to withdraw deposits at the same time (*b*) all depositors may be required to give advance notice of their intention to withdraw their deposits (*c*) deposits are the property of the bank and are therefore carried as "assets" on the balance sheet (*d*) depositors will not withdraw all their deposits at the same time.
3. Which of the following would *not* be classified as a thrift institution? (*a*) a commercial bank (*b*) a credit union (*c*) a mutual savings bank (*d*) a savings and loan association.
4. Commercial banks differ from savings banks in that (*a*) only savings banks can accept time deposits (*b*) commercial banks can "manufacture deposits" (*c*) savings banks specialize in short-term loans whereas commercial banks specialize in long-term loans (*d*) commercial banks pay higher rates of interest to their depositors than savings banks.
5. The major source of income for banks is (*a*) service fees charged on their deposit accounts (*b*) fees from the sale of government bonds (*c*) income from services such as safe deposit boxes, life insurance, and notary fees (*d*) interest earned on their loans.
6. The process of deducting interest in advance from a loan is known as (*a*) discounting (*b*) charging (*c*) liquidating (*d*) certifying.
7. Lila Gallo borrowed $10,000 from her bank to build up the inventory of her stationery store. The loan was payable in six

months at 12 percent interest, which the bank deducted in advance. How much money did Lila actually receive? (a) $10,000 (b) $8,800 (c) $9,400 (d) $9,600.

8. Most bank reserves are kept in (a) the vaults of other banks where they can earn interest (b) Federal Reserve banks (c) miscellaneous investments so as to earn income (d) very safe long-term government bonds.

9. A principal function of commercial banks is to (a) lend money for home mortgages (b) provide businesses with checking accounts and loans (c) sell traveler's checks (d) trade stocks and bonds.

10. With a reserve ratio of 25 percent and deposits of $4 million, what is the total amount of money that a commercial bank is permitted to lend? (a) $3 million (b) $8 million (c) $1.6 million (d) $1 million.

11. The Federal Deposit Insurance Corporation guarantees deposits (a) with funds provided entirely by the federal government (b) with funds provided equally by the federal and state governments (c) out of premiums paid into an insurance pool by participating banks (d) for up to $100,000 in all banks, financial institutions, and mutual funds in the United States.

12. A central bank (a) is a bank that is conveniently located in a business and financial district (b) coordinates a nation's banking system and money supply (c) is a relatively new concept first developed by the United States (d) directs the activities of all the financial institutions in a country.

13. The Federal Reserve System provides for the pooling of the nation's bank reserves (a) through the actions of the Open Market Committee (b) by establishing legal reserve ratios (c) through the creation of an elastic currency (d) by requiring that reserves be kept on deposit in district banks.

14. Federal Reserve notes are an "elastic currency" because (a) their total value is fixed by Congress in accordance with the needs of business (b) their supply automatically expands and contracts with the needs of business (c) the Board of Governors can expand or contract the supply as needed (d) their value may be adjusted to the cost of living.

15. All of the following are component parts of the Federal Reserve System *except* the (a) Board of Governors (b) Federal Advisory Council (c) Open Market Committee (d) Treasury Department.

16. If Powers, living in New York, draws a check on a local bank and sends it to Thomas, who deposits it in a Los Angeles bank, Thomas's bank will (a) deduct a small service charge to cover the cost of collection (b) send it to the clearinghouse in its own district (c) send it to the district bank in New York for collection (d) not be able to accept it because Los Angeles is in the Twelfth Federal Reserve District, while New York is in the Second.

17. The Federal Reserve System acts as a fiscal agent for the United States government by (a) supervising the collection of income taxes (b) maintaining a part ownership in all the nation's commercial banks (c) receiving deposits and making payments on the government's behalf (d) printing all the nation's paper money.
18. Monetary policy refers to the Federal Reserve System's power to (a) provide an elastic currency (b) supervise the practices of the member banks (c) regulate the nation's supply of money and credit (d) clear checks.
19. In which section of a balance sheet would a bank's deposits be summarized? Among the (a) capital stock (b) assets (c) liabilities (d) net worth.

Essay Questions

1. Suppose that banks were required to keep 100 percent of their deposits on reserve. How would banking differ from the way it is currently practiced in the United States?
2. "Bank reserve requirements affect the size of the nation's monetary supply." (a) Prove this statement by showing the effect on the money supply of an increase in the reserve ratio from 10 percent to 20 percent. (b) Describe the effect on the money supply if a person were to withdraw $100,000 from a commercial account and bury it in the backyard. For purposes of illustration, assume a reserve ratio of 25 percent.
3. The balance sheet of the Third National Bank for December 31 is summarized in Table 14.3. (a) Explain the meaning of *each* of the balance sheet entries (numbered 1–8). (b) In the week that followed, cash deposits that were kept on hand increased by $10 million. In addition, the bank increased its loans by $7 million, all of which was credited to deposit accounts. Summarize the

TABLE 14.3 **Balance Sheet, Third National Bank**
December 31, 19____

Assets		Liabilities and Net Worth	
(1) Cash in vault	$ 7,500,000	(6) Deposits	$24,000,000
(2) Reserves	12,500,000	(7) Capital stock	5,500,000
(3) Loans	9,750,000	(8) Surplus and profits	10,000,000
(4) Securities	8,500,000		$39,500,000
(5) Other assets	1,250,000		
	$39,500,000		

changes that took place in the bank's balance sheet as a result of these transactions.

4. Figure 14.2, on page 280, illustrates the principal components of the Federal Reserve System. In your own words, describe the ways in which each one contributes to the Fed's work.

5. One of the principal functions of the Federal Reserve System is to provide the nation with an elastic currency. (a) Define "elastic currency." (b) Describe how the Federal Reserve System fulfills this responsibility. (c) Suppose that the nation's money supply were required by law to be equal to the amount of gold held by the government, and that paper money and coin were circulated strictly in accordance with this formula. How would this differ from an elastic currency? What problems would be created by such a system?

CHAPTER 15

The Fluctuating Value of Money

"No, sir, a dollar just isn't worth a dollar anymore."

"You're telling me? Do you know what I just paid for a pack of chewing gum? I mean, *chewing gum!*"

"Don't tell me about chewing gum. When I was your age, we could buy a whole pack of gum for a dime, and when Grandma was your age she bought a pack for a nickel."

"A *nickel?* I heard a comedian on a talk show last night say that prices are so high these days even a nickel costs a quarter."

When people complain that "a dollar isn't worth a dollar anymore" they are not suggesting that there is anything less than 100 cents in every dollar. What they really mean is that most things cost more now than they once did. This trend, with which most of us are familiar, serves to illustrate how the *value* of money can change.

When the general price level rises, we have a period of *inflation*. During periods of inflation, the dollar's value may be said to be falling because it cannot buy as much as it once did. There have also been times when quite the opposite took place: prices, in general, declined. During such periods of *deflation*, money increased in value.

In this chapter we shall examine some of the ways in which the value of money (its "purchasing power") is measured, why it tends to fluctuate, and the impact of these fluctuations on various groups in our economy.

HOW THE VALUE OF MONEY IS MEASURED

1. Index Numbers. When we speak of rising and falling prices, we are, of course, referring to the general level of prices, rather than to the price of any individual commodity. Statisticians have devised various techniques for computing the overall average of prices and expressing it in terms of an *index number*. This number shows the percentage of change from a base year (or average of years), which is assumed to be 100. Thus, if the index number for a particular year is 135, we know that whatever is being measured has increased by 35 percent since the base year (135 − 100 = 35). Similarly, an index number of 87 would mean that there had been a decline of 13 percent since the base year.

(Note, however, that, although an index number of 110 in 1983 would indicate an increase of 10 percent since the base year, an index number of 115 in 1984 would *not* mean that there had been a 5 percent increase from 1983 to 1984. This increase would actually be only 4.5 percent because 115 is 4.5 percent larger than 110.)

In matters pertaining to the value of money and the level of prices, the most frequently used indexes are the *Wholesale Price Index* and the *Consumer Price Index*. Both are prepared by the Bureau of Labor Statistics of the United States Department of Labor. As the names suggest, the Consumer Price Index (also known as the "Cost of Living Index") measures the price of goods and services purchased by consumers, and the Wholesale Price Index measures the prices paid by business.

The preparation of these indexes is quite a complicated procedure because, if it is to be meaningful, each index must include the average price paid for all major categories of goods and services. In preparing the Consumer Price Index, therefore, the Department of Labor finds out the prices of about 400 goods and services. It also has to consider how much of each of these items average consumers purchase in filling their "market baskets." This information was determined by an extensive study of the spending habits of some 40,000 families living

TABLE 15.1 Consumer Prices and Purchasing Power, 1940–1982

| | I | II |
| | | Purchasing Power of the |
Year	Consumer Price Index (1967 = 100)	Consumer Dollar (1967 = $1)
1940	42.0	$2.38
1950	72.1	1.39
1960	88.7	1.27
1965	94.5	1.06
1970	116.3	.86
1974	147.7	.67
1978	195.4	.51
1982	289.1	.34

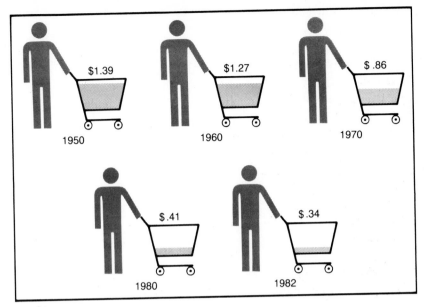

FIGURE 15.1 Purchasing Power of the Dollar: What a 1967 Dollar Was Worth in Selected Years

in 216 urban areas of the United States. The department calculates the Consumer Price Index by comparing the cost of this "market basket" today with its cost during the 1967 base period. Table 15.1 shows the CPI for selected years between 1940 and 1982. A similar procedure is used to calculate the Wholesale Price Index.

2. Purchasing Power. Sometimes the value of money is expressed in *purchasing power*. This is a way of expressing the cost of living in dollars and cents. Thus, if the cost of living has doubled since the base year, one might say that the value of the dollar is now 50 cents. In other words, it would now take twice as many dollars to purchase certain typical goods and services as it took to purchase the same goods and services during the base year. Figure 15.1 illustrates how the purchasing power of the dollar declined during the years indicated. (See also Table 15.1.)

HOW INFLATION AFFECTS THE ECONOMY AND PEOPLE'S LIVES

Although money may increase as well as decrease in value, there has not been a long-term period of *deflation* since the 1930s. *Inflation*, however, has been a fact of life for as long as most people can remember. With the exception of 1949 and 1955, when living costs actually declined, consumer prices have risen in every year since 1939. Prior to 1965, however, the annual cost of living increase was

The Fluctuating Value of Money

Runaway Inflation. In the 1920s German marks were worthless as currency, so people used them to paper their walls. What can individuals do to protect themselves against inflation?

rarely more than 1.5 percent. Although even in those years people grumbled about rising prices, most Americans seemed to accept a modest inflation rate as the price of economic growth and relative prosperity. Beginning some time around 1965, however, inflation began to accelerate. Consumer prices increased at a 4 percent annual rate between 1965 and 1970, and this rate increased by 7 percent per year from 1970 to 1975 and to 9 percent from 1975 to 1980. In 1974 the nation experienced its first "double-digit" inflation, when the cost of living increased by 11 percent. Double digits struck again in 1979 and in 1980, when the inflation rate reached 13.5 percent.

In its more extreme forms, inflation can wreck an economy and even an entire society itself. The experience of Germany in the years following World War I stands as a terrible example of the consequences of a runaway inflation. In 1913, the year before the war, 4 marks (the German unit of currency) could be exchanged for a dollar. By 1923 it took 4,000,000,000,000 (that is 4 *trillion*) marks to buy a dollar. The cost of living in Germany had increased 1 *trillion* times. So, for example, the price of a pound of butter had climbed to 1.5 million marks and that of a loaf of bread to 200,000 marks. Newspapers printed photographs of people with wheelbarrows and baby carriages on their way to market to buy bread. Why the wheelbarrows and carriages? To carry the money needed for their purchases. Other stories told of people who had buried their life's savings in their backyards to protect them from the ravages of war. In an ironic twist of fate, they found that inflation had destroyed what the bombs and bullets of World War I had missed—the value of their money.

Not everyone is adversely affected by inflation, however. Depending upon their circumstances, some people may actually *profit* from inflation. Here is a summary of inflation's likely impact upon a variety of people in your community.

1. Savers and Investors. For a wide variety of reasons, people set aside a portion of their incomes as savings. Some save for a "rainy day" when the unexpected will put special demands upon the family purse. Others save for a new car, a musical instrument, or a college education. Whatever our reasons, we all would like to feel that our savings are secure and are earning a nice return in the form of dividends or interest. If the cost of living should increase at a rate higher than the return on our savings, however, the money we withdraw will be worth less than it was when we deposited it. Suppose, for example, that in 1979 you deposited $1,000 in a savings account that paid 6 percent interest. Two years later, in 1981, you withdrew the deposit along with $123.60 in accumulated interest, for a total of $1,123.60.

"Not bad," you thought. "I put in $1,000 and got back $1,123.60. Not bad at all."

But wait. The inflation rate during those years averaged 12 percent a year. This rate meant that in 1981 it took $1,254 to buy as much as $1,000 bought in 1979. But you, the saver, received only $1,124 in principal and interest and therefore were worse off by about $130.

Because money loses its purchasing power during inflationary times, people with surplus funds frequently look for investments that will increase in value as fast as or faster than the cost of living. Among the most popular "hedges" (or insurances) against inflation have been real estate, gold, and precious gems. For similar reasons, rare postage stamps, antiques, and works of art have also enjoyed popularity as vehicles for anti-inflationary investment. There are no guarantees accompanying these investments, however, and, as many people discovered when the time came to sell, many so-called "inflation hedges" were worth less than their initial costs.

2. People on Fixed Incomes. Retired persons, widows with young children, the seriously disabled, and others who depend on fixed incomes for financial support suffer during periods of inflation. When prices go up, there is nothing that people on fixed incomes can do but spend less.

Fixed incomes are derived from pensions, insurance annuities, and social security payments. In recent years efforts have been made to tie social security benefits into the cost of living. This relationship has meant that, as the Consumer Price Index increased, so too did

ALFRED MARSHALL
Principles of Economics (1890)

As the nineteenth century drew to a close, the world described by economists like Adam Smith, Thomas Malthus, and David Ricardo had undergone considerable change. The Industrial Revolution had transformed England from a primarily agricultural society into an industrialized nation whose very survival was dependent upon its international trade. Political power, which in Smith's day was totally in the hands of the landed aristocracy, was now shifting to the middle class of the world of business, industry, and finance.

In the world of economics, critics of classical theory asserted that it failed to reflect these changes. Others, whom we would now describe as "socialists" and "Communists," called for the replacement of the existing order with a new kind of economic system. The publication by Alfred Marshall of his *Principles of Economics* in 1890 came as a tonic to the "silent majority" of the day who were looking for a restatement in modern terms of the theoretical basis of their economic order.

Alfred Marshall (1842–1924), whose work became a bible for what came to be known as "neoclassical" economics, was a member of the faculty of Cambridge University from 1885 until his death. He became a legend in his own time, and his lecture hall the center of economic thought and education for the English-speaking world. Even before the publication of his *Principles,* it was said that at least half the professors of economics in England's universities had been his pupils. Marshall's

---

social security benefit payments. There is no guarantee that this policy will be continued, however.

3. *Business Firms.* The extent to which individual firms are affected by inflation depends upon a firm's ability to cover its increased costs. Suppose, for example, that as a result of an inflationary trend a firm is able to raise its selling prices by 20 percent without any loss in its volume of sales. If, at the same time, the firm's costs of doing business have increased by less than 20 percent, it will be better off than it was before the inflation. If the increased cost of doing business cannot

influence became international as universities in England and America made the *Principles* required reading. Not until the 1940s was the *Principles* supplanted by other works.

What Marshall had accomplished was a revitalization of the classical economics of writers like Smith and Ricardo by modernizing it and fleshing out areas of weakness in its theoretical framework. For example, Marshall developed the concept of *elasticity of demand* in order to explain price behavior.

For many years, too, classical economists had been debating whether supply or demand was the more important determinant of price. Marshall's introduction to his position on this issue is worth quoting as an example of his skill at slicing through complex issues with easy-to-grasp logic. "We might as reasonably dispute whether it is the upper or the under blade of a pair of scissors that cuts a piece of paper, as whether value is governed by *utility* or *cost of production* [demand or supply]. It is true that when one blade is held still, and the cutting is effected by moving the other, we may say with careless brevity that the cutting is done by the second; but the statement is not strictly accurate and is to be excused only so long as it claims to be merely a popular and not a strictly scientific account of what happens."*

Although today's economic students are no longer required to read the *Principles,* Marshall's theories and methods are reflected in the works of all modern textbook authors and are part of the education of the practicing economists of the English-speaking world.

---

* Alfred Marshall, *Principles of Economics* (New York: The Macmillan Company, 1948, 8th ed.), p. 348.

be offset by higher prices, however, the firm will be hurt by the inflation.

4. People Who Owe Money. Debtors will generally profit from inflation, providing that the value of the money they must repay is less than the amount of their loans. Suppose that you borrowed $1,000, which you promised to repay in two years, and inflation averaged 10 percent per year over those two years, for a total of 20 percent. You would be able to repay your $1,000 loan with dollars that had the purchasing power of only $800 (because $1,000 − 20 percent = $800). As one economist aptly put it: "It's rather like borrowing steak and repaying the loan with hamburger."

You will recall from your study of American history that certain groups, like the farmers, have favored inflationary, or "cheap-money," policies. The farmers relied heavily on borrowed funds to finance their businesses, and they saw inflation as a means of easing their burden of debt. In recent years, however, farmers have generally suffered from inflation because the cost of borrowing has increased even faster than the cost of living. (For a detailed discussion of the plight of the farmer, see Chapter 22.)

5. People Who Lend Money. Lenders can be hurt by inflation for the same reason that borrowers may profit because the value of the money that they lend is worth less than the value of the money that is repaid. Lenders can, and frequently do, protect themselves from the impact of inflation by building that cost into their interest rates. So, for example, if the average cost of a loan was 20 percent over a period of time when the inflation rate was 8 percent, lenders would continue to earn a profit despite inflation.

WHAT ARE THE CAUSES OF INFLATION?

Economists offer a number of reasons why we have inflation. Virtually all of these reasons fall into one of two categories: *demand-pull* and *cost-push.*

1. Demand-Pull. Demand-pull inflation is brought on when the demand for goods and services outraces the economy's ability to produce them. In this situation prices will necessarily increase. One economist may have described demand-pull best as a situation in which "too much money was chasing too few goods."

What, you may ask, is the source of all this excess demand? One source is the federal government. Sometimes, the government spends more than it earns in taxes and other revenues. The net effect of excess spending is to leave the public with more money and greater purchasing power than it had before the government actions.

The government also has the power to increase the money supply through the Federal Reserve System. The Fed issues virtually all the paper money that passes through our hands. If, as a result of Federal Reserve policies, the supply of money is increased fast enough, the excess demand that results will lead to a general rise in prices.

But the government is not the only source of demand-pull inflation. Changes in the spending habits of individuals and business firms can also result in "too much money chasing too few goods." A classic example of this process followed the end of World War II. Although personal income was high during the war, production was geared toward military goods and so there were few consumer goods for people to buy. Since savings were viewed as both practical and patriotic, most people set aside a portion of their earnings toward the day when consumer goods would again become available. When the war ended, the rush was on to buy the new appliances, cars, homes, and radios as fast as they became available. As a result, consumer prices, which had risen by only about 10 percent during the four war years, quickly escalated by an additional 30 percent over the following three years.

Still another source of demand-pull inflation is a psychological factor that, for want of a better term, we may call "public expectation." If individuals and business firms *believe* that prices will be rising in the near future, they may rush to buy today what they might otherwise have postponed buying until a later time. Ironically, if a large enough section of the public acts on this expectation, the prophecy will be fulfilled. Why? Because the rising demand will lead to an increase in prices.

2. Cost-Push. Not all inflation can be explained as "too much money chasing too few goods." The inflation of 1979–1981, for example, saw prices increasing at a record rate at a time when industry was operating at barely 80 percent of its capacity and one worker out of fourteen was out of work. In other words, Americans did not have "too much money," the economy could have produced more, and yet we had inflation. According to economists, the cause in this and other recent rising price spirals was *cost-push inflation.* This is the name given to the run-up in prices that results as sellers raise their prices because of an increase in their costs.

Cost-push inflation occurs because large segments of the nation's economy do not operate under conditions of pure competition. Thus some labor unions can achieve wage increases without increasing their members' productivity. And producers in certain key industries have the power to increase prices even though shortages do not exist.

Management and labor are frequently at odds as to which was the first cause of a cost-push inflation. Management is likely to charge that the principal cause of inflation was unions' demand for wage increases which outran productivity. In the absence of additional output, business was compelled to offset its higher wage costs with price increases. For their part, unions are likely to argue that their wage demands were merely an effort to make up for increases in the cost of living. "Don't blame us," unions seem to say. "Business raised its prices first."

Some liken the question to the age-old puzzle about which came first, "the chicken or the egg." Without attempting to settle the argument, we can say that the *wage-price spiral* has led to a series of inflationary price increases in the past and is likely to do so again in the future.

In recent years the type of cost-push inflation that has been most troublesome is known to economists as *commodity inflation*. This term identifies run-ups in the prices of certain key commodities as the source of general price increases. The most dramatic example of commodity inflation in the 1970s took place in the petroleum industry. Foreign suppliers operating through the Organization of Petroleum Exporting Countries were able to use their monopoly power to push prices from under $4 a barrel in 1973 to over $21 in 1980. As the price increases radiated out to gasoline and other petroleum by-products, the inflationary spiral seemed to affect virtually every one of the economy's goods and services.

HOW THE GOVERNMENT FIGHTS INFLATION

"One of the Administration's long-run objectives is the elimination of inflation" (President Ronald Reagan, 1982).

Controlling or eliminating inflation has been a goal of the federal government ever since World War II. Much of the effort toward meeting these goals has been directed at the two principal causes of inflation, *demand-pull* and *cost-push*.

Aiming at Demand-Pull as a Cause of Inflation. Government programs to limit the effect of demand-pull as a cause of inflation seek to control the growth of business and consumer purchasing power. Two approaches are available for that purpose: *monetary policies* and *fiscal policies*. As you have learned, monetary policies are administered by the Federal Reserve System. The Fed can use its powers to slow the rate of growth of the money supply, make it more difficult for individuals and firms to borrow, or some combination of the two.

Fiscal policies are in the hands of Congress, which has the power to levy taxes and spend government funds. Any combination of reduced spending and increased taxes will reduce the spending power of consumers and business. When consumers and business have less to spend, demand will usually decline and prices should therefore level off.

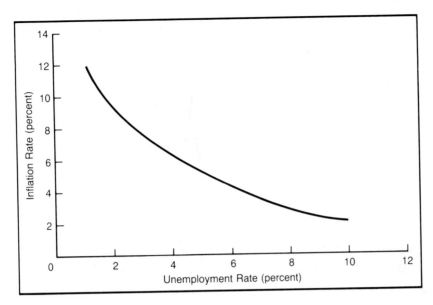

FIGURE 15.2 Phillips Curve

And now for the bad news . . . While reductions in consumer and business demand will take the pressure off price increases, reduced demand is also likely to add to unemployment. As sales decline, factories and other businesses tend to lay off workers. The process can also lead to an unhappy cycle, for as unemployment grows, spending is likely to decline still further and lead to another round of layoffs. This concept can be represented visually by a *Phillips Curve,* named in honor of A. W. Phillips, the British economist, who first demonstrated the relationship between the inflation rate and unemployment. (See Figure 15.2.) In this illustration, unemployment increased from one percent of the labor force to 10 percent as the inflation rate fell from 12 percent to 2 percent.

Efforts to reduce demand are especially hard on groups that rely heavily on borrowed funds. One such group is the housing industry. Since virtually all housing is constructed in part with mortgage loans, government efforts to reduce the money supply make borrowing more difficult. As a result, many people are unable to buy new homes because they cannot obtain mortgages. Meanwhile, as the rate of new housing starts plummets, building contractors, suppliers, and construction workers fall on hard times.

Aiming at Cost-Push as a Cause of Inflation. Government programs to deal with cost-push as a cause of inflation are known as *incomes policies.* Incomes policies seek to limit wage and price increases in one or more of the following ways: voluntary controls, reducing monopoly power, or direct controls.

The Fluctuating Value of Money   **299**

Voluntary Controls. In recent years Presidents Nixon, Ford, and Carter have called upon labor leaders and industry to limit voluntarily their wage demands and price increases to certain guidelines. These efforts to obtain self-regulation have generally failed. Most people seem fearful that while they may follow the President's request, the "other person" will not and will benefit from the sacrifices of others.

Limiting Monopoly Power. Cost-push is most likely to occur in those industries in which management or labor is so strong that it can dictate prices. Therefore, by limiting the market power of labor and management, government could reduce their ability to fix prices. But practical experience has shown that it is extremely difficult to tighten antitrust laws. Moreover, many economists argue that big business and big labor are essential if America is to compete successfully with foreign business.

Direct Controls. During World War II, and part of the Korean War and Vietnam War, the federal government imposed wage and price controls on the nation. These controls established maximum prices on many items, and also fixed wages. Direct controls were generally effective during World War II because the war was a popular one and the public supported the controls program. At other times, however, controls were not well received. Many regarded them as inconsistent with a democratic society and a free enterprise system. Controls were also very costly to administer because thousands of workers had to be hired to enforce them.

Aiming at Inflation From the "Supply Side." Market price, you will recall from Chapter 2, is a function of both demand *and* supply. In the 1970s a group of economists suggested that price increases could be limited if the output of goods and services were increased. As these "supply-side" economists saw it, the biggest hindrance to increased output was the federal government, whose tax rates were so high as to discourage investment and production. The supply-siders' key to reducing inflation was to reduce taxes. The increase in take-home pay, they reasoned, would enable consumers to increase both their spending and savings. Increased sales would then encourage business to expand. Meanwhile, the additional savings would add to the pool of funds available for investment. The proposal created a sensation, because heretofore a tax cut had been regarded as a way to *increase*, not decrease, prices. (See reading, pages 362–363.)

In the early 1980s, the government used a combination of monetary policy and supply-side techniques to combat a very serious inflation. Results of the effort were mixed. By limiting the growth of the money supply (monetary policy) and reducing taxes (a supply-side strategy), cost-of-living increases were slowed to the lowest rate in nearly twenty years. Unemployment, however, climbed to nearly 10 percent of the labor force, its highest level since the Great Depression.

EXERCISES

Multiple Choice

1. During periods of inflation, the value of the dollar (*a*) decreases (*b*) remains the same (*c*) decreases for a while and then increases (*d*) increases.

2. An increase in average weekly income does *not* result in a higher standard of living if it is caused by (*a*) increased purchases of consumer goods (*b*) increased private investment (*c*) rising prices (*d*) increased productivity.

3. Which would generally have a tendency to create inflation? (*a*) low wages and a surplus of consumer goods (*b*) a limited supply of money and an expanding population (*c*) a high rate of employment and a shortage of consumer goods (*d*) an increase in taxes and a decrease in government spending.

4. Which groups generally would find inflation advantageous? (*a*) bankers with 80 percent of their deposits on long-term loan (*b*) retired teachers living on social security benefits (*c*) investors whose holdings are mostly in bonds (*d*) farmers repaying long-term debts.

5. The purchasing power of the dollar (*a*) tells us the price of a good or service (*b*) is the same as the foreign exchange rate of the dollar (*c*) compares the value of the dollar in one period with its value in another period (*d*) never changes.

6. If the Consumer Price Index today stands at 125, this means that (*a*) prices have risen by 125 percent this year (*b*) prices have risen by 25 percent this year (*c*) there has been a decrease in the cost of living (*d*) the cost of living has increased by 25 percent since the base year.

7. When prices are forced upward because there is "too much money chasing too few goods," economists describe this as (*a*) spiraling deflation (*b*) demand-pull inflation (*c*) cost-push inflation (*d*) push-pull inflation.

8. All other things being equal, each of the following events *except* one will tend to force prices up. Which one will *not*? (*a*) Labor

wins a 10 percent wage increase. (b) Factory output is increased by 15 percent. (c) Government increases the size of its payments to the unemployed by 15 percent. (d) Taxes are reduced by 10 percent.

9. If the yearly inflation rate is 10 percent, prices will double in approximately (a) ten years (b) nine years (c) eight years (d) seven years.

10. Which of the following groups is likely to be the hardest hit by inflation? (a) people in debt (b) people living on fixed pensions (c) factory workers whose pay includes a cost-of-living benefit (d) salespeople who work on *commission* (a percentage of their sales).

11. A major problem in the government's efforts to control inflation is that (a) people do not like to see government increase its level of spending (b) efforts to reduce prices often add to unemployment (c) such efforts require a reduction in taxes (d) no one knows how to measure inflation.

12. In its efforts to support the purchasing power of the dollar, the government is most likely to (a) reduce spending (b) reduce taxes (c) reduce interest rates (d) reduce taxes *and* interest rates.

Essay Questions

1. Jones deposited $1,000 in a savings bank account and received 5 percent interest annually. Three years later Jones withdrew this deposit plus the accrued interest. During that same period, the cost of living rose 20 percent. (a) In terms of the bank deposit, how did the events of the three-year period affect Jones? Explain. (b) How might Jones have invested the $1,000 more profitably?

2. Base your answers to the questions on Table 15.1 on page 290. (a) (1) What information is given by the figures in Column I? (2) Explain the meaning of the notation "1967 = 100." (3) What is the meaning of the figures in Column II? (b) What has happened to the purchasing power of the dollar in the years since the end of World War II? How would you account for this trend?

3. Some economists have argued that the best way to fight inflation is to increase the production of goods and services. They recommend that the government use its taxing powers to stimulate production. In that way, it will avoid repeating the errors of past policies, which added to the unemployment rolls and created hardships for the housing industry. (a) How would an increase in production reduce inflation? (b) How did past policies add to unemployment and create hardships for the housing industry? (c) How might the government use its power to tax (or not to tax) to stimulate production?

4. "In seeking the causes of inflation, one ought not to overlook the *expectation* of future price increases, for therein lies a *self-fulfilling prophecy*." Explain this statement.

302

5. A recent victim of runaway inflation has been Argentina. When World War II ended, the Argentine peso was about equal in value to the American dollar. By 1983, however, some 12 million pesos were needed to buy a single dollar.

Identify and explain the likely effect of such an inflation on three of the following groups of Argentines: (*a*) retirees living on pensions (*b*) young married couples (*c*) people with their savings in banks (*d*) people who own their own businesses (*e*) farmers (*f*) landlords.

The millions of dollars tennis players spend on new equipment amount to only a tiny fraction of the gross national product.

UNIT VII

Promoting Economic Stability

CHAPTER 16

Measuring the Nation's Economic Performance

Every good driver knows to keep an eye on the dashboard gauges. From these instruments, the driver can judge the speed that the car is traveling, the fuel level, and the relative health and performance of the engine. In this way trouble can often be prevented before it occurs.

Just as experienced motorists keep an eye on their dashboards, so do economists, people in business, bankers, and others monitor the nation's economic performance. In this way they are better able to answer such questions as: How does this year's production compare to last year's? Is our economy growing, declining, or stagnating? What is the outlook for the economy in the months ahead?

Although there is no such thing as an "economic dashboard," there are certain widely published statistical studies, or *economic indicators*, that tell us where the economy has been and where it seems to be going. Best known and most widely followed of these indicators is the gross national product.

THE GNP: TOTAL OUTPUT OF GOODS AND SERVICES

What is the gross national product (GNP)? It is the total market value of all the goods and services produced by the economy in a single year. Now, all this production had to have been purchased by some individual or institution. Therefore, every American who spends money—including yourself—contributes to the enormous sum that is the GNP.

For example, think of the purchases of a typical consumer on a typical day. We may call this person Barbara Byer. Let us say that these were the total of Ms. Byer's purchases on a certain Tuesday in 1980:

Lunch (pizza and soda)	$ 3.50
Drugstore items	6.80
New dress	63.00
Commutation (bus fares)	6.00
Gift for a friend	15.75
Total Expenses	$95.05

Add to this sum all the other expenditures made by our typical consumer, Ms. Byer, for the other 364 days of the year. (If she was indeed typical, she and her family spent about $16,188 after taxes.) Then add to this sum the *total yearly expenditures of all other American consumers* (including you and members of your family).

To the billions of dollars in this consumer total, add more billions spent by *all American businesses* on such things as new cash registers, office copiers, computers, stationery supplies, and delivery trucks.

Then add the huge number of purchases that *government agencies* make for such things as new schools, police uniforms, military equipment, and file cabinets.

Finally, add the dollar value of all the American-made cars, books, clothes, and other *goods sold abroad in foreign markets.* (Subtract from this exports total the amount spent by Americans on foreign-made goods and services.)

Adding up all these colossal sums gives us the total value of the year's economic output: the GNP. In 1982, the GNP exceeded a whopping *$3 trillion.* Of course, most economists and business leaders hope that this figure, immense as it is, will grow even larger in each succeeding year. They regard an increase in the GNP as a good sign of healthy economic growth. On the other hand, a decrease in the GNP may mean economic decline or recession—as well as a decline in the standard of living.

THE GROSS NATIONAL PRODUCT AS TOTAL EXPENDITURES

There are, as you know, three principal sectors of the nation's economy: (1) individual consumers, (2) private businesses, and (3) governments of various kinds (state, local, and federal). Economists who measure the GNP try to determine the dollar amount that each of these sectors contributes to the total. The purchases made by these sectors in one

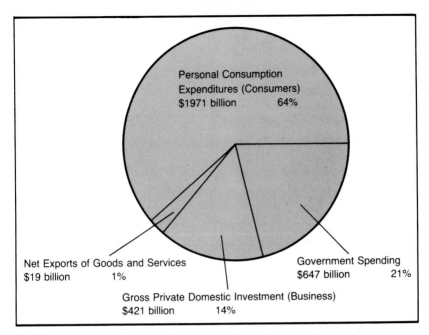

FIGURE 16.1   Purchasers of the Gross National Product, 1982

year (plus the purchases of foreigners—or "net exports") represent the amount of new goods and services created in that year.

In reading about these components of the GNP in the newspapers or hearing about them on radio or television, you are likely to see or hear them referred to by their technical names: personal consumption expenditures (consumers), gross private domestic investment (business), government spending (government), and net exports of goods and services. Figure 16.1 shows these components of the GNP in 1982.

1. Personal Consumption Expenditures: The Consumers' Share. The technical name given to the purchases made by the nation's consumers is *personal consumption expenditures.* Consumer expenditures usually constitute about two-thirds of the GNP. The government divides personal consumption expenditures into three categories:

a. Durable goods. Long-lasting items, such as automobiles, refrigerators, and furniture, are durable goods. These goods accounted for $243 billion of the 1982 GNP.

b. Nondurable goods. Food, clothing, gasoline, and medicine are typical of the quickly consumed items in this category. In 1982, $762 billion was spent on nondurable goods.

c. Services. Consumers in 1982 spent $967 billion on services such as medical care, recreation, and housing.

2. Gross Private Domestic Investment: Business Purchases. Business purchases, which are classified as *gross private domestic investment*, totaled $421 billion in 1982. Most of this sum was spent for construction and new equipment. As we shall soon see, this segment of the GNP is particularly important because its activity affects not only present conditions but future GNP as well.

In order that all production be included in the GNP, those goods that have not been sold must be accounted for. Accordingly, the retail value of unsold goods produced during the year for which the GNP is being calculated is added to gross investment under the category "business inventories." When the goods are sold in succeeding years, their value is deducted from the GNP for the year in which they are sold so that they will not be counted a second time. In this way, only current production is accounted for.

Also included in gross private domestic investment are changes in the stock of raw materials and partially finished goods held by the nation's businesses at the end of the year.

3. Government Spending: Purchases of Goods and Services. In Figure 16.1 on page 307, the amount of $647 billion includes purchases by all levels of government—federal, state, and local. These purchases constituted 21 percent of the total GNP. By contrast, government purchases in 1948 accounted for only 12 percent of that year's GNP. (The reasons for this increase in government's share of total expenditures were described in Chapter 11.)

Not included in government purchases is $361 billion paid by all levels of government in transfer payments: old-age pensions, welfare benefits, unemployment insurance, and veterans' benefits. The people who received this money were not being paid for any goods or services that they helped produce. Rather, the money was "transferred" from one group of citizens to another.

4. Net Exports of Goods and Services. Not all the goods and services purchased by Americans were produced in the United States. If we were to include in our total GNP the money spent on imports, by consumers, government, and business, the GNP would no longer be an accurate measure of United States production. At the same time, that portion of our production that is purchased by foreigners should be included in the GNP. This problem is disposed of in the category of net exports of goods and services in which imports are subtracted from exports. The difference (when exports are greater than imports) is added to the total GNP. When imports are greater than exports, the difference is subtracted from the GNP. In Figure

16.1 the $19 billion under "Net Exports" was obtained by subtracting imports of $330 billion from exports of $349 billion.

THE GROSS NATIONAL PRODUCT AS TOTAL INCOME

You recall from Chapter 3 that there is an endless flow of money among the three major sectors of the economy. For example, whatever consumers spend on clothing automatically turns into income for clothing merchants and manufacturers. What businesses spend on wages and salaries automatically becomes income for the consuming public. Any expense for one group becomes income for another. Because of the circular flow of money, total expenditures are exactly equal to total income.

Thus, the GNP can be measured in two ways. It can be the *total expenditures* of the three sectors of the economy. Or it can be the *total income* of the same three sectors. This is true because total income and total expenditures are always equal. To summarize:

Expenditures	=	GNP	=	Income
(total spent on year's output)		(total market value of goods and services)		(total income received by those in the production process)

So far, we have analyzed GNP as the total sum of expenditures. We can also analyze it as the total income of businesses, governments, and consumers. How do economists measure the portion of the GNP which each sector receives as income? They do this by subtracting one item after another and proceeding in orderly steps from a total sum (GNP) to smaller components. They finally arrive at the sum (considerably smaller than GNP) which consumers may put in their bank accounts as their own money to be spent or saved. Let's follow the economists' calculations step by step.

Finding the National Income. Of the total goods and services produced in a year (GNP), not all is received by individuals and industry. With time, machinery, tools, and factories wear out or *depreciate* in value. Funds must be set aside to replace them. The total depreciation deducted by businesses during the year is known as the capital consumption allowance. Economists deduct this sum from the Gross National Product to obtain what they call the *Net National Product (NNP)*.

From this subtotal, economists subtract sales taxes and excise taxes which businesses pay to the government. The new subtotal is what

TABLE 16.1	National Income in 1982 (in billions)	
Gross National Product		$3,057.6
minus Capital Consumption Allowance		356.3
equals Net National Product		2,701.3
minus Indirect business taxes		264.7
equals National Income		$2,436.6

we call the *national income (NI)*. It is the total of all incomes earned by individuals and businesses in the production of the GNP.

In 1982 the national income totaled $2,436.6 billion, which was calculated as is shown in Table 16.1 and Figure 16.2.

National income can be used to evaluate the share of the GNP received by the various components of the economy. It can also be used to study changes in the distribution of the nation's income over the years. National income is thus an indicator of who is receiving the goods and services produced by the economy.

FIGURE 16.2 National Income Accounts, 1982

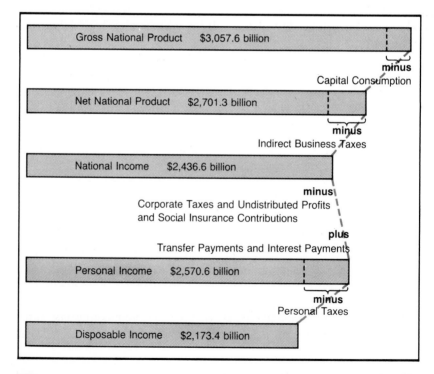

In 1982 the national income, in billions of dollars, was distributed as follows:

Compensation of employees	$1,856.4
Proprietors' income	120.4
Corporate profits	160.5
Rental income	34.1
Net interest	265.2

Compensation of Employees. Counted as compensation are all types of income earned by persons who work as employees. Wages, salaries, bonuses, tips, and other cash payments are included, as well as payments in the form of room and board. Also counted are any other payments made by the employer to benefit the worker, such as payments for Old Age and Survivors Insurance, pensions, and unemployment insurance. Compensation of employees usually amounts to about three-quarters of the total national income.

Proprietors' Income. The $120.4 billion listed as proprietors' income represents the earnings of unincorporated businesses, cooperatives, and farms.

Corporate Profits. This figure includes the profits of all nongovernment corporations.

Rental Income. Income from rent includes not only rent paid for the use of property, but also royalty payments to holders of patents and copyrights.

Net Interest. The $265.2 billion net interest earned in 1982 represents the difference between the total interest received and paid out by the business sector.

Personal Income. How much of the national income is distributed to families and individuals as *personal income*? The answer is most of it, but not all. As you see in Figure 16.2, the income taxes that corporations pay directly to the government are *not* counted as personal income. These corporate taxes must be subtracted from the national income.

At the same time, economists count as personal income the checks that are regularly issued by the government in the form of social security benefits, welfare payments, and veterans' pensions. Such *transfer* payments are added to national income (after corporate taxes have been subtracted). The final result of these calculations is the total income received in one year by all individuals—the total personal income.

Is every dollar of personal income available to consumers to spend or save as they wish? No, a sizable sum is deducted by the government as income taxes. Subtracting these taxes from personal income, we arrive finally at the figure for *disposable personal income (DPI)*. This is all that remains from the GNP for individuals to put into their own bank accounts.

In 1982 consumers paid $397.2 billion in taxes and kept $2,173.4 billion in disposable personal income. Of this amount they spent $1,971.2 billion on goods and services. The rest went into savings ($142.7 billion), interest on consumer loans ($58.6 billion), and payments to people living abroad ($0.9 billion).

Problems of Measuring the GNP. Measuring the GNP both as total income and total expenditures can be extremely complicated. Economists must exercise great care to avoid making errors and distorting the data. For example, how can they avoid counting the same product or service two or three times as it is sold and resold in the course of the year? Secondly, in a year of inflated prices, how do they determine the *real* value of goods and services, instead of their inflated and distorted value?

Counting Only Final Goods and Services. The mistake of counting something twice is avoided by including only final goods and services in the GNP. The value of intermediate goods and services is not counted. Intermediate goods and services are those that went into

"I certainly hope they don't include this stuff in the gross national product!"
Drawing by Dana Fradon; © 1961 *The New Yorker Magazine, Inc.*

the production of final goods and services or that changed hands on their way to becoming final goods and services.

Suppose, for example, that it cost a firm $15 to produce a pair of shoes, which it sold to wholesalers for $25. The wholesalers sold the shoes to retail outlets for $35, and the retailers offered the shoes for $65 a pair. If we were to include each of those transactions in computing the gross national product, we would end up with a figure of $140 for each pair of shoes produced ($15 + $25 + $35 + $65 = $140). But the market value of the shoes was only $65, and it is that figure that concerns us in computing the GNP. For the purposes of the GNP, the shoes are considered intermediate goods until their final sale. To avoid double counting, only the market value of the *final* good or service is counted in figuring the GNP.

Expressing the GNP in Constant Dollars. A second problem concerns the constantly changing value of the dollar. While there are always a hundred cents in a dollar, its value fluctuates in terms of what it can buy. Because of the general rise in prices in recent years, a dollar cannot buy as much today as it did even in the recent past. For that reason, comparisons of the GNP for different years can be misleading.

For example, let us suppose that in a certain year the GNP stood at $3 trillion. In the following year, prices increased by 10 percent, but the output of goods and services remained the same. Exactly the same number of automobiles, pens, haircuts, and everything else that was produced the first year was also produced in the second year. Prices, however, had increased by 10 percent so that the GNP now stood at $3.3 trillion. Thus, our economic gauge would show a $300 billion increase in the GNP, even though the output of goods and services had not increased at all.

Such misleading results occur when the GNP is figured using *current dollars*—that is, the actual number of dollars spent during the year, regardless of how many items each dollar could purchase. Reports based on current dollars do not take into account the changing *value* of the dollar.

To solve this problem, the United States Department of Commerce uses a more realistic standard of measurement known as *constant dollars*. Constant dollars express the value of dollars in terms of what they can purchase rather than the actual number of dollars spent. Amounts given in constant dollars have been adjusted to compensate for changes in the level of prices. This adjustment is accomplished by selecting a base year—currently 1972—and expressing the GNP in terms of the prices of that year.

Constant Dollars and Current Dollars. What was the purchasing power of this $10 bill in 1970 as compared to its purchasing power in 1982? (Refer to Table 15.1.)

Let us assume that prices increased 90 percent between 1972 and 1983. An item that sold for $100 in 1972 would therefore cost $190 in 1983. But in constant dollars the 1983 price would also be given as $100, since that was the price at which that item could be purchased in 1972. Constant dollars thus give some idea of the *amount* of goods and services produced in a given year, relative to the base year. Table 16.2 shows the GNP for selected years expressed in current dollars and in constant dollars (the base year is 1972). The table shows that the GNP as expressed in constant dollars was greater than its current dollar value in the years before 1972. The reason is that before 1972 prices were relatively low. Thus fewer dollars were required to

TABLE 16.2   Gross National Product for Selected Years, 1929–1982 (billions of dollars)

Year	Current Dollars	Constant Dollars (1972)
1929	$103.4	$315.7
1933	55.8	222.1
1940	100.0	344.1
1950	286.5	534.8
1960	506.5	737.2
1972	1,185.9	1,185.9
1980	2,614.1	1,480.7
1982	3,058.0	1,485.0

TABLE 16.3 Gross National Product of Selected Countries, 1980
(in constant 1979 dollars)

	Total GNP (in billions)	Per Capita GNP
United States	$2,370.0	$10,408
Sweden	108.2	13,032
France	575.1	10,709
Soviet Union	1,290.8	4,861
Greece	40.5	4,215
India	144.5	208
Ethiopia	4.0	134
Japan	1,044.9	8,946

purchase the same amount of goods and services that could be purchased in 1972.

Per Capita GNP. GNP data are often used to compare the output of two or more nations in order to estimate standard of living. If all other things are equal, the nation with the larger GNP will have more goods and services available for its people. Before any comparisons can be made, however, the data must be adjusted for population differences. This is usually done by dividing a nation's gross national product by its population in order to arrive at its GNP *per capita* (per person). Table 16.3 shows the sometimes surprising difference between a nation's total GNP and its per capita GNP, in constant dollars. Of the eight countries in the table, Sweden ranked sixth in total GNP in 1980. Did this low rank mean that the Swedish people were among the world's poor? Certainly not. On a per capita basis, Sweden outproduced all the other nations in the table, including the United States.

Per capita adjustments are also valuable in comparing a nation's output from one year to the next. For example, suppose you learned that a country's GNP had increased by 15 percent over a three-year period. Could you assume there would be 15 percent more goods and services available per person? Not necessarily. If the population had increased by 20 percent over the same period of time, there would actually be less available per person. By comparison, learning that the GNP had grown by 15 percent per capita in constant dollars would be more informative. Why? Because these data take into account changes in both population and purchasing power.

Measuring the GNP. The volunteers who cooked and served this church supper received no income for their services. Consequently, their labor was not included in the GNP. Is volunteer labor important to the United States standard of living?

LIMITATIONS OF THE GNP

Although the GNP is the most talked-about measure of a nation's economic activity, it has its limitations. Two of the most serious defects of the GNP are its failure to include transactions that take place outside the market economy, and its inability to measure the economic well-being of the nation in qualitative terms.

1. The GNP fails to include "nonmarket" economic activities. While the GNP is supposed to represent the total value of all goods and services produced by the economy, a large chunk is not included. Homemakers, for example, who spend their days caring for children, cleaning the home, and preparing food and cooking for the family are performing services whose value is not included in the GNP. Meanwhile, the services of housekeepers, cooks, cleaning service workers, and other household help who are paid to perform the same duties as homemakers *are* included in the GNP. Similarly, the earnings of gardeners who care for lawns are included in the GNP, whereas the value of the labor performed by those who take care of their own gardens is not.

In addition, there is an entire category of illegal and unrecorded economic activity that is not included in the GNP. Known as the "underground economy" (see pages 243–245), these transactions include activities like narcotics sales and gambling, as well as purchases and sales that people fail to report properly to the government.

2. The GNP fails to measure economic well-being. Although the GNP tells us whether total output is increasing or decreasing, it does not tell us anything about the *quality* of that output. So, for example, $1 billion worth of cigarettes and $1 billion worth of grain receive equal value in the GNP totals, even though the former product is harmful to the nation's health.

Similarly, the increased production of things that we all want often leads to the production of those that we do not. In these circumstances, GNP will count the "good things" but it will not include the bad ones. When increased factory output leads to a greater quantity of goods and services, these totals are included in the GNP. If, however, the output creates a greater amount of environmental pollution, the cost of that pollution is not reflected in the GNP.

EXERCISES

Multiple Choice

1. Between 1920 and 1957, the nation's gross national product more than doubled. This means that the (a) amount of wages earned increased over 100 percent (b) total value of goods manufactured increased over 100 percent (c) total value of new goods and services increased over 100 percent (d) government included intermediate goods and services in the GNP.
2. Which one of the following will give the best measure of the nation's economy? (a) national income in current dollars (b) common stock prices (c) total employment (d) gross national product per capita in constant dollars.
3. The maximum GNP that a nation can produce in any one year is determined by (a) its productive resources (b) consumer demand for products (c) disposable personal income (d) its natural resources.
4. Which of the following groups accounts for almost all purchases of the nation's total output? (a) government, business, and farmers (b) business, consumers, and government (c) households, consumers, and business (d) government, consumers, and foreign buyers.
5. Assume that since 1982 the GNP has increased from $3 trillion to $4.5 trillion and that prices have increased by 50 percent. Which of the following would express today's GNP in terms of 1982 dollars? (a) $4.5 trillion (b) $5.75 trillion (c) $3 trillion (d) $2.25 trillion.
6. Which of the following events would be included in the GNP as gross private domestic investment? (a) the purchase of a private

home by a family (*b*) the purchase of common stocks in a corporation (*c*) the purchase of new machinery by a business (*d*) a deposit of $1,000 into a savings account.

7. The largest item on the expenditure side of the GNP is (*a*) personal consumption expenditures (*b*) gross private domestic investment (*c*) government purchases of goods and services (*d*) net exports.

8. One way to avoid counting an item in the GNP more than once is to (*a*) count only the wholesale cost of the item (*b*) include only the final retail price of the item (*c*) deduct the capital consumption allowance (*d*) count each resale only once as the item passes from producer to retailer.

9. Intermediate goods and services are omitted from the GNP in order to (*a*) make the GNP easier to calculate (*b*) avoid overstating the value of the nation's output (*c*) avoid confusing expenditures with income (*d*) allow for exports.

10. The function of "constant dollars" is to (*a*) keep the value of the dollar stable (*b*) control the level of spending (*c*) allow for changes in the level of prices (*d*) make adjustments for taxes and interest.

11. In the national income accounts, the item "net exports of goods and services" represents (*a*) the profits of the nation's exporters over a given year (*b*) the total value of the nation's exports as expressed in constant dollars (*c*) the total value of the nation's exports in current dollars (*d*) the difference between the nation's exports and imports in a given year.

12. Which of the following items would *not* be included in the GNP for a particular year? (*a*) the construction of a factory by the government (*b*) the purchase of a hot dog on a roll with mustard (*c*) the sale of 1,000 shares of AT&T stock (*d*) the sale of a new automobile.

13. A farmer sold a crop of potatoes to a wholesaler for $7,000. The wholesaler, in turn, sold the crop to a manufacturer of potato chips for $8,000. The potato chips were sold to a chain of supermarkets for $10,000. The supermarket chain sold the chips to the public for $15,000. What effect did these sales have on the GNP? (*a*) GNP increased by $7,000. (*b*) GNP increased by $15,000. (*c*) GNP increased by $40,000. (*d*) They had no effect on GNP.

Base your answers to questions 14 to 16 on the following data from last year relating to the economy of the tiny nation of Cosmo:

Total consumption	$167 million
Total investment	40
Government spending	53
Exports	25
Imports	35

14. What was Cosmo's GNP last year? (a) $250 million (b) $260 million (c) $295 million (d) $320 million.
15. Total consumption in Cosmo last year was what fraction of the GNP? (a) one-quarter (b) one-third (c) one-half (d) two-thirds.
16. Cosmo's net exports totaled (a) $35 million (b) $25 million (c) −$10 million (d) −$20 million.

Essay Questions

1. In comparing the economies of two nations, economists frequently use per capita GNP figures. (a) Why is per capita GNP rather than total GNP used? (b) What other factors are important in such a comparision? Explain.
2. (a) Briefly define each of the following accounts: (1) gross national product (2) national income (3) personal income (4) disposable personal income. (b) For *each* of the above accounts, name one person or institution that might be interested in the current figures and explain one reason for this interest. (*Note*: Do not use the same person or institution more than once.)
3. Study the graph and answer the questions. (a) What is the purpose of Figure 16.3? (b) Why are the figures for current GNP greater than those expressed in 1972 dollars? (c) What happened to GNP between 1978 and 1982 (1) in current dollars? (2) in 1972 dollars? (3) How do you account for these differences?

FIGURE 16.3 United States Gross National Product in 1972 Dollars and Current Dollars, 1978–1982

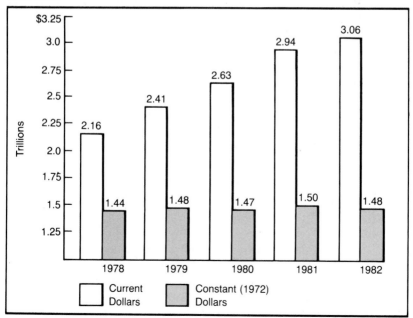

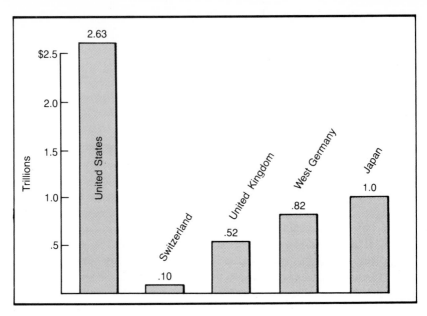

FIGURE 16.4   Gross National Product for Five Countries, 1980

4. Study the graphs and answer the questions. (*a*) List the countries depicted in Figure 16.4 in order of decreasing GNP. (*b*) List the countries depicted in Figure 16.5 in order of decreasing per capita GNP. (*c*) How do you account for the differences between the ranking for Figure 16.4 and Figure 16.5?

FIGURE 16.5   Per Capita Gross National Product for Five Countries, 1980

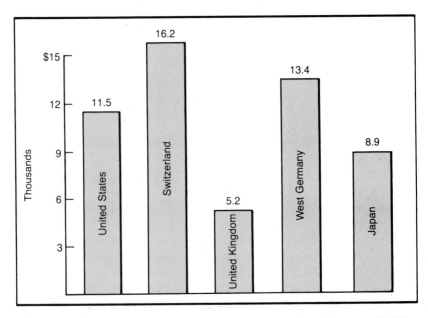

CHAPTER 17

The Level of Economic Activity

America's economic history has been marked by both good times and bad times. In good times, jobs are plentiful, stores are busy, and the nation's factories hum with activity. In bad times, just the opposite is true. Jobs are scarce, business is slow, and factories and machines stand idle. These changes are shown in Figure 17.1, which illustrates business activity since 1905. As you can see, changes in the level of the nation's economic activity have been the rule rather than the exception.

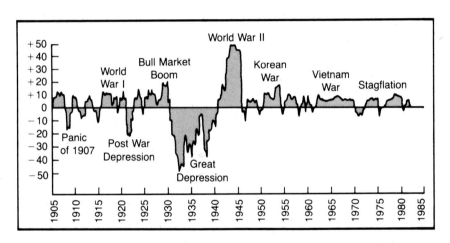

FIGURE 17.1   United States Business Activity Since 1905 (*AmeriTrust*, Cleveland)

THE BUSINESS CYCLE: THE UPS AND DOWNS OF THE AMERICAN ECONOMY

The ups and downs in the level of economic activity are commonly referred to as the *business cycle*. In Figure 17.1, the 0 line represents what economists decided should have been the normal level of activity for a particular year. The jagged line indicates the extent to which actual economic activity was above or below the norm.

The graph shows that, although no two cycles have been identical in either duration or intensity, there has been a consistent up-and-down pattern through the years. Economists studying business cycles

321

have identified four phases through which these cycles pass as they swing down, up, and back again. Figure 17.2 shows that these phases are (1) *recession*, (2) *trough*, or *depression*, (3) *expansion*, or *recovery*, and (4) *peak*, or *prosperity*.

1. Recession. During a recession, economic activity goes into a decline. Consumers buy less than before. The decline in consumer demand prompts firms that service consumers to cut back on their own orders. The pace of manufacturing slows. As workers are laid off, the unemployment rate rises. Salaries and wages fall, consumer demand is further reduced, and the recession intensifies.

Contrary to your expectations, prices do not necessarily fall during a recession. In those industries in which competition is keen, prices do come down with a decline in sales. Where there is little competition,

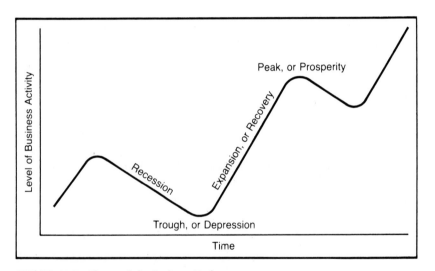

FIGURE 17.2 Phases of the Business Cycle

however, prices are likely to be "sticky," the economists' way of saying that prices tend to stay where they are. With little or no competition to undercut them, managers are able to maintain prices by laying off workers and reducing output.

2. Trough, or Depression. Sooner or later, a recession will bottom out into what economists refer to as the trough of the cycle. When the recession is mild and short-lived, the trough will be reached before the levels of unemployment and business shrinkage become serious. At other times, recessions have reached very low levels of output and employment and extended over long periods of time before running their course. This pattern was especially persistent in the years before World War II. Economists in those years were likely to use the term "depression" in describing the trough of the business cycle.

Exactly at what point a recession could be declared a depression is never very clear. A popular comedian in the 1930s explained: "A recession is when *you* are out of work. A depression is when *I* am out of work."

3. Expansion, or Recovery. In time, optimism creeps back into the economy. The level of spending begins to increase as consumers and business firms expand their buying and production. As more and more workers find jobs, unemployment drops. This process leads to an increase in income and the further growth of spending.

4. Peak, or Prosperity. As the upper turning point of the business cycle is reached, the economy closes in on its capacity. As sales increase, business firms expand their operations. Meanwhile, factories that may have been idle or only partly utilized will again produce at or near their capacities. This in turn will reduce unemployment as workers are hired to handle the increased output. Prices are likely to rise during peak periods because, as incomes increase, so too do business and consumer demand, thereby fueling inflation.

If the recovery climbs high enough, the economy will reach the point of *full employment.* By this we mean that the nation's productive resources will be working to capacity. If, however, the recovery is short-lived, the peak may be reached at something less than full employment.

THE GREAT DEPRESSION

Values have shrunk to fantastic levels; taxes have risen; our ability to pay has fallen; government of all kinds is faced by serious curtailment of income; the means of exchange are frozen in the currents of trade; the withered leaves of industrial enterprise lie on every side; farmers find no markets for their produce; the savings of many years in thousands of families are gone. More important, a host of unemployed citizens face the grim problem of existence and an equally great number toil with little return. Only a foolish optimist can deny the dark realities of the moment.

These words, which described the worst economic crisis ever faced by the United States, were spoken by President Franklin D. Roosevelt during his Inaugural Address in March 1933. They were hardly an exaggeration. With 13 million workers unemployed (representing one out of every four persons in the labor force), 4,000 banks failing, production at its lowest point since 1900, and business failures at an all-time high, times were hard indeed.

DEVELOPING ECONOMIC UNDERSTANDING

The Business Cycle and Economic Indicators: How Do We Know Where We Are?

In tracking the business cycle, economists and other forecasters rely on a number of measures or *indicators*. The best-known and most widely followed of these indicators is the gross national product. But the GNP is only one of several economic indicators that can give us a picture of where the economy is today. Others tell us something about where we are going and where we have been.

As a matter of convenience, economists place these statistics into three groups: *coincident indicators, leading indicators,* and *lagging indicators.* Coincident indicators move up and down along with the economy, leading indicators move ahead of the economy, and lagging indicators follow behind the nation's general economic trends.

COINCIDENT INDICATORS. Like the GNP, the index of industrial production is a coincident indicator. This index shows changes in the output of America's factories, mines, and utilities. Similarly, personal income (described in Chapter 16) is another widely followed measure of the status of the economy. Other coincident indicators include the retail sales index and the wholesale price index.

LEADING INDICATORS. The leading indicators generally move ahead of the economy. Economists discovered that soon after there was an increase in the construction of new homes the entire economy seemed to improve. Similarly, an increase in employment in manufacturing was likely to be followed by an upturn in business in general. By contrast, a decline in new housing or manufacturing employment was often a sign that the economy as a whole would soon decline.

Other leading indicators include corporate profits, common stock prices, business failures, commercial and industrial construction, and manufacturers' new orders for durable goods.

The Great Depression of 1929–1939 profoundly disturbed economists. Some explanation had to be found for those awful years. True, swings from good to bad times were nothing new. You may have read about Joseph's Egypt and the seven fat and seven lean years. But such fluctuations were brought about by obvious physical causes, such as droughts and plagues. No such cause could be identified for

The leading indicators are particularly important because they enable us to predict the future. By way of increasing their usefulness, the federal government's Department of Commerce publishes a monthly *Index of Leading Economic Indicators*. The index measures changes in each of the above series as well as several others.

LAGGING INDICATORS. Measurements that seem to move behind the general economic trends are the *lagging indicators*. So, for example, an increase in unemployment will usually follow the onset of a recession. Similarly, unemployment will not decline until a recovery is already under way. As you look through this list, you might consider the reasons why these indicators tend to follow rather than lead the economy: unemployment rate, current expenditures for plant and equipment, manufacturers' inventories, and consumer installment debt.

1. Define each of the following: (a) leading indicator (b) lagging indicator (c) coincident indicator.
2. (a) Identify two *leading*, two *lagging*, and two *coincident* indicators. (b) Explain why *three* of these indicators are so classified.
3. With reference to one or more of the *coincident, leading,* and *lagging* indicators (refer to at least one indicator from each category), identify and explain: (a) At what point on the business cycle do you believe the economy to be at the present time? (b) What do you believe will be the economic trend over the next six months to a year?
   (Hint: You will find many of the economic indicators featured in the financial pages of your daily newspaper and the business periodicals on file in your school and public libraries. These periodicals include such newspapers and magazines as *The Wall Street Journal, Business Week, Fortune, Barrons,* and *Forbes.*)

America's miseries in the 1930s. Although the production of goods and services had fallen by one-third from 1929 to 1933, the nation's capacity to produce was at an all-time high. Why then should a nation rich in resources and technology be so stricken? What remedial measures could be taken to restore the prosperity of the 1920s? What could be done to prevent the recurrence of such a depression?

The Level of Economic Activity   325

In seeking the answers to these questions, economists tried to develop a better understanding of economic forces and their impact upon human well-being. Several theories as to the causes of economic fluctuations were formulated, along with the steps that might be taken to keep them under control.

THEORIES ON THE CAUSES OF BUSINESS CYCLES

For as long as economists have been aware of the periodic ups and downs of the economy, they have searched for reasons to explain and predict them. W. Stanley Jevons, a noted British economist, created quite a stir in 1878 with his announcement that business cycles were caused by sunspots. These dark patches on the sun, Jevons believed, affected global weather patterns, which, in turn, had a direct influence on crops. Worldwide crop failures raised food prices, lowered living standards, and triggered recessions and depressions. It was an interesting idea, but the science of astronomy later proved that Jevons' theory had little basis in fact.

External Causes. Since Jevons' day, there has been no shortage of theories and explanations for the causes of business cycles. The most widely accepted explanations focus on two categories of causes, *external* and *internal*. External causes, such as sunspots, are those at work outside the economic system. Other external causes would include such things as *innovations* and *political events*.

Innovations. Some economists have attributed the development of certain innovations as a principal cause of fluctuations in the economy. The shift from hand labor to machine labor in the textile industry, which opened the Industrial Revolution in England, is a case in point. Similarly, the introduction of the "horseless carriage" (the automobile) in the early 1900s and the computer in the 1950s set off a series of events that changed the trend of the economy in this country.

Because innovations involve new ways of doing things, the theory goes, they require investment to pay for new capital, or plant and equipment. This new investment puts additional income into the hands of business and its employees. This income leads to additional business and consumer spending, which in turn stimulates expansion and prosperity. In time, the expansion fostered by the innovations comes to an end, leading to a leveling off of business activity, a contraction in consumer spending, and recession.

Political Events. Major political events, such as a war or an economic boycott either at home or abroad, can so affect the nation's economy as to reverse its course. Perhaps the most dramatic case in recent years was the successful effort by the Organization of Petroleum Exporting Countries to increase the price of crude oil. Starting in 1973, with an embargo on oil shipments, OPEC pushed the price of oil up from $2 to more than $20 a barrel. The immediate effect of this 1000 percent price increase was to pay to foreign oil suppliers billions of dollars that would otherwise have been in the hands of Americans. With so much less business and consumer spending power available, the sales of goods and services in this country declined sharply. This lack of capital in turn led to the nation's most serious recession since the 1930s.

Internal Causes. Internal causes of business cycles relate to factors *within* the economy that are likely to trigger either an expansion or a contraction of business activity. Some of the more widely held internal theories are described below.

Psychological Factors. If business *believes* that conditions are going to improve, this belief will lead to a series of events that will make the prophecy come true. For example, if in the *expectation* of increased sales most firms increase their investment in new plant, equipment, and merchandise, their actions will add to employment and personal income. With more to spend, consumers will in fact spend more, thereby stimulating additional business investment and personal income. Thus, as the economy expands, business will enjoy the fulfillment of its prophecy.

If, on the contrary, business believes the future to be bleak, firms are likely to reduce production and lay off workers. This belief too could become a self-fulfilling prophecy, for with reduced employment consumer spending will decline and business will continue to contract.

Psychological theory can also be applied to the behavior patterns of consumers. When they believe that hard times are approaching, consumers are likely to postpone major purchases and spend less money. The business community will then have to reduce the level of its operations. As unemployment increases and personal income declines, the recession will gain momentum and consumers will witness the fulfillment of their prophecy. Consumer optimism, in contrast, will have the opposite effect. Increased spending will trigger increased business activity, employment, and earnings, and the business cycle will swing into its recovery phase.

Underconsumption. According to the theory of underconsumption, forces within the business cycle itself reverse its trend. During periods of prosperity, both business and consumer savings are relatively high. Meanwhile, production levels increase until business discovers that it is outpacing consumption. At that point, business activity is reduced,

JOHN MAYNARD KEYNES
The General Theory of Employment, Interest, and Money (1936)

The ideas of economists and political philosophers are more powerful than is commonly understood. Indeed, the world is ruled by little else. Practical men, who believe themselves to be quite exempt from any intellectual influences, are usually the slaves of some defunct economist.

In these words from the final pages of his most famous work, *The General Theory of Employment, Interest, and Money*, John Maynard Keynes (pronounced Kay-NZ) correctly anticipated the impact of his own writings on later generations. Keynes' *General Theory* now stands with Smith's *Wealth of Nations* and Marx's *Capital* as one of the most influential statements of economic philosophy of the modern age.

Keynes was born into academic surroundings in Cambridge, England. His father was an economist at the University, and his mother was one of its first women graduates. At Cambridge, Keynes was considered Alfred Marshall's most brilliant student. After graduation and a brief stint with the British civil service, Keynes joined the Cambridge faculty. He left the university in 1915 to undertake a successful career in the British Treasury. In 1919, Keynes attended the Versailles Peace Conference that followed World War I. His dismay with the direction that those talks were taking led him to resign his post in protest. As the chief British representative to the Bretton Woods Conference following World War II, Keynes helped to shape the course of international trade during the postwar years. But it was his *General Theory*, published in 1936 during the Great Depression and for which he is best remembered, that heralded what has come to be known as the "Keynesian Revolution."

Prior to the appearance of the *General Theory*, most economists held that, left to its own devices, the economy would achieve equilibrium (a state of balance) at *full employment*. This theory was in accord with the ideas of the French economist Jean Baptiste Say (1767–1832), who had suggested that supply creates its own demand, that is, whatever the economy produced would be purchased. Moreover, prices would seek whatever level was necessary to bring about this supply-demand rela-

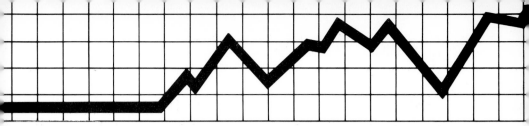

tionship and full employment. If there was unemployment at any point in time, it existed only because wages were too high. In such circumstances, market forces could be expected to drive down wages to whatever level was necessary to enable employers to hire all those willing and able to work. Naturally, it followed from this reasoning that the worst thing government could do would be to interfere with the economy, for to do so would prevent the market forces from restoring the full-employment equilibrium.

One did not have to be an economist in the 1930s, however, to know that the full-employment theory simply did not work. Millions of workers were unable to find jobs, while factories lay idle for want of orders. Similarly, farm products rotted unsold in the midst of worldwide hunger. Keynes pointed out that the economy had indeed reached equilibrium, but it had done so at a point well below full employment. There simply was no self-correcting mechanism that would put people back to work in the short run.

"Perhaps not," said many economists. "But in the long run, the system will come into balance and unemployment will disappear."

"In the *long run*," Keynes replied, "we are all dead."

The key ingredient in Keynes' analysis was *aggregate demand,* the collective spending by all elements of the economy. There is, he argued, a level at which aggregate demand will support full employment. Anything below that level would simply result in less than full-employment equilibrium. At levels higher than full employment, there would be inflation.

The challenge, then, in times of unemployment and idle capacity, was to find ways to *increase* aggregate demand. Keynes' solution called upon government to "prime the pump" of consumer spending and business investment through appropriate taxing and spending policies.

This program was a revolutionary break with the *laissez-faire* thinking of the time, which vigorously opposed government intervention in economic affairs. Indeed, Keynes ignited a controversy that continues to this day between those who favor government participation and those who oppose it.

One of those influenced by Keynes' ideas was United States President Franklin D. Roosevelt. His New Deal program marshaled the resources of the American economy in an unprecedented effort to fight the Great Depression. Following World War II, the Employment Act of 1946 made the participation of government in efforts to stabilize the economy part of the overall economic policy of the United States.

layoffs follow, and income levels decline. On the downswing side of the cycle, the opposite takes place. With less to spend, savings as a percent of total income decline. Meanwhile, consumer and business spending will increase. This upswing moves business to increase the level of production and thereby brings the recession to an end.

While economists tend to agree that there is some validity in each of these explanations, they also hold that no one in and of itself is sufficient. Instead, they suggest that some combination of these and other factors working together is responsible for specific turns of the economy. Most important are the changes that take place in *aggregate demand* and its relationship to *full employment*.

AGGREGATE DEMAND, FULL EMPLOYMENT, AND THE PRICE LEVEL

The nation's total output of goods and services, its gross national product (GNP), is purchased by three principal groups: consumers, producers, and government. (For purposes of this discussion, we have included *net exports*—purchases by foreigners—with business spending.) As you learned earlier, economists refer to the total sum as *aggregate demand. Full employment* refers to the total amount of goods and services that the economy could produce *if its resources were fully employed.* The level of aggregate demand as compared to that of full employment goes a long way toward explaining why the economy is undergoing a period of recession, expansion, or inflation.

For example, during periods of recession, aggregate demand declines so that the spread between it and full employment increases. As business closes down its factories, stores, and offices, workers are laid off and total income falls.

The reverse happens during periods of recovery. At these times consumer, business, and government demand is greater than current production levels. Producers expand their activities, leading to more employment, increased purchases of raw materials, and expanded production facilities.

As aggregate demand increases, it may exceed the capacity of the economy to satisfy it. If the nation's factories, shops, and workers are fully employed, increased spending would not add to employment or production. With "too much money chasing too few goods," prices would probably increase. Conversely, a reduction of aggregate demand in those circumstances is likely to lead to lower prices rather than to a reduced output of goods and services.

In its efforts to stabilize the economy and promote its growth, the federal government will seek to adjust aggregate demand at levels sufficient to keep the economy fully employed without promoting

Aggregate Demand and Full Employment

Figure 17.3 illustrates the economic importance of aggregate demand and its relationship to full employment. In this hypothetical illustration, we have assumed that with its resources *fully employed* the economy will be able to produce $4 trillion worth of goods and services at *current prices*.

In *Case I* aggregate demand stands at $3 trillion. This level will leave the nation with unused capacity in the form of idle plants, shops, and, of course, workers. Economists refer to the $1 trillion spread between the actual GNP and its potential as the *recessionary gap*. How would you describe economic conditions at this time?

In *Case II* aggregate demand exactly equals the economy's ability to produce at full employment. How would you describe economic conditions at this time?

In *Case III* aggregate demand is running at $5 trillion. This level is 25 percent greater than the economy's ability to produce at full employment. Economists refer to the $1 trillion spread as the *inflationary gap*. How would you describe economic conditions in these circumstances?

FIGURE 17.3   Aggregate Demand and Its Significance

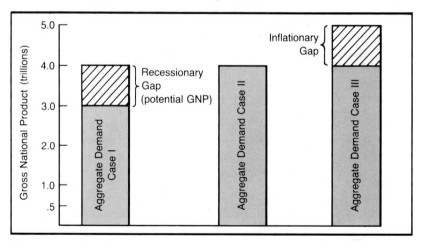

inflation. Toward that end economists have spent a great deal of time studying the gross national product and its components in an effort to discover ways in which to turn the government's dream into a reality. As recent history has shown, much remains to be done before that goal can be achieved. Nevertheless, a number of significant discoveries have been made.

ANALYZING THE GROSS NATIONAL PRODUCT

In studying the spending patterns of two of the three principal purchasers of the gross national product, consumers and producers, economists found that these patterns differed sharply. While consumer spending as a proportion of the GNP varied hardly at all over the years, there were wide swings in expenditures by the business sector. These patterns are illustrated in Figure 17.4. Since the purpose of the research was to better our understanding of the business cycle, the discovery was a promising one. After all, once the causes of the economy's ups and downs are isolated, it might then be possible to

FIGURE 17.4 Fluctuations in Demand by Consumers and Producers, 1951–1981

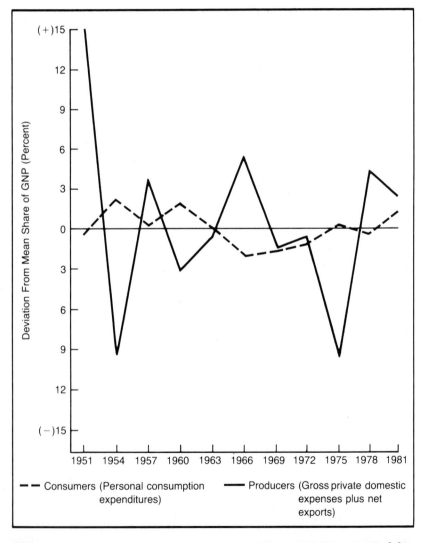

do something about them. As the results of the research came in, a clearer picture of the roles played by consumers and producers and their impact upon the economy began to emerge.

Consumers and Consumption. Consumer spending makes up the largest share—about 63 percent—of the GNP. It is also the most consistent component. As indicated by Figure 17.4, consumer spending has not strayed above or below 3 percent of its average share since 1951. Meanwhile, other studies revealed that consumers have consistently spent from 90 to 93 percent of their *disposable income* (their income after taxes). The remainder went into savings.

It was evident that consumer spending was a *result* rather than a cause of fluctuations in the economy because the amount that consumers spent depended on how much they earned. An examination of *investment* (business spending), by comparison, revealed a different picture.

Business Spending (Investment). Business spending on plant, equipment, and inventories (goods held for later sale) is called *investment*. Unlike consumption, investment is anything but stable. In fact, investment fluctuates widely.

The relative instability of investment as compared to consumer spending can be seen in Figure 17.4. This comparison is also demonstrated in Figure 17.5 on page 334, where you will note that, while consumer spending increased every year since 1951, business investment rose and fell over those years.

Fluctuations in the level of spending by business are clearly a major cause of the ups and downs of the business cycle. But why does business spending fluctuate so much more than consumer spending? The following summarizes the principal forces affecting the level of investment.

Why Business Investment Fluctuates. As long as production methods and sales volume remain the same, there will be little reason for business to add to its supply of plant, equipment, or inventories. Whatever investment takes place under those circumstances would be to replace worn-out capital and inventories that had been sold. Any or all of the following factors, however, would affect the level of business spending:

The Cost and Availability of Investment Funds. Business firms obtain the money they need for investment out of savings or from loans. Sometimes, *investment capital* (the money used to purchase capital goods such as plant, equipment, and inventories) is relatively inexpensive and easy to borrow. At other times, however, interest rates are high. Since business firms have to take the cost of borrowing

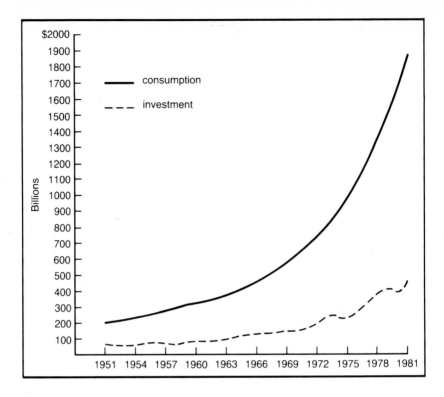

FIGURE 17.5   Personal Consumption Expenditures and Gross Investment, 1951–1981

into consideration in making their investment decisions, interest rates will affect the level of investment.

The Expectation of Larger Sales.   If, for any reason, business thinks that it can increase its sales, it will purchase more equipment to increase its capacity. If the business outlook is bleak, investment will be reduced.

New Discoveries.   When new products are developed, business invests in the plant and equipment necessary to produce them. For example, the development of computers has led to the heavy investment by certain industries in automation equipment.

Population Growth.   If the market for goods and services is increased, business will have to expand its output in order to satisfy the new customers. Thus normal population growth will provide a demand for a constantly expanding output.

New Tax Laws.   Government tax policies can either encourage or discourage investment. When, for example, the government allows businesses to deduct a large portion of their investments from taxable income, businesses will be encouraged to invest a large part of their profits. In addition, the mere expectation of government action may influence business spending. Thus, if business people thought that the government was about to reduce tax concessions for investments, they might be stimulated to make their investments before the law was enacted.

(Another example of tax legislation designed to stimulate investment would be a provision permitting businesses to reduce the depreciation period of their capital. For example, if a machine that cost $100,000 was calculated to have a life of ten years, $10,000 could be deducted from taxable income each year. If, on the other hand, it could be written off in five years, the firm could deduct $20,000 from its taxable income each year.)

Expected Price Changes. If industry believes that a general price increase is on the way, it is more likely to invest in new capital and inventory. In that way industry would hope to save on costs by buying now, and increasing its profits by selling its wares after prices had risen. If, however, prices were expected to fall, business could be expected to follow the opposite course by delaying new investments.

ECONOMIC FLUCTUATIONS MAY BE CUMULATIVE

Frequently, economic fluctuations feed upon themselves: Expansion creates further expansion and recession begets more recession. One explanation for this can be found in the *multiplier*.

The Multiplier. Two weeks ago Friday was your lucky day. You received a birthday gift of $1,000 from rich Uncle Louis. You had no difficulty deciding what to do with the money. You put $200 in the bank and spent the remaining $800 on the video recording and play-back equipment you had wanted for a long time. WAM Electronics, from which you bought the equipment, used $640 of your money to have its store painted, and banked the rest. Meanwhile, painter Paul Carmino used $512 of the money he received for his work to pay for a week's vacation at the shore. The remaining $128 went into Paul's money market fund.

Let us freeze the action right here, because something interesting has been happening that we do not want you to miss. Uncle Louis' $1,000 gift has already led to total spending of $1,952 (because $800 + $640 + $512 = $1,952). Moreover, if we assume that as the process of spending and saving goes on, people will continue to spend 80 percent of their additional income, another $3,048 in income will be generated, bringing the total amount of spending begun by Uncle Louis' $1,000 to $5,000. Economists refer to the increased income generated by additional spending as the *multiplier effect,* or simply, the *multiplier.* Since in this instance total spending was increased by $5,000, the multiplier will be said to have been 5.

The size of the multiplier depends upon the public's inclination to spend. If, on the average, people spend 75 percent of any additional income that comes their way, the multiplier would be higher than it would be if their inclination to spend, or as the economists put it, their *marginal propensity to consume,* were but 50 percent.

Suppose, for example, that a new length of highway is to be built at a cost of $1 million. As the work progresses, the sum will be disbursed to workers, suppliers, contractors, and others. Let us suppose that, during the course of construction, the marginal propensity to consume is 50 percent. Accordingly, the recipients of the $1 million in construction funds will spend $500,000 of that amount and save the rest. Those receiving the $500,000 will then spend half that amount, as will those receiving the $250,000, and so on down the line until there is nothing additional remaining to be spent. By that time, some $2 million will have changed hands. The multiplier was 2.

Had buyers been willing to spend three-quarters of their additional income, the multiplier would have been 4, and the $1 million that went into building the highway would have added $4 million to national income.

The multiplier also works in reverse. A decrease in spending will reduce total income by a multiple of the amount of the reduction. Thus, if total spending were to decrease by $50 billion at a time when the multiplier was 3½, there would be a decrease of $175 billion in national income.

Aggregate Demand and the Government. While the amount spent by consumers and business is the result of millions of private decisions, government, or public, spending can be planned and controlled in such a way as to benefit society as a whole. For example, when the economy is functioning at less than full employment, the government can increase its spending in order to increase aggregate demand. Similarly, the government can deliberately curtail the level of its spending to reduce aggregate demand during a period of inflation. In either case, the government's efforts will be aided by the multiplier, which will magnify the impact of the increase or decrease in spending.

The government can also affect aggregate demand through its power to tax. Tax increases reduce the ability of consumers and business to spend, while tax cuts have the opposite effect. In Chapter 18, we shall take a closer look at these and other techniques available as part of the government's efforts to regulate the economy.

The Multiplier, the Accelerator, and the Paradox of Thrift

The magnitude of the multiplier is directly related to the public's inclination to spend or save additional income. Just as the *marginal propensity to consume* (MPC) describes the public's inclination to spend, the *marginal propensity to save* (MPS) describes its willingness to save. Since income not spent is considered to be savings, MPC + MPS = 1.

THE MULTIPLIER.   The multiplier can be expressed mathematically as the reciprocal of 1 minus the marginal propensity to consume, *or* the reciprocal of the marginal propensity to save:

$$\text{multiplier} = \frac{1}{1 - \text{MPC}} = \frac{1}{\text{MPS}}$$

Thus, if the marginal propensity to consume were 80 percent, the multiplier would be 5 because:

$$1 - {}^{80}\!/_{100} = {}^{1}\!/_{5}$$

and the reciprocal of $^{1}/_{5}$ is 5.

THE ACCELERATOR.   Just as the multiplier describes the effect of changes in spending upon total income, so the acceleration principle describes the effect of changes in spending upon the purchase of new plant and equipment, or *investment*. As consumer demand increases, business will strive to expand its productive capacity so as to earn additional profits. This expansion leads to an investment in capital goods that is proportionately greater than the increase in consumption. If consumption declines, or even levels off, the opposite will take place. There will be a decline in the production of capital goods that will be proportionately greater than the decline in consumption.

For example, let us assume that national production of rotary lawn mowers totaled 100,000 in 1980 and 1981. The mowers had been manufactured with the aid of 100 automated milling machines that automatically fashioned their engine blocks. Let us also assume that ten of these milling machines wore out every year and had to be replaced.

In 1982, mower sales increased by 10 percent to 110,000 units. Since the existing machinery could have produced only 100,000 units (one for every 1,000 mowers), the manufacturers had to purchase ten additional engine-block machines to meet the increased demand. This number was in addition to the ten that were normally bought to replace

TABLE 17.1   Impact of Lawn Mower Sales Upon the Engine-Block Milling Machine Industry, 1980–1984 (hypothetical)

Year	Mowers Sold (consumption)	Milling Machines Required	Additional Machines Purchased	Percent Change From Previous Year
1980	100,000	100	10 (replacements)	0
1981	100,000	100	10 (replacements)	0
1982	110,000	110	20 (10 replacements + 10 additional)	+ 100
1983	120,000	120	20 (10 replacements + 10 additional)	0
1984	120,000	120	10 (replacements)	− 50

those that had worn out. Thus the 10 percent increase in consumer demand resulted in a 100 percent increase in sales over the previous year for manufacturers of engine-block milling machines.

In 1983 mower sales increased once more by 10,000 units, to a total of 120,000. Consequently ten milling machines were again ordered in addition to the ten needed to replace worn-out equipment. From the machine industry's standpoint, the twenty machines produced and sold that year represented no increase over the previous year's sales.

In 1984 lawn mower sales again totaled 120,000 units. Purchases of new engine-block machines were limited to the ten needed to replace those that had worn out. This purchase represented a 50 percent decline in business to the milling machine industry, as sales slumped from twenty to ten units. The sequence of events may be summarized in Table 17.1.

From the discussion and table, we can see why capital-goods industries need an ever-increasing demand for consumer goods just to remain stable. But like everything else, consumer demand will fluctuate, and when it does, it will trigger still wider swings in the capital-goods industries.

INTERACTION OF THE MULTIPLIER AND THE ACCELERATOR.   Just as two or more members of the same family can pass a cold back and forth in a cycle of illness, so can the multiplier and the accelerator feed upon one another. Thus a recession will be aggravated and economic expansion will be promoted.

As a result of the multiplier effect, a small increase in spending will increase total income by a greater amount. This effect will generate an even greater increase in investment as producers respond to increased consumer demand. The investment increase generated by the accelerator will lead to another round of additions to income, spending, and *multiplier effects,* and the economy will continue to climb toward prosperity, full employment, and (if the trend should continue) inflation.

On the downside, a leveling off of consumer demand will result in a still greater decline in the capital-goods industries. The reduction in investment and the decline in income that result will lead to a reduction in consumer spending. National income will be reduced by a multiple of the initial reduction in spending, and the recession will pick up momentum.

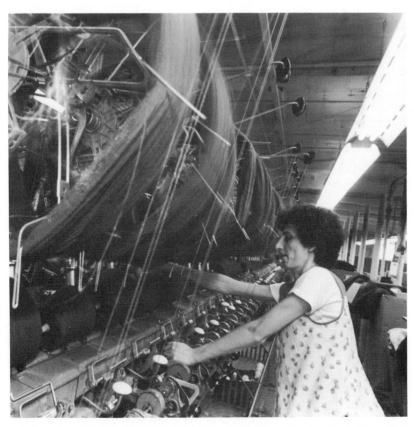

Consumer Demand and Full Employment. How might this worker be affected by a slight decline in consumer demand?

The Level of Economic Activity

THE PARADOX OF THRIFT

"A penny saved is a penny earned."—Benjamin Franklin

paradox—a statement that is seemingly contradictory or opposed to common sense and yet is perhaps true. (Webster's *Collegiate*)

We have mentioned that, when the economy is producing at a level below its capacity, any increase in spending will result in a still greater increase in output. But suppose that, instead of increasing its spending, society as a whole were to apply Benjamin Franklin's advice and increase its *savings*. Since more savings would reduce total spending, the multiplier would serve to decrease production by an even greater amount. This sequence would add to unemployment, reduce earnings, and compel some people to dip into their savings in order to survive. In other words, by increasing its savings, *society as a whole would have less to save*. But, as everyone knows, an increase in savings is frequently a desirable course for *individual families* to follow. Were society as a whole to do the same, however, it would reduce the amount available for savings.

This concept, which defies the common-sense proposition that saving is a worthy activity for every individual, is described by economists as the *paradox of thrift*.

1. Define each of the following: (a) marginal propensity to consume (b) marginal propensity to save (c) the accelerator.
2. According to Table 17.1: (a) What happened to the number of lawn mowers sold in 1983 as compared to 1982? (b) What effect did this have on the sale of new engine-block milling machines in 1983 as compared to 1982? (c) What effect did the 10 percent increase in mower sales in 1982 have on the sales of milling machines?
3. In its efforts to stabilize the economy, the government frequently attempts to influence the level of aggregate demand. It is assisted in this by multiplier and accelerator effects, which magnify the impact of its efforts. (a) Identify and explain two steps that the government might take to fight a recession. (b) What effect will the multiplier and the accelerator have on these efforts?
4. What did a prominent economist mean by this statement: "If too many people 'save for a rainy day,' you can be sure of one thing: that is just what they will bring about—a rainy day"?

EXERCISES

Multiple Choice

Questions 1–3 are based upon Figure 17.6 below:

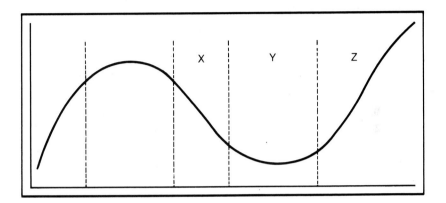

FIGURE 17.6

1. Phase *X* represents the (*a*) peak (*b*) trough (*c*) recovery (*d*) recession.
2. Phase *Y* represents the (*a*) peak (*b*) trough (*c*) recovery (*d*) recession.
3. Phase *Z* represents the (*a*) peak (*b*) trough (*c*) recovery (*d*) recession.
4. Economists refer to the sum total of consumption, investment, and government spending as (*a*) the multiplier (*b*) the acceleration principle (*c*) the sunspot theory (*d*) aggregate demand.
5. The component of the GNP that fluctuates *most* is (*a*) consumer spending (*b*) business spending (*c*) government spending (*d*) national income.
6. The component of the GNP that fluctuates *least* is (*a*) consumer spending (*b*) business spending (*c*) government spending (*d*) net exports.
7. If the economy's resources are fully employed, an increase in total spending is most likely to result in (*a*) a decline in tax receipts (*b*) an increase in production and employment (*c*) an increase in income and prices (*d*) an increase in exports.
8. When is the economy most likely to operate at less than full employment? (*a*) during periods of inflation (*b*) when there are shortages of unskilled labor (*c*) when total spending is falling (*d*) when consumer spending is increasing.

9. Consumer spending is most likely to fall when (a) taxes are reduced (b) consumer income is reduced (c) a general increase in prices is expected (d) social security payments are increased.
10. Which condition would exert an inflationary influence on the economy? (a) Aggregate demand for goods exceeds the aggregate supply. (b) The federal government is operating with budgetary surpluses. (c) Tax receipts are at high levels. (d) The currency in circulation has a low rate of turnover.
11. If aggregate demand declines as compared to the productive capacity of the economy as a whole, which of the following events is likely to occur? (a) Employment will increase. (b) The growth rate will decline. (c) Prices will rise. (d) Tax receipts will increase.
12. As a stabilizing influence, the most important component of the GNP is government spending because (a) it is the largest component (b) it fluctuates the least (c) it is the only component that can be deliberately adjusted in the public interest (d) it is the smallest component of the GNP.
13. Changes in the level of spending by any sector of the economy (consumers, business, or government) will be magnified in their effect upon the total economy. One explanation for this is contained in (a) the law of diminishing returns (b) Engel's Law (c) the theory of the multiplier (d) the innovation theory.
14. Which of the following is *not* likely to lead to an increase in business investment? (a) an increase in taxes (b) an improvement in the sales outlook (c) a decline in interest rates (d) population growth.
15. The size of the multiplier is directly affected by (a) government spending (b) business spending (c) business inventory (d) the marginal propensity to consume.

Essay Questions

1. In the midst of a deep recession, the President of the United States called upon the nation's consumers to "spend their way" out of the slump. What did the President mean?
2. Assume that the nation has just reached the bottom of a long recession. Summarize the probable effect of the recession upon: (a) prices (b) wages (c) employment (d) investment (e) profits.
3. "The trouble with *recessions and recoveries* is that they *feed upon themselves*. This may be fine for a while, but sooner or later they *create more problems than they solve*." Explain the *italicized* portions of this statement.
4. (a) "Economists are in agreement as to where the economy was in the *past*, but the *present* and the *future* are not likely to generate such unanimity." Explain this statement. (b) At what stage in the business cycle would you say the economy is today? Do you see any signs indicating that there will be a change in the trend of the economy at any time in the near future? Explain.

CHAPTER 18

Managing the Nation's Economy

In the early 1980s, as the nation's unemployment rate approached 10 percent, the Republican administration of President Ronald Reagan came under fire from the Democrats. President Reagan wasted no time in reminding his critics that the inflation rate, which had reached record highs under President Jimmy Carter, a Democrat, was now down to acceptable levels.

The dispute about unemployment and inflation had its origins during the New Deal of the 1930s, when economists recognized that the policies which promoted inflation could also be used to reduce unemployment. Conversely, inflation could be reduced by inducing mild recessions, which—as you would expect—added to unemployment. Every President from Franklin D. Roosevelt to the present has had to steer a course between inflation and unemployment in an effort to achieve the economic goals of his administration.

In this chapter we shall describe the tools that are available to the government to achieve its economic goals. In the course of the discussion, we shall try to show why the solution of one economic problem frequently creates another.

WHAT ARE THE GOALS OF ECONOMIC POLICY?

In 1946, shortly after the end of World War II, Congress passed the landmark Employment Act. This law committed the federal government to an active role in managing the nation's economic affairs and identified the government's economic goals. As stated in the act:

> It is the continuing policy and responsibility of the federal government to use all practical means . . . to foster and promote *free, competitive enterprise . . . maximum employment, production*, and *purchasing power*.

Although the exact meaning of the goals that we have italicized has been interpreted in a variety of ways, most economists would agree that they include the following:

Free, Competitive Enterprise. Given a choice, it is in the public interest for economic tasks to be performed by private enterprise rather than by the government.

Maximum Employment. Government policy ought to promote conditions that would enable everyone willing and able to work to find a job. This policy was further defined in 1978 by the Full Employment and Balanced Growth Act (Humphrey-Hawkins Act), which specified a 4 percent unemployment rate as the equivalent of full employment.

Production (economic growth). At any point in time, the economy's ability to satisfy wants is limited by its human, capital, and natural resources. As new resources are developed and technology improves, the economy's capacity to produce can increase in a process described as "economic growth." The promotion of economic growth is another of government's economic goals.

Purchasing Power. Most Americans would like to know that the money they set aside in savings will be able to buy as much tomorrow as it can buy today. *Price stability* is a goal toward which many government actions have been directed.

The federal government's efforts to achieve its economic goals are based on the assumption that the key to full employment and economic stability lies in maintaining appropriate levels of aggregate demand. This demand, you will recall, is the total of spending required to purchase the gross national product. It consists of spending by consumers (C), business (I), and government (G), or C + I + G.

When aggregate demand exactly equals the economy's ability to produce, the economy is said to be at *full employment*. When aggregate demand is running at something *less* than its capacity, the difference is described as a recessionary gap. When aggregate demand is *greater* than the economy's capacity to produce, the difference will be accommodated with higher prices and is referred to as an inflationary gap. (Review the boxed feature on page 331.)

During periods of recession and inflation, the government's actions will be directed toward correcting these imbalances. Thus the government will seek to increase aggregate demand during periods of recession and to *dampen* it during periods of inflation. Toward that end, the government can avail itself of two broad categories of programs, known as *fiscal policy* and *monetary policy*. Congress and the President share the responsibility for administering fiscal policy. Monetary policy is administered by the Federal Reserve System, which regulates the nation's supply of money and credit. (The role of the Fed was described in Chapter 15.)

FISCAL POLICY

Fiscal policy is the use by the federal government of its powers to tax and spend for the purpose of regulating the economy. The target of fiscal policy is total, or aggregate, demand (C + I + G).

By increasing or decreasing its own spending (G), when spending, or consumption, by consumers (C) and business investment (I) is constant, the government can *directly* affect the level of total demand. By using its power to tax to affect C and I, the government can *indirectly* influence the direction of aggregate demand. When taxes are reduced, both business and consumers will have more to spend, thus increasing aggregate demand. Tax increases have the opposite effect. With less to spend, C and I will fall along with aggregate demand. Remember, too, that any changes in C, I, and G will be magnified by the multiplier.

Let us suppose government economists have determined that at full employment the economy could produce $3 trillion in goods and services. If aggregate demand is running at $2.4 trillion, it thereby leaves a *recessionary gap* of $600 billion. In such a situation, unemployment is likely to be high and business prospects poor. Let us also assume that the multiplier in these times is 4. It therefore follows that if government could find a way to increase spending by $150 billion, aggregate demand would be increased by $600 billion because of the multiplier effect, and the economy would be restored to full employment. This level could be achieved in theory by an increase in government spending, a decrease in taxes, or some combination of the two.

In applying its powers to tax and spend, government had developed two types of stabilizers. One type, used as Congress and the President consider them necessary, includes *discretionary tools*. The other type involves government-related measures that go into effect automatically so as to increase or decrease taxes and spending in accordance with the needs of the economy. These measures are known as *automatic stabilizers*.

Discretionary Fiscal Policy. The most important discretionary fiscal policies are taxation and government spending.

Taxation. "As a result of passage of the historic Economic Recovery Tax Act of 1981, we have significantly restructured the tax system to encourage people to work, save, and invest more." Thus wrote President Ronald Reagan in his Annual Economic Report to Congress in February 1982. The law of which the President wrote provided for tax reductions that were specifically designed to encourage consumer spending and business investment. The 1980s had opened with a serious economic recession. The new law sought to move the economy back to full-employment levels by increasing both consumer and business spending as a means of increasing aggregate demand. (Review the discussion on pages 330–336.)

Government Spending. In a 1980 speech, President Jimmy Carter asked Congress to "fight inflation by holding down federal spending." At earlier times, other Presidents have called upon Congress to increase spending as a means of combating a recession and have sought tax increases as a way of fighting inflation.

The actions of Presidents Reagan, Carter, and their predecessors stand as examples of the application of discretionary fiscal policies to specific economic problems. President Reagan called for a tax reduction as a way of increasing aggregate demand during a recession. President Carter sought a reduction in government spending as a means of reducing aggregate demand so as to end a period of "double-digit" inflation. (A period of double-digit inflation is one when prices are increasing by 10 percent or more per year.)

The very nature of discretionary policies burdens them with two weaknesses. The first weakness is the difficulty of knowing exactly when the economy has turned up or down. Although economic statisticians can draw a fairly accurate picture of what has happened to the economy in the *past*, their ability to predict the *future* leaves much to be desired. The second weakness of discretionary policies has to do with the time and effort needed for Congress to enact fiscal policy into law. For these reasons, discretionary policies are frequently applied too late to be effective.

Automatic Stabilizers. Not all fiscal programs share the weaknesses of discretionary fiscal policies, however. Some government-related measures automatically change the level of spending and taxation so as to support the business cycle when it would otherwise sag and hold it down when it would otherwise surge ahead. These are the so-called built-in, or automatic stabilizers. The most important of the automatic stabilizers are unemployment compensation and progressive income taxes.

Unemployment Compensation. Unemployment-compensation laws require the collection of taxes from those who are working. These funds are pooled for payment to workers who lose their jobs. When unemployment is on the rise during a period of recession, government payments in the form of unemployment benefits *automatically* increase. In this way, money is pumped into the economy exactly when it is needed most. As employment increases, just the opposite happens: Payments to unemployed workers decline while taxes increase.

Progressive Income Taxes. The amount that individuals and firms pay in income taxes varies directly with their earnings. During periods of national economic expansion, when business activity is increasing along with employment and prices, income tax collections also increase. Increased tax collections lessen the ability of consumers and businesses to spend more, and in that way serve to slow the boom. Just the opposite takes place during a recession. As incomes fall, so too do income tax payments. This leaves consumers and business firms with an increasing share of their income, which, if they choose to spend it, will help restore aggregate demand.

FISCAL POLICY AND THE NATIONAL DEBT

In the election campaign of 1984, the national debt was a major issue because of its immense size. In that year, the United States government owed more than *one trillion dollars* to banks, corporations, and citizens from whom it had borrowed money. And it was expected that this frightening burden of debt might double—and double again—in only a few years. Economists pointed out that the national debt had already grown nearly a thousand times since 1910. The staggering increase was caused in part by the wars of this century. Two world wars, the Korean War, and the war in Vietnam cost billions of dollars in borrowed money. In a sense, these wars and other expenses of government are still being paid for.

The national debt has been increasing in recent years because the government has run a *deficit* (spent more than it earned) in forty-two of the last fifty years. The two principal causes of deficit spending have been wars and recessions. Since 1776 it has been United States policy to spend whatever it took to win its war and worry about paying the costs afterward. Only since the Great Depression of the 1930s, however, has the government used its powers to tax and spend, that is, *fiscal policy*, to fight recessions. During economic downturns, the government seeks to stimulate aggregate demand by reducing taxes, increasing its own spending, or both. All of these options are likely to add to the national debt.

How large is the national debt? At the end of 1981, for the first time in our history, the debt passed the astonishing figure of $1 trillion, and it has been climbing ever since.

Huge as it is, certain aspects of the national debt whittle it down to size. Government agencies purchase about one-third of the bonds and notes that the Treasury sells when it borrows. So, for example, of the $1.03 trillion debt in 1982, $343 billion was held by the government itself. This sum reduced the total debt outstanding to less than $700 billion.

Is a $700 billion debt too large? One is tempted to respond:

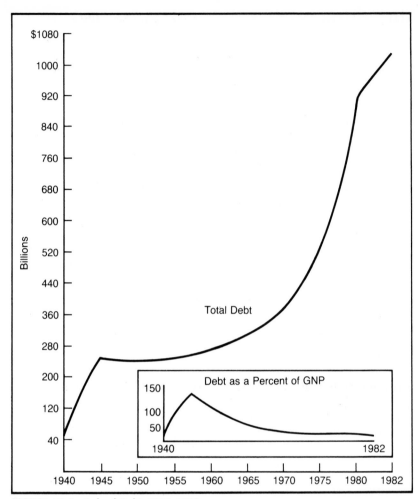

FIGURE 18.1   Federal Debt, 1940–1982

"Compared to what?" To a student whose only income is a $10 weekly allowance, even a $700 debt might seem unmanageable. Given a part-time job with an income of $80 a week, however, it might be possible for a student to carry such a loan.

Just as an individual looks to earning capacity to bear the burden of debt, so does a nation rely upon productive output, or gross national product (GNP), to carry it through. When World War II ended in 1945, the United States GNP was running at $212 billion. The national debt that year stood at $259 billion, or 122 percent of the GNP. While the debt has continued its climb since 1945, the GNP has risen at an even faster rate. Consequently, when the public debt reached the $1.03 trillion level in 1982, it was but 34 percent of the nation's $3 trillion GNP. These trends are summarized in Figure 18.1.

THE CONTROVERSY OVER DEFICIT FINANCING

Few topics in economics are likely to stir up as much debate as that of the national debt. Much of the discussion includes the following accusations:

1. Individuals who fail to balance their budgets and *liquidate* (pay off) their debts will, sooner or later, face bankruptcy and ruin. The same fate is in store for the federal government unless it too revises its spending habits and learns to live within its income.

2. Our children and grandchildren will be saddled with the burden of paying for the excesses of today.

3. Government deficits fuel inflation.

Most economists dismiss as naive the attempt to liken the consequences of individual behavior to the activities of the federal government. Unlike people, who age and die, the United States government will (we all hope) go on forever. There is, therefore, no reason for it to liquidate its debts. Interest payments must, of course, be made regularly. As long as the nation's productivity remains high and borrowing is kept within reason, meeting those payments ought not to present insuperable problems. Moreover, unlike individuals who might reach the point where they could no longer repay their debts, it is impossible that the federal government will be unable to pay its debts. The government, as you know, has the sole power to *print money*. If all else failed, it could "resort to the printing press" to repay its debts.

There is, however, disagreement among economists over the effect of budget deficits on future generations. Those who favor deficit financing concede that the debts we contract today to fight a war, build a bridge, or end a recession will add to the taxes of future generations. But, they remind us, throughout history, future generations also benefited from the wars that were won, the bridges that were built, and the additional wealth that was produced because recessions were ended. Moreover, the interest payments that go on generations after the money was first borrowed will be paid by Americans to *other Americans* who happen to be holding the bonds and notes that represent the national debt.

Economists who disagree view these arguments differently. While it was once true that 95 percent or more of the national debt was in the hands of Americans, since the 1970s the debt has been shifting into foreign hands. As of the early 1980s, 25 percent of the national debt was held by foreigners. If this trend continues, future generations will have to ship a substantial portion of America's wealth to foreign lands in payment for the interest and principal on those loans.

Economists also argue that there is but a limited amount of capital available to be borrowed at any one time. Consequently, government loans sometimes have the effect of denying private enterprise the opportunity to borrow the funds it needs to expand production. Future generations are thus deprived of the benefits they might have received from the increased output of goods and services.

Will government deficits fuel inflation? They will if the government decides to repay its debts by printing money. In this circumstance, there would be more money competing for the same quantity of goods and services, and prices would simply have to go higher. Similarly, government borrowing when the economy is at full employment would also fuel inflation because, as the money is spent, it will be competing with the private sector for goods and services. Deficits will not be inflationary if they are financed out of taxes. Similarly, if the funds are used to finance government spending at a time when the economy is functioning at less than full employment, the addition to spending will not be inflationary.

Two other problems created by the huge national debt concern the effect it has on attitudes toward government spending, and on the redistribution of wealth that this borrowing fosters.

1. Politicians rarely achieve popularity by raising taxes. They often prefer to pay for government projects out of borrowed funds rather than increased taxes. Some economists and political scientists have argued that this attitude has led to wasteful spending programs in the past and is likely to foster more of the same in the future.

2. In repaying its debts, the government levies taxes on individuals and business firms and uses the proceeds to meet its interest payments. Since large blocks of government bonds and notes are usually in the hands of financial institutions and wealthy individuals, the effect of the process is to transfer wealth from the taxpayers in general to the rich.

MONETARY POLICY

The government has a second set of tools with which to keep the nation's economy healthy. These tools are known as *monetary policy* and are the actions taken by the Federal Reserve System (the Fed) to regulate the nation's supply of money and credit. The principal objective of monetary policy is to promote full employment, stable prices, and economic growth. Monetary programs do not need the prior approval of the President or Congress, as do fiscal policies. For this reason many economists feel that monetary policy is the more effective of the two.

In conducting its monetary programs, the Fed decides how much money ought to be circulating at a particular time. Ideally, under conditions of full employment and price stability, the Fed will seek to maintain the *status quo* (present state of affairs) by allowing the money supply to grow exactly as fast as the GNP. Sometimes, however, the Fed will adopt an *easy-money* policy. This policy will allow the money supply to grow faster than the GNP. At other times the Fed may employ a *tight-money* policy, in which growth in the money supply is slower than that of the GNP. Easy-money policies stimulate aggregate demand and, for that reason, are more likely to be adopted during times of recession. Tight-money policies reduce aggregate demand and thereby dampen business activity. They are most often applied during periods of inflation.

THE FEDERAL RESERVE REGULATES THE MONEY SUPPLY

The responsibility for conducting the nation's monetary policy is in the hands of the Board of Governors of the Federal Reserve System. The Fed exercises its powers in two ways. First and foremost, the Fed regulates the supply of available credit. Second, the Fed uses its powers to affect *how* credit may be used.

How the Fed Regulates Credit. The amount of money that people spend depends upon how much they have and how much they can borrow. If you manage to save $2,000 at a time when you need $9,000 to buy an automobile, you would have to find someone to lend you $7,000. If you can get a $7,000 loan, you would then be able to purchase your new car, and the nation's money supply would be increased. But if you cannot get the loan, the money supply would not be increased, and you would not have a new car. The point is that the availability of credit affects both the money supply and the level of business activity. When loans are easily obtained, the money supply will expand and business will sell more goods and services. When loans are difficult to obtain, the money supply will decrease as old loans are paid off. Prices are likely to decline or remain the same, and business activity will falter.

With these relationships in mind, let us see how the Fed's Board of Governors goes about its task of regulating the nation's supply of money and credit. There are three major methods whereby the board can set monetary policy. First, it may change its reserve requirements. Second, it may change the discount rate. Third, it may take actions through the work of its Open Market Committee. These three methods are described in the pages that follow.

The Quantity Equation of Exchange

The economic theory underlying much of monetary policy can be summarized in the simple mathematical equation known as the *quantity equation of exchange*. This equation is written as

$$MV = PQ$$

where P = the average *price* paid for final goods and services,
     Q = the *quantity* of goods and services produced,
    M = the *money* supply, and
    V = the *velocity,* which is the number of times the money supply changes hands over the course of the year.

Money changes hands as it is spent. For example, the $5 bill that you use to pay for the record album you find on sale does not simply sit in the store's cash register. It is given in change to another customer, who uses it to purchase a movie ticket. From there the bill continues its journey in similar fashion until it is finally withdrawn from circulation.

P, the average price paid for the final goods and services produced by the economy, multiplied by *Q,* the quantity produced, gives us the total value of all the goods and services produced in a year. This total value is, by definition, the gross national product. Thus we can say that $MV = PQ$ can also be expressed as $MV = GNP$. With this equation in mind, we can now define velocity as equal to the gross national product divided by the money supply (because $V = \dfrac{PQ}{M}$). For example, in 1980, when the GNP totaled $2,626 billion and the money supply was $416 billion, velocity was 6.3 (because $2,626 divided by $416 equals 6.3).

Economists known as *monetarists* rely on the quantity equation of exchange to demonstrate how monetary policy can be used to achieve

Changing Reserve Requirements. A major part of a bank's income comes from interest on the loans that it makes. But a bank cannot lend unlimited amounts of money to the public. It is required, instead, to keep a certain percentage of its deposits on reserve at all times. This percentage, or *reserve ratio,* is established by the Federal Reserve System and may be altered within certain limits set by

the goals of full employment, price stability, and economic growth. Assuming, as the monetarists do, that velocity is fairly stable in the long run, then any increase in the money supply will increase PQ by a similar amount, while a decrease will have the opposite effect. It therefore follows that when the economy is functioning at something less than full employment, an increase in the money supply (M) will lead to a corresponding increase in the output of goods and services (Q). Once the economy has reached capacity, however, increases in the money supply will lead to inflation. Why? Because, with Q at its limit, increases in the GNP will have to be absorbed by higher prices (P).

When written as $P = \dfrac{MV}{Q}$, the equation gives us a picture of the forces directly affecting price levels. We can see, for example, that prices vary *directly* with changes in the money supply and velocity, and *inversely* with changes in the output of goods and services. We can see, too, why the Fed seeks to reduce growth of the money supply during periods of inflation *and* how V and Q might prevent the success of its efforts.

1. According to the quantity equation of exchange, $MV = PQ$. Explain the meaning of each of the four elements in the equation.
2. According to the *quantity theory of money,* what would be the effect on prices following: (a) an increase in the money supply (b) an increase in velocity (c) an increase in the output of goods and services?
3. Assume that the money supply and the rate at which it is changing hands is increasing. How will this affect prices and production if: (a) productive resources are fully employed (b) productive resources are not fully employed?
4. With reference to the final sentence in the reading: (a) Why would the Fed seek to reduce growth in the money supply during periods of inflation? (b) How could V and Q prevent the success of the Fed's efforts?

Congress. Obviously, when the reserve ratio is raised, a bank's ability to lend money is decreased because it must keep more money on hand. When reserve requirements are lowered, the opposite is true. Thus if a bank had $1 million on deposit and the reserve ratio was 15 percent, it would have to keep $150,000 on reserve against up to $850,000 in loans. If the reserve ratio were raised to 20 percent, the bank would have to keep $200,000 on reserve, thereby reducing its lending ability by $50,000.

The effect of a change in reserve requirements on the banking system as a whole is even more dramatic. You will recall that in Chapter 14 (see pages 275–277) we demonstrated how a deposit of $10,000 could lead to an expansion of deposits through the banking system of $50,000 when the reserve ratio was 20 percent. If the reserve ratio was 25 percent, a deposit of $10,000 could lead to only $40,000 in total new deposits.

At one time, bank reserves were required by law primarily to give depositors a feeling of confidence that if they went to their bank to make a withdrawal, there would be funds waiting for them. With the advent of the FDIC and the improvement of banking techniques, the likelihood of bank failure has been sharply reduced. Therefore, the reserve ratio has come to be regarded primarily as a tool that the Fed can use to influence the supply of money. During periods of "boom" when resources are fully employed and prices are moving up, the Fed's Board of Governors may decide to move against the inflationary trend by raising reserve requirements. In a recession, a lowering of the Fed's reserve requirements would enable banks to increase their loans.

Changes in reserve requirements are regarded as drastic and are infrequently used. For one thing, it is felt that such a move would "change the rules of the game" in the middle of the contest because banks base their operations on one set of reserve requirements. If these requirements were altered, it would be quite difficult for banks to make the changes that such a shift would require. For this reason, this tool is used in a limited way and only when the Fed feels the need for extreme measures.

Changing the Discount Rate. When their reserves get low, member banks may replenish them with loans from the central bank of their Federal Reserve district. In doing so, they pay interest that is *discounted* (deducted in advance) at the time of the loan. The interest rate charged by the Fed on loans to member banks is called the *discount rate*. If the discount rate is 10 percent and a member bank borrowed $100,000 payable in six months, it would receive $95,000 credited to its account (after signing a promissory note for $100,000). The interest was calculated as follows: 10 percent of $100,000 equals $10,000; six months is half a year, and one-half of $10,000 is $5,000.

Banks are influenced by the discount rate when they set the rates they will charge their customers for loans. If banks are to earn a profit on their loans, they must charge more than the discount rate. For

Effect of Discount Rate Changes on Homeowners. What effect would a one percent increase in the Federal Reserve's discount rate have on the sale of private homes?

example, if commercial banks charged 14 percent on the money for which they paid 10 percent, they would earn a profit of 4 percent. Thus, if the bank lent $100,000 to a customer for six months at 14 percent, it would deduct $7,000 in interest, leaving the bank with a profit of $2,000 on the transaction.

We can see then that, if the Fed raises or lowers the discount rate, member banks are likely to follow suit. Thus, if the rate is lowered from 10 to 8 percent, banks would be able to lower the rate they charged their customers while maintaining their margin of profit. If the rate is raised, we would expect the opposite to happen.

The amount of money that consumers and business firms borrow is affected in part by the rate of interest that they will have to pay. As loans become more costly, the public is likely to borrow less. When interest rates come down, however, borrowing becomes more attractive. Thus the authority to regulate the discount rate can be used to affect the volume of credit available in the economy.

Open Market Operations. The most important tool available to the Federal Reserve System for regulating the amount of available credit is its *open market operations*. These operations are supervised by the Open Market Committee, consisting of the seven members of the

Board of Governors and five presidents of Federal Reserve district banks.

There is an open market for the purchase and sale of government securities, just as there is for corporate stocks and bonds. Government securities, which consist of both bonds and notes, are bought and sold by government agencies as well as by private institutions such as banks, insurance companies, and large corporations.

If the Open Market Committee determines that prices have been rising too fast and that it would be desirable to stop the inflationary trend, it could elect to sell securities to the public. This sale would be accomplished by lowering the selling price to a point that would make the securities an attractive buy.

Does Federal Borrowing "Crowd Out" Business?

When the federal government spends more than it takes in, it has to borrow to make up the deficit. One source of funds is the Federal Reserve System. The Fed has the power to print money and lend it to the government. The government does not care much for that method, however, because the additional dollars add to the money supply, thereby raising prices and fueling inflation.

The government can also borrow from the same places from which business borrows: banks, insurance companies, and private firms. It does this by selling its securities—bonds and Treasury bills. The public buys up all these securities because the government will pay as much interest as is necessary to cover its debts. Naturally, the more that government needs to borrow, the more it must pay in interest.

But when interest rates increase, private enterprise finds it difficult to borrow the funds it needs to conduct its affairs. In other words, the more that government borrows, the less there is available for business. In the 1980s, government's need to borrow became so great that economists began to write about the crowding-out effect of the federal deficit. We can illustrate this effect with a few statistics.

In 1970 federal borrowing totaled about 19 percent of all the funds that were lent that year. This figure grew to 34 percent in 1981. In the next few years, government deficits reached record peacetime highs. As a result government borrowing reached 68 percent of all loans in 1983 and 62 percent in 1984. This enormous government debt, many experts predicted, would soon "crowd" private firms out of the credit markets and bring on a recession. It remains to be seen whether these predictions are accurate.

When private institutions such as corporations purchase government bonds or notes, they customarily pay for them by check. Naturally, this reduces the size of their bank deposits. When banks buy government securities, they pay for them out of their reserve accounts on deposit with their district bank. In both cases, the purchase of securities reduces the size of bank reserves. This reduction has a pronounced effect upon the money supply because a decrease in reserves may be reflected several times over in a contraction of credit. Assuming a reserve ratio of 20 percent, for example, a decrease in bank reserves of $1 million could lead to a reduction of $5 million in deposits throughout the nation's banking system. This reduction in the supply of money would in turn apply downward pressure on the price level.

In times of recession or falling prices, the Open Market Committee might elect to buy securities. This would be accomplished by offering to pay a high enough price. Those persons and businesses who sold their securities would deposit the money that they received in their accounts, and bank reserves would increase. Similarly, bank reserves would grow as banks sold their government securities and deposited the money in their accounts at the district bank. Thus, when the Open Market Committee buys securities, bank reserves increase, and an increasing amount of credit becomes available.

Open market operations are relatively easy to apply and are quite effective. They are therefore the most frequently used monetary tool of the Federal Reserve.

The Fed Uses Its Qualitative Controls. The three methods described above are the most important monetary tools available to the Federal Reserve System in its efforts to regulate the money supply. There are, however, several other strategies that the Fed can apply in selected areas to affect the use of credit.

Moral Suasion. The term "moral suasion" refers to attempts by the Federal Reserve System to "put pressure" on the member banks either to increase or decrease all or certain kinds of loans. Moral suasion may take the form of news releases, letters of appeal, and conferences.

Margin Requirements. Margin refers to the amount of cash that an investor must put up when buying securities. The investor may borrow the rest of the purchase price. The margin ratio is established by the Fed's Board of Governors. When margin requirements are raised, borrowing is restricted. When they are lowered, borrowing may be increased.

TABLE 18.1   Fiscal and Monetary Policies and the Business Cycle

	Recession	*Inflation*
Fiscal policies	1. Lower taxes 2. Increase government spending 3. Increase private spending (by automatic stabilizers)	1. Raise taxes 2. Decrease government spending 3. Decrease private spending (by automatic stabilizers)
Monetary policies	1. Lower the reserve ratio 2. Buy securities 3. Lower the discount rate 4. Lower margin requirements	1. Raise the reserve ratio 2. Sell securities 3. Raise the discount rate 4. Raise margin requirements

Temporary Controls. At times the Federal Reserve System has been given the power to regulate consumer and home mortgage loans. During periods of special need, such as times of war, it could, of course, be given these powers again if that became necessary.

MONETARY AND FISCAL POLICY SUMMARIZED

At this point, let us summarize the ways in which the federal government could move to stabilize the economy in the various phases of the business cycle. (See Table 18.1.)

The application of economic theory to real-life situations frequently yields moderate to disappointing results. Although the principles underlying fiscal and monetary theory have been applied for over fifty years, recession, inflation, and unemployment have not disappeared. Indeed, inflation reached record levels in the 1970s while unemployment and business failures in the early 1980s were at their highest levels since the Great Depression of the 1930s.

Clearly, then, the tools of monetary and fiscal policy have certain weaknesses that prevent their fully achieving what they set out to do. These weaknesses are summarized in the section that follows.

LIMITATIONS OF FISCAL POLICY

1. Forecasting and Timing Difficulties. The success of fiscal programs depends upon how quickly and accurately the government is able to recognize economic trends. The problem is that business trends cannot be measured with absolute accuracy. Though economists are able to describe in general terms how well or poorly the economy is doing, no one has discovered how to predict the future of the economy with certainty. If, for example, we are in a recession, who can really say that the next day will not bring an upward turn? If that happened and recovery set in before the government recognized the shift, any effort to increase total demand, such as a tax cut or a spending program, could prove to be inflationary.

2. Political Considerations. During periods of recession, the government may lower taxes and increase spending. These actions are quite popular politically because voters almost always favor lower taxes, and many persons benefit directly from government spending. A problem arises, however, during periods of boom and inflation when the opposite actions are called for. Members of Congress do not like to associate themselves with higher taxes. Nor is it politically helpful to reduce or eliminate spending programs that would have benefited the people "back home." For this reason, fiscal policy is more popular when it is used to combat recession than when it is used against inflation.

Space Programs and the Economy. What would happen to the economy if the federal government suddenly tripled its rate of spending on space-shuttle technology without making any other changes in its taxing or spending policies? Would this extra spending have an inflationary effect, a recessionary effect, or no effect? Explain.

An additional problem is created by the sometimes agonizingly slow pace of the democratic process. In many instances Congress has taken so long to act that necessary legislation was passed too late to achieve its fiscal goals.

3. Inflexibility of the National Budget. Ideally, government spending should increase during periods of recession and decrease during inflation. Currently, however, about two-fifths of the budget goes for national defense and interest on the national debt. Defense needs and interest payments must be met regardless of economic conditions, as must many other expenditures that pay for essential government services. These fixed expenses leave but a fraction of the total budget that can be manipulated to stabilize the economy.

4. Lack of Coordinated Fiscal Policies. In the best of all worlds, state and local governments would mesh their budgets with that of the federal government so as to launch a coordinated attack on the nation's economic woes. In practice, quite the opposite is likely to take place. With tax receipts on the decline, as they are in times of recession, states and localities can be expected to reduce their level of spending. During periods of inflation, however, tax receipts will increase, as will spending by the state and local governments.

Increased spending is quite the opposite of what is called for by fiscal theory. In times of recession, the theory says, government spending should be increased as a way of increasing aggregate demand. More government spending, in turn, would lead to increased spending by consumers and businesses. During times of inflation, the opposite medicine is called for: Government spending should decrease so as to reduce total demand.

But, during times of recession, state and local governments receive less revenue from taxpayers. While these governments might like to increase their spending during hard times, they face major obstacles. First, unlike the federal government, the states do not have the power to print money. Second, states and localities often find borrowing difficult during recessions, and are left with little choice other than to do their heaviest spending during times when their economies are flourishing. Unfortunately, inflationary periods are just such times.

LIMITATIONS OF MONETARY POLICY

1. Forecasting and Timing Difficulties. The same problems described in connection with fiscal policies apply as well to monetary policies (see above).

The Laffer Curve: How to Cut Taxes and Increase Government Revenues

Cut taxes yet increase revenues? Absolutely, argued Arthur Laffer, of the University of Southern California, who demonstrated the proof of this seeming paradox with a graphic model, the now famous "Laffer Curve." At point A in Figure 18.2, the income tax rate is zero; consequently, the government earns no revenue. As tax rates are levied and increased at B, C, and D, government revenues also increase. But something happens beyond point D. People begin to find taxes so high that they look for other uses for what had been their working time. Some will work fewer hours, some may drop out of the labor force, while others may look for ways to hide all or part of their income from the tax authorities. At point E on the scale, we see that revenues are less than they were at C and D. At F revenues are the same as they were at B where tax rates were much lower. At 100 percent, revenues are again back to zero since no one would work if all earnings were taken in taxes.

Laffer concluded from this study that as long as taxes remained within the normal range, increased rates of taxes would earn the government additional income. But beyond that lay a region of decreasing revenue. Within that broad range government could increase its income tax revenue *only by reducing tax rates.*

FIGURE 18.2 Laffer Curve

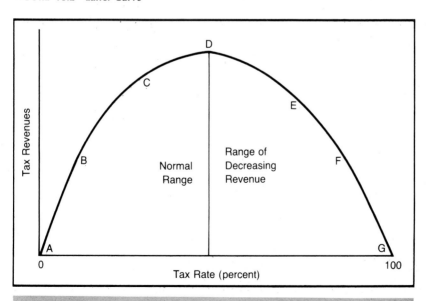

Supply-Side Economics

The efforts of the federal government to stabilize the United States economy were for many years based upon the theories of the British economist John Maynard Keynes (see pages 328–329). Keynes had identified *aggregate demand* as the key to ending a recession or bringing inflation under control. Accordingly, in times of recession, government used its monetary and fiscal powers to *increase* spending by consumers, business, and itself. In times of inflation, government followed an opposite course in order to reduce spending and bring down prices.

Keynesianism worked well enough during those years in which either recession *or* the rise in the price level was troublesome. In the 1970s, however, the nation found itself in the midst of both recession *and* inflation. Economists coined the term "stagflation" (for economic *stag*-nation plus in*flation*) to describe those times but seemed at a loss to suggest how the government could deal with both problems at one and the same time.

There was, however, one group of economists, including Arthur Laffer of the University of Southern California, who claimed to have found a solution to the dilemma. These economists were dubbed the "supply-siders" because they saw production (that is, *supply*) as the key to ridding the nation of stagflation. The goal of the supply-siders was to "unleash free enterprise" so as to increase investment, productivity, and production. If production was increasing, they argued, prices would have to come down. Meanwhile, the additional investment in new equipment and enterprises would put the unemployed back to work, increase personal and business earnings, and bring the recession to an end.

In the supply-siders' view, there were three obstacles to achieving these goals. These were:

1. Income taxes were so high that they discouraged capital investment in new plant, equipment, and business enterprises.

2. Government-sponsored welfare programs discouraged individual initiative. Why, the supply-siders asked, would people look for work if they knew that they could have as much money simply by going on welfare?

3. Government regulatory agencies discouraged innovation and creativity.

The remedies proposed by the supply-side economists included the following:

1. Reduce income taxes, particularly for those in the upper-income brackets. This reduction would leave business people and others with additional after-tax income, which could be invested in productive enterprises.

2. Reduce government spending for social programs so as to limit assistance to those who were "truly needy." This provision would encourage the less needy to find jobs.

3. "Get government off the backs of business" by reducing the number of and powers of the regulatory agencies.

Critics of supply-side economics said that the tax proposals would serve only to enrich the wealthy. There was no guarantee that people with additional after-tax income would really invest the money in business enterprises. Supply-siders were also accused of being indifferent to the needs of the millions of Americans sorely in need of government assistance, and wrong in their assessment of the value of regulatory agencies.

Ronald Reagan was the first American President to apply supply-side economics to his programs. In an effort to slow inflation and revive the economy, income taxes were reduced, government participation in many social programs was cut back, and the activities of a number of regulatory agencies were narrowed. The results of the effort were still being debated in 1984. Those who supported the President pointed with pride to an inflation rate that had been brought down to its lowest point in many years. Critics deplored the fact that nearly 9 million workers, or approximately 8 percent of the labor force, were unemployed.

1. (a) What is "stagflation"? (b) Why do the supply-side economists believe that *production* is the key to fighting stagflation? (c) Compare the Keynesian approach to correcting a recession to that advocated by supply-side economists.

2. With respect to each of the following, explain the policy favored by supply-side economists and their reasons for those policies: (a) income taxes (b) welfare programs (c) the regulatory agencies.

3. (a) Summarize the information contained in the Laffer Curve on page 361. (b) Why do supply-side economists use the Laffer Curve to support their positions?

4. Critics of supply-side policies say that they (a) discriminate against the poor (b) favor the rich (c) lead to record deficits in the federal budget. Explain each of these criticisms.

2. Variable Effectiveness. The Fed has had more success in combating inflation than recession because the decision to spend or not to spend rests with consumers and businesses. In times of inflation the Fed can push interest rates up so high as to make it virtually impossible for people to afford to borrow. So, for example, the inflation of 1979–1980 was finally brought to an end, but only after interest rates on business and consumer loans had been pushed to levels ranging from 15 to 20 percent.

Recessions are another matter. Although the Fed will do what it can to reduce interest rates and make it easier for banks to grant loans, it cannot *force* businesses and consumers to spend money. The problem is that, when the economic outlook is bleak, caution and fear may prove more effective in determining spending patterns than easy-credit conditions. Just this sort of pattern took place during the Great Depression when, despite very low interest rates, there was relatively little business activity.

3. Discriminatory Tight-Money Policies. When the Fed tightens credit, it affects some industries more than others. Few people, for example, can afford to pay cash for the homes they buy. They rely instead upon mortgage loans to fund their purchases. When the Fed tightens up on credit, the interest rates on mortgages, along with other loans, are increased. This increase discourages housing sales because fewer people are able to afford the monthly carrying charges.

4. Fed Policies and Velocity Changes. The impact of monetary policy may be lessened by changes in velocity. The amount of money in circulation is dependent upon the money supply and its *velocity* (that is, the number of times money changes hands in a given period of time). Remember that the goal of monetary policy is to increase the money supply during times of recession and to decrease it to offset a period of inflation.

Unfortunately, changes in velocity can neutralize the effect of changes in the money supply. Suppose that, in an effort to reduce prices, the Fed decreased the money supply to 10 percent when, at the same time, spending by consumers and businesses increased by 10 percent. The net effect of the decrease in the money supply in this instance would be offset by the increase in velocity, and prices would remain where they were.

EXERCISES

Multiple Choice

1. The statement that the federal government has the responsibility to use its powers to promote stability, growth, and full employment is contained in the (a) Constitution (b) Employment Act of 1946 (c) Social Security Act of 1935 (d) National Labor Relations Act.
2. When aggregate demand is less than the economy's capacity to produce the difference, it (a) will bring on a general increase in prices (b) will stimulate production (c) is described as a "recessionary gap" (d) is described as an "inflationary gap."
3. During periods of inflation, government efforts are likely to seek to (a) decrease production (b) dampen aggregate demand (c) increase spending by C, I, and G (d) stimulate aggregate demand.
4. Which is likely to be an effective use of federal power to control inflation? (a) increasing personal income taxes (b) use of moral suasion to lower interest rates (c) decreasing personal income taxes (d) increasing social security payments.
5. Which step might be taken to stimulate business activity during a recession? (a) lower the discount rate (b) increase margin requirements (c) decrease spending for public works (d) raise corporate income tax rates.
6. The term "open market operations" refers mainly to (a) speculation in stocks and bonds by members of the stock exchange (b) the purchase and sale of government securities by Federal Reserve banks (c) discounting of notes by Federal Reserve banks (d) regulation of margin requirements by the Federal Reserve's Board of Governors.
7. Discretionary fiscal policies (a) depend upon the skills of the Federal Reserve System for their success (b) are more effective during periods of inflation than recession (c) call for the adjustment of interest rates on loans to business (d) require accurate forecasting and timely application to be effective.
8. Which statement is true of the national debt? (a) About one-half of it is held by the government itself. (b) It has declined as a percentage of the gross national product over the years. (c) It has passed the $10 trillion mark. (d) All of the above.
9. Monetary policies are administered by (a) the Treasury Department (b) the President (c) the Federal Reserve System (d) the Congress.
10. The federal government's fiscal policy differs from its monetary policy in that its fiscal policy is concerned mostly with (a) taxing and spending (b) reserve ratios and discount rates (c) economic stability in the short run (d) the management of "checkbook money."

11. The burden of the public debt on the taxpayer increases when (a) interest rates fall (b) both the public debt and the population are increasing (c) the size of the debt is increasing proportionately more rapidly than national income (d) national income is increasing and prices are relatively stable.

12. Which is an automatic stabilizer? (a) income tax (b) workers' compensation (c) compulsory arbitration (d) maximum hours law.

13. Government spending that creates a deficit in the federal budget is most desirable when (a) business profits are too high (b) the cost of living has gone up (c) there is a rapid expansion in private spending (d) there is a threat of a depression.

14. A major effect of the lowering of reserve requirements for member banks by the Board of Governors of the Federal Reserve System would be (a) a decrease in margin requirements for stock purchases (b) a decrease in the supply of checkbook money (c) an increase in commercial bank loans (d) an increase in "tight money."

15. When the Open Market Committee sells securities, the effect of this action is to (a) increase the reserves of member banks (b) reduce interest rates (c) increase the supply of money and credit in circulation (d) reduce the reserves of member banks.

16. Fiscal tools have been more effective during periods of recession than periods of inflation because (a) people like to see the government reduce its spending (b) it is easier for Congress to reduce taxes and increase spending than to adopt the opposite course of action (c) the Open Market Committee finds it easier to buy bonds than to sell them (d) a tax increase is relatively easy for the President to obtain.

17. When the Federal Reserve raises the discount rate, member banks usually raise their interest rates because (a) as members they must go along with the wishes of the Federal Reserve (b) they are required to do so by law (c) it now will cost them more to borrow the funds that they will be lending out (d) they want to take the opportunity to increase their volume of loans.

18. The use of monetary policy to combat inflation has been criticized because (a) it calls for additional government spending (b) it places too heavy reliance upon the Treasury Department (c) it calls for higher taxes (d) it discriminates against certain industries, such as the home building trades, that rely most heavily upon consumer borrowing.

Essay Questions

1. Occasionally, the assertion is made that "full employment is not possible without inflation." (a) Explain the meaning of this statement. (b) Do you agree with it? Why or why not?

2. Assume that the nation has entered a period of recession and that the federal government has decided to bring fiscal and monetary

tools to bear upon the problem. (*a*) Explain *three* ways in which the government could use its monetary tools to reverse the trend. (*b*) Explain *two* fiscal policies that the government might adopt to reverse the trend. (*c*) Explain *three* built-in stabilizers that would automatically serve to slow down or reverse the trend of the recession.

3. The national debt passed the $1 trillion mark in 1981. At its present rate of growth, the debt will reach $2 trillion by 1986, bringing the average debt to something over $7,000 for every man, woman, and child in the country. This huge amount of debt has sparked a bitter controversy. Some people regard the debt as an evil that should be reduced and eventually eliminated. Others argue that the debt is necessary to the nation's economic health. Identify and explain two of the arguments advanced for each point of view.

4. Events in the late 1970s and early 1980s have shown that neither monetary nor fiscal policy can guarantee *full employment, a stable dollar,* and *economic growth.* Identify and explain four reasons why monetary and fiscal policy may fail to achieve their goals.

Consumers who spend their money wisely will have more goods and services than those who spend it carelessly.

UNIT VIII

Personal Economics

CHAPTER 19
Personal Savings and Consumer Credit

In and of itself, money is of little value. You cannot wear it. It cannot be eaten, and it certainly will not keep you warm and dry in foul weather. The real value of money lies in the goods and services it can buy in the marketplace. The money that people spend usually comes from one or more of the following sources: (1) current income, (2) personal savings, or (3) credit. It is likely that in your lifetime all of these alternatives will be available to you. That is, you will be earning an income and you will have to decide how much of it you will spend and how much you will set aside as savings. You will also have the opportunity to borrow in order to buy something today that you will pay for in the future. How you use future income, savings, and credit opportunities will directly affect the amount of goods and services you will be able to buy. In this chapter, we shall explore the variety of ways in which most consumers save and borrow.

PERSONAL SAVINGS

After paying their taxes, people can do one of two things with their income: spend it or save it. *Personal savings* are that portion of their income that consumers do not spend. Just how much individuals and families save depends upon the size of their incomes and their tastes. In 1981, the personal savings of Americans amounted to $107 billion out of their $2.015 trillion in *disposable personal income* (the income remaining after the payment of taxes). This averaged out to a little more than 5 cents of savings for every dollar earned.

Why People Save. Those who set aside a portion of their income in savings do so for a variety of reasons. Among most frequently cited reasons are the following:

369

For a "Rainy Day." Many people set aside a portion of their earnings so that they will have something to fall back upon in the event of emergencies such as accidents, illness, or the loss of a job.

For Purchase of Costly Things. Some goods and services cost too much to be bought out of current income. A bicycle, a camera, a winter coat, a summer vacation, and an automobile are the kinds of things that some people prefer to save for rather than buy on credit.

For Additional Income. Most savings earn a return. This return may be in the form of *interest*, as it is in certain kinds of savings accounts and bonds, or *dividends* if the savings were placed in shares of stocks or mutual funds. (Strictly speaking, *dividends* are the share of earnings paid to stockholders, while *interest* is the payment made for the use of money.)

For Retirement. Most workers would like to be able to retire when they reach a certain age. Retirement usually requires that workers undertake a savings program during their earning years to establish a fund upon which they can draw at the time of retirement.

What Consumers Want From Their Savings. As you may have gathered from the many television commercials and newspaper ads clamoring for your business, there are a variety of ways in which one can save. Commercial banks, savings banks, money-market funds, and brokerage houses try very hard to sell you their services. In deciding which savings vehicle best suits their needs, wise consumers will consider each of the following:

Relative Safety. Some forms of savings are more secure than others. Money placed in United States Savings Bonds, for example, is as secure as the government itself. Similarly, most bank deposits are insured by an agency of the federal government, so that even if a bank should fail, its depositors are not likely to lose their savings. Corporate securities (stocks, bonds, and notes) are no sounder than the firms that issue them. It is therefore possible to lose part or all of the savings one invests in securities.

Anticipated Return, or Earnings. People may receive a wide range of returns—in the form of dividends, interest, and capital gains—on the investment of their savings. Depending upon what kind of account one chooses to open, bank interest can range from 5 to 14 percent. Stocks, by comparison, offer dividends that fluctuate with the fortunes of the corporation. In addition, investors may receive *capital gains* (profits earned from the sale of the stock). Similarly, bonds, money-market funds, and other investment vehicles promise a variety of returns for consumers.

Liquidity. The ease with which a form of savings can be converted into cash is described as its *liquidity*. Some banks have automated teller services that process both deposits and withdrawals on a twenty-four-hour, seven-day-a-week basis. This feature provides for greater liquidity than the more traditional bank account, where banking hours limit transactions to daytime hours on weekdays only. Savings invested in real estate (land and buildings) or other property such as rare stamps and coins are far less liquid than bank accounts because finding a buyer for them can be quite time consuming.

How important liquidity is will depend upon the goals of one's savings program. Clearly, funds that may be needed to meet emergencies will have to be kept in a more liquid state than those earmarked for long-term purposes such as marriage or retirement.

WHERE DO CONSUMERS KEEP THEIR SAVINGS?

Savings Institutions. Most consumer savings are kept in accounts maintained by savings-and-loan associations, savings banks, commercial banks, and credit unions. Deposits in these institutions are insured by agencies of the federal government for up to $100,000 per depositor.*

Savings institutions offer a wide choice of plans including passbook and checking accounts, certificate of deposit, and retirement accounts. Money needed to pay bills and meet current expenses is best kept in passbook, checking, or NOW accounts. Passbook accounts give easy access to funds but pay relatively low interest rates. Checking accounts allow you to pay bills merely by writing a check, but pay no interest at all. NOW (for *negotiable orders of withdrawal*) accounts are interest-bearing checking accounts. Interest paid on NOW accounts is usually even less than that paid on passbook accounts. Because these accounts pay such small returns, it is advisable to keep as little of one's savings as possible (say, two months' income) in them and put the rest into accounts that pay more.

One high-yield option is a *certificate of deposit* (CD). A CD offers significantly higher rates of return than a regular savings account. But

---

* The Federal Savings and Loan Insurance Corporation (FSLIC) insures deposits in the savings-and-loan associations. The Federal Deposit Insurance Corporation (FDIC) insures savings and commercial bank deposits. The National Credit Union Administration insures credit union deposits.

TABLE 19.1 Options for Savings in Banks and Credit Unions

Name of Account	Term	Minimum Deposit	Recent Rate of Return	Advantages	Disadvantages
Passbook savings	Can be withdrawn at any time	Usually none	5¼% commercial banks; 5½% savings-and-loans and savings banks; up to 12% in credit unions	Easy access to funds	Very low rate of interest
Regular checking	Can be withdrawn at any time by check	None; however, there may be a charge for checking when balance falls below a minimum	None	Provides instant access to money wherever checks are accepted	Pays no interest on deposits
Interest-bearing checking (NOW)	Same as regular checking	$25 to $50 to qualify for interest. Minimum balance required for free checking	5¼%	Same as regular checking	Low rate of return
Money-market CD	6 months	$500	9%; actual rate is based on most recent monthly auction of Treasury Bills plus .25%	High rate of return; money can be withdrawn after only 6 months	Since rates are for 6 months only, one cannot "lock in" high rates. Many do not have $500
3-Month CD	91 days	$500	8.25% (same as Treasury Bill rate as set by weekly auction)	High rate of return	Ties up funds for 91 days
2–3 year CD 3–5 year CD	2–3 yrs; 3–5 yrs	$500	10–11%	High return, low minimum deposit	Penalty for early withdrawal of principal (interest may be withdrawn)
IRA and Keogh plans	Funds must remain on deposit until depositor is at least 59½ years of age	Varies from bank to bank Maximum contribution is $2,000 for an individual; $4,000 for a married couple if both are working; $2,250 if one spouse is not working	No ceiling; rate depends upon plan selected and market price of money	Can deduct contribution to plan from income and not pay taxes on either the contribution or the interest it earns until one starts receiving benefits	Funds are tied up until contributor is 59½ years of age

a CD ties up your money for a certain period of time (from three months to five years) and requires a minimum deposit, starting at $500, depending upon the account.

For the long term, all savings institutions offer retirement plans such as *Individual Retirement Accounts* (IRAs) and *Keogh Plans*. Employed persons and their spouses set aside a limited amount of funds in special IRAs and Keogh Plan accounts until they are fifty-nine and a half years of age or older. At that point, they are eligible to withdraw all or part of these savings. Money put into IRAs and Keogh Plans can be deducted from one's income, and taxes on that amount and on the interest earned by the account need not be paid until the benefits are actually received.

Savers using IRAs and Keogh Plans have a wonderful opportunity to cash in on the power of compound interest. Suppose, for example, that a twenty-five-year-old worker put aside $2,000 a year in an IRA that paid 12 percent interest compounded daily. At that rate, the account would have over $1 million when the worker reaches age sixty. Table 19.1 summarizes the principal options offered by the savings institutions.

Money-Market Funds. Second only to banks in popularity among consumers as a place to invest their savings are the money-market funds. A *money market* is a place where short-term securities such as Treasury bills, bankers' acceptances, and promissory notes (in other words, interest-bearing IOUs) are purchased and sold. By "short term" we mean that the securities mature in a year or less. Since individual money-market instruments typically sell for $10,000 or $100,000 and up, only the wealthiest individuals, major corporations, financial institutions, and government agencies can afford to trade in them. Moreover, through most of their history, the difference in interest paid by money-market instruments and the thrift institutions (banks and credit unions) was slight. In the 1970s, however, interest rates began to soar. As a result, savers who were earning a mere 4 or 5 percent on their deposits in thrifts began to wonder how they could share in the interest rates offered in the money market, which were then approaching 10 percent.

The answer came with the creation of a new kind of mutual fund, the *money-market fund*. A *mutual fund* is a corporation that uses its stockholders' capital to buy stocks, bonds, or other securities. With millions, even billions, of dollars at their disposal, individual mutual funds can spread the risk of speculative investments over many different securities. The funds can also afford to hire professional money managers, investment counselors, and other specialists.

In exchange for their services, the mutual funds levy a small annual fee, which is deducted from the income and profits (if any) earned by the fund. The balance is distributed to the stockholders in accordance with the number of shares owned.

Money funds invest primarily in *money-market instruments* (interest-bearing IOUs issued by government agencies, banks, and corporations). The interest earned by the funds is then distributed to their shareholders. Since interest rates fluctuate daily, shareholders income will rise and fall with the prevailing rates of interest.

Money-market funds are highly liquid. Funds can be withdrawn without penalty at any time. Many funds offer check-writing privileges, thus giving investors instant access to their money.

Before transferring savings from a bank to a money-market fund, however, investors should know about the *risks* that are involved. Unlike bank deposits, money funds are *not* insured. Therefore, it is possible to lose money if, for some reason, a fund should go bankrupt. Investors should also know that the high rate of interest that attracted them in the first place is not locked in. Rates may fall, and with them the earnings of the fund.

Bonds. Bonds are long-term obligations issued by governments and private corporations. Most bonds provide for the repayment of principal at the end of a specified period of time along with the periodic payment of interest. Interest paid by state and local government bonds is exempt from federal income taxes.

Unlike bank deposits, corporate bonds and government bonds (except United States Savings Bonds) do not guarantee the return of principal *before* maturity. Bonds sold in the open market will receive a price that may be more or less than their face value. How much bonds are worth will depend upon the length of time remaining until maturity, the financial strength of the corporation or agency issuing the bonds, and the prevailing rate of interest.

United States Savings Bonds are unique in that they may be redeemed at any time at a rate stated in advance and guaranteed by the United States government. The interest paid by these bonds ranges from 5½ to 8 percent.

Pension Plans. Many firms and government agencies require that their employees place a portion of their incomes in retirement programs. Frequently, the employers also contribute to the plan.

Pension funds are invested in a variety of ways in order to provide both security and growth for their eventual beneficiaries. Upon retirement, the workers will receive pensions that are usually based upon length of service and level of income during their working years. Because the payments are deducted from paychecks, pension plans

The Power of Compound Interest

Bank deposits and certain other forms of savings have a mighty force working for them called "compound interest." Compound interest is interest earned on the original deposit *and* the interest already earned. Suppose, for example, you deposited $1,000 in a savings account that paid 5¼ percent interest compounded annually. At the end of the first year, your account would be credited with $52.50 in interest, giving you a new balance of $1,052.50. At the end of the second year, the 5¼ percent would be *compounded*, that is, it would be calculated on the basis of the new balance, with interest now amounting to $55.26. The additional dollars in interest may not sound like much now, but let us suppose that the deposit had been made by a 15-year-old who decided to leave the money in the bank until retirement at age 65. After fifty years of compounding at 5¼ percent, the $1,000 would have grown to $12,915.31. Compare this compounding process to *simple interest*, in which interest is earned on the principal alone. In that case the $1,000 would have grown to only $3,625 after fifty years.

Compound interest becomes spectacular at higher levels. If, instead of 5¼ percent, the account had paid 12 percent in compound interest, the $1,000 deposit would have grown to $289,001.90 in fifty years!

SPECIAL NOTE.   Compound interest can be computed quite easily on your pocket calculator. Simply add 1 to the interest rate; multiply it by the principal; and strike the (=) sign once for each year to be compounded. For example: Suppose that you wanted to calculate the balance after seven years of a deposit of $800 in an account that paid 9.5 percent in compound interest. This would be entered in your calculator as follows:

$$1.095 \times 800 = \quad 876.00$$
$$= \quad 959.22$$
$$= 1050.35$$
$$= 1150.13$$
$$= 1259.39$$
$$= 1379.03$$
$$= 1510.04$$

The final readout is the correct balance: $1,510.04.

---

are regarded as "forced savings." This feature makes them especially advantageous to those who find it difficult to save on their own.

Common Stocks. Some people invest a portion of their savings in the stocks of publicly held corporations. Many of these stocks yield a return in the form of dividends. Investors may also receive a capital gain if the value of their stocks should increase over the years.

Your Checking Account

Some day soon, you may decide that it would be a good idea to have a personal checking account. Banks today offer many services to their customers, and all banks do not offer the same services. Therefore, it will pay you to shop around before opening an account. Table 19.2 shows the different accounts that four large banks recently offered their customers. At these banks, the minimum required balances and the checking charges vary, depending on the type of account.

Once you have opened a checking account, your bank will issue a supply of checks with your name and account number printed on them. The checks will also be imprinted with the name of your bank and its identifying numbers. Many of the identifying numbers will be printed in

TABLE 19.2   Types of Checking Accounts: A Comparison of Four Banks

Type of Account	Minimum Balance Required to Avoid Monthly Maintenance Fees and Per-Check Charges		Monthly Maintenance Fee		Per-Check Charge		Interest Earned	
Personal Checking	Bank A	$ 1,000	A	$ 6	A	25¢	A	
	Bank B	2,000	B	6	B	25	B	none
	Bank C	1,500	C	8	C	50	C	
	Bank D	600	D	3	D	25	D	
NOW Account	A	$ 4,000	A	$ 8	A	25¢	A	
	B	4,000	B	8	B	25	B	5¼%
	C	3,000	C	10	C	50	C	
	D	1,200	D	5	D	25	D	
Super NOW	A	$ 5,000	A	$12	A	25¢	A	Same as
	B	10,000	B	10	B	none	B	money
	C	5,000	C	15	C	50	C	market
	D	*	D	10	D	none	D	rates

* A monthly maintenance fee of $5 is charged to accounts with an average monthly balance of $2,500 or more; $10 is charged to accounts with an average monthly balance of less than $2,500.

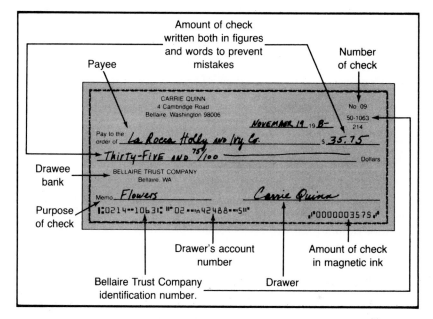

FIGURE 19.1 Check Drawn by Carrie Quinn on Bellaire Trust Company

magnetic ink so as to enable the bank's machines and those of the clearinghouse to process the checks.

A check is a *draft*, or written order, in which a person or a business directs a bank to pay a sum of money to a third party. The person or business writing the check is the *drawer*; the bank is the *drawee*; and the party receiving the money is the *payee*.

In Figure 19.1, Carrie Quinn has ordered flowers for her daughter's Sweet Sixteen party and paid for them by check. Carrie has the legal right to order the Bellaire Trust Company to pay $33.75 because the bank is holding at least that much money in her account.

People receiving checks generally deposit them shortly after they are received into their bank accounts. They may, however, pass them on to another party. In either case, it is necessary for the *payee* to endorse the check by signing his or her name on the back. Endorsements generally fall into one of three categories: *blank, special,* or *restrictive.* In Figure 19.2 on page 378, Carrie Quinn has endorsed three checks that were paid to her.

A *blank endorsement* gives anyone holding the check the right to cash it or pass it on to someone else. To protect yourself against loss or

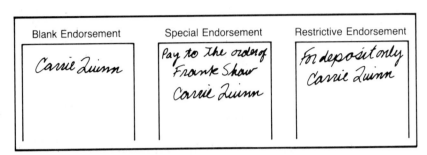

FIGURE 19.2 Check Endorsements by Carrie Quinn

theft, you should never endorse a check in blank until you are ready to cash it or submit it for deposit.

A *special endorsement* passes ownership of a check to a specific person or business that will then be free to do with it as it sees fit.

A *restrictive endorsement* is usually used to send a check by mail to a bank for deposit to an account. Since checks with restrictive endorse-

No.	Date	Issued to or Description of Deposit	Amount of Check			Amount of Deposit		Balance Forward	
								672	31
								25	15 -
108	11/17	TO MYRA MAPLE	25	15				647	16
	11/18	TO DEPOSIT				175	-	175	—
								822	16
								35	75
109	11/19	TO La Rocca Holly and Ivy Co.	35	75				786	41
110	11/20	To Washington Savings BANK MASTER CHARGE	98	36				98	36
								688	05

FIGURE 19.3 Check Register Entries Kept by Carrie Quinn

There is considerable risk attached to stock ownership as a form of savings. The ability of a firm to earn profits and grow will directly affect the size of the dividend it can afford to pay and the value of its stock. The failure of the firm either to produce a profit or to grow could, therefore, result in financial loss to the individual investor.

Mutual Funds. While some mutual funds provide vehicles for the investment of savings in the money market, others specialize in

ments cannot be used for any purpose other than the one specified, they are not likely to be stolen.

Banks are not obligated to pay checks if there is not enough money in the account to cover them. If you should write such a check, your bank will "bounce" it back to the payee and charge you a fee for the service. To avoid the cost and embarrassment of a bounced check, it is essential to keep careful and accurate records of every checking transaction. To help you maintain your records, banks provide record-keeping devices, such as *check registers* or check *stubs*, with their checkbooks. (See Figure 19.3.)

1. Define each of the following: (a) bank draft (b) blank endorsement (c) restrictive endorsement (d) special endorsement (e) check register.
2. Checking accounts generally pay no interest or a lower rate of interest than other kinds of bank accounts. Why then do people choose to keep funds in checking accounts since the money could earn more elsewhere?
3. Clarence Rouge, who lives in Columbus, Georgia, purchased a dozen United States maps from the Magna Carta Map Company in Bleu City, Indiana. He paid for the maps with a personal check for $33.75. Describe the route followed by Mr. Rouge's check from the time he wrote it until its final return to him.
4. Marie Quinones will be living on campus when she enters the state university next fall. Her mother gave Marie this advice about handling her money. "One of the first things you should do is open a checking account at a bank near the campus. But before you do that, Marie, be sure to *shop around* for the best deal." (a) Why did Marie's mother advise opening a checking account at college? (b) What did Mrs. Quinones mean when she said, "Be sure to *shop around* for the best deal"?

corporate securities, that is, stocks and bonds. These funds enable small investors to share in the ownership of hundreds of securities. In this way, these investors can afford both to spread the risk associated with "playing the stock market" and to have full-time professionals manage their investments. Mutual funds have the added advantage of liquidity because investors have the right to sell their shares back to the fund at their current market value whenever they so choose.

Critics of the mutual funds say that their fees are too high. Some

Investment Options. Why do some people think that buying works of art is a better investment than buying stocks and bonds?

funds charge commissions on sales to the public that are from four to six times higher than those levied on the sale of corporate stocks. In addition, the critics maintain, the management fees levied by all mutual funds are frequently excessive. Some funds also are much more profitable than others because managerial competence varies. People thinking about investing in mutual funds should investigate and compare them before investing their money.

Real Property. The category of real property includes buildings, land, jewelry, and works of art, all of which have value in themselves. People who invest a portion of their savings in real property do so in the hope that this investment will provide a *hedge* (insurance) against inflation. An *inflation hedge* is an investment that is likely to increase in value during times of inflation and thereby offset its effects on savings and real income.

PROVIDING FOR FINANCIAL RISK THROUGH INSURANCE

What Is Insurance? Insurance is a means of sharing the risk of financial loss with others. Let us suppose that a community of 1,000 persons owning cars, each of which was worth $5,000, knew that one of its automobiles was going to be stolen during the year. The people in this community could protect themselves from financial loss by putting $5 apiece into a fund that would be given to the unlucky person whose car was stolen. In this way, no one would lose more than $5, whereas each person's potential loss had been $5,000.

All insurance, be it life, fire, theft, or liability, is based upon this same principle of risk sharing. That is, insurance companies calculate the probability of loss during a period, and divide the risk among the number of people sharing it.

Life Insurance. With life insurance, the risk of dying in a particular year is shared by people in the same age group. The money put into the pool by each person is called the *premium.* Naturally, the older a person is, the greater the risk of death. Thus, in theory, the premium ought to increase with age. For the sake of convenience, however, most policies have a *level premium.* That is, insured persons pay the same premium for the life of the policy rather than an increasing amount as they grow older. Included in an insurance premium is a sum large enough to cover the insurance company's expenses, provide for unforeseen losses, and, in some cases, to leave the company with a profit.

In addition, most life insurance policies have a cash value. This is a sum that will be paid to policyholders if they choose to surrender their policies. They may also borrow against this amount. Because the cash value increases with time, as additional premiums are paid and dividends are added, insurance provides the insured persons with an opportunity to add to their savings. Some of the more common types of life insurance are described below.

Term Life Insurance. Term insurance provides for the payment of benefits only in the event of the policyholder's death before a certain date. Because there is no provision for cash value in this type of policy, it is the least expensive form of insurance.

Straight Life Insurance. The holder of a straight, or ordinary, life insurance policy pays premiums until death, at which time the *beneficiary* (the person who will receive the benefits) will receive the *face value* (the amount for which the policy is written). Straight life insurance has a cash value that builds up over the years.

Limited-Payment Life Insurance. Premiums for a limited-payment policy are paid for only for a certain number of years (perhaps twenty or thirty). Since the cash reserve must be built up to a substantial point in a limited period, this policy is more expensive than straight life.

Endowment Policy. An endowment policy offers a lump-sum payment at the end of a specified number of years. Should the insured die before that time, his or her beneficiaries receive the face value of the policy.

Annuity Policy. An annuity is an agreement that provides for the payment of money at regular intervals. Annuities may be purchased with a lump-sum payment, and paid out when the purchaser reaches a certain age. Annuities may also be purchased on the installment plan for a number of years, at which time the periodic payments will begin. Since both endowment and annuity policies require large cash reserves, their premiums are substantially higher than those required for term and straight life policies.

Saving Through Life Insurance: An Evaluation. Insurance programs offer people the opportunity to establish a compulsory savings plan for themselves. Before undertaking such a program, it might be wise for each person to ask, "How much am I willing to pay to enforce my need to save?"

Suppose, for example, that instead of buying an endowment policy, a person bought a term-insurance plan and put into a long-term savings account the difference between the cost of the term insurance and the endowment premium. In all probability, the saver would have far more money in the savings account at the end of twenty or thirty years than the proceeds from the endowment policy. Meanwhile, the term insurance would have protected the saver's family in the event of death.

It certainly makes sense for people to protect themselves and their families wherever they can from the hardships imposed by financial loss. Toward that end, everyone should explore the kinds of protection offered by the life and casualty insurance companies and seek the advice of qualified experts.

THE ECONOMIC IMPLICATIONS OF SAVINGS

Savings, while important to both individuals and families, also play a vital role in the nation's economy. Here is why. In order for any society to increase its output, it must devote part of its production to the manufacture of capital goods and services. The automobile industry, for example, could not increase its total output unless some companies built new machinery and tools. What is true for the automobile industry is true for all industries. New capital must be constantly produced to expand production and to replace equipment that has worn out.

To pay for this investment, businesses may set aside part of their earnings in the form of savings, sell stock, or borrow. In other words, business investment is paid for out of the savings of business itself or of others. Remember that when businesses borrow money from commercial banks, insurance companies, investment banks, or other financial agencies, they are in fact borrowing the money that savers deposited with these institutions. Thus, we see that savings institutions enable those persons who are willing to save and thus postpone their purchases to pool their funds. This money is then made available for loans to business or government and thus permits our economy to continue to function and expand.

The process of saving and investing is voluntary in our economy. No one tells consumers or business people how much they may spend or save. Although the government may use its powers to influence these choices, the final decision rests with individuals.

It is the sum total of the millions of individual decisions as to whether to spend or save, to produce or invest, that will ultimately affect the kind and quantity of goods and services produced. Savings are an important link in the economic process because savers, by giving up the opportunity to enjoy goods and services in the present, are making possible increased production in the future.

CONSUMER CREDIT

"Neither a borrower nor a lender be." Until about fifty years ago, most people would have agreed with the advice given in *Hamlet*. Borrowing by individuals was looked upon as a human frailty, one with terrible long-term consequences. Attitudes have since changed drastically. The use of credit has become a way of life for millions of American consumers. (See Figure 19.4 on page 384.) Despite credit's popularity, however, the excessive use of debt can cause personal hardship and unhappiness. For that reason, it would pay us all to learn how to use credit properly.

People use credit because it enables them to buy things now that they would otherwise have to save for before buying. Consider the case of the young married couple who would like to embark on their new life with a variety of appliances, a car, and their own home. They calculate that, by setting aside a portion of their income each week, they will have saved enough by the end of the year to buy the appliances they want. The car will take about three years more. But a home will take at least twenty years to achieve by saving. They decide, instead, to borrow the money and buy the appliances, the automobile, and the home now.

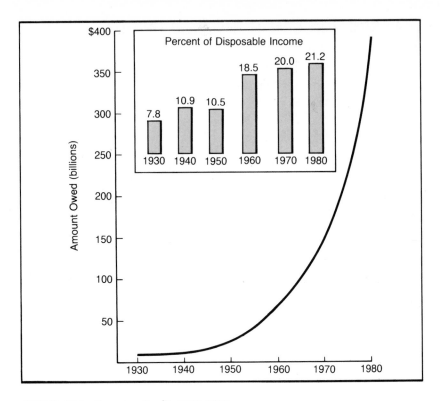

FIGURE 19.4 Consumer Credit, 1930–1980

Much the same decision to use credit was made by the high school graduate who elected to take a student loan to pay for a college education. Then there were the two friends in the word-processing department at a midtown business office who decided to "fly now and pay later" by using credit to finance a two-week summer vacation in Europe.

Credit, while usually costly, can sometimes save people money in the long run. One might, for example, find it cheaper to buy a car on the installment plan than to rent it, or to buy a washer and dryer on credit rather than to continue using the coin-operated machines to wash the family laundry.

Consumer credit also serves to keep up the high level of consumer spending on which our economy relies to support its level of activity. It is unlikely that all the goods bought with credit would have been purchased for cash. Experience has shown that people will spend far more in their lifetime when they are able to borrow against future earnings than when they have to pay out of past savings. We can, therefore, see that the availability of credit for consumers increases their total level of spending, which, in turn, benefits the economy as a whole.

WHAT KINDS OF CREDIT ARE AVAILABLE TO CONSUMERS?

Consumer credit is generally available in any or all of the following forms: *installment plans, charge accounts, credit cards, personal loans,* or *home mortgages.*

1. Installment Plans. The "installment plan" or "time payment plan" is most frequently used to finance the purchase of large items such as household appliances and automobiles. At the time of sale, installment buyers will be required to make a down payment and sign a contract. The contract will include the following:

1. A statement showing the selling price of the item, the size of the down payment, all the finance charges that will be added to the selling price, and the total cost of the purchase after the charges are added to the selling price.
2. The number, amounts, and due dates of all payments.
3. The penalty for failure to make the regular payment on time.

An installment contract is usually a *conditional sales contract* or a *chattel mortgage contract.* In a conditional sales contract, *title* to the goods (that is, *ownership*) remains with the seller until the final payment is made. In a chattel mortgage contract, title passes immediately to the buyer, but the seller retains a legal claim to the goods until the final payment is made. In both cases, the contracts are designed to make it relatively easy for the seller to *repossess* (take back) the merchandise if the buyer fails to live up to the terms of the contract. In addition, some installment contracts allow the seller to *attach* (take a portion of) the buyer's wages should he or she fail to meet the payments. You should always read and understand an installment contract *before* you sign it.

2. Charge Accounts. Whenever you hear a shopper say "Charge it, please" to a salesperson, it is safe to assume that the shopper has a charge account with the store. Charge accounts are services offered by most large department stores as well as many smaller ones. Under a charge account, title to the merchandise passes to the buyer in exchange for the promise to pay. Those who pay their charge account bills on time (usually within 30 days of the billing date) do not have to pay finance charges. Late payers, however, are subject to additional charges.

Some stores provide special kinds of charge accounts for customers who prefer not to pay the full amount of their purchases within a month. These *extended-credit,* or *revolving charge,* accounts entitle

Credit Cards. What are the advantages and disadvantages of using credit cards to delay payments for goods and services?

buyers to repay only a portion of the outstanding balance in accordance with the terms set by the store.

3. Credit Cards. Credit cards, those little plastic cards that so many people carry these days, came into their own with the computer revolution of the 1960s and 1970s. The most popular cards permit their holders to charge purchases at thousands of stores, restaurants, and hotels, both at home and abroad.

Many of the nation's banks offer credit cards through either the MasterCard or VISA programs. Customers are billed monthly. Those who pay promptly are not charged for the service. Those who pay a portion of their bills are subject to a service charge of about 1½ percent of the monthly balance. In addition, some banks levy an annual fee for the use of their cards. After deducting their fees, the banks forward the balance of the cardholders' payments to the appropriate merchants.

Credit cards similar to bank cards are issued by organizations such as American Express and Diners Club. Like the banks, these services deduct a percentage of the charges sent on to them by the participating businesses. Cardholders are expected to pay their outstanding balances in full at the end of each monthly billing period. In addition, they are charged an annual fee for the use of the card.

4. Personal Loans. Banks, personal-finance companies, and other lending agencies also make loans that are secured by the consumers' general credit rather than any specific merchandise. Most are *personal installment loans*, so called because they are paid off at regular intervals over a specified period of time.

5. *Home Mortgages.* Home mortgage loans finance the single biggest investment in most people's lives: their homes. Mortgage loans are long-term loans, usually running from fifteen to thirty years. Security for the mortgage loan is the home that it finances. After making a sizable down payment, the new homeowner will pay equal monthly installments until the mortgage is paid in full. One portion of the payment, known as amortization, is used to reduce the principal of the loan. The rest represents interest on the outstanding balance.

SHOPPING FOR CREDIT

It costs money to borrow money. Lenders charge interest on their loans. They may also levy charges to cover the cost of credit investigations, insurance, and other expenses. Since interest costs and other charges vary, it is wise to compare costs before deciding upon a particular kind of financing. The federal Truth-in-Lending Law has simplified the task of comparing the cost of loans by requiring that lenders tell you the *annual percentage rate (APR)* and the *finance charge* of their loans. The APR is the percentage cost of credit on a yearly basis. The finance charge is the total dollar amount you pay to use credit.

Suppose you decide to buy a new car that sells for $7,500. You have saved $1,500 for the down payment and plan to finance the $6,000 balance with a loan. The car dealer offers to arrange the financing, as do two of your town's banks. Each lender offers somewhat different terms, which are summarized in Table 19.3.

Which of these arrangements would be best for you? The lowest cost loan, over all, is available at Bank X, where you will pay back a total of $7,279.20 for a loan of $6,000. You could, however, lower your monthly cost by taking a longer term loan from Bank Y or the dealer. These loans, however, would be more costly than one from Bank X. A loan from Bank Y would add nearly $450 more to the cost

TABLE 19.3   Credit Options in a New-Car Purchase

Lender	APR	Length of Loan	Monthly Payment	Finance Charge	Total Cost
Bank X	13%	3 years	$202.20	$1,279.20	$7,279.20
Bank Y	13%	4 years	$160.98	1,727.04	7,727.04
Car Dealer	14%	4 years	$163.98	1,871.04	7,871.04

of the loan over the four-year term, and a loan from the dealer would add nearly $600 more.

GETTING AND KEEPING A GOOD CREDIT RATING

Nobody *has* to lend you money. Creditors—the people in the business of making loans—have a right to expect to be repaid promptly and in full for the use of their money. They also have the right to investigate applicants for loans in order to determine if they are good credit risks. Sooner or later, you are likely to need some kind of credit, and it would be wise to take steps to establish your credit worthiness before that need arises.

What Creditors Look For. In looking into the qualifications of a person applying for a loan, credit investigators usually apply the "Three C's" test of credit worthiness. These are *character, capacity,* and *capital.* Character refers to the applicant's responsibility and reliability. These traits are important to a creditor because they can be used to measure the intensity of a borrower's desire to repay a loan. Capacity measures a person's ability to meet obligations when they fall due. It weighs income now and in the future against basic expenses. Capital refers to the financial resources (income and savings) behind the applicant's promise to repay the loan.

If you want to establish yourself as a good credit risk, a logical first step is to open savings and checking accounts in your own name. These accounts, plus a charge account at a local store, will provide you with several financial references when the need for them arises.

The rest is up to you. If you pay your bills on time and maintain a balance in your checking account, you will gain the reputation you are seeking: a person who is a good credit risk. In all likelihood, your record will be passed along to one or more credit bureaus. These institutions maintain files on virtually everyone who has ever used bank or charge account credit in the United States. Lenders pay these bureaus for information about the people who apply for loans. If your file indicates that you are a good credit risk, you are likely to get your loan. If it does not, you may be out of luck.

Federal Laws Protect Those Who Borrow or Wish to Borrow. Creditors have the right to deny you a loan because you are a poor risk. However, federal laws prohibit lenders from turning you down because of your sex, race, color, religion, national origin, marital status, age (provided that you are old enough to make a legal contract), or receipt of public assistance.

If you are turned down for a loan, the law requires that the lender notify you within thirty days and explain the reason why. At your

TABLE 19.4   Consumer Credit-Protection Laws

Law	Year Enacted	Provisions
Civil Rights Act	1968	Prohibits discrimination because of race, color, religion, national origin, or sex when you try to obtain financing for your home.
Truth-in-Lending Act	1968	Requires that certain disclosures of the terms of consumer loans be given to you so that you may compare the cost of credit among different financial institutions.
Fair Credit Reporting Act	1971	Requires procedures for keeping your credit information accurate, relevant, and confidential.
Equal Credit Opportunity Act	1974	Prohibits discrimination in any aspect of your credit transaction because of race, color, religion, national origin, sex, marital status, age, or receipt of public assistance.
Fair Credit Billing Act	1974	Requires prompt correction of billing errors involving your credit or charge account.

request, credit bureaus holding files on you must make the contents of those files available for your inspection. The credit bureau must make corrections if the files contain any errors.

Some of the more important laws protecting users of consumer credit are shown in Table 19.4.

Credit: Master or Servant? A pamphlet written for the members of the armed forces and their families concludes with this advice:

> Credit can be a powerful force in your life. If you use it with intelligence and restraint, it can help you to obtain the things you want. If you stay its master, it can serve you well.
>
> But if you use credit carelessly, without due regard for the obligations it creates for you, credit can become your master and you its servant. You can find yourself working not for the things you want for yourself and your family, but to pay for the privilege of having used someone else's money.*

---

* Reprinted from "Credit: Master or Servant?" U.S. Department of Defense, 1978.

EXERCISES

Multiple Choice

1. Which of the following forms of saving offers the greatest *liquidity?* (*a*) savings account (*b*) corporate stock (*c*) real estate (*d*) individual retirement account (IRA).

2. Which of the following types of investment would consumers be most likely to use if they were interested in *growth?* (*a*) savings account (*b*) life insurance (*c*) corporate stock (*d*) government savings bond.

3. Which of the following forms of savings offers the greatest degree of *safety?* (*a*) a mutual fund (*b*) corporate stock (*c*) real estate (*d*) a government savings bond.

4. Mutual funds are attractive to small investors because (*a*) the funds offer a guaranteed return on investment (*b*) the funds are insured by an agency of the United States government (*c*) the funds offer the opportunity to share in the investment in a variety of stocks and bonds (*d*) investors know that at the end of a specified number of years their investment will be worth more than it would have been if they had put it in one of the thrift institutions.

5. Which of the following investments offers the *highest rate of return?* (*a*) a corporate bond paying $72 per year in interest that is selling for $600 (*b*) a money market fund paying 8 percent interest (*c*) a corporate stock selling for $40 that pays dividends of $2 per share (*d*) a 9½ percent CD (certificate of deposit).

6. Insurance is frequently described as a method of "sharing the risk" because (*a*) risk of loss is shared with the insurance company (*b*) people can share the risks with themselves by spreading the payments over a number of years (*c*) those who insure themselves share the risk with all of society (*d*) an insured person shares the risk of loss with all the other policyholders.

7. Savings are essential to the nation's economic health because (*a*) thrift is a sign of responsibility (*b*) they provide a pool of resources that can be used to expand the nation's output (*c*) the cost of government can be reduced because the Treasury Department need not print as much money (*d*) everyone ought to set something aside "for a rainy day."

8. Why do some people put all or part of their savings in an "inflation hedge"? (*a*) A hedge offers the greatest liquidity. (*b*) A hedge fixes the dollar value of one's savings regardless of what happens to the cost of living. (*c*) A hedge protects people against the loss of purchasing power that accompanies inflation. (*d*) A hedge offers the greatest safety of principal and highest rate of return.

9. Which of the following is *not* a form of consumer credit? (*a*) charge accounts (*b*) installment plans (*c*) credit cards (*d*) checking accounts.
10. "Amortization" is usually associated with (*a*) charge accounts (*b*) home mortgages (*c*) credit cards (*d*) installment plans.
11. At the end of the month, Mr. Jones had an unpaid balance of $50 on his department store charge account. The store notified him that it was charging him 2 percent of this amount (or $1) because this was its regular monthly service charge on all unpaid balances. The true interest rate on this charge account is (*a*) 2 percent (*b*) 10 percent (*c*) 24 percent (*d*) 100 percent.
12. Three months ago, Carol and Henry Fuegos purchased a freezer on the installment plan. A week ago, the company at which they both worked closed down, and they may not be able to meet their installment payments. What is likely to occur? (*a*) One of the two may have to go to jail for failing to meet the installment payments. (*b*) The freezer may be repossessed. (*c*) They will be excused from further payments until they find new jobs. (*d*) The finance company will try to find them jobs.

Essay Questions

1. Compare the following kinds of savings alternatives by describing their advantages in one column and their disadvantages in another: (*a*) passbook savings account (*b*) certificate of deposit (CD) (*c*) money-market fund (*d*) NOW account.
2. "Everyone, whether young, old, or somewhere in between, needs life insurance." With reference to the people in each of the following categories, discuss the extent to which you agree or disagree with this statement. (*a*) A single young adult who lives alone (*b*) A married couple with no children (*c*) A married couple with three children (*d*) A retired couple in their seventies with no dependents.
3. "People who want to borrow money would be well-advised to shop as carefully for their credit as they would for costly merchandise." (*a*) Explain this statement. (*b*) What should one look for in shopping for credit?
4. It has been argued that lenders should be limited by law as to the amount of interest they can charge for their loans. Others, however, say that setting ceilings on interest rates makes no more sense than placing limits on the amount that sellers can charge for their merchandise. What is your opinion in this debate? Explain your answer.
5. In a recent advertisement, a savings bank suggested that it could transform young workers into millionaires if they would open IRA accounts at the bank. (*a*) What is an IRA? (*b*) How could the bank expect to make its depositors rich?

CHAPTER 20

How Can Consumers Get More for Their Money?

The Smith and the Jones families are as similar as two unrelated families can be. Both consist of two men and two women who are in the same age group, earn almost identical incomes, and live in the same neighborhood. But unlike the Smiths, the Joneses will not be going on vacation this year, nor will they do much on weekends.

The Joneses have over the years developed the habit of charging most of their nonfood purchases to their bank credit cards. The interest charges have been rising, as have the monthly payments. Mr. and Mrs. Jones cannot really explain how they got so far into debt. They also know, however, that although gambling is fun, their interest in racetrack gambling cost them dearly last year. More and more out of each week's pay seems to go toward paying off their creditors.

How well people live depends largely upon the goods and services they are able to buy. And how much people can buy depends, in turn, on how much they earn *and* how wisely they spend their money. Clearly, the Smiths have been spending money far more wisely than the Joneses. And the Joneses' situation is a shame. Although many of us have little control over how *much* we earn, we all have a great deal of control over how we *spend* our money. All it takes is some attention to income management and to our shopping habits.

INCOME MANAGEMENT FOR CONSUMERS: THE PERSONAL BUDGET

Nearly all of us are limited in what we can spend by our income. Experience has shown that a most effective way to manage our income is to develop a plan, or *budget*, for that purpose.

Preparing a Budget. A budget has two major parts: income and expenses. (See Table 20.1.) As a first step in preparing a budget, we usually list our income from all sources. Total income provides the basis on which our spending plan will be prepared. The second step

392

TABLE 20.1   Monthly Household Budget for _____, 19___

Income
  Wages (Salary)
  Dividends and interest payments
  Gifts
  Other
                                   Total Income _____
Expenses
  Housing (rent or mortgage)
  Taxes
  Insurance
  Utilities (gas, electric, phone, water)
  Auto payments and repairs
  Food and beverages
  Clothing
  Transportation
  Education
  Household operation and maintenance
  Health and drugs
  Savings and investments
  Recreation and entertainment
  Donations and contributions   _____
                                   Total Expenses

in budget-making is to summarize the spending we will do during a certain period. Spending includes *fixed* expenses, *flexible* expenses, and savings. Fixed expenses are those that must be met every month, such as rent, utilities, insurance, and the like. Flexible expenses can vary from month to month, depending on our needs and income. In order to save money regularly, some people find it helpful to pretend that savings are a fixed expense. In this way, they are more likely to save a set amount and less likely to find an excuse to spend it.

A personal budget enables us to see at a glance whether we are living within our means. A budget also gives us an opportunity to put our priorities in order so that our more important expenses are met first. Similarly, budgets tend to reduce the amount of "spur-of-the-moment," or *impulse*, buying that frequently hits us on payday, during holiday shopping, or at other times when we are carrying more money than usual. Table 20.2 on page 394 shows how consumers in three different income brackets spent their dollars in 1980.

How Can Consumers Get More for Their Money?   **393**

Impulse Buying. How would a carefully prepared budget help this consumer to resist a shop window's signs and lures?

SHOPPING GUIDELINES FOR CONSUMERS

As you filled your shopping cart in the local supermarket, did you ever wonder about the wisdom of your choices? There were four to five brands and a variety of sizes from which to choose among the laundry detergents. What made you pick the brand you selected?

TABLE 20.2   How Consumers Spent Their Dollars in 1980

	Lower Budget ($14,000 income)	Intermediate Budget ($23,000 income)	Higher Budget ($34,000 income)
Consumables			
Food	31¢	24¢	20¢
Housing	19¢	22¢	23¢
Transportation	8¢	9¢	8¢
Clothing, personal care	9¢	8¢	7¢
Medical care	9¢	6¢	4¢
Other	4¢	5¢	5¢
Other items	4¢	4¢	5¢
Social security	6¢	6¢	5¢
Personal income taxes	10¢	16¢	23¢

Source: Bureau of Labor Statistics. Based on a four-person family with one employed person.

Personal Economics

the computer we just got shows we can't afford the Christmas we just had!

Reprinted by permission: Tribune Media Services, Inc.

Although all ground meats looked more or less the same, they were packaged under a variety of names such as "chuck," "ground round," "filet," and "top sirloin." Could you explain the differences between them all? And which toothpaste did you decide upon? The tastiest? The least expensive? The one you saw advertised on television last night? Much the same could be asked of your clothing selections, the athletic equipment you recently purchased, and your portable cassette player. Did you know what you were doing, and do you think you got the most for your money?

There are five steps you can take that will aid you in making intelligent shopping choices. These steps ask that you know what you want before you shop, gather information, read labels, do comparative shopping, and read over bills and contracts before you sign.

1. Know What You Want. A budget will help you set a limit on the amount you can spend for each purchase. To know what you want means deciding in advance what you will be looking for when you go shopping. You also will know how much you are prepared to spend, based on your budget, before you go into a store.

2. Gather Information. Private and public agencies and organizations publish data describing products and comparing their features. Read as much as you can before making a purchase that involves considerable effort and expense.

3. Read Labels. You can learn a great deal simply by reading the labels and other descriptive matter accompanying goods that are

How Can Consumers Get More for Their Money?

offered for sale. In many cases, a label will tell you something about the weight or volume contained in a package, the product's grade or quality, and the nature of the contents. Labels may also inform you about the use and care of the product and its price.

4. Do Comparison Shopping. Although some products sell for the same amount in all stores, many items will vary from 10 to 20 percent in price at different stores. It usually pays to check prices in a number of outlets, particularly for expensive items, before you buy.

5. Read Over All Bills and Contracts. Anyone can make a mistake, so whenever someone hands you a bill, check it for errors before you pay. If a purchase requires that you sign an agreement or a contract, read it over carefully. Make sure that (*a*) you will be receiving everything you expected, and (*b*) the total cost and the method of payment are what you believed they would be.

INFORMATION FOR CONSUMERS

With the wide choice of brands and the conflicting advertising claims, shopping can at times be a confusing experience. Fortunately, there are a number of sources of information, both public and private, which consumers can consult before making their purchases.

Federal and State Agencies. Nearly all the states and many local governments provide services to inform and protect consumers. Among the most helpful services are the publications of the many agencies of the federal government. These publications contain a wide range of information for consumers. For example, they will advise you about repairing your car, how to save money on food, health care, energy, and other household expenses, and how to slim down and trim up. Many of the booklets are free or cost just a few dollars. You will find them listed, with a brief description of their contents, in the "Consumer Information Catalog." The catalog is free from the Federal Consumer Information Center, Pueblo, Colorado, 81009.

Private Organizations. The Life Insurance Institute, Better Business Bureau, American Laundry Institute, and American Gas Association are examples of the kinds of institutions maintained by private industry that can inform or protect the public.

The Better Business Bureau is made up of leading business people in the community. Among its primary concerns are the maintenance of fair business practices and the prevention of fraud. Consumers who feel that they have been treated unfairly by a local business can take the matter up with their Better Business Bureau. The bureau will investigate the matter and, if necessary, press the business concern into making amends.

The other private agencies named above are maintained by their respective industries and are of value to the consumer seeking information. If you are interested in buying life insurance, for example, the Life Insurance Institute will send you a great deal of information concerning the different kinds of insurance available.

PROTECTION FOR CONSUMERS

Many of the things we buy are inside wrappings, packages, and other containers. Similarly, most of the appliances, clothing, furniture, and other goods we buy are "blind items." We, as consumers, have no way of really knowing how they are made. How, for example, can we know if a watch is water-resistant, as the label claims? Can you be sure that the "cotton blend" shirt you bought recently is not really synthethic fiber? How can we be certain that the five-grain aspirin tablet really contains five grains of aspirin?

For some time, it has been recognized that consumers are usually at a disadvantage in the marketplace. For that reason, many governmental agencies, on all levels, were assigned the responsibility of providing consumers with some kind of protection.

State and Local Protection. State and local governments have passed laws to ensure true weights and measures. In many communities this is evidenced by the stamps that are affixed to scales in food stores. Local communities and state governments are also concerned with protecting the public's health. In this effort, they inspect perishable foods for purity and check business establishments to determine if they are sanitary. They also require that many persons, such as doctors and insurance agents, obtain licenses before they are permitted to sell their services to the public. In this way, certain minimum levels of competency are established.

Federal Protection. There are today more than fifty federal agencies that provide some form of protection and information services to consumers. Some of the more important agencies are described below.

The Food and Drug Administration (FDA) is responsible for protecting the public against dangerous foods, drugs, and cosmetics. If the FDA determines that a food, drug, or cosmetic is unsafe, impure, or mislabeled, it may take steps to ban the item's sale.

The Office of Consumer Affairs (OCA) coordinates federal activities in the field of consumer affairs and seeks ways to aid and protect the consumer. OCA publications inform the public of current and pending legislation, and the activities of various consumer groups.

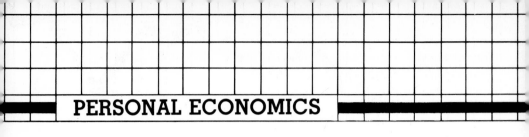

PERSONAL ECONOMICS

How to Write a Letter of Complaint

Sometimes, the things we purchase are defective or do not perform in the ways they should. In most instances these problems can be resolved simply by returning the items to the sellers for exchange or refund. There are times, however, when those steps may not resolve the problem. Then it may be helpful to write a letter of complaint.

There is no single way to write a complaint letter. What is important, however, is to pack as much relevant information into the document as possible. According to the Office of Consumer Affairs, this information should include the following:

1. A description of the problem.
2. A statement of what you believe would be a fair settlement of the problem (for example: getting your money back, having the product repaired, or receiving an exchange).
3. Copies of all documents necessary to substantiate (support with proof) your case. These would include such things as sales slips, repair orders, warranties, cancelled checks, etc.
4. Your name, address, and telephone number.

Frequently, large corporations maintain offices that deal directly with consumer problems. These offices are usually indicated in the book of instructions or warranties that accompanied your purchases. If there is such an office you will save time by sending your letter directly to it. Otherwise, send it to the president of the firm.

Always remember that the person reading your letter was not personally responsible for your problem, but he or she may be responsible for resolving it. Therefore you ought not to write a sarcastic, threatening, or angry letter. Figure 20.1 shows a sample letter of complaint.

Finally, keep copies of your letter and all related documents and information.

I. *True or False?* If, according to the reading, the statement *in italics* is correct, write "true." If the statement is incorrect, write "false" and complete the sentence in such a way as to make it correct.

1. If something that you have purchased is defective or not performing in the way that you expected, one of the first things that you should do is *write a letter of complaint.*

2. When writing a letter of complaint, *you should not be too specific about what is wrong.*

```
                         Your Address
                         City, State, Zip Code
                         Date


    Appropriate Person
    Company Name
    Street Address
    City, State, Zip Code

    Dear (Appropriate Person):

    I recently purchased a (name of product or service
    including model number).  I made this purchase at
    (place, date, and other important details of the
    transaction).

    Unfortunately, (the product or service) has not per-
    formed satisfactorily because (state the problem).
    Therefore, I would like you to (state the specific
    action you want, such as "return my deposit" or "take
    back my purchase in exchange for undamaged goods").
    Enclosed are copies (do not send originals) of my
    records of this transaction.

    I am looking forward to your reply and to a prompt
    resolution of this matter.  Please contact me at the
    above address or by phone at (your telephone number).

                         Sincerely,

                         Your Name
```

FIGURE 20.1   Letter of Complaint

3. It is a good idea to *keep a copy of any letter that you send as well as the original sales slip.*

4. If your letter is to a large department store, you ought to *give your letter to one of the salespersons.*

5. A letter of complaint ought to include your name, address, and *telephone number.*

II. *Write a Letter of Complaint.* You purchased a sweater last month and the colors faded badly after just one washing. You immediately brought the sweater back to the department store and were prepared to accept either a refund of the purchase price or another sweater. Instead, a salesperson told you that there was nothing the store could do about the faded sweater. Store policy was not to give refunds or exchange merchandise after two weeks from the purchase date. You feel that the store's policy is unfair and you are entitled to your money back. On a separate sheet of paper, write a letter of complaint that you would send in these circumstances.

The Department of Agriculture inspects and grades meat, and it regulates the grading and labeling of fruits and vegetables that enter into interstate commerce. You have probably noticed the purple stamp of the Department of Agriculture on some of the meat your family has purchased. The department also disseminates information on the preparation of food and the maintenance of balanced diets.

The Federal Trade Commission (FTC), in addition to its many other responsibilities, attempts to combat false or misleading advertising. Of course, great leeway is granted to the advertisers in making claims for their products. When they state in their advertising that "Only one can be the best, and that's our orange juice," no one expects that the manufacturer will really have to prove the claim. However, when claims are made for the effectiveness and superiority of certain over-the-counter drugs, such as pain relievers, the FTC will demand clinical proof.

The Consumer Product Safety Commission seeks to protect consumers against unreasonable risks associated with consumer products. It sets certain safety standards and produces materials on proper product use. In certain instances, the commission may take action to remove unsafe or dangerous products from the marketplace.

CONSUMERISM—THE CONSUMER-ACTION MOVEMENT

In the early 1960s, there developed a popular movement whose goal was to educate and protect American consumers. Known as *consumerism,* the movement for over a decade was a major force on the American political scene. As a result of the consumer-action movement, both industry and government took steps to develop beneficial laws and programs.

As the decade of the 1980s opened, the nation was in the grip of the worst period of inflation in its peacetime history. Prices were increasing at the rate of one percent a month. This inflation was blamed, in part, by the Reagan administration, on excessive government regulation. These regulations, it was argued, added to the business process unnecessary costs which had to be passed along to consumers. While recognizing that certain government regulations were essential to consumer interests, the Reagan administration moved to reduce or eliminate those it felt were costly or ineffective. In their place, the administration called for vigorous competition between firms and voluntary programs as the best way to serve consumer interests. Market forces, it was claimed, can resolve most consumer problems without government involvement. If a product is inferior or unsafe, declining sales will force the manufacturer to make improvements. If a product really causes injury, lawsuits and court judgments will punish the wrongdoers and compensate the injured.

Those holding the opposite view argue that competition does not work if the market is dominated by only one or two firms or the government. Moreover, competition, when it exists, can be effective only if consumers are well-informed and choose wisely.

Differences of opinion between those favoring active government participation in and regulation of the market and those advocating a minimum of involvement are not likely to disappear soon. Consumers will need to keep themselves informed and politically active.

ADVERTISING AND THE CONSUMER

The purpose of advertising is to create, increase, and sustain demand for a product or service. We have seen that firms with high overhead costs can reduce these costs on a unit basis through mass production. But mass production requires mass demand. The creation of that mass demand is the special responsibility of advertising.

Advertising is big business in this country. As indicated by Figure 20.2, advertisers spent about $240 for every man, woman, and child in the United States in 1980. This amount will probably continue to increase, as it has in the past. Few of us can escape the messages that advertisers send out. About fifteen minutes out of every hour of television is devoted to commercial advertisements, and a major portion of newspapers and daily mail is advertising. Advertisements offer for sale items ranging from everyday necessities to exotic luxuries.

FIGURE 20.2 Advertising Expenditure per Person, 1940–1980

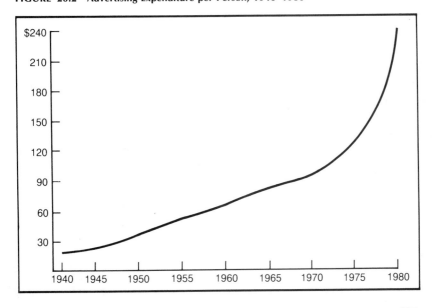

We have noted that where there is monopolistic competition (see Chapter 7) a producer will strive to create an image of the product which sets it apart from others in the industry. The success of the quest for *product differentiation,* that is, the extent to which the public believes one product is different from the rest, will directly affect the producer's freedom to price it.

The Controversy Over Advertising. Advertising has been one of the more controversial features of the free enterprise system. Summarized below are the principal arguments of (1) those who praise it and (2) those who condemn it.

Advertising has been praised.

1. Without advertising, it would be next to impossible for new products and inventions to break into the market. Advertising has made possible the introduction of many new and beneficial products and services to the general public. In the early 1980s, for example, the personal computer for home use appeared. The extent to which Americans accept this innovation will depend, in part, on advertising.

2. Advertising provides product information that enables consumers to make intelligent choices and spend their money wisely.

3. Advertising helps industry as well as consumers. The high level of demand that advertising creates brings about economies of scale and lowers costs, thus reducing prices and raising living standards.

4. The advertising industry has a significant effect upon the nation's economy. Advertising provides jobs and income for thousands and helps support newspapers, magazines, radio, and television.

Function of Advertising. A recruiting ad for the United States Army. Are such ads helpful sources of information to readers?

Advertising has been condemned.

1. Most advertising is more interested in "creating an image" of the product than providing information. Were you to take a close look at magazine ads and television commercials, you would probably find that they tell you little about the quality, special features, or price of the products they are trying to sell.

2. While increased sales and production may follow from a successful advertising campaign, unit costs may not decrease because of the high cost of the advertising.

3. Some advertising is misleading or, worse still, deceptive. Although regulatory agencies such as the Federal Trade Commission and the Federal Communications Commission supervise the industry, certain advertising continues to mislead consumers. In one well-publicized incident, a leading soup company attempted to deceive the public by putting marbles in the bowls of soup featured in its television commercials. Because the marbles went to the bottom, the vegetables and other ingredients rose to the top, thereby giving the dish a "hearty" appearance.

4. The money spent on advertising could serve a better purpose elsewhere. Suppose that no one advertised. Then, it is argued, the $61.3 billion that was spent on advertising in 1981 might have been used to improve existing products and develop new ones. Or, if less money had been spent on advertising, the savings could have been used to reduce prices. Those who disagree argue that without advertising, consumers would have spent far less than the $1.8 trillion that they put into goods and services in 1981. As past experience has shown, a substantial reduction in consumer spending could trigger a recession. (See Chapter 17 for a discussion of the effect of the reduction of consumer spending on the business cycle.)

5. "If a man can make a better mousetrap than his neighbor," said the American writer Ralph Waldo Emerson, "the world will make a beaten path to his door." Although spoken over a century ago, Emerson's words express what is still thought of as the essence of the free enterprise system. That is, in the competition between sellers to produce the best goods at the lowest prices, consumers will seek out the victors. Living standards will rise as more and better goods and services become available to all. Successful producers will receive their financial rewards in the form of profits.

Emerson, of course, wrote before the era of the television commercial and the ad campaign. All too frequently, advertisers ignore the criteria of quality and price. They focus instead upon emotional appeals to sell their wares. Money that might have been spent in research to produce a better frozen food goes, instead, to finding a catchy tune to accompany a new commercial. While this kind of competition may benefit the advertising industry, it does little for consumers' living standards.

Learning to Live With Advertising. For better or worse, advertising is a fact of modern life, and you might just as well learn how to live with it. As a consumer, you will find some advertising helpful, some harmless, and some deceptive, or misleading. A careful analysis of the helpful type of advertising will enable you to learn where particular goods and services may be purchased and how they compare in quality and price. You will also be informed about new products that are coming on the market and the features that they offer.

More difficult to evaluate are the advertisements that appeal to emotions rather than to reason. The need to feel part of one's group is common to us all. Advertisers therefore appeal to this need with messages suggesting that "everyone is buying it."

Testimonials, ads in which a celebrity endorses a product or service, have a double-edged appeal. On one level, they suggest, "Here is a successful person who uses our product. Wouldn't it make sense for you to use it too?" On a more subtle level, testimonials appeal to the subconscious by suggesting that, by using the endorsed product, we might *become* the celebrity.

Another factor influencing what people buy is what Thorstein Veblen, an American economist writing at the turn of the century, called "conspicuous consumption." By this term Veblen meant the tendency of many consumers to purchase goods in order to impress others. Thus a family may buy an expensive automobile in order to impress the neighbors. Others may shop in expensive stores because the labels and packages show the names of the stores. For this reason, advertising firms try to create an image of affluence for their products. That is, through packaging, advertising, or some other promotion, they try to identify their products with a high income level. Next time you are looking through a magazine, see what methods are used in ads to convey this feeling of affluence.

Although the vast majority of advertising is honest, there are those who would intentionally use it to mislead or deceive the consumer. A widespread fraud is called bait-and-switch. This tactic usually involves an advertisement in which a well-known product is offered at a low price (the "bait") so as to attract customers into the store. Once in the store, they are "switched" by salespeople to a competing brand at a price that will earn the dealer a larger profit. Customers who stick to their guns and insist on the advertised product are likely to be told that the "last one was just sold."

A second form of deception is the phony contest in which consumers are congratulated on having won prizes. All they need to do to collect

Government Regulatory Agencies: When Does Regulation Become "Too Much Regulation"?

Ever since 1887, when the Interstate Commerce Commission (ICC) was created, the federal government has looked to *regulatory agencies* or *commissions* to assist in protecting the public against many aspects of economic life. These agencies, now about fifty in number, make up what some have come to call the "fourth branch of government." (The legislative, executive, and judicial branches are the other three.) Some of the regulatory agencies with which you may already be familiar are the Federal Communications Commission (FCC), the Securities and Exchange Commission (SEC), the Consumer Product Safety Commission, and the Federal Trade Commission (FTC).

While many people have praised the regulatory agencies' work in protecting the public interest, others, particularly in the business community, have complained that the agencies often go too far. Over-regulation, they argue, increases the cost of doing business and leads to higher prices and lower living standards. In the late 1970s and early 1980s, Congress seemed to side with the argument against regulation. To limit the agencies' powers, Congress enacted a series of laws giving itself the power to veto many regulatory agency actions.

A dramatic illustration of this scenario began in 1980 when the FTC issued a ruling that required used-car dealers to post on each car a sticker listing its major defects. Also required was a notice informing consumers of their warranty rights. Used-car dealers complained to Washington about the ruling saying, among other things, that it was unfair because it would require them to make costly inspections of every car they sold. Their pleas won the sympathy of Congress, and in 1982 it vetoed the FTC action. In 1983 the Supreme Court stepped into the controversy with a landmark decision that declared Congressional vetoes of regulatory agencies' policies unconstitutional. This decision restored the FTC's regulations for used car sales. It also restored the independence previously lost by the regulatory agencies to Congressional vetoes.

---

the "prizes" is buy the seller's product or listen to a sales pitch. Fictitious pricing is a third common advertising fraud. And advertisers offer their goods at substantial discounts from "original list prices" that were, in fact, inflated or simply created by the seller.

Of course, no list, however long, can recite all the kinds of deceptions one may come across, for the creation of misleading advertising is an ongoing process. The best protections against it lie in the knowledge that these deceptions do exist, common sense, and the age-old caution, *caveat emptor* ("let the buyer beware").

EXERCISES

The Household Budget:
A Practical Approach to Financial Planning

"Annual income twenty pounds, annual expenditure nineteen nineteen six, result happiness. Annual income twenty pounds, annual expenditure twenty pounds ought and six, result misery." (Mr. Micawber in *David Copperfield,* by Charles Dickens) (*a*) Explain the meaning of the quotation. (*b*) What is the purpose of a family budget? (*c*) Use the headings listed in Table 20.1 on page 393 to prepare a *monthly* budget for each of the following families. All three couples are in their early twenties and have no dependents.

	Annual Income
George and Martha Greentree	$16,000
James and Dolly Bluestone	26,000
Abe and Mary Gray	45,000

(*d*) Summarize the principal differences between the three budgets.

Have You Read Any Good Labels Lately?

The questions that follow are based on information in the canned food label below. If the information is *not* contained on the label, write the words "not available" on the appropriate line.
1. What does the can contain?
2. What is the retail price of this can?
3. Louis Lean is on a high-protein, low-fat diet. Will the contents of the can suit him?
4. Fran Fine does not eat anything that contains artificial coloring. Is there anything in this product Fran should know about?

5. How many calories does one serving of this product contain?
6. What vitamins are contained in this can of food?
7. What is the purpose of the vertical lines printed above the numbers 24000 01101?
8. What other important information concerning the contents of the can is contained in the label?

Comparison Shopping

Prepare a table with the following headings: *Product   Brand Name   Net Contents   Total Cost   Cost per Ounce* (a) Complete the table by visiting your local supermarket or grocery store. Obtain the information required about three brands of each of the following products: coffee, laundry detergent, mouthwash, and canned peas. (b) Which of the products had the greatest price differential? Which had the least differential? How do you account for the differences?

Government in the Marketplace

The argument between those who favor greater participation by government in programs to protect the consumer and those taking the opposite view has gone on for many years. (a) Summarize the reasons advanced by those who favor government protection for the consumer. (b) Opponents of government intervention frequently argue that the greatest protection for consumers lies in their knowledge of the marketplace and in the American system of competitive free enterprise. Explain this point of view. (c) To what extent do you agree or disagree with the views expressed in (a) and (b)?

Advertising and the Consumer

Sellers use a variety of techniques to create demand for their products. (a) Clip three advertisements from newspapers and magazines and describe the appeal that you believe is being used to make the reader want to buy the product. (*Note:* Each advertisement should illustrate a different type of appeal.) (b) Analyze the packaging of one super-market item by describing how the design was created to help sell the product. (c) List three of the most appealing commercials that you have seen recently on television. Describe how the producers combined both audio and visual effects to sell their products. (d) There are those who argue that the public would be better served if the money spent on advertising went instead to produce better products. What is your view of this argument? (e) In defense of advertising, the following points are usually made: (1) advertising keeps consumers informed about products and prices (2) advertising increases competition (3) advertising enables sellers to market new products (4) advertising supports the media (5) advertising provides many job opportunities. To what extent do you agree or disagree with each of these points?

Congested subways and abandoned farms are two signs of rapid economic change.

UNIT IX

Living Issues in the United States Economy

CHAPTER 21

The Economics of Cities

The United States today is a far cry from the nation it was when George Washington was President. In 1790 only 5 percent of the population lived in cities, or *urban areas*. (An urban area is defined by the government as a community of 2,500 or more people.) As Figure 21.1 on page 410 indicates, things are much different today. Nearly three-quarters of the population now lives in urban areas. Moreover, if current estimates are correct, over 90 percent of the population will be city dwellers by the year 2000.

In making the transition from a rural to a predominantly urban society, the nation has encountered a host of problems, many of which are economic in nature. In this chapter, we shall describe the more pressing of these economic problems, along with the remedies that have been suggested or tried.

OUR GROWING URBAN POPULATION

The transition from a basically rural, agricultural nation to one dominated by cities was stimulated by each of the following developments in American life.

1. Increases in Farm Productivity. The principal reason why so many Americans lived on farms in Washington's day is that it took many farmers to feed and clothe the nation. Since then, there has been a revolution in farm technology that has increased productivity to a level at which fewer and fewer farmers are needed to satisfy the nation's demand for food and fiber. Millions of former agricultural

409

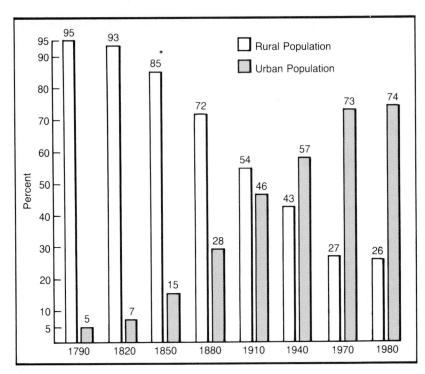

FIGURE 21.1 Rural-Urban Population Changes, in Percentages, 1790–1980

workers were thus able to work in the production of nonagricultural goods and services. (The problems of farmers and of farming in general are described in Chapter 22.)

2. Population Growth. At the same time that the proportion of the population living in the cities has been increasing, the population as a whole has been growing. With this population "explosion" has come a corresponding increase in the size of the cities. In 1790, the nation's population totaled fewer than 4 million. In the mid-1980s it exceeds 235 million people. While not a single American city exceeded 100,000 in population until 1820, there are now more than 150 such cities.

A great part of the population increase came from immigration. During the fifty-year period from 1881 to 1930, some 28 million people immigrated to this country, and most of them settled in cities. Although the tide of immigration has subsided since that time, an average of some 365,000 people have arrived yearly over the past twenty years, adding to urban population growth.

3. Advances in Science and Technology. Modern advances in medicine and hygiene that have reduced the threat of epidemics have been an important factor in urban growth. So, too, was the Industrial Revolution, in which machines and improved farming efficiency led to the development and expansion of the factory system. Laborers who were no longer needed to work the farms moved on to where the jobs were: in the factories and trades of the cities.

Urban growth was also stimulated by the revolution that took place in transportation. The development of the railroads, the automobile, and the trucking industry facilitated the transcontinental shipment of food, fuels, and raw materials to urban centers.

4. The Emergence of Metropolitan Areas. As city populations grew, the need for additional space for business and housing could be met by either the construction of taller buildings or the opening of new areas in or around the city. The first solution was provided by the construction of skyscraper office buildings and high-rise apartment houses. The second evolved as business moved "uptown" into new sections of the city or into one of the many suburban communities outside its borders.

Although the suburbs are governed separately and apart from the cities that spawned them, their fortunes are very much tied to the urban centers. The federal government refers to the central cities of 50,000 or more people and their surrounding suburbs as *metropolitan areas*. There are now over 300 metropolitan areas or, as they are officially called, *Metropolitan Statistical Areas (MSAs)*. These areas range in size from Enid, Oklahoma's 63,000 people to the New York metropolitan area's population of 17.5 million.

In time, the growth of some metropolitan areas led them to overlap and become integrated with one another. In the early 1980s the government recognized over twenty Consolidated Metropolitan Statistical areas. The seven leading metropolitan areas in Table 21.1 on page 412 are consolidated areas, with a total population of over 56 million persons. Thus nearly one-quarter of the population of the United States lives in just seven areas of the country.

5. Flight to Suburbia. Suburbs have existed ever since the development of the commuter railroad and the automobile. Even before World War I, Americans were singing George M. Cohan's "Only Forty-five Minutes From Broadway." The lyrics of this popular song extolled the virtues of New Rochelle, one of the first of New York City's affluent suburbs.

In 1946, with the end of World War II, however, the rush to the suburbs began in earnest. After the Great Depression and the war, jobs were again plentiful, people had money to spend, and the nation's factories were tooled up and ready to satisfy the pent-up demand for their goods. At the top of the wish lists for many Americans were cars and their own homes. The suburbs, or "suburbia," offered them

TABLE 21.1 Population of the Twenty Largest Metropolitan Areas, 1980 (in millions)

	Population	Percent Change Since 1970
New York–N. New Jersey, Long Island	17.5	−4
Los Angeles	11.5	+15
Chicago	7.9	+2
Philadelphia	5.6	−2
San Francisco	5.4	+12
Detroit	4.7	−2
Boston	3.9	+2
Washington, DC	3.2	+7
Houston	3.1	+43
Dallas	2.9	+25
Cleveland	2.8	−5
Miami–Ft. Lauderdale	2.6	+40
Pittsburgh	2.4	−5
St. Louis	2.3	−3
Baltimore	2.2	+5
Atlanta	2.1	+28
Minneapolis–St. Paul	2.1	+8
Seattle	2.0	+12
San Diego	1.8	+38
Cincinnati	1.6	+4

the prospect of a dream fulfilled, and, as they flocked to buy, the nation witnessed a dramatic population shift. Some of the results of the exodus from central city to suburb are reflected in Table 21.2.

Businesses, too, have moved to the suburbs. Some firms left the city to serve the needs of suburbanites. This shift led to the development of shopping malls and cultural centers at convenient locations in the metropolitan areas. Other firms moved to the suburbs for a variety of reasons, including cheaper land, less vehicular traffic, a suitable labor force, lower taxes, and the absence of labor unions.

CURRENT PROBLEMS OF THE METROPOLITAN AREAS

1. Transportation. The traffic jam has become an accepted part of the American scene. Each morning and evening, suburban commuters take to the roads in their journey to and from their jobs in the cities or other suburbs. Heavy commuter traffic on already overburdened

TABLE 21.2 Population of the Suburbs of Five Major Cities, 1950 and 1980 (in millions)

	1950		1980	
	Population	*Percent of Total*	*Population*	*Percent of Total*
New York City				
central city	7.9	83	7.0	78
suburbs	1.6	17	2.0	22
Los Angeles				
central city	1.9	45	1.9	40
suburbs	1.6	55	4.5	60
Chicago				
central city	3.6	70	3.0	42
suburbs	1.5	30	4.1	58
Philadelphia				
central city	2.0	56	1.6	36
suburbs	1.6	44	3.0	64
Detroit				
central city	1.8	61	1.2	28
suburbs	1.2	39	3.1	72

streets means more congestion, noise, and pollution. Most city planners agree that if people would forego their autos in favor of public transportation, they would take a large step toward improving urban traffic problems. One bus, for example, can replace forty or fifty cars, just as a single commuter train can replace several hundred cars. Unfortunately, public transportation has been losing riders. Although the population has been increasing, fewer people have been using mass transit facilities.

In response to the problem, the cities have tried to improve driving conditions, while, at the same time, they have sought to increase public acceptance of mass transit. The first approach involves construction of more and better highways along the principal commuter routes, and parking facilities within the central city. These efforts have been made difficult by the enormous costs of construction. Another difficulty is the cities' shortage of space. New roads, parking lots, or garages are likely to displace people or firms, which, for that reason, frequently oppose the project. Some urban economists have also claimed that successful highway and parking programs are really self-defeating. By making driving attractive, they lure still more motorists into the central city. Planners would prefer to see programs that discourage the use of private cars within the city limits and encourage the use of mass transit.

Toward that end, many communities have sought to improve existing mass transit facilities or to acquire new ones. For its part, the federal government has lent extensive assistance through the Urban Mass Transit Administration of the Department of Transportation as well as through other agencies and programs.

Some economists have suggested that one reason why so many motorists prefer to drive rather than use public transportation is that their travel is being subsidized by government. The costs of roads, traffic controls, tunnels, bridges, city streets, and cleanup are borne by all taxpayers, even those who do not own or drive cars. Let the motorists bear their fair share of the full cost of their driving, economists claim, and many will give up driving in favor of mass transportation. Although there have been specific suggestions for "user fees," "parking permits," and increased tolls that would be imposed on those who drive into crowded cities, few communities have actually adopted any of these approaches.

2. Revenue. The nation's cities have had to wrestle with a very difficult fiscal problem. The demand for municipal services has been growing at the very same time that the cities' ability to raise revenue has been dwindling. The principal causes of this problem are: the influx of low-income groups, the growth of the suburbs, and the number of tax-exempt activities functioning within the cities.

Influx of Low-Income Groups. According to the Census Bureau, those who moved from the central cities to the suburbs after World War II were predominantly middle-income white families. At about the same time, huge agricultural businesses moved into the deep South, bringing with them sophisticated farming machinery that replaced many workers, who were predominantly black. These workers and their families, along with other low-income groups from Mexico, Puerto Rico, and other Caribbean regions that were facing similar job displacements, began a mass migration into the cities in search of jobs and better lives.

Table 21.3 summarizes some of the more significant results of this population shift. We see that nearly two-thirds of the nation's white families now live in suburbs, whereas two-thirds of its nonwhite families live in the central cities. Over one-half of these nonwhite urban families earned less than $15,000 per year. About one-third of the urban whites earned less than that amount. In all, some 43 percent of the families living in the cities earned less than $15,000 as compared to 27 percent of those living in the suburbs.

TABLE 21.3 Money Income of Families in Metropolitan Areas, 1980 (percent distribution, by income level)

Income Level	LIVING IN CITIES			LIVING IN SUBURBS		
	White	Black	Hispanic	White	Black	Hispanic
Under $5,000	6.2	19.9	15.3	3.5	11.8	7.5
$5,000– $ 9,999	13.4	23.1	21.5	9.1	20.9	15.4
$10,000– $14,999	16.1	18.0	20.5	12.7	17.2	18.7
$15,000– $19,999	14.6	12.8	13.0	14.1	12.0	18.0
$20,000– $24,999	15.0	9.9	12.2	15.4	10.9	13.1
$25,000– $29,999	11.5	7.2	7.2	13.6	10.1	9.5
$30,000– $39,999	11.9	6.1	6.2	16.4	11.7	10.6
$40,000– $49,999	5.4	2.1	1.9	7.6	4.1	4.4
$50,000 and over	7.5	.9	2.1	7.5	1.4	2.8
Median Income	$19,891	$11,596	$12,974	$23,318	$15,092	$17,094
Number of Families (000's omitted)	11,700	3,431	1,495	21,851	1,295	1,092

As the low-income urban population grew, so too did the need for public health, housing, and welfare services. But many of those whose taxes might have helped pay these services were now living in the suburbs and paying few if any city taxes. Thus the population shifts of the 1950s and 1960s left the cities with the problem of finding ways to provide more and more services with fewer and fewer tax dollars.

Suburban Growth. Suburbia has added to the fiscal problems of the cities in a number of ways. Suburbanites are entitled to the same services provided to the cities' full-time residents. Police and fire protection, utility services, and, of course, transportation facilities must be maintained for all. Suburbanites also enjoy the cities' many benefits, such as their museums, theaters, libraries, and universities.

Municipal leaders have complained that those who earn their living

in the cities, or enjoy the use of their facilities, do not pay their fair share toward the cities' support. Although most cities do attempt to tax commuters through business, income, and sales taxes, these levies rarely, if ever, cover the cost of the services provided.

"Why then," you ask, "don't the cities simply increase the taxes they are already collecting from those whose homes are in the suburbs?" To increase taxes, cities fear, would drive many people into moving away or worse: prompt the firms for which they work into relocating. Either consequence would reduce tax revenues still further for the financially distressed cities.

Tax-Exempt Activities. Government agencies, religious organizations, and certain charitable and nonprofit groups are exempt from taxation. They are nevertheless entitled to the services provided for everyone else, and for that reason are a costly drain on the financial resources of many cities.

3. Housing. With the departure of the middle class and the influx of the poor, there has developed in most large cities the problem of the rapidly expanding slum. As housing formerly used by the middle class was occupied by poor families, the buildings tended to be neglected by their owners. Physical decay on one block will cause families in the next one to move away, and as their place is taken by the poor, the cycle is repeated and continued. As a result, there developed in the central cities areas in which buildings and stores lie as abandoned eyesores in scenes reminiscent of the aftermath of World War II's destruction.

Compounding the problem of deteriorating neighborhoods and housing shortages are racial discrimination, rent controls, and public housing. Although it is against the law to prevent people from owning or renting a home because of their race or nationality, discrimination persists against members of certain minority groups. Discrimination has led to the continued development of *ghetto* areas (a ghetto is a slum section occupied by one or more minority groups) with their high concentration of substandard housing.

Rent-control laws were enacted during World War II to protect tenants from exorbitant rent increases at a time of housing shortages. Critics of the policy claim that the laws fail to give landlords a fair profit, or any at all, on their investments. As a result, these landlords are compelled to neglect and even abandon their buildings rather than operate them at a loss. Little or no new housing is built in the face of rent controls, and so the housing shortage worsens.

Subsidized public housing has also had its share of critics. (The term refers to housing in which government funds are used to subsidize—that is, pay for the cost of—construction *and* part of the

The Economics of Cities

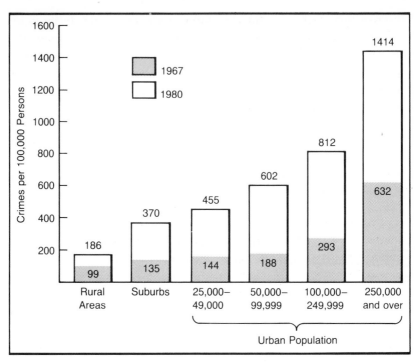

FIGURE 21.2 Rates of Violent Crime in Rural Areas, Suburbs, and Urban Areas, 1967 and 1980

monthly rentals.) Shortly after World War II, the federal government became active in massive slum-clearance projects under what came to be known as urban renewal programs. Entire city blocks were razed and replaced with high-rise public housing projects surrounded by green spaces. "Bulldozer renewal," as some critics termed the effort, frequently took place on land once occupied by many smaller buildings and resulted in a *reduction* in the number of available housing units. Urban renewal was also said to have destroyed neighborhood community values, wiped out many small single proprietorships, and caused psychological problems for displaced residents (who had to find new homes). Moreover, for lack of funds, much public housing is poorly maintained and policed by the cities, and new slums are often the result.

4. Crime. Crime, and the fear of becoming crime victims, are further burdens borne by the populations of many cities. As indicated in Figure 21.2, the rate of *violent crime* (murder, rape, robbery, and assault) has been increasing and is significantly higher in the cities than in the suburbs and rural areas.

Urban crime is a financial burden to city governments. Rising crime rates mean that the cities need more police protection, courts, prosecution, and correctional facilities. Crime also adds to the cost of doing business in the city. Stolen merchandise and crime-prevention systems represent expenses that firms will generally be compelled to pass along to consumers in the form of higher prices. These costs make it more difficult for companies in high-crime areas to compete with firms in safer locations.

Other crime costs are more difficult to measure. No one can really determine how many people who might otherwise have chosen to live in the cities were prompted to move away by the high crime rates. Nor can one put a dollar value on the physical and psychological damage suffered by the victims of crime.

5. Deteriorating Capital, or "Infrastructure." Like the human skeleton, a city's *infrastructure* provides the structural framework and support for its activities. Roads, bridges, water and waste systems, power plants, and rail lines are but some of the elements of a city's infrastructure. In recent years, the infrastructure of most cities has been deteriorating for lack of needed repairs and replacements. In the early 1980s, the federal government found that only one-third of all community water-treatment systems were operating at full capacity and that one-fifth of all bridges had decayed to the point that they were no longer safe. Other reports told that New York City was losing millions of gallons of water daily because of leaky watermains; waste watermains in Albuquerque could no longer handle the truck traffic driving over them; and whole sections of Pittsburgh were fast becoming isolated as deteriorating bridges were closed.

Maintaining a City's Infrastructure. Who pays the cost of keeping city streets in good repair?

The Economics of Cities

MEETING THE CITIES' PROBLEMS

Two realities compound the cities' fiscal problems: Like everything else, the cost of government has been increasing over the years, and it costs more to govern large cities than small ones. (See Figure 21.3.)

Unfortunately for the cities, their ability to collect revenue is limited when compared to that of the state or federal governments. As indicated by Table 21.4, taxes provide about one-third of city revenues, while state and federal contributions add another 30 percent to their budgets.

Adding to the cities' fiscal problems are the limitations of their primary source of income, the property tax. This tax is unable to keep up with changes in living costs because it is usually based upon out-of-date assessed valuations. Another limitation is that people can simply move away whenever they feel that property taxes have become too burdensome.

Sales taxes, too, have their shortcomings. These taxes are regressive in that, in proportion to income, they fall more heavily on the poor than the rich. Moreover, sales taxes must be levied with one eye on nearby communities lest their rates drive shoppers away.

The income tax, which is the federal government's principal source of revenue, has many advantages over property and sales taxes. The

FIGURE 21.3   City Government Expenditures per Person, by Population Size, 1981

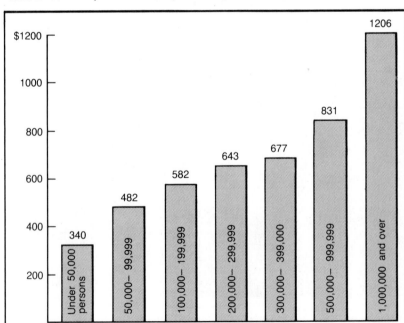

**TABLE 21.4   City Government Revenues, 1980
(in billions)**

Taxes		
Property	$ 16.9	
Sales and gross receipts	8.2	
Licenses and other	6.2	
	Total Taxes	$ 31.3
Intergovernmental Revenue		
Federal government	$ 12.4	
State government	15.9	
	Total Intergovernmental Revenue	28.3
Utilities		15.5
Other		19.8
	Total Revenues	$ 94.9 billion

income tax is progressive, so that wealthier taxpayers pay a higher portion of their income in taxes than do poorer ones. Moreover, tax revenues will increase automatically as the general level of income increases. Thus we find that, as one economist put it, "the federal government has the money, while the cities have the problems." In

Energy-Saving Dome. Building a gigantic dome over parts of New York City could greatly reduce heating costs in winter and cooling costs in summer. Why has such a dome not yet been built?

recognition of this situation, the federal government has been contributing to urban programs on a large scale ever since the days of the New Deal in the 1930s.

The principal federal agency that administers the government's urban programs is the *Department of Housing and Urban Development (HUD)*, created in 1965. HUD's activities are carried out by a number of agencies, the two most important of which are the following:

The *Federal Housing Administration* (FHA) promotes the construction of housing by guaranteeing the repayment of loans made for that purpose.

The *Government National Mortgage Association* (GNMA) (Ginny Mae) makes funds available for certain kinds of housing loans. In the course of its operations, GNMA raises funds through the sale of bonds that are commonly known as "Ginny Maes."

HUD also administers the federal government's community development and urban development programs. Community development grants fund improvements such as housing rehabilitation, streets and roads, water and sewer facilities, and other public facilities. Urban development funds are awarded to local governments that work with both public and private groups to promote local economic development projects.

Revenue-Sharing. In 1972 the federal government instituted revenue-sharing. This arrangement was a break with the past in that huge amounts of money were allocated to the states and local governments to spend more or less as they saw fit. (See Figure 21.4.) Before 1972, federal funds were usually allocated in the form of *restricted grants*, that is, they were awarded on the condition that they be used for a specific purpose, such as building a highway or a school.

There are two kinds of revenue-sharing: *general revenue-sharing grants* and *block grants.* General revenue-sharing grants enable the recipients to use the funds in any way they wish. Thus, in one year Baltimore built a subway while Miami applied its funds to solving some of the problems created by the sudden influx of Cuban refugees. Block grants restrict spending to certain categories of activities. These categories include public safety (police, fire, and corrections) and environmental protection (waste disposal and water supply).

> I am proposing a major effort to restore American federalism. This transition over nearly ten years will give States and localities the time they need to plan for themselves when and how to meet State and local needs that are now being met with Federal Government funds.—President Ronald Reagan, Budget Message to Congress, 1982.

New Federalism. While campaigning for the presidency in 1979, Ronald Reagan promised to "get the government off our backs" by

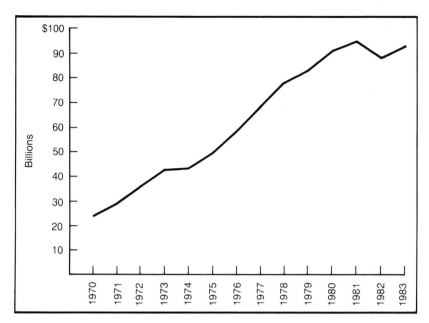

FIGURE 21.4 Federal Aid to State and Local Governments, 1970–1983

turning many federally created programs over to the states and localities. Once elected, President Reagan sought to fulfill this promise in a program that he described as the "New Federalism." At the heart of the New Federalism is the idea that the states and localities know their needs better than the politicians in Washington do and are more concerned about how they spend their money. Programs designed to deal with local rather than national problems ought to be paid for and administered by the states and localities rather than by the federal government. That approach would, in the President's view, "insure that these programs will be more responsive to both the people they are meant to help and the people who pay for them." As proposed, the new program would run for ten years. During that time, state control would gradually replace federal control over a wide array of public works and welfare programs. Similarly, the states were expected gradually to assume responsibility for the financing of these programs.

The impact of the New Federalism was felt almost immediately as the upward march of federal aid to state and local governments was ended. This change put pressure on the cities and states to reduce spending or raise taxes.

Opponents of the New Federalism argue that most federal programs were federal because they dealt with problems that went beyond state boundaries. They also say that the effect of turning those problems over to the states would put groups like the poor and the handicapped—and the central cities themselves—at the mercy of the state legislatures. These bodies, which are often controlled by suburban and rural interests, have generally resisted taxes whose proceeds were targeted for the poor and the cities.

It remains to be seen how much of the New Federalism will be accepted and adopted by the states. What can be said now, however, is that any shift of power away from Washington will pose new challenges for city and state governments across the nation.

EXERCISES

Multiple Choice

1. What percentage of the total United States population lives in urban areas? (a) 75 (b) 50 (c) 25 (d) 15.
2. A metropolitan area is (a) a very large city (b) an average-sized city (c) a cluster of big cities (d) a city and its surrounding suburbs.
3. Which of the following has *not* been a factor in the shift of the population from rural to urban areas? (a) increased farm productivity (b) population growth (c) the decline in urban crime (d) the industrialization of America.
4. In the years between 1950 and 1980, (a) most large American cities increased substantially in population (b) rural regions increased in population faster than metropolitan regions (c) most large American cities did not increase in population as rapidly as their suburbs did (d) the suburban population declined.
5. All of the following reasons would account for the movement of people out of the central cities and into the suburbs *except* (a) the increasing ownership of automobiles (b) the increase in personal wealth since the end of World War II (c) the desire to raise one's children away from the problems of the cities (d) the desire to live in a cultural center among people of differing backgrounds, interests, and points of view.
6. In the United States, an important result of the movement of people from the cities to the suburbs has been a reduction in (a) the number of middle-income families living in the central cities (b) the urban crime rate (c) urban renewal (d) the cost of public transportation systems in cities.
7. City planners have called for increased federal assistance in solving the problems of the city because (a) government programs are more efficient than private programs (b) the federal government is more efficient than local governments (c) local governments do not understand their problems as well as federal experts (d) many of the problems of the city are national in origin and too costly for any single city to solve.

8. The principal source of income for city governments is the (*a*) income tax (*b*) property tax (*c*) lottery (*d*) sales tax.
9. "Urban renewal" refers to (*a*) the reduction of crime in the cities (*b*) the removal of people from slums to suburbs (*c*) the improvement of suburban housing (*d*) the rebuilding of the decaying sections of a city.
10. On a *per capita* basis, large cities are, on the average (*a*) more expensive to govern than smaller cities (*b*) less expensive to govern that smaller cities (*c*) neither more nor less expensive to govern than smaller cities (*d*) less expensive to govern than the suburbs or rural areas.
11. One of the reasons why commuters have resisted shifting from private automobiles to mass transit is that (*a*) most cities have eliminated rush-hour traffic jams (*b*) much of the cost of automobile commuting is paid for by government (*c*) no community has improved its mass-transit facilities since 1950 (*d*) parking is plentiful in downtown centers.
12. The proposal known as the "New Federalism" calls for (*a*) greater control over the affairs of cities by the federal government (*b*) federal programs to deal with each of the major categories of urban problems (*c*) the substitution of state and local control over what had been federal programs to aid the cities (*d*) the creation of a federal agency to coordinate national efforts to aid the states and localities.

Essay Questions

1. During World War II, a completely new city—Oak Ridge, Tennessee—was created in order to develop an atomic bomb. Unlike most cities, in which institutions and services developed as they were needed, the planners of Oak Ridge had to provide complete facilities for an "instant city." (*a*) Assuming that you were planning a total city "from scratch," what major categories of services would you have to provide? (*b*) What major problems might arise from this kind of city planning? (*c*) What advantage would such a city have over a city of equal size that had evolved in the traditional way?
2. One of the major problems confronting cities has been the need to find adequate sources of revenue to meet their ever-increasing costs. (*a*) Name *three* factors that have added to the financial burdens of the cities in recent years. (*b*) Explain *one* proposal that has been advanced to solve each of these problems. (*c*) Summarize the reasons why the federal government is better able to finance its activities than city governments can finance theirs.
3. (*a*) Do you think that the suburbs ought to become more involved in solving the problems of the cities? (*b*) Should persons living in

the suburbs but earning their living in the city be required to pay taxes to the city? (c) Should "supergovernments" covering the entire metropolitan region be established? (Give *two* arguments to defend *each* of your answers.)

4. An examination of the tables and graphs contained in this chapter will reveal many of the problems faced by America's cities today. With reference to any two tables in this chapter, (a) identify one urban problem suggested by these data and (b) describe a possible solution for the problem that you have identified.

5. In the early 1980s a new approach to city problems, calling for urban *enterprise zones*, was introduced in Congress. This proposal would target for economic improvement a deteriorated, blighted city area, or "zone." Businesses would be encouraged to locate there by certain federal tax incentives. In this way, it was hoped, jobs and income would help to rehabilitate some of the worst slums in the nation. (a) Why does the government want to attract business into poor urban areas? (b) How could the tax law be changed to attract business into undesirable neighborhoods? (c) Supporters of the enterprise zone concept argue that the federal government will get more for its dollars in such a program than it would if the money were used to build low-income housing. What is your opinion? Explain your answer.

CHAPTER 22
The Economics of Farming

The harvests were as bountiful as they had ever been in Illinois' McLean County in September 1982. For the third year in a row, farms all across the western United States were registering record yields of corn, wheat, and soybeans. But, like other farmers from one end of the Plains to the other, McLean's farmers were worried.

"One more year like this and we'll all be out of business," said Harold Stewart. His 500 acres had never produced so much corn.

What had happened was this: Grain prices had fallen so low that, despite the record yields, farmers were having difficulty meeting their costs of production. Indeed, in *constant dollars*, net farm income had fallen to its lowest point in years. (See Figure 22.1 on page 428.) The year was also a bad one for the firms whose fortunes were tied to the farm economy. Everyone—from the tractor sales agent and the feed and fertilizer supplier to the local grocer and the clothing merchant—was hurting as farmers did what they could to reduce their expenses.

It had not always been like this. A decade earlier, farm income had reached record highs as farmers and those in allied industries enjoyed a golden age of prosperity. Said Mr. Stewart, "It seems that farming in America has always had its ups and downs. It's just my bad luck to be stuck on one of its downhill legs."

Mr. Stewart was right. Farm income had fluctuated widely over the years. But why? And what has been and is being done about it?

In order to answer these questions, it is necessary to know something about the special nature of farming and its recent history.

THE MIRACLE OF UNITED STATES FARM PRODUCTION

Throughout the history of the United States, the population has been increasing. Despite this increase, however, fewer and fewer farmers are required to produce the food we need. As recently as 1940, for example, 23 percent of the population (about one person in four) lived on farms, but only 2.7 percent (one out of 37) lived there in 1981. Moreover, of the 6½ million farms in 1940, fewer than 2½ million remained in 1981.

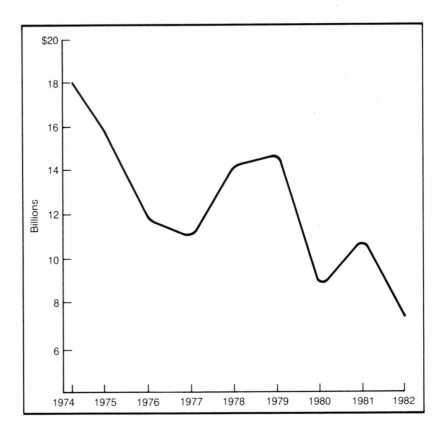

FIGURE 22.1 Net Farm Income, in 1967 Dollars, 1974–1982

To put it another way: In 1850 the average farm worker produced enough food and fiber for four people. By 1940 the number had risen to 12. Today, each farm worker produces enough to feed 78 people.

How is it possible for so few to provide enough for so many? The answer lies in the technology that enables farm productivity to achieve levels that few people would have dreamed possible forty years ago.

Farm productivity (farm output per hour of work) owes its growth to developments in science and technology. Highly specialized machinery and equipment now perform tasks that until the recent past could be done only by hand. For example, 95 percent of the work necessary to harvest the sugar beet crop in 1944 was performed by hand. Since 1958 the entire crop has been harvested by machine. Chemical fertilizers, pesticides, and seeds have been improved to increase the quantity and quality of crop yields. Farm animals, too, have been affected by the new technology, and the production of livestock has accordingly increased. Some of the results of this agricultural revolution are summarized in Figure 22.2.

The mechanization of agriculture—the replacement of human labor

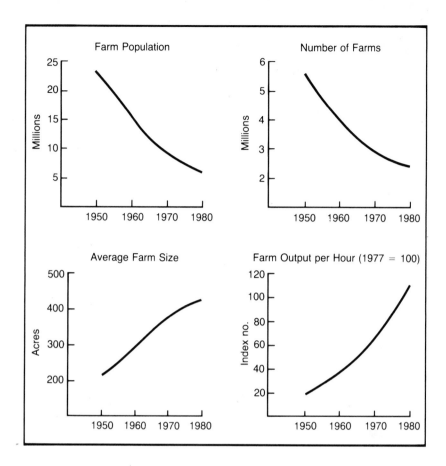

FIGURE 22.2   Changes in American Farming, 1950–1980

by machines—which has increased productivity and enabled so few farmers to feed so many of us, has also been a source of farmers' financial difficulties. In 1981 the average investment in machinery and equipment ran to more than $40,000 per farm, as compared to only $8,500 in 1947. Farmers who cannot afford the equipment necessary to operate a modern farm have been doomed from the start to sales that barely exceed their costs. Others, forced to borrow to pay for their equipment, must earn enough to offset their additional financing costs. This burden became particularly onerous in recent years when interest rates climbed to all-time highs.

One consequence of the high cost of modern farming is that the size of the average farm has been increasing. This increase in size is the result of efforts by farmers to reduce their overhead costs on a per-unit basis by increasing their output.

But to many economists, the most disturbing result of the high cost of farming is the unequal distribution of income. As indicated by

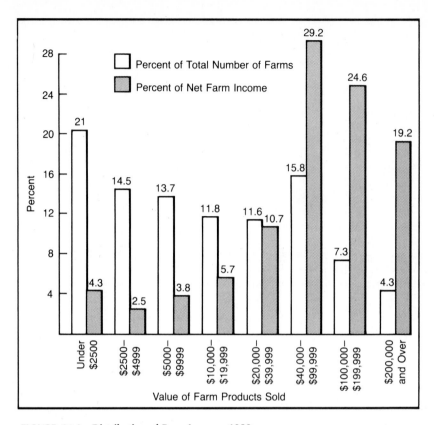

FIGURE 22.3   Distribution of Farm Income, 1980

Figure 22.3, one-quarter of the nation's farms earned three-quarters of the total farm income in 1980. The remaining three-quarters of farms were left to share but one-quarter of the income.

Farmers have also had to face economic problems that are unique to their industry. These problems involve demand and the immobility of resources.

SUPPLY, DEMAND, AND RESOURCE USE OF AGRICULTURE

Economists describe the supply of, and the demand for, agricultural products as *relatively inelastic*. Inelasticity, you recall, means that price changes will have only a slight effect upon supply and demand. In other words, if the price of corn were to fall by 25 percent, there would be an increase of something less than 25 percent in the amount of corn purchased. Similarly, an increase in prices would not be followed either by a substantial increase in corn offered for sale or a decrease in corn purchased.

Demand for Farm Products. Between 1965 and 1981, the number of dairy-farm animals declined by 50 percent. But in the same period, the number of gallons of milk sold to consumers increased slightly. How does this illustrate both farm productivity and inelastic demand?

Inelastic Demand for Farm Products. Though families will adjust their eating habits somewhat as prices for particular foods rise or fall, their total consumption will remain about the same regardless of food prices. So, for example, if the price of a loaf of bread were to fall from 90 cents to 45 cents, the average family would not be likely to double its bread consumption. This unresponsiveness of demand to price also applies to income changes. As its income increases, a family's consumption of agricultural products will increase far less than its consumption of most other goods and services. There is, after all, a limit to the amount of food one can eat.

One result of this pattern is that in 1920 the farmers' share of the gross national product ran to 13 percent. While American industrial production increased over the next sixty years, per capita consumption of farm products remained more or less stable. As a result, the farmers' share of the GNP had slipped to only 2½ percent by 1980.

In summary: There is little aside from population growth that will increase the demand for food. While manufacturers have created demand for their new products, farmers have had relatively little success in product innovation. An apple has remained an apple, and today's farmers still produce essentially the same products that were grown and raised by their parents and grandparents.

Inelastic Supply of Farm Products. When automobile sales slump, manufacturers can lay off workers, shut down plants, and thereby cut back production until the demand for their product revives. Meanwhile, reduced output will serve to maintain prices at current levels.

Much the same is true of many other manufacturing industries: Prices can be maintained by reducing output during times when the demand for the product falls. Similarly, when the demand for products rises, manufacturing output can be increased. Farmers, however, do not have these options. Once their crops are planted or the size of their herds is established, farmers can do little to increase or decrease production until the next growing or breeding season. Moreover, even if individual farmers could reduce the amount of acreage planted in a particular crop in a given year, this would have little effect on prices. The reason is that no single farmer or group of farmers controls a sufficient supply of any commodity to the extent that enables them to set prices.

Today's farmers also face high overhead costs. Mortgages, taxes, and depreciation costs must be paid regardless of economic conditions and commodity prices. Typically, farmers will conclude that it is in their own best interest to produce as much as they can at whatever price they can get.

Perhaps more than any other industry, farming depends on the weather. In years when nature has favored them with just the right combination of sun and rain, farmers have had to accept relatively low prices for their bountiful crops. In other circumstances, when bad weather has reduced the size of the year's harvest, the laws of supply and demand have served to push up prices. But higher prices did not aid farmers who had little to sell.

To summarize: The supply of food and fiber is influenced more by natural forces and the desire of farmers to produce as much as possible than by the prevailing level of prices.

Immobility of Resources. Farm income is lower than nonfarm income because there are too many farmers. If the less efficient farmers were to change jobs, the average income of those who remained would necessarily increase. But most people are farmers because they like the life and are reluctant to give it up. Work in the fresh air, free of the hustle, crowds, dirt, and temptations of the city, holds an attraction for many Americans, particularly those who were born into it. Also, many farmers have had little training for any other kind of work and are fearful of leaving the work for which they know they are qualified. Still another reason why people hesitate to abandon farming is the feeling that in really hard times they will always be able to feed their families out of the food they raise.

Economists describe this reluctance to leave the farm as the *immobility* of farm labor. Still another relatively *immobile* resource in the farming industry is its land. Unlike land in the metropolitan regions, which can be used for any number of productive purposes or developed for housing, much of the nation's farmland is unsuited for other uses.

Net Result: The Farm Problem. The "farm problem" refers to the relatively low income of the agricultural sector of the economy. This problem has a number of causes:

1. The huge increase in agricultural productivity, which led to the production of far more food and fiber than farmers could profitably sell.
2. The inelasticity of supply, which contributed to the overproduction of farm goods.
3. The inelasticity of demand, which made it difficult to dispose of excess production.
4. The immobility of farm labor, which kept more people on the farm than were needed to satisfy the demand for farm products.
5. The immobility of farmland, which could not be economically transferred to industrial production or housing.
6. The high cost of modern farming, which placed the small farm at a competitive disadvantage.

In the years following the Civil War, American farmers increasingly looked to the federal government for assistance in solving their problems. The struggles for lower tariffs, monetary reform, and antitrust legislation all received the active endorsement of the nation's farmers. The Great Depression of the 1930s wreaked great hardships on the nation's farmers and spurred the enactment of legislation specifically designed to relieve their suffering.

GOVERNMENT AND THE FARMER

During World War I, American farmers expanded their production as rapidly as they could in order to satisfy the demands of the Allies. With the armistice in 1918, however, European farmers returned to work, and American farmers soon found that they were producing far more than they could profitably sell. In accordance with the laws of supply and demand, this overabundance led to a decline in American farm prices, and many farmers found themselves unable to meet their mortgage payments.

The decline in farm prices continued until 1933, when, as part of Franklin D. Roosevelt's New Deal, Congress established the *Agricultural Adjustment Administration (AAA)*. The AAA was empowered to enter into agreements with farmers to reduce the amount of their acreage. In this way the total output of such crops as wheat, cotton, corn, and tobacco was reduced. For their cooperation, farmers were paid subsidies. The deliberate reduction in supply had its desired effect, and farm prices climbed during the years that followed.

The AAA came to a temporary end in 1936 when the Supreme Court ruled that the method used to finance the subsidies was unconstitutional. Nevertheless, the concept of limiting acreage for particular crops was continued in the *Soil Conservation and Domestic Allotment Act* of 1936. This law required farmers to plant the acreage that they withdrew from production with soil-conserving crops. In 1938 a new Agricultural Adjustment Act was passed. By introducing the idea of government acquisition and storage of surplus production, this law established a pattern of farm assistance that was generally followed up to 1973. The 1938 law established the following programs:

1. Benefits were provided to farmers who withdrew acreage from production and planted soil-conserving crops in their place.

2. The government was empowered to set limits on the amount of crops that farmers could sell.

3. If farmers were unable to sell all their produce, the government was authorized to store the surplus crops until they could be sold. In the meantime, farmers were given "loans" on their crops in storage. The amount of these "loans" was based upon some percentage of "parity" (see below).

From 1945 to the early 1970s, the government continued to rely upon production controls and price supports to help the farmer. In addition, it sought to dispose of the surplus production.

Price Supports: Parity. Farmers in general complained that the prices they were receiving for their products were "too low." As we have seen, their cries for assistance led the federal government in the 1930s to introduce a program of minimum prices for some (but not all) of their products.

But to guarantee a fixed price for all time—for example, $1 per bushel for corn—would not really have been helpful because of the problem of inflation. We have already mentioned how people on fixed incomes tend to suffer during periods of rising prices. For this reason, the government's support programs were designed to protect *purchasing power* rather than *prices*. Toward that end, the concept of *parity* was evolved. Parity was a price that would give farmers the same purchasing power from the sale of their goods that they had during the years 1909–1914. These years had been good ones for farmers and for that reason were selected to provide the statistical base for parity prices.

Let us suppose, for example, that during the 1909–1914 period the average price of wheat was 50 cents a bushel and that by 1980 the cost of living had increased six times. If farmers were still receiving 50 cents a bushel for their wheat in 1980, they would certainly have a problem since it would take six bushels to buy what one could buy back in 1910. To maintain their purchasing power, the growers would have had to receive $3 a bushel, the *parity price*, for their wheat.

In guaranteeing farm prices, the government usually aimed toward a figure of something less than 90 percent of parity. If, as in the above example, wheat were being supported at 80 percent, farmers would be guaranteed $2.40 per bushel (80 percent of $3).

How Farm Prices Were Supported. In supporting farm prices, the government relied upon three strategies: crop loans, outright purchase, and acreage controls.

Under the loan program, the Commodity Credit Corporation permitted farmers to borrow money on crops that they had placed in storage. The amount of the loan was based upon the value of the stored crop at the prevailing support price. Farmers took such loans when they were unable to obtain a higher price in the open market. If the market price later rose above the amount of their loans, farmers had the option of taking the crop out of storage and selling it. If the price failed to rise above the support price, the farmers kept the loans and the government retained the crop.

The government has also supported farm prices through the outright purchase of certain commodities. Under this procedure, farmers had the option of selling their goods to the government whenever the market price fell below its support price.

A third approach to price supports was directed at the supply side of the market. Farmers were paid to divert to other uses acreage that formerly had been planted in certain crops. In this way, it was hoped, production of those crops would decrease and prices would rise.

Price-support programs have been in effect in one form or another for the past fifty years. In that time critics have focused on what they believe are the programs' most serious weaknesses:

1. Price supports, it is charged, increase the cost of living by raising food prices above free-market prices. Supports also impose higher taxes on us all, for we pay for the cost of farm subsidies and loans.

2. The commodities acquired by the government through its price-support programs have, at times, reached unreasonably high levels. Indeed, stocks of certain commodities stored by the government have been so huge that they had to be destroyed.

3. Acreage controls have not successfully reduced farm output because farmers generally withdraw only their least productive land from cultivation. Moreover, further improvements in farm technology

Price of Farm Products. In 1980 farmers received $3.11 per bushel of corn. In 1982 they received only $2.32 per bushel. What factors may have caused this price decline?

increased productivity so that use of the remaining land restored production to its former levels.

4. The most generous support programs seem to be awarded to those commodities whose producers have the greatest political clout. Critics cite tobacco growers who, despite the health hazard presented by their product, have continued to win government endorsement of price supports.

Recent Innovations. Two new approaches to the farm problem are target pricing, along with efforts to increase the demand for farm products both at home and abroad.

Target Pricing: Innovation of the 1970s. Introduced by Congress in 1973, target pricing was an attempt to support farm income without increasing consumer prices. Under this approach the government establishes "target prices" for the commodities it wishes to support. Whenever the market price falls below the target price, farmers are paid a "deficiency payment" to make up the difference. So, for example, if the target price for wheat is $4 a bushel and a farmer sells 1,000 bushels at $3.50 a bushel, the government will make up the

$500 difference (1,000 bushels @ $4/bu = $4,000, but at $3.50, the farmer would have earned only $3,500).

Under target pricing, consumers can pay the free-market price for the commodities they buy, while farmers are assured a minimum return on their investment.

Reinforcing Demand. The government has introduced a number of programs that would increase the demand for farm products. Should these programs succeed, they would serve to maintain farm prices at current levels. In a recent example, the Agriculture and Food Act of 1981 established a credit refund that would encourage shipments of farm goods to markets abroad. The act also provided for the continuation of the multibillion-dollar food stamp program. Efforts to expand the export of American farm products have involved the State Department and other government offices in seeking to persuade foreign nations to reduce their trade barriers.

The Farm Problem in the 1980s and Beyond. Throughout much of the 1950s and 1960s, it appeared that the huge stockpiles of farm commodities that had been amassed as part of the government's price support programs would always be with us. Worldwide crop failures in the mid-1970s brought that thinking to an end as government-owned surpluses were sold off and farm incomes boomed. (See Figure 22.4 on page 438.) The related run-up in food prices was soon felt by shoppers at supermarket checkout counters all across the country. In the aftermath of consumer protests over the high food prices, serious consideration was given to suggestions that the government abandon its long-standing policy of price supports and acreage controls.

Then, as the decade of the 1970s drew to a close, farm production the world over improved. Indeed, this improvement reached such proportions by the 1980s that United States farm prices declined once more and income plummeted. The government again entered the market to restrict production, support prices, and purchase and store surplus commodities. Toward those ends, in 1983 it introduced the payments-in-kind (PIK) program. PIK offered farmers commodities in government warehouses if the farmers agreed to keep acreage unplanted. (See reading, page 440.)

On the one hand, agriculture must be considered among the most successful of American industries. The 3 percent of the American labor force that works on farms produces about 20 percent of the nation's exports. Indeed, no other country is as efficient in the production of food and fiber as the United States. On the other hand, many of the farmers' problems seem as difficult to solve today as they ever were. While it is impossible to predict the future of farming in

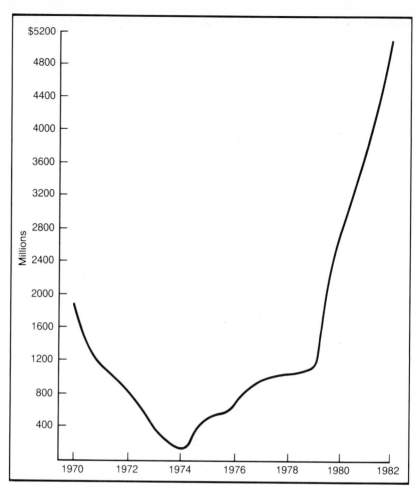

FIGURE 22.4   Value of Price-Supported Farm Products Owned by the Government, 1970–1982

the United States, it seems reasonably certain that the partnership between the farmer and the government will continue. As the old problems of declining farm income and overproduction reappear, we may also assume that the time-tested strategies of price supports and demand creation will continue to be applied.

EXERCISES

Multiple Choice

1. To keep farm income on the same level as the income of the rest of the economy, the federal government instituted (a) equalization

fees (b) parity payments (c) marginal farming (d) pesticide programs.

2. Which statement best describes a trend in agriculture during the past 35 years? (a) The number of farmers has remained the same, but they constitute a smaller percentage of the total population. (b) The number of farmers has declined, but the number of farms has remained about the same. (c) Small farms and large farms have increased their productivity at about the same rate. (d) Large farms produce an increasing percentage of the farm output.

3. President Franklin D. Roosevelt's agricultural policy (a) concentrated primarily on farm cooperatives (b) was opposed by a majority of the farmers affected (c) used soil conservation as a device to extend aid to farmers (d) aimed to increase productivity by intensive cultivation of the soil.

4. With respect to agriculture in the United States, which of the following was the basic cause of the other three? (a) parity payments to farmers (b) scientific and mechanized methods of farming (c) overproduction of farm products (d) decline in farm population.

5. A major difference between farmers and industrial producers is the (a) existence of overhead costs for the industrialist (b) need for credit by the farmer (c) need for skilled labor in the factory (d) difficulty of adjusting farm production to meet market demand.

6. Which phrase best describes long-term agricultural trends in the United States? (a) reduced farm acreage and reduced crop production (b) increased farm acreage and reduced crop production (c) reduced farm acreage and increased crop production (d) increased use of farm acreage and increased crop production.

7. When harvests are good, farmers may experience difficulty in selling their crops because (a) prices will rise and consumers will therefore buy less (b) the reduction in prices may not result in a corresponding increasing in the consumption of farm products (c) consumers buy less when prices fall (d) the demand for farm products is highly elastic.

8. By the 1980s, United States farm production was (a) greater than ever before (b) one-half of what it had been in the 1940s (c) one-third of what it had been in the 1940s (d) about equal to the 1940s.

9. Farmers as a group are particularly concerned about interest rates because (a) farmers tend to speculate more than others (b) farmers tend to have more money to invest in stocks and bonds than other economic groups (c) farmers rely heavily on credit to finance their operations (d) there is a direct correlation between interest rates and food consumption.

10. The demand for farm produce is relatively inelastic. For that reason, a relatively small increase in the supply of a commodity will result in a relatively sharp (a) decrease in market price and

farm income (b) increase in market price and farm income (c) increase in price, but a fall in farm income (d) increase in the cost of doing business on the farm.

11. Which of the following statements best describes the distribution of income among the nation's farms? (a) About 25 percent of the wealthiest farms earn 75 percent of all farm income. (b) Income is more equally distributed among farmers than any other economic group. (c) The increased use of machinery has all but eliminated bankruptcy and business failure among the ranks of farmers. (d) All of the above are true.

12. The farm problem is a result, in part, of (a) increasing farm productivity (b) the relative immobility of farm labor (c) the high cost of farming (d) all of the above.

13. Suppose that: the cost of living increased six times since the base years of 1909–1914; wheat sold for an average price of 85 cents a bushel during the base years; and the government today has decided to support wheat at 80 percent of parity. What will be the government support price for wheat? (a) 68 cents per bushel (b) $4.08 per bushel (c) $5.10 per bushel (d) $5.95 per bushel.

Essay Questions

1. Read the selection and answer the questions that follow.

Payments-in-Kind: A New Approach to an Old Problem

By 1983, the combined forces of abundant crop yields and declining world prices for grain had left federal government warehouses awash in grain. Overabundant stocks also threatened to depress prices to the point of disaster for thousands of the nation's farmers.

In an effort to meet the problems head-on, the White House introduced a new "payments-in-kind" agricultural subsidy plan, known as PIK. With PIK, farmers could choose to idle some lands that might otherwise have been planted in grain or cotton. In return, the farmers were to receive payment in commodities drawn from government inventories. For example, a farmer whose lands might have produced 10,000 bushels of corn would be entitled to receive 80 percent of that amount, or 8,000 bushels, from government warehouses for agreeing not to plant corn.

Farmers obviously approved of the plan, for in its first year, 1983, some 36 percent of the nation's acreage usually planted in cotton and grain was taken out of production. PIK's advocates claimed the following advantages:

a. PIK would reduce the costly storage program for surpluses in government stockpiles.

b. PIK would prevent a further decline in farm prices.

Critics warned, however, that PIK might create more problems than it solved because:

a. PIK might cause prices to rise so high that foreign buyers would no longer purchase American farm produce.

b. The industries supplying American farmers might be hurt if PIK were continued over any extended length of time.

(*a*) Explain why government warehouses were "awash in grain" before the PIK program went into effect in 1983. (*b*) What was the PIK program's greatest strength? Explain. (*c*) Why did critics see PIK as a threat to the industries supplying the farmers? (The farm-supply industry includes producers of tractors and other heavy machinery, tools and equipment, and fertilizers.) (*d*) In 1984 the government paid dairy farmers for milk that they *did not produce*. Under the terms of that new program, farmers received a fixed sum for every gallon less than their average production the previous year. (1) In what way was this similar to the PIK program? (2) In what way was it different from PIK?

2. Base your answers to this question on the information contained in Figure 22.2 on page 429. (*a*) Summarize the changes that took place in farming between 1950 and 1980. (*b*) Why did these changes occur? (*c*) Identify and explain one problem created by these changes for: (1) the farmer, (2) the federal government, and (3) the cities.

3. Over the years, farmers have argued that their problems are quite different from those of the rest of the economy. One of the principal causes of farmers' difficulties is the inelasticity of demand for, and supply of, farm products. (*a*) Explain why both the supply of and the demand for farm products are inelastic. (*b*) What special problems have inelastic supply and demand created for farmers? (*c*) How has the federal government attempted to solve these problems?

4. The federal government's program of farm assistance has long been a source of discussion and debate. (*a*) Explain *three* reasons that have been advanced to justify farm assistance programs by the federal government. (*b*) Explain *three* arguments that have been advanced in criticism of these programs. (*c*) Identify and explain one way in which government has attempted to help the farmer in the years *since* 1980.

5. "The troubles of America's farmers have as much to do with harvests in Europe, Africa, and Asia as they do with conditions in this country." (*a*) Explain the quotation. (*b*) What efforts has the government made in the past to help farmers sell their products abroad? (*c*) Some Americans have complained that the sale of farm products to foreign countries has created shortages and high prices at home. Therefore, the government ought *not* to encourage the sale of farm products abroad. What is your opinion of this argument? Explain your answer.

CHAPTER 23

Economic Growth and the Quality of Life

Economic growth—the ever-increasing output of goods and services—may be society's oldest economic goal. This goal is hardly a surprising one, since the dream of a better tomorrow is part and parcel of the human condition. For that reason, economists have studied and written about the process, and every presidential administration in modern times has supported policies and programs to promote growth.

In recent years, however, questions have been raised about the basic assumptions of economic growth. As evidence of the relationship between production and environmental decay mounted, some people questioned whether society could afford to pay the price of growth. The controversy has yet to be resolved.

In this chapter, we shall survey the process of economic growth by describing:

What growth is
Why growth is important to our economy and to the global economy
The ingredients of economic growth
The role of government in promoting growth

Finally, we shall summarize the views of those who would limit or eliminate growth as well as of those who continue to support the process as a goal worthy of the American economy.

WHAT IS ECONOMIC GROWTH?

Economic growth is an increase in the output of goods and services over a period of time. The easiest way to measure growth is by means of the gross national product. Thus, if the GNP in one year were greater than that of the preceding year, we *might* say that there was economic growth. By now, however, you know that it would not necessarily follow that more goods and services were actually produced in the second year, because the value of the dollar is not fixed. In other words, if the GNP had shown a 5 percent increase in a year in which inflation had reached 10 percent, then *fewer* goods and services were actually produced in the second year. For that reason, economists prefer to use the GNP as expressed in *constant dollars* (or *real GNP*) as a measure of economic growth.

While real GNP enables us to compare the economy's total output in one year with that of another, it does not tell us much about living standards. For example, if the population were to increase by 10 percent while the real GNP was increasing by only 5 percent, there would actually be fewer goods and services available *per capita* (for each person). Thus, living standards would have declined, even though real GNP had registered an increase. This, then, is the reason why economists developed a second measure of economic growth: *real GNP per capita*. This measure eliminates both fluctuations in the value of the dollar and population differences as factors in comparing the output of one period of time with another.

From what we have just said, we can now define economic growth as an increase over a period of time in either real GNP *or* real GNP per capita.

WHAT IS THE IMPORTANCE OF ECONOMIC GROWTH?

1. Higher Living Standards. Because there will be more of everything to go around, living standards will be improved whenever the economy's real GNP per capita increases.

2. Aid to the Needy. Growth enables us to help the depressed sectors of our economy. Throughout history, there have been some groups in society that have been in need of help. Today, the unemployed, the aged, the sick, those lacking in basic skills, and the victims of discrimination occupy the common category of "needy." Society has two choices to help these citizens: It can either take goods and services away from those who have them and give them to the needy, or it can produce more and share the increased output with everyone. The first choice is repugnant to many who feel it is wrong for one group to benefit at the expense of another. They prefer to see everyone's living standards improved through a sharing of the increased bounty produced by economic growth.

3. Free World Political Leadership. Growth enables us to continue to lead the free world. Ever since the end of World War II, the United States has led the free world in its ideological and military confrontations with the Soviet Union and its Communist allies. Costly as these programs have been, we have been able to maintain them out of the surplus created by our growing economy without reducing American living standards.

4. *Aid to Poor Countries.* Growth is the only means by which less developed countries can rid themselves of poverty.

The term *less developed countries* (LDCs) is usually applied to the poor countries of the world. Current estimates indicate that, by the year 2000, two-thirds of the world's 6 billion people will be living in the LDCs. The fundamental challenge facing these countries will be to find ways in which to extricate themselves from the poverty that plagues them. The amount of growth necessary to move a less developed country into a developed status varies from place to place, but without growth poverty will persist. (The special problems of the less developed countries are discussed in Chapter 27.)

WHAT ARE THE INGREDIENTS OF ECONOMIC GROWTH?

Each of the following is an essential ingredient in the process of economic growth: an expanding capacity to produce goods and services, a willingness to buy the increased production, and a favorable political and social climate.

1. *Expanding Production Capacity.* At any time, there is a limit to the amount of goods and services the economy is capable of producing. This limit, you will recall from Chapter 1, is shown in what economists call the production possibilities curve. Exactly what this limit is will depend upon the supply of productive resources and society's ability to use them—that is, its *productivity.*

Productive resources, the things such as raw materials, labor, management, and capital that go into the production of goods and services, are limited. Once resources are fully employed, output cannot be increased unless a new supply of resources is made available *or* new and more efficient production techniques are applied. For a discussion of productivity and its components, see Chapter 4.

2. *Increasing Demand.* Regardless of what the economy is capable of producing, its actual production will depend upon how much consumers, business, and government are willing to buy, or as you have learned, what economists call aggregate demand. When aggregate demand is running at anything less than the economy's ability to produce, business will lay off workers and operate at less than capacity. In these circumstances, government may choose to apply fiscal or monetary policies in an effort to restore demand to more favorable levels and stimulate economic growth.

Automation: Promises and Problems

In recent years, one of the key elements leading to increased productivity and economic growth has been *automation,* which is described in the following excerpt.

> At first glance, the factory looked like many other machine-parts factories. There on the work floor were the complex machines noisily at work transforming steel blanks into finished gears. The factory was like many others, but with one major exception: All of the jobs were being done by robots. No people were to be seen at all. (*Summary of a recent news report*)

The workerless factory is no longer a figment of a science fiction writer's imagination. This so-called factory of the future is the latest development in the phase of industrialization known as *automation.* During the period of mechanization that followed the Industrial Revolution, human labor came to be replaced by machines. The machines, however, were directly controlled by workers. For example, a worker using a power-driven lathe shaped a piece of metal in accordance with design specifications. By the 1950s, a whole new generation of machines

Automation. Robots weld car chassis in this St. Louis plant. What are the positive and negative consequences of substituting machines for workers?

Economic Growth and the Quality of Life **445**

that could be operated without human hands had been developed. Thus, lathes could be programmed to shape parts by themselves.

DEVELOPMENTS IN THE 1980s

In the 1980s, the pace of change in automation quickened. Spectacular developments were made in five industries: computers, fiber optics, robotics, satellites, and videodiscs.

COMPUTERS. The cost of information-processing equipment fell dramatically in the 1980s. Microchips capable of storing enormous amounts of information in an area smaller than a fingernail have reduced computers from room size to typewriter size. As a result, the use of computers in offices and homes is expanding rapidly.

FIBER OPTICS. In fiber optics, thin strands of special glass are used to transmit information on beams of light. These beams carry audio or video signals much faster than metal wires. Although the cost is still prohibitive, present estimates are that, by the end of the century, fiber optics will enable people to transmit great masses of information at low cost, anywhere in the world.

ROBOTICS. The systematic development of robot workers is a rapidly expanding field. In Japan, the world's leading user of robots, over 14,000 factory robots were in operation in 1982. In the United States, robot use is expected to double every three years, thereby bringing the total number of these mechanical workers up to 268,000 by 1993.

SATELLITES. Telecommunication satellites are earth-orbiting structures that transmit signals to and from earth stations. In the 1980s, the costs of both the satellites and the earth stations will continue to fall. Lower costs will reduce the cost of communications between two or more points anywhere in the world. The increased use of satellites will make electronic mail feasible because the same links that carry voice, picture, and data will also transmit documents.

VIDEODISCS. Videodiscs have the capability of inexpensively storing printed, visual, and audio information. When linked to computers, they enable users to retrieve information easily on command. With this capability, the use of videodiscs by libraries, museums, schools, homes, and industry is likely to increase as the technology is improved and the cost reduced.

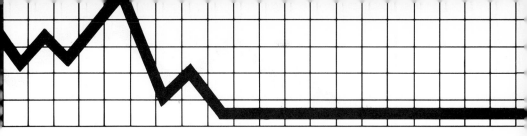

New systems integrating the elements described above enable engineers to use computers to assist them in the creation of designs. These, in turn, are passed on to computer-controlled centers where the robots that handle the parts, the carts that deliver the materials, and the machines that fabricate them into finished products are directed and controlled. Meanwhile, all the components are linked electronically so that each stage of the process can be monitored.

The substitution of machines for human workers has enriched the lives of everyone. The ever-increasing output of goods and services offers us all the promise of higher living standards and the elimination of poverty from our land. It is wonderful to note, too, that all these gains in production and productivity can be had with fewer hours of work and fewer workers. But therein lies one of automation's perils. With fewer jobs available, how are people to earn the money that they will need to improve their living standards? This and the other questions raised by technology's advance deserve a closer look.

QUESTIONS FOR LABOR AND BUSINESS

First to feel the effect of automation is likely to be the worker whose job is lost to a machine or an automated procedure. This problem—sometimes called technological unemployment—has prompted economists and others to raise the following questions:

1. What can be done to find jobs for workers displaced by machines?

2. How will automation affect the total number of jobs available? Will increased total output be enough to make up for the jobs lost through automation? How many new jobs will be created to build and service the new equipment?

3. Can ways be found to retrain workers for the jobs created by automation?

4. What can be done to increase the mobility of labor? Traditionally, people like to work in familiar surroundings. However, as automation replaces human labor in one section of the country, new jobs may open in other industries somewhere else. The problem then is to find ways to inform those who have lost their jobs about opportunities elsewhere, and to help those who are willing to make the move.

5. For business, the conversion to automation is costly. Entrepreneurs must therefore ask themselves: Can we afford to convert to automation, and if so, how?

HOPEFUL SIGNS FROM THE PAST. Experience has shown that jobs lost as a result of technology and change were often offset by new job openings flowing from them. In the thirty-five-year period between 1947 and 1982, for example, the labor force grew from 60 million to 105 million people, an increase of over 75 percent. One of the reasons for this growth has been the stream of new inventions that created new markets and more jobs. For example, today's high-technology industries, such as computers and satellite communications, were unheard of thirty-five years ago. Now they are major producers and account for many jobs and billions of dollars of our gross national product.

WHAT SHOULD GOVERNMENT'S ROLE BE?

The fundamental problem posed by automation has been described as a race between the forces that tend to eliminate jobs and those that create them. In this race, the government has a special role to play. Instead of restricting the expansion of automation, it would seem far wiser for government to do what it can to promote those activities that create jobs and help workers. Toward these ends, government can support research, encourage foreign trade, and promote training programs to qualify workers for today's jobs. Government policy can also stimulate demand for goods and services.

As one economist has put it, automation today poses society with a

3. Favorable Political and Social Climate. Economic growth is more likely to occur in a favorable political and social setting. Among the more important elements needed for growth are the following:

Political Stability. Economic growth is more likely to occur in nations where the government is stable and capable of maintaining order. In such an atmosphere, business is more likely to accept the risks of expansion.

Government Concern for the Needs of Business. There is much that government can do to assist business and thereby promote economic growth.

Willingness to Save and Invest. *Capital formation*, the acquisition of additional and more efficient tools and machinery, is essential to

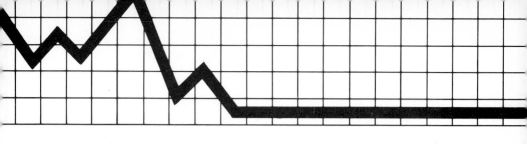

promise, a *threat*, and a *challenge*. The promise of automation lies in the ever-increasing volume of goods and services it can provide human-kind. The threat, as we have seen, is directed principally at the workers whose jobs will be lost to the machine.

Herein, then, lies the challenge: Will society reject automation and its many benefits in order to preserve the "good old days and their grand old ways"? Or will society adapt itself to the new technology and so reap the benefits of its material promise?

1. Prepare an outline of the information contained in the reading.
2. How does automation differ from *mechanization?*
3. A manufacturer of garden tools currently employs about a hundred workers. Recently, the firm learned that it could replace its old-fashioned plant with automated equipment and double its output of tools while, at the same time, reducing its labor force to thirty-five workers. The new equipment would cost $3–$4 million. (a) What reasons might the tool firm have for automating its production? (b) Identify and explain one problem that the decision to automate might create for the manufacturer. (c) Identify and explain one problem that the decision to automate might create for the workers. (d) Identify and explain one solution to each of the problems you described in answer to (b) and (c) above.

increasing productivity and growth. But capital cannot be acquired unless there is a sufficient amount of savings available for investment. Some societies are so poor that any savings set aside for the purchase of productive facilities must come out of funds that would otherwise be used to clothe, house, or feed their people. Frequently, those few people with money available for investment would prefer to do so abroad, where the financial returns are more certain. Other rich individuals may choose to use their wealth to acquire land or luxuries, neither of which will add to the nation's productive capacity.

National Health. A healthy society is more productive than an unhealthy one. Absenteeism is lower, working years are longer, and job efficiency is greater in the healthy nations of the world.

GOVERNMENT AND ECONOMIC GROWTH

The federal government plays a special part in fostering economic growth. The government strives to maintain aggregate demand at appropriate levels, promotes full employment, and supports research, development, and educational and training programs.

1. Adjusting Aggregate Demand. The federal government relies on its monetary and fiscal powers to maintain a healthy balance between the total demand of business, individuals, and government and the economy's ability to satisfy that demand. If the economy is to grow, aggregate demand will have to increase along with it. If demand does not grow, expansion will slow down and eventually grind to a halt. But if the opposite happens and demand increases faster than the economy's ability to satisfy it, prices will rise in what could be an inflationary spiral. As the record of the 1970s indicated, inflation too can discourage economic growth.

2. Promoting Full Employment. Full employment, a job for every American who is willing and able to work, has been a primary goal of government for over fifty years. Since unemployment often has multiple causes, the government has tried a number of ways to relieve the problem.

Economists have identified three types of unemployment: *frictional*, *structural*, and *cyclical*.

Frictional Unemployment. When is unemployment *not* unemployment? When it is *frictional unemployment*. The term frictional unemployment describes the status of workers who have left one job and are in the process of finding another. The jobs these workers are seeking are available, and it is only a matter of time before they will be employed again. Since frictional unemployment is a normal, often voluntary, event, economists allow for it in their definition of *full employment*. Exactly how many workers are frictionally unemployed at any time is uncertain. Most economists, however, would agree that unemployment of 4–6 percent of the labor force is a reasonable estimate, and for that reason would regard anything less as "full employment."

Since frictional unemployment is seen as a normal economic condition, the federal government has not done much to reduce it. Some workers would like to see established a federally sponsored employment service that would serve as a clearinghouse for information about job openings and employee availability. This type of service, it is claimed, would reduce frictional unemployment by speeding up the process by which people find jobs.

Structural Unemployment. Like frictional unemployment, structural unemployment refers to workers who have left their jobs and are seeking others. Unlike the frictionally unemployed, however, workers who are structurally unemployed are not likely to be rehired in the near future at the types of jobs they had before. The reason for the difference is that structural unemployment is caused by changes in the nature or location of employment opportunities.

Structural unemployment may occur in certain areas of the labor force when new technology makes certain skills obsolete, as when farmhands are replaced by automatic harvesting machinery, and white-collar clerical workers are replaced by computers. Or structural unemployment may occur on a regional or sectional basis, as when the textile industry left New England for the South. States like Michigan and West Virginia, which had been centers of the automobile and coal-mining industries, were especially hard hit during the economic recession of the early 1980s. So, for example, when in 1983 the national jobless rate was averaging about 10 percent, unemployment stood at nearly 15 percent in Michigan and 18 percent in West Virginia.

Prejudice and discrimination, which make it more difficult for some Americans than others to find jobs, are yet additional causes of structural unemployment. (See Figure 23.1.)

FIGURE 23.1   Unemployment Rates for Selected Groups, 1982

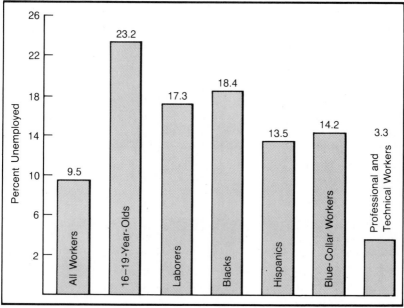

The reduction of structural unemployment is extremely difficult and costly. At the least, it requires:

1. Retraining workers whose skills are no longer in demand
2. Moving people to where the jobs are or enticing industry into areas of high unemployment
3. Changing the social values of those who would discriminate against others because of their race, age, religion, or sex

Cyclical Unemployment. The name given by economists to unemployment caused by insufficient demand is cyclical unemployment. Whenever the demand for goods and services is running at something less than the economy is capable of producing, business will operate at less than its capacity, and workers who might otherwise be employed will be laid off. In its efforts to reduce cyclical unemployment, government will rely upon its fiscal and monetary powers to maintain aggregate demand at full-employment levels.

3. Supporting Research, Education, and Training. Productivity is one of the keys to economic growth. As output per worker increases, total output, too, may be expected to grow. Much of the increased productivity will come from the invention of new machines and the development of new production processes. The federal government has played an important role in stimulating innovation. This effort has often taken the form of direct participation by the government in research projects that resulted in the discovery of new techniques and inventions. Indirectly, the government fosters research by awarding patents and granting tax concessions.

> Federal education, training, and employment programs . . . share one common goal: to assist all citizens to lead fulfilling and productive lives. . . . Government expenditures on these programs are considered investments . . . whose return will be an improved ability of people to contribute to the nation's well-being by increasing their participation in the labor market and society in general.

This statement accompanied President Ronald Reagan's request for funds to support the nation's education programs through the year 1983. The federal government's call for a massive commitment to education signified its belief in the value of that approach to economic growth.

THE CONTROVERSY OVER ECONOMIC GROWTH

Economic growth has its opponents. They charge that economic growth may be a principal cause of *the depletion of our natural resources* and *environmental decay.* Here are some of the specifics of these charges.

Economic Growth and the Depletion of Our Natural Resources.
The ever-increasing output of goods and services, which we call
"economic growth," consumes inputs of human, capital, *and* natural
resources. Some of these natural resources are *renewable* in that,
once consumed, they can be replaced. For example, with proper
conservation, forests can be replanted and fish and wildlife stocks
restored to former levels. Other resources, such as coal, copper, and
petroleum, are nonrenewable and, once consumed, cannot be replaced. Since the demand for nonrenewable resources is ever-
increasing and the earth's supply is limited, these resources will
inevitably be exhausted one day. How long the depletion process
takes depends upon the rate at which resources are consumed and
on the available supply.

In 1980 a presidential commission reported the results of its study
of the "probable changes in the world's population, natural resources,
and environment through the end of the century." One of the studies
contained in the commission's *Global 2000 Report* calculated the life
expectancy of the world's supply of certain mineral resources. The
results of the study are seen in Table 23.1.

TABLE 23.1   World Reserves of Selected Mineral Resources, 1976

Commodity	Life Expectancy in Years Based on Current Consumption Levels
Fluorine	18
Silver	20
Zinc	26
Mercury	22
Sulfur	34
Lead	37
Tungsten	52
Tin	41
Copper	63
Nickel	86
Platinum	110
Phosphate	240
Manganese	164
Iron in ore	172
Aluminum in bauxite	312
Chromium	377
Potash	470

Source: *The Global 2000 Report to the President*, Vol. I, page 29.

The Economics of Pollution

One of the underlying principles upon which our economy is built is that individual firms, in their effort to maximize profits, will strive to keep their costs down and their customers happy. The never-ending quest for ways to reduce costs serves to benefit us all in increased ouput, lower prices, and higher living standards.

Pollution, too, is a cost of production, but, unlike the others, those who cause pollution do not have to pay for it. Water and air pollution, for example, have reduced the supply of fish, ruined building exteriors, and caused physical damage to the lungs of countless citizens. As a result, food prices have risen, as have the costs of building maintenance and medical care. But these costs will be borne first by those directly affected: the fish lovers, building owners, and lung-disease victims. Nothing in our market system could pass the costs back to the power plants and factories that caused the pollution in the first place. The water and air into which they pumped their wastes were always free to be used for that purpose. (See Figure 23.2.)

Economists refer to the costs paid by society as a whole rather than by those creating them as *external* or *social costs*. Those costs normally paid by firms in the course of their business activities are *internal costs*. The principal difficulty with external costs is that they do not provide an incentive for efficiency, as do internal costs.

If the local hamburger drive-in thinks it can increase the speed of service by rearranging the way in which its customers line up, it will bend every effort toward finding the best possible arrangement. Not so, however, with respect to cleaning up the empty wrappers and drink containers from the drive-in that are found littering the countryside. Someone else will have to pay to have the refuse picked up.

Another problem of environmental economics is that of growth. In the past, economic growth was regarded as a worthy goal. However, the process of increasing the output of goods and services that goes into economic growth also generates increasing levels of pollution.

Most economists agree that because pollution costs are external, government will have to step in to do something about them. One proposed solution is to attempt to internalize pollution costs by passing them back to those who caused them. This could be achieved, for example, by charging the factory a fee for the amount of pollutants it pours into the atmosphere. This would make the polluter's production

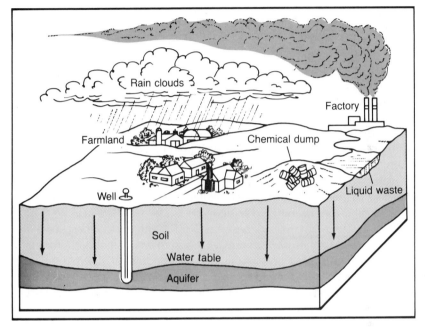

FIGURE 23.2   External or Social Costs of Pollution

costs more realistic and provide a cost incentive to reduce pollution levels. Other approaches involve requirements that firms change their production procedures and modify or replace their machinery, and programs sponsored by the government to clean up the damage that has already been done to the environment.

Naturally, the costs of all these approaches will ultimately be passed on to the consumer. With higher prices, fewer goods and services will be sold and the nation's rate of growth will be slowed.

1. What is the difference between an *internal* cost and an *external* cost?
2. Why is it that internal costs provide an incentive for efficiency, but external costs do not?
3. Critics of the market system point to its inability to deal with harmful external costs (or *externalities*) as a major weakness of the system. (a) Cite one example of a harmful external cost. (b) Why does the market system fail to deal with harmful external costs?
4. (a) Why has it been argued that economic growth adds to the pollution of the planet? (b) Assuming that growth does indeed add to pollution, would you say that we should abandon economic growth? Explain.

MAKERS OF ECONOMIC THOUGHT

The First Nobel Prize in Economics Is Awarded (1969)

The growing importance of economics and the influence of economists were given international recognition in 1969 with the award of the first Nobel Memorial Prize in Economic Science to Ragnar Frisch of Norway and Jan Tinbergen of the Netherlands. Since 1901 the Nobel Prizes, which are financed out of the estate of the Swedish inventor of dynamite, Alfred Nobel, have been given for outstanding achievement in physics, chemistry, medicine, literature, and international peace. The award for economics was the first new category to have been added since the creation of the prize. Frisch and Tinbergen were recognized for their pioneering efforts in the field of econometrics. (See page 507.)

In 1970 Paul Samuelson became the first American to receive the Nobel Prize in Economics. Samuelson was singled out for his contribution toward the application of mathematics to economic theory, although he is best known to college students as the author of a widely read economics textbook. A kind of latter-day Alfred Marshall, Samuelson brought Keynesian economics into college classrooms in much the same way that Marshall had popularized the work of Adam Smith and his followers.

The Nobel Prizes have not been limited to economists of just one school of economic thought, however. In 1976 the award went to Milton Friedman, a leading American monetarist. Friedman has been as vigorous in his assault upon Keynesian economics as Samuelson has been in its defense. Another American Nobel Laureate who shares Friedman's distrust of government is George Stigler, winner of the 1982 award.

Diversity was also evident in the 1974 and 1975 prizes. The 1974 award was shared by Friedrich von Hayek, of Austria, and Gunnar Myrdal, of Sweden. Hayek is a sharp critic of planned economies, while Myrdal has long advocated government involvement in the economic process. The 1975 award was shared by the American Tjalling Koopmans and the Russian Leonid Kantorovich for their "contributions to the theory of optimum allocation of resources." Koopmans' world, however, assumes the motivating power of the "invisible hand" of free enterprise, whereas Kantorovich's is directed by the rulers of a Communist state.

The Nobel prizes have also reflected the growing world concern about the economies of less developed nations. In 1979 the prize was shared by Theodore W. Shultz of the United States and Sir Arthur Lewis of Great Britain. Sir Arthur, the first black to win a Nobel prize other than the Peace prize, was honored for his study of economic growth in the transition from agricultural to industrial society.

Renewable resources might also be exhausted should society fail to apply the kind of conservation techniques required to preserve them. "If present trends continue," the commission predicted, "regional water shortages will become more severe. . . . Growing stocks of commercial-size timber are projected to decline 50 percent per capita. . . . Extinctions of plant and animal species will increase dramatically."

Growth as a Cause of Environmental Decay. By now everyone is aware of the environmental problems created by the increased output of goods and services. Of course, pollution is nothing new. Citizens of ancient Rome, medieval Paris, and Victorian London all complained about the foul wastes created by animals, households, and industries. Never before, however, have the problems of pollution reached such terrifying proportions as they have today, when the continued existence of life on the planet appears to be in jeopardy.

In today's world, the consequences of pollution range from the esthetic to the cataclysmic. Littered parks and highways are unsightly and deprive us of all the enjoyment they might otherwise provide. Polluted air and water can make us ill. They can also kill. For some years now, scientists have known that prolonged inhalation of certain mineral and metallic dusts (such as coal and asbestos) can cause lung disease and cancer. Most ominous, however, are those forms of pollution that threaten the survival of the planet itself.

One case in point is the "greenhouse effect" created when carbon in the emissions of countless factories, automobiles, and utility plants combines with water in the atmosphere to create a mantle of carbon dioxide around the globe, turning the earth into a vast greenhouse. (A garden greenhouse allows the sun's rays to enter the atmosphere, and its light to be reflected out while its heat is trapped within.) This type of pollution, it is feared, could increase global temperatures. As little as 5°–10° C increase in polar temperatures could result in the melting of the Greenland and Antarctic icecaps. The release of so much water, in turn, would raise the level of the oceans high enough to force the abandonment of many of the world's coastal areas (which are often the most densely populated areas of a continent). Since this flooding would not happen overnight, people would perhaps be prepared for it.

Because of the obvious correlation between output and pollution, some critics have suggested that the GNP be increased only enough to accommodate population growth. In this way, say the advocates of *zero economic growth*, available supplies of natural resources will last longer, and pressures on the environment will be reduced.

Others take the opposite point of view by endorsing continued

To Grow or Not to Grow

It is said we must abandon economic freedom because our frontier is closed; because our biosphere is strained; because our resources are running out; because our technology is perverse; because our population rises; because our horizons are closing in. We walk, it is said, in the shadow of death, with depleted air, poisoned earth and water, and a fallout of explosive growth showering from the clouds of our future in a quiet carcinogenic rain. In this extremity we cannot afford the luxuries of competition and waste and freedom. . . .

But quite to the contrary, these problems and crises are in themselves the new frontier; are themselves the mandate for individual and corporate competition and creativity; are themselves the reason why we cannot afford the consolations of planning and stasis [stagnation]. The old frontier of the American West also appeared closed at first. It became an open reservoir of wealth only in retrospect, because the pioneers dared to risk their lives and families in the quest for riches. . . .[1]

If the present growth trends in world population, industrialization, pollution, food production, and resource depletion continue unchanged, the limits to growth on this planet will be reached sometime within the next one hundred years. The most probable result will be a rather sudden and uncontrollable decline in both population and industrial capacity.[2]

[1] George Gilder, *Wealth and Poverty* (New York, Basic Books, 1981), pp. 267–268.

[2] D. H. Meadows, et. al., *The Limits to Growth* (New York, Universe Books, 1972), p. 23.

growth in whatever way market forces deem best. We are reminded that predictions of doom and gloom have been with humans throughout recorded history, and in each instance humankind found a way to overcome the menace and ease the threat. For example, Thomas Malthus was proved wrong in his prediction that population growth would outstrip the food supply (see page 178). Malthus did not foresee that the technological revolution would increase farm productivity and that millions of acres of new farmland would be opened in the Americas. In the same way, we today are uable to predict the discoveries and adaptations that later generations will make to solve their problems.

Somewhere between the two positions lies a middle ground occupied by those who, while opposed to zero growth, favor some restrictions on the market economy in the interest of environmental protection. They liken the zero-growth strategy to that of a passenger ship's captain who stops his fog-enshrouded vessel in the middle of the ocean until such time as the fog lifts. While the tactic may lessen the chances of collision at sea and suit the people who are occupying the comfortable staterooms, the poorer passengers, whose cramped, damp quarters deep in the bowels of the ship are difficult to bear, would much prefer to move on to their destination.

In the real world, it is argued, a growing economy is the poor's best hope to improve their lot. For this reason, it would be better to "continue the journey" by striving for economic growth while, at the same time, seeking ways to eliminate its dangers. The goal ought to be one of "clean economic growth." Generally favored is modification in the rules of free enterprise so as to allow for government regulation that would protect the environment and conserve resources. The statements in the reading "To Grow or Not to Grow" represent the views of those who stand at opposite ends of the growth controversy. Where do you stand?

EXERCISES

Multiple Choice

1. *Economic growth* may be defined as a change in (*a*) national income (*b*) population (*c*) the amount of goods and services produced (*d*) the money supply.

2. If the population of the nation should grow at the rate of 5 percent per year while production increases at the rate of 4 percent, (*a*) living standards are likely to increase (*b*) living standards are likely to decrease (*c*) living standards will remain the same (*d*) inflation is inevitable.

3. Which of the following is the most reliable measure of economic growth? (*a*) total GNP in current dollars (*b*) GNP per capita in current dollars (*c*) total GNP in constant dollars (*d*) GNP per capita in constant dollars.

4. Economic growth may be expected to provide a nation with all of the following *except* (*a*) more consumer goods and services per citizen (*b*) the ability to continue aiding foreign nations (*c*) more unemployment (*d*) the ability to reduce poverty at home.

5. All of the following are necessary ingredients in economic growth *except* (*a*) increasing productivity (*b*) reduction of aggregate demand (*c*) stable government (*d*) a highly motivated work force.

6. Savings are important to economic growth because (*a*) when everyone saves there is less wasteful spending (*b*) savings provide investment capital which can be used to increase future production (*c*) consumers can use their savings to buy the things they really need (*d*) when savings are ample, the government can afford to reduce its expenditures.

7. Emerging nations seeking rapid economic growth would be best advised to (*a*) increase consumer spending (*b*) discourage all saving (*c*) concentrate on the production of consumer goods (*d*) concentrate on the production of capital goods.

8. Which category of unemployment can best be reduced by worker retraining programs? (*a*) structural unemployment (*b*) frictional unemployment (*c*) cyclical unemployment (*d*) seasonal unemployment.

9. If aggregate demand declines while the nation's productive capacity is unchanged, (*a*) economic growth will decline (*b*) economic growth will increase (*c*) prices will increase (*d*) unemployment will decline.

10. Which of the following is an example of an *external* cost of operating a paper mill? (*a*) the cost of the raw materials used to make paper (*b*) the cost of the fuel used to drive the mill's machinery (*c*) the wages paid the mill workers (*d*) the cost of cleaning up a river polluted by the mill's wastes.

11. Which of the following proposals seems to offer the best hope of reducing the depletion of nonrenewable natural resources? (*a*) Increase the production of natural resources. (*b*) Increase the rate of economic growth. (*c*) Seek ways to substitute renewable resources for the nonrenewable ones. (*d*) Increase government subsidies for the cleanup of toxic-waste sites.

12. Advocates of *zero economic growth* favor (*a*) a freeze of the GNP at present levels (*b*) a reduction in the GNP (*c*) a freeze in real GNP per capita (*d*) a rapid increase in real economic growth.

Essay Questions

1. (*a*) In describing economic growth, economists most frequently speak of *per capita GNP in constant dollars.* Summarize the reasons why this statistic is preferred to total GNP in current dollars. (*b*) However, GNP as expressed in constant dollars is not a perfect measurement of the nation's economic health, for there are things that are important to a society's economic well-being that are not reflected in the GNP. Explain this statement.

2. (*a*) What benefits can economic growth offer the nation as a whole? (*b*) How does its economic growth put America in a position to help the world's emerging nations? (*c*) Show why *each* of the following has been a necessary ingredient in America's economic growth: (1) increasing productivity, (2) increasing aggregate demand, (3) political and social stability.

3. "One of the key ingredients in economic growth is *investment.*" (*a*) Explain this statement. (*b*) Identify and explain two steps that the government might take to promote investment. (*c*) Why is the shortage of investment capital more of a problem for the less developed countries than for the world's industrialized nations?

4. Read the selection and answer the questions that follow.

LOVE CANAL: A Landmark in the History of Environmental Pollution

Modern society could not exist without the chemical industry. Virtually everything we buy is made with one or more chemical products. But the use of chemicals in manufacturing also creates waste, and some of these wastes are extremely hazardous. For many years there was little general interest in the methods for disposing of chemical wastes. In many instances, wastes were simply taken to public dumps and buried. Then, in 1978, events in Love Canal focused national attention on the problems and dangers surrounding the hazardous waste dumps.

Love Canal took its name from its original developer, William Love, who had hoped to build an industrial complex and canal on a tract of land outside Niagara Falls. With the canal only partially completed, the project ran into financial difficulties and was abandoned. About fifty years later, in 1947, the property was purchased by the Hooker Chemical and Plastics Company. After burying tons of chemical wastes in the canal, the company donated the site (in 1953) to the Niagara Falls Board of Education. The board built an elementary school on part of the property and sold the rest to a developer who built and sold hundreds of single-family homes.

As the 1970s drew to a close, Love Canal residents found chemicals bubbling to the surface of their lawns and seeping through the walls of their basements. In 1978 the New York State Department of Health declared the Love Canal area a health hazard and urged that all persons living there be evacuated. Health department studies also revealed that the people living near the canal were suffering from an unusually high incidence of birth defects, cancers, and other serious diseases. In 1979 President Carter declared the contamination a "federal emergency," enabling homeowners to sell their properties to the government and move to safer areas.

Love Canal is not the only American community threatened by the presence of a nearby hazardous waste dump. In a study by the Environmental Protection Agency (EPA) published in 1980, it was shown that there could be as many as 12,000 more hazardous waste sites threatening the public health and safety all across the United States.

It remains to be seen whether ways can be found to minimize the dangers of toxic wastes to the environment and to the general population.

(a) Why did the people of Love Canal have to leave their homes? (b) Why are there so many hazardous waste sites in the United States? (c) Some have argued that until the problem of what to do about hazardous wastes is solved, economic growth should be suspended. (1) What is *economic growth*? (2) What does economic growth have to do with the creation of hazardous wastes? (3) What is your opinion of the proposal to halt economic growth as a way of reducing the creation of hazardous wastes? (d) How did the Love Canal disaster call attention to the problem of *externalities*?

In an economically interdependent world, Japanese trucks and American soft drinks are seen on every continent.

UNIT X

The Global Economy

CHAPTER 24
International Trade

Although most of us think of ourselves as Americans, living and working within the American economy and producing and consuming American goods and services, we are in fact also part of a much larger unit: the *global economy.* In this century, the nations of the world have become increasingly interdependent, and many of the goods and services that we consume come to us either in part or in their entirety from foreign lands. Similarly, the rest of the world has looked to the United States for many goods and services.

We might also consider the case of a simple candy bar that can be purchased over the counter at a local store or market. Let us suppose that the candy bar is one of the chocolate-coated varieties with almonds. On examining the paper and aluminum foil wrapper, we see that the candy bar was produced by a *multinational corporation,* a giant firm that conducts business activities in two or more countries. (See pages 478–483.) As for the paper, it was manufactured from wood pulp produced in Canada. The aluminum foil was made of bauxite mined in Jamaica and processed in an American factory.

Sugar, the principal ingredient in the candy bar, was produced out of Philippine cane, while the chocolate had its origins in cacao beans that were grown in Ghana. The almonds came from southern Italy. In the candy-making process, many cargo ships were used to bring the ingredients to the United States. One of these ships, built in a Japanese shipyard for a Greek company, sailed under Liberian registry with an Indonesian crew.

Trade takes place between nations for the same reasons that it occurs within nations. Florida oranges, Nebraska wheat, California semiconductors, and New York clothing are purchased by Americans from other parts of the nation because it makes more sense to buy the out-of-town products than to attempt to produce them locally. Americans *import* (purchase from abroad) goods and services that they are either unable to produce in this country or that are less expensive than the same or similar goods and services produced here.

INTERNATIONAL TRADE AND ECONOMIC SPECIALIZATION

Two hundred years ago, Adam Smith wrote that the wise head of a household will never attempt to make at home that which can be bought for less. Smith went on to explain that it made more sense for people to work at whatever they do best, and use their earnings to buy the things they want.

Smith's advice to individuals to *specialize* in some economic activity applies equally well to localities and to nations. Consider, for example, the case of New York and Kansas. Much of the clothing sold in Kansas was made in New York, just as many of the wheat products consumed in New York had their origin in Kansas. The reason is that, among other things, New York has extensive facilities for the manufacture of clothing and a large and experienced labor force, while Kansas has the necessary soil, climate, capital, and labor to produce wheat. For similar reasons, West Virginia is a major producer of coal, Florida of citrus fruits, and California of semiconductors.

In similar fashion, nations tend to specialize in the production of certain goods and services. Brazil concentrates on the production of coffee beans, and Honduras on bananas. Australia has a sizable wool industry, and France produces much of the world's perfume. Meanwhile, the American passenger airline and the British insurance industries are example of the kinds of service exports that are concentrated in certain countries.

Nations specialize in the production of certain goods and services for a number of reasons. These are related to the *uneven distribution of resources, absolute and comparative advantage,* and *political considerations.*

1. Uneven Distribution of Resources Around the Globe. Just as individuals differ in size, strength, talent, and ability, so do nations and regions differ in their resources. These differences, which limit the kinds of economic activities that nations can successfully engage in, include climate, factor supply, and demand.

Climate. The effect of climate upon the economy of a nation is, in many cases, quite apparent. Coffee is produced in large quantities in Brazil because the moderate temperature and heavy rainfall in certain regions of Brazil favor its growth. Citrus trees need frost-free areas, such as Florida, Israel, and Spain, while grains thrive in cooler climates, as in the Great Plains and Argentina. Rubber requires a damp, hot climate, as in Indonesia, while many fruits and vegetables rely on the alternating cool-damp, hot-dry type of Mediterranean climate, as in Italy and California.

In recent years, climate has lost much of its former importance in determining the course of a nation's economy. Our ability to control indoor temperature has enabled us to establish mines and factories in regions that were formerly considered either too hot or too cold for normal production. The air-conditioned offices and factories of the American Southwest and the rapidly growing industrial complexes of the eastern Soviet Union bear witness to our control of our physical environment. In addition, synthetic fibers have been used as substitutes for such natural products as silk and cotton, which can be produced only in certain climates.

Another factor limiting the effect of climate upon international specialization has been the development of new strains of agricultural products. New types of wheat with a very short growing season can now be raised in regions that were formerly considered too cold. Beet sugar, which can be grown in temperate regions, is being widely used in place of the cane sugar of the tropics. Similarly, the development of elaborate irrigation programs, as in Israel, has enabled even desert regions to develop an agriculture.

Climate, however, will continue to affect international trade. Despite all the recent developments we described, certain items can still be produced only in certain climates. The cost of maintaining an artificial climate for their growth would be prohibitive. For this reason, nations will continue to produce goods for which their climate is most suitable.

Factor Supply. The factors of production (land, labor, capital, and management) are not equally distributed. This explains why one region of our country tends to specialize in the production of farm products (because the ratio of land to labor is high) while another leans toward manufacturing (for the opposite reason). Texas, with its ample supply of land in relation to its population, can afford to allow cattle to roam over thousands of acres of range, while Chicago has the people and facilities necessary to slaughter these animals and pack their meat. On the international scene, too, the factors of production are unevenly distributed. Argentina and Australia are similar to Texas in that the ratio of people to land is relatively low. As a result, these nations can engage in extensive cattle and sheep grazing. England and Japan, on the other hand, with their relatively concentrated populations, have developed manufacturing industries that rely upon ample supplies of labor and capital.

The quality of labor also varies from one nation to another. Western Europe, Japan, and the United States have relatively more skilled labor than other parts of the world. These countries are therefore able to support industries requiring highly trained workers and complex technology.

Capital, in the form of plant and equipment, is also unevenly distributed throughout the world. The countries with the highest concentration of capital per worker tend to have the greatest productivity. Abundant capital enables these nations to concentrate on producing goods that lend themselves to mass production. For this reason, Sweden, with a relatively small population, is able to support an automobile industry, and Japan, with little or no iron ore resources, can undersell the rest of the world in finished steel. Meanwhile, countries like Costa Rica, Ghana, and Sri Lanka, with their limited industrial capacities, must emphasize preindustrial activities such as farming.

Management, too, is a vital ingredient in production. Those nations that lack an adequate supply of industrial managerial talent tend to concentrate on the production of nonindustrial goods. This explains, in part, the difficulties that many of the less developed nations have had in industrializing. These nations have been short of managerial personnel and therefore have had either to delay their programs or "import" managers from abroad.

Mass Production and Mass Demand. Even if a wondrous genie were to provide Ghana, Costa Rica, and Sri Lanka with automotive factories, it is unlikely that many cars and trucks would be produced. The relatively small and poor populations of those lands could not afford to buy enough of the output to take advantage of the economies of scale. Mass production can proceed only if there is a market for its output. The need for a market explains why only a small handful of nations produce commercial aircraft. Only a nation with markets large enough to support an aircraft industry can afford to have one.

2. *Absolute Advantage and Comparative Advantage.* When one nation can produce a good or service at a lower cost than another, the former is said to have an *absolute advantage* in that item. It therefore follows that nations would do well to specialize in the production of those things in which they have an absolute advantage, and use the surplus from their sale to buy other goods and services from nations that have an absolute advantage. Thus, the United States buys rubber from Indonesia and tin from Bolivia, and sells its refrigerators to both countries.

Basis for Trade. Why do some countries specialize in the production of bananas?

Under certain circumstances, however, it pays for a nation to import goods and services from abroad *even though they could be produced more cheaply at home.* The reason is contained in the principle of *comparative advantage.*

Consider the physician who, while a college student, became highly proficient at typing. The physician, who has a receptionist to assist her around the office, has been deluged with paperwork and has considered hiring a part-time typist to ease the burden. The doctor estimates that the typist, who earns $50 a day, would be needed two days a week. At the same time, the doctor knows that she could probably handle all the work in one day's time and thereby save the expense of the typist. As you may already have guessed, however, the doctor chose to hire the typist. Why? She knew that she could earn several times the typist's salary by attending to her medical practice on the day she would have had to devote to typing.

Economists explain the logic of the doctor's choice in light of comparative advantage and opportunity costs. Opportunity costs, you recall, are the amount of goods and services one must forego to obtain more of something else. To the physician, the opportunity cost of doing her own typing was the income from one day's medical practice. These earnings were far greater than the $100 salary she would have to pay the typist for two days' work. Since the opportunity cost of doing her own typing was greater than attending to her practice, we

International Trade

say that the physician had a *comparative advantage* in medicine even though she enjoyed an *absolute advantage* in both fields.

What is true of typists and physicians may also be applied to nations. First stated early in the nineteenth century by the English economist David Ricardo (see pages 78–79), the Law of Comparative Advantage may be summarized as follows:

If two nations have different opportunity costs in the production of two goods or services, the nations should: (1) specialize in the one in which their opportunity costs are lower; (2) leave the production of the alternate item to the other country; and (3) trade with each other.

To illustrate how the Law of Comparative Advantage applies to nations, suppose that the United States is more efficient than Canada in the production both of maple syrup and copper wire. American workers can produce a barrel of syrup in five hours and a mile of wire in six, while Canadian workers take eight hours to produce the syrup and seven to produce the wire. Let us also suppose that one barrel of syrup can be exchanged for a mile of wire and vice versa. We may summarize the situation as follows:

	Hours of Labor Required	
	United States	Canada
Maple syrup (per barrel)	5	8
Copper wire (per mile)	6	7

The United States has an absolute advantage in producing both wire and syrup because it can produce both products with fewer hours of labor. Despite this advantage, it would pay the United States to specialize in the production of syrup and trade with Canada for the wire. Without trade it would take eleven hours of labor in the United States to produce a barrel of syrup and a mile of wire. If, however, the United States were to produce *two* barrels of syrup at a cost of only ten hours of labor, it could exchange one of those barrels for a mile of wire, thereby saving one hour of labor. Canada would also benefit from specialization. Without trade, it takes fifteen hours of labor to produce a barrel of syrup and a mile of wire. By specializing in the production of wire, however, Canada could produce two miles with but fourteen hours of labor. Canada could then exchange a mile of wire for a barrel of American syrup and also save an hour of labor.

In terms of opportunity costs, both the United States and Canada gain one hour of labor by specializing in the production of those goods in which they were most efficient—the one in which they had a comparative advantage. This hour could be used by both Canada and the United States to produce additional goods and services, thereby raising their standards of living. It therefore follows that if all countries produced those things at which they were most efficient, the world's output would be *maximized* (raised to the greatest possible level). Thus, everyone's living standards would rise.

3. Political Considerations. The decision to trade or not to trade is sometimes based on political rather than economic reasons. Because of Cuba's hostile foreign policies, the United States no longer trades with that nation. (At one time, Cuba was our leading source of sugar and a major market for our exports.) Also for political reasons, the United States has virtually no trade with Kampuchea, Vietnam, and Albania.

By contrast, we sometimes go out of our way to trade with nations simply because we want to support their governments, their policies, or both. When it appeared that the Polish Communist government was preparing to introduce democratic reforms, the United States government encouraged private banks to make loans to Poland. For similar reasons, our government encouraged American business to trade with South Korea but prohibited trade with North Korea. For many years, too, trade with the Chinese Nationalist government on Taiwan was encouraged, while trade with the Communist government on the mainland was prohibited. This trade policy changed when President Richard Nixon made his historic trip to Peking in 1972, and normal diplomatic and trade relations began between the United States and the world's most populous land. Even today, however, many restrictions remain in effect on trade between China and the United States.

How Important Is Foreign Trade?

How do we measure the value of foreign trade in American life? Consider the following:

1. Over 20 percent of United States manufactures are exported.

2. One in every six workers in the manufacturing sector owes his or her job to exports.

3. Some 40 percent of American farm acreage produces goods for export.

4. One-third of United States corporate profits are derived from international activities.

BARRIERS TO WORLD TRADE

From what we have said thus far, you might think that nations would be eager to promote international trade and take advantage of the benefits of specialization and comparative advantage. You know, however, that all nations, including our own, have imposed restrictions on imports, and sometimes on exports. In the discussion that follows, we shall examine the ways in which these restrictions have been applied and then the reasons why foreign trade has been subject to this treatment.

Tariffs. The most common form of restriction on foreign trade is the *tariff*, a tax placed on imports. In order to protect profits, the importer usually adds all or part of this tariff to the selling price of the goods. If this tax brings the price of the item to a point where it is more expensive than an identical domestic product, consumers may hesitate to purchase the imported item. In this instance, the duty is described as a *protective* tariff, because it serves to protect the domestic industry from the competition of foreign goods.

Tariffs are also used to raise money for the government. This is generally accomplished by limiting the tax to a point where the increased price resulting from the duty is still lower than that of the goods produced at home. Such a levy is described as a *revenue* tariff because it is designed to provide income for the national government.

Tariffs are also classified by the manner in which they are computed. A *specific* tariff assesses a certain amount of money per unit, such as $2 per ton. An *ad valorem* tariff is expressed as a percentage of the value of the goods.

Quotas. Quotas limit the quantity of a particular good that may enter a country in a particular year. Once that limit is reached, no more of the product may be imported until the following year.

Currency Controls. In order to import goods from a particular country, the importer must have that country's currency. Thus, for example, a Moroccan importer must usually pay in francs when buying French perfume. By limiting the amount of foreign currency that importers may buy, the government can limit trade with other nations.

Administrative Red Tape: The "Invisible Tariff." Administrative red tape, sometimes called the "invisible tariff," refers to the practice followed by some governments of making the process of importing so complicated as to discourage businesspersons from attempting to purchase goods from abroad. By requiring the filing and processing of complicated forms, governments can discourage trade as effectively as by levying a protective tariff.

Export Controls. Exports, too, may be restricted. The United States today forbids most trade with certain nations, such as Albania and Cuba. Similarly, certain kinds of goods may not be sold unless an export license is first obtained. In this way strategic materials, such as weapons and high-technology products, can be prevented from reaching specific nations.

WHY DO NATIONS RESTRICT INTERNATIONAL TRADE?

Most economists agree that trade restrictions are harmful because they increase prices, waste resources, and therefore reduce living standards. This view was seconded by President Ronald Reagan, who wrote:

> I see an expansion of the international trading system as the chief instrument for economic growth in many of the less developed countries as well as an important factor in our own future and that of the world's other major industrial nations. To this end, I reaffirm my Administration's commitment to free trade. (*Economic Report of the President, 1982*)

Despite economists' views, a substantial body of opinion in most nations, ours included, favors tariffs, quotas, and other curbs on foreign trade. The section that follows is a summary of the principal arguments advanced by groups that favor such restrictions.

Mercantilism: The Quest for a "Favorable Balance of Trade." You will recall from your study of American history that, during the colonial period, American trade was closely regulated by Great Britain. Laws were passed requiring that "enumerated articles" (mostly raw materials) be sent only to British ports; prohibiting the manufacture of certain goods in the colonies; and requiring that imports and exports be carried in English or colonial ships. A major purpose of these laws was to enable the colonial power, England, to have a "favorable balance of trade"—an excess of exports over imports. According to *mercantilist* doctrine, popular from the sixteenth through the eighteenth century, achieving this balance would lead to financial happiness.

The mercantile theory said that the wealth of a nation could be measured by the amount of gold and silver it possessed. A favorable balance of trade would bring this result because foreigners would pay for exports with gold and silver and because these precious metals could be kept at home if imports were limited. Accordingly, Great Britain and other nations that were committed to mercantilism resorted to protective tariffs and other restrictions to limit imports, while doing whatever they could to help domestic industry compete for foreign markets.

Colonies that could be compelled to trade with the country that controlled them were quite important. These colonies could furnish raw materials and precious metals at relatively low cost, and they could provide markets for finished products.

Few economists today measure a nation's wealth by the amount of gold and silver it possesses. Precious metals alone cannot feed or clothe a people. Nevertheless, one still hears what might be characterized as "neomercantilist" (revived mercantilist) arguments endorsing a "favorable balance of trade." Neomercantilists say that we should keep our dollars at home by exporting more than we import, and they support legislation restricting imports and promoting exports.

In truth, foreign nations do not want American dollars for their own sake but because they can be used to buy goods from the United States. So, for example, the dollars that we spend for clothing manufactured in India will be returned to us when India buys something, like American wheat, from us. And, because of the principle of *comparative advantage*, both nations will gain from the exchange to an extent that they could not have enjoyed had they attempted to produce both items on their own.

The "Americans Cannot Compete With Cheap Foreign Workers" Argument. Domestic manufacturers who are unable to compete with foreign competitors frequently argue that their troubles are due to "cheap foreign workers" who earn less than their American counterparts. In this argument, the manufacturers are likely to be supported by the workers whose jobs are threatened. Together, the two groups will pressure the government to pass legislation preventing the competitive foreign goods from entering the domestic market.

It is true that American wages are higher than those paid to workers in most (but not all) nations of the world. It is also true that, because of labor cost differences, certain goods can be produced abroad for less than in America. If those items were allowed to enter the country freely, American entrepreneurs might be forced out of business and American workers might lose their jobs.

It is *not* true, however, that *all* American industries will be unable to compete with foreign producers, because labor is only one of the factors of production. Even though American farmers are perhaps the best paid in the world, America is a leading exporter of food. Similarly, American machinery, transportation equipment, and office systems are major export items, and the workers in those industries are well paid even by American standards.

High or Low Tariffs? At one time, the United States had a thriving motorcycle industry. Today, most of the cycles sold here are made in Japan. Should the government take steps to protect American manufacturers from foreign competition?

Well-paid American workers can compete in some industries largely because of their high productivity. Suppose, for example, that workers in a toothbrush factory in a foreign country who earn $1 an hour can produce 100 toothbrushes in that hour. The labor cost of those brushes would be one cent. Suppose, too, that American workers who are paid at the rate of $7 an hour can turn out 1,400 toothbrushes. Unit labor costs would be only one-half a cent per brush. The differences are accounted for by the kind of capital and the quality of labor available to the American and the foreign producers. As a result, the American toothbrush manufacturers will be able to undersell foreign producers despite wages running seven times higher than the competition.

As the opponents of protective laws point out, tariffs and other restrictions that compel consumers to purchase more expensive domestic goods benefit the few at the expense of the many. It makes about as much sense, they continue, for the United States to put a tariff on knitted woolen goods in order to protect American industry and workers as it would for New York State to put a tariff on wheat from the Midwest. Although in both cases certain persons might benefit from this protection, consumers would have to pay more for the goods they bought and therefore could afford less. It would be preferable to let those industries that are unable to meet foreign competition disappear and to assist the displaced workers in finding new jobs in more efficient industries.

Relocation programs could be quite complicated, however, because available jobs might require skills the displaced workers did not

International Trade

possess or might be located far from the workers' homes. Recognizing these problems, opponents of protectionism have argued that it is the responsibility of the government to find ways of helping workers whose lives are so affected. They recommend that training programs be established to teach these workers marketable skills, and that special unemployment compensation be made available to prevent some of the financial hardship resulting from the loss of jobs.

The "We Need to Protect Our Infant Industries" Argument. Another argument for trade barriers is to promote economic development by protecting "infant industries." According to this argument, newly developed industries should be given time to grow and become efficient. These new industries grow only if the government keeps foreign competition out of the country.

There is nothing new about the "infant industry" argument; Alexander Hamilton advocated it in the late 1700s. Most historians agree that a large measure of the success of American industry in the years prior to the Civil War came about because Congress passed a series of protective tariffs. Many of today's less developed nations that are seeking to build up their industrial capacity have quite naturally relied upon similar reasoning to justify protecting their industries. Here again, it could be argued that the living standards of the general population will be lowered as tariffs make goods more expensive. This fact is readily conceded by those favoring protection. However, they argue that, when the "infant industries" mature, they will benefit the whole economy by increasing total output and providing more jobs. In addition, these industries will become more efficient and will ultimately be able to compete with foreign companies.

Critics of this argument have pointed out that, in the United States today, "infants" rarely are protected because they cannot put the necessary pressure on Congress. The industries that usually are protected have been in business a long time and are willing to spend the money needed to get Congressional action. The "infants" today are vigorous new industries that do not need protection.

The "We Have to Think of National Security" Argument. It has been argued that certain industries are so vital to our nation's defense that their preservation is a matter of national security. Thus, for many years, foreign petroleum was subject to a protective tariff. Such a tax was thought necessary to guarantee the existence of a domestic oil industry and thus assure adequate supplies in wartime.

For similar reasons, the American shipbuilding industry was supported through direct subsidies and special regulations requiring that American ships carry certain goods destined for export. Here again, it was believed that, in the event of a national emergency, the nation's supply of shipping would be assured.

Most people agree that industries directly associated with the national defense should be closely protected and regulated. Clearly, the manufacture and sale of the weapons of war ought to be conducted in such a way as to assure the nation of the supplies it needs. Criticism falls on those who argue the national defense to justify protecting industries that are less directly involved. In the nuclear age, long global wars like World Wars I and II are no longer possible. Therefore, it does not make sense to waste precious resources by supporting inefficient industries that are not part of our defense program.

The "Tariffs Are a Great Source of Revenue Because They Are Paid by Foreigners" Argument. In the early days of our republic, tariffs provided the federal government with its principal source of income. In 1800, for example, total federal income was $10.8 million. (That *million*-dollar figure is no mistake; the nation did not have a billion-dollar budget until 1917.) Nearly 85 percent of this total, or $9.1 million, came from customs duties. Tariffs provided almost one-half of the federal government's income as recently as 1907.

Tariffs are popular because they give the appearance of being paid for by the foreign exporters. In reality, of course, the import duties are added to the prices of the goods and are passed along to the domestic consumers.

Nowadays, the United States no longer expects tariffs to provide substantial income. In 1983, slightly over 1 percent of our tax receipts came from this source. Other countries, however, still rely on revenue tariffs as a major source of income.

EVOLUTION OF AMERICAN TRADE POLICY

The tariff issue has provoked many political battles through the course of American history. In 1816 Congress passed America's first protective tariff, chiefly to protect our "infant industries." In time, the "infant industries" grew up, but they continued to clamor for protective tariffs. Since most of these industries were concentrated in the North, their insistence on tariff protection was an important cause of the sectionalism that existed in the years before the Civil War. For its part, the South, which was largely agricultural, feared that high American tariffs would lead to retaliation by the nations of Europe. This would mean that tariffs would be raised on American exports, thereby making it more difficult to sell cotton and tobacco abroad. In addition, Southerners preferred to buy the less expensive goods manufactured in Europe that were being kept out by protective tariffs.

Through much of American history, the protectionists generally had their way. Tariff rates were raised in 1824 and again in 1828. From 1832 to 1857, tariffs were lowered slightly, but they remained mostly protective. Beginning with the Civil War, the tariff renewed its upward trend for over seventy years with only a few exceptions, notably the years 1909–1920. Protectionism reached its peak during the Great Depression of the 1930s. In an effort to protect American jobs and increase sales by reducing foreign competition, Congress passed the *Smoot-Hawley Tariff Act* of 1930, which raised duties to an all-time high.

Instead of promoting American industry, Smoot-Hawley nearly destroyed it. Because they were no longer able to sell to us, foreign nations lacked the dollars to *buy* from us. Moreover, the high United States tariffs so outraged our former trading partners that many retaliated by raising their own tariffs. High foreign tariffs thus led to a decline in American exports (particularly of farm products and machinery) and increased unemployment and business failures.

The protectionist trend was reversed in 1932 in the landslide election that swept Franklin D. Roosevelt, the Democrats, and the New Deal into office. In 1934 the Roosevelt administration secured passage of the *Reciprocal Trade Agreements Act*. This law permitted the President to lower tariffs by up to 50 percent for imports from any nation that would grant similar concessions to us.

WORLD TRADE SINCE 1945

The General Agreement on Tariffs and Trade (GATT). When World War II ended, the United States and the other victorious powers vowed to avoid the mistakes of the past by promoting trade between nations. Toward that end, twenty-three of the world's trading nations created the General Agreement on Tariffs and Trade (GATT) in 1947. Today there are nearly four times the original number of members.

Unlike the Reciprocal Trade Act, which provided for *bilateral* (two-nation) negotiation, GATT established the machinery for *multilateral* (many-nation) negotiations. Since 1947, some eight "rounds" of negotiations have dismantled the tariff barrier system of the 1930s. As a result, tariff levels today are far lower than they were half a century ago.

Perhaps the most dramatic of these international trade discussions was the Kennedy Round, named for the American President whose administration inspired it. The Kennedy Round of discussions, completed in 1967, resulted in the largest tariff reductions in our history.

An important round of GATT-sponsored negotiations was the Tokyo Round, which was concluded in 1979. This round took place during

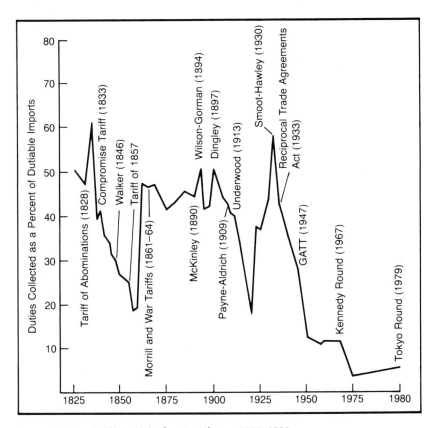

FIGURE 24.1 Tariffs in United States History, 1820–1980

a time of worldwide recession and inflation. In times of economic distress, people tend to call for tariffs and other trade barriers as cures for national problems. The 1970s were no exception, and many nations gave in to the protectionist sentiment by adopting strategies to reduce imports and subsidize exports. (See Figure 24.1 for a graphic summary of United States tariff policies.)

The Tokyo Round of discussions attempted to reverse the protectionist trend. In the agreement that was finally prepared, the industrial nations agreed to reduce tariffs over an eight-year period beginning in 1980, and the member nations agreed to restrict the use of *nontariff* barriers.

In November 1982 another meeting of the eighty-eight member nations of GATT was held in Geneva, Switzerland. The meeting was called by the United States because of its concern over the growing wave of *protectionism* (movement to raise tariffs) that was circling the globe at that time. Although not much was accomplished at the meeting, the nations did pledge to continue their efforts to reduce tariffs and promote international trade.

The European Economic Community (EEC). Ever since the Roman empire fell in the fifth century, Europe has been a continent divided. Political and economic rivalries have engaged European nations in an apparently endless round of turmoil. It was against this background that history was made in 1957 when six nations—France, Italy, Germany, Belgium, the Netherlands, and Luxembourg—agreed to form a trading group called the "European Economic Community," which became better known as the "Common Market."

A *common market* is an association of nations that agree to: (1) eliminate trade barriers between one another, (2) permit workers from each of the members to cross national borders at will, (3) impose trade restrictions on nations *outside* the common market, and (4) develop similar policies on a variety of economic matters.

Since 1957, four more nations have joined the Common Market: Great Britain, Ireland, Denmark, and Greece. Over the years, too, the goals set forth above have become a reality as the EEC developed into a single trading unit.

The United States has viewed the EEC with mixed emotions. On the one hand, the Common Market represents the end of the age-old rivalries among West European nations. Germany and France, which had fought each other in three wars within seventy-five years, now became commercial allies. In this way, the cause of peace has been advanced. Moreover, the removal of tariffs and other barriers to trade has made for a more efficient allocation of resources. All the member nations have benefited as output increased and living standards improved. Increasing wealth has also enabled the Common Market countries to increase their purchases from the United States.

On the other hand, the creation of a single trading bloc has locked some American goods out of competition. For example, at one time American cars exported to Holland were subject to the same tariffs as French, Italian, and British cars. Now, the European cars imported into Holland pay no tariff, while American cars are subject to the tariff as before.

MULTINATIONAL CORPORATIONS AND THE "GLOBALIZATION" OF BUSINESSES

International trade has been booming ever since the end of World War II. The removal of many of the trade barriers that were in place before 1939 has made it much easier for nations to import and export. As a result, the value of American merchandise exports went from $10 billion in 1950 to $224 billion by 1980. But that is only part of the picture, for along with the change in the volume of business there was also a dramatic change in its character.

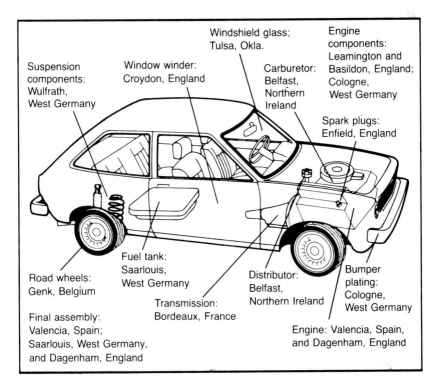

Suspension components: Wulfrath, West Germany

Window winder: Croydon, England

Windshield glass; Tulsa, Okla.

Carburetor: Belfast, Northern Ireland

Engine components: Leamington and Basildon, England; Cologne, West Germany

Spark plugs: Enfield, England

Road wheels: Genk, Belgium

Fuel tank: Saarlouis, West Germany

Transmission: Bordeaux, France

Distributor: Belfast, Northern Ireland

Bumper plating: Cologne, West Germany

Final assembly: Valencia, Spain; Saarlouis, West Germany, and Dagenham, England

Engine: Valencia, Spain, and Dagenham, England

FIGURE 24.2   The Ford *Fiesta*'s international flavor
Copyright © 1980 by The New York Times Company. Reprinted by permission.

Growth of Multinationals.   Ever since the 1950s, American business has been investing heavily in foreign assets. In 1950 direct investment—the value of foreign assets owned by American firms—was $12 billion. By 1980 the figure had grown to $214 billion. The firms that bought these stores, factories, mines, and offices overseas are known as *multinational corporations* (MNCs). Multinational corporations may be defined as firms with home offices in one country and subsidiary offices in a number of others, which conduct their business on a global scale *as if there were no national boundaries.* The illustration of the Ford *Fiesta* (Figure 24.2) is a case in point. All the labeled components were manufactured or purchased by Ford subsidiaries in the listed countries.

Why do firms become multinationals? There are three principal reasons:

1. They increase the markets for their products. By opening a subsidiary in, say Ghana, a shoe manufacturing company will not have to pay whatever tariffs Ghana may levy on imported shoes.

2. They take advantage of lower production costs. If the cost of labor, land, or materials is lower abroad than it is at home, the foreign subsidiary will be able to produce goods at a lower cost.

International Trade   **479**

**TABLE 24.1   Gross Yearly Sales and Foreign Revenues of
Leading Multinational Corporations Compared to Gross National
Products of Selected Nations, 1980
(billions of dollars)**

Country or Company	GNP or Gross Sales	Foreign Revenues	Foreign Revenues as Percent of Total Sales
Brazil	$225.2		
Belgium	118.0		
Exxon	103.1	$73.3	71.1
Switzerland	103.1		
Mobil	60.4	38.0	62.8
Argentina	59.6		
General Motors	57.7	16.1	27.9
Ford Motor	37.1	18.7	50.3
Thailand	28.8		
IBM	26.2	13.8	52.6
General Electric	25.5	5.7	22.5
ITT	23.8	12.3	51.8
Portugal	23.6		
Egypt	22.2		
Peru	15.3		
Citicorp	14.2	9.1	64.1
Morocco	14.9		
E.I. Du Pont de Nemours	13.7	3.9	28.3
Xerox	8.2	3.8	46.7
Burma	6.2		

Source: *Forbes,* July 5, 1982, pp. 126–128; reprinted by permission of *Forbes* Magazine, © Forbes Inc., 1982.

3. They gain access to raw materials at lower costs. This is probably the oldest reason why American firms have invested in foreign lands. It has been going on ever since the first American trapper purchased from the local Indian tribes the right to conduct a fur business.

The largest of the multinationals are enormous in size. Exxon, Mobil, and General Motors, for example, register total yearly sales that are larger than the gross national products of every South American country with the exception of Brazil. This is illustrated further in Table 24.1.

Foreign-Owned Multinationals. Just as American multinational corporations operate in foreign lands, so too do foreign multinationals operate in the United States. Table 24.2 lists a number of those corporations with which you may be most familiar.

Multinational Corporations—Pros and Cons. The multinationals have been subjected to intense scrutiny and criticism. The following section summarizes the principal charges that have been leveled against them and the arguments that have been presented in their support.

1. Multinational corporations export American jobs. In their efforts

TABLE 24.2 Major United States Companies With Foreign Ownership

Company	Foreign Investor	Country	Industry/ Product	Percent Foreign- Owned
Scott Paper	Brascan, Ltd.	Canada	paper products	21
American Motors	Regie National des Usines Renault	France	automobiles	46
A&P	Tengelmann Group	Germany	supermarkets	50
Shell Oil	Royal Dutch Shell	Netherlands	oil	69
Grand Union	Générale Occidentale SA	France	supermarkets	100
Nestlé	⎫		food	100
Libby, McNeill & Libby	⎪		food	100
Stouffer	⎬ Nestlé SA	Switzerland	food, restaurants	100
Beech-Nut Foods	⎭		baby food	100
Miles Laboratories	Bayer AG	Germany	health care	100
Lever Brothers	Unilever NV	Netherlands	consumer goods	100
Hygrade Food Products	Hanson Trust, Ltd.	United Kingdom	meat processing	100
Joseph Seagram & Sons	Seagram Co., Ltd.	Canada	spirits, wine, oil, gas	100
Howard Johnson	Imperial Group, Ltd.	United Kingdom	hotels, restaurants	100
A. B. Dick	General Electric, Ltd.	United Kingdom	office equipment	100
Timex	Olsen, Lehmkuhl families	Norway	watches	100
Hills Brothers Coffee	COPERSUCAR	Brazil	coffee	100

to reduce production costs, it is argued, MNCs are quick to transfer their operations to places where labor costs are lowest. For that reason virtually all bicycles, radios, and television sets are now manufactured outside the United States. With them went thousands of American workers' jobs.

While those who defend the MNCs concede that many jobs no longer exist in this country, they argue that the *total* number of jobs has increased as a result of multinational operations. Overseas subsidiaries of multinationals purchase their parts and other components from the parent firm and therefore create additional jobs in those industries. (For example, the General Motors plants in Canada buy their engines and transmissions from GM producers in Michigan.) This view was also borne out by a study published by the Harvard Business School in the 1970s, which demonstrated that American corporate activity abroad had resulted in a net increase of 700,000 jobs for American workers.

2. American technology is being exported to other lands where it is used against us. The point of this argument is that after American industry has invested billions of dollars in research and development (sometimes with government assistance), the new products and technologies resulting from that research have been used by foreign subsidiaries of the MNCs to undersell domestic producers. Living standards have been raised in host countries at the expense of the American standard of living.

Defenders of the MNCs concede that foreign subsidiaries have benefited from American technology and that the living standards of the host countries have indeed been raised. But these benefits have also been passed on to the American economy because the technology that raised foreign incomes has also enabled those economies to buy more from us. Trade is also a two-way street, and American firms have benefited from the technology developed by other people. For example, the American steel industry has hired Japanese consultants, and it has sent observers to Japan to learn about that nation's steel-manufacturing techniques.

3. Multinationals are so large and powerful that they represent a threat to the economies of their host countries. We have already noted that the sales of some multinational corporations are greater than the GNPs of their host countries. This size difference has created a number of fears, particularly among the less developed countries. Although they are grateful for the technology and capital that the MNCs bring with them, these nations know that their goals and those of the corporations are different. They also know that unlike domestic corporations, which are easily regulated, the multinationals can pull up stakes and move out whenever they feel it in their interest to do

so. Finally, international scandals have damaged the reputation of the MNCs and added to the fears of some host countries. One investigation revealed that Lockheed, in its efforts to secure defense contracts, made payments to influential people in the Japanese and Dutch governments. Other scandals implicated United Brands and the government of Honduras, Gulf Oil and certain Arab states, Exxon and the Italian government, and ITT and Chile.

Supporters of the multinational concept agree that corruption in industry ought to be stamped out as ruthlessly as it would be in government or labor. They question whether it is any more likely to occur in multinationals than in domestic corporations. As for the tremendous power attributed to the multinationals, their supporters argue that total sales are no substitute for *sovereignty*. Even the smallest of nations has rights and powers denied to the greatest of corporations. With a police force, an army, and the power to seize the property of *anyone*, the national state exercises a kind of authority difficult, if not impossible, for a corporation to defy.

EXERCISES

Multiple Choice

1. Who really bears the cost of a tariff? (*a*) the retailer (*b*) the government of the exporting country (*c*) the importer (*d*) the consumer.
2. Suppose the United States were to abolish its tariffs. What would be a probable result? (*a*) There would be fewer job opportunities in American exporting industries. (*b*) The American standard of living would be considerably lowered. (*c*) Some workers in presently protected industries would lose their jobs. (*d*) Most farmers would be hurt.
3. When nations specialize in certain products and engage in international trade to obtain other products, (*a*) the total output of goods and services will be increased (*b*) fluctuations in the business cycle will be eliminated (*c*) the likelihood of worldwide unemployment will be increased (*d*) the living standard of wealthy nations will be lowered.
4. A protective tariff is most effective in (*a*) allowing a nation to make the best use of its economic resources (*b*) increasing the export of goods to foreign nations (*c*) safeguarding the interests of particular domestic industries (*d*) raising the national standard of living.
5. According to the infant-industry argument, tariff protection is legitimate if (*a*) the protected industry is very small (*b*) there is

TABLE 24.3   Output per Worker per Day
(in pounds)

Country	Fish	Fowl	Ratio of Fish to Fowl
A	200	100	2:1
B	80	20	4:1

fierce competition from abroad (*c*) the industry is trying to market a new product (*d*) once it is established, the unprotected industry will be able to compete effectively with foreign corporations.
Base your answers to questions 6 and 7 on Table 24.3.

6. According to the information contained in the table, (*a*) Country B has an absolute advantage in the production of both fish and fowl (*b*) Country B has an absolute advantage in the production of fowl only (*c*) Country A has an absolute advantage in the production of both fish and fowl (*d*) absolute advantage cannot be determined because there is no mention of price.

7. According to the Law of Comparative Advantage, (*a*) trade should not take place between Countries A and B (*b*) Country A should buy its fish from B and raise only fowl (*c*) Country A should buy fowl from B and devote all its energies to fishing (*d*) Country B should buy both its fish and fowl from A.

8. In the mythical country of Parthia, skateboards can be produced and sold for $11 per unit, while the mythical country of Dacia can produce and sell them for $9 each. The major exporting country, Cartia, can deliver skateboards to Parthia and Dacia for $7 per unit. Both Parthia and Dacia have levied a $3 per unit tariff on imports of skateboards. What kinds of tariff did Parthia and Dacia levy? (*a*) Both countries levied a protective tariff. (*b*) Parthia levied a revenue tariff; Dacia levied a protective tariff. (*c*) Both countries levied a revenue tariff. (*d*) Parthia levied a protective tariff; Dacia levied a revenue tariff.

9. The economic theory that nations should regulate their international trade so as to maintain an inflow of precious metals was known as a (*a*) laissez-faire (*b*) capitalism (*c*) mercantilism (*d*) free trade.

10. Which of the following has an effect different from that of the other three? (*a*) reciprocal trade agreements (*b*) import quotas (*c*) currency controls (*d*) protective tariffs.

11. All of the following have brought about the reduction of tariffs between nations *except* the (*a*) Kennedy Round (*b*) General Agreement on Tariffs and Trade (*c*) Hawley-Smoot Tariff Act (*d*) European Common Market.

12. From 1816 until the 1930s, America's tariff policy could best be described as (*a*) one of free trade (*b*) protectionist (*c*) reciprocal (*d*) nonexistent.

13. An economic common market has all of the following advantages *except* (*a*) lowers trade barriers among its member nations (*b*) allows workers from one member nation access to jobs in another member nation (*c*) permits nonmember nations unlimited trading advantages (*d*) develops economic policies for the economic advantage of all its members.

14. A multinational corporation is a business that (*a*) sells its products only to foreign governments (*b*) has operations in many countries (*c*) avoids tariffs and business taxes (*d*) takes economic advantage of less developed nations.

Essay Questions

1. Economists frequently cite the law of comparative advantage to show why nations should engage in international trade. (*a*) State the principle of comparative advantage. (*b*) Is it possible for one nation to have an *absolute advantage* in the production of all goods and services? Explain. (*c*) Is it possible for one nation to have a *comparative advantage* in everything? Explain.

2. An American appliance manufacturer recently told a friend, "When Japanese manufacturers undersell my fans, American workers lose their jobs as I lay them off. What's more, the profits that I lose because of this foreign competition and the salaries that my workers are not paid are lost forever from the American economy. The only answer to this problem is to raise tariffs on Japanese goods." (*a*) Should American appliance manufacturers be protected against foreign competition that undersells them here? Give *two* arguments to support your point of view. (*b*) Assuming that the manufacturer quoted above was located in Peoria, Illinois, why would he not be likely to use these arguments against a competitor in Denver? (*c*) Under what circumstances would you say that governments are most justified in protecting domestic producers?

3. "To many Americans, the Common Market represents both a triumph and a challenge. On the one hand the long-sought-after goal of European unity has been brought a giant step closer, while, on the other, it has created a formidable competitor in American markets." (*a*) Why do many Americans regard the Common Market as an important instrument of international unity and peace? (*b*) How has the Common Market created a "formidable competitor in many American markets"?

CHAPTER 25

Financing International Trade

"Hey, Alice, how did the European trip go this summer?"

"It was fantastic. I just loved seeing all those countries. But let me tell you, it sure is easy to get confused over foreign currency. *Marks, liras, francs, pounds!* I had a time keeping track of my money."

Americans traveling abroad soon learn that they will have to exchange their dollars for the currency of the country they are visiting. Stores, restaurants, and hotels expect to be paid in the local unit of money. At the end of their trip, travelers can change whatever foreign money they have not spent back into dollars.

EXCHANGE RATES

How much foreign money Americans can purchase with their dollars depends upon the *exchange rate*—that is, how much each unit of foreign currency is worth in American money. In July 1984, as indicated by Table 25.1, the Canadian dollar was worth 75 cents, the Mexican peso one-half of a cent, and the Norwegian krone 12 cents. With this knowledge, you can now calculate, for example, that the sweater you admired last summer, which was priced at 163 kroner in the Oslo department store, costs about $20 in American money.

Exchange rates play a crucial role in international trade. Suppose that the rate of exchange for Norwegian money were to jump from 8.2 kroner to the dollar to 10 to the dollar. This change would make Norwegian goods less expensive to Americans (that sweater would now cost only $16.30), while Norwegians would have to pay more for goods produced in the United States.

Because exchange rates have a direct effect upon international trade, this section will focus upon how these rates are determined, why they are subject to change, and some of the things that are being done to keep rates reasonably stable.

TABLE 25.1   Foreign Exchange Rates on July 11, 1984

Country	Dollar Value per Unit of Foreign Currency	Units of Currency per Dollar
Australia (dollar)	.8247	1.21
Austria (schilling)	.0505	19.79
Belgium (franc)	.0172	58.21
Brazil (cruzeiro)	.000565	1770.00
Britain (pound)	1.3090	.76
Canada (dollar)	.7490	1.33
Denmark (krone)	.0964	10.38
France (franc)	.1146	8.73
Italy (lira)	.000572	1745.50
Japan (yen)	.004125	242.45
Mexico (peso)	.0051	194.00
Norway (krone)	.1221	8.19
Spain (peseta)	.0062	161.30
Switzerland (franc)	.4158	2.41
W. Germany (mark)	.3517	2.84

Exchange Rates. Imagine that you were traveling through Mexico in July 1984. A restaurant charged you 1,940 pesos for lunch. Using Table 25.1, calculate the cost of your meal in United States dollars.

HOW ARE EXCHANGE RATES DETERMINED?

Why was the Japanese yen worth less than half a cent, the French franc 11½ cents, and the British pound $1.30 in July 1984? Exchange rates have been established in a variety of ways over the years. In this century, the most significant patterns were the *gold standard*, the *gold exchange standard* or *Bretton Woods system*, and most recently, the *floating exchange rates system*.

The Gold Standard. At one time, particularly during the seventy-five-year period preceding the Great Depression of the 1930s, most of the world was on the *gold standard*. Under this arrangement, anyone could convert a nation's currency into a fixed amount of gold. In the United States, this amount was 23.22 grains of gold for each dollar. Since the English pound was convertible into 113 grains of gold, or 4.87 times as much as the dollar, the rate of exchange was one pound equaled $4.87. No Americans would have to pay more for their pounds, since they could always exchange their dollars for gold and use it to buy pounds from the British government. Similarly, no English people would take less than $4.87 for a pound.

The gold standard, when it functioned as it was supposed to, also tended to keep international trade in balance. That is, no country could indefinitely have a "favorable" balance of trade. If a nation exported more than it imported, it would have an influx of gold. This increase in the money supply would tend to raise prices. Meanwhile, in the country that was losing gold, prices would fall. Because of the higher prices in the first country, exports would decline. Imports, on the other hand, would increase as foreign prices became more attractive. Gold would flow away from those nations with large supplies and toward those with small gold balances.

There were two weaknesses in the gold standard that eventually brought about its demise. First, the gold standard made it difficult, if not impossible, for a government to regulate its money supply. Second, the gold standard placed international commerce at the mercy of the gold supply.

As we discussed in Unit VII, the money supply has a direct effect upon the level of economic activity. For that reason, most governments now rely on a variety of monetary tools to regulate their economies. Under the gold standard, however, there was little that nations could do to control the money supply because, in the final analysis, the supply depended upon the amount of gold in their treasuries. This latter amount, in turn, was dependent upon the level of exports as compared to imports and the output of the world's gold mines. Increases in the gold supply had an inflationary effect, while decreases were deflationary in their impact. Either event, if it came at the wrong time, could have a disastrous effect upon a nation's economy.

Nations thus had little control over their economic destinies. Therefore, it is not surprising to learn that, during the Great Depression of the 1930s, most nations abandoned the gold standard. From that time until the end of World War II, international trade was reduced to a trickle of its former volume.

The Bretton Woods System, or Gold Exchange Standard. In the summer of 1944, while World War II was still raging, the major industrial nations of the free world met at Bretton Woods, New Hampshire, to establish a new international economic order. Out of these meetings emerged a system for setting exchange rates that has become known as the *Bretton Woods system,* or the *gold exchange standard.*

The new system called for fixed exchange rates, like those that had existed under the gold standard, for all currencies. Since by 1944 most of the world's gold had been acquired by the United States, the dollar became the standard upon which to base exchange rates. Nations following the Bretton Woods system agreed to buy or sell dollars at a fixed rate, or "peg." For its part, the United States agreed to permit any foreign nation to convert its dollars into gold at the rate of $35 to the ounce. In this way, nations could continue to base the value of their currencies upon gold without actually owning any of the metal. For example, the Mexican peso was pegged at 12½ to the dollar, while the French franc was valued at 5 to the dollar. Since the dollar was convertible to gold at 35:1, 175 French francs equaled one ounce of gold (because 5 times 35 equal 175), and 437.5 pesos equaled one ounce of gold. This exchange rate also meant that one franc equaled 2½ Mexican pesos.

Role of the International Monetary Fund (IMF). The gold exchange standard promised to be effective as long as member nations were willing and able to exchange their own currencies for those of other nations or for American dollars *and* were willing to convert those dollars to gold at 35:1. But what would happen if a government was in danger of running out of dollars or other foreign exchange? And who would supervise the system and attempt to resolve problems affecting international payments? The answers to these questions were to be provided by the International Monetary Fund (IMF). The IMF was empowered to make loans to nations in need of foreign exchange, dollars, or gold. Such loans were considered temporary ones until the flow of a nation's exports restored its supply of reserves.

When the payments problem proved to be a long-term one, the IMF would permit *devaluation*, the deliberate reduction in the value of a nation's currency. If, for example, the value of the French franc were halved from 5 francs to the dollar to 10 to the dollar, buyers in other nations would be able to acquire twice as many francs for their money. The effect of such a move would be to make French goods cheaper to foreigners and therefore promote exports out of France and the flow of foreign exchange into France. In the 1930s, currency devaluations were viewed as attempts to steal business. Such attempts led to rounds of retaliation as the devaluation of one currency led to the successive devaluation of a number of others. For this reason the IMF was assigned the added responsibility of supervising the process so as to limit the number of currency devaluations among its members.

The Bretton Woods system worked fairly well until the late 1960s. In the end it was the inability of the United States to continue exchanging gold for dollars that led to the system's demise. When the end finally came in 1973, the world learned that international trade could function without gold and without fixed exchange rates. And two new terms were added to the jargon of foreign exchange: "SDRs" and the "float."

Special Drawing Rights and Floating Exchange Rates. The flow of American spending abroad increased dramatically during the Vietnam War. This spending, added to the normal demand by Americans for imported goods, served to place more dollars in the hands of foreigners than they were willing to keep. As the call for gold and foreign currencies in exchange for dollars mounted, it became evident that the United States had insufficient reserves to meet the demand. Unfortunately, there was nothing in the original Bretton Woods agreement that would allow for a devaluation of the dollar.

Special Drawing Rights (SDRs). In 1968, in an effort to relieve the pressure, the International Monetary Fund created Special Drawing Rights. SDRs, or "paper gold" as they were frequently called, represented an attempt to provide another reserve currency for international trade that could substitute for gold and dollars. SDRs were created out of a pool of foreign exchange deposited by the sixteen leading member nations of the IMF. SDR balances were credited to the member nation, which could then use them in place of dollars or gold to settle accounts with other countries.

By 1971, it was evident that, despite the availability of SDRs, confidence in the dollar had been badly shaken. Investors and countries the world over that had formerly been content to hold on to their dollars were now seeking to convert them to gold or other currencies.

In the face of this pressure, the United States was finally compelled to abandon its support of gold and to devalue the dollar. In 1971, President Richard Nixon made the historic announcement that the government would no longer exchange gold for dollars. In 1973, the policy was further expanded to allow the value of the dollar to "float" to whatever level the laws of supply and demand would permit. With the dollar "cut loose," so too were the rest of the world's currencies. The Bretton Woods system was finished.

The "Float" Explained. Floating exchange rates are determined in accordance with the laws of supply and demand in much the same way that securities are priced in stock exchanges. Demand in this case comes from the desire of foreigners to obtain a country's goods and services, while supply is derived from the desire of that nation's citizens to import the goods and services of others. As the demand for Portuguese goods increases, so too will the demand for escudos to pay for them. If, at the same time, there is no change in the pattern of Portuguese imports, the price of escudos is likely to rise. Similarly, if Venezuela's imports exceed its exports, the supply of bolivars in foreign hands will increase, and the price of that currency is likely to fall.

Although the float is capable of functioning without government direction or supervision, many nations keep a close watch on foreign exchange markets so as to keep their own currencies from fluctuating too widely in price. They do this by using government assets to buy or sell their own currencies as the circumstances dictate.

The International Monetary Fund no longer buys and sells gold in exchange for foreign currencies. In its stead, SDRs have become the primary reserve among the member nations. Meanwhile, the dollar has continued to function as the single most important foreign currency despite the fact that its exchange rate, like all the others, is subject to change.

THE BALANCE OF PAYMENTS

We have seen that international trade is complicated by the fact that payments are made in foreign money, or currency. We have also noted that a currency's exchange rate—the price one must pay for a particular currency—depends upon the supply of and the demand for that currency.

But what determines the supply of or the demand for a particular currency? And how could a private citizen, who might be engaged in international trade, avail him or herself of such information? The information one needs for these purposes is found in a *balance of payments statement* (Table 25.2). Just as an individual firm's income statement summarizes the sources of its earnings and expenditures, so a nation's balance of payments summarizes its transactions with the rest of the world. Some of those transactions, like the importing of foreign oil by the United States, result in the outflow of dollars and/or foreign exchange. Others, like the exporting of wheat by the United States, bring funds into the country. When more funds are flowing out of the United States economy than are flowing in, pressure builds up on the dollar. This pressure will be relieved when the dollar "floats" down to a new level, so that it becomes less expensive to foreign buyers. The pressure could also be relieved by the United States government, which, if it wished, could enter the market and support the dollar.

In this country, the data that make up the balance of payments are collected and published quarterly by the United States Department of Commerce. Although a full treatment of these data is beyond the scope of this text, it is worth our while to summarize their principal features. These features are the *current account*, the *capital account*, the *official settlement account*, and the *statistical-discrepancy adjustment*.

The Current Account. Most, but not all, of the economic activity in international trade involves the importing and exporting of goods and services. At the same time, a steady flow of funds is exchanged between nations as buyers pay for their purchases. This activity is summarized in that portion of the balance of payments known as the *current account*.

Merchandise makes up the largest portion of the current account. Imports of merchandise are paid for with foreign exchange and are recorded as an outflow of funds. For example, when Daring Dan's Datsuns spent $100,000 for a shipment of automobiles, payment was made to the Japanese manufacturer with yen obtained from Daring Dan's bank. This $100,000 item was included in the $247.3 billion outflow in the merchandise imports account. Merchandise exports, on the other hand, produce a flow of funds into the United States. When a Venezuelan manufacturer purchased a $60,000 knitting machine from an American firm, this sum was included in the $211 billion item that summarized merchandise exports.

Current account items are sometimes classified as either "visible" or "invisible." A knitting machine and an automobile are obviously included in the category of "visible" items of trade. It is easy to visualize how the purchase and the sale of visible items lead to an

TABLE 25.2 United States Balance of Payments, 1982 (billions of dollars)

	Inflow	Outflow	Net
Current Account			
Merchandise trade			
exports	$211.0		
imports		$247.3	−$36.3
Investment income	85.9	57.2	28.7
Net military trans- actions		0.6	0.6
Net travel and transport		1.3	−1.3
Other services, net	8.1		8.1
Pensions, gifts, and grants		7.9	−7.9
	Balance on current account		−8.1
Capital Account			
U.S. assets abroad			
private		107.5	
government		10.7	
Foreign assets in the U.S.			
private	81.5		
government	3.0		
	Balance on capital account		−33.7
	Balance on current and capital account		−41.8
Adjustment for Statistical Discrepancy			43.7
Official Settlement Account			
U.S. official reserve assets		5.0	
Foreign official assets in U.S.	3.1		
	Change in U.S. Reserves		−$1.9

inflow and outflow of foreign exchange. Services, however, cannot be seen or touched: They are "invisible." Nevertheless, they have value and may be imported or exported. Invisible items therefore affect the balance of payments in much the same way as visible ones. For example, the American traveling on an Indian-owned airline to Bombay has *imported* a service (passage to India). The airfare of $750 will be included in the category of *travel and transportation* as an outflow of funds. Similarly, the $600 dividend recently received by an American investor in a Swiss chocolate factory will be included as an inflow of funds in the *investment income account.*

Can you think of a transaction that would create an outflow of funds from the investment income account?

There was a time, particularly during the seventeenth and eighteenth centuries, when economists were especially interested in comparing merchandise imports to exports. This relationship, which they called the "balance of trade," was described as *favorable* when exports exceeded imports and *unfavorable* when imports were greater than exports. Favorable balances enabled nations to add to their hoards of gold and silver. Economists today no longer attach much importance to the balance of trade or to hoards of precious metals. They much prefer to examine an entire balance of payments for the more complete picture it provides of a nation's international transactions.

The Capital Account. Loans or investments made abroad by individuals and governments are recorded as either outflows or inflows in the *capital account* of the balance of payments. Saudi Arabian investment in Iowa farmland creates an inflow of funds, just as the American purchase of an oil refinery in West Africa would create an outflow of funds. (Over the years, the income, if any, generated by these investments will be noted as a reverse flow in the current account.)

In the course of a year, some Americans sell off their overseas assets while others purchase new ones. Similarly, some foreigners will sell their holdings while others will add to theirs. The net result of these transactions in 1982 is summarized in the table.

The Official Settlement Account. Payments in foreign trade are facilitated by banks that buy and sell the pounds, francs, yen, and other currencies required by their customers. For their part, the banks look to the Federal Reserve System for the same kinds of services. Surplus currencies are sold for dollars, while those in demand are purchased. In the final analysis, then, it is the United States government that attends to providing the balance in the balance of payments. How the government does this is summarized in the Official Settlement Account.

Suppose that, on the one hand, in a given year there was a surplus in the balance of payments, and the flow of funds into the banks was greater than the flow out. Eventually, this surplus of foreign currencies will find its way to the Federal Reserve System, where it will be added to the government's official reserves. If, on the other hand, outflows are greater than inflows, American banks may be asked to sell more foreign exchange to importers than they purchase from exporters. In that event, they will have to go to the government for the difference. In those circumstances, the government either will dip into its foreign exchange reserves or, if necessary, liquidate some of its SDRs in order to satisfy the needs of the member banks.

In 1982, the United States reduced its reserves by $1.9 billion so as to cover the deficit in the balance of payments.

The Statistical-Discrepancy Adjustment. The balance of payments is an extremely complicated statement, which, for a variety of reasons, usually contains a sizable error ($43.7 billion in 1982). This error is usually entered as a "statistical discrepancy."

Deficits, Surpluses, and Equilibrium in the Balance of Payments. As long as there is *equilibrium* in the balance of payments—that is, as long as currency outflows are equal to inflows—the dollar will maintain its value in relation to foreign currencies. If there is a *surplus* because inflows are greater than outflows, however, the dollar will increase in value. Just the opposite happens during years in which there are *deficits* in the balance of payments. A deficit appears whenever outflows of foreign exchange are greater than inflows. During deficit years, the dollar is likely to decline in value in comparison to foreign currencies.

Contrary to popular opinion, surpluses in the balance of payments are not always desirable, and deficits are not always undesirable. On the one hand, a surplus could mean that, as a result of its vigorous export trade, a nation is enjoying a high level of income, employment, and production. On the other hand, a surplus could be the opening event in a round of inflation. Why? Because increased production will also increase income and consumer spending. With more dollars chasing fewer goods (at home), prices are likely to rise.

Deficits, in contrast, usually result from an imbalance in which the flow of goods and services entering a country is greater than the flow of those leaving. These inflows could serve to raise living standards as those at home share in more of the good things in life. As the deficit persists, however, the dollar will be less welcome abroad. The dollar's decline will increase the cost of foreign exchange and therefore imports. At this point, living standards may decline as fewer Americans are able to afford to buy goods from abroad. In the 1970s, the sudden increase in the price of petroleum forced many Americans to reduce their driving, turn down their thermostats, and cut back on their consumption of electricity.

Of course, the dollar's decline will make that currency and, therefore, American products, more attractive to foreign buyers. As exports expand, foreign exchange will return to these shores and the dollar will increase in value.

The Money Without a Country: Eurodollars, Petrodollars, and Other Eurocurrencies

As you know from Chapter 14, the carrying out of federal monetary policy and the regulation of American banking are the responsibility of the Federal Reserve System. A major goal of the Fed's efforts is to keep the purchasing power of our money stable. In recent years, however, the Fed's ability to achieve this goal has been weakened. Hundreds of billions of American dollars have been transferred out of United States government control and transformed into *Eurodollars* and *petrodollars*. (See Figure 25.1.)

FIGURE 25.1   United States Money Supply and Supply of Eurodollars, 1972–1982

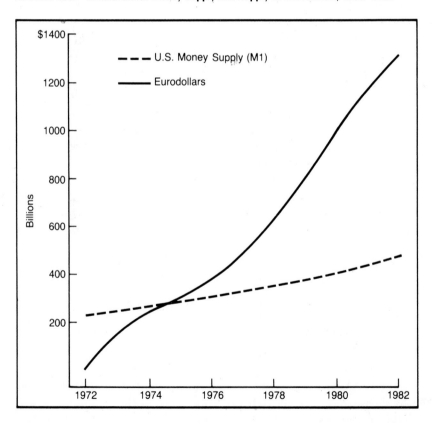

No magical genie has been at work casting spells over American currency. What has happened is that a number of governments in Europe, the Middle East, Asia, and the Caribbean have permitted both domestic and foreign banks to carry accounts in currencies other than their own. "Eurodollars" is the name given to any dollar accounts carried in banks outside the United States, and "petrodollars" describes the dollar balance accumulated by the OPEC nations. Because European banks were the first to carry these deposits, moneys may also be known as "Eurocurrencies," "Europounds," "Eurofrancs," and even "Euroyen."

Eurodollar deposits are beyond the control of the Federal Reserve System, which is one of the principal reasons for their popularity abroad. The Fed's reserve requirements and its other regulations to which domestic banks are subject add to the cost of doing business. But these restrictions do not apply to dollar accounts in American bank branches or to foreign banks outside the United States. For that reason, foreign-based banks have been able to offer dollar loans at lower rates of interest than American-based banks. Similarly, it has also been possible at times for Eurobanks to offer higher interest rates to their depositors than domestic banks were able to offer.

Major American corporations have been active Eurodollar customers. During those times when the Federal Reserve was using its powers to limit domestic bank loans, many firms in need of money got around the Fed's restrictions by borrowing in the Eurodollar market.

There are those who say that the Eurodollar market is harmful to American interests. They would like to see the overseas branches of American banks subject to the same requirements as domestic banks. Critics are also concerned about the size of the Eurodollar market. Present estimates put the supply of Eurodollars at about twice the domestic money supply (currency plus demand deposits).

Others argue, however, that the Eurocurrency market serves a useful and vital function in the global economy. By providing a ready source of supply for dollars and other currencies, this market promotes international trade and stability. Were it not for the Eurodollar market, for example, foreigners would be less willing to hold on to their accumulated dollars. The United States would then have to come up with sufficient foreign currencies, SDRs, or gold to redeem Eurodollars. Moreover, as long as other foreign banks can do so, it is not possible to accomplish anything simply by prohibiting American banks from trading in Eurodollars. Such a step would only put the American banks abroad out of business while the foreign banks continued to trade in dollars.

1. What are Eurodollars?
2. Why has there been a huge flow of Eurodollars (petrodollars) to the Middle East in recent years?
3. For what reasons have American corporations kept surplus funds in overseas bank accounts?
4. The Eurodollar market has been the subject of controversy among economists. (a) How is the Eurodollar market seen as harmful to American interests? (b) How is the Eurodollar market seen as helpful to American interests?
5. With reference to Figure 25.1, (a) What does the solid line represent? (b) What does the dashed line represent? (c) In what way did the years after 1974 differ from prior years? (d) True or false: According to the graph, the supply of Eurodollars will continue to exceed United States money supply at least until the year 2000. Explain your answer.

The Value of the Dollar in the 1980s. In the early 1980s, something unusual happened. The dollar increased in value in comparison to foreign currencies even though merchandise imports had been greater than exports. The principal reason for the dollar's climb was the unusually high level of American interest rates. When foreigners discovered that they could earn more on their savings by investing them in the United States than they could in their own lands, they clamored for dollars. With foreign currencies relatively cheap, Americans continued to import goods in record amounts. This left American exporters hard-pressed to sell their goods because the dollar had become so expensive. Meanwhile, as long as American interest rates remained high, there did not seem to be anything that anyone could do to bring down the value of the dollar.

EXERCISES

Multiple Choice

1. Which is the best explanation of why the Mexican peso has value outside of Mexico? (*a*) Anyone can walk into a bank and exchange the peso for gold. (*b*) Merchants throughout the world will accept the peso in exchange for their goods. (*c*) The peso can be used to buy Mexican goods and services. (*d*) There is an ample supply of pesos.

2. Assume that the exchange rate for the Chilean peso is $1 = 135 pesos. How much would an American importer pay in dollars for 202,500 pesos' worth of wool? (*a*) $15,000 (*b*) $1,500 (*c*) $150 (*d*) $15.

3. Suppose that a few days before the American importer made payment on the wool purchased in question 2, the Chilean peso was devalued. What effect would this have had on the importer? (*a*) It would have had no effect. (*b*) It would have made the wool more expensive. (*c*) It would have made the wool less expensive. (*d*) It would have made it impossible for him to make payment.

4. Assume that exchange rates are allowed to float and that the demand for German marks has been increasing. Under these circumstances, which of the following is most likely to occur? (*a*) It will take fewer dollars to buy German marks. (*b*) The price of German goods in terms of dollars will fall. (*c*) Germans will find that imported goods are getting more expensive. (*d*) Americans will have to pay more for goods made in Germany.

5. If a nation's reserves of dollars or other foreign currencies were running low, it might look to the International Monetary Fund for (*a*) a loan of foreign exchange (*b*) the printing of any foreign currency it needed (*c*) an investment loan to build up-to-date production facilities (*d*) a market for its surplus production so as to restore a "favorable balance of trade."

6. Special Drawing Rights (SDRs) were created to provide all of the following *except* (*a*) an international monetary reserve currency (*b*) an alternative to gold (*c*) currency that can be used by tourists as they travel from one country to another (*d*) a substitute for American dollars as a "reserve currency."

7. Which was the most serious weakness of the gold standard? (*a*) Gold made it difficult to determine rates of exchange. (*b*) Gold based a nation's currency on a standard that was not widely accepted. (*c*) As the supply of gold in any nation increased, imports became more costly. (*d*) Gold made a nation's money supply dependent upon gold rather than the national interest.

8. What would be likely to happen to the Italian lira if Italy replaced Japan as the world's leading exporter of automobiles and electronic

equipment? (a) The lira would increase in value, thereby making imports less expensive in Italy. (b) The lira would decrease in value, thereby making imports more expensive in Italy. (c) The change would not affect the value of the lira. (d) The change would compel the Italian government to devalue the lira.

9. A nation's balance of trade describes (a) the total flow of money into and out of the country (b) its exports and imports of merchandise (c) its overall economic health (d) how well it is doing in international trade.

10. A nation's balance of payments summarizes the nation's business transactions (a) with multinational corporations based in that country (b) with the European Common Market (c) with the International Monetary Fund (d) with the rest of the world.

11. If there is a surplus in a nation's balance of payments, the value of that nation's currency will (a) decline (b) remain the same (c) increase (d) increase, then decline.

Essay Questions

1. Sweater Trends, Inc. distributes sweaters manufactured to its specifications to department stores and boutiques around the country. In seeking a manufacturer for its latest design, Sweater Trends narrowed down its choices to three firms. One, an American company, has offered to deliver the sweaters for $10 each. A Hong Kong firm can do the same, including delivery to the United States for 48 *Hong Kong dollars* each. The third, an Italian manufacturer, offered to deliver the sweaters for 7,500 *lire* each.

   Exchange rates at the time stood at $1 = 6 *Hong Kong dollars*
   $1 = 1250 *lire*

   Since the initial order was to be for 10,000 sweaters, Sweater Trends selected the manufacturer that made the lowest bid.
   (a) Which manufacturer did the distributor select? (b) Suppose that by the time Sweater Trends was ready to place its order, exchange rates had shifted so that $1 was now equal to 4 *Hong Kong dollars* and 625 *lire*. (1) Which manufacturer would Sweater Trends have then engaged? (2) What happened to the value of the American dollar as a result of the shift in exchange rates? (3) How did the shift in exchange rates affect American living standards? (4) What might have caused such a shift in exchange rates?

2. "A nation's exports pay for its imports." Explain this statement.

3. Today there are economists who argue that the world's trading nations ought to return to the gold standard. (a) What was the gold standard? (b) Identify and explain one advantage that the gold standard offers in international trade. (c) Identify and explain a principal weakness of the gold standard.

4. In discussing the balance of payments, economists occasionally refer to "invisible" items of import or export. (*a*) What is meant by an "invisible" import or export? (*b*) Tell whether each of the following events does or does not affect our nation's balance of payments. For each event that has an effect, explain whether it is as an *import* or as an *export*. (*1*) An American travels to London on a British airline. (*2*) A French tourist spends $500 during a visit to the United States. (*3*) A retired American has social security payments sent to her in Mexico. (*4*) An American exporter pays a United States airline $1,000 to ship goods abroad. (*5*) A Japanese automobile manufacturer rents a factory in California to assemble trucks.

5. "During the 1980s, the dollar appreciated in value as compared to most foreign currencies. The reason was the eagerness of many foreign investors to cash in on the very high interest rates being offered on American securities." (*a*) Why would high interest rates on American securities be of interest to investors in other lands? (*b*) Why did the dollar *appreciate* in value as compared to most foreign currencies? (*c*) What effect did the appreciation of the dollar have on *imports?* on *exports?*

CHAPTER 26
Other Economic Systems

Somewhere in the United States, a young father and mother have decided that the time has come to buy their baby his first pair of shoes. Before they do so, they will have to make some decisions. Which stores will they visit? What brand will they buy? How much of their income are they willing to spend for a pair of baby shoes?

Somewhere in Sweden, a Swedish couple have to buy their infant his first pair of shoes. They, too, will visit a number of stores before deciding on which pair of shoes to buy. The money for the shoes will come in part from children's benefits provided to parents by the government.

Meanwhile, Hungarian parents are about to do the same thing: buy baby her first pair of shoes. Before they do so, they too will have to make some decisions. Although the leather and other raw materials used in manufacturing the shoes are produced in government-owned factories, the stores that sell the shoes are privately owned. Since these stores differ as to quality of service and variety of goods they sell, these parents will shop around to find the shoe store that best satisfies their needs.

And somewhere in the Soviet Union, a Russian father and mother have made the same decision. They will go to the government-owned store and buy a pair of government-made baby shoes.

The desire of parents to provide their babies with shoes is no different in the United States, Sweden, Hungary, or the Soviet Union. What is different is the way in which that want is satisfied, because the economic systems of these four nations are different from one another.

Before the Russian Revolution in 1917, there was just one kind of economic system in the industrialized world, and that system was capitalism. The overthrow of the czarist government in Russia, however, led to the establishment of a Communist regime. Since that time, many nations have adopted economic systems that have been described as *communism* or *socialism*. Capitalism now finds itself in the minority among the world's economic systems.

In this chapter we shall examine some of these other economic systems. You will learn about the ways in which they differ and how to measure one against the other. Finally, we shall describe the economic systems of several nations so as to identify their successes and failures, similarities and differences.

Can the United States learn anything from the economic systems of other nations? We shall leave that for you to decide.

HOW WE COMPARE ECONOMIC SYSTEMS

In Chapter 1 we described how all societies are called upon to solve the problem of scarcity by deciding *what* should be produced, *how* it should be produced, and *who* should receive the goods and services produced. We also noted that societies have relied upon *tradition*, *command*, or the *market* to answer those questions and *coordinate* activities within their economies.

How a nation coordinates its activities is one way in which we can compare its economic system to that of another. Who owns the means of production is another. Let us explore this a little more closely.

Who Owns the Means of Production? Capitalism vs. Socialism. The rules governing the ownership and use of the means of production vary from one economic system to another. The *means of production* refers to capital used to create goods and services and thus includes tangible things of value like land, buildings, and trucks, as well as intangibles like copyrights and patents. Economic systems in which the means of production is privately owned are known as *capitalist systems*. Those systems in which the state owns the means of production are called *socialist systems*. Later we shall also describe *communism*, which in its popular usage refers to the economic and political systems of the Soviet Union, China, and a number of other countries in which a Communist party is in power. For their part, Communist nations tend to use the terms "socialist" and "Communist" interchangeably in describing their *economic* systems.

Actually, in no modern industrial state is *all* property in public or private hands. When economists refer to the United States and Canada as *capitalist* economies and the Soviet Union and China as *socialist* economies, what they really mean is that *most* of the property in the capitalist states is privately owned, and *most* of the property in the socialist states is publicly owned. Although the United States is a capitalist society, the government, as we have already noted, accounts for about 20 percent of the gross national product. And, while both the Soviet Union and China stress the public ownership of property as a cornerstone of their socialist systems, there is nevertheless an increasing tendency to permit some private ownership.

A third category of economic system is the *mixed economy*. Mixed economies are defined as those in which both public ownership and private ownership of property exist to a significant degree. Just about all non-Communist countries, including our own, would fall into this category because they provide for both public and private ownership of property.

COORDINATING ECONOMIC ACTIVITY: THE MARKET vs. THE PLAN

The process of gathering together the factors of production in order to create goods and services along with distributing them to society is the essence of *coordination*. This process provides the answers to the universal questions of *what, how,* and *who*. You will recall from our earlier description (in Chapter 1) that in ancient and medieval times people relied upon tradition to answer these questions. Goods were produced according to time-honored customs by people who were born into their roles as farmers, laborers, or nobility.

Today's world, however, is dominated by those nations that rely upon either some form of central planning (that is, *command*) or *markets* to coordinate their economies. Here again it is difficult at times to draw distinctions because every society relies to some extent upon government planning and the marketplace to answer the basic economic questions. We can say, however, that in the capitalist countries of Western Europe, Japan, and the United States, the market dominates economic activity. In the Communist world of Eastern Europe and Asia, government planning is the rule.

What Goods and Services Shall Be Produced and in What Quantity? In a market economic system, the key factor is price. Consumers cast their votes in the form of the price they are willing to pay for a particular good or service. Producers seek to satisfy the demand as best they can. If not enough of a good is produced, its price will be forced upward until supply and demand are about equal. If, however, too much is produced, the price will fall and output will be reduced. In the final analysis, consumers have the last word in a market economy, and for that reason, when describing their role, we speak of "consumer sovereignty."

In a planned economy, government experts are "sovereign" because they decide what goods will be produced. Advocates of central planning argue that when government experts are allowed to decide what to produce, the welfare of society as a whole is more likely to be considered than if the decisions are made by consumers and producers alone. By contrast, those who favor the market system point out that, since people know best what they want and need, systems that are free to ignore consumers' desires are likely to produce goods that no one wants. In the real world, of course, prices are not the sole determinants of what will be produced. Government power is frequently used to tax some goods and services and subsidize others, thereby influencing what goods and services will in fact be produced. Similarly, planned economies can and frequently do take into account consumer wishes before deciding what goods to produce.

How Should Goods and Services Be Produced? Price, as established by the forces of supply and demand, is the key ingredient determining how goods are produced in a market economy. Producers will attempt to combine those *inputs* (factors of production) that give them the greatest production at the lowest possible price. For example, manufacturers of loose-leaf paper will try to use their machines, labor, and raw materials in such a way as to produce the greatest quantity of paper at the lowest cost so as to reap the greatest profit. Meanwhile, the suppliers of those inputs (the lumber, chemicals, and machinery) that go into the manufacture of paper will also strive to offer their goods and services at the lowest prices so as to beat out the competition and earn a profit.

In planned economies, government employees make the decisions that determine how land, labor, and capital will be combined in the production process. In some instances, the process is *centralized:* The planning applies to similar industries throughout the economy. Other systems are *decentralized:* Local plant or store managers are allowed to make the decisions that determine how goods and services will be produced.

One of the questions often asked when comparing one economic system to another is, "Which system produces goods and services at lower costs?" The reason for the question is that if one society can produce goods at lower costs than another, there will be more of everything to go around, and living standards will therefore be higher. Supporters of the market system claim that the profit motive is the greatest single incentive for keeping costs down, while socialists argue that the real costs to society are hidden by the profit motive. The factory that pollutes the environment or endangers its employees' health and safety may appear to produce goods at a lower cost than one that operates safely. But if one were to add in the costs to society of cleaning up the environment and caring for the sick and disabled, a different picture might emerge.

Who Shall Receive the Goods and Services That Are Produced? In a market economy, a person's standard of living depends to a large

Soviet Supermarket. How do the packaging and display of goods in this Soviet supermarket compare to the way goods are packaged and displayed in your neighborhood store?

extent upon his or her income and the level of prices. How much one earns and the prices one pays depend, in turn, upon the laws of supply and demand. In the Soviet Union, China, and other centrally planned economies, incomes and prices are the two principal factors in determining *who* will receive the goods and services that are produced. The difference, however, is that in centrally planned economies incomes and prices are likely to be determined by the government.

In the Soviet Union most industries (and this includes *all* factories making automobiles and household appliances) are owned by the state. If the Russian government believed that automobile workers were entitled to higher wages than workers in household appliance factories, it would simply direct the auto and household appliance plants to put those beliefs into practice. By contrast, in the United States market economy government preferences have little or nothing to do with wages in the automobile and appliance industries. We must look to the forces affecting supply and demand to explain wage differences.

As for prices, in a centrally planned economy they too are set by the government, and in some respects they have the same kind of effect as do prices in the United States. So, for example, when prices are high, fewer people can afford to buy goods than when prices are low. But, as we have already learned, prices have a very special role to play in a capitalist system: They are the key to the allocation of resources. High prices attract workers into fields they might otherwise have avoided and entice producers into increasing their output, while low prices have the opposite effect.

506

We have also seen that when the laws of supply and demand are allowed to operate freely, the market will be "cleared." That is, all the goods and services available at the market price will be bought up by those willing and able to pay the price. This is not the case under central planning. Since it is the government and not the forces of supply and demand that sets prices, there is no guarantee that the market will be cleared. If government planners miscalculate consumer demand and prices are set too high, unsold goods will sit on dealers' shelves. But if prices are set too low, so many consumers will be able to pay the price of the things they want that there will not be enough to go around.

When shortages do appear, planned economies often look to some form of *rationing* to distribute their output fairly. Rationing is a system that allots fixed amounts of goods and services to individuals and families. In some instances, rationing provides the same amount of the item to everyone. So, for example, a book of coupons entitling the holder to six ounces of meat each week might be issued to every adult in a household. In other circumstances, the government might elect to give a select group of people rations that are more generous than those allotted to the general public. In the Soviet Union, for example, virtually all housing is owned by the government, and rents are relatively low. The housing itself, however, varies in size and quality, and is in short supply. For that reason, housing is rationed. Workers who perform what the Soviet government considers to be the more important tasks in Russian society are entitled to bigger and better apartments than those whose work is considered less important.

WHAT TOOLS ARE AVAILABLE TO ECONOMIC PLANNERS?

Since they do not have the price system and profits to guide them in their decision making, how do planners in socialist economies arrive at their decisions? Two of the most frequently used economic tools for this purpose are *econometric models* and *input-output analysis*.

Econometric models employ mathematical equations as a means of applying theory and statistics to explain economic behavior. (*Econometric* is a fairly new word that was created by combining the words "economics" and "metric.") Both government and private industry have utilized econometric models to forecast economic conditions. For example, if government economists wanted to know what effect a 10 percent increase in interest rates would have on the rest of the economy, they would feed this question into their model. In response, they would receive an estimate of the changes that would take place in areas like business investment, consumer spending, and savings.

Input-Output Analysis

An input-output table shows how the industries within an economy depend upon one another. For simplicity, think of a hypothetical economy in which there are but three major industries: paper, lumber, and chemicals. Reading down Table 26.1, we see where the materials that went into the production of the output of each of the industries came from. Economists describe these materials as the *inputs*. Thus, the first entry in the first column tells us that $50 million worth of paper products was used by the paper industry in producing its total output. The paper industry also needed $200 million in lumber, $200 million in chemicals, and $100 million in other resources. (*Other resources* include labor, natural resources, capital goods, and services.)

Reading from left to right tells who *bought* the output of each industry. Thus, the paper industry sold $100 million worth of its products to the lumber industry, $50 million to the chemicals industry, and, as we have already noted, another $50 million in paper products to its own industry. The total value of paper sold to industry was $200 million. Add to this total some $350 million in sales that were made to other "final consumers"

TABLE 26.1   Input-Output Table for an Economy With Three Industries
(millions of dollars)

	Paper Industry	Lumber Industry	Chemical Industry	Total Sales to Industry	Final Consumption	Total Output
Paper Industry	$ 50 (.09)	$100 (.30)	$ 50 (.13)	$ 200	$350	$ 550
Lumber Industry	$200 (.36)	$ 50 (.15)	$ 40 (.11)	$ 290	$ 40	$ 330
Chemical Industry	$200 (.36)	$ 30 (.09)	$100 (.27)	$ 330	$ 40	$ 370
Other Resources	$100 (.18)	$150 (.45)	$180 (.49)	$ 430		$ 430
Total Input	$550	$330	$370	$1,250	$430	$1,680

such as households, government, and foreign buyers. Thus, paper industry production totaled $550 million for the year.

Input-output tables are of particular value in a planned economy because they show the government how much of each input would be affected as a result of changes in production in a particular industry. For an illustration, let us turn to the lumber industry, where inputs totaled $330 million. One of these inputs was paper worth $100 million. For every dollar of lumber that was produced, 30 cents worth of paper products were needed (because $\frac{\$100}{\$330}$ = $0.30). Economists refer to the value of each input needed to produce one dollar's worth of output as the industry's *input coefficient*. The industries' input coefficients are shown in parentheses in the table.

Suppose, for example, that the centrally planned economy represented by this table wanted to increase the production of chemicals for its final consumers by 30 percent. By how much would the production of inputs have to be increased in order to achieve this goal?

A 30 percent increase in the production of chemicals would raise final consumption to $52 million (because $40 million + 30 percent × $40 million = $52 million), or by an additional $12 million. The additional $12 million in chemicals would also require additional inputs, as follows:

Paper:	.13 × $12,000,000	= $ 1,560,000
Lumber:	.11 × 12,000,000	= 1,320,000
Chemicals:	.27 × 12,000,000	= 3,240,000
Other:	.49 × 12,000,000	= 5,880,000
	Total value of inputs =	$12,000,000

If the production of chemicals is to be increased by $12 million, more inputs will be consumed in the process than before. Input-output analysis in this instance tells us that the paper industry would have to provide an additional $1.56 million worth of its products, lumber an additional $1.32 million, and all the other resources going into paper production will have to be increased by $5.88 million. In addition, the chemicals industry would have to increase its own production by another $3.24 million to round out the inputs for this additional output.

Naturally, this kind of information is essential in a planned economy. Not only does it tell planners how changes in production in one industry will affect other sectors of the economy, it also indicates where, if there are shortages, bottlenecks are likely to appear.

1. What is an input-output table?
2. Why is input-output analysis particularly important in a planned economy?
3. With reference to the information contained in Table 26.1, suppose it was decided to increase the production of paper by $55 million. How much more lumber, chemicals, and paper inputs would be needed to produce the additional paper?
4. Suppose that at the time it was decided to produce the additional

Econometric models are generally used to measure the effect of changes on the economy as a whole. But suppose we want to see how specific industries within the economy are related to one another. For this purpose, economists use *input-output analysis*. (See the reading above, pages 508-509.)

The manufacturer of paper in our theoretical example needs lumber and chemicals. But, just as the paper industry looked to chemicals and lumber for its raw materials (or inputs), so too the chemicals industry and the lumber industry need paper, the lumber industry needs chemicals, and the chemicals industry needs lumber. In the real world of modern industrial nations, relationships are far more complex, of course, because there are literally hundreds upon hundreds of interconnected industries.

Input-output analysis, in combination with modern computers, has made the planning task much simpler. First developed by Wassily Leontief, an American economist who later received a Nobel Prize in Economics for his efforts, a table of inputs and outputs was constructed that demonstrated the interdependence of the industries within an economy. Aided by the input-output table, planners can now calculate the effect of changes in demand in one industry on other industries within the economy.

KARL MARX'S ECONOMIC THOUGHT

Contrary to popular thinking, Karl Marx did not describe the Communist state in detail but, rather, concentrated his attention on capitalism and its weaknesses. Marx went on to predict the replacement of capitalism by another system in which the workers would control

$55 million worth of paper, the chemical industry was operating at capacity. Could the additional paper be manufactured? Explain your answer.

5. Is there a need for input-output analysis in a market economy? Explain your answer.

6. "The value of input-output analysis is limited by the fact that it is based on information about *past* rather than *future* events." Explain this statement.

all wealth and the means of production. It was left to later writers and to the leaders of the Communist countries to work out the details of the new society that was to replace capitalism.

Major Theories. Some of the major theories advanced by Marx were the following:

1. The history of society has been a "history of class struggle." Throughout history, Marx argued, one class has dominated the others. Thus, during the period of feudalism in Western Europe, the landed classes (church and nobility) were triumphant. These were, in turn, overthrown by the bourgeoisie, or capitalists, who grew fat through the exploitation of their workers, the *proletariat*—Marx's term for people who must work for wages. Marx predicted that the proletariat would bring about a final upheaval through its overthrow of capitalism.

2. Workers are paid less than the value of the goods they produce. Marx called the difference between the value of what the workers' wage can buy and the value of the goods the workers produce *surplus value*. You have probably already recognized that what we are talking about is *profit*. The Marxists suggest that this profit, or "surplus value," rightfully belongs to the workers.

3. Capitalism will inevitably lead to an endless round of economic depressions. Marx argued that, because of competition from other firms, capitalists are under constant pressure to reduce their costs. They accomplish this by investing in laborsaving machinery (thereby adding to unemployment), reducing wages, or both. Meanwhile, those firms unable to compete successfully are forced out of business, and their workers are added to the rolls of the unemployed. As unemployment mounts and wages decline, depression is the inevitable

KARL MARX
Das Kapital (1867)

For the people of China, the Soviet Union, Eastern Europe, and the rest of the Communist world, *Das Kapital* is a kind of bible and Karl Marx is its prophet. Who was this dark-eyed, bewhiskered man, whose face peers down from walls in homes and offices wherever communism is the official state doctrine?

Karl Marx was born in the German city of Trier in 1818. Educated in the universities of Bonn and Berlin, he became a journalist but was forced to leave Germany because of his radical views. In Paris, Marx met Friedrich Engels (1820–1895), the son of a wealthy textile manufacturer. The two men became lifelong friends, a fact that is significant for several reasons. First, Marx and Engels collaborated on writing the *Communist Manifesto* (1848), which set forth a declaration of principles for a newly created Communist group first known as the *League of the Just* and later as the Communist League. Second, had it not been for Engels' financial aid, it is unlikely that Marx would have finished his greatest work.

Because of his support of the 1848 revolution in Austria, Marx was banished from the continent. In 1849, Marx moved his family to London. There he spent nearly all his working days in the reading room of the British Museum in research and writing. Marx and his family lived in wrenching poverty for many years. What little income he had came from articles he wrote for an American newspaper, the New York *Tribune,* and from money that Engels gave him.

In 1864 Marx helped to organize the *International Workingmen's Association.* The *First International,* as the association was commonly known, was a forerunner of today's Communist parties. Finally, in 1867 the first volume of his massive work, called *Das Kapital (Capital),* was published. After Marx's death in 1883, two more volumes of the work were edited by Engels and published in 1885 and 1894. Karl Marx's economic theories are discussed at length on pages 510–514.

It is probably true that more people today point to the writings of Karl Marx as the source of economic wisdom and inspiration than to the work of any other economist living or dead. Authorities differ as to the reasons for Marx's wide appeal. Perhaps many find his elaborately detailed descriptions of the evils of capitalism and his predictions of inevitable doom to be appealing. Whatever the reason, about a third of the people of the globe describe their economic system as *Marxist.*

result. The trend is reversed as wealthier businesses buy up those that have failed. As time goes by and surplus stocks are consumed, the remaining businesses hire increasing numbers of workers, and prosperity returns. Eventually, however, the cycle is repeated, more economic power is concentrated in fewer hands, and the proletariat endures greater suffering.

This is the logic that led Marx to predict that, under capitalism, the rich would get richer, the poor poorer, and with the increasing reliance upon machinery the army of unemployed would grow and grow.

4. Revolution is inevitable. The mounting discontent among the workers will unite the proletariat, said Marx. They will rise up, overthrow their capitalist oppressors, and establish the Communist state.

5. In achieving the Communist state, the new society will have to advance through two stages:

Dictatorship of the Proletariat. Communist nations have argued that in their early stages of development they are surrounded by capitalist enemies. It is therefore necessary to establish a Communist dictatorship to organize the state along socialist lines and stamp out capitalism.

Communism and the Withering Away of the State. The dictatorship of the proletariat will permit the government to establish a socialist state in which the workers will own all the means of production. Ultimately, the system will advance far enough technologically so that it will supply sufficient quantities of goods and services to satisfy everyone. All workers will work to the best of their abilities and will be paid in accordance with the principle, "to each according to one's needs." Thus, the absence of want and of any struggle between classes will make government superfluous, and the state will "wither away."

Theory and Reality. Although most Americans would reject the theories and conclusions of Karl Marx, his ideas can hardly be ignored since they influence the economic thinking of such a large portion of the world. Certainly, some things that Marx predicted about capitalism proved to be true. He was right when he predicted that there would be recurring depressions and that giant firms would come to dominate the industrial scene. Nevertheless, Marx's most important conclusion—that capitalism would inevitably collapse—has not been borne out.

Why was Marx wrong? Why did capitalism survive? The answer is that Marx pictured capitalism as a system that was completely dominated by the greed of the capitalist. As Marx saw it, a society so dominated would be incapable of reforming its economic system to give workers a greater share of the goods and services they produce. As a result, this exploited group would rise up and overthrow its masters. Beginning in the late nineteenth century, however, the governments of many capitalist countries did many things to help workers. You are familiar with much of this social and economic legislation that protects consumers and workers and promotes the more equitable distribution of income. Our government and the governments of many other capitalist nations have not acted merely as the tools of the capitalist class but have sought to protect all their citizens. Moreover, contrary to Marx's predictions, labor and management have learned to work together within the framework of the capitalist system.

Some of the most powerful countries in the world regard Marxism as the theoretical basis of their economies. In the pages that follow, we shall take a closer look at how the Soviet Union applied Marxist philosophy.

COMMUNISM IN PRACTICE: THE SOVIET UNION

The Russian Revolution. Prior to 1917, communism existed only in the minds of persons who had read Karl Marx and his followers. In 1917, however, following the collapse of Russia's armies in World War I, two revolutions took place in Russia, with the Communist party (or "Bolsheviks") seizing control at the end of the second. Thus began the first and most successful Communist state. Although many observers predicted the imminent downfall of the Russian experiment, the Russian economy developed to such an extent that, within three decades after the revolution, Russia had become the second most powerful nation in the world. Communism has also spread to a number of other nations, mostly in Eastern Europe and Asia.

War Communism and the New Economic Policy. Although the Communists seized power in Russia in 1917, they were unable to institute planned socialism until 1928, when the first of the five-year plans was introduced. The delay was a consequence of two factors: civil war and a temporary retreat to capitalism.

During the years 1917–1920, Russia was plunged into civil war. This was the era of "war communism," in which the leadership of the nation, headed by Nikolai Lenin and Leon Trotsky, attempted to run the economy through a system of direct controls over the existing industries and farms. However, because of the breakdown of communications and coordination resulting from the war, the triumph of the Communist troops in 1920 found the nation on the brink of economic disaster.

To restore order and prepare for the introduction of full-scale communism, Lenin announced the introduction, in 1921, of the New Economic Policy (NEP). This was, in effect, a return to a limited form of capitalism. It permitted the maintenance of privately owned retail stores, farms, and small industries. The state, meanwhile, operated large industries, banking, and foreign trade. During the years between 1921 and 1928, the NEP successfully restored order to the Soviet economy.

Five-Year Plans. When Josef Stalin rose to power in Russia in the mid-1920s, he found himself at the head of an industrially backward nation. In an attempt to modernize the Russian economy as rapidly as possible, Stalin instituted a series of *five-year plans.* These plans are detailed statements of the nation's economic objectives for the succeeding five years and they apply to all aspects of the economy, including industry, agriculture, trades, and the professions. Lawyers are expected to try their quota of cases, taxi drivers must log so many miles, and barbers must perform their minimum number of haircuts.

The five-year plans not only set forth production goals but also allocate the resources necessary to achieve them. If, for example, it is determined that steel production should be increased, the plan provides for the construction of additional production facilities and provides other resources and labor needed to meet that goal.

With the exception of the war years (1939–1945), five-year plans or their equivalent (there was one seven-year plan) have been in force since 1928. The most recent plan went into effect in 1981.

Special Role of Government in the Soviet Economy. Because the Soviet state owns almost all the means of production and distribution (including industries, mines, farms, and stores), it determines how the basic questions of *what, how,* and *who* will be answered in Russia. Moreover, as the only legal political party, the Communist party exercises the ultimate power over the nation's political and economic life. Thus it is the Communist party that decides what the general economic goals for the coming years are to be. The Soviet government's principal responsibility is to prepare the detailed plans to achieve these goals.

Deciding What Will Be Produced in the Soviet Union. The Soviet Union, as we have said, relies on government planning to decide what goods and services will be produced, and the government either owns or closely controls most of the nation's productive resources. Individuals do own their personal possessions, like household goods, savings accounts, and insurance policies, and some people in the trades, such as carpenters, domestic servants, and tailors, may legally work for themselves. In addition, there is a considerable amount of "moonlighting" in which people who normally work for the state take on private jobs after hours. But the value of privately owned property and labor represents a tiny fraction of total Soviet economic output.

The task of carrying out the economic programs contained in the five-year plans is assigned to various agencies, the most important of which is the State Planning Committee, or the *Gosplan*. The Gosplan prepares a detailed agenda of the economy's goals for the following year. Since it is beyond the scope of the Gosplan or any other single agency to set down in detail how the tens of thousands of items will be produced, the task is subdivided into major commodity categories (such as motor vehicles, textiles, and ferrous metals). Each of these categories (there are about forty in all) is the responsibility of economic ministries and regional Gosplans, which prepare output targets for each of the 350,000 enterprises that make up the Soviet economy.

The manager of each individual enterprise estimates the inputs that he or she needs to meet the state's quotas. These input estimates are sent to the ministries where they are combined with requests from other enterprises and forwarded on to the Gosplan. Since requests for inputs rarely match the available resources, the Gosplan must modify quotas and reassign tasks among the enterprises until a final plan is achieved. This plan, which is binding upon all the units in the economy, sets forth target quotas for sales, costs, profits, and productivity increases for the coming year.

Deciding How Goods Will Be Produced in the Soviet Union. The task of carrying out the annual plan is the major responsibility of the people who direct the economic units or "enterprises" in the Soviet economy. These managers of factories, stores, farms, and offices share a common goal: to meet their quotas. While many of the problems that the managers must face in the day-to-day conduct of their businesses are similar to those confronting American managers, there are also a number of significant differences. The tale that follows will illustrate several of these differences.

Soviet Management Problems. Pyotr Zantepolski heads the management team of a factory that manufactures gas ranges. Like every other manager of a Soviet enterprise, Pyotr is assigned a quota—the number of units his plant is expected to produce. For that purpose,

Pyotr also is assigned a budget that will pay for the labor and materials necessary to do the task.

To Pyotr, his quota is all-important. If he meets or surpasses it, he will be rewarded with honors and bonuses. But if the factory fails to produce enough to meet its quota, Pyotr could be fined, fired, or both. Pyotr does not have to worry about sales, marketing, or competition, however, because all the factories in the gas range industry are owned and operated by the government.

Last June, Pyotr's factory faced a crisis. Although his workers were keeping up with the production schedule, nearly half of the ranges they produced lacked oven controls. These controls were to have been provided by a manufacturer in another town, but the shipment was late. To make matters worse, even if the controls that the planners allotted to Pyotr's factory had arrived before the end of the month, there was no way of knowing whether or not they would fit the oven model that the factory produced. Since the only place to buy oven controls in the Soviet Union is from the state-owned enterprise that produces them, Pyotr could not "take his business elsewhere."

What then could Pyotr do to meet his quotas? One alternative was to take some workers off the assembly line and assign them the task of making oven controls. The major drawback with this scheme was that making controls would bring the production of ranges to a near standstill. Another alternative was for Pyotr to call some of the managers of kitchen range factories around the country to see if they had any controls to spare. The problem with this approach was that many managers concealed their surpluses for fear that the planning authorities would reduce their allotments in the future, thereby making it more difficult to meet quotas. Finally, Pyotr could seek the assistance of a *tolkach*. The *tolkachi* ("pushers") are people who earn their living by locating hard-to-get materials for enterprises in need. The tolkachi use methods that are not always ethical or legal, but they do perform a valuable function by enabling managers to meet their quotas. For its part, the Russian government prefers to look the other way rather than put the tolkachi out of business.

More often than not, a plant manager will use all the available options to fulfill a quota. That is, the manager will borrow from other plants, produce as much as possible without disrupting the plant's production lines, and use the services of a tolkach to obtain needed parts when they are not available through regular sources.

SWEDEN: THE MIDDLE WAY

Gunnar Ulsten and Ingrid Ulsten (ages sixteen and twelve) live in Sweden's capital city of Stockholm. Their parents work for a division of Volvo, a major manufacturer of automobiles, trucks, and engines. Like most of Sweden's business and industry, Volvo is privately owned.

Life for the Ulsten family is much like that of millions of middle-class urban Americans. The apartment in Stockholm is roomy and boasts the kinds of modern conveniences that Americans have also come to take for granted (central plumbing and heating, telephones, television, and refrigeration). The Ulstens also own a small summer cottage on a lake, which the family can reach by car in three to four hours. As you may have guessed, Sweden, like the United States, is a wealthy country. Indeed, since 1974 Sweden has had a higher per capita gross national product than the United States.

Although he was quite young at the time, Gunnar can still remember what fun it was when his sister was born. Swedish law permits either parent to take a paid leave in order to care for a new baby. For personal reasons, the Ulstens decided it would be better if Mr. Ulsten took the leave so as to allow Mrs. Ulsten to return to her job at Volvo. In school, Gunnar and Ingrid have learned that, for a capitalist country, Sweden has an unusually large number of social welfare programs. As a result, the Swedish government plays a large role in the nation's economy. In the United States, for example, government spending usually accounts for about 20 percent of the GNP; in Sweden, by comparison, government spending comes to 65 percent.

Medical Care in Sweden. When patients leave this hospital in Sweden, who pays the costs of their therapy and care? Does this differ from medical-care practices in the United States?

Some economists refer to the Swedish economy as the "middle way," meaning that the nation has adopted many Socialist programs while maintaining the kind of private ownership normally associated with capitalism. One of these social programs paid for all of Mrs. Ulsten's maternity expenses. Another program pays the entire cost of Ingrid and Gunnar's medical and dental care. All Swedish children also are entitled to a free education from kindergarten through college. Their meals, books, and school supplies are provided without charge until they are sixteen. Thereafter, they receive a monthly allowance of $30 for as long as they remain in school.

When they enter the world of work, Gunnar and Ingrid will be eligible for different kinds of government-sponsored benefits. Unemployment insurance will reimburse them if they lose their jobs, and government programs will train them for new ones. Free transportation is available if the new job requires that they travel to another town. When they retire, Gunnar and Ingrid will receive pensions and other forms of government assistance, such as housing and health care.

In recent years, the Swedish economy began to falter, and the middle way became a rocky road. The Swedish government had always relied on tax revenues to pay for its social programs. As long as the economy did well, the burden of these taxes was kept within reason. For many years following World War II, the Swedish economy did extremely well. The nation had remained neutral throughout the war, so that, at the war's end, unlike the other industrial nations of Europe, Sweden's factories were intact. The demand for Swedish goods boomed, and for the next twenty-five years the government had little difficulty in paying for its social programs.

But conditions changed after the oil crises in the mid-1970s. The cost of imported oil, which had averaged about $2.6 billion before that time, jumped to $7 billion by 1981. Meanwhile, labor unions won a 50 percent increase in their wages. These events served to push up the prices of Swedish goods in world markets, and exports declined.

Today, Sweden has the world's highest income tax rate. But despite taxes, the government has had to borrow additional funds to pay for its costly social programs. These borrowings, in turn, have fed inflation at home and made Swedish goods even more expensive abroad.

In the face of these pressures, it remains to be seen whether Sweden will be able to continue providing its costly social services without increasing taxes still further. If continuing in the same fashion is not possible, Sweden must reduce some services, increase some taxes, or apply a combination of the two measures.

HUNGARY: MARKET COMMUNISM AT WORK

Hungary is one of the Communist nations of Eastern Europe. Hungary invariably supports the Soviet Union's positions in the United Nations and is a member of the Warsaw Pact, the military alliance of Communist nations, and COMECON, the Soviet-sponsored economic association of those countries. The economic system of Hungary, however, is quite different from that of the Soviet Union. Although most of Hungary's resources are owned by the government, the allocation of those resources is largely determined by the *market* rather than the *government*. The system requires that managers of government-owned enterprises show a profit on their operations or risk being fired. This system is quite different from the one in the Soviet Union, where managers are assigned production *quotas*. In other words, if a manager of a door factory in the Soviet Union were told that his or her quota for a month included one thousand 80-centimeter doors, the production of that number would be crucial (to the manager) regardless of whether or not anyone wanted to buy them. The manager's Hungarian counterpart, by comparison, would first want to predict what size doors would sell before setting out to produce them. Thus, if it appeared that the demand for 80-centimeter doors had dried up, but that there was a shortage of 65-centimeter doors, the manager would be likely to order that the latter size be cut. Why? Because at the end of the period the plant would show a bigger profit.

The Hungarian economy also differs from the Soviet economy in the extent to which the former permits private ownership of the means or production. Since 1982, the Hungarian government has allowed firms with as many as 150 employees to incorporate and compete with state-owned industries.

This system, which some describe as "market socialism" or "market communism," was first developed by Yugoslavia, and was successfully introduced into Hungary in 1968. By the 1980s, average Hungarians were living better than their counterparts in any other nation of Eastern Europe. Indeed, there are predictions that the time will come when all the nations now dominated by the Soviet Union will function under a system of "market communism."

COMPARING ECONOMIC SYSTEMS

We have noted that among the socialist nations the means of production are principally owned by the state, and coordination of economic activities is principally carried out through government planning. In capitalist countries, private ownership is predominant, and coordination is the principal responsibility of the marketplace.

But labels can be confusing, because in reality all the countries that call themselves "capitalist" rely to some extent on government ownership and planning. Conversely, even Communist countries like the Soviet Union and China, both of which claim to be "socialist," allow some private ownership of the means of production, and permit free-market activities.

Adding to this confusion is the labeling of certain western democracies (such as Sweden, England, and France) as "socialist." This labeling is done even though in each country most of the means of production are in private hands, and the government's role in the economy is rarely more influential than that of ours.

Clearly, then, labels cannot be relied upon to compare the economic systems of two or more nations. Instead, we would recommend that you ask the two questions upon which the chapter has focused:

1. Who owns the means of production in these nations?
2. How are these nations' economic systems coordinated?

Once you have answered these questions, you will be able to apply labels of your own.

EXERCISES

Multiple Choice

1. The first major nation to adopt communism as an economic system was (a) Russia (b) Germany (c) France (d) China.
2. Which statement about capitalism is *false?* (a) Today most of the world's people live in countries that describe themselves as "capitalist." (b) In capitalist societies, most of the productive resources are privately owned. (c) America is a capitalist country. (d) Capitalism offers consumers more power than any other economic system.
3. In which respect does the economy of the Soviet Union *differ* from that of the United States? (a) the emphasis on technological progress (b) the use of money as a medium of exchange (c) the emphasis given to the problem of continued economic growth (d) the manner of deciding what goods and services will be produced.
4. Which statement about socialism is *false?* (a) The concept of socialism has changed since the time of Karl Marx. (b) Socialists today no longer advocate government ownership of the means of production. (c) Socialism permits the government to compensate private owners for property nationalized by the state. (d) Socialism permits greater political freedom than communism.

5. Which of the following is true of both the American and the Soviet economy? (*a*) Most of the means of production are owned by the state. (*b*) Wages and salaries are used as an incentive to work. (*c*) Labor unions play a significant part in determining conditions of work. (*d*) Consumer demand largely determines what will be produced.

6. The means by which the economic questions of *what, how,* and *who* are answered in any society is called (*a*) coordination (*b*) capitalism (*c*) input-output analysis (*d*) socialism.

7. What goods will be produced in a Communist economy is determined chiefly by (*a*) supply and demand (*b*) government planning (*c*) labor unions (*d*) the people by means of referendums.

8. Which of the following statements abut Russian history is *true?* (*a*) The NEP represented a return to harsh dictatorial government. (*b*) Trotsky introduced "war communism" to modify the harsh communism of Stalin. (*c*) "War communism" was an attempt to increase Russian production during World War II. (*d*) The NEP represented a return to a limited form of capitalism.

9. A significant difference between the economies of the Soviet Union and Hungary is (*a*) The Soviet Union is a communist state, while Hungary describes itself as "semicapitalist." (*b*) Unlike the Soviet Union, there is no central planning in Hungary. (*c*) Hungary relies far more heavily on the marketplace in determining what goods and services to produce than does the Soviet Union. (*d*) Unlike the Soviet Union, in which most of the farms, factories, and mines are owned by the government, most of these are privately owned in Hungary.

10. In what way did the five-year plans affect the Russian people? (*a*) The plans established the constitutional framework for the government of the USSR. (*b*) The plans established all retail prices. (*c*) The plans set forth what goods and services would be available for public consumption. (*d*) The plans set forth the books, plays, and other cultural media that would be available to the public.

11. Sweden is said to follow a "middle way" because (*a*) it maintains elements of both socialism and capitalism (*b*) it combines a blend of totalitarian dictatorship with democracy (*c*) it follows an economic path somewhere between communism and socialism (*d*) it is as likely to support the Soviet Union in United Nations debates as it is to support the United States.

12. Why might Soviet citizens want to read their nation's most recent five-year plan? (*a*) The plan will tell them who is likely to succeed their present leader. (*b*) The plan sets forth the kinds of subjects that Russian children will be studying in school. (*c*) The plan will give them insight into the nation's economic priorities. (*d*) The plan enables them to compare their nation's progress with that of the United States.

13. Which is the most important agency for carrying out the Soviet Union's economic plan? (*a*) the Communist party (*b*) the secret police (*c*) the tolkachi (*d*) the Gosplan.
14. Which of the following is true of the Soviet Union today? (*a*) There is consumer sovereignty and consumer choice. (*b*) There is no consumer sovereignty but there *is* consumer choice. (*c*) There is no consumer sovereignty and no consumer choice. (*d*) There is consumer sovereignty, but no consumer choice.

Essay Questions

1. According to one economist, "The major problems of American factory managers are labor costs and prices. The major problems for their Soviet counterparts are raw materials and quotas." Explain this statement.
2. Identify and explain two differences between the economies of Hungary and the Soviet Union.
3. "Although first developed by an American economist, input-output analysis is of greatest value in the socialist and communist economies." Explain this statement.
4. Interpreting a Cartoon. Look at the cartoon, read the paragraph below it, and answer the questions that follow.

Beattie in *The Daytona Beach News-Journal*

In the Siberian city of Irkutsk (population 568,000), ration coupons, red for one kilo (2.2 pounds) of meat and green for two-thirds of a pound of butter, are distributed monthly by the local housing administration. The possession of a ration coupon does not guarantee that the shopper will be able to buy meat or butter, because the item may not be available.

(a) Explain the meaning of the cartoon. (b) Would you agree that the economic system of each nation is responsible for the conditions portrayed? Explain your answer.

5. Suppose that the Soviet Gosplan wanted to increase the production of bicycles. In order to gather together the necessary productive resources and to sell the increased output, this increase will involve many economic decisions. (a) Identify and explain four things that will have to be done to increase the production of bicycles in the Soviet Union. (b) Describe three steps that might be taken to increase bicycle sales. (c) How might the increased production of bicycles affect the entire Soviet economy?

6. Analyzing Statistical Data. The questions are based on Table 26.2. (a) Summarize the purpose of the table. (b) Which items require less work time in Moscow than in Washington? How would you account for these differences? (c) For which item is the discrepancy greatest between the work times required in Moscow and in Washington? How would you account for these differences?

TABLE 26.2 Average Work Time Required to Purchase Selected Consumer Goods in Washington and Moscow, 1982

Item	Quantity (kg.)	Washington	Moscow
		(minutes of work time)	
Flour	1.0	5	28
Bread	7.0	112	119
Noodles	2.0	28	68
Beef	1.0	69	123
Hamburger	1.0	37	123
Sausages	1.0	33	160
Codfish	1.0	61	47
Sugar	3.3	30	191
Butter	0.5	28	111
Margarine	2.0	46	222
Milk	12.0 liters	72	264
Cheese	2.0	200	370
Eggs	18.0	14	99
Apples	1.0	10	92
		(hours of work time)	
Rent, monthly		51	12
Color television		65	701
		(months of work time)	
Small car		5	53
Medium-size car		9	86

Source: *Forbes Magazine*, Dec. 6, 1982, p. 140. Reprinted by permission of *Forbes Magazine*, © Forbes Inc., 1982.

The Global Economy

CHAPTER 27

The Less Developed World

More than half the people of the world are living in conditions approaching misery. . . . Their poverty is a handicap, and a threat both to them and to more prosperous areas.

Little has changed since President Harry S. Truman spoke these words in 1949. The planet is still divided between what are now called the "less developed countries," of the poor world, and the "more developed countries," of the rich. There is, of course, some poverty in all nations, including our own, but there is much more, and much worse, poverty in the less developed countries.

WHY ARE MANY COUNTRIES "LESS DEVELOPED"?

According to the United Nations, the thirty-three *more developed countries* (MDCs) are the nations of Europe and North America (Canada and the United States), and include Australia, New Zealand, Japan, and the USSR. The remaining countries, over a hundred and twenty, in all, are "less developed." How do these *less developed countries* (LDCs) compare to the more developed ones?

The quality of life in the United States and in the other developed countries is a reflection of humankind's scientific, technological, and cultural achievements. People eat better, live longer, are better educated and cared for, and have more of the material things of civilized life than at any other time in history. A few statistics, summarized in Table 27.1 on page 526, will serve to illustrate these differences. The following discussion is based on the contents of the table.

1. Per Capita GNP. A nation's *per capita gross national product* is determined by dividing the total GNP by the population. The resulting figure enables us to compare one nation's output with another's. Among the more developed countries, per capita GNP averaged $6,260, as compared to $560 for the LDCs.

2. Daily Per Capita Calorie Supply. The second group of four statistics, known as *social indicators*, tells us something of the quality

TABLE 27.1 The More Developed and the Less Developed Countries—Measuring the Differences in 1980

Region or Country	Per Capita GNP ($)	Daily Calorie Supply per Capita (% of MDR)	Infant Mortality Rate (per 1000)	Life Expectancy (yrs)	Literacy Rate (%)	Energy Consumption per Capita*	Population in 1980 (millions)	Rate of Yearly Population Growth (%)	Estimated Population Year 2000 (millions)
More developed countries	6,260	n.a.	20	72	99	n.a.	1,131	0.6	1,272
Less developed countries	560	n.a.	110	57	52	n.a.	3,283	2.0	4,884
Bangladesh	90	78	153	46	22	43	90.6	2.6	156.7
Brazil	1,570	107	109	64	76	1,050	122	2.1	42.2
China (People's Republic)	460	n.a.	56	64	n.a.	850	975	1.2	1,212.3
Egypt	400	109	90	55	44	463	42.1	2.7	64.9
Ethiopia	120	75	162	39	15	20	32.6	2.5	55.3
India	180	91	134	52	36	176	672.2	1.9	976.2
Indonesia	360	105	91	50	62	278	144.3	2.0	210.6
Japan	7,330	126	8	75	99	3,825	116.8	0.9	129.4
Kenya	320	88	83	56	40	139	15.9	3.9	32.3
Malaysia	1,090	112	44	61	60	716	14.0	2.5	20.7
Mexico	1,290	114	70	65	76	1,384	68.2	3.1	128.9
South Korea	1,160	119	38	62	93	1,359	38.2	1.6	51.1
Soviet Union	3,700	n.a.	31	70	99	n.a.	266.0	0.8	311.0
Switzerland	12,100	130	10	73	98	3,690	6.3	0.2	6.4
United States	9,700	135	13	73	99	11,374	226.5	0.7	260.4
West Germany	9,600	127	15	72	99	6,015	61.1	-0.2	59.8

Source: Data adapted by the author from the *Statistical Yearbooks* of the United Nations, and publications of the World Bank.   *kg coal equivalent   n.a.: not available

of life in a particular country. The indicators we have chosen focus on certain aspects of the diet, health, and education of the sample populations. *Daily calorie supply per capita* measures how well people are eating by telling us what percentage of the minimum daily requirement of food energy the average person is consuming. Remember, the figure is an *average*. While some people in a country are consuming more than the amount indicated, *others are consuming less*.

3. *Medical Services*. The next two columns tell us something about the state of medical and public health services. *Infant mortality rate* is the number of babies out of every 1000 live births who die before their first birthdays. *Life expectancy* is the number of years the average child within the designated nation may expect to live. Here again, there is a sharp difference between the more developed and the less developed countries. Infant mortality is only 20 per 1000 in the MDCs as compared to 110 per 1000 in the LDCs. Life expectancy averages 72 years in the MDCs as compared to 57 years in the LDCs.

4. *Literacy Rate*. This figure measures the percentage of the adult population that can read and write. In the more developed countries, where compulsory education is a fact of life, virtually everyone is literate. But in the less developed world, over a billion people have never had the opportunity to learn to read and write.

5. *Energy Consumption per Capita*. Energy is needed for heat, light, power, and transportation. Energy is created with the help of a variety of fuels, including petroleum, coal, and nuclear varieties. *Energy consumption per capita*, a nation's total energy consumption divided by its population, enables us to compare the relative availability of this vital resource. The averages in this table are stated in terms of the kilograms of coal required to produce the equivalent amount of power.

6. *Population Data*. The final three columns show how the populations of the selected nations are changing. The first column lists the country's total population in 1980, the second shows its present rate of population growth, and the third estimates the population, based on the given rate of growth, for the year 2000.

WHY ARE THE LESS DEVELOPED COUNTRIES POOR?

Because we are discussing three-quarters of the world's peoples, any summary of the reasons for their poverty must be generalized. One way to simplify the discussion is to separate those nations whose holdings of a natural resource are so extensive that it is reasonable to

Improving the Standard of Living. What can be done to make this farm in India yield a larger crop?

assume they will not be poor for long. One such group includes the nations of the Organization of Petroleum Exporting Countries (OPEC), whose wealth from the sale of oil gives them an enormous advantage over the other LDCs in the development race. (OPEC includes Abu Dhabi, Algeria, Ecuador, Gabon, Indonesia, Iran, Iraq, Kuwait, Libya, Nigeria, Qatar, Saudi Arabia, and Venezuela.) Other LDCs, such as Israel, Mexico, and several South American countries, also seem to fall outside the kind of generalizations that follow. As for the remaining LDCs, in their fight against poverty, they tend to suffer from some or all of the handicaps discussed below.

1. Traditions That Are Obstacles to Economic Growth. In many of the poorer nations, deeply ingrained customs and traditions limit their ability to increase production. In certain Moslem countries, for example, half of the adults are excluded from the labor force because religious custom prohibits the employment of women. Other customs lock many people of the Indian subcontinent in the caste, or social class, into which they were born. And in regions where the great majority of the people are devout Buddhists, the quest for peace of mind and the preparation for the afterlife often have wider appeal than accomplishments in the world of work. Tradition also makes the adoption of new methods of production, particularly in agriculture, difficult to achieve. Farmers who barely eke enough out of their lands to feed their families are understandably reluctant to try a new fertilizer or plowing technique because they know that failure could mean starvation.

2. *Unfavorable Social and Political Conditions.* Many less developed countries are dominated by an aristocratic elite with large landholdings. Sometimes, a few industrial, professional, and business leaders share this control. Most of the people are unable to influence the course of their lives because they lack the political or economic power to do so. In many cases, too, political leadership is maintained through the armed forces. With this kind of social and political system, public administration is generally corrupt and inefficient. Jobs are rarely awarded because of merit, and even the best plans may fail because of the absence of an organization capable of carrying them out. Of even greater seriousness is the general hostility to change frequently exhibited by those in power. This hostility discourages the much-needed foreign investment and innovation necessary for industrialization. Tied in with unfavorable social conditions in most LDCs is the absence of a physical infrastructure. The public facilities or installations essential for economic development, such as roads, water supplies, and public utilities, do not exist.

3. *Rapid Population Growth.* As you can see in Table 27.1, the population in the less developed world is growing at a much faster rate than it is in the more developed world (2.0 percent vs. 0.6 percent). At these rates, the average population in the less developed nations will double in thirty-four years, while it will take over a hundred years to double in the developed nations. Think of the kinds of problems this population explosion will create. Production in less developed countries will have to double in the next thirty-four years just to maintain living standards at present levels!

Remember, too, that life expectancy in the less developed countries is about fifteen years less than in the developed societies. Combined with their high birthrates, lower life expectancy means that the LDCs have a predominantly young population. As a result, over half the population of a typical LDC is too young to work and another quarter is too busy rearing children to work. Thus only one person in four is available to work and must in addition earn enough to care for the other three.

4. *Shortage of Capital.* Because they possess the kinds of factories, tools, and technical know-how necessary to the task of modern production, the developed nations can turn out vast quantities of goods and services. The less developed countries, by contrast, are woefully short of capital. To obtain capital, they must set aside a portion of their production in the form of savings and, at the appropriate

time, *invest* in plant and equipment. The problem is that few people in poor countries can afford to save anything. Saving reduces the meager supply of goods and services even further, thus adding to the people's misery.

Some economists have called the conditions we have just described the "vicious circle of poverty." Because production levels are low, the public must consume the bulk of whatever is produced. Under these circumstances, little can be set aside for savings and investment, and so production remains low. In looking at this "vicious circle of poverty," one economist was moved to comment that the "curse of the poor is their poverty."

5. Poorly Trained Labor Force. In the less developed nations, illiteracy is a major problem. Ways must be found to train workers who can neither read nor write to operate and maintain modern tools and equipment. Technical workers and managers are also in short supply because few people in the work force have had an opportunity to receive long formal training or on-the-job experience.

A PROGRAM FOR THE LESS DEVELOPED COUNTRIES

Economists suggest that the less developed countries follow a number of measures in their efforts to reduce poverty. You may wish to add your own suggestions to the list.

1. Increase Farm Productivity. More than half the total labor force in the LDCs works in agriculture; in the poorest nations, the average is closer to 70 percent. Contrast these percentages with the 6 percent figure for the industrialized world's agricultural labor force. Productivity accounts for the difference. Whereas farms in the more developed nations typically produce a surplus, much of the agriculture in the LDCs consists of *subsistence farming.* Farms operating at subsistence levels produce just enough to feed the farmers and their families. Modern technology enables farmers in the more developed countries to produce far more than their counterparts in the LDCs. If poor nations modernize their farming methods, they will free many workers for service in other forms of production, which in turn could lead to an overall improvement in living standards.

In addition to improved technology, agricultural-productivity programs in the less developed world frequently involve *land reform.* The process of land reform gives those who formerly worked as tenant farmers an opportunity to own the land on which they work. The belief is that farmers who own their land are likely to be more productive than those who work for others.

Old and New Technologies. In Nigeria, a woman carries home a bundle of firewood while others are employed in drilling and extracting oil. How does this picture illustrate both the problems and opportunities of the LDCs?

2. Reduce Population Growth. If a nation's per capita gross national product is to grow, total GNP must increase faster than the population. For this reason, a number of developing nations have introduced family-planning programs. These programs vary from simple publicity campaigns and information sessions to a variety of government-sponsored birth-control programs. Convincing people in poor countries to limit the size of their families is not an easy task. For many people, their children represent a kind of social security. By the time they are ten or eleven years old, these children will be helping the family earn its living. In later years, when the parents are too old to care for themselves, the children will be expected to attend to their parents' needs. Without children to care for them, many elderly people die of hunger or neglect.

3. Accumulate Capital Goods. Modern production requires the application of machinery and tools. Since the less developed countries are unable to manufacture their own equipment, they have to purchase it abroad. They can do so in one of three ways: buy the equipment with their own funds; permit foreign investors to establish businesses on their soil; or accept loans from international agencies or foreign banks.

The Less Developed World

HOW LESS DEVELOPED COUNTRIES PAY THE COSTS OF DEVELOPMENT

LDCs look to the following to provide the capital for their development projects: their own savings, foreign governments, international organizations, and private sources.

1. Savings. About 80 percent of the capital needed for development in less developed countries comes out of their own savings. Closely related is some kind of master plan in which the central government sets forth the goals of its development program.

2. Foreign Governments. The LDCs frequently look to the developed nations for grants and loans to finance development projects. In 1981 the leaders of twenty-two nations met at a conference in Cancun, Mexico, to discuss ways in which help to the developing world could be more effectively distributed. This "North-South" Conference, as it came to be called ("North" for developed, "South" for less developed), failed to arrive at a consensus. But the willingness of the President of the United States and other heads of state to discuss these matters at an international conference was an indication of the seriousness with which they viewed the LDCs' problems.

3. International Organizations. International organizations provide grants, loans, and technical advice to developing nations. A major source of this aid is the United States and its affiliated organizations. Another agency, the International Monetary Fund (IMF), makes loans to solve temporary economic problems. In the early 1980s, a number of LDCs were in deep financial trouble because of their inability to repay loans. (See boxed feature, page 533.) In their plight they looked to the International Monetary Fund for relief. The IMF approach involved two strategies. One was to make loans which enabled financially troubled nations to meet their debt repayments. The other was to require that the nations seeking help take steps to put themselves on a sound financial footing before the loans were granted. These steps involved such things as increasing taxes and reducing expenditures.

The largest single provider of development loans, however, is the World Bank. Low-interest World Bank loans are granted for periods of from fifteen to twenty years. In addition, the International Development Association, a bank affiliate, can make interest-free loans available to the *least* developed nations for as long as fifty years. Other agencies, such as the Asian Development Bank and the African Development Bank, are prepared to make loans to nations in their particular regions.

The Debt Crisis of the Less Developed Countries

In 1982 many less developed countries found themselves hopelessly in debt. They had borrowed some $500 billion from the industrialized nations, and now were unable to repay. In this crisis, the developing nations sought additional financing from foreign banks. "Nothing doing," said the banks. "We can't afford to lend any more money until you pay back what you owe us." To which the LDCs in effect replied, "Unless you grant us additional loans, we will not be able to make payments on our debts."

Three factors had created this crisis. One was the recession in which the world found itself in 1981. This led to a drying up of demand for imports from the LDCs and other nations. A second factor was the record high interest rates available in the United States. This led to a "flight of capital" out of the LDCs as people with surplus funds withdrew them for investment in American securities. The third factor adding to the crisis of the LDCs was the appreciation in the value of the dollar. In effect, this rise made the currencies of the LDCs less valuable since it would now take more of these currencies to buy dollars than before. But most of the loans made to those nations had been in dollars. This meant that the nations had to sell far more of their goods in order to earn enough to pay off their debts.

"Why," you ask, "should it have been our nation's concern if the LDCs were unable to pay their debts?" One very good reason was that in 1983 much of that money was owed to five of our nation's largest banks. Indeed, the amount involved was so large that it was estimated that if Brazil, Mexico, and Argentina were to *default* (fail to meet their obligations), the banks would be put out of business.

In this crisis the world looked to the International Monetary Fund (called by President Reagan the "linchpin of the international financial system") to create a plan for rescuing the debtor nations.

4. *Private Sources.* Private banks and corporations, *if they feel that they have a reasonable chance to earn a profit*, also invest in the less developed countries. For this reason, private sources generally prefer to do business with the stronger economies.

Finally, agencies such as the United States Peace Corps and a variety of church and privately sponsored groups also contribute to the development process. By teaching, assisting in health projects, working on construction sites, and consulting with local leaders, they bring the benefits of technology to the developing nations.

EXERCISES

Multiple Choice

1. Which of the following characteristics does *not* describe an aspect of life in the less developed countries (LDCs)? (*a*) high birthrate (*b*) shortage of capital goods (*c*) widespread poverty (*d*) large industrial labor force.

2. Roads, water supply, and communications networks are part of a nation's (*a*) physical infrastructure (*b*) governmental facilities (*c*) public utilities (*d*) social order.

3. Land reform is frequently suggested as a key to solving some of the economic problems of the LDCs. This reform involves (*a*) the application of scientific farming to agriculture (*b*) the use by farmers of only their most fertile lands (*c*) programs to enable farmers to own land (*d*) soil conservation programs.

4. As compared to the more developed countries, LDCs have (*a*) a larger proportion of children (*b*) a larger proportion of elderly people (*c*) a smaller proportion of children (*d*) a larger proportion of people over forty.

5. Which of the following is an international organization that lends capital to needy nations for development projects? (*a*) Common Market (*b*) International Monetary Fund (*c*) World Bank (*d*) OPEC.

6. In many of the poor, less developed nations, it is frequently necessary for the government to (*a*) encourage people to have large families (*b*) bring about forced savings (*c*) stamp out all private enterprise (*d*) produce only consumer goods.

7. As compared to the developed nations, the population of the world's less developed nations (*a*) has grown somewhat less rapidly (*b*) has grown at about the same rate (*c*) has grown at a faster rate (*d*) has declined.

8. Agriculture is frequently an obstacle to industrialization in a less developed nation because (*a*) a relatively small percentage of the nation's population works on farms (*b*) inefficient methods keep the labor force tied to farms and unavailable for industrial work (*c*) the farms are usually owned by the government (*d*) the farmers do not want to produce more than they need.

9. What is true of labor force participation in the less developed countries as compared to that in the more developed countries? (*a*) It is greater in LDCs. (*b*) It is smaller in LDCs. (*c*) It is about the same in both. (*d*) There is no pattern of labor force participation that distinguishes one group of countries from the other.

10. According to the United Nations, (*a*) more developed countries outnumber less developed countries by about two to one (*b*) more developed countries outnumber LDCs by about four to one (*c*)

there are about the same number in both categories (*d*) LDCs outnumber more developed countries by about four to one.

11. Why do the more developed countries have higher *literacy rates* than the less developed countries? (*a*) People in the LDCs have fewer books to read than people in more developed countries. (*b*) There are more people in more developed countries. (*c*) There are greater educational opportunities in more developed countries. (*d*) Education is not a high priority in the LDCs.

12. Which of the following steps should less developed countries take to break the "vicious circle of poverty" that plagues most of them? (*a*) increase consumption (*b*) accumulate capital goods (*c*) increase loans to foreign countries (*d*) all of the above.

Essay Questions

1. One of the major problems confronting less developed nations is how to amass the capital goods necessary to increase productive output. Capital formation may be financed through *personal savings, taxation, deficit financing,* or *aid from abroad.* (*a*) With reference to *three* of the *italicized* items, explain how they serve to finance capital formation. (*b*) Summarize the problems that a less developed nation seeking to amass capital will have in applying *each* of the methods discussed in (*a*).

2. In seeking solutions to the problems of the less developed nations, economists have focused on the following four areas: (1) population growth (2) land reform, (3) foreign aid, and (4) technical assistance. Describe how *each* of the four items listed above is related to the problems of less developed nations.

3. Use Table 27.1, Measuring the Differences, on page 526. (*a*) Compare the data for *one* less developed country with the data for the United States. (*b*) What do these data indicate about the difference between life in the two countries? (*c*) Identify and explain one step that the less developed country might take to improve unfavorable conditions.

4. A major dilemma facing the less developed countries has been described as the "vicious circle of poverty." (*a*) Describe this problem. (*b*) Identify and explain one solution to this problem. (*c*) With reference to your answer to (*b*), what problems will the LDCs have to overcome in order to implement your suggestion?

5. Identify and explain three reasons why people in more developed countries should be concerned with the problems of people in less developed countries.

Illustrations and Tables

Illustrations

Circular Flow of Money Between the Public and Business (3.1)   53
Circular Flow of Goods and Services (3.2)   53
Circular Flow of Money, Goods, and Services (3.3)   54
Circular Flow of Money, Goods, and Services Between the Government
   and the Public (3.4)   55
Circular Flow of Economic Activity Among the Public, Business, and
   the Government (3.5)   56
Role of Markets in Our Economy (3.6)   58
Business Organizations and Receipts, 1980 (5.1)   100
Organization of a Typical Corporation (5.2)   102
Sources of Corporate Funds, 1980 (6.1)   107
How to Read Stock Market Tables (6.2)   111
How to Read Bond Market Quotations (6.3)   116
Market Price Under Conditions of Monopoly (7.1)   124
Administered Price Under Conditions of Falling Demand (7.3)   135
Interlocking Directorate (8.4)   146
Growth of the Labor Force, 1950–1980 (9.1)   166
Women in the Labor Force, 1900–1980 (9.2)   166
Occupations of Employed Workers, 1950–1980 (9.3)   167
Median Weekly Earnings of Full-Time Workers, 1982 (9.4)   173
Lorenz Curve (9.5)   176
People Living Below the Poverty Line, 1960–1981 (9.6)   177
Women in Selected Occupations, 1982 (9.9)   188
Major Issues in Strikes, 1981 (10.1)   199
Labor Union Membership, as a Total and as a Percent of Nonfarm
   Employment, 1950–1981 (10.2)   203
Work Time Lost Because of Strikes, 1945–1981 (10.3)   204
Work Time Lost Because of Strikes and Unemployment, 1981 (10.4)   204
Growing Importance of Government: 1932, 1957, 1982 (11.1)   214
Combined State and Local Government Budgets, 1980 (11.2)   225
Tax Revenues per Capita, 1960–1981 (12.1)   238
The Underground Economy, 1981 (12.3)   245
Measures of the Money Supply, 1981 (13.2)   262
Number and Assets of Banking Institutions, 1980 (14.1)   268
Structure of the Federal Reserve System (14.2)   280
Districts of the Federal Reserve System (14.3)   282
Purchasing Power of the Dollar: What a 1967 Dollar Was Worth in
   Selected Years (15.1)   291
Phillips Curve (15.2)   299
Purchasers of the Gross National Product, 1982 (16.1)   307
National Income Accounts, 1982 (16.2)   310
United States Gross National Product in 1972 Dollars and Current
   Dollars, 1978–1982 (16.3)   319
Gross National Product for Five Countries, 1980 (16.4)   320
Per Capita Gross National Product for Five Countries, 1980 (16.5)   320
United States Business Activity Since 1905 (17.1)   321

536

Phases of the Business Cycle (17.2)   322
Aggregate Demand and Its Significance (17.3)   331
Fluctuations in Demand by Consumers and Producers, 1951–1981 (17.4)   332
Personal Consumption Expenditures and Gross Investment, 1951–1981 (17.5)   334
Federal Debt, 1940–1982 (18.1)   348
Laffer Curve (18.2)   361
Consumer Credit, 1930–1980 (19.4)   384
Advertising Expenditure per Person, 1940–1980 (20.2)   401
Rural-Urban Population Changes, in Percentages, 1790–1980 (21.1)   410
Rates of Violent Crime in Rural Areas, Suburbs, and Urban Areas, 1967 and 1980 (21.2)   418
City Government Expenditures per Person, by Population Size, 1981 (21.3)   420
Federal Aid to State and Local Governments, 1970–1983 (21.4)   423
Net Farm Income, in 1967 Dollars, 1974–1982 (22.1)   428
Changes in American Farming, 1950–1980 (22.2)   429
Distribution of Farm Income, 1980 (22.3)   430
Value of Price-Supported Farm Products Owned by the Government, 1970–1982 (22.4)   438
Unemployment Rates for Selected Groups, 1982 (23.1)   451
External Costs of Pollution (23.2)   455
Tariffs in United States History, 1820–1980 (24.1)   477
The Ford *Fiesta*'s International Flavor (24.2)   479
United States Money Supply and Supply of Eurodollars, 1972–1982 (25.1)   496

Tables

Competition in Selected Industries, 1981 (7.2)   141
Principal United States Antitrust Laws (8.1)   163
Median Weekly Earnings of Full-Time Workers, 1981 (9.1)   168
Median Income of Families, by Selected States, 1979 (9.2)   174
Median Personal Income, by Sex and Educational Attainment, 1970–1980 (9.3)   174
Percent of Income Received by Each Fifth and the Top 5 Percent of Families, 1950–1981 (9.4)   175
Poverty Status, by Households, 1981 (9.5)   177
Average Weekly Earnings of Nonagricultural Workers (10.1)   206
Receipts and Outlays of the Federal Government (11.1)   218
Federal Budget, 1982 (11.2)   219
Government Spending in Postwar Years (11.3)   224
State and Local Government Finances, 1946 and 1980 (11.4)   227
Tax Rate Schedule Y, Married Taxpayers and Qualifying Widows and Widowers (12.1)   235
Tax Table for Persons With Taxable Incomes of Less than $50,000 (12.2)   236
Federal Personal Income Taxes Collected, by Income Range, 1980 (12.3)   237
Money Supply, 1982 (13.1)   261
Progress of $10,000 Through the Banking System (14.2)   276
Consumer Prices and Purchasing Power, 1940–1982 (15.1)   290
National Income in 1982 (16.1)   310
Gross National Product for Selected Years, 1929–1982 (16.2)   314

Gross National Product of Selected Countries, 1980 (16.3)   315
Fiscal and Monetary Policies and the Business Cycle (18.1)   358
Options for Savings in Banks and Credit Unions (19.1)   372
Types of Checking Accounts (19.2)   376
Credit Options in a New-Car Purchase (19.3)   387
Consumer Credit-Protection Laws (19.4)   389
How Consumers Spent Their Dollars in 1980 (20.2)   394
Population of the Twenty Largest Metropolitan Areas in 1980 (21.1)   412
Population of the Suburbs of Five Major Cities, 1950 and 1980 (21.2)   413
Money Income of Families in Metropolitan Areas, 1980 (21.3)   415
City Government Revenues, 1980 (21.4)   421
World Reserves of Selected Mineral Resources, 1976 (23.1)   453
Gross Sales and Foreign Revenues of Leading Multinational
    Corporations Compared to Gross National Products of Selected
    Nations, 1980 (24.1)   480
Major United States Companies With Foreign Ownership (24.2)   481
Foreign Exchange Rates on July 11, 1984 (25.1)   487
United States Balance of Payments, 1982 (25.2)   493
Average Work Time Required to Purchase Selected Consumer Goods in
    Washington and Moscow, 1982 (26.2)   524
The More Developed and Less Developed Countries—Measuring the
    Differences, 1980 (27.1)   526

Glossary

accelerator   the effect of changes in spending upon investment.

administered price   a selling price established by business, labor, or government, rather than by the forces of supply and demand.

advantage   the ability of one nation to produce a good at lower cost than another nation.

aggregate demand   the total of all the spending by all sectors of the nation's economy: consumers, business and government.

antitrust law   a federal act that prohibits business monopoly and promotes competition.

arbitration   the process of settling a labor-management dispute in which an impartial third party renders a binding decision.

asset   anything of value that is owned by an individual or a business.

automatic stabilizer   a feature built into the economic system that automatically compensates for changes in the business cycle.

automation   the substitution of modern machinery for human labor in the production process.

balance of payments   a financial statement that summarizes a nation's economic transactions with the rest of the world.

balance of trade   the difference between the cost of a nation's merchandise imports and the value of its merchandise exports.

balance sheet   a financial report that summarizes the assets, liabilities, and net worth of an individual or organization.

barter   the exchange of a good or service for another good or service.

base year   a year assigned a value of 100, to which an index number is compared.

board of directors   the elected representatives of the stockholders of a corporation.

bond   a certificate issued by units of government and corporations in exchange for long-term loans.

budget   a plan for dealing with future income and expenses.

bulls and bears   the nicknames given to stock market speculators. *Bulls* expect to profit from an increase in stock values while *bears* expect to profit from a decrease in stock values.

business cycle   the fluctuations in a nation's economic activity.

buying long   a speculative transaction in which an investor hopes to profit by selling securities at a higher price than originally paid for them.

capital   the machines, tools, buildings, and other things created by people that are used to produce goods and services. Capital may also refer to money or other financial assets of a business.

capital gain   the profit realized from the sale of an asset.

capitalism   an economic system in which most of the resources of production are privately owned, and most economic decisions are made by individuals and business firms.

cartel   a group of sellers who formally agree among themselves to restrict output so as to control the prices of their product.

certificate of deposit (CD)   a savings instrument, similar to a bond, that is available to depositors in banks and thrift institutions.

check   a depositor's order directing a bank to pay a specified sum to a designated party.

checkable account   a bank account that gives the depositor the privilege of writing checks against deposits. Common checkable accounts are demand deposits and negotiable orders of withdrawal.

closed shop   a business in which, as agreed upon in a contract, only workers belonging to a specified union may be hired.

collective bargaining   a series of discussions between representatives of a union and representatives of management to arrive at a contract that will spell out the terms of employment.

command economy   an economic system in which most decisions are made by a central authority.

commercial bank   a privately owned bank that provides a wide array of financial services, especially to business customers.

common stock   a share of ownership in a corporation.

communism   the economic system of the Soviet Union, China, and other Communist countries. It stresses public ownership of the means of production, and decision-making by a central authority.

comparative advantage   the principle that a nation should specialize in the production of those goods and services in which its *opportunity costs are lowest* (it is most efficient) and trade its surplus goods and services for the things it needs.

competition   the rivalry among buyers and sellers for goods and services.

concentration ratio   the percentage of an industry's output that is produced by its four largest firms.

conglomerate merger   a merger which combines firms that produce unrelated products.

constant dollar   the value of the dollar, which has been adjusted to eliminate the effects of inflation or deflation.

consumer   a person who uses goods and services to satisfy needs and wants.

Consumer Price Index (CPI)   the series of index numbers measuring changes in the level of prices over a period of time; also frequently described as the "cost of living index."

consumerism   a movement that seeks to educate American consumers as to their legal rights in the marketplace.

corporation   a business chartered under state or federal law and owned by its stockholders.

cost-push inflation   a rise in the level of prices caused by an increase in the cost of doing business.

countervailing power   the theory that the market power of one powerful economic group may offset the power of another group.

creditor   a person or institution (such as a bank) to whom money is owed.

currency   the money issued by the federal government.

current dollar   the value of a dollar at a particular point in time.

debt   the money owed by a person, institution, or nation.

deflation   a general decline in prices.

demand   the quantity of a product or service that would be purchased at a particular price.

demand deposit   a deposit in a commerical bank which can be withdrawn at once (on demand) upon presentation of a check; a checking account.

demand-pull inflation   a rise in the level of prices caused by an increase in demand.

depreciation   a decline in the value of a capital asset caused by use, the passage of time, or both.

depression   a serious, long-lasting decline in a nation's business activity.

devaluation   a reduction in the price of one currency in terms of the currencies of other nations.

diminishing marginal utility   the principle that each added unit of a product or service will be less satisfying than the previously added unit.

diminishing returns   the point at which the extra output resulting from the addition of more units of a productive factor (natural resources, labor, capital, or management) will begin to decline.

direct tax   a tax paid to the government by the person or business that is taxed; a tax that cannot be shifted.

discount rate   the interest rate on loans that the Federal Reserve charges its member banks.

discretionary stabilizer   a monetary or fiscal tool that the government may use in order to regulate the economy.

diseconomy of scale   an increase in the cost of doing business that results when a business has grown too large.

disposable personal income   the amount left to individuals after taxes are deducted from their earnings.

dividend   a share of profits paid by a corporation to its stockholders.

division of labor   the breaking down of the production process into small tasks, each performed by a different worker.

durable good   a product that is expected to last several years.

econometrics   a branch of economics that uses mathematics and statistics in solving economic problems.

economic growth   an increase in the output of a nation's goods and services.

economic indicator   a set of statistics about the performance of a sector of the nation's economy; often classified as *coincident, leading,* and *lagging.*

economic system   the way in which a nation organizes itself to answer the fundamental economic questions of *what* to produce, *how* to produce, and *who* shall receive its goods and services.

economy of scale   a reduction in the cost of doing business that results from increases in the size of operations.

elasticity of demand   the extent to which total spending for an item will fluctuate with changes in price.

elasticity of supply   the extent to which the total spending for an item will fluctuate with changes in supply.

eminent domain   the right of government to acquire private property for public use by paying a reasonable price to the owner.

entitlement program   a government social program that provides monetary payments whose purpose is to relieve individuals of the burdens associated with old age, unemployment, and illness.

entrepreneur   a person who gathers together the factors of production to create and operate a business enterprise in the hope of earning profits.

equation of exchange   MV = PQ, where M equals the money supply, V equals velocity, P equals the average price paid, and Q equals the quantity of goods and services produced.

equilibrium price   the price at which the supply and demand curves intersect. At this price the quantity of a good or service supplied equals the amount demanded.

Eurodollar   a dollar account carried in a bank outside the United States.

exchange rate   the amount of one currency that can be purchased for a certain amount of another currency.

excise tax   a tax on the manufacture, sale, or use of a good or service.

externality   a cost or benefit of economic activity that is paid for or enjoyed by those who neither produced or consumed it.

factor of production   a resource that is used to produce goods and services. Human resources, natural resources, capital, and management are factors of production.

Federal Deposit Insurance Corporation (FDIC)   the federal government agency that insures checking account deposits and savings.

Federal Reserve System (Fed)   the United States central banking system.

fiscal policy   the use by the government of its powers to tax and spend in order to regulate the economy.

five-year plan   a long-range projection of national economic activity, used by many socialist countries.

fixed cost (overhead cost)   a cost of doing business that remains more or less constant regardless of the volume of business.

floating exchange rate   the value of a nation's currency, which moves up and down through the interaction of the laws of supply and demand.

free enterprise system   *see* capitalism.

fringe benefit   the compensation received by employees in addition to wages; benefits include pensions, vacations, and health insurance.

full employment   the condition in which all of an economy's resources are being used.

General Agreement on Tariffs and Trade (GATT)   an organization of over a hundred nations that promotes trade among nations.

good   a tangible item of value.

grant-in-aid   a payment by one level of government to another that is "earmarked" (to be used) for a particular purpose.

Gresham's Law   the principle that "cheap money drives out dear money." When two or more kinds of money are in circulation, the one that is deemed more valuable will be hoarded and disappear from circulation.

gross national product (GNP)   the total value of all goods and services produced by a national economy in a single year.

holding company   a corporation that has controlling interest in the shares of one or more other corporations.

horizontal merger   a merger of two or more firms producing competing products.

imperfect competition   a market situation that combines elements of pure competition and monopoly.

index number   a number that shows percentage change from a base.

indirect tax   a tax that can be shifted from the person or business taxed to someone else, who is frequently unaware of that fact.

infant industry   an industry which, because it is newly developed, is unable to compete with the same industry of other nations.

inflation   a general rise in prices.

inflationary gap   the excess of aggregate demand over total output at full employment.

infrastructure   the physical capital that supports a society's activities; includes roads, power lines, water facilities, and schools.

injunction   a court order to cease a certain activity.

input-output analysis   an examination of the ways in which the industries within an economy affect one another.

interest   the money that borrowers must pay for the use of someone else's money.

interlocking directorate   a situation in which the same people sit on the boards of directors of competing firms.

International Monetary Fund   an international agency that seeks to promote global trade by facilitating the exchange of one nation's currency for that of another.

investment   an expenditure that adds to the supply of capital; includes spending for factories, machinery, tools, equipment, and inventories.

invisible hand   a concept stated by Adam Smith in *The Wealth of Nations:* in their pursuit of profits, business people are often led into activities that benefit society as well as themselves.

L   the broadest measure of the nation's money supply; consists of *M3* plus savings bonds and certain private and government securities.

Laffer Curve   the graphic model used to prove that, under certain circumstances, a tax cut will generate increased revenue.

laissez-faire   a French expression ("let them do") given to an economic doctrine popularized by Adam Smith: government ought not to interfere with the running of the nation's economy.

legal tender   the currency that must by law be accepted in payment of debt; sometimes referred to as "lawful money."

less developed country (LDC)   a nation in which the quality of life—as seen in life expectancy, per capita GNP, literacy rate, infant mortality rate, and daily calorie supply—is significantly poorer than it is in a more developed nation. The countries of North America and Europe, the Soviet Union, Japan, Australia, and New Zealand are classified as "more developed"; all others are classified as "less developed."

liability   an obligation or debt.

limited liability   the legal exemption of stockholders from the debts of the corporation. Therefore, the losses that they might suffer are *limited* to the amount of their investment.

liquidity   the ease with which a form of savings can be converted to cash.

lockout   the shutting down of a plant by management in the hope of bringing the workers to agree to its contract terms.

Lorenz Curve　a graph that compares income distribution as it actually is with what income distribution would be if everyone received an equal share.

M1　the nation's money supply, as measured by the total currency, checkbook money, and traveler's checks in circulation on any given day.

M2　the nation's money supply, as measured by M1 plus individual savings accounts, money market funds, and certain foreign assets.

M3　the nation's money supply, as measured by M2 plus business and other large savings accounts.

macroeconomics　the study of forces affecting a nation's economy as a whole; deals with aggregate (total) quantities and economic growth.

margin　a down payment required when purchasing securities on credit.

marginal utility　the additional usefulness received from each added unit of a product or service.

market　a place where goods and services are bought and sold.

market price　*see* equilibrium price.

market system　an economic system in which the free operation of supply, demand, and market price will determine how goods and services are produced and distributed.

mediation　the process in which an impartial party, or mediator, tries to bring both sides in a labor dispute into agreement; suggestions offered by the mediator are not binding.

mercantilism　a set of economic theories and practices that were generally accepted from the sixteenth to the eighteenth centuries. Mercantilism held that a nation's wealth could be measured by its stock of precious metals (gold and silver).

merger　the absorption of one or more firms by another.

Metropolitan Statistical Area　an urbanized region consisting of cities of 50,000 or more people and their surrounding suburbs.

microeconomics　the study of those economic forces that act upon individual parts of the economy such as its business firms, households, and work force.

minimum wage　the lowest wage that an employer may by law pay an employee.

mixed economy　an economic system that encompasses private and public ownership of the means of production, and central planning and the free market, in allocating the nation's resources.

monetary policy　the actions taken by the Federal Reserve System to regulate the nation's supply of money and credit.

money　anything that is generally accepted in payment for goods and services; *see* M1.

money-market fund　a mutual fund that buys and sells money market instruments (interest-bearing IOUs issued by government agencies, banks, and corporations).

monopolistic competition　a market situation in which there are many firms selling similar items on the basis of product differentiation.

monopoly　a market situation in which there is only one seller.

monopsony　a market situation in which there is only one buyer.

mortgage　a pledge of property as security for a loan.

multinational corporation　a firm that conducts its business in two or more countries.

multiplier   a numerical factor by which an increase in investment or spending is multiplied to find the effect on national income.

mutual fund   a corporation that uses the proceeds from the sale of its stock to purchase the securities of other corporations.

national debt   the money owned by the federal government.

national income   the total of incomes earned by individuals and business firms in the production of the GNP.

natural monopoly   an industry in which competition would be wasteful or against the public interest.

natural resource   a material obtained from land, sea, and air; a factor of production.

negotiable order of withdrawal (now account)   an interest-bearing checking account offered by banks and thrift institutions.

net worth   the value of a business as measured by the excess of its assets over its liabilities.

oligopoly   a market dominated by only a few sellers.

oligopsony   a market dominated by only a few buyers.

open market committee   the agency of the Federal Reserve System that directs the purchase and sale of government securities.

open shop   a business or factory in which the employer is free to hire either union or nonunion workers.

opportunity cost   the amount of goods and services that must be forfeited (done without) in order to obtain another good or service.

Organization of Petroleum Exporting Countries (OPEC)   a cartel of non-Western oil-producing nations.

overhead cost   a fixed cost.

paradox of thrift   the assertion that if individuals increase the level of their savings, society as a whole will have less to save.

parity   the price that will give farmers the same purchasing power from the sale of their goods that they enjoyed during certain base years.

partnership   an unincorporated business owned by two or more people.

Phillips Curve   a graph illustrating the tradeoff between inflation and unemployment; when one is reduced, the other increases.

preferred stock   the shares of stock that are entitled to a fixed dividend before profits are distributed to holders of common stock. Holders of this stock receive their shares of the proceeds of liquidation before holders of common stocks.

price   *see* equilibrium price.

price leadership   a characteristic of an industry that is an oligopoly: the firms match each other's price increases and decreases.

private property   a basic right in capitalist societies which allows individuals to own property and use it in any lawful manner that they choose.

product differentiation   the creation by sellers of the appearance that their products are different from those of their competitors, while they in fact are not different.

production possibilities curve   a graph showing the various combinations of goods and services that an economy might produce if all its resources were fully and effectively employed.

productivity   a measure of the efficiency of production; most often expressed in terms of *output per worker per hour.*

profit   the income that remains after the costs of doing business have been deducted from receipts of the sale of goods and services.

profit motive   the incentive that leads people to accept the risks of doing business.

progressive income tax   a tax that increases in the percentage paid as the taxpayer's income increases.

promissory note   a written promise to pay a specific sum of money at a particular place and time.

proportional tax   a tax that applies the same rate to all persons' taxes regardless of income.

protective tariff   a tax whose primary purpose is to protect domestic production from foreign competition

proxy   a certificate signed by a stockholder authorizing others to cast ballots belonging to the shares of stock.

public utility   an industry legally considered to be in the public interest. Typically, public utilities provide electrical power, communication services, and transportation.

purchasing power   the measure of the amount of goods and services that the dollar can buy.

pure (perfect) competition   a market situation in which there are many buyers and sellers; no one of them acting alone can affect the price.

real income   the purchasing power of income, expressed in constant dollars.

real property   land or anything more or less permanently attached to it, such as buildings.

recession   a period of general decline in the nation's economy.

recessionary gap   the amount by which aggregate demand falls short of the total needed to sustain full employment.

regressive income tax   a tax that takes a larger proportion of the earnings of people with lower incomes than it does of those with high incomes.

rent   the payment for use of an asset, especially land.

resource   *see* natural resource.

reserve ratio (reserve requirement)   the percentage of its total deposits that a bank is required to keep in its Federal Reserve district bank or as cash in its vaults.

revenue-sharing   the funds collected by one level of government that are shared with another level.

revenue tariff   a tax whose primary purpose is to generate income.

right-to-work law   a state law that makes it illegal to require that workers join labor unions.

S corporation   a small corporation with a partnership's tax benefits.

selling short   a stock transaction in which a speculator (commonly called a "bear") hopes to profit from a decline in the price of a security.

service   an intangible item of value, such as medical care.

single proprietorship   an unincorporated business owned by one person.

socialism   an economic system in which the means of production are owned by the state.

Special Drawing Rights (SDRs)   the credits to the accounts of member nations in the International Monetary Fund, which can be used to purchase foreign currencies.

stagflation   a period of recession and inflation.

standard of living   the quantity and quality of goods and services available to an individual or a society.

stock   a certificate representing ownership in a corporation.

strike   a work stoppage by a firm's employees.

supply   the quantity of a product or service offered for sale at a particular price.

supply-side economics   an economic theory that calls for a shift in the focus of government from the demand (consumption) side of the economy to the supply (production) side.

tariff   a tax on imports.

tax   a monetary assessment imposed by the government on people or property for public purposes.

technology   the use of tools, materials, machines, and power sources to enable workers to perform tasks more easily and productively.

thrift institution ("thrift")   a savings institution specializing in home mortgage loans as well as many other banking services.

tight money   a Federal Reserve policy that attempts to slow down the growth of the money supply.

traditional economy   an economic system in which resources are allocated in accordance with long-established procedures.

transfer payment   a money payment by the government to an individual for which nothing is received in return. Welfare, social security, and unemployment insurance are transfer payments.

union shop   a firm under contract with a union in which nonunion members may be hired on condition that they join the union.

unlimited liability   a disadvantage of the single proprietorship and the partnership: the personal property of any or all of the owners may be taken to pay the debts of the business.

velocity   the number of times that a unit of currency is spent in a given period.

vertical merger   a consolidation of two or more businesses that are each other's suppliers or customers.

Index

Ability to pay, and taxes, 233
Absolute advantage, 466–469
Accelerator, 337–338
Ad valorem tariff, 470
Administered prices, 134–135
Advantage: absolute, 466–469; comparative, 466–469, 472
Advertising: and consumer, 401–405; controversy over, 402–404; living with, 404–405
Affirmative action, 183
African Development Bank, 532
Agency shop, 194
Aggregate demand, 330–331, 360, 362, 444; adjustment by government, 336, 450; Keynes on, 329
Agricultural Adjustment Administration (AAA), 433–434
Agricultural products, *see* Farm products
Agriculture: *see* Farm entries
Agriculture and Food Act of 1981, 437
Aid to Families with Dependent Children (AFDC), 181
American Federation of Labor (AFL), 191, 192–193
American Telephone and Telegraph Company (AT&T), 152, 154
"Americans versus cheap foreign workers" argument, 472–474
Annual percentage rate (APR), 387
Annuity policy, 382
Anticipated return, of savings, 370–371
Antitrust laws, 149–154
Arbitration, in strikes, 195, 202
Asian Development Bank, 532
Assets: of a business, 117; of a commercial bank, 273–274
Attachment of wages, 385
Automatic stabilizers, 345, 346–347
Automation, 445–449

Balance of payments, 491–495; favorable, 494; unfavorable, 494
Balance of payments statement, 492, 493
Balance of trade, 471–472
Balance sheet, 117–118; of commercial bank, 272–275
Balanced budget, 217

Balanced Growth Act (Humphrey-Hawkins Act), 344
Banks: commercial, *see* Commercial banks; district, of Federal Reserve System, 281, 282–285; and economy, 279; investment, 110; members, of Federal Reserve System, 281; regulation of, 278–279; safety of, 277–279; savings, mutual, 270
Banking: business of, 268–269; central, 280; origins of, 267–268; *see also* Federal Reserve System
Banking reserves, 282–283
Banking system: contraction of deposits by, 277; expansion of deposits by, 275–277
Barter, 255
"Bears," 115
Benefits received, and taxes, 232
Better Business Bureau, 396–397
Big business, and government control, 142–160; *see also* Economies and diseconomies of scale
Bimetallic money standard, 264
Blank endorsement, 377–378
Block grants, to cities, 422
Board of directors, of corporation, 101
Board of Governors, of Federal Reserve System, 281
Bonds, 109–110, 374; government, 110; purchase and sale of, 110–113, 115–116
Boycott, 199–200
Bretton Woods system, 489–490, 491
Brokerage firm, 113
Budget: federal, *see* Federal budget; personal, 392–394
Budget Office, 218
"Bulls," 114
Bureau of Printing and Engraving, 259, 263
Business(es): automation and, 447–448; of banking, 268–269; big, *see* Big business; crowding-out effect on, 356; government concern for, 448; opposition of, to labor unions, 191; S corporation, 99–100
Business combinations, 143–149
Business cycle(s), 321–323; causes of, 326–327, 330

Business firms: inflation and, 294–295; organization of, 93–103

Business investment, fluctuation of, 333–335

Business organizations, and receipts, 100

Business spending: GNP and, 308, 333, 334; influencing of, through taxation, 231

Business tax, 249

Buying long, 114

Calorie supply, daily, per capita, 527

Capital: and credit, 388; definition of, 3–4; deteriorating, in metropolitan areas, 419; human, government investment in, 182–185; as resource, 72; shortage of, in LDCs, 529–530

Capital account, 494

Capital formation, 4, 448–449

Capital gains, 237

Capital goods, 3; in LDCs, program for accumulation of, 531

Capital growth, 114

Capital investment, and productivity, 75

Capital stock, 274

Capitalism: definition of, 46; versus socialism, 503

Cartels, 146

Carter, Jimmy, 300

Caveat emptor, 117, 405

Celler-Kefauver Antimerger Act (1950), 151–152

Census Bureau, 414

Central banking, see Federal Reserve System

Certificate of deposit (CD), 371, 373

Chamber of Commerce of the United States, 202

Charge accounts, 385–386

Chattel mortgage contract, 385

Checkbook money, 260, 283

Checking accounts, 376–378

Checkoff, unions and, 194

Checks: collection by district banks, 283–284; traveler's, 260–261

Chrysler Corporation, 50, 208

Circular flow, of economic activity, 52–54; government and, 54–56

Cities, economics of, 409–424; see also Metropolitan areas

Civil Rights Act of 1964, 183

Clayton Antitrust Act of 1914, 144, 150–151, 153

Closed shop, 198

Coincident indicators, 324

Coins, 259, 263

Collective bargaining, 190, 195–197

Collusion, under oligopoly, 134

COMECON, 520

Command economy, 9, 504

Commercial bank(s), 269; balance sheet of, 272–275; and creation of money, 270–277; expansion of deposits by, 274–275

Commissions, regulatory, 405

Commodity inflation, 298

Common Market (European Economic Community), 478

Common stocks, 108, 375, 378

Communism: market, in Hungary, 520; in Soviet Union, 514–517; and withering away of state, 513

Communist League, 512

Communist Manifesto, 512

Comparative advantage, 466–469, 472

Comparison shopping, 396

Compensation of employees, and GNP, 311

Competition, 48; and economic policy, 343; imperfect, 123; monopolistic, see Monopolistic competition; pure, 34, 122–123

Compound interest, 375

Computers, 446

Concentration ratio, 140–141

Conditional sales contract, 385

Congress of Industrial Organizations (CIO), 192–193

Conspicuous consumption, 404

Constant dollars, 427, 443; GNP in, 313–315

Consumer(s), 1; advertising and, 401–405; and GNP, 307–309, 333; income management for, 392–394; information for, 396–397; protection for, 397, 400; and savings, 370–375, 378–380; shopping guidelines for, 394–396; and utility regulation, 158–159

Consumer credit, 383–384; kinds of, 385–387

Consumer Price Index, 290–291

Consumer Product Safety Commission, 400, 405

Consumer sovereignty, 48–49

Consumerism, 400–401

Consumption, 1

Contract(s): and consumers, 396; freedom of, 47; tying, 151; union, 196–197

Control(s): currency, 470; direct, 300; export, 471; government, big business and, 142–160; qualitative, of Federal Reserve System, 357–358

Coolidge, Calvin, 205
Copyrights, 124–125
Corporate profits, and GNP, 311
Corporate securities, 108–110
Corporation(s), 96–103; advantages of, 97–99; disadvantages of, 99–100; funds obtained by, 106–119; large, organization of, 100–103; multinational, see Multinational corporations
Corn Laws, 79
Corporate income tax, 242, 244–246
Cost(s): of development, of LDCs, 532, 534; external or social, of pollution, 454; of government, paying for, 230; internal, of pollution, 454; opportunity, 5–6, 14; of resources, 88; selling, under monopolistic competition, 133
Cost of living, rising, wages and, 194
Cost-push inflation, 297–298; government and, 299–300
Council of Economic Advisers, 184
Counterfeiting, 257
Countervailing power, 158–160
Credit: consumer, see Consumer credit; big business access to, 83; regulation of, by Federal Reserve, 351–357; shopping for, 387–388
Credit cards, 386
Credit rating, 388–389
Credit unions, 270
Creditors, of corporation, 99
Crime and corruption, in metropolitan areas, 418–419
Crowding-out effect, on business, 356
Cumulative preferred stock, 109
Currency, 257–260; district banks and provision of, 283; production and distribution of, 263
Currency controls, 470
Current account, 492–494
Current dollars, 313
Cycles, business, 321–323, 326–327, 330
Cyclical unemployment, 452

Debenture bonds, 109
Debreu, Gerard, 11
Debt, national, fiscal policy and, 347–348
Debt, personal, and inflation, 295–296
Debt crisis, of LDCs, 533
Deductions, on taxable income, 238
Defense, national, 213–214, 220
Deficit spending, controversy over, 349–350
Deficits, in balance of payments, 495
Deflation, 289, 291
Demand, 20–30; aggregate, see Aggregate demand; decrease in, 27–29; elasticity of, 24–30; for farm products, 437; for goods and services, and demand for labor, 170; increase in, 27–29, 444; inelastic, see Inelastic demand; for labor, 170; Law of, 21–23, 169; and market price, 37–38; mass production and, 466; supply and, see Supply and demand
Demand curve, 21, 22
Demand deposits, 260, 269, 271, 283
Demand-pull inflation, 296–297; government and, 298–299
Demand schedule, 21
Department of Agriculture, 400
Department of Housing and Urban Development (HUD), 422
Department of Justice, 152, 153, 161, 162, 208
Department of Labor, 290
Department of the Treasury, 259, 263
Department of Transportation, 414
Deposit insurance, 277–278
Deposits: contraction of, by banking system, 277; demand, see Demand deposits; expansion of, 274–277; as liabilities, 274; time, 269
Depreciation, 4, 106
Depression, economic, 13, 322–323; see also Great Depression
Development: of LDCs, costs of, 532, 534; research, and by-products, 83
Dictatorship of the proletariat, 513
Diminishing marginal utility, 23–26
Diminishing Returns, Law of, 77, 80–81
Direct taxes, 250
Disability payments, under social security, 222
Discount rate, changing of, by Federal Reserve, 354–355
Discounts, 271–272; quantity, 83
Discretionary fiscal policy, 345–346
Discrimination: and wages, 173–174; efforts to reduce, 182–183
Disposable Personal Income (DPI), and GNP, 312, 333
District banks, of Federal Reserve System, 282–285
Dividends, 108, 114, 370
Division of labor, 81–83
Double taxation, of corporation, 99
Draft (check), 377
Durable goods, 307

Econometric models, 507, 510
Economic growth, 13; controversy over, 452–453, 457–459; definition of, 442–

443; government and, 450–452; growth of government and, 217; importance of, 443–444; ingredients of, 444, 448–449; zero, 457

Economic indicators, 305, 324–325

Economic planners, tools of, 507, 510

Economic Recovery Tax Act of 1981, 345

Economic society, interdependence of, 51

Economic system, United States, institutions of, 46–49

Economic systems, comparison of, 503–504, 520–521

Economics, definition of, 1

Economics of Imperfect Competition, The, 130

Economies and diseconomies of scale, 81–83, 88

Education: and determination of wages, 174, 175; in federal budget, 220; support of, by government, 452; state and local expenditures for, 226, 227

Elasticity: of demand, 24–30, 295; of supply, 33–34

Elderly, the, poverty and, 180

Eminent domain, 47

Employees: compensation of, and GNP, 311; public, and right to strike, 205–207

Employment, and economic policy, 344

Employment Act of 1946, 13, 184, 329, 343

Endorsements, 377–379

Endowment policy, 382

Energy consumption, in LDCs, 527

Engel, Ernst, 233

Engel's Law, 233, 234

Engels, Friedrich, 512

Entrepreneurs, 4

Environmental decay, 452, 457–459, 461

Equal Employment Opportunity Commission, 183

Equal pay for equal work, 193

Equilibrium price, 34, 35

Equity financing, 107–108

Escalator clause, 194

Essay on the Principle of Population, An, 178–179

Estate taxes, 246

Eurodollars, 496–498

European Economic Community (EEC), 478

Exchange, quantity equation of, 352–353

Exchange rates, 486–487; determination of, 488–491; floating, 490, 491

Excise taxes, 246

Exemptions, 238

Export controls, 471

Exports, net, 308–309, 330

Extended-credit accounts, 385–386

External costs, of pollution, 454

Externalities, 66

Exxon, 480, 483

Fact-finding, in strikes, 202

Factor supply, 465–466

Factors of production, 1, 2–4; proper proportions of, 76–77, 80–81

Fair Labor Standards Act of 1938, 192

Fair return, to utilities, 156

Fairness, in tax system, 231

Farm problem, 430–433; in 1980s and beyond, 437–438

Farm production, United States, 427–430

Farm productivity: increasing, 409–410; in LDCs, programs to increase, 530

Farm products: inelastic demand for, 430, 431, 437; inelastic supply of, 431–432

Farmers, government subsidies and, 433–438, 440

Farming, subsistence, 530

Fed, *see* Federal Reserve System

Federal agencies, and consumers, 396

Federal budget, 217–221, 224; expenses in, 218–221, 224; inflexibility of, 360

Federal Communications Commission (FCC), 403, 405

Federal Deposit Insurance Corporation (FDIC), 278, 371

Federal Housing Administration (FHA), 422

Federal Insurance Contributions Act (FICA), 246

Federal Open Market Committee, 281

Federal protection, for consumers, 397, 400

Federal Reserve notes, 259

Federal Reserve System (Fed), 259, 263, 279–285, 296, 298, 350–351, 494, 496; economic activity and, 285; historical background of, 279–280; operation of, 282–285; qualitative controls of, 357–358; regulation of money supply by, 351–358; reserve account with, 273; structure of, 280–282

Federal Savings and Loan Insurance Corporation (FSLIC), 371

Federal taxes, 234–239, 242, 244–247
Federal Trade Commission (FTC), 50, 400, 403, 405
Federal Trade Commission Act of 1914, 150, 151, 152, 153
Fiat currency standard, 264
Fiat money, 258, 264
Fiber optics, 446
Fifth Amendment to Constitution, 47
Finance charges, 387
Finances, state and local, 224–226
Financial statements, 117–119
First-level holding companies, 145
Fiscal assistance, in federal budget, 221
Fiscal policy, 344–347; limitations of, 358–360; and national debt, 347–348; summary of, 358
Fiscal year, 217
Five-year plans, 515
Fixed incomes, inflation and, 293–294
Flat tax, 239
Food and Drug Administration (FDA), 397
Food Stamps Program, 181
Ford, Gerald, 300
Forecasting and timing difficulties: and fiscal policy, 358–359; and monetary policy, 360
Foreign governments, and development costs of LDCs, 532
Foreign-owned multinational corporations, 480–481
Foreign trade, importance of, 469; *see also* International trade, World trade
Fractional currency, 259
Fractional reserve banking, 271
Franchise(s), 50, 155
Franklin, Benjamin, 340
Free enterprise system, 46, 47, 343
Free world political leadership, economic growth and, 443–444
Freedom, economic, 12
Freedom of contract, 47
Frictional unemployment, 450
Friedman, Milton, 456
Fringe benefits, unions and, 195
Frisch, Ragnar, 456
Full employment, 323, 330–331; Keynes on, 328–329; promotion of, by government, 450–452
Funds: money-market, 373–374; mutual, 378–380; obtained by corporations, 106–119; transfer of, district banks and, 284–285

Galbraith, John Kenneth, 158

General Agreement on Tariffs and Trade (GATT), 476–477
General Motors, 153, 480, 482
General revenue-sharing grants, 422
General Theory of Employment, Interest, and Money, The, 328–329
Ghetto areas, 417
Gift taxes, 246
Gilder, George, 458
Ginny Maes, 422
"Givebacks," economic recession and, 207–208
Global economy, 463
Global 2000 Report, 453
Globalization of business, multinational corporations and, 478–483
GNP, *see* Gross National Product
Goals, economic, of society, 12–13
Gold exchange standard, 489–490, 491
Gold standard, 264, 488–489
Gompers, Samuel, 191, 205
Goods, 1; durable, 307; nondurable, 307
Goods and services: demand for, and demand for labor, 170; and GNP, 305–306, 312–313; government purchase of, 308; net exports of, 308–309; production of, 5–7, 8, 61–63, 72–74
Government(s): automation and, 448–449; and circular flow of economic activity, 54–56; concern for business, 448; cost of, paying for, 230; and economic growth, 450–452; and farmer, 433–438; foreign, and development costs of LDCs, 532; growing importance of, 213–217; opposition of, to labor unions, 191–192; regulation of business by, through antitrust laws, 149–152; regulatory agencies of, 405; role of, 49–51, 215–216; in Soviet economy, 515; versus inflation, 298–301; *see also* Federal *entries*
Government bonds, 110
Government control, big business and, 142–160
Government investment, in human capital, 182–185
Government legislation, and determination of wages, 173
Government monopolies, 125
Government National Mortgage Association (GNMA), 422
Government ownership, public enterprise as, 157
Government regulation, of public utilities, 154–155

Government spending: as fiscal policy, 346; and GNP, 308; impact of, on economy, 226

Grant-in-aid programs, 250–251

Grants, to cities, 422

Great Depression of 1930s, 50, 184, 192, 264, 301, 323–326, 329, 347, 411, 476, 488

Gresham's Law, 257

Grievance machinery, unions and, 195

Gross National Product (GNP), 56–57, 71–72, 305–306, 324, 351, 442–443, 457; analysis of, 332–335; in constant dollars, 313–315; of LDCs, 525; limitations of, 316–317; per capita, 315; problems measuring, 312–315; as total expenditures, 306–309; as total income, 309–315

Gross private domestic investment, 308

Gross receipts taxes, 247

Growth: capital, 114; economic, see Economic growth; of government, 213–217; of labor force, 166; production, as goal of economic policy, 344; population, see Population growth; suburban, 415–416; of urban population, 409–413

Hamilton, Alexander, 474

Hayek, Friedrich von, 456

Health insurance, under social security, 222

Holding companies, 144–146

Home mortgages, 269–270, 387

Hours of work, unions and, 194

Housing: in metropolitan areas, 417–418

Human capital, government investment in, 182–185

Human resources, 2

Hungary, market communism in, 520

Imperfect competition, 123, 129, 131–138

Incidence of taxes, 249–250

Income(s): additional, saving for, 370; disposable, GNP and, 312, 333; distribution of, 175–176; fixed, inflation and, 293–294; national, 309–311; not subject to taxation, 237; personal, and GNP, 311–312; of proprietors, and GNP, 311; redistribution of, 230–231; rental, and GNP, 311; total, GNP as, 309–315; work and, 168–169

Income maintenance approach, to poverty, 180–182

Income management, for consumers, 392–394

Income statement, 118–119

Income tax(es): corporation, 242, 244–246; individual, 234–239, 242; opinions on, 239, 242; progressive, as fiscal policy, 346–347; state and local, 247–249

Income tax credits, 239

Income tax return, filing of, 240–241

Incomes policies, 299–300

Index numbers, 289–291

Indicators, economic, 305, 324–325

Indirect taxes, 250

Individual income tax, 234–239, 242

Individual Retirement Accounts (IRAs), 373

Industrial Revolution, 294

Industries, promotion of, through taxation, 231

Industry rates, regulatory agencies and, 156

Inelastic demand: characteristics of, 26; for farm products, 430, 431

Inelastic supply, of farm products, 431–432

"Infant" industries, and tariffs, 474

Inflation, 13, 289, 362; causes of, 296–298; government versus, 298–301; and growth of government, 216; and personal lives, 291–296

Inflation hedge, 380

Inflationary gap, 331

Injunction, 201

Innovations, and business cycles, 326

Input-output analysis, 507, 508–511

Installment plans, 385

Institutions, of United States economic system, 46–49

Insurance, 380–382; deposit, 277–278; health, under social security, 222; life, 381–382; social, 180

Intercorporate stockholding, 151

Interdependence of economic society, 51

Interest, 370; compound, 375; in federal budget, 220; on business loans, 271–272; net, and GNP, 311

Interlocking directorates, 146, 151

Internal costs, of pollution, 454

Internal Revenue Service (IRS), 237

International Business Machines Corporation (IBM), 153, 161–162

International Development Association, 532

International Monetary Fund (IMF), 489–490, 532

International organizations, and development costs of LDCs, 532
International trade, 463–483; and economic specialization, 464–469; financing of, 486–498; restrictions on, 471–475; *see also* World trade
International Workingmen's Association, 512
Interstate Commerce Commission (ICC), 405
Interstate Commerce Commission Act of 1887, 143–144, 149, 150
Inventory, business, 271
Investment: business, fluctuation of, 333–335; capital, and productivity, 75; economic growth and, 448–449; GNP and, 333, 334; government, in human capital, 182–185; by utilities, value of, 157
Investment bank, 110
Investment funds, cost and availability of, 333–334
Investors, inflation and, 293
"Invisible hand," Adam Smith and, 11
Invisible tariff, 470–471

Job security, unions and, 195
Job training, 172, 220, 452
Johnson, Lyndon, 185
Jurisdictional strike, 201

Kantorovich, Leonid, 456
Kapital, Das, 512
Kennedy Round, of GATT, 476
Keogh plans, 373
Keynes, John Maynard, 328–329, 362, 456
Knights of Labor, 190–191
Koopmans, Tjalling, 456

L (money supply), 262
Labels, and consumer, 395–396
Labor, 72; automation and, 447–448; demand for, 170; division of, 81–83; New Deal for, 192; supply of, 171–172
Labor force: growth of, 166; occupations in, 165–167; overview of, 165–167; poorly trained, of LDCs, 530; size of, 165, 166; trends of, 167; women in, 166
Labor-Management Relations Act of 1947, 198, 200, 201
Labor-Management Reporting and Disclosure Act of 1959, 198, 200, 201
Labor-market strategies, poverty and, 182

Labor unions: basic aims of, 193–195; corruption and crime in, 203, 208; current problems of, 202–208; and determination of wages, 172–173, 206–207; federal laws regulating, 198; history of, 190–193; membership decline in, 202–203; pressuring of, by management, 201–202; pressuring of management by, 198–201; recognition by management, 195–196
Laffer Curve, 361
Lagging indicators, 324, 325
Laissez-faire, 11, 178, 329
Land, 2, 72
Landrum-Griffin Act of 1959, 198, 199, 201, 203
Law of Comparative Advantage, 79, 468
Law of Demand, 21–23, 169
Law of Diminishing Returns, 77, 80–81
Law of Supply, 31–33, 169
Laws: antitrust, 149–154; and business investment, 334–335; federal, *see* Federal laws
Layoffs, economic recession and, unions and, 204
LDCs, *see* Less developed countries
Leading indicators, 324–325
Legal monopolies, 124–125
Legal tender, 257
Legislation, government, and wages, 173
Lenin, Nikolai, 514, 515
Less developed countries (LDCs), 179; aid to, 444; costs of development of, 532, 533; debt crisis of, 533; definition of, 525–527; program for, 530–531; reasons for poverty of, 527–530
Lewis, John L., 192–193
Liability(ies), 117; of commercial bank, 274–275; limited, 97–98; unlimited, 94, 95–96
Life, unlimited, of corporation, 98
Life expectancy, 527
Life insurance, 381–382
Limited liability, 97–98
Limits to Growth, The, 458
Liquidation, 349; of corporation, 109
Liquidity, 371
Literacy rate, in LDCs, 527
Living standards, 216
Loans, 271–272; as assets, 273–274; to corporations, 106; personal, 386; short term, 269
Local government finances, 224–226
Local taxes, 247–249
Lockout, 201

Lorenz curve, 175–176
Low-income groups, in metropolitan areas, 414–415

M1, M2, M3 (money supply), 262
Machinery, specialized, availability of, to big business, 83
Macroeconomics, 57
Malthus, Thomas Robert, 178–179, 294
Management, 4; of big business, 88; pressuring of, by labor unions, 198–201; pressuring of unions by, 201–202; skills of, and productivity, 75
Management problems, Soviet, 516–517
Margin requirements, 115, 357
Marginal productivity, 170
Marginal propensity to consume, 336
Marginal utility, 23–24
Market(s): definition of, 57–59; money, 373; over-the-counter, 110, 111–112; securities, 110–112; specialized, 116; stock, 107–108; free versus planned, 504–507
Market communism, in Hungary, 520
Market economy, 9; dollars as votes in, 59
Market price: effect of change in demand on, 37–38; effect of change in supply on, 38–39; under monopolistic competition, 132–133; under monopoly, 125–127; under oligopoly, 134; supply and demand and, 34
Market system: advantages of, 63–67; disadvantages of, 65–67; price-directed, 59–63; and production of goods and services, 61–63; United States as, 57–59
Marshall, Alfred, 294–295, 456
Marx, Karl: and *Das Kapital,* 512; economic thought of, 510–511, 513–514
Mass production, and mass demand, 466
Maximum employment, as goal of economic policy, 344
McClellan Committee, on labor unions, 200–201
Meadows, D. H., 458
Mediation, 202
Medicaid, 181–182
Medical services, in LDCs, 527
Member banks, of Federal Reserve System, 281
Mercantilism, 10, 471–472
Merchandise, in balance of payments current account, 492
Mergers, business, 146–149

Metropolitan areas: current problems of, 412–419, 420–424; emergence of, 411, 412
Metropolitan Statistical Areas (MSAs), 411, 412
Microeconomics, 57
Minimum wage, 173
Minority groups, and poverty, 177
Mixed economy, 49, 504; Sweden as, 517–519
Mobil Oil, 480
Mobility of workers, 172
Modified gold standard, 264
Monetary policy(ies), 281, 344, 350–351; limitations of, 360, 364
Monetary standards, in United States history, 264
Money(s): characteristics of, 257; checkbook, 260, 283; creation of, commercial banks and, 270–277; fiat, 258, 264; functions of, 256–257; historical background of, 255–256; kinds of, 257–261; lending of, inflation and, 296; near, 261–263; owing of, inflation and, 295–296; paper, 264; printing of, 349; token, 259; value of, 289–291
Money-market funds, 373–374
Money supply, regulation of, by Federal Reserve, 351–358
Money wages, 194
Monopolistic competition, 129, 131–133; market price under, 132–133
Monopoly(ies), 123–129; government, 125; market price under conditions of, 125–126; natural, public utilities as, 125, 154–155; power of, limitation of, 300
Monopsony, 136–138
Moral suasion, 357
More developed countries (MDCs), 525
Mortgage bonds, 109
Mortgages, home, 269–270, 387
Multinational corporation(s): definition of, 463; foreign-owned, 480–481; and globalization of businesses, 478–483; growth of, 479–481; pros and cons of, 481–483
Multiplier, 335–336, 337–339
Mutual funds, 378–380
Mutual savings banks, 270
Myrdal, Gunnar, 456

Nader, Ralph, 158
National Credit Union Administration, 371
National debt, fiscal policy and, 347–348

National defense, 213–214, 220
National health, and economic growth, 449
National Income, 309–311
National Labor Relations Act, 192, 195
National Labor Relations Board (NLRB), 192, 195–196, 208
Natural monopolies, public utilities as, 125, 154–155
Natural resources, 2–3, 221; depletion of, 452–453, 457
Near moneys, 261–263
Net exports, 308–309, 330
Net interest, and GNP, 311
Net National Product (NNP), 309
Net worth, of commercial bank, 274–275
New Economic Policy (NEP), 515
New Deal, 329, 422, 433, 476; for labor, 192
New Federalism, 422–424
Nixon, Richard, 300, 469, 491
Nobel Memorial Prize in Economic Science, 11, 456
Nondurable goods, 307
Nonmarket economic activities, GNP and, 316
Nonmarket forces, and determination of wages, 172–175
Norris-La Guardia Act, 201
NOW (negotiable order of withdrawal) account, 371

Occupational Safety and Health Administration (OSHA), 182
Occupations, in labor force, 165–167
Office of Consumer Affairs (OCA), 397
Officers, of corporation, 101
Official settlement account, in balance of payments, 494–495
Old Age, Survivors, Disability, and Health Insurance (OASDHI), 222–223
Oligopoly, 129, 133–134
Oligopsony, 136, 138
Open Market Committee, 281
Open Market operations, of Federal Reserve, 355–357
Open shop, 194
Opportunity cost, 5–6
Organization: of business firms, 93–103
Organization of Petroleum Exporting Countries (OPEC), 146, 298, 497, 528
Output, of goods and services, 72–74; see also Productivity
Over-the-counter markets, 110, 111–112

Paper currency, 259–260

Paper money standard, 264
Paradox of thrift, 340
Parity, 434–435
Partnership, 94–96
Patents, 124–125
Pattern bargaining, 197
Pay, equal, for equal work, 193
Payee, 377
Payments-in-kind (PIK), 437, 440
Payments, balance of, see Balance of payments
Payroll taxes, 249
Peace Corps, 533
Pension plans, 374–375
Personal consumption expenditures, 307–309
Personal income, and GNP, 311–312
Personal loans, 386
Personal property taxes, 247–248
Personal savings, 369–371
Petrodollars, 496–498
Phillips Curve, 299
Picketing, 199
Planned economy, versus market, 504–507
Political events, and business cycles, 326–327
Political leadership of free world, economic growth and, 443–444
Political stability, economic growth and, 448
Pollution, 454–455, 461
Pools, 143–144
Population data, for LDCs, 527
Population growth: and business investment, 334; and growth of government, 215; programs to curb, in LDCs, 531; Malthus on, 178–179; rapid, in LDCs, 529; urban, 409–413
Pound, British, 264
Poverty: 176–185; programs to fight, 180–185
Power, countervailing, 158–160
Preferred stock, 108–109
Price(s): 20, 60–61; administered, 134–135; equilibrium, 34, 35; market, see Market price; under monopolistic competititon, 133; parity, 435; and supply and demand, 35–37, 40
Price changes, expected, and business investment, 335
Price controls, 300
Price-directed market system, 59–63
Price discrimination, 151
Price leadership, under oligopoly, 134
Price level, aggregate demand, full employment and, 330–331

Price rigidity, 129
Price stability, as goal of economic policy, 344
Price supports, 434–436
Price wars, 143
Pricing, target, 436–437
Primary boycott, 199
Principles of Economics, 294–295
Principles of Political Economy and Taxation, The, 78–79
Private organizations, and consumers, 396–397
Private property, 46–47
Product differentiation, 131, 132, 133, 134, 136, 402
Production: factors of, *see* Factors of production; farm, United States, 427–430; of goods and services, 5–7, 8, 61–63, 72–74; mass, and mass demand, 466
Production capacity, expanding, 444
Production growth, as goal of economic policy, 344
Production possibilities curve, 14–16
Productive resources, 1
Productivity, 73–74, 444; and demand for labor, 170; farm, *see* Farm productivity; increase of, 75–76; marginal, 170; wages and, 193
Professional Air Traffic Controllers Organization (PATCO), 207
Profit(s), 106, 511; and ability to pay, wages and, 193; corporate, and GNP, 311; undistributed, 106; undivided, as liabilities, 274
Profit motive, 47–48
Progressive income taxes, 233; and fiscal policy, 346–347
Promissory note, 271
Property, private, 46–47
Property taxes, 247–249
Proportional taxes, 233–234
Proposition 13, 248–249
Proprietors, income of, and GNP, 311
Prosperity, 322, 323
Protection, for consumers, 397, 400
Protectionism, 477
Protective tariffs, 473–474, 475–477
Proxies, 103
Public assistance, 180–182
Public domain, 125
Public employees, and right to strike, 205–207
Public enterprise, 157
Public goods and services, 65
Public housing, subsidized, 417–418
Public ownership, 150

Public relations, of management, 202
Public Service Commission (PSC), 158
Public utilities, 125, 154–155
Purchasing power, 291; as goal of economic policy, 344
Pure competition, 122–123
Pyramiding, 145

Qualitative controls, of Federal Reserve System, 357–358
Quantity discounts, 83
Quantity equation of exchange, 352–353
Quesnay, François, 11
Quotas: in market communism, 520; in world trade, 470

Rates, industry, regulatory agencies and, 156
Rationing, 507
Reagan, Ronald, 298, 345, 346; on education assistance, 452; on international trade, 471; on New Federalism, 422–423
Real GNP, 443
Real property, 380
Real property taxes, 247
Real wages, 194
Receipts, business organizations and, 100
Recession, 322; and "givebacks," 207–208; and layoffs, unions and, 204
Recessionary gap, 331, 345
Reciprocal Trade Agreements Act of 1934, 476
Redistribution of income, 230–231
Regional development, 221
Regressive taxes, 234
Regulation: of banks, 278–279; of business, by government, through antitrust laws, 149–152; of money supply, by Federal Reserve, 351–358; of unions, federal laws for, 198; utility, 154–155, 158–159
Regulatory agencies, 156–157, 405
Renewable resources, 3, 453
Rental income, and GNP, 311
Research and development, 83; support of, by government, 452
Reserve account, with Federal Reserve, 273
Reserve ratio, 352
Reserves, banking, 271, 282–283
Resources: ability to use, 73; amount and quality of, 72–73; cost of, to big business, 88; farm, immobility of, 432–433; human, 2; natural, *see* Natural resources; nonrenewable, 3, 453;

productive, 1; renewable, 3, 453; uneven distribution of, 464–466
Restraint of trade, 161–162
Restricted grants, to cities, 422
Restrictive endorsement, 378–379
Retained earnings, 106
Retirement, saving for, 370
Retirement payments, under social security, 222
Return(s): anticipated, on investments, 370–371; Diminishing, Law of, 77, 80–81; fair, to utilities, 156
Revenue(s), 25; marginal, 170; in metropolitan areas, 414–416; sources of, for state and local governments, 226, 227
Revenue-sharing, 422
Revenue tariff, 470
Revolving charge accounts, 385–386
Ricardo, David, 78–79, 294, 468
Right to strike, public employees and, 205–207
Right-to-work laws, 198
Rising cost of living, wages and, 194
Rising living standards, and growth of government, 216
Robinson, Joan, 130
Robinson-Patman Act (1936), 151
Robotics, 446
Rockefeller, John D., 144
Roosevelt, Franklin, 191, 192, 329, 433, 476; on Great Depression, 323
Roosevelt, Theodore, 192
Russian Revolution, 514

S corporations, 99–100
Sales taxes, 247
Samuelson, Paul, 456
Satellites, 446
Saving(s): consumers and, 371–375, 378–380; and economic growth, 448–449; economic implications of, 382–383; inflation and, 292, 293; in LDCs, 532; through life insurance, 382; personal, 369–371
Savings and loan associations (S&Ls), 269–270
Savings banks, mutual, 270
Savings bonds, 374
Savings institutions, 371–373
Say, Jean Baptiste, 328
Scarcity, 1, 14–16
Science: in federal budget, 221; and growth of government, 216; and technology, 410–411
Second Bank of the United States, 280
Second-level holding company, 145–146
Secondary boycott, 199–200

Securities: as assets, 274; corporate, 108–110
Securities and Exchange Commission (SEC), 117, 405
Securities markets, 110–112
Security: economic, 13; income, in federal budget, 220
Selling costs, under monopolistic competition, 133
Selling short, 115
Service(s), 1; in GNP, 307; goods and, see Goods and services
Sherman Antitrust Act of 1890, 144, 150, 151, 152, 161, 192
Shifting of taxes, 250
Shopping guidelines, for consumers, 394–396
Single proprietorship, 93–94
Skilled workers, 2
Skills: and productivity, 75; requirements for jobs, 171
Slowdown, work, 200
Smith, Adam, 10–11, 50, 78, 142, 178, 294, 328, 456, 464; on role of government, 49; on tax system, 231–232
Smoot-Hawley Tariff Act of 1930, 476
Social costs, of pollution, 454
Social indicators, in LDCs, 525, 527
Social insurance, 180
Social security system, 222–223
Social security tax, 246–247
Socialism, capitalism versus, 503
Soil Conservation and Domestic Allotment Act of 1936, 434
Soviet Union, communism in, 514–517
Special Drawing Rights (SDRs), 490–491
Special endorsement, 378
Specialization: and big business, 81–83; economic, international trade and, 464–469; and economy, 52
Speculation, 114–115
Spending: business, see Business spending; consumer, influencing of, through taxation, 231; deficit, controversy over, 349–350; government, see Government spending
Stability: economic, 12–13, 184; political, economic growth and, 448; price, as goal of economic policy, 344
Stagflation, 362
Stalin, Josef, 515
Standard of living, 2–3
Standard of value, money as, 256
Standard Oil Company, 144, 149
State agencies, and consumers, 396
State Department, 437
State finances, 224–226

State protection, for consumers, 397
State taxes, 247–249
Statement(s): balance of payments, 492, 493; financial, 117–119
Statistical-discrepancy adjustment, in balance of payments, 495
Stigler, George, 456
Stock(s), 98, 108–109; capital, as liability, 274; common, 375, 378; purchase and sale of, 110–115
Stock exchanges, 110, 112
Stock market, 107–108
Stockholding, intercorporate, 151
Store of value, money as, 256–257
Straight life insurance, 381
Strike(s), 198–199, 204–205; jurisdictional, 201; right to, public employees and, 205–207; settlement by third parties, 202
Strikebreakers, 201
Structural unemployment, 451–452
Subsistence farming, 530
Suburban growth, as problem of metropolitan areas, 415–416
Suburbia, flight to, 411–412, 413
Supplemental Security Income (SSI), 180–181
Supply, 20, 30–34; changes in, 33, 38–39; elasticity of, 33–34; inelastic, of farm products, 431–432; of labor, factors affecting, 171–172; Law of, 31–33
Supply and demand: determination of price by, 34, 35–37, 40; and wages, 169
Supply curve, 32–33
Supply schedule, 30, 31, 32
Supply-side economics, 300–301, 362–363
Surplus value, 511
Survivors benefits, under social security, 222
Sweden, as mixed economy, 517–519
Syndicate, 110

Taft-Hartley Act of 1947, 198, 199, 201, 205
Target pricing, 436–437
"Tariff revenue paid by foreigners" argument, 475
Tariffs, 470–471
Tax(es): business, 249; direct, 250; estate, 246; excise, 246; federal, 234–239, 242, 244–247; flat, 239; gift, 246; gross receipts, 247; highway, 249; incidence of, 249–250; income, see Income tax(es); indirect, 250; inheritance, 249; local, 247–249; payroll,

249; progressive, 233; property, 247–249; proportional, 233–234; qualification for payment of, 232–234; regressive, 234; sales, 247; social security, 246; state, 247–249
Tax laws, new, and business investment, 334–335
Tax system: assessment of, 251; good, 231–232
Taxation: double, of corporation, 99; as fiscal policy, 345; functions of, 230–231; income not subject to, 237
Technological revolution, 167
Technology: advances in, and growth of government, 216, 221; and productivity, 75–76; and science, 410–411
Tennessee Valley Authority (TVA), 157, 230
Term life insurance, 381
Thrift, paradox of, 340
Thrift institutions, 269–270
Tight-money policies, 364
Time deposits, 269
Tinbergen, Jan, 456
Token money, 259
Tokyo Round, of GATT, 476–477
Trade, see Foreign trade, International trade, World trade
Trade policy, American, evolution of, 475–476
Traditional economy, 8–9
Traditions, and LDCs, 528–529
Transfer of funds, district banks and, 284–285
Transfer payments, 216
Transferability of shares, 98
Transportation: in federal budget, 221; in metropolitan areas, 412–414
Traveler's checks, 260–261
Trotsky, Leon, 514
Truman, Harry, on poor countries, 525
Trusts, 144
Tying contracts, 151

Underconsumption, and business cycles, 327
Underground economy, 243–245
Underwriters, of stocks and bonds, 110
Undistributed profits, 106, 274
Unemployment, 450–452
Unemployment compensation, 222; as fiscal policy, 346
Unincorporated businesses, 93
Union contract, 196–197
Union label, 195
Union shop, 194, 198
Unions, labor, see Labor unions

United Automobile Workers (UAW), 207
United States: history of monetary standards in, 264; as market system, 57–59
United States Copyright Office, 124
Unlimited liability, 94, 95–96
Unlimited life, of corporation, 98
Urban Mass Transit Administration, 414
Urban population, growth of, 409–413
Urban society, and growth of government, 217
Utilities, public, 125, 154–155; regulation of, 158–159
Utility, marginal, diminishing, 23–26

Value: of investment by utilities, 157; of money, 289–291; standard of, money as, 256; store of, money as, 256–257
Veblen, Thorstein, 404
Velocity, of money, 352, 353, 364
Videodiscs, 446

Wage controls, 300
Wage-price spiral, 298
Wages: determination of, 168–169, 172–175; higher, unions and, 193–194, 206–207

Wagner Act of 1935, 192
War communism, 514–515
Warsaw Pact, 520
Wealth and Poverty, 458
Wealth of Nations, The, 10–11, 142, 231–232, 328
Welfare, expenditures for, on state and local levels, 226, 227
Welfare programs, 180–182; criticisms of, 184
White-collar workers, growing number and importance of, 203
Wholesale Price Index, 290–291
Wilson, Woodrow, 192
Women: in labor force, 166; households headed by, in poverty, 180
Work, and income, 168–169
Workers' skills, and productivity, 75
World Bank, 532
World trade: barriers to, 470–471; since 1945, 476–478; *see also* Foreign trade, International trade

Young people, poverty and, 180

Zero economic growth, 457